Why Islam Is Greater Than Your Religion In Philosophy

A
Work In
American Pragmatism

By
Nick Ruderman

First Edition, 2009

Copyright © 2009 by Nick Ruderman

Printed in the United States of America.
Printed on acid-free paper by Lightning Source.
www.lightningsource.com

No part of this book may be copied or reprinted without written permission by the publisher.

Published by Ruderman Publishers, 2009
Nick_Ruderman@email.com
South Woodstock, Vermont

Ruderman, Brian Nicholas.
Why Islam Is Greater Than Your Religion In Philosophy:
A Work in American Pragmatism

1. Philosophy, General. 2. Philosophy, Religion. 3. Philosophy, Pragmatism. I. Title.

ISBN-978-0-615-31612-3 paperback

Manufactured in the United States of America.

To my parents:
Mary Ellen McCue, Barry Ruderman
And of course,
Paul Lenett

Contents

	Preface	
1)	Strategic Pragmatism	13
2)	"The Separation of Church and State" and Other Political Misnomers	42
3)	Why Islam Is Greater Than Your Religion In Philosophy	71
4)	Living As If There Were No Tomorrow	133
5)	Black Nationalism and International Justice	179
6)	Many Forms of Justice	217
7)	The Politics of Faith and The Justification of Suffering	274
8)	The Good Life and the Problem of Evil	300
	Acknowledgements	345
	Index	346

Preface

"The future is the only kind of property that the masters willingly concede to the slaves."
Albert Camus, "State Terrorism and Rational Terror", 1951[1]

I grew up with a firm belief in the maxim that 'more people die in the name of religion than from starvation'. Whether this maxim is true or is not true, wars from the Crusades, two World Wars, the troubles in Northern Ireland, and the current wars on Afghanistan and Iraq have only helped reinforce this prejudice.

While a preponderance toward war may be held by religious people themselves, not all atheists believe that religion is the root of all wars. Karl Marx, for example, believed that wars were fundamentally economical in motivation and were not religious or faith-based. Of course, Marx may have been wrong here, as he was in many other places, but this belief in the economic causal-basis for war is also shared by the most decorated Marine in United States history, Major General Smedley Butler.

The General was born in 1881, the son of two generations of US Congressmen. He had bravely fought in many wars and was highly honored by those whom he led during his exemplary time in the service. In a speech delivered shortly before his death in 1940, the retired General said of his military career:

"I spent 33 years and four months in active military service and during that period I spent most of my time as a high class muscle man for Big Business, for Wall Street and the bankers. In short, I was a racketeer, a gangster for capitalism. I helped make Mexico and especially Tampico safe for American oil interests in 1914. I helped make Haiti and Cuba a decent place for the National City Bank boys to collect revenues in. I helped in the raping of half a dozen Central American republics for the benefit of Wall Street. I helped purify Nicaragua for the International Banking House of Brown Brothers in 1902-1912. I brought light to the Dominican Republic for the American sugar interests in 1916. I helped make Honduras right for the American fruit companies in 1903. In China in 1927 I helped see to it that Standard Oil went on its way unmolested."[2]

During his career General Butler received tremendous recognition including two-Congressional Medals of Honor, two Distinguished Service Medals, and many others. His men called him 'The Fighting Quaker', and his gravestone in Pennsylvania reads, "WAR IS A RACKET, A FEW PROFIT AND THE MANY PAY". In his great anti-war book of the same title he says:

"Out of war nations acquire additional territory, if they are victorious. They just take it. This newly acquired territory promptly is exploited by the few –the self-same few who wrung dollars out of blood in the war. The general public shoulders the bill. And what is the bill? This bill renders a horrible accounting. Newly placed gravestones. Mangled bodies. Shattered minds. Broken hearts and homes. Economic instability. Depression and all its attendant miseries. Back-breaking taxation for generations and generations."[3]

Many people say that the War on Terror is really a war for oil. If the War on Terror appears to be a religious war or if the interim laws written therein seem to be based upon religion –it ain't necessarily so. The British counter-terror laws of the last century, for example, tended to focus on Catholics and Hindus. This may only have been coincidental to the locality of their colonial and military occupation. Those who were defenders happened to have one religion while the aggressors had another. Be that as it may, the confusion of war and religion is often sustained and confounded further by institutions like governmental-bureaucracy and the mass-media of television, cinema, newspapers, magazines, internet blogs, as well as the interests of one's friends and one's social surroundings.

In this century British and American laws have come to focus primarily on the religion of Islam and the Arab peoples in general.[4] Under this gaze across more than one quarter of the world's population, our White House and English-speaking media would have us believe that Arabs and Muslims are set against our democratic way of life and are enemies of the free world. According to such generalizations we are to believe that people such as the five-time presidential-nominee, consumer's-advocate, American lawyer Ralph Nader, a man who has testified more times before Congress than any other non-governmental official, and who drafted the Clean Air and Clean Water Acts, who put seat-belts in cars, is a terrorist. We are to believe that the Gold-medal Olympian, Vietnam War resister, and American Heavyweight Champion of the World, Muhammad Ali is a terrorist. We are to believe this of such people as the folk-singer Cat Stevens, the NBA star and actor Kareem Abdul-Jabar, President Barrack Obama's father, as well as millions of Americans and nearly two billion people in the world.

The first democratically elected president of South Africa, Nelson Mandela, and the Hindu pacifist Mohandas Gandhi have both been listed by the British and American governments as terrorists. Why is it that the non-violent activist and revolutionary leader Gandhi studied the holy book of Islam, the Quran, when he prayed?[5]

Was Gandhi a believer in the right to fight for freedom of religion, or was Gandhi a terrorist? -a label used by the English-speaking and Western media a hundred years ago. Still today there is a bureaucratic response to those people who resist occupation- whether it be justified as a war of preemption, or as simply the 'cost' of freedom.

Freedom is one of the great foundations of America –freedom from the arbitrary rule of a King, freedom of the press, freedom of religion, freedom of the courts, and freedom to politically organize and demonstrate. But a problem that concerns us today in the age of freedom is the problem of conformity. The love of freedom, or the belief that freedom is the greatest good, has led to a belief in the rights of certain individuals over the rights of communities and others. Some call this free trade, the free market, libertarianism, or the survival of the fittest, all of which stand for the justification of the unequal distribution of goods such as healthcare, resources, and well-being. With moneyed corporate television and the media telling us on a regular basis what to believe and what not to believe thousands of times a day, the problem of conformity has become essentially a problem for freedom loving people.

Freedom and Credulity

According to different polls Americans are predominantly religious, and for the most part, Christian. The US has never had a non-Christian president (or a female, or an atheist, etc..). Since the Second World War, the military budget has taken up half the US spending budget. The president who started the current US wars with Muslim nations, Bush II's favorite self-portraits is his Christian faith. According to Former President Bush, the Christian religion defines who he is and what his values are. Are we to believe that Bush is in earnest or that he totally misunderstands Christianity? Or is it a little bit of both –that he is both right and wrong, that he is prone to human error like the rest of us?

Whether or not President Bush actually knows what he believes, we cannot doubt his own conviction that he is a deeply religious man. And, this is representative of the majority of US citizens, as well as people in the world, who also identify themselves as religious. In fact, many people who do not identify themselves as religious often share many of the same religious convictions. How many 'non-religious' people do you know who actually believe in such secular superstition as ghosts, spirits, angels, demons, magic, reincarnation, past-lives, benign karma, fate, evil, immortality, or the existence of a supra-moral world-order? It might be better to ask how many people do *not* believe in such hocus-pocus and superstition. Not many it seems, though there are a few people who don't know everything and will keep reading.

How do we arrive at our beliefs anyway? By freewill? Is it possible that we do not always choose what we believe? And if that's so, how much of what we believe is voluntary?

For example, some say that our beliefs are significantly based upon our social group or class. If my family, friends, or social group-class believe or practice something, like say, driving on the right side of the road, then it in all likelihood follows that I believe and practice the same thing. Such beliefs and practices are institutionally either right or wrong, but they are not universally right or wrong. Or internationally as it were-some cultures do not drive on the right side of the road, but neither do they drive on the wrong side of the road.

Many people think that what we believe depends upon who our parents are or how we were raised by them. George Bush Sr. and George Bush Jr., for example, are nearly identical in their beliefs, spiritually and politically. One of them thought Saddam Hussein wasn't a threat to the United States and one pretended he was. Differences do occur.

Some might concede that while we often have beliefs that are similar to our parents, like say, faith or political-affiliation, our beliefs are also be based on our age, gender, hair and skin color, race, height, economic status, religion, class, nationality, species, and on and on. Such institutional beliefs are notoriously based upon generalization and popular conformity, the acceptance without questioning of what we are told is true. Be that as it may, many theories exist which try to explain how we arrive at our beliefs, and many people disagree with each other. For pragmatists the many differences are essential to a healthy and functioning democracy.

American Pragmatism

Pragmatism as a philosophy was first explicated in the late 19th century by a New England mathematician named Charles Sanders Peirce (1839-1914). Peirce (pronounced like 'purse') was the son of a mathematician, and during his life he had done a great deal of surveying for the United States Coast and Geodetic Survey. He described the task of the pragmatist philosopher to be "Just as a civil engineer… [who] will think of the different properties of all materials, so in… pragmatism the properties of all indecomposable concepts were examined and the ways in which they could be compounded."[6] For Peirce there was no arbitrary split between science and faith, fact and value, theory or practice.[7] "Practical consequences" are the import of pragmatism, and not conformity to some prejudicial belief or superstition.

In a study of the classical writings of the pragmatists, the American philosopher H.S. Thayer says that pragmatism was primarily a 'movement' and not a 'doctrine'. He notes that: "The movement is no longer active, having largely succeeded in its critical and positive aims." The positive aims of pragmatism were not confined to the human mind or college classroom and accordingly "not only affected academic philosophy but had a profound impact upon the study of law, education, political and social theory, religion, and the arts."[8]

The most famous proponent of pragmatism and also the most influential, was a man born and raised in Vermont named John Dewey (1859-1952). During his lifetime he was dubbed "America's Philosopher" by the *New York Times*. Dewey's 1918 book, *Democracy and Education*, is indisputably the most influential treatise on education ever written by an American and is usually required reading for students of education in both secular and religious schools alike. Dewey spent a good deal of his life setting up experimental 'laboratory' schools in which more progressive and creative techniques were used and tried in pedagogy, the science of education. Dewey's experimentalist approach to education is in sharp contrast to the bureaucratization and centralization of public schooling as it exists today and increasingly so over the last 8 years in America, under the no child "Left Behind" Bush novelty (some might add, his best seller). Much of the 21st century has witnessed a governmental attempt at dumbing-down the public schools of our children, in which test-taking has become the paradigm of learning and not those activities that spark human curiosity and imagination, or the experimentalism that marked Dewey's legacy.

In its heyday, pragmatists could be found to be of great influence in institutions of diverse proportion. A profound influence on semiotics, symbolic and formal logic was made by Peirce, the physician and psychologist William James (1842-1910) "established experimental psychology in North America"[9], and wrote an influential treatise on the plurality of religions in his study *The Varieties of Religious Experience*. In jurisprudence and legal studies a large influence was made by the pragmatist Supreme Court Justice Oliver Wendell Holmes (1841-1935), who has forever changed the thousand years-old Common Law. The pacifist and mother of the Progressive Party, Jane Addams (1860-1935) established one of the earliest settlement houses in the United States, taking in immigrants, minorities, the poor, single mothers, and others. She educated and empowered many people, helping inaugurate a strong tradition of virtue and community in Chicago. An insatiable opponent of war and imperialism, in 1931 she was the first American woman awarded the Nobel Peace Prize. Until her death in 1935, Jane had founded and chaired international anti-war movements and had sat as president of the Women's International League for Peace and Freedom (WILPF). Dewey influenced both the fields of education and political philosophy as well, starting teachers unions and helping found the National Association of American Colored People, (NAACP) and the American Civil Liberties Union (ACLU). There were many, many others who refused to separate knowledge and action as well.

With the death of John Dewey in 1952 and the beginning of the Cold War, pragmatism as a philosophy in America had been eclipsed by two then popular non-historical and culturally based European philosophies called existentialism and positivism, both of which have been refuted by contemporary pragmatists. It was through the influence of such writers as W.V. Quine (1908-2000) and Richard Rorty (1931-2007) and others that pragmatism began to reemerge in the 1970's. Today our contemporary pragmatists often stand at the head of their fields of discipline such as Hilary Putnam (semantics, mathematics), Cornel West (race studies, democratic socialism), and Justice Richard Posner (legal pragmatism).[10] Pragmatism also enjoys popularity along the literary philosophies of such influential writers as George Santayana, Lionel Trilling, and Louis Menand.

What exactly is pragmatism? The standard definition of the word calls it "a practical approach to problems and affairs" and it is not suprising that once upon a time to call someone 'pragmatic' was to call them artless or opinionated. As an American school of thought it can be linked to the nature writers like Ralph Waldo Emerson and the surveyor Henry David Thoreau who were both from New England and whose naturalism inspired the social and environmental aspects of pragmatism. Moreover, pragmatism emerged in a democratic polity following the bloodiest Civil War. There was great talk at the time about 'reconstruction' both politically and ideologically and John Dewey made the reconstruction of philosophy one of his central tasks.

America was very much still the New World and democracy was still a new political experiment, with great struggles making room for different people and different cultures from the four corners of the earth. Pragmatists believed that social experimentation ought to continue as the very virtue of the American experiment with democracy. For this reason pragmatism's most important contribution to the world is its theory of pluralism. Pluralism is a word/concept that means multiplicity, as in many, and pragmatists believe that a true democracy is a vehicle for this multiplicity, or the multiple realization of the many faces of reality

Democracy and Modernity

Democracy was used in the Greek city-state of Athens some 2500 years ago. At the time the Athenian philosopher Plato warned his fellow citizens that an excessive love of freedom leads to tyranny. Or, as we call it in our modern democracy –Homeland Security.

If in a democracy every person is a part of the government, we might hope that our fellow citizens are all well-versed in moral and ethical matters, and that their love of wisdom was at least as vigilant as their love of politics. We might expect the democratic political system that produced Socrates, Plato, and Aristotle to produce a nation of philosophers. Although the American public is comprised of a rich diversity and broad range of cultural backgrounds, the modernizing tendency has been to universalize or institute only one type of institution of thought and belief, while eliminating the rest. This monotony is true of all modern institutions.

The four most popular political institutions of the modern world are capitalism, socialism, anarchism, and nationalism. While it is popular cliché to represent these four institutions as pairs of opposites, as in 'capitalism vs. socialism', or 'nationalism vs. anarchism', like 'republican vs. democrat' or 'liberal vs. conservative', 'right vs. left', etc, such black and white pictures often obscure what is common and eliminate what is diverse.

For example, each of these four modern institutions seeks to make itself universal. Socialism, Capitalism, Anarchism, and Nationalism (call it SCAN) all commonly believe they represent people's true interests and true human nature. SCAN seeks to eliminate each of those institutions which are different from their own and which cannot be assimilated. By reducing the totality through conformity to one social institution, SCAN is opposed to the pragmatic principle of pluralism or multiplicity. This 'totalization' or conformism by SCAN is called imperialism.

Imperialism is a word usually used in politics to either justify the arbitrary use of power, as for example in the expansion of a nation or empire. Or it is used to criticize the arbitrary abuse of power, as stemming from unreason, or lack of morals. Imperialism can be found not just in political institutions as we saw with SCAN, but in social institutions as well. 'Cultural imperialism' is the name for the conformity to these social institutions such as age discrimination, sexism, racism, homophobia, and economic and class war.

Class war, or class struggle as it is sometimes called, is the name given to the economic struggles which occur within modern society —the battle between the haves and the have nots, or in French, the 'bourgeois' and the 'proletariat'. Like a Charles Dickens novel, the factory owners are few but have a lot of wealth and political clout, while the workers are many but are poor and unorganized. Thus ensues the struggle between classes

Described at this level, class war can be clearly understood —it's the rich versus the poor. However, ever since the theory of class war was invented in the 19th century, there has been another more positive understanding which holds that this class war *should* exist. This is because there remains a confusion over whether such a war between classes is descriptive of society in general (taking all societies existing in the present, past, and those which could exist in the future as being fundamentally the same), or whether this war is of necessary and universal importance and value.

So it is no wonder that all four of the SCAN institutions not only believe in class war, but support it as well. Indeed, the SCAN institutions try to escalate this class war, to make it more prevalent and affecting. It is held accordingly that this class war is the only way for society to reach its goal, be it found in revolution (socialism), hegemony (capitalism), utopia (anarchism), or tightened borders (nationalism).

If class war is the product of the imperialist method of 'divide and conquer', those who fight this war just as often work to maintain the status quo or to distract people from the problem of imperialism itself. In this sense the class war describes the general in-fighting amongst a given society or in any class or strata therein.

And this is where the theory of class war is most accurate —in describing the attempt not to be as unbiased as possible or as objective as possible, or as reasonable, intellectual, or scientific as possible, but to squabble over only what is of little or no consequence, making instead personal differences to be of supreme importance, and to root out all of those who don't conform. Supporters of class war make everyone's business their own business and extensively micro-manage other people's personal lives and private affairs, much like a soap-opera. Through this miniaturism of concern a general blindness of the big picture is ensured. Such petty indiscretion and muddling inevitably works to the advantage to those in power, and further disempowers and discourages those who don't conform or enlist in a war of class.

In this sense the SCAN ideologies often function as a 'Fifth Column', and this is not a controversial remark. The 'Fifth Column' refers to any person or persons who secretly work against their own community or country, say during an attack by an 'enemy', like Benedict Arnold during the revolutionary war who fought on both sides in the attempt to help the English against the Americans. Such duplicitous faith would have us love our enemies and hate our friends.

Accordingly, such advocates of class war tell us to hate those who aren't disaffected, decadent, or cynical. Acknowledgement of others must be disrespect or dishonor, while compromise and solidarity are seen as disloyalty to one's own party. We are to hate the government, the military, the police, the incorrigible, or those who 'just don't get it'. It is little wonder that such proponents of class war have been the worshipful devotees of such quislings as Heidegger, Wittgenstein, or Rushdie, and proponents of class war have been the unabashed enemies of such revolutionaries as Thomas Paine, Gandhi or reformers like Nader, each of whom support diversity and solidarity.

What is more, the SCAN institutions are all guilty of illogical thinking and that weak reasoning that is sometimes called 'magical thinking'. It is magical thinking to believe that class war is necessary for progress. It is magical thinking to believe that social and political institutions are an ultimate or metaphysical reality and are not human creations. It is magical thinking to believe that just two classes exist, or that people's minds are so simple and binary. Members of the SCAN institutions often dedicate themselves to such inessential and impractical magical theories as various as preaching knowledge of the imminent end of the world, or an impending social cataclysm, or the cryptography of the mind and the world -the preposterous belief that reality is magically represented in secret codes or some allegorical riddle, or some other form of kitsch.

While the world of make-believe can be entertaining and the arts help in teaching our children and assisting us in living the good life, art is also one of the greatest progenitors of stereotype and false-presentation. At the beginning of the Reagan-era in 1981, Hilary Putnam noted that, "The arts have been exalted by us to a place much higher than any they occupied in Plato's day or in the middle ages. As a number of authors have remarked, for a certain sort of educated person, art today is religion, i.e. the closest thing to salvation available."[7] Through the popular works of war-advocates such as Carl Jung and Joseph Campbell we are to believe that a hero and moral can be found in any and every dunghill art form. Its not enough that injustice exists in the real world, but every primitive myth, stereotype, or 'novel' contrivance, or such cinema as Star Wars, James Bond, or the Lord of the Rings stand as a tale of bravery and heroism, according to such sentinels of image and servants to mediocrity. As it is a large amount of art and entertainment serves as a great distraction for people, and this works to the advantage of those in power.

Probably the greatest contributor to conformity in our society, or distraction from democracy is alcohol, and it is a wonder that right before the 19th Amendment gave women the vote, the 18th Amendment banned the sale of alcohol.[11] Beer and hard liquor serve as the greatest placaters to political machinations, and those who are alcoholics (meaning those who drink on a regular, or nightly basis), are thorough conformists and political non-entities through ritual self-poisoning and mind-numbing. Likewise, it is no great wonder that the US is the number one importer and consumer of cocaine, that those coke-heads are political and ethical nobodies, with no regard for local and unrefined responsibility.

Every country, whatever its current political form, is comprised of individuals, no matter how much freedom each person really has. Conformity to modern institutions is a problem whether a country is democratic or whether it is a dictatorship. Credulity persists, despite the strength of political freedom, where wisdom is not solicited. An ancient Celtic proverb says that, "He who is not strong must be clever." Its not that there isn't a time and place for institutions like socialism, capitalism, anarchism, and nationalism. It's that these modern institutions are not tolerant of those realities from which they ideologically differ. Such is the disinheritance of imperialism.

The Green Party nominee Ralph Nader is quick to point out that the Bush family, like many other patriarchal families, is the product of generations of sons who were pushed around by their fathers. But he also points out that we have to overcome such personal and childhood struggles if we want to become part of the solution and not remain part of the problem.[12]

Philosophy vs. Imperialism

The American philosopher Harry Frankfurt begins his book, *On Bullshit*, by noting that, "One of the most salient features of our culture is that there is so much bullshit."[13] According to this theory there is a "widespread conviction that it is the responsibility of a citizen in a democracy to have opinions about everything, or *at least* everything that pertains to the conduct of his country's affairs."[14] I take it that Frankfurt here is referring to the busy-bodying of those who watch day-time television or are given to discouragement and unedifying complaint. Luckily, having the courage for ones convictions is not limited to mere opinion or personal affronts.

The principles of democracy were perhaps best exemplified by a retired soldier named Socrates. At some point in his later years Socrates got sick of all the bullshit and decided to do something about it. In retirement he made it his job to publicly argue with the bigots of his democracy and in the process make his fellow citizens aware of the contradictions of those bullshit artists of the day, whether they were politicians, lawyers, poets, priests, or sons of bitches.

In Socrates' day the kind of professional who taught this art of bullshit was called a sophist. Sophists were teachers who for a fee, would teach people how to persuade others to believe something, regardless of whether or not it is really true. Socrates pointed out to his fellow Athenians that the sophistical method of the sophists doesn't distinguish between belief and knowledge, between having an opinion or a grasp of the truth. Today the sophist is popularly replaced by the relativist.

Relativism is the belief that there is no absolute truth, only what is true for one's self or one's class. According to such a general prejudice there is no getting at the 'real' truth to the matter, only adherence to one's own preference or the force of whatever is felt to be true. Most often when confronted with a contradiction in their values, relativists will reply that, indeed, everyone is biased in their values, beliefs, and judgment, so there isn't really a truth to the matter, only preference. The relativist, however, usually does not specify whether this 'universal bias' exists because of such opposing motives as selfishness or allegiance. Most of the relativists I have met are really, unbeknownst to themselves, defending their relatives, as the name 'relativism' implies, for they offer no disagreement to what they were raised to believe, whether it be in some prejudice or a general apathetic indifference.

William James makes such an assumption in a lecture he gave in Cambridge, Massachusetts in 1896 titled, "The Will to Believe". James tried to convince his audience members that their choice of philosophy or religion is one that may ultimately be settled by the force of passion or the desire for reward, given the limits of reason and the intellect, (and we might suppose), the length of Bill's sermon. This flies in the face of what was written a hundred years earlier by the Lutheran philosopher Immanuel Kant (1724-1804), who taught that faith is just a kind of reason. If James' will to believe seems to imply that reason is just a kind of faith or belief, this does not sit well with logic-workers, or logicians.

In fact, Peirce sought to distance himself from the pragmatism of James though the two remained life-long friends, just as Plato and Aristotle disagreed with each other on a very similar matter, but remained life-long friends. Aristotle had simply said, "Plato is my friend, but truth a greater friend."

Plato held that logic, or the *logos*, is a universal principle that governs everything in the universe, whether regarding celestial navigation (astrology) or the human mind. To this proposition Aristotle points out a paradox that Plato had dismissed as illusory. This is the philosopher 'Meno's paradox' concerning matters of which people do not know. For example, every time I've checked to see if 2 and 2 really equal 4 I've always gotten the same positive results. Meno's paradox states: "Either a man will learn nothing at all or he will learn only what he already knows."[15] If logic is universal how is ignorance possible? How is learning possible? For Aristotle, Plato's theory of logic is too general to be applicable as a research program and since the time of Plato, the *logos* has been used in Europe and beyond as the ultimate principle of conformity and imperialism, as the Austrian philosopher Karl Popper showed in his 1943 work, *The Open Society and Its Enemies*.[16]

Thus, it was Aristotle who demonstrated to the Western reader for the first time the difference between belief and logic, between faith and reason. Relativists deny any distinction, holding instead that either all beliefs are relatively logical, or that all logic is genetic or innate. William James is corrected by this non-citizen of Athens who will revisit us throughout this book.[17] The logic of Aristotle, and not the *logos* of Plato, begins the tradition of Western logic as we understand it today: the science of reason. As we shall see, this only happened through the work of medieval Arab and Muslim scholars, and not through the death of Socrates or Plato's successors.

Like Aristotle, pragmatists hold that some philosophies are greater than others. Some philosophies are more reasonable than others, more realistic, more practical, more consistent, and more ethical. This does not mean that some philosophies don't really exist or aren't really real. Pragmatism is not an instance of negation or imperialism but of practical valuation. To advocate something does not entail opposing other things. The pragmatist works strategically and not according to such simple class allegiances or black and white pictures of reality. To the question of the purpose of pragmatism, its strategy, we turn to in Chapter 1.

If in America religion is kept out of public schools and philosophy is relegated to the college classroom alone, it is no surprise that in a secular democracy there is a tendency to think that all philosophies are elitist or that all religions are the same simple thing. Beyond this construct, what roles do religion and philosophy play in America? Is there in America a separation of church and state or is America a 'secular' state, secular meaning worldly and mundane. To this question we turn to in Chapter 2.

Although each philosophy and religion have divergent histories and some have been more or less politically tolerant than others, this book will not by and large be based upon history. Because many religions, like many philosophies, are based upon books, there is a fact of the matter over which religion is the most philosophically or scientifically tolerant. To this matter we turn to in Chapter 3.

The world is becoming homogenized and monotonized more and more each year through the process of modernization and globalization. The economic decisions that humans make over the next years will have drastic consequences over our environment, as they have more and more so since the industrial revolution. Our future on earth is heavily dependent upon our ecological ethics. What are the philosophies that enable such an ethics and what can we hope of the future? To this question we turn to in Chapter 4.

If the philosophers care about truth, truth is often found in the same place as justice and many theories and practices of justice exist. Whose justice is most important, if not my own? Is there one universal truth which is the truth for everyone? Is there one kind of justice which is the most ideal –an ideal justice? How are we as a nation to deal with other nations, or nationless peoples? Can there be one law, or one universal justice that applies to everyone? To these questions we turn to in Chapters 5 and 6.

Philosophy has been more popular in some places than others and some traditions promote and esteem wisdom more than others. As long as there has been language and dialogue there has been argument and debate. It is no coincidence that those people who are the quickest to dismiss philosophy as idle talk, are those who are most often dim-witted conformists, afraid to think for themselves or disagree with what they were taught as children. Those in particular who end arguments by saying that "its all relative", are supporters of imperialism and the justice that does not exist. Chapters 7 and 8 deal with questions about the relationship between ethics and knowledge and the relationship between philosophy and religion.

There are many traditions in the world, and the American ideal at its best is that of tolerance of different cultures and different traditions. This is highlighted by pragmatism, America's most remarkable contribution to the world and the human search for truth and understanding. This book celebrates the non-relativity of ethics and celebrates those movements which celebrate diversity.

Philosophy itself is a precarious field in America or has been since at least 1492. Be that as it may, America is one of the hardest working countries in the world, and there are many here for whom self-sacrifice is the norm and working hard is the standard. This book attempts to reintroduce Americans to the crucial link between work and study, action and knowledge, practice and theory, fact and value, and truth and love –a combination of which are needed in order to properly complement America's diligence and fortitude with better reason and greater and greater wisdom.

Preface 11

Nick Ruderman
Cas-Cad-Nac *(Abenaki for 'mountain with a rocky summit')*
Ascutney, Vermont
4 October, 2008
Revised 17 October, 2009

---

[1] Albert Camus, *The Rebel*, trans. Anthony Bower, (New York, Alfred A. Knopf, 1954) p165
[2] Smedley D. Butler, Major General, United States Marines (Retired), *War Is A Racket*, (Gainesville, Florida, Crises Press, 1995), VII
[3] Butler, p7
[4] This was legalized by passing the USA PATRIOT Act in 2001. The preliminary work on the subject is Nancy Chang's, *Silencing Political Dissent,* (New York, Seven Story Press, 2002). The Patriot Act was just renewed for 2010 by the Senate Judiciary Committee. See Charlie Savage's, "Judiciary Panel Approves Patriot Act Sections", *New York Times*, October 8, 2009
[5] *Gandhi: Selected Writings*, ed. Ronald Duncan, (London, Harper & Row, 1972) p192
[6] Charles Sanders Peirce, *The Architectonic Construction of Pragmatism*, originally published in the 1902 *Dictionary of Philosophy and Psychology*, ed. J.M. Baldwin, quoted in *Pragmatism: The Classic Writings*, ed. H.S. Thayer, (Indianapolis, Hackett Publishing Company, 1982), p50-51
[7] Hilary Putnam, *The Collapse of the Fact/Value Dichotomy and Other Essays*, (Cambridge, Massachusetts, Harvard University Press, 2002) p30-31
[8] Thayer, p11
[9] Charlene Haddock Seigfried, in *The Cambridge Dictionary of Philosophy*, Second Edition, ed. Robert Audi, (Cambridge, Cambridge University Press, 1999) p731
[10] West has also written a great deal about Christian philosophy as well, beginning with his first book *Prophesy Deliverance! An Afro-American Revolutionary Christianity* (1982). Putnam's latest book is an excellent discussion of Jewish philosophy titled, *Jewish Philosophy as a Guide to Life* (2008). Many of the classical pragmatists were Christian such as William James and Josiah Royce, while Peirce came to prefer Buddhism. Dewey and Santayana were raised Calvinist and Catholic respectively but became apostate. Jane Addams was of Quaker descent. Holmes may or may not have been an atheist.
[8] Hilary Putnam, *Reason, Truth and History*, (Cambridge, Cambridge University Press, 1981) p151
[11] The 20th Amendment unamended the 18th.
[12] On the Daily Show with Jon Stewart. 2/7/07. See also Nader's, *The Seventeen Traditions*, (New York, Harper, 2009)
[13] Harry Frankfurt, *On Bullshit*, (Princeton, Princeton University Press, 2005)
[14] Frankfurt, p63-64. Italics mine.
[15] Aristotle, *Posterior Analytics*, Book I, Chapter 1, 71a28, in *The Philosophy of Aristotle*, trans. Sir W.D. Ross, ed. Renford Bambrough, (New York, Mentor Books, 1963), p161
[16] People often don't realize that Socrates, Plato, and Aristotle were all fallibilists.
[17] "We can agree that decision follows or implies belief. But this is irrelevant... For decision involves reason and thought... for what we decide to do is what we have judged as a result of deliberation." Aristotle, *Nicomachean Ethics*, trans. Terence Irwin, (Indianapolis, Hackett Publishing, 1985), 1112a11, 16, 1113a

1

Strategic Pragmatism

"Here, starting from this third person, is the proximity of a human plurality. Who, in this plurality comes first? Here is the hour and birthplace of the question: a demand for justice! Here is the obligation to compare unique and incomparable others; here is the hour of *knowledge* and, then, of the objectivity beyond or on the hither side of the nudity of the face; here is the hour of consciousness and intentionality."
-Emmanuel Levinas[1]

    The verb 'refute' is defined in Webster's Dictionary as "to overthrow by argument, evidence, or proof: to prove to be false or erroneous: Confute." To begin this merriment lets start with some refutations while having the reader's full attention. There is an all-too powerful assumption that those who are critical of the US government are anti-American. Or as the President of the Free World decreed: *If you are not for us, you are against us*. This is an error in reasoning called a False Dilemma, or as it is sometimes referred to -the Either/Or Fallacy.

    In Classical American Logic, however, there isn't just an either/or of reasons but there are three types of reasoning, or forms of inference. Deductive Reasoning: where the conclusion follows necessarily from the premise(s). Inductive Reasoning: where the conclusion follows probabilistically from the premise(s). And Abductuve Reasoning (or Retroduction): where the conclusion follows hypothetically from the premise(s). A Fallacy is universally an error in reasoning.

    What kind of error in reasoning did President George W. Bush commit when he said that *If you are not for America, you are for the terrorists?* Again the Either/Or Fallacy, wherein reality is falsely represented as being only one of two or more possibilities. For example, someone might say you are either black or you are white, or either you speak Greek or you are a Barbarian, you're either left-handed or you're right-handed, either you're a republican or you're a democrat, either you're for America, or you are for the terrorists.

    According to this *False Dichotomy*, as it is sometimes called, there is a mutual exclusivity where choice is falsely limited to one of two options. We are made to believe that reality is so neatly divided between binary opposites, good vs. evil, an omnipotent God who grapples with the Devil.

    There is another popular adage from the leaders of the free world: *Freedom Isn't Free*. Freedom isn't free. Freedom isn't free? Hey, if freedom isn't free -what *is* freedom? how much does it cost? It's like saying that independence is dependent. Or, infinity is finite. Oh, so good isn't the opposite of evil, they are really the same thing? Rather, this political adage that 'freedom isn't free' is a violation of the Law -the Law of Non-Contradiction. It can't be raining and not raining, simultaneously. The conviction that it could was called by the English novelist George Orwell, *doublespeak*.

    After all what about the Mexicans who are trying to come across the border but are being shot? Aren't these North American Mexicans for America, and not against

---

[1] Emmanuel Levinas, "Diachrony and Representation" in *Time and The Other,* trans. and ed. by Richard Cohen, (Pittsburgh, Duquesne University Press, 1987) p106

America? Didn't they democratically agree to opening up the North American borders for Free Trade?

Another crooked line of reasoning by the executive 'branch' runs like this: There are people critical of the US government. Terrorists are critical of the US government. Therefore people critical of the US government are terrorists. This error in reasoning is called the Fallacy of the Undistributed Middle, and is another violation of the Law. By the very same reasoning, the Executive branch would also infer that: All US citizens are North American. All Mexicans are North American. Therefore, all Mexicans are US citizens. Vraiment? (Really, I live closer to French Canada, Les Quebecois.) In all actuality, the Law of the Distributed Middle exists because of reason and not nationality.

There are perhaps millions of bumper stickers on petroleum-burning cars that tell us that we as US citizens don't support our own army if we don't support a war declared by the Executive Branch. This is a formal Error in Reasoning known in Logic as the Fallacy of Denying the Antecedent. This two-premise fallacy can be stated:

1) If A then B; 2) Not A. Therefore Not B.

An example of Denying the Antecedent can be: 1) If you fly then you travel. 2) You don't fly. Therefore, you don't travel. One does not need to go to college to know that this type of reasoning is perfectly false. NFL commentator John Madden did not fly, but traveled all over the United States analyzing and announcing football games, and as you read these words a Marine is in most likelihood low-crawling across Parris Island.

Many fans of President Bush said that in order to support our own troops we must support the war. Their argument runs: *1) If you support the war, then you support the troops. But because 2) you don't support the war, you don't support the troops.* This is the opposite of true, and is false. It is false reasoning to think that it doesn't probably follow that people who are anti-war are anti-military. One of America's greatest war protestors, Major General Smedley Butler, is the most decorated United States Marine in American History, having fought on nearly every continent in the world, receiving many wounds in the process. He was one hell of a model American. Butler courageously delivered many speeches denouncing war and racism, and in 1935 wrote an anti-war book titled, *War Is a Racket*. At the outbreak of the current US Wars on Afghanistan and Iraq, Retired Generals Anthony C. Zinni and Wesley Clark, among many other distinguished experts in their craft, stood as great examples of US citizens opposed to the US War on Iraq. Or are we to believe that the information given to us by the US Commander in Chief from 1988-1992, George Herbert Walker Bush –that Iraq is no longer a threat- was in fact a cover-up? This seems to be the presumption of the son.

In political thought there is often a confusion between individuals and institutions. This is the most common problem with all bureaucracies: the problems of representation and accountability. In a democracy the governing is supposedly done by the people, especially the majority of the people. The United States, however, has a representative democracy, which means it is a particular kind of democracy - a bureaucratic democracy. In America there is a bureau of officials –senators, presidents, and judges, etc… who decide if the American people want to go to war. Sometimes the majority are represented, often times they are not, as we saw for example in the 2000 election, where the majority of votes did not win the election.

The reliance on an ambiguity or confusion between citizens and their so-called representatives, or ambivalence between these two forms of democracy rests upon two types of fallacious reasoning. These are called the Fallacy of Division and the Fallacy of Composition. It is these two complimentary types of bad reasoning which seem to govern political rhetoric, often creating a great deal of false nationalism and patriotism, revealing the commonality between the declaration that who is not for us is against us, the imperialist trope, 'Divide and Conquer'.

This error in reasoning consists of the confusion between parts and the whole, depending upon the direction of fit. For example, Shaquille O'Neill is a great basketball player. But even if all his teammates are great basketball players, this doesn't make them a great team. This is a Fallacy of Composition, where it is believed the parts equal the whole. Similarly, a great team mustn't necessarily be made up of great players. Thinking so would be an example of the Fallacy of Division, or the belief that the whole is equal to its parts.

In the outbreak of the US entering the Second World War, it was said that the Japanese attacked Pearl Harbor. Now it would certainly be hard to believe that every Japanese man, woman, and child traveled thousands of miles across the Pacific Ocean to attack Pearl Harbor. This is the Fallacy of Division. In fact, it was Japanese soldiers under the orders of Japanese bureaucrats who attacked Pearl Harbor on December 7, 1941. When on August 6th and November 15th, 1945 the US dropped two nuclear bombs on Japanese people who had not attacked Pearl Harbor, this was the error of reasoning called the Fallacy of Composition[2], because the US was not us, but Harry Truman.[3]

All logic aside, what does it mean to be an American? Does it mean only to pursue the American Dream? To get rich or die trying? Or is America something that is fantastic –like the celebration of what is great, or standing up for those who are oppressed, as say the American revolutionary Thomas Paine who stood for women's rights, or Henry David Thoreau who stood up for Mexicans during America's war on Mexico, or President Abraham Lincoln, who put an end to slavery?

One of the greatest living American heroes is Muhammad Ali. Not only was Muhammad Ali a gold-medal Olympian and a three-time Heavyweight Champion of the World: he was one of the most vocal opponents of US imperialism. When in 1966 word began to spread that Muhammad Ali had been drafted to fight in the Vietnam War, Ali refused to go, and told reporters among other things, "I ain't got no quarrel with them Vietcong."

Many of those who are opposed to the current US war with Afghanistan and Iraq are starting to learn something, not in spite of our efforts. We are learning that we must work toward overcoming our own racism before we can begin to work toward overcoming war. And the reason the anti-war movement of the 60's was so much stronger than the anti-war movement of today was because of the civil-rights movement. The anti-war movement in the 60's rode the back of the civil rights struggles that had been going on for at least a decade. From the bus boycotts in Montgomery, Alabama in

---

[2] My thanks to Robert M. Johnson for introducing me to the fundamentals of Formal and Informal Logic, and William E. Mann for his discussions on these two modes of logic. See Robert M. Johnson's, *A Logic Book*, Third Edition, (Belmont, Wadsworth Publishing Company, 1999) and William E. Mann's, *The Languages of Logic*, (Lanham, University Press of America, 1979)

[3] Truman gave the orders to drop the bomb without Congress knowing.

1956, to the demonstrations in Birmingham in 1963, to the millions who marched on Washington where Martin Luther King addressed America and the world via radio and television. Under the banner of the civil rights movement millions of people had begun to march and demonstrate against the imperial policies of the US government. This civic arousal became the motivation for millions of Americans to find the will and moral strength to oppose the US war on Vietnam.

If Muhammad Ali had not disobeyed the law and had joined the army, it is more than likely that he would have never seen combat. Like celebrities who had been drafted before him, Ali would have been a troop celebrity, entertaining the men in boxing exhibitions, as well as furthering his stardom once he'd finished his two years. Or he could have chosen to join the Army Reserves or National Guard, as say President George W. Bush did to avoid combat, though not all reservists are the sons of CIA chiefs.

Muhammad Ali, however, was not motivated by fear. To the contrary, Ali presented unprecedented bravery. Ali was a trained fighter, rated number in the world with his fists, yet he now chose pacifism and civil disobedience. This is because he was guided by a very strong ethic that was new to America, or at least forgotten since the League of the Iroquois ruled New York. In 1967, Ali was arrested for pacifism and sentenced to five years in prison at the height of his career, banned from the sport he loved.

Forty years later there is a very similar treatment of Muslims in America. Like Muhammad Ali, Muslims today are under constant FBI surveillance. In the last 8 years alone, thousands of American Muslims have been arrested, harassed, intimidated, and their phones tapped and homes invaded by a Homeland Security that begs all reasoning.[4]

The path of civil disobedience had been chosen by others before Muhammad Ali, and Martin Luther King (1929-1968) stood as one of its greatest proponents. Martin Luther King was in turn influenced by the Hindu lawyer Mohandas Gandhi (1869-1948) who studied the English Common Law in London to lead a successful revolution against the British in the first half of the 20th century. This was achieved through nonviolence and civil disobedience in opposition to the imperialism and foreign occupation of the British Empire. Gandhi's philosophy of *ahisma,* or non-violent civil disobedience, helped join Hindus and Muslims together in the struggle to overcome the imperial methodology of 'divide and conquer', and end the violent occupation.

Before Gandhi, civil disobedience had been practiced in early 19th century Massachusetts by the land-surveyor Henry David Thoreau (1817-1862). Thoreau first used the phrase "civil disobedience" in his opposition to the imperialism of both slavery in America and the US war on Mexico. In 1849 Henry wrote:

"When a sixth of the population of a nation which has undertaken to be the refuge of liberty are slaves, and a whole country is unjustly overrun and conquered by a foreign army, and subjected to military law, I think that it is not too soon for honest men to rebel and revolutionize. What makes this duty the more urgent is the fact, that the country so overrun is not our own, but ours is the invading army."[5]

The practice of civil disobedience is a choice of action. While some might call civil disobedience 'theoretical', just an impractical ideal that cannot have political effect,

---

[4] An early documentation of this phenomenon was done by Nancy Chang, who is the senior litigation attorney at the Center for Constitutional Rights in New York City. Check her informative study, *Silencing Political Dissent*, (New York, Seven Stories Press, 2002), though of course the numbers have only increased in the last eight years.
[5] Henry David Thoreau, *Civil Disobedience,* (New York, Dover Publications, 1993) p4

historically, it has been effectively practiced, working through strategy and forethought, creating upheavals of social prejudice, ushering social cohesion and solidarity. Civil disobedience is a practical philosophy with its origin in America and should be understood as a form of pragmatism: an American philosophy that has changed the world.

Pragmatism emerged from the very place where Thoreau had studied in his youth: Cambridge, Massachusetts. The philosophy of pragmatism began in the late 19th century with the mathematician and logician Charles Sanders Peirce (1839-1914). If the opening of this essay demonstrated the poor logic of a person such as Bush II, this is certainly not the case here. Peirce (pronounced 'purse') is one of the greatest and most influential logicians and his work helped to revolutionize and formalize logic and introduce new categories of reasoning. Peirce both directly and indirectly influenced many other pragmatist thinkers of his generation, as for example the psychologist William James (1842-1910), the philosopher Josiah Royce (1855-1916), the pacifist and feminist Jane Addams (1860-1935), the sociologist George Herbert Mead (1862-1931), the writer George Santayana (1863-1952), the educational reformer John Dewey (1859-1952), and Supreme Court Justice Oliver Wendell Holmes (1841-1935).[6]

Pragmatism means 'practicalism' and is founded on three basic tenets: 1) naturalism, 2) pluralism, and 3) fallibilism. Naturalism in philosophy denotes a commitment to explanations that are not magical or super-natural. All environmentalists are naturalists, but some naturalists are more interested in sociology: the study of peoples. This brings in the second basic tenet of pragmatism: pluralism. Pluralism is the belief that along with there being many peoples there are many truths, many kinds of truths, and some truths are perspectival -they depend on one's perspective, like a personal truth. This perspectivism helps introduce the third tenet of pragmatism: fallibility. If some truths are dependent upon a certain perspective, claims to universality are fallible, which means they are capable of being wrong. For example, I think it is a fact that William Shakespeare wrote *Hamlet*. However, someone more skilled in the art of literary authentication, or philology, might disagree with me. And who knows what DNA evidence will uncover in the future -maybe Julius Caesar wrote the play? I could be wrong.

It is the pragmatist tenet of fallibility that is most often criticized. Critics of fallibility claim that the only alternative to dogmatism and certainty is the impossibility of knowledge, aka, skepticism. This was the position of Bush II and Cheney and all spoiled-brats who are too self-righteous to admit when they've been proven wrong. From a misunderstanding of the tenet of fallibilism, or the practical belief that error is possible, some have gone so far as to argue that skepticism is a possible psychical reality –in other words, it is imagined that there could be a person who could truly doubt everything. This is also the most common critique of pragmatism -that the principle of fallibility leans too

---

[6] Peirce had credited the philosopher Immanuel Kant as in influence, who used the word 'pragmatism' (*pragmatisch*) in *The Metaphysics of Morals*, albeit in a more definite and narrow sense. Bertrand Russell believed that pragmatism "was first promulgated by [Karl] Marx" in 1845. Dewey had credited the English philosopher Francis Bacon (1561-1626) as the "prophet of a pragmatic conception of knowledge." John Dewey, *Reconstruction in Philosophy* (1920), (Boston, Beacon Press, 1957) p38; Bertrand Russell, *Human Knowledge: Its Scope and Limits*, (New York, Simon and Schuster, 1948) p421-422; Charles S. Peirce, "What Pragmatism Is" (1905), from *Selected Writings: (Values in a Universe of Chance)*, ed. Philip P. Weiner, (New York, Dover Publications, 1958) p183

heavily on skepticism and leads to either faithlessness, or skepticism's corrosive neighbor –ethical relativism.

Whether such criticism is significant, pragmatists usually find that such global skepticism is a nuisance and is both impractical and unrealistic. Moreover, most pragmatists claim that such an absolute skepticism is inconsistent and contradictory. As Santayana simply put it, "Believe, certainly; we cannot help believing; but believe rationally, holding what seems certain for certain, what seems probable for probable, what seems desirable for desirable, and what seems false for false."[7]

Live Free or Die?

Because of the three tenets of pragmatism: naturalism, pluralism, and fallibilism, pragmatism tends to be in opposition to imperialism, as we saw in the case of Henry David Thoreau. Imperialism, or the wanton use of power -that is, the abuse of power -at first glance seems to counter at least the latter two tenets of pragmatism: pluralism and fallibilism. Imperialism as a force eliminates any questioning or reasoning that might reveal the possibility of error. This in turn works to eliminate plurality and diversity so that only the one goal remains: the imperialist ideology (be it a kind of socialism, capitalism, anarchism, nationalism, racism, homophobia, or some combination therein).

It is sometimes argued that the ultimate goal of imperialism is peace or utopia. For example, the feminist Charlotte Gilman supposedly sought to eliminate all non-European races and create a paradise where only women lived. Such a vision has peace and happiness as its goal, but is guided by hatred and stupidity. The tenets of pluralism and fallibilism leave us to wonder at what price such peace is worth, and whether anything of value would remain once violence had been justified. As the Buddha (563-483 BCE) said, "Not by enmity are enmities quelled, whatever the occasion."[8]

Early in their lives, both Gandhi and the English logician Bertrand Russell (1872-1970) had advocated imperialism, particularly British Imperialism. When they came to change their minds, they became opposed to imperialism and became advocates for non-violence. For example, when the Boer War began in 1899, a war between the imperial army of the British against the Dutch colonists in South Africa, Russell described himself as a Liberal Imperialist, living comfortably in England. When in 1901 Bertrand returned home from a poetry reading and witnessed a friend suffering from "an unusually severe episode of pain", he was stricken by the experience and underwent an immense realization.

"Suddenly the ground seemed to give way beneath me, and I found myself in quite another region. Within five minutes I went through some such reflections as the following: the loneliness of the human soul is unendurable; nothing can penetrate it except the highest intensity of the sort that religious teachers have preached; whatever does not spring from this motive is harmful, or at least useless; it follows that war is wrong, that a public school education is abominable, the use of force is to be deprecated, and that in human relations one should penetrate to the core of loneliness in each person and speak to that."

---

[7] George Santayana, *Character & Opinion In the United States*, (Garden City, Doubleday Anchor Books, 1956) p54
[8] Siddharta Gotama Buddha, *The Dhammapada*, trans. John Ross Carter and Mahinda Palihawadana, (Oxford, Oxford University Press, 1987) 1:5

"...Having been an imperialist, I became during those five minutes a pro-Boer and a pacifist."[9]

In the years to come, Bertrand Russell would be arrested for preaching pacifism at the outbreak of the First World War in 1914. Following World War II Russell protested nuclear proliferation with Albert Einstein[10], and was banned from teaching at the City College of New York because of his pluralist conception of marriage. Along with the French existentialist *philosophe* Jean-Paul Sartre, they led a mock-trial on US foreign policy, known as the Russell Tribunals, which set an example for the International Law of the future. In Bertrand Russell's influential work, *A History of Western Philosophy*, written shortly after the Second World War, he warned his Western audience of the invidiousness of imperialism:

"There is an imperialism of culture which is harder to overcome than an imperialism of power. Long after the Western Empire fell –indeed until the Reformation –all European culture retained a tincture of Roman imperialism. It has now, for us, a West-European imperialistic flavour. I think that, if we are to feel at home in the world after the present war, we shall have to admit Asia to equality in our thoughts, not only politically, but culturally. What changes this will bring about, I do not know, but I am convinced that they will be profound and of the greatest importance."[11]

Gandhi too, was arrested practicing civil disobedience, or *Satyagraha*, which was called a "threat" by the British government. When the English declared war on the Zulu people Gandhi was practicing law in South Africa and volunteered to be a medic and tend to the wounded Zulus. He said at the time that he "believed that the British Empire existed for the welfare of the world."[12] He soon changed his mind. In his autobiography, Gandhi stated:

"The Boer War had not brought home to me the horrors of war with anything like the vividness that the [Zulu] 'rebellion' did. This was no war but a man-hunt, not only in my opinion, but also in that of many Englishmen with whom I had occasion to talk."[13]

In 1909 Gandhi wrote a revolutionary treatise titled *Hind Swaraj, or Indian Home Rule*, in which he formally turned away from the British Empire. He explained: "I bear no enmity towards the English but I do towards their civilization."[14] When Gandhi returned home at the end of World War I he began the civil disobedience and non-cooperation movement which would end British occupation over the people and territories that are now referred to as Bangladesh, India, and Pakistan. Gandhi taught that "Before one can be fit for the practice of civil disobedience one must have rendered a willing and respectful obedience to the state laws."[15] Under this banner of non-violence,

---

[9] Written by Bertrand Russell in 1951, *The Autobiography of Bertrand Russell: The Early Years: 1872-World War 1*, (New York, Bantam Books, 1969) p194

[10] Albert Einstein himself had written, "It is easier to win over people to pacifism than to socialism. Social and economic problems have become much more complex, and it is necessary that men and women first reach the point where they actually believe in the possibility of peaceful solutions. Once this has been accomplished, they may be expected to approach economic and political problems in a spirit of cooperation. I would say that we should work first for pacifism, and only later for socialism." From "Einstein on Peace," p124, quoted in *Albert Einstein: The Man and His Theories*, ed. Hilaire Cuny, trans. Mervyn Savill, (New York, Paul S. Eriksson, Inc., 1965) p118-119

[11] Bertrand Russell, *A History of Western Philosophy*, (New York, Simon and Shuster, 1945) p400

[12] Mohandas Gandhi, *An Autobiography: The story of My Experiments With Truth*, trans. Mahadev Desai, (Boston, Beacon Press, 1993) p313

[13] Gandhi, *Autobiography*, p315

[14] Mohandas Gandhi, *Hind Swaraj, or Indian Home Rule*, (Ahmedabad, Navajivan Publishing House, 1938) p92

[15] Gandhi, *Autobiography*, p470

millions of Muslims and Hindus effectively worked together for revolution, routing the imperialists and the promoters of class division.

In this spirit occurred the Iranian Revolution of 1979. *Time* magazine's Man of the Year, the Muslim scholar and cleric Ayatollah Ruhollah Mousavi Khomeini successfully led a non-violent revolution against the White Revolution of the King of Iran, Shah Pahlavi. The Shah of Iran had been the longest standing dynasty, stretching 2,500 years, having somehow survived the pagan conquests of Alexander the Great, the wars with Byzantine, the Christian crusades of the Holy Roman Empire, as well as the reaches of the Muslim Ottoman Empire of Turkey. Although exiled from Iran for 16 years, Khomeini spread his word of revolution through pamphlets and books, and the distribution of recorded lectures on tape. Khomeini's non-violent revolution has often been called the "Cassette Revolution", and it successfully ended Western imperialism in Persia. Preaching a message against the imperialism of divide and conquer, the non-division between Shia and Sunni, he told the Iranian people:

"We must fight the army from within. We must fight from within the soldier's hearts. Face the soldier with a flower. Fight through martyrdom, because the martyr is the essence of history. Let the army kill as many as it wants, until the soldiers are shaken to their hearts by the massacres they have committed. Then the army will collapse, and thus you will have disarmed the army."[16]

Living a few miles from the state of New Hampshire, I see that all of the foreign-oil burning cars have two license plates, both of which say, "Live Free or Die". This is much like a phrase uttered by Patrick Henry during the American Revolutionary War, "Give me liberty or give me death". These are justifications for martyrdom, and it is hard to think of one war wherein many of the participants were not positive that they would die in battle. Without sacrifice, ethics is illusory. Though we may not believe in aggression and advocate pacifism, we should understand that someone would be willing to sacrifice their life in the name of freedom and liberty, or some other cause that is foreign to us autonomists and libertarians. This was the understanding of those involved in the trench warfare of World War I, the kamikaze pilots of World War II, and the martyrs who carry explosives on themselves in an effort to end foreign occupation. As Gandhi told the occupying British forces, "I beg you to accept that there is no people who would not prefer their own bad government to the good government of a foreign power."

One of the most influential of recent proponents of civil disobedience was the first democratically elected president of South Africa, Nelson Mandela. Mandela and the African National Congress worked to end apartheid, which had been a power structure set up by the British even before Gandhi had lived in South Africa. Mandela told his followers that, "peace is a more effective way of gaining a new South Africa than the use of violence."[17] For many years Nelson Mandela was listed as a terrorist by the US government, as for example, during the Reagan administration.

The Cold War and The War on Terror

If Muhammad Ali was arrested for pacifism, one cannot imagine a Muslim in America today being arrested for pacifism, if only because we have been made to think of

---

[16] Quoted by Dilip Hiro, *Iran Under the Ayatollahs*, (New York, Routledge & Kegan Paul, 1985) p100
[17] Nelson Mandela, *Nelson Mandela Speaks*, (New York, Pathfinder Press, 1993) p233

Islam as violent and dangerous by the US government, the co-opted US media, and the inherited imperial European tradition. Within just a few months after September 11th thousands of Muslims were arrested without charges, and thousands of more innocent people have been falsely arrested and harassed in the name of Homeland Security since the fall of 2001. This had happened to 110,000 American's of Japanese descent who were placed in concentration camps for the entirety of the Second World War, as suspected terrorists.[18]

The Bush administration, like the Reagan administration used the word 'terrorism' in order to describe the enemies of the state. This is much like the US Declaration of Independence, after admitting it be self-evident that all men are created equal and that humans all have inalienable rights, ends by warning against the "merciless Indian savages". This is called 'State Terrorism'. As the French-Algerian writer Albert Camus put it in his study on "State Terrorism and Rational Terror" –"as long as enemies exist, terror will exist".[19] In fact, the US General William Yarborough who led Special Forces on missions in Columbia admitted to having been a terrorist.[20] Israel's first Prime Minister Moshe Dayan called the Irgun Zvai Le'ummi organization, which was commanded by the future Prime Minister Menahem Begin, a terrorist organization, saying it took part in terror activities and reprisals.[21]

The War on Terror has an uncanny resemblance to the Cold War, and the one came right after the other. The Cold War began at the end of World War II in Europe with the Russians toppling Berlin and the defeat of the Nazis by the American, British, and Russian armies in 1944. The Allied nations divided Germany into several sections with the Russians controlling the East, and the victors of World War II instilled different political forms. On the one hand there was the communism of Russia and the Maoist revolution of China, which were socialist and anti-capitalist. And there was capitalism of the US, which marshaled a Western Europe that was in tatters at the end of the war. Co-opted by the US under and Marshall Plan, the Western European nations were enlisted to help fight off the spread of socialism.

This post-World War II era, (sometimes called the 'Third-World War' because of wars by developed countries on the third-world), is called a "Cold" War because, while there were real casualties over it's 50 years, the battles were to a large extent *ideological*. The Cold War and the War on Terror are similarly ideological wars, meaning they are/were based to a great extent on labels, stereotypes, rhetoric, and misrepresentations.

The violent side of the Cold War consisted of a nuclear arms race between the US and Russia, wherein thousands of nuclear missiles were manufactured and are still stored away, as well as the US sponsorship of third world revolutionary and counterrevolutionary factions in Korea, Vietnam, as well as the Taliban in Afghanistan, and any number of South American dictators. In the Russian-Afghanistan War that lasted

---

[18] For the facts check Nancy Chang's, *Silencing Political Dissent*, (New York, Seven Story Press, 2002). Some died during interrogation –check Akbar S. Ahmed, *Islam Under Siege*, (Cambridge, Polity Press, 2003) p40
[19] Albert Camus, "State Terrorism and Rational Terror", *The Rebel*, trans. Anthony Bower, (New York, Alfred A. Knopf, 1954) p154
[20] Noam Chomsky, *Hegemony or Survival: America's Quest for Global Dominance*, (New York, Henry Holt and Company, 2003) p192
[21] Moshe Dayan, *Moshe Dayan: The Story of My Life*, (New York, William Morrow and Company, 1976) p78

through the 1980's, Muslims were persecuted and killed. It was during this conflict that the US sponsored the Taliban to fight against the Russian aggressors.

On the surface the Korean and Vietnam Wars appear to have been civil wars between the northerners and the southerners, like the American Civil War. However, in reality they were manifestations of the Cold war between the US and Russia, who picked sides, supplying weapons, oil, and military training. The troubles which occurred in parts of Africa and Asia, as for example, in Rwanda, Sudan, Uganda, Israel/Palestine, Afghanistan, Pakistan, India, and many, many other places, all stem from problems created by the victors of World War II, though it would be safe to say this was also resultant of the five-hundred year colonial movement in general which began with Columbus.

One of the most famous ordeals of the Cold War occurred during the early 1950's, in what is popularly known as the McCarthy Hearings. Named after the US senator Joseph McCarthy, the McCarthy Hearings were conducted in an attempt to vilify and defame Americans who were accused of being communists by McCarthy himself. This list of "communists" was sometimes in the hundreds and included members of government, military generals, celebrities, and citizens of notoriety. McCarthy and his fellow inquisitors took on the most grave persona and heir of indubitable certainty concerning an immanent danger at hand.

Through the use of fear and intimidation and an unthinking conviction of their own righteous infallibility, it was determined that those labeled as communists were subversive, plotting, dangerous, and a threat to homeland security. Any American "soft on communism", including the media and citizens and government-officials alike, were cowed into submission as the government violated citizens rights.

The resemblance between the Cold War and the War on Terror becomes even uncannier when we are reminded of how many people were pushed around by the US government in the days following September 11, 2001. If the Vietnamese were labeled as terrorists by the US government at the height of the Cold War, the War on Terror has Muslims playing the role of scapegoat (or an oily Red Herring), more than 10 years after the fall of the USSR and the end of the Cold War. One might even say that in the 21st century Muslims are either attacked, arrested, or killed in nearly the same way as the Jews of Europe during World War II.[22]

What is unseeming about the US government and media during the entirety of the US wars on Afghanistan and Iraq thus far, is the necessity of labeling each non-American according to their religion, even if the occurrence is seemingly unrelated. To cite just one headline in an American newspaper: "Rival Sunni Factions Battle".[23] With such precision as the goal in reporting, we are left to wonder how anyone could be called a racist. Why during the US wars with Afghanistan and Iraq are all non-American combatants characterized by their religion, and not vice-versa? Can it be imagined that during the American Civil War each troop and casualty was labeled by their religion? A newspaper headline of 1863 might have read: "Rival Christian Factions Battle", or "Rival Baptist Factions Battle", or "Three Catholics and three Protestants Died in Battle".

---

[22] For this interpretation see Oren Jacoby's 2007 documentary *Constantine's Sword*, based on James Carroll's book of the same title. http://constantinessword.com
[23] From *The Valley News*, 11/11/07

It is popularly understood that the Irish Revolution was, like the genocidal Thirty-Year War during the 17th century, a war between Catholics and Protestants.[24] Whether these labels hold true or not, like the labels 'communist', 'terrorist', 'faction', or 'insurgent' it seems such designations are capable of distracting us from appreciating the plain fact that revolutions are often against imperialism and insurgents are often against foreign conquest and occupation, and are not just violent ideological and religious disagreement.

But perhaps we ought to turn such a mirror around and see if perhaps the US war on Afghanistan and Iraq could be viewed as a religious war. A retired Colonial from the Army recently told me it doesn't help that the US troops are Christians invading a Muslim country. President Bush himself, with the infallibility of executive fiat, called the War on Terror a "Crusade". What are crusades? How many have there been? When were they? Why did they happen? When did they end?

Proposed Roads to Zion: Crusade or Jihad?

Perhaps paradoxically it is popularly claimed that religious wars have been around for some time. Within the Hebrew and Christian Bibles there are many wars that take place, and this is true of most other religions as well. Are we to infer that God is pro-war? In discussing the question of the religiousness of war we should ask whether 'religious wars' are religious in the sense of their being fought for religious causes, or if a 'religious war' is referred to as thus because it is fought by groups of people who happen to be religious.

For example, the British fought against the Germans in both World Wars yet both nations are Christian, or were ruled by democratically elected Christian officials. Both World Wars were instigated by Christian nations, and some 80 or 90 million Christians died, in what some have called the most suicidal events in world history. The Crusades, on the other hand, were fought because of religious bigotry and through religious justification. The Crusaders fought believing they had a moral obligation to do the work of God, though some earnest historians argue that the Crusades were fought for plunder and piracy. We should not be so romantic as to forget that of 8 or 9 Crusades, the Christians lost nearly 100% of the time.[25] History is writ thus.

The Crusades were Holy Wars issued by various popes, monarchs, clergy, as well as citizens. Their scope included conquering the 'Holy Land' (which plays a significant role as the location of the second coming of Jesus) as well as the biblical call to spread Christianity. This mission of spreading Christianity entailed the forced conversion and execution of Pagans, Muslims, Jews and the elimination of 'bastardized' forms of Christianity such as that of the Gnostics, Donatists, and Catharis, among other believers.

---

[24] Check James Carroll, *Constantine's Sword*, (New York, Mariner Books, 2001) p407; Ronald H. Bainton, *Christian Attitudes Toward War and Peace*, (Nashville, Abingdon Press, 1960) p151. Bertrand Russell, *New Hopes for a Changing World*, (New York, Simon and Schuster, 1951) p91. Russell writes that by the end of the Thirty-Years War (1618-1648) the population of Germany had been halved. British historian Norman Davies puts the numbers as having gone from a population of 21 million to 13 million, or a death toll of roughly 33 percent. *Europe: A History*, (New York HarperCollins, 1998) p568

[25] This is not true of the Northern Crusades where Norway, Sweden, and Finland were crushed and forced to convert. (Davies, p362)

When the Christians took Jerusalem in 1096 for the last time before World War I, not a woman or child was spared.

According to the Western governments and media there is an Islamic equivalent to the Christian crusade: it is called *Jihad*. Jihad is an Arabic word that is often translated by the US Executive branch and much of the Western media as meaning 'war'. Similarly, a Hebrew word that is applied to both Jewish and Christian soldiers alike, is *Zionist*. Could these three concepts –crusade, jihad, and Zionism –be seen in some way as being the same?

Zionism as an ideology has existed before the time of the Babylonian Exile, eight centuries Before the Christian Era (BCE). When the Babylonians, led by Nebuchadnezzar, conquered Judea in 586 BCE the Jews were exiled from Palestine/Israel. This lasted some 50 years until the year 536 BCE when the Zoroastrian Cyrus the Great and the Persians, or modern day Iranians, (Iran means 'the land of the Aryans'), defeated the Babylonians and provided for Jews to return to Palestine/Israel. The quest for and proof of Zion is described by the pre-exilic prophet Isaiah:

"For out of Zion shall go forth the law, and the word of the Lord from Jerusalem. And He shall judge between the nations, and shall decide for many peoples; and they shall beat their swords into plowshares, and their spears into pruning-hooks; nations shall not lift up sword against nation, neither shall they learn war any more." (Isaiah 2:3-4)[26]

Isaiah describes a Zion where humans no longer fight, animals no longer quarrel, lions feed on grass, and wolves and sheep dwell together. Isaiah prophesies a utopian Zion, saying: "They shall not hurt or destroy in all My holy mountain [Mt. Zion]; For the earth shall be full of the knowledge of the Lord, as the waters cover the sea." (Isaiah 11:9)

Modern Zionism, as opposed to that of the original biblical or prophetic vision, according to the Palestinian refugee Edward Said, is the child of "Western ideological parents".[27] The theory of Modern or Western Zionism was created in 1896 by Theodor Herzl, and put into practice by the British Empire in November of 1917. Since 1516, Palestine had been a province of the Muslim Ottoman Empire. Following the end of World War I and the fall of the Ottoman Empire, the Middle East was for the most part split into different European colonies. In 1917 the British government drafted the Balfour Declaration after years of planning between Chaim Weizmann and the British Lord Arthur Balfour. Lord Balfour had already worked in many of the British colonies including India, Egypt, and Sudan and had fought in such wars as the British wars against Afghanistan, the British wars against the Zulus, the British wars against the Boers in South Africa, and Balfour had also been involved in the Russo-Japanese War.[28]

Modern Zionism is, according to Edward Said's study, *The Question of Palestine:*

"Zionism essentially saw Palestine as the European imperialist did, as an empty territory paradoxically 'filled' with ignoble or perhaps even dispensable natives... Zionism and European imperialism are epistemologically, hence historically and politically, coterminous in their view of resident natives, but it is how this irreducibly imperialist view worked in the world of politics and in the lives of people for whom epistemology was irrelevant that justifies one's looking at epistemology at all."[29]

---

[26] All references to the Torah and the Tanach will be from the Masocretic Text, (trans. and published by The Jewish Publication Society of America, 1917)
[27] Edward W. Said, *The Question of Palestine*, (New York, VintageBooks, 1992), p26
[28] Edward W. Said, *Orientalism*, (New York, Vintage Books, 1979) p31
[29] Said, *The Question of Palestine*, p81, 83

By the end of World War II there was a dire question over the repatriation of the European Jews, two-thirds of whom had been killed in the *Shoah*, or Holocaust.[30] The millions of European Jews who survived were at first put in camps by the British. This lasted until an 'illegal' exodus began to the British controlled Palestine, which at the time, already had a considerable number of residents, a little less than 33% of whom were Jewish.[31] In 1947 the United Nations voted to make Palestine/Israel into just Israel, a region that the English had been militarily occupying for 30 years already. The author of *The War of the Worlds* wrote that before this UN vote, an anti-occupation guerilla war had been going on between the British Empire and the native Palestinians for some time. H.G. Wells wrote that "even before 1939 it was clear that the worse was yet to come."[32] Edward Said explains the changing global importance that the Israel/Palestine region was to play for the rest of the 20th century, and which has been the case in the 21st century, thus far.

"It was perfectly apparent to Western supporters of Zionism like Balfour that the colonization of Palestine was to be made a goal for the Western powers from the very beginning of Zionist planning: Herzl used the idea, Weizmann used it, every leading Israeli since has used it. Israel was a device for holding Islam –and later the Soviet Union, or communism –at bay."[33]

There are Zionists who do not believe that Zionism entails the imperialism of the Crusades. And as we saw in its original context in Isaiah, Zionism was a longing for freedom, peace, and universal law, all of which were guaranteed to occur according to the prophetic tradition. Interestingly both the original Zionism of Isaiah and the Modern Zionism of the Balfour Declaration were buttressed by foreign powers: on the one hand the Persian Empire, and on the other hand the British Empire and the United Nations. However, the Zionism that was created eight centuries before Christianity differs from the Zionism that followed Christianity. This is for several reasons, including the new nationalist vision of *Messianism*, or belief in the Divine Right of Kings.

Arabic is an ancient language, thousands of years old and Islam began fourteen centuries ago. The Arabic word *jihad* does not have a specific or 'special' reference to it in either the Quran or in the Arabic literature that come before or after Islam emerged. Although President Bush II believed jihad literally means "war", for those who are more linguistically affluent jihad is more accurately translated as "striving" or "exertion".[34] If we look at a contemporary use of the word jihad in the Islamic world, for example, in the Islamic Republic of Iran, we find there is an organization called *Jihad-I sazandigi*. This literally means, "jihad for construction", and works to build houses for the poor. As a verb and not a noun (or institution, such as war), jihad is similarly used during prayer, in fasting, in overcoming ignorance, and attaining knowledge.[35]

A *Crusade* on the other hand, is more along the lines of 'divide and conquer'. As Ronald Bainton put it in his classic study, *Christian Attitudes Toward War and Peace:*

"The crusade suffers from the assurance not to say the arrogance of all elitism. It is the war of a theoretically minded community which seeks to impose the pattern of the Church upon the world... Those

---

[30] Two-thirds of the 18 million who died in the Holocaust were a mix of Poles, Germans, Russians, and Roma (Gypsies).
[31] Said, *The Question of Palestine*, p11
[32] H.G. Wells, *The Outline of History*, Volume II, (New York, Doubleday & Company, Inc., 1956) p903
[33] Said, *The Question of Palestine*, p29
[34] David Waines, *An Introduction to Islam*, (Cambridge, Cambridge University Press, 1995) p283
[35] Seyyed Hossein Nasr, *The Heart of Islam*, (San Francisco, HarperCollins, 2002) p257, 259

who have fought in a frenzy of righteousness against the enemies of God –or of the democratic way of life- are disposed to demand unconditional surrender..."[36]

The present US Crusade against the natives of the "Holy Land" comes in lieu of the 'Millennium' or end of a thousand year period, a belief that the Western calendar is aligned with vague, if magical, interpretations of the New Testament, Modern Zionism, and of course the desert Messiah: oil.

Religion and Philosophy

To a non-religious person such as myself, there can be a kind of perplexity over why there are so many different religions, and more importantly, why they can't all 'just get along'. A look at both history and current events forces us to ask the question whether all of these religions are compatible or whether they are just 'a cauldron of animosities'.

Some religions, especially the most popular ones, seem to be ridden with histories of violence, while other religions which seem to have had fewer conflicts, are often marked by their own peculiarities. Some religions seem more tolerant while others, less so. Each religion has different particularities and different generalities. Some religions hold that there is one God or Goddess, some hold there are two gods, some hold there are many gods and goddess's, and some religions hold that there are no gods or goddess's at all.

In philosophy it is perhaps more simple. Philosophers have at least since the time of the ancient Chinese or Greeks argued and debated, proving and refuting each other in questions over what is good, right, just, and true. Of course not all arguments are won or lost and many problems and questions are never solved or resolved. Be that is it may, since the dawn of thought people have at times successfully used reason to change their minds and the minds of others for the better or greater good.

Why should someone be religious? How often do people choose their religion, anyway? Why should someone study philosophy? Which philosophy ought one to study? What is so practical about thinking or arguing for that matter? Aren't philosophy and religion completely separate entities, or are there places where they overlap?

In southern Italy in the 6th century BCE, the influential mathematician and philosopher Pythagoras started his own religion based on mathematics and philosophy. The 'Pythagoreans', as his followers are called, believed that all reality was mathematical, or was comprised somehow of numbers. Pythagoreans were vegetarians as well, believing that people are sometimes reborn as animals, and we should therefore not eat our ancestors.

The 5th century BCE Greek philosopher Heraclitus criticized the followers of the god Bacchus (sometimes called Dionysus) for being alcoholics and for being shameless, idolatrous, and decadent. The 5th century BCE philosopher from modern day Turkey, Anaxagoras, was invited to Athens to teach philosophy and was found guilty of impiety by the democratic citizens. This also happened to Protagoras (d.420) who was found guilty of impiety and was exiled. Socrates and Plato were critical of the mythical stories surrounding the Greek gods. They believed that the popular stories told about the gods

---

[36] Bainton, *Christian Attitudes Toward War and Peace*, p243

and goddesses which depicted them as scheming, ignorant, and dishonest were, like so many of the popular decadent art forms: irrational, unrealistic, and appealing to what is most trivial and childish. Socrates himself was accused of worshiping false gods as well as corrupting the Athenian youth. He was found guilty by a jury of five hundred and was sentenced to death 399 years before the birth of Jesus.

The last of the ancient Greek philosophers, the Skeptics, were critical of and uncommitted to religion. Typically the best doctors and physicians belonged to one of the schools of skepticism.[37] Their schools were closed in the year 529 by the Christian Holy Roman Emperor Saint Justinian I, because of Christian protest and his own bigotry. Historians believe this to be the beginning of the Dark Ages of Europe. However, their medical practice was continued in Spain, or Andalusia as it was called, less than two centuries later. During the time of the Dark Ages, religion and philosophy flourished together in Africa, Asia, the Middle East, and Spain due to the spread of Islam.

Philosophy reentered Europe when Christian scholars such as the Italian theologian Thomas Aquinas (1225-1274) began studying the Islamic commentaries on Aristotle. Aquinas' major work, *Summa Theologiae*, quotes Aristotle some 3,500 times.[38] Logic then became an integral part of Scholastic, or Medieval European Philosophy. However, the skeptical or fallibilist aspect of philosophy would not return until the 16th or 17th centuries with such thinkers as the Englishman Francis Bacon (1561-1626) and the Frenchman Rene Descartes (1598-1650).

One of the first European philosophers to reconsider the position of fallibilism was the son of three generations of Christian Lutheran Pastors, Friedrich Nietzsche (1844-1900). While studying theology in Germany in 1865, Nietzsche came to wonder why he should be religious given the possibility of skepticism. In a letter to his sister, Nietzsche concluded that one's choice in religion is arbitrary and inscrutable.

"If we had believed since youth that all salvation came not from Jesus but from another –say, from Mohammed –is it not certain that we would have enjoyed the same blessings? To be sure, faith alone gives blessing, not the objective which stands behind the faith. I write this to you… only in order to counter the most usual proofs of believing people, who invoke the evidence of their inner experiences and deduce from it the infallibility of their faith. Every true faith is indeed infallible; it performs what the believing person hopes to find in it, but it does not offer the least support for the establishing of an objective truth."

"Here the ways of men divide. If you want the achieve peace of mind and happiness, then have faith; if you want to be a disciple of truth, then search. Between, there are many halfway positions. But it all depends on the principal aim."[39]

Nietzsche argued that the question of whether one ought to be religious and the question of what religion one ought to choose are both indeterminable for the same reason: he held the search for truth to be a totally different affair, given the possibility of skepticism.[40]

One of the most celebrated arguments in favor of religious belief by any writer is that of the American pragmatist William James in his 1896 lecture, "The Will to

---

[37] The three Skeptic schools of medicine, the Logical, Empirical, and Methodical, are discussed by Philip Hallie in his edition of selected writings by *Sextus Empiricus*, (Indianapolis, Hackett Publishing, 1985)
[38] James Carroll, *Constantine's Sword*, p305
[39] Dated June 11, 1865, *Selected Letters of Friedrich Nietzsche*, ed. and trans. by Christopher Middleton, (Chicago, University of Chicago Press, 1969) p7
[40] Although Nietzsche's hero Arthur Schopenhauer (1788-1860) had argued in favor of Buddhism over Western religions, Nietzsche eventually did go on to praise such religions as Hinduism, Buddhism, and Islam.

Believe". In this lecture James argues that religiosity is preferable to skepticism. He argues that if certain truths are for the time being unknowable, one is better to adopt a believing attitude because, whether or not the belief is really true, the rewards are potentially extravagant and no bad consequences can result if one is wrong. Either believe in heaven and be rewarded or in truth there is no heaven and one with a believing attitude loses nothing. How many converts this argument has made is uncertain. Perhaps the orthodox would consider such an argument blasphemous.

As for the question over *which* religion to choose, James argues that we ought to go with the decision that has the greatest appeal to force. He offers such dilemmas someone might have, such as whether to: "Be an agnostic or be a Christian" or "Be a theosophist or be a Mohammedan [Muslim]".[41] Whichever side of the argument has the greatest and most genuine force will be the best answer, in lieu of the evidence.

James would later (1901-1903) deliver a much greater and more pluralistic work aptly titled, *The Varieties of Religious Experience* in which he attempted to interrelate the many different religions. This was accomplished through psychological analysis of the different religious practices. However, James' attitude of there being a separation between philosophy and religion remained. He wrote: "The question, What are the religious propensities? And the question, What is their philosophical significance? Are two entirely different orders of question from the logical point of view…"[42] Under James' pragmatism, one religion cannot be more philosophical or reasonable than another. He writes:

> "Philosophy in this sphere is thus a secondary function, unable to warrant faith's veracity… In all sad sincerity I think we must conclude that the attempt to demonstrate by purely intellectual processes the truth of the deliverances of direct religious experience is absolutely hopeless."[43]

This question over the comparability of philosophy and religion was handled by the 20th century philosopher Ludwig Wittgenstein (1889-1951).[44] Wittgenstein held to the view that the religious cannot be explained or reduced to the philosophical because religion and philosophy are essentially foreign to one another. For Wittgenstein religious belief does not need, and more significantly, cannot have justification. This conception is known as 'Fideism'. For a Fideist certain beliefs and practices do not need justification, because where faith is concerned, logic is inapplicable and irrelevant. As Wittgenstein himself had early on garrulously said, "Whereof one cannot speak, thereof one must remain silent."[45]

For the Fideist there are ways of thinking which are fundamentally foreign to one another and which cannot be translated or interrelated. The rationale of fideism is similarly used in the philosophy of science and is called the 'incommensurability thesis'. This is the idea that certain theories, systems, or classes of ideas are fundamentally

---

[41] William James, "The Will to Believe", in *Essays in Pragmatism*, ed. Alburey Castell, (New York, Hafner Press, 1948) p89. As has been pointed out by others, James' "Will to Believe" is almost identical to an argument for belief made by the French philosopher Blaise Pascal (1623-1662), called "Pascal's wager".
[42] William James, *The Varieties of Religious Experience*, (New York, Macmillan Publishing, 1961) p23
[43] James, *The Varieties of Religious Experience*, p355
[44] See Ludwig Wittgenstein, *Lectures and Conversations on Aesthetics, Psychology, and Religious Belief*, ed. Cyril Barrett, (Oxford, Blackwell, 1966)
[45] Ludwig Wittgenstein, *Tractatus Logico-Philosophicus*, trans. D.F. Pears and B.F. McGuinness, (London, Routledge, 2000) First published in 1922.

incomparable and different ; there are some things that cannot be compared or judged and are thus 'incommensurate'. Its like apples and oranges.

Whether or not one finds the arguments for Fideism and incommensurability to be arbitrary and capricious, the notions of separate and discreet classes of incomparability became fundamental to the work of Karl Marx (1818-1883) and Friedrich Engels (1820-1895). Marx and Engel's *Communist Manifesto*, written in 1848, has influenced billions of people, as well as countless political and social revolutions. The *Manifesto* begins by explaining that the "history of all hitherto existing society is the history of class struggles."[46] For Marx and Engels human history is comprised of a struggle between two opposing classes, between the haves and the have-nots, or the Bourgeois and the Proletariat.

For Marx and Engels, as well as the new philosophy *anarchism* that emerged after the *Manifesto*, reality is made up of two incommensurable classes that struggle with one another. This "class war" is one between factory owners and workers, the rich and the poor, and not one between religions, which for Marx are all commonly "opiate[s] of the masses".

Marx and Engels were influenced by the writings of the scientist Charles Darwin (1809-1882) who believed that the wars of culture and civilization would result in genocide.[47] Marx and Engels and the anarchists, believed the class war would become increasingly more violent, though this must occur in order that the classless society, or utopia, to emerge.

One thing that has emerged, as we can see with all of these individuals, is the widespread belief that religion and philosophy are two totally different things. If Karl Marx, Friedrich Engels, and the anarchists are right that human reality consists of class war, or if Nietzsche was right that faith is opposed to the search for truth, or if William James was right and the choice of one's religion only extends to the level of cultural or emotional enforcement, or if Ludwig Wittgenstein is right that religious belief does not licit justification -it seems there can be no relation of reason to faith, or faith to reason.

Under the view of these thinkers who all agree that religion and philosophy are unrelated, there is an appeal to non-rational criteria and a belief that reality is inscrutable to reason. This seems to be what results from the belief that reality is a totality of facts, or that faith is purely subjective and indiscernible to philosophers. Apparently all we are left with is conformity and allegiance, if we are looking to explain peoples belief systems.

The question of the propensity toward conformity was explored by the psychologist Sigmund Freud (1856-1939). Freud held an opposing view to these thinkers just mentioned, believing that in fact religion and philosophy have a great deal to do with each other. Freud had spent a good part of his life talking with and listening to non-philosophical people, in the attempt to help them explain how they arrive at their beliefs and problems. In his later writings especially, Freud applied all he had learned from his studies in an effort to account for this phenomena of conformity.[48]

In his 1913 study, *Totem and Taboo*, Freud compared the studies of different non-European societies with his own studies in the psychoanalysis of his fellow Europeans.

---

[46] Karl Marx and Friedrich Engels, *The Communist Manifesto*, (New York, Bantam Books, 1992) p17
[47] Charles Darwin, *The Descent of Man*, in the selections from *On Evolution*, ed. Thomas F. Glick and David Kohn, (Indianapolis, Hackett Publishing, 1996) p246
[48] My thanks to Charles Guignon for introducing and discussing with me the works of Freud and others.

Freud made an effort to bridge the gap between the social and psychological, between the studies of societies and cultures as a whole, and his own psychological studies of the individual mind. He finds, for example, that his fellow Europeans current in his day were just as given to superstition as those foreign cultures considered at the time to be "savages".

Freud was particularly curious over which had primacy: the individual mind or the structure and norms of society? His own studies in Europe showed:

> "The psycho-analysis of individual human beings, however, teaches us with quite special insistence that the god of each of them is formed in the likeness of his father, that his personal relation to God depends on his relation to his father in the flesh and oscillates and changes along with that relation, and that at bottom God is nothing other than an exalted father."[49]

Something that has been pointed out is the number of philosopher's without a parent. Descartes (1598-1650) lost his mother when he was 2. Pascal's (1623-1662) mother died when he was 10. Thomas Hobbes (1588-1679) was abandoned by his father at a young age. Spinoza's (1632-1677) mother died when he was 6. The co-inventor of the calculus Gottfried Leibniz (1646-1716) was 6 when his father died. The skeptic David Hume (1711-1776) lost his father at 3. At 13 both Kant's (1724-1804) and Hegel's (1770-1831) mothers died. Jeremy Bentham's (1748-1832) mother died when he was 11. When Arthur Schopenhauer (1788-1860) was 17 years old his father committed suicide. Nietzsche (1844-1900) lost his father when he was 4. Bertrand Russell (1872-1970) lost his mother and father when he was 2. When Malcolm X (1925-1965) was 6 years old his father was murdered. Jean-Paul Sartre's (1905-1980) father died when he was 2.

Similarly, Confucius (551-479) and Aristotle (384-322) were orphaned at a very young age, Moses' (13th century BCE) father was forced to abandon him when he was an infant, during his life Jesus was considered by many to be fatherless, and Muhammad (570-632) never knew his father.

The Catholic historian James Carroll notes that etymologically the Latin word *Emancipation* "refers to a son's being set free from the domination of his father".[50] Although Zeus killed his father Cronus, we need not conclude that freethinking requires parricide. Zeus was, for example, dishonest, unfaithful to his wife, and a slave of passion who secretly impregnated mortal women. Anyone familiar with the story *Lord of the Flies* already has an understanding of why we would not want children making our political decisions. As it is, Mother Earth seems to be in tough enough of a predicament with those humans that she has nourished through generations of adolescence.

Because of the problem of conformity, or the inheritance and spread of bad habits and weak beliefs, 2500 years ago Plato favored the city-state of Sparta over his own democratic city-state of Athens. This was because of the Spartan practice of parental-anonymity, so that a child did not know its parents. This ensured that individual prejudices were not handed down through generations, and that some children were not loved less than others. It is tempting to reply to this Spartan view of Plato's that it is probable such a social structure created an even greater atmosphere of conformity, if not fraternity.

---

[49] Sigmund Freud, *Totem and Taboo*, trans. and ed. by James Strachey, (New York, W.W. Norton & Company, 1989) p182.
[50] James Carroll, *Constantine's Sword*, p414

There is a pervasive ignorance of the role that philosophers and their philosophies and religions have played in shaping history, both politically and ideologically. A better way of discussing the relationship between religion and philosophy is to discuss the relationship between faith and reason. For example, both philosophy and religion come together is in their aspiration for truth, truth being justified true belief. And discussing the link between faith and reason gets more to the heart of the question over which kind of philosophy or religion is most practical or the most realistic. This is exemplified in the study of logic.

Logic was studied by the ancient Hindus as well as the followers of Confucius. The Confucian school of logic, *Ming-chia,* was started in 4th century BCE by the philosopher and Prime Minister Hui Shih (380-305). The Hindu Mimamsa school of logical analysis was started somewhere between the 5th-4th centuries BCE by the philosopher Jaimini, who authored the *Mimamsa Sutra.* It was sometime in the 4th century that Aristotle began to study logic.

In 431 of the Common or Christian Era (CE) the writings of Aristotle were banned from Christian Europe by the Council of Ephesus, and the tradition of logical analysis inaugurated by Aristotle went with it. Although the Roman philosopher Boethius (480-525) worked to translate the logical work of Aristotle into Latin, he was shortly thereafter found guilty of treason and was executed by the state. However, from this time forward the logic of Aristotle was studied in Syria (5th century) and then in Spain by Arabic, Jewish, and Islamic philosophers and mathematicians.[51]

Logic was disseminated through the works of such religious thinkers as Abu Yusuf al-Kindi, or in Latin, *Alkindus* (800-870 CE) often called "the philosopher of the Arabs"; from Turkestan Abu Nasr al-Farabi, or in Latin *Abunaser* (870-950 CE); the Persian Ibn Sina, or in Latin *Avicenna* (980-1037), from Iran Abu Hamid al-Ghazali, or in Latin *Algazelis* (1058-1111); the Arabic Ibn Rushd, or in Latin *Averroes* (1126-1198) who was referred to by the medieval Christian philosopher Thomas Aquinas as "the Commentator"; the Jewish philosopher Moses ben Maimon, or in Latin *Maimonides* (1135-1204) who wrote a *Treatise On The Art of Logic,* and was called by Aquinas, "the Rabbi"; the French theologian and philosopher Peter Abelard (1079-1144) who wrote works on *Logica ingredientibus* and *Dialectica* and used the works of Aristotle and Boethius; the Scottish philosopher Duns Scotus (1266-1308), who was greatly influenced by the writings of the Muslim philosopher Ibn Sina (Avicenna); and lastly the Italian Thomas Aquinas (1225-1274) himself, who made thousands of references to Greek, Muslim, and Jewish philosophers.

Notice that all of these Arabic names are Latinized. This is due to the heavy influence that Semitic philosophers had on the West. This was true in the area of logic, medicine, mathematics, and science. The German philosopher Josef Pieper, for example, has concluded that Ibn Rushd's (Averroes') "influence in the Latin West was so tremendous that the philosophy of the European Renaissance has with some degree of justice been called 'Averroism' –in itself an indication of the direction in which that influence operated."[52]

---

[51] Josef Pieper, *Scholasticism: Personalities and Problems of Medieval Philosophy,* trans. Richard and Clara Winston, (New York, McGraw-Hill Book Company, 1960), p103
[52] Pieper, p104

One thing that has traditionally separated philosophy from religion is the attitude toward things like superstition, magic, and the paranormal. Belief in magic, for example, can be found in religious and non-religious people alike. However, some religions are more philosophical than others. In fact, some religions are opposed to the belief in magic, as we see with the Chinese and Hindu philosophic schools of Ming-chia in China, and the Mimamsa in the Asian-subcontinent.

Judaism is also opposed to the belief in magic. When we look in the Torah, we find toward the end of the book of Genesis that the Egyptian Pharaoh is having a reoccurring dream that his magicians cannot decipher or dispel. The Pharaoh is both King of Egypt and head of the Egyptian religion and when Joseph correctly interprets Pharaoh's dream, the Jews are given a place above all others in Egypt. For some generations the Jews prosper there until there came a Pharaoh who knew not Joseph. The Jewish people became enslaved for 430 years, until Moses confronts the Pharaoh. The book of Exodus depicts the Pharaoh's magicians being defeated in battle by the brothers Aaron and Moses.

This contempt for the belief in magic is also true of belief in ghosts, spirits, oracles, or myths. The third book of the Torah, Leviticus, forbids the practices of divination and soothsaying (19:26) as well as the belief in ghosts and spirits (19:31). Yhwh (the Hebrew word for 'God') is against those who believe in ghosts and spirits. (20:6) Holding such beliefs is deemed unlawful (20:27). The last book of the Torah, Deuteronomy, lists as abominations the belief in divination, soothsaying, enchantment, sorcery, charming, and necromancy (18:10-11).

The prophet Isaiah condemned soothsaying (2:6) belief in ghosts (8:19), clairvoyance, and astrology. (47:13) The inefficacy of magic is pointed out several times in the Hebrew passages of the writings of Daniel. The writing Ecclesiastes says that the dead are no longer conscious (9:5), and the end of the Hebrew Bible, the Tanach, repeats the condemnation of soothsaying, enchantment, sorcery, or the belief in ghosts or spirits.[53] (2Chronicles 33:6)

However, as the Talmudist Louis Ginzberg points out, Judaism is also opposed to mythology, myth, and allegory as well. He writes that: "The hostility of the Jew to myth was continuously on the increase, and that which was objectionable to Israel in Biblical times became still more so in the rabbinic period."[54] According to Ginzberg, the aim of all allegorical interpretation of scripture is to "spiritualize mythology", and this type of reading is in opposition to there being a literal truth intended by an author, be they mortal or otherwise. For this reason Ginzberg is critical of writings such as the Hellenistic writings of Daniel, which Jews do not consider to be divine, and which interprets prophesy allegorically, like all mysticism and myth-mongering, something Ginzberg calls a "thoroughly Jewish dread".[55]

The holy book of Hindus, the Bhagavad-Gita, teaches us that people who are boring believe in spirits and ghosts (17:4). The question of magic, sorcery, ghosts, and spirits is a point of contention in Christianity. For example, Jesus is said to have cast out

---

[53] It should be noted that in the first book of Samuel, that Saul is depicted as asking a witch to summon the ghost of Samuel. (1 Samuel 28:8) Though this does sound impious, it should be noted that some Philistines kill Saul the next day.
[54] Louis Ginzberg, *On Jewish Law and Lore*, (New York, Atheneum, 1970) p63
[55] Ginzberg, p127-128

devils (Matthew 8:32, 12:27, 17:18, Mark 5:13, 9:25, Luke 8:29, 9:42, 11:19), to have walked on water (Matthew 14:26, Mark 6:49, John 6:19), to have increased five loaves of bread and a couple of fish to feed 5,000 people (Matthew 14:19, Mark 6:41, Luke 9:16, John 6:11), and to have turned water into wine (John 2:9).[56] The New Testament is critical of at least one 'magic-user' named Simon (Acts 8:9), one 'sorcerer' named Bar-Jesus (Acts 13:6), and something called 'spiritism' which is witchcraft (Galatians 5:19, Revelation 21:8, 22:15). The emphasis on the split between body and soul, however, does seem to point toward the belief in spirits after all. Jesus tells us: "The spirit, of course is eager, but the flesh is weak." (Matthew 26:41)[57]

The Quran of Islam condemns sorcery (2:96, 7:117), recounting how Moses defeated the Egyptian sorcerers (10:81, 26:44), and how Jesus was accused by many of being a sorcerer (5:110, 26:153, 185, 61:6). The Quran also opposes belief in demons (4:54) and something called 'divining-arrows' along with gambling. (5:4, 93)

Both the sociologists Max Weber and Maxime Rodinson agree that people who believe in magic are bad with money.[58] The Quran informs us, "the sorcerer prospers not, wherever he goes." (20:72) Rodinson notes that, "In so far as magic is used in trial by ordeal, it obstructs the rationalization of law." In Christianity, on the other hand, at least during the European middle ages, "magical notions obtained for a long time in the domain of law, with practices like trial by combat, 'the judgment of God', and the various forms of ordeal. Nothing of this kind ever existed in Islam."[59]

Freud found through his studies that there is a certain kind of primitive intellect that believes that thoughts have magical powers. He called this belief in magical thinking the "omnipotence of thoughts". Omnipotence is a concept that means "all-knowing" and Freud found this to be the mental state of neurotics –their knowledge claims are not very realistic. Freud wrote that, "What characterizes neurotics is the fact that they prefer psychical [or mental] reality to factual reality and react just as seriously to thoughts as normal persons do to realities."[60] In so many words: if it can be believed then it must be true.

The pragmatist Hilary Putnam uses Freud's analysis of the phenomenon of magical thinking to discuss how there are also people who believe in a 'magical theory of reference'. Such a person will believe, for example, that the utterance of certain names

---

[56] The historian of Native Americans Francis Jennings discusses how much more superstitious the Christian colonists were than the Native Americans. Puritans, for example, believed in the efficacy of magic, the exorcism of demons, and of course the importance of executing 'witches'. See, *The Invasion of America: Indians, Colonialism, and the Cant of Conquest*, (New York, W.W. Norton, 1975) p50-51

[57] Martin Luther King, Jr., was critical of the moral separation of body and soul. He was also critical of supersticious belief and the belief in magic.

[58] The incapacity of all claims to magic is at least empirically verifiable in that no one claiming to have magical power has been able to win the million dollar reward promised by James Randi's non-profit organization which works to debunk magic. The One Million Dollar Paranormal Challenge was started in 1964 with a single donation of $1000. You'd think some poor schlep magician would go win the money already, at least for some charity. www.randi.org

[59] Maxime Rodinson, *Islam and Capitalism*, trans. Brian Pearce, (Austin, University of Texas Press, 1978) p97, 107

[60] Freud, *Totem and Taboo*, p198. He writes: "'Superstition' –like 'anxiety', 'dreams' and 'demons' –is one of those provisional psychological concepts which have crumbled under the impact of psycho-analytic research." (p121)

bestows them with magical powers.[61] Thoughts of the mind, under this magical conception, are corresponding representations of reality and one's own beliefs cannot fail to be truths.

What is so alarming about these arguments of Freud and Putnam is that 'magical thinking' and 'thought omnipotence' are seemingly as common today in self-proclaimed "civilized" nations as it was in medieval times or as is said to be the case in Third World countries. Contemporary examples of 'magical thinking' are found in the pervasive belief in the Divine Right of Kings –the belief that kings are divinely appointed. Magical thinking is found in those who claim knowledge of the immanent End of Times, and so many other instances of nationalism, imperialism, racism, sexism, classism, age discrimination, and religious discrimination. If people believe it then it must be true: such is the rule of conformity.

When President Bush told the world that he knew just who had committed the atrocities of September 11th and who was to be held responsible, though every possible hijacker was dead, he was using this kind of 'magical thinking'. Or when President Bush and Vice-President Dick Cheney claimed to know for a fact that Saddam Hussein and the Iraqi government had a hand in the atrocities of September 11, as well as stores of WMD's, or Weapons of Mass Destruction –was all, as it turns out, magical thinking. Eight years and thousands upon thousands of bodies and shattered families later, no WMD's have been found. When President Bush told voters that God spoke through him, Bush made use of this magical theory of reference.[62] And this is the type of specious reasoning which inspired Bush to tell the world that *if you are not for America you are for the terrorists.*

Strategic Pragmatism

As we see, magical thinking is also found in people's beliefs about history, about the future and the concept of time in general. This can take the form of *clairvoyance*, or belief in the infallibility of knowledge of the future. Or, as is not uncommon, belief in knowledge of the day and time of the apocalypse. The father of the Jehovah's Witness sect Charles Russell (1852-1916) (not to be confused with the earliest and strongest critic of the Vietnam War, Bertrand), aggressively evangelized his convictions of precisely which year would be the last, though he lived to be proven an ignoramus each time until his prophetic death.

Conversely, another version of magical thinking that has become particularly popular is the idea of the necessity of progress. This belief in the law of necessary progress has been an assumption in the Western world, at least since the Enlightenment of the 17th and 18th centuries. The belief in the necessity of progress was of course a step-forward from the magical thinking of the not too distant medieval times a few centuries earlier, when scholastics had a pessimistic understanding of human nature.[63]

---

[61] Hilary Putnam, *Reason, Truth and History*, (Cambridge, Cambridge University Press, 1981) p3
[62] Kevin Phillips, *American Theocracy*, (New York, Viking, 2006) p208
[63] All except the Catholic philosopher Peter Abelard (1079-1144) –my thanks to William E. Mann for making me aware of this.

According to such a magical theory of the necessity of progress we are to believe that humanity is along for a historical ride or journey to universal enlightenment. For those people who are still fighting against the aggressive occupation of a foreign army, or who happen to have some religion we do not understand, well, there is a learning curve. Those who don't get it, will sooner or later, realize they are wrong. Whether we call this the law of evolution or evangelism we, perhaps unintentionally, adopt the attitude that our 'race' or 'culture', or 'nation', or religion is further progressed, more civilized and further evolved than those of the less sophisticated and technocratic "third-world" countries.

We find the belief in the necessity of progress in William James' *Will to Believe*, as well as in the work of other philosophers of the modern era such as Georg Wilhelm Friedrich Hegel (1770-1831), Karl Marx, Friedrich Engels, the French sociologist Auguste Comte (1798-1857), and the Russian anarchist Mikhail Bakunin (1814-1876), as well as the followers of Darwin, including Thomas Huxley (1825-1895) and Herbert Spencer (1820-1903).[64] In 1831 Hegel wrote:

"But the Africans have not yet attained this recognition of the universal; their nature is as yet compressed within itself: and what we call religion, the state, that which exists in and for itself and possesses absolute validity –all this is not yet present to them. The circumstantial reports of the missionaries fully bear this out, and Mohammedanism [Islam] seems to be the only thing which has brought the negroes at all nearer to culture."[65]

No doubt, Hegel was an obedient conformist. And it seems the further we get from our own revolutions and civil wars the further we get from understanding the meaning and importance of other people's current struggles for independence. Or perhaps we are being lied to. When the media shows us footage from some of the many struggles still underway in the world, we are often left to think of these rebels or insurgents as barbaric or primitive, if only because the technology was not available at the time of our own revolution and civil war to record some of these gruesome images. Americans should know that there were perhaps thousands of summary executions during the revolution, and more Americans died in the Civil War possibly than in all other US wars combined. Truly, war is still a popular institution.

In a sense, it is difficult to imagine what people believe about the future if they do not believe in the necessity of progress, or as we saw with the scholastics and the Russelites (Jehovah's Witnesses), something more misanthropic or anti-human. We must ask then what prejudices this belief in progress thus creates in our conception of 'uncivilized' peoples of the third-world. The belief in progress becomes a belief in one kind of civilization. This is imperialism.[66]

Can pluralism be applied to the question of our own destiny? The pragmatist Hilary Putnam offers a more practical ethic concerning the belief in progress: he believes in the *possibility* of progress.[67] This is not a trivial distinction, but highlights the role that reason plays in the real world. This is best summarized by several clarifications made in

---

[64] To his credit and in contradistinction to his followers, Darwin did not believe in the necessity of progress. He believed there were going to be many more wars. Check his study, *The Descent of Man*.
[65] Georg Wilhelm Friedrich Hegel, *Lectures on the Philosophy of World History*, trans. H.B. Nisbet, (Cambridge, Cambridge University Press, 1975) p177
[66] Albert Camus' book *The Rebel*, shows the link between those with a revolutionary spirit and their belief in the necessity of progress. (p164-165)
[67] Hilary Putnam, *Ethics Without Ontology*, (Cambridge, Harvard University Press, 2004) p110

his book, *Reason, Truth and History*.[68] After arguing against the 'magical theory of reference' as being false, Hilary says that while "the determination of reference is social and not individual", "one's understanding of one's own thoughts –is not an *occurrence* but an *ability*." The belief that consciousness is (at least in part) an ability and not an occurrence, seems to counter the modernists who believe in an ostensibly supernatural justification for the mechanical necessity of progress. Putnam's account is of progress as an ability or possibility and not an occurrence or law of necessity. This is much more naturalistic, pluralistic, feasible as well as fallible. Perhaps this is why Putnam is known as the philosopher famous for having 'changed his mind', becoming a pragmatist.

If we look for precedent of progress in American history through the belief and practice of pragmatism, we will find that there have been many achievements. For example, prior to the signing of United States Declaration of Independence on July 4th, 1776, there had been a functioning democracy, America's first, for hundreds, perhaps thousands of years before Western progress had reached such succession. This first 'American' democracy was the Six Nations or Iroquois Confederacy: the Senecas, Cayugas, Onondagas, Oneidas, Mohawks, and the Tuscarora. Each tribe had made compromises that were viewed as practical in order to further their ecology, safety, and well-being. Speaking of pragmatism, the Iroquois were for centuries by and large a woman-run, or matriarchal society, a phenomenon still very uncommon amongst the more 'civilized' cultures. And in terms of ecological pragmatism, we in the 21st century United States have a great deal to learn from the Native Americans as industrial progress has practically over-polluted the US and the world.

The first pragmatics applied to religion were those of the man of two revolutions: the American Founding Father Thomas Paine (1737-1809). While his lengthy study from 1794-1795 of the Christian bible in the two-part *Age of Reason* had been mostly critical, in a later (1804) and lesser known pamphlet, Paine sought to highlight the reasonableness of a belief in a transcendent deity in, *The Religion of Deism Compared With The Christian Religion, and The Superiority of the Former Over the Latter*. He wrote:

"There is a happiness in Deism, when rightly understood, that is not to be found in any other system of religion. All other systems have something in them that either shock our reason, or are repugnant to it, and man, if he thinks at all, must stifle his reason in order to force himself to believe them... Here it is that the religion of Deism is superior to the Christian Religion... it avoids all presumptuous beliefs, and rejects, as the fabulous inventions of men, all books pretending to revelation."[69]

Pragmatists, however, have generally sought to show what is common or diverse amongst the various religions. William James, for example, sought to show that each religion equally shared in the holism, or sense of connectedness, in religious experience, and Josiah Royce sought to demonstrate that the concerns of religions are the same as the concerns of the community. Gandhi who, though he was Hindu, often read from the Quran during prayer, and Martin Luther King, who similarly fought against an unjust legal system, also utilized this pluralistic aspect of pragmatism. Both Gandhi and King studied Henry David Thoreau and found success through the practicality of nonviolent resistance and civil disobedience.

And even if we are as pragmatist's non-theists, as is my case, we do well to heed the advice of pluralism given in John Dewey's 1934 lecture, *A Common Faith*. He brings

---

[68] Hilary Putnam, *Reason, Truth and History*, p18,19
[69] www.deism.com/paine_essay01.html

to our attention a distinction between religion, on the one hand, and what is religious on the other, in advocating pluralism over universalism.

Dewey says that, "there is no such things as religion in the singular. There is only a multitude of religions." Attempts to prove religious universality "prove too much or too little", while any differences in religions can be so 'shocking' what remains common is 'meaningless'. For this reason Dewey concludes that: "Choice among religions is imperative, and the necessity of choice leaves nothing of any force in the argument from universality."[70]

John Dewey thus sets up a preference model for the pragmatism of religiosity that attempts to accommodate the three tenets of pragmatism: naturalism, pluralism, and fallibilism. Dewey believes that what is religious can best do without the belief in supernaturalism, which retards progress, and can do without the belief that only one religion exists, which then would hold a monopoly over values and ideals. Supernaturalism and the magical belief that there is only one religion strongly go against the three pragmatic tenets of naturalism, pluralism, and fallibilism.[71] He writes: "All religions…involve specific intellectual beliefs, and they attach –some greater, some less –importance to assent to these doctrines as true, true in the intellectual sense."[72]

Dewey found that since the First World War a general disorder, "has led to a revival of the theology of corruption, sin, and need for supernatural redemption."[73] Because of the different roles that moral responsibility plays, or the role that moral responsibility cannot play because of our sinful human nature:

"… it is inferred, we must resort to supernatural control. Of course, I make no claim to knowing how far intelligence may and will develop in respect to social relations. But one thing I think I do know. The needed understanding will not develop unless we strive for it. The assumption that only supernatural agencies can give control is a sure method of retarding this effort. It is as sure to be a hindering force now with respect to social intelligence…"

"The point to be grasped is that, unless one gives up the whole struggle as hopeless, one has to choose between alternatives. One alternative is dependence upon the supernatural; the other, the use of natural agencies."

Dewey believed that the best thing to do during the age of science is to emphasize the natural strengths of traditional belief. What is important is natural

"Were the naturalistic foundations and bearings of religion grasped, the religious element in life would emerge from the throes of the crisis in religion. Religion would then be found to have its natural place in every aspect of human experience that is concerned with estimate of possibilities, with emotional stir by possibilities as yet unrealized, and with all action in behalf of their realization. All that is significant in human experience falls within this frame."

"Men have never fully used the powers they possess to advance the good in life, because they have waited upon some power external to themselves and to nature to do the work they are responsible for doing… It involves no expectation of a millennium of good."[74]

These remarks were an echo of what Dewey had written in a 1930 reflection titled, *What I Believe*. The themes of naturalism, pluralism, and fallibilism can be found therein as well.

---

[70] John Dewey, *A Common Faith*, (New Haven, Yale University Press, 1934) p7-8
[71] However, as Louis Menand points out, William James tried to the end of his life to believe in mental telepathy among other forms of mysticism, though never unreservedly. In, *The Metaphysical Club*, (New York, Farrar, Straus and Giroux, 2001) p372
[72] Dewey, p29
[73] Dewey, p74
[74] Dewey, p76, 81, 57, 46

"It is impossible, I think, even to begin to imagine the changes that would come into life –personal and collective- if the idea of a plurality of interconnected meanings and purposes replaced that of *the* meaning and purpose. Search of a single, inclusive good is doomed to failure."

"A philosophic faith, being a tendency to action, can be tried and tested only in action. I know of no viable alternative in the present day to such a philosophy as has been indicated."[75]

What Is Greater

"Enlightened Moslems, accordingly, have often been more Epicurean than Stoical; and if they have felt themselves (not without some reason) superior to Christians in delicacy, in *savoir vivre,* in kinship with all natural powers, this sense of superiority has been quite rationalistic and purely human. Their religion contributed to it only because it was simpler, freer from superstition, nearer to a clean and pleasant regimen of life. Resignation to the will of God being granted, expression of the will of man might more freely begin." –George Santayana, 1905, *The Life of Reason*[76]

In a collection of dialogues titled *Breaking Bread*, the Christian feminist bell hooks and Christian pragmatist Cornel West offer a rich discussion about many current problems and ethical questions concerning institutions such as racism, sexism, politics, and religion, and they discuss ways in which we can make possible a resistance to these instances of imperialism. One principle that guides the openness and depth of their conversation is their commitment to what they call "vulnerability". Through this unguarded vulnerability hooks and West mean something like being emotionally 'available' or 'sensitive' to the other person so that one can learn about themselves and each other, and learn how to "promote non-market values such as equality, justice, love, care, and sacrifice in a society, culture, and world in which it is almost impossible to conceive of a[n]…alternative."[77]

hooks discusses how, for example, "the work of intellectuals is rarely acknowledged as a form of activism". She argues to the contrary of such a prejudice:

"Oftentimes intellectual work compels confrontation with harsh realities. It may remind us that domination and oppression continue to shape the lives of everyone, especially Black people and people of color. Such work not only draws us closer to the suffering, it makes us suffer… When intellectual work emerges from a concern with radical social and political change, when that work is directed to the needs of the people, it brings us into greater solidarity and community. It is fundamentally life-enhancing."[78]

As hooks and West's discussion makes plain -this avail-ability, or vulnerability, or openness, or fallibility -is the secret of pragmatism. When there is a pragmatic of ethics, such as that of Henry David Thoreau who sacrificed his own freedom for the lives of Mexicans and Africans, or Thomas Paine who assisted the French in their revolution, which got him imprisoned and nearly cost him his head during the Reign of Terror, or when Paine made the sacrifice to get published declarations of the rights of women, Native Americans, and Africans -there is a substitution, a one-for-the-other, of putting

---

[75] John Dewey, *What I Believe*, in *The Essential Dewey, Volume 1*, ed. Larry A. Hickman and Thomas M. Alexander, (Bloomington, Indiana University Press, 1998), p25, 28
[76] George Santayana, *The Life of Reason, Or The Phases of Human Progress*, (New York, Charles Scribner's Sons, 1955) p471
[77] bell hooks and Cornel West, *Breaking Bread: Insurgent Black Intellectual Life*, (Boston, South End Press, 1991) p101
[78] hooks and West, p164

another above oneself. This was done by John Dewey during the trial of the Communist exile Leon Trotsky, though Dewey was not a Marxist, and Dewey had stood up for Bertrand Russell, who was banned from teaching at the City College of New York because of his tolerance for open-marriages. Though not a minority, Dewey was instrumental in developing the NAACP, or the National Association for the Advancement of Colored Persons. This book is a call for substitution.

Although he was not a pragmatist, the 20th century philosopher Emmanuel Levinas inspires the strategy of this work in pragmatism.[79] To sum up Levinas' philosophy in three words: Truth Presupposes Justice. Accordingly, ethics comes before all other concerns and pursuits and could demand my own self-sacrifice. As Levinas tells us: "My freedom does not have the last word; I am not alone."[80] In his 1984 publication, *Ethics As First Philosophy*, Levinas's prologue confers:

"My being-in-the-world or my 'place in the sun', my being at home, have these not also been the usurpation of spaces belonging to the other man whom I have already oppressed or starved, or driven out into a third world; are they not acts of repulsing, excluding, exiling, stripping, killing?"[81]

"In the face of the other man I am inescapably responsible and consequently the unique and chosen one." For Levinas, ethics lies in a "capacity to fear injustice more than death, to prefer to suffer than to commit injustice, and to prefer that which justifies being over that which assures it."[82]

"...what I permit myself to demand of myself is not comparable with what I have the right to demand of the Other. This moral experience, so commonplace, indicates a metaphysical asymmetry: the radical impossibility of seeing oneself from the outside and of speaking in the same sense of oneself and of others, and consequently the impossibility of totalization..."[83]

Under such exigencies, according to Levinas, I must substitute myself for the other person who is the persecuted. This is exemplified in the face-to-face relation with the other person, where sincerity is found in making one's self-available to the other's suffering. Through the import of sincerity, Levinas shows that justice is victory over rhetoric.

"Truth is thus bound up with the social relation, which is justice. Justice consists in recognizing in the Other my master. Equality among persons means nothing of itself; it has an economic meaning and presupposes money, and already rests on justice –which, when well-ordered, begins with the Other. Justice is the recognition of his privilege qua Other and his mastery, is access to the Other outside of rhetoric, which is ruse, emprise, and exploitation. And in this sense justice coincides with the overcoming of rhetoric."[84]

This ethical substitution and work of strategic pragmatism was made by the Frenchman Emile Zola who in the 1890's came to the defense of Captain Alfred Dreyfus, a man accused of treason. Captain Dreyfus had been one of the first Jewish citizens to become a high-ranking officer in the French navy. He was conspired against by some conniving officers and accused of giving away French military secrets to Germany. The trial gained international attention and many French newspapers turned the whole

---

[79] Hilary Putnam finds a link between Levinas and pragmatism in his work *The Collapse of the Fact/Value Dichotomy*, (Cambridge, Harvard University Press, 2002) p132n36
[80] Emmanuel Levinas in 1961, *Totality and Infinity*, trans. Alphonso Lingis, (Pittsburgh, Duquesne University Press, 1969) p101
[81] Emmanuel Levinas, *Ethics As First Philosophy*, in *The Levinas Reader*, trans. Sean Hand and Michael Temple, ed. Sean Hand, (Oxford, Blackwell Publishers, 1989) p82
[82] Levinas, *Ethics As First Philosophy*, p84, 85
[83] Levinas, *Totality and Infinity*, p53
[84] Levinas, *Totality and Infinity*, p72

Dreyfus affair into a racist campaign.[85] Although Zola was not Jewish, he and other *Dreyfusards* became outraged by the ignorance and bigotry of some of their countrymen. It was Zola's book, *J'accuse...* ("I Accuse") that worked to dispel the racism and anti-Semitism that were on the rise due to the Dreyfus Affair. Zola too, was in turn found guilty of defamation by the French courts and he escaped to England for his own safety, though of course both he and Dreyfus were eventually exonerated.

The ethics of substitution had been made early in American history when the Dutch clerk Edward Hart who along with other citizens of Flushing, Queens, New Amsterdam (now called New York) petitioned on December 27th, 1657 against a law banning Quakers from living in the area. Although they were thrown in jail, as well as the farmer John Browne in 1662, their substitution of themselves for those being discriminated against stands as an example of ethical substitution, for none of them were Quakers themselves.[86]

Such an ethic lives in the spirit of the Danish King who wore the yellow badge during the Nazi occupation of Copenhagen.[87] The yellow badge, or *Sciamanno,* was a piece of clothe with the star of David which Jews were required to wear by the Nazi law and before then by the Catholic church, upon the decree of the Fourth Lateran Council of 1215. This decrial lasted until 1799 when Napoleon and the French conquered Europe, making illegal any law that discriminated against people according to their religion or race, ending the Inquisition against Muslims and Jews.

This ethical substitution was made by the French existentialist *philosophe* Jean-Paul Sartre, who fought in the French Resistance during World War II. Sartre had also, as we saw at the behest of Bertrand Russell, co-conducted the 'Russell Tribunals' in 1966, also known as the 'International War Crime Tribunals', which sought to make the world aware of atrocities being committed in the Vietnam War. Though Sartre was an atheist, born of parents who were Protestant Christian, his book, *Anti-Semite and Jew,* worked to refute anti-Semitism and end hatred against Jews. He argued that the anti-Semite as a conformist "attaches himself to a tradition and to a community –the tradition and community of the mediocre." Accordingly, "there is a passionate pride among the mediocre, and anti-Semitism is an attempt to give value to mediocrity as such, to create an elite of the ordinary."[88]

This ethical substitution was done in the work of James Carroll whose book, *Constantine's Sword*, is written with a great deal of knowledge and sympathy about the history of Christian European laws against other religions such as Judaism and Islam. He writes for "everyone who recognizes in the Holocaust the dark heart of our civilization."[89] Carroll was himself a priest for several years and writes as a dedicated Catholic ethicist.

When in 1967 Muhammad Ali was arrested for pacifism and for defying the US law, he told a reporter from *Sports Illustrated:*

"Why should they ask me to put on a uniform and go ten thousand miles from home and drop bombs and bullets on brown people in Vietnam while so-called Negro people in Louisville are treated like

---

[85] Carroll, p462
[86] Kenneth T. Jackson, "A Colony With a Conscience", in the *New York Times,* December 27th, 2007
[87] Davies, p121
[88] Jean-Paul Sartre, *Anti-Semite and Jew*, trans. George J. Becker, (New York, Schocken Books, 1965) p22, 23
[89] Carroll, p63

dogs? If I thought going to war would bring freedom and equality to twenty-two million of my people, they wouldn't have to draft me. I'd join tomorrow. But I either have to obey the laws of the land or the laws of Allah. I have nothing to lose by standing up and following my beliefs. We've been in jail for four hundred years." [90]

Ali chose the Semitic law of *Sharia* over the Common and Roman laws of the Western world, as did Muammar Muhammad Qaddafi when his country gained independence in the 1970's after years of French occupation. Of the 400 or so laws stated in the Quran there is one which differs significantly from American or European law: *There is no compulsion in religion.* (Surah 2:256)

In America and England, sadly, there is compulsion in religion. Namely, if you are Islamic you are a suspect. Since the USA PATRIOT Act was drafted in September 2001, thousand of Arabs and Muslims have been pushed around, arrested, harassed, and have been profiled by the governments of England and America as being dangerous and threatening.

This of course is nothing new. Anti-Semitism is often thought of as being reserved for discrimination against Jews. However, this scope should be widened to understand that anti-Semitism is against Semites such as Arabs and Muslims as well. This raises an important question for a democracy, namely, what are the political conditions of religion in America? To this question we immediately turn.

---

[90] Quoted by David Remnick, *King of The World: Muhammad Ali and the Rise of an American Hero*, (New York, Random House, 1998) p289-290

2

"The Separation of Church and State"
–and other Political Misnomers

A topic which has reared its head in America, particularly over the last 8 or 9 years, is the question of the 'separation of church and state.' While some believe that there can be a civil union between church and state, others believe that there cannot, and that church and state ought to be segregated. Some view the separation of religion and politics as stemming from a concern for toleration; others believe that this disjunction causes more problems than it solves. Who is right, if anybody? Is there today a separation of church and state in America, or are politics and religion somehow intermingled in the United States, for better or worse? This essay will focus on the relation and/or separation of church and state as concerns several particular issues that most notoriously have a bearing on the subject. These being the issues of women's rights, slavery, the capital punishment, and the so-called Divine Right of Kings.

Two of the most influential events for church and state relations in the Western world over the last 500 years have been the Enlightenment and the Protestant Reformation. The Protestant Reformation was a movement led by certain 16th century Christian leaders who were against the medieval church of the Holy Roman Empire, both politically and ideologically. The Enlightenment came later in 17th and 18th centuries.

Both the Enlightenment and the Protestant Reformation in turn came after something more fundamental which had occurred in medieval Europe through Spain: this is where our narrative begins, in the Renaissance. 'Renaissance' is a word that is derived from Latin and means something like 'being born', or 'being born again'. When someone is said to be of the Renaissance this is meant to say that this person is learned, intellectual, or is well-versed in a broad range of things.

The Medieval Ages of Europe are often called the 'Dark Ages' because of the prevalence of wars of conquest and empire and the decline of literacy and science and intellectualism as well. During this time of the Dark Ages, another culture had been thriving around the world, that of the Muslims. If the Dark Ages of Europe lasted from the 5th to the 14th centuries, the Muslim 'Golden Age' had begun in the 7th century and by the 8th and 9th the Muslims had an enormous expanse –from Asia, Africa, to Spain and southern Italy, up until the 14th and 15th centuries.

During the Golden Age of Spain, which at the time was called *al-Andalusia*, religious tolerance was greater than at any other time in Western history. Science, medicine, and philosophy achieved a synthesis beyond anything the ancient Greeks or Romans could have imagined. In turn, the Muslims of Spain reintroduced Europeans to the ancient studies of the Greeks and Romans, as well as the new medicine, science and mathematics of Asia and the Middle East. The 19th century Swiss historian Jacob Burckhardt (1818-1897) tells us of this narrative in his classic study, *The Civilization of the Renaissance In Italy*:

"The worldliness, through which the Renaissance seems to offer so striking a contrast to the Middle Ages, owed its first origin to the flood of new thoughts, purposes and views which transformed the medieval conception of nature and man... To the study of man, among many other causes, was due the tolerance and indifference with which the Muhammadan religion was regarded. The knowledge and admiration of the remarkable civilization which Islam... had attained, was peculiar to Italy from the time of the Crusades... It can be shown that in the thirteenth century the Italians recognized a Muhammadan ideal of nobleness, dignity and pride, which they love to connect with the person of the sultan."[1]

The power of the Holy Roman Empire, which had ruled over Europe for centuries, had been steadily weakening as they lost every subsequent crusade, of which there were around a dozen. As the state power of the Holy Roman Empire decayed, there began a separation of church and state. Literature, art, and science became rejuvenated and the studies of logic and philosophy were reintroduced. It was during the days of the Renaissance of Italy that Martin Luther (1483-1546) began the Protestant Reformation.

If the Italian Renaissance had begun a separation of church and state, the Protestant Reformation had the opposite effect. While the papacy weakened, the three Protestant patriarchs –Luther, John Calvin (1509-1564), and Henry VIII (1491-1547) held to a strong vision of the Christian state. This greatly helped in creating the modern phenomenon of nationalism and solidifying the unbending Divine Right of Kings. This Protestant fusion of church and state held sway in Europe until the Enlightenment.

'Enlightenment' is a term given to a period in Western history in the 17th and 18th centuries during which the ideals of the Renaissance were born again, and intellectuals and freethinkers (and not just monarchs) generally became influential. This reborn spirit of enlightenment was by no means uniform and oftentimes was not tolerated, depending on the given society or community[2]. Revolution swept across Europe during this time: some were successful, some unsuccessful. Where was the Enlightenment most brightly shown and practiced, this rebirth of renaissance? In the very place where the Enlightenment had begun: Scotland.

The Scottish Enlightenment was the most successful in achieving the widest range of thought and innovation as well as sustaining the longest fruition. This was because the Scottish had strong relationships amongst its communities. In Scotland the colleges, churches, and communities often worked together and the literacy rates were high. And it was in Scotland where some of the most original and most influential thinking was done.[3]

The names and figures that are most often associated with the Enlightenment are usually not Scottish. Rene Descartes (1598-1650), Jean-Jacques Rousseau (1712-1778), and Voltaire (1694-1778) were French; Gottfried Leibniz (1646-1716), Wolfgang Mozart (1756-1791), and Immanuel Kant (1724-1804) were Eastern-European –German, Austrian, and Prussian respectively; John Milton (1608-1674), John Locke (1632-1704), and Jeremy Bentham (1748-1832) were English; Benedict Spinoza (1634-1677) was

---

[1] Published in 1860. Jacob Burckhardt, *The Civilization of the Renaissance In Italy*, trans. S.G.C. Middlemore, (London, Penguin Books, 1990) p314
[2] In fact, English historian Norman Davies raises the question as to "why the age of the Renaissance and the Reformation proved so much more vicious... than the so-called Dark Ages, why superstition came to a head when humanism and the scientific revolution were supposedly working in the opposite direction." Davies notes that historians "usually attribute it to the pathological effects of religious conflict." Norman Davies, *Europe: A History*, (New York, HarperCollins, 1996) p567
[3] Alasdair MacIntyre, *After Virtue*, (Notre Dame, University of Notre Dame Press, 1981) p37; Arthur Herman, *How The Scots Invented the Modern World*, (New York, Three Rivers Press, 2001) p21, 23

Dutch-Jewish; and Benjamin Franklin (1706-1790), Thomas Paine (1737-1809), and Thomas Jefferson (1743-1826) were American. Most of these figures had to compromise either their philosophy or their politics during their lifetime. This was not the case in Scotland, where the philosophers sometimes took views which in other countries would have been politically heretical. For this reason the Scottish Enlightenment went the farthest and lasted the longest.

The Scottish Enlightenment most famously included such figures as David Hume (1711-1776), Adam Smith (1723-1790), and Thomas Reid (1710-1796). The Scottish Enlightenment was given impetus by two friends: John Knox (1513-1572) and George Buchanan (1506-1582). Knox himself had convinced many Scotsman to convert to the religious faith of the Genevan Protestant reformer John Calvin. Knox taught that the bible is the literal word of God and in 1560 he wrote that a national education system should be put in place in Scotland. 80 years later this became state law, and programs were set up so that all women and men could learn to read. Scotland became Christian Europe's first literate society.[4] Because of the strong communities that were formed in Scotland, they were able to avoid a class war, which some theorists contradictorily hold to be necessary in building a strong community.

In 1579 George Buchanan wrote, *The Law of Government Among the Scots*, which taught that while political authority is a God-given right, this right resides in the Scottish people and not in any King or monarch.[5] This type of government is also known as 'democracy'.

By 1638 the Scottish people –citizens, ministers, intellectuals –signed a National Covenant, which challenged the power of the King of England, who was himself originally a Scotsman, Charles I (1600-1649). One of the chief complaints against the King was his declaration of Martial-law, which gave all legal power to one person –the King himself. Under Martial-law, the head of state can rewrite laws and sentence to death, independently of the courts. 10 months after signing the National Covenant, the General Assembly in Glasgow declared war on King Charles and his bishops. The two wars that followed are known as the Bishop's War(s), and King Charles' English troops were defeated by the Scots. Charles was forced to 'sue for peace'. This of course led to the short-lived Puritan revolt in England, wherein Charles was defeated in 1644 and lost his head 5 years later. The English were able to abolish the monarchy for almost 20 years, though there was little complaint among them when Charles' son, Charles II (1630-1685) was made King of England in 1660.

Thus while the Protestant Reformation reified the belief in the Divine Right of Kings, the Scottish Enlightenment began the attack on the Divine Right of Kings. The Enlightenment culminated in the American and French revolutions, where in both instances, the divine monarchy was disestablished. This was a separation of church and state.

---

[4] Herman, p23. One of the greatest medieval philosophers was the Scotsman John Duns Scotus (1266-1308) who studied and taught about Aristotle and the Muslim Aristotelian Ibn Sina (Avicenna) (980-1037) in London, Paris, and Cologne.
[5] Herman, p18

After American Enlightenment

During the American Revolutionary war the greatest critic of the belief in the Divine Right of Kings and most vocal advocates for the separation of church and state was Thomas Paine. Prior to the Revolutionary War Thomas Paine had come to America from England through the invitation of Benjamin Franklin. Upon reaching the New World, Paine worked primarily on opposing slavery, finding in Thomas Jefferson a fellow devotee of the cause, as Paine championed women's rights. In 1775 Paine wrote an early criticism of slavery, *African Slavery in America,* and shortly thereafter Paine helped pass the first American anti-slavery laws in Pennsylvania,[6] though Vermont was the first state to abolish slavery.

The very same year Thomas Paine also either wrote or edited and published works defending women's rights. In *An Occasional Letter On The Female Sex*, it is written,

"If we take a survey of ages and of countries, we shall find the women almost –without exception –at all times and in all places, adored and oppressed. Man... has never neglected an opportunity of exerting his power... Yet such, I am sorry to say, is the lot of women over the whole earth. Man with regard to them, in all climates, and in all ages, has been either an insensible husband or an oppressor..."[7]

Thomas Paine, however, is primarily known as having been an important figure in the American Revolution. With the outbreak of the revolution he wrote the most widely published manuscript of the time called, *Common Sense,* which argued against the British Monarchy and the Divine Right of Kings. Appealing to 'common-sense', Paine wrote:

"[I]t is not so much the absurdity as the evil of hereditary succession which concerns mankind. Did it ensure a race of good and wise men it would have the seal of divine authority, but as it opens a door to the *foolish,* the *wicked,* and *improper,* it hath in it the nature of oppression. Men who look upon themselves born to reign, and others to obey, soon grow insolent; selected from the rest of mankind their minds are early poisoned by importance; and the world they act in differs so materially from the world at large, that they have but little opportunity of knowing its true interests, and when they succeed to the government are frequently the most ignorant and unfit of any throughout the dominions."[8]

After the American Revolution, Paine traveled first to England as an engineer, and then to France as a revolutionary. He attempted to assist the British in political reforms and the French in their revolution, both times barely escaping with his life. The English Tories sought to lynch Paine and reportedly just missed him by a few a minutes in Dover when he sailed for France. In France he participated in their Revolution, drafting his popular book on English and French politics, *Rights of Man.* He was opposed to executing the former King, Louis XVI (1754-1793), whom Paine saw as having been more of a bystander. Because Paine was opposed to the death penalty, he himself was imprisoned and put on death row. Though George Washington ignored his letters written from the Bastille pleading for amnesty, after a dozen or so months Paine was released, near dead with illness.

---

[6] Thomas Paine, "African Slavery In America", *Writings of Thomas Paine*, ed. Philip S. Foner, (New York, The Citadel Press, 1945) p15-19
[7] Thomas Paine, "An Occasional Letter On The Female Sex", *Writings of Thomas Paine*, p34-36
[8] Thomas Paine, *Common Sense*, (London, Penguin Books, 1976) p79

When Paine finally returned to the United States times had changed. His friend Thomas Jefferson was then president and was no longer opposed to slavery.[9] Jefferson had written as early as 1779 that "Slaves guilty of any offence punishable in others by labor in the public works, shall be transported to such parts in the West Indies, South America, or Africa, as the Governor shall direct, there to be continued in slavery."[10]

Thomas Paine, on the other hand, found an increasing importance in the need of educating the young Americans on matters of justice in the U.S. as seen in his book, *Agrarian Justice* (1795). After completing the second volume of his treatise, *The Age of Reason*, Paine's celebrity status had disappeared and he became more and more 'unpopular' in the US. Toward the end of his life he focused his attentions toward attempting to further ensure the separation of church and state in the United States.[11]

In 1832 a French lawyer named Alexis de Tocqueville (1805-1859) visited a very young United States to learn how the democracy was faring. He noted in his study, *Democracy in America*, "The thirteen Colonies, which simultaneously threw off the yoke of England towards the end of the last century, had… the same religion, the same language, and same customs, and almost the same laws…"[12]

De Tocqueville did not think this repetition was intentional but was part of the moral tradition that the Americans had inherited from their English fathers. He wrote of his travels in America:

"…Christianity itself is an established and irresistible fact, which no one undertakes either to attack or to defend. The Americans, having admitted the principal doctrines of the Christian religion without inquiry, are obliged to accept in like manner a great number of moral truths originating in it and connected with it."[13]

He concluded that the United States had developed a very centralized form of political power, even more so than any self-centered monarch of Europe. He wrote: "the United States form not only a republic, but a confederation; yet the national authority is more centralized there than it was in several of the absolute monarchies of Europe."[14]

De Tocqueville foresaw with clear vision the likelihood of "the most horrible of civil wars", and he stands as prophetic to the great collision of conscience that would

---

[9] It seems Jefferson eventually lost a belief in the separation of church and state. "I trust that there is not a *young man* now living in the United States who will not die an Unitarian." –Thomas Jefferson, letter to Dr. Benjamin Waterhouse, June 26, 1822. Quoted in Walter Kaufmann, *The Faith of a Heretic*, (Garden City, Anchor Books, 1963) p287. Unitarianism, now called the Unitarian Universalist Association, is an American Christian church. Their purpose statement is "to cherish and spread the universal truths taught by the great prophets and teachers of humanity in every age and tradition, immemorially summarized in the Judeo-Christian heritage". Quoted by R.E. Richey in *The Perennial Dictionary of World Religions*, ed. Keith Crim, (San Francisco, HarperCollins, 1981) p776

[10] "A Bill for Proportioning Crimes and Punishments", in Walter Kaufmann, *Without Guilt and Justice*, (New York, Peter H. Wyden, Inc., 1973) p42

[11] Paine also wrote the essay, "Of the Religion of Deism Compared with the Christian Religion and the Superiority of the Former over the Latter". It is popularly understood that the Founding Fathers were Deists. Deism is the belief in an impersonal god who does not interact with the world, but who designed the world and humans in a rational sense. This is comparable with Aristotle's conception of the Divine who is unconcerned with the world of change.

[12] Alexis de Tocqueville, *Democracy in America*, trans. Henry Reeve, ed. Andrew Hacker, (New York, Washington Square Press, 1973) p52

[13] de Tocqueville, p131

[14] de Tocqueville, p55

culminate in the American Civil War which ended slavery in the United States, one of the bloodiest wars in the history of the world.

In the southern states slavery remained in full swing and de Tocqueville, although a foreigner, was aware of the difficult situation this created for the unity of the United States. Vermont was the first state to abolish slavery and soon after other states in the north of the US followed. Some 30,000 Vermonters fought in the Civil War, leading the battle of Gettysburg, which many site as the turning point in the war.

Scotland was among the first Western nations to abolish slavery. Although the Scotsman Francis Hutcheson (1694-1746) had condemned slavery in his early 1700's study, *A System of Moral Philosophy*, it was another Scotsman, Chief Justice Lord Mansfield (1705-1793) who had ruled that slavery was contrary to the law. When an African-born Jamaican slave, Joseph Knight, was taken to Scotland in 1769, he successfully won his freedom in the highest court in Scotland.[15]

In America a one-time slave, Frederick Douglas (1817-1895), wrote extensively about the situation in the US. Douglas had been born into slavery and was able to escape to the North in 1838. He became particularly influential in helping to build the abolition movement in the United States. In 1845 Frederick Douglas wrote:

"I assert most unhesitatingly, that the religion of the south is a mere covering for the most horrid crimes, -a justifier of the most appalling barbarity, -a sanctifier of the most hateful frauds, -and a dark shelter under, which the darkest, foulest, grossest, and most infernal deeds of slaveholders find the strongest protection. Were I to be again reduced to the chains of slavery, next to that enslavement, I should regard being the slave of a religious master the greatest calamity that could befall me. For of all slaveholders with whom I have ever met, religious slaveholders are the worst."[16]

Frederick Douglas was also very active in the early days of the women's suffrage movement. When in 1871 Victoria Woodhull (1838-1927) became one of the first female candidates for President of the United States, nominated by the Equal Rights Party, she chose Frederick Douglass as her vice-president, without his knowledge.[17] And when the civil rights and women's' rights activist, Ida B. Wells-Barnett (1862-1931) wrote a study against the practice of lynching in America, she had Douglass write the introduction.[18]

In her study titled *Century of Struggle*, Eleanor Flexner (1908-1995) gives an account of the forces that worked for and against giving women the right to vote. It began in 1848 with two women who lived in upstate New York at Seneca Falls. Lucretia Mott (1793-1880) and Elizabeth Cady Stanton (1815-1902) published an invitation in the local newspaper, inviting women only to a "Women's Rights Convention –A convention to discuss the social, civil and religious rights of woman…" The women had to break into a locked church to hold the meeting. They rephrased the US Declaration of Independence to read:

"We hold these truths to be self-evident: that all men and women are created equal; that they are endowed by their Creator with certain inalienable rights: that among these are life, liberty, and the pursuit of happiness."[19]

---

[15] Herman, p104-105
[16] Frederick Douglass, *Narrative of the Life of Frederick Douglass, an American Slave*, (Penguin Books, 1986) p117
[17] Eleanor Flexner, *Century of Struggle: The Women's Rights Movement in the United States*, (Cambridge, Harvard University Press, 1975) p157
[18] Flexner, p147
[19] Flexner, p74-75

When the Women's Christian Temperance Union was formed in 1874, it was initially opposed to women's suffrage in its inception. When a few years thereafter the WCTU underwent a regime change, support for women's rights to vote became standard. Women who wished to become members who were not white were told to form their own chapters.[20]

While the women's suffrage movement had faired best in Wyoming, Kansas, New York, and New Jersey, it suffered the greatest defeat in Massachusetts. This was for several reasons. In her work *Womanhood In America: From Colonial Times to Present*, Mary Ryan notes that:

"The New England colonies took considerable pains to educate American youth, but their enthusiasm flagged when it came to women. Females were banned from institutions of higher learning and were commonly admitted to the public schoolhouse only during those hours and seasons when boys were occupied with other affairs or were needed in the fields."[21]

In the 1830's, the General Association of Ministers of Massachusetts forbid women to speak in pulpits.[22] Massachusetts, in 1837, was the last New England state to disestablish congregationalism, which had long connected church and state.[23] Moreover, Massachusetts was the birthplace of the anti-suffrage movement, and had the largest Catholic population. While the Catholic Church was neutral on the question of women's suffrage, many of the clergy had spoken and written against any such reform, working through such groups as the Massachusetts Anti-Suffrage Committee and the National Association Opposed to Woman Suffrage. One Massachusetts Cardinal Gibbons wrote an address for the National Anti-Suffrage Convention which was held in Washington in 1916.[24]

Not all feminists supported equal rights and women's suffrage. Charlotte Gilman (1860-1935) for example, was a white supremacist and supported eugenics, and the anarchist/feminist Emma Goldman (1869-1940) had been against women's suffrage at the time, though her reasons are revealing.[25]

"I do not believe that women will make politics worse; nor can I believe that she could make it better. If, then, she cannot improve on man's mistakes, why perpetrate the latter? ...There is no reason whatever to assume that woman, in her climb to emancipation, has been, or will be, helped by the ballot...

"Her development, her freedom, her independence, must come from and through herself. First, by asserting herself as a personality. Second, by refusing the right to anyone over her body; by refusing to bear children, unless she wants them; by refusing to be a servant to God, the State, society, the husband, the family, etc. by making her life simpler, but deeper and richer... Only that, and not the ballot, will set woman free..."[26]

One of the most effective advocates of women's rights and equal rights was the pragmatist/feminist Jane Addams (1860-1935). Jane Addams was an influential proponent of the women's suffrage movement and a lead figure in the founding of the

---

[20] Flexner, p186-187, 196
[21] Mary P. Ryan, *Womanhood In America: From Colonial Times To Present*, (New York, New Viewpoints, 1975) p69
[22] Howard Zinn, *A People's History of the United States*, Revised and Updated Edition, (New York, HarperPerennial, 1995) p119
[23] Kevin Phillips, *American Theocracy*, (New York, Penguin Books, 2006) p112
[24] Flexner, p280, 309
[25] For example in Gilman's book, *HERLAND*. Goldman was an early, if unpopular lecturer on eugenics. http://sunsite.berkeley.edu/goldman/Guide/chronology0119.html
[26] Emma Goldman, "Woman Suffrage", from *Anarchism and Other Essays*, (New York, Dover Publications, Inc., 1969) p209, 211

Progressive Party in 1912.[27] At the time of the First World War, Addams worked to set up international peace organizations, just as she had set up national political conventions, and in 1931 she became the first American woman awarded the Nobel Peace Prize.[28] She had been friends with and had worked in close association with John Dewey (1859-1952) and the social pragmatist George Herbert Mead (1863-1931), both of whom taught at the University of Chicago.

In 1889 Addams set up one of the first social settlement houses in US history, called the Hull House in Chicago. This settlement worked as a center for education and offered community services for minorities, immigrants, and the poor. These free services included room and board, and things as such as healthcare, language classes, as well as education in the arts and sciences. In 1889 a significant portion of Chicago was inhabited by African-Americans and 60% of Chicago residents were foreign-born.[29] By 1910, over 400 settlement houses had been established in America.[30]

"Socializing Democracy" was the goal of the pacifist Addams and she sought to bring the different classes into a "harmonious relation". She noted from her work at the settlement house with people from all walks of life and all racial backgrounds, cultures and traditions that such a diverse settlement was not a possibility but a reality. In her 1899 work, *A Function of the Social Settlement*, she writes, "We are not willing, openly and professedly, to assume that American citizens are broken up into classes…" Such thinking creates "the suspicion that intellectual and moral superiority too often rest upon economic props…"[31] Her 1910 work, *Twenty Years at Hull-House* reported that, "The dependence of the classes on each other is reciprocal, it gives a form of expression that has peculiar value."[32] This was an extension of what she had written in 1903 in her work, *Democracy and Social Ethics*.

"We have learned to say that the good must be extended to all of society before it can be held secure by any one person or any one class; but we have not yet learned to add to that statement, that unless all men and all classes contribute to a good, we cannot even be sure it is worth having."[33]

Addams was very aware of the role that sexuality played in politics and discourse. She was concerned about the "masculinization" of women and "observed remorsefully that the uninhibited young women of the 1920's were too concerned with personal freedom and self-development to devote themselves to the cause of social freedom and justice for all Americans."[34] Addams prided herself on her teetotalism, celibacy and strength as a single woman and from a young age she had demanded her friends refer to her as Miss Addams.[35] She explained the post-19th Amendment disintegration of the women's rights movement through the breakdown of sex taboos and the preoccupation with sexual gratification and self-fulfillment.[36]

---

[27] Flexner, p266
[28] Ryan, p230; Louis Menand, *Pragmatism: A Reader*, (New York, Vintage Books, 1997) p272
[29] Louis Menand, *The Metaphysical Club: The Story of Ideas in America*, (New York, Farrar, Straus and Giroux, 2001), p308
[30] Ryan, p229
[31] Jane Addams, *A Function of the Social Settlement*, in Louis Menand's, *Pragmatism: A Reader*, p273
[32] Quoted by Ryan, p233
[33] Jane Addams, *Democracy and Social Ethics*, quoted by Menand in *The Metaphysical Club*, p312
[34] Ryan, p253
[35] Menand, *The Metaphysical Club*, p307
[36] Ryan, p255

Until 1830 most teachers in America were men and there was a general opposition toward women teachers that was held. This lasted until it was realized that women could be paid to teach for one third or one half of what men were paid, and in Massachusetts women teachers were paid less than women factory owners. By 1860 more women were teaching than men, and by 1870 the ratio was at 60%. By 1900 over 70% of teachers were women, and by 1925 the ratio reached beyond 83%. In his work *Anti-Intellectualism in American Life*, Richard Holfstadter (1916-1970) notes that in America "teaching has been identified as a feminine profession," and there is an "American masculine conviction that education and culture are feminine concerns."[37]

This is the case in politics as well. According to Holfstadter, fundamentalist religion and fundamentalist Americanism are similarly concerned with "toughness" and "masculinity" and their own infallibility. Holfstadter writes that, "One reason why the political intelligence of our time is so incredulous and uncomprehending in the presence of the right-wing mind is that it does not reckon fully with the essentially theological concern that underlies right-wing views of the world." This attitude affects the understanding of gender and politics.

"What the politicians relied upon, as the basis for an unspoken agreement about the improper character of the reformers, was the feeling, then accepted by practically all men and by most women, that to be active in political life was a male prerogative, in the sense that women were excluded from it, and further, that capacity for an effective role in politics was practically a test of masculinity. To be active in politics was a man's business, whereas to be engaged in reform movements (at least in America) meant constant association with aggressive, reforming, moralizing women –witness the case of the abolitionists… If women invaded politics, they would become masculine, just as men became feminine when they espoused reform."[38]

The Declaration of Independence and the US Constitution

The U.S. *Declaration of Independence* had boasted, in the Enlightenment tradition, that because human beings have equal rights, each person has certain "inalienable rights." Interestingly, an original draft written by Jefferson had called for the abolition of slavery. But this is not so in the U.S. Constitution, which does not mention "inalienable rights". There is another popular misconception that written in the U.S. Constitution is the phrase stating, "separation of church and state". Not only does the Constitution not say this, it also did not state any justification for the perpetuation of the slavery practice that had been going on for hundreds of years before the writing of the Constitution.

The U.S. Constitution states:

"No religious test shall ever be required as a qualification to any office or public trust under the United States." –Article VI, Section 3

Article VI, Section 3 of the Constitution removes religiosity as a requirement to citizenship; it is a law barring what a religion can do for the state. But what about what the state can do for religion? The so-called 'Establishment Clause' of the 1st Amendment attempts to prohibit this as well:

---

[37] Richard Holfstadter, *Anti-Intellectualism in American Life*, (New York, Vintage Books, 1962) p316-317, 319, 320
[38] Holfstadter, p119, 134, 189-190

"Congress shall make no law respecting an establishment of religion, or prohibiting the free exercise thereof; or abridging the freedom of speech, or of the press; or the right of the people peaceably to assemble, and to petition the government for a redress of grievances." -1st Amendment

In fact, the first 10 Amendments to the US Constitution, also known as the 'Bill of Rights', were by and large adaptations from the Constitution of the Republic of Vermont, which had been the first state to join the union after the American Revolution, making it the 14th state.[39] Although the 1st Amendment attempted to further separate religion and the state, it was not successful in making a clean sweep. It wasn't until the 13th Amendment that slavery was Constitutionally banned in the United States. In 1920, the 19th Amendment gave women the vote. Just last year (2008) Supreme Court Justice John Paul Stevens offered a dissenting opinion on the question of the Constitutionality and ethicality of capital punishment, or the death penalty.[40]

Any country that is a true democracy of course has variety: its not just one thing. In particular, the 'opinion' of the majority decides upon the laws of the land. One of the problems with the belief in the separation of church and state is that it can be anti-democratic. It runs along the contemporary rhetoric of those who say "government is bad" and should be limited. This is mirrored by the libertarian belief that the government that governs least governs best. However, if we are a democracy the government is run by the people and for the people. If it just so happens that the majority of Americans are Christian then too bad for the minorities, maybe they ought to convert or move on.

This may be a permanent tension. No society or person can completely re-create or reinvent themselves. Each of us comes from a tradition –it is a bourgeois philosophy that would tell us otherwise. A democracy should not discriminate over which race or religion makes one eligible to become a citizen, though perhaps we ought to just close the borders.

However, we are a constitutional democracy. The Founding Fathers, as best they could, wrote the constitution so that the two democratic vices: oligarchy, or rule by the wealthy, or Dictatorship, or rule by the military, would not occur. This is also supposed to mean that the minorities (such as the wealthy, or the well-armed) ought not to tyrannize over the majority.

Moreover, the American democracy is in many ways only democratic to the extent that it is bureaucratic, which is by and large the case. Not only did the Founding Fathers invent the democratic laws, but to this day it is politicians, representatives, and judges almost always make the laws for us as a people. It is not very often that we can feel that "we the people" have made most of or any of the decisions that our government makes, even though we are part of that government.

The US Constitution and US History

It has been argued both that the Founding Fathers were religious men, and it has been argued that they were not. A popular interpretation is that they were all Deists – believers in a God that is transcendent and separate from the world. For this reason the

---

[39] www.usconstitution.net/vtconstexp.html
[40] Linda Greenhouse, "Justice Stevens Renounces Capital Punishment", *New York Times*, 4/18/08. Capital punishment typically costs states anywhere from half a million to three-quarters of a million dollars. See Ian Urbina's, "Citing Cost, States Consider End to Death Penalty", *New York Times*, 2/24/09

Founding Fathers are often called "naturalists", meaning, they did not justify their morality in supernatural terms, but in terms of human nature, and the nature of the world. They of course were arguing against the Divine Right of Kings and they believed in truths which were 'self-evident' and which could be discovered through the natural abilities of human nature.

This is in stark contrast to the presidential run of 2008. For example: all of the candidates running for both the Republican or Democratic nomination were Christian. For the Republicans there was the former governor of Massachusetts, Mit Romney. In one of his speeches in late 2007 Romney said that he believes every word in the Bible, believing it to be the word of God. Thus he goes further than his own church, the Mormons, who believe that the Bible contains a few errors.[41] He later said:

"I will take care to separate the affairs of government from any religion, but I will not separate us from the God who gave us liberty. Nor would I separate us from our religious heritage... In recent years, the notion of the separation of church and state has been taken by some well beyond its original meaning [by those who] seek to remove from the public domain any acknowledgement of God. Religion is seen as merely a private affair with no place in public life. It is as if they are intent on establishing a new religion in America –the religion of secularism. They are wrong."[42]

Another serious contender for the Republican nomination was the former mayor of New York City, Rudolf Giuliani, who had the backing of Christian leader Pat Robertson. Giuliani had told voters not that he will be guided by the Constitution, which is the law of the land, but that he "prays to Jesus for guidance and for help."[43]

Although Senator John McCain wound up getting the Republican nomination, the runner up was the Governor of Arkansas, the former Baptist minister Mike Huckabee, who describes himself as a "Christian leader". In a December 2007 rally Huckabee said that, "There is a maturing of Christian involvement in politics in this generation." Moreover: "We cannot change the world if we refuse to participate in the institutions of society that dictate its directions."[44]

The Republican nominee John McCain said in September 2007, "I just have to say in all candor… this nation was founded primarily on Christian principles…" McCain said he believes that "the Constitution established the United States of America as a Christian nation," though he did not specify in which country's Constitution he had read this.[45]

On the Democratic ticket the runners there have had identical tests of qualification. Both Hilary Clinton and Barack Obama have described themselves as sincere Christians, as did John Edwards. President Bill Clinton and Vice-President Al Gore are both Southern Baptists. In fact, besides the questionable religiosity of the Founding Fathers (Jefferson was a Unitarian), every president in the history of the United States has been a Protestant Christian, with the exception of one president [who was assassinated], John F. Kennedy, who was a Catholic.

In their study, *The Western Intellectual Tradition*, authors J. Bronowski and Bruce Mazlish are careful to point out that while Founding Fathers such as George Washington

---

[41] Michael Luo, "Mormons And the Bible, Every Word", *New York Times*, 12/1/07
[42] Michael Luo, "Romney, Eye on Evangelicals, Defends His Faith", *New York Times*, 12/7/07
[43] David D. Kirkpatrick and Michael Cooper, "In a Surprise, Pat Robertson Backs Giuliani", *New York Times*, 11/8/07
[44] Jodi Kantor and David D. Kirkpatrick, "Pulpit Was the Springboard for Huckabee's Rise", *New York Times*, 12/6/07
[45] Stephen Labaton, "McCain Casts Muslims as Less Fit to Lead", *New York Times*, 9/30/07

(1732-1799) and Alexander Hamilton (1755-1805) may have been great revolutionaries, Thomas Jefferson (1743-1826) was certainly not just a revolutionary but was a genuine thinker and intellectual.[46] It was Jefferson who in 1781 had said, "It does me no injury for my neighbor to say there are twenty gods, or no god. It neither picks my pocket nor breaks my leg."[47] Jefferson had also drafted the *Declaration of Independence*, founded the University of Virginia, and had written the "Statute of Virginia for Religious Freedom".

During the early days of the Cold War, President Dwight D. Eisenhower (1890-1969) said, "Our government makes no sense unless it is founded in a deeply felt religious faith –and I don't care what it is."[48] As a General in WWII Eisenhower had said, "This war was a holy war more than any other in history this war has been an array of the forces of evil against those of righteousness."[49] When running for President Ronald Reagan (r. 1981-1989) had sworn his obedience to the Bible saying, "all the complex and horrendous questions confronting us at home and worldwide have their answer in that single book."[50]

In fact, politicians today act as if their religious or spiritual faith was a kind of duty with very important political, not to mention ethical, consequences. When President Bush II was asked what he would do if he won the election, he replied rhetorically that he would ask himself this simple question, 'What would Jesus do'? In 1999 when Bush was running for office he told an assembly of Texas pastors that God had called on him to run for office. In 2004 George Bush II told Amish in Pennsylvania, "I trust God speaks through me. Without that, I couldn't do my job."[51] How this differs from the Divine Right of Kings which our Founding Fathers rebelled against it is difficult for some of us to discover.

As the majority of US citizens are possibly aware there are probably dozens, maybe hundreds, of violations of the Constitution and the Establishment Clause that exist today. Just as the Kings of England had declared themselves to be the head of state, declaring Martial-Law, President Bush overrode the system of checks and balances found in the Constitution, in order to give himself supreme power over the senate and the judiciary.

From 1989 to 2007 the US Congress approved nearly 900 "earmarks" for religious groups and institutions, a cost exceeding over $318 million dollars. From 1998 to 2005, the number of religious organizations which are clients to Washington tripled.[52] This was largely due to Bush's introduction of "Faith-Based Initiatives". The faith-based initiative is the attempt to replace work done by social services with similar work done by religious institutions. Hilary Clinton has said that there isn't a contradiction in "support for faith-based initiatives and upholding our constitutional principles", Barack Obama has called them a "uniquely powerful way of solving problems", and both Mitt Romney

---

[46] Bronowski and Mazlish, p391
[47] Quoted by Fawn M. Brodie, *Thomas Jefferson: An Intimate History*, (New York, W.W. Norton & Company, Inc., 1974) p157
[48] Dwight D. Eisenhower, December 1952, in Walter Kaufmann, *The Faith of a Heretic*, p276
[49] Dwight D. Eisenhower, quoted in James Carroll, *Constantine's Sword*, (Mariner Books, 2002) p256
[50] Kantor and Kirkpatrick, 12/6/07
[51] Phillips, p192, 207-208
[52] Diana B. Henriques and Andrew W. Lehren, "Religious Groups Reaping Share of Federal Aid for Pet Projects", *New York Times*, 5/13/07

and Mike Huckabee created faith-based initiatives while they were governors.[53] A suspicion of financial incentive could be the reason why some European nations have refused to recognize the existence of certain religions, as for example Scientology, which is viewed seemingly as a tax-haven.[54] Moreover, in many European countries there is discrimination against a non-Christian religion such as Islam as well, where dress codes and mosques are monitored and limited by the state governments.

Natural Law vs. Religious Law

In searching for the roots of the American Founding Father's understanding of ethics it is argued that they believed in something called the 'natural' law. The Natural Law is a theory that came out of possibly the Persians or the Greek Stoics. The early Christian theologian, Augustine's (354-430) 'discovery' of natural law came out the attempt to explain the question as to how it could be possible that humans were ethical before there was revealed religion. During the Enlightenment a new use and understanding for the concept of Natural Law found a purpose in explaining morality in natural terms, rather than supernatural. The argument is usually stated thus:

Be it the nature of humans or of physical reality, there is a natural law which all nature obeys or follows. This was the thinking of the Founding Fathers who believed that all they needed to do was to appeal common sense or human desire to see what the laws of government ought to be like. The legal philosopher A.P. d'Entreves sums up the magnanimity of this point.

"But when we read the American or the French Declarations we know that we are confronted with a complete architecture, about the style of which there can be no mistake. It is a political philosophy based upon a particular notion of the individual, of society and of their mutual relationship. What Jefferson called the 'station' to which nations and men are entitled under 'the laws of Nature and of Nature's God' has become the determining factor in political obligation. It is a pattern of ideas for which it is difficult to find precedents in history, and it has left an indelible mark upon our civilization."[55]

Thus, some might ask whether certain laws are part of 'common-sense' or 'human nature', in which case they are just or correct laws according to the natural law of our Founding Fathers, or whether a given law is in fact a religious law, which might then be specific to a particular religion and the given revelation. In the 1830's de Tocqueville, as we saw, believed that Americans had rather uncritically adopted the laws of Christianity as the basis for their own set of laws. However, in light of the Constitution it seems that this cannot be done. The following are some examples of a dissonance between Natural and Religious law and the US Constitution.

There are ongoing issues with the religious representations made by the government and government officials. As it is, religious institutions in the United States are excused from paying taxes on their income. Perhaps this is because all U.S. currency has printed on it, "In God We Trust"? One of the first bills which Bush II was able to

---

[53] David Kuo and John J. DiIulio Jr., "The Faith To Outlast Politics", *New York Times*, 1/29/08

[54] Scientology is banned in several European countries, there is a legal case in Belgium currently. Check *New York Times*, 9/5/07. There is currently a move to ban Scientology in Germany. *New York Times*, 12/8/07

[55] A.P. d'Entreves, *Natural Law: An Introduction to Legal Philosophy*, (London, Hutchinson & Co., 1961) p54-55

pass, the so-called "faith based initiative", which as we saw, works to give tax-payer dollars to religious institutions. In what ways are these instances of the Establishment Clause?

If the context is missing, this statement of James Inhofe, former chair of the Senate Environment and Public Works Committee is itself revealing, "I don't believe there is a single issue we deal with in government that hasn't been dealt with in the Scriptures." Former Republican House majority leader, Tom Delay, said, "God is using me all the time, everywhere, to stand up for a biblical world view in everything that I do and everywhere I am. He is training me." [56]

The American-Filipino Wars (1899-1913), unofficially went on for well over a dozen years, the purpose of which President William McKinley (r.1897-1901) said was to "civilize and Christianize" the Filipinos. Theodore Roosevelt (1901-1909) also supported the occupation of the Philippine islands and was particularly pleased when 600 Muslim Filipino's, or *Moros*, were massacred in 1906. Some 600,000 Filipinos were killed in total.[57]

The military is an important venue of patriotism and one way we citizens can participate and give back to our country. However, there too there is often contention concerning religious intermingling. An investigation in 2005 of the US Air Force found that higher-ranking staff officials used their position to "evangelize cadets".[58]

According to the US Constitution one would expect state or public schools to be non-specific toward a particular religious ideology. The issue is obviously contentious because of the differences between state and federal law. In 2007 the American Civil Liberties Union (ACLU) won a federal case, stopping the Christian group Gideons International from spreading bibles in 5th grade classes as well as during lunch hours in schools in Missouri.[59] Although it is not against the law to teach the Christian Bible in Texas public schools, once the ACLU had filed suits, Texas district schools switched their curriculum, which had originally promoted Protestant Christianity and a literal reading of the Bible.[60]

Public schools have also been a point of contention concerning school prayer as well as the Pledge of Allegiance. I personally can remember as a child being told to recite the Pledge of Allegiance each day at the beginning of school. Although the US Supreme Court ruled in 1962 that endorsement of prayer in schools violated the First Amendment, in schools in Chicago, Illinois today there is a mandatory silence for prayer, as well as the recitation of the pledge of allegiance.[61]

The Texas Republican Party runs on the purposive slogan: "dispel the myth of the separation of church and state."[62] In 2004 they stood on the Christian Nation platform and promised to abolish the Environmental Protection Agency.[63] As the former Republican analyst Kevin Phillips surmises: just look at how many of the issues concerning religious freedom and the violation of the Constitution are decided. He writes:

"National opinion surveys and the priorities expressed since the late 1970's by church, religious-right, and Republican grassroots organizations give precedence to the life-and-death, sex-and-family issues

---

[56] Quoted in Phillips, p96, 216
[57] Quoted in *The People Speak: American voices, Some Famous, Some Little Known*, ed. Howard Zinn, (New York, HarperCollins, 2004) p25
[58] Neela Banerjee, *New York Times*, 3/8/08. For a just account of these events see Oren Jacoby's 2007 documentary *Constantine's Sword*, based on Carroll's book of the same title. http://constantinessword.com

over any others. Endless confrontations have arisen over abortion, women's rights, assisted death and the right to die, the promotion of sexual abstinence, contraception, and the question of gay marriage. The spur is the scriptural belief patterns that significantly influence 60 to 65 percent of Americans and appear to dominate the views of roughly half that number. ... viewpoints on these issues closely reflect the influence of religious denominations, not just religiosity in general."[64]

Such issues as the Terri Schiavo case where Bush II and his brother, the governor of Florida, Jeb Bush, stepped in and denied her the right to die (2004), or Bush II's attempt at a Constitutional Amendment banning gay marriage, stand as obvious cases where legislation is founded upon religious belief. Policies such as 'Don't Ask, Don't Tell', which are still controversial and equivocal, do not necessarily resemble a religious agenda, but their obscurity makes it hard to rule out. Moreover, in US courtrooms to this day, witnesses are made to swear an oath while placing their hand on the Christian Bible and must consent to the words, "so help you God." While a list might be long a few other laws which seem to hearken to such a value system are the Sunday Laws or Blue Laws, such as in Massachusetts where it is illegal to sell alcohol on the first day of the week, and in most states public nudity is illegal (however, not in Vermont), as well as nudity and sexuality on television, though of course there is plenty of violence depicted. What value system might these laws be informed by?

One of the central fronts of the battle between religion and secularism is in science. The theory of evolution, which dates back a thousand years before Charles Darwin (1809-1882) revamped the field, has been banned in some US schools and has resulted in some famous trials. 2008 marks the first year that children who attend public schools in Florida will learn anything about the "theory" of evolution.[65] For some time the National Park Service sold books that placed much doubt upon evolutionary theory.[66] In 2004 62 preeminent scientists complained that the Bush administration was tampering with scientific evidence.[67] In 2007 Vermont Representative Peter Welch cited some 181 edits and changes to scientific studies on the environment and Global Warming made by the White House's Council on Environmental Quality.[68]

Corporations such as Exxon/Mobil and Coors Brewing Company have for years funded and supported the religious-right as well as organizations that work against environmentalism. Directly and indirectly, Coors and Exxon/Mobile have supported some of the following organizations: the Interfaith Council for Environmental Stewardship, the Action Institute for the Study of Religion and Liberty, the Heritage Foundation, the Mountain States Legal Foundation, the Council for National Policy, the Coalition on Revival, the Christian Reconstructionists, and the Christian Coalition.[69]

---

[59] AP Press, *New York Times*, 11/10/08
[60] Neela Banerjee, *New York Times*, 3/6/08
[61] P.J. Huffstutter, *Los Angeles Times*, printed in, *The Valley News*, 1/1/08
[62] Quoted by Paul Krugman, *New York Times*, 4/13/07
[63] Phillips, 232n38, 233n39
[64] Phillips, p239
[65] Editorial, *New York Times*, 3/6/08
[66] Phillips, p246
[67] Phillips, p247
[68] Daniel Barlow, "Welch grills former White House Staffer on changes to climate reports", *The Times Argus*, 3/20/07
[69] Phillips, p65n80, p238

The USA PATRIOT Act and Religious Legislation

Pope Nicholas V (Roman Pontiff 1447-1455) had decreed the Papal Bull (or law of the Holy Roman Empire) *Romanus Pontifex* in 1455, which gave economic and military license to the Kingdom of Portugal to take the lands of pagans, Muslims, and other non-Christians and to enslave them. Just a few years earlier in 1452 Muslims had taken the capitol of the Eastern wing of the Roman Empire, Constantinople, which they renamed Istanbul. Pope Nicholas V issued a Crusade after the fall of Constantinople in 1452.[70] The Bull gave authority:

"...to invade, search out, capture, vanquish, and subdue all Saracens [Muslims] and pagans whatsoever, and other enemies of Christ wheresoever placed, and the kingdoms, dukedoms, principalities, dominions, possessions, and all movable and immovable goods whatsoever held and possessed by them and to reduce their persons to perpetual slavery, and to apply and appropriate to himself and his successors the kingdoms, dukedoms, counties, principalities, dominions, possessions, and goods, and to convert them to his and their use and profit."[71]

Guided by the Vicar of Christ, the Portuguese set out raiding the African coast along the Mediterranean and Atlantic Coast, beginning the African slave trade.[72] Columbus discovered the New World in 1492 and his plans for enslaving the native tribe (the Arawaks) is recorded in his diary.[73] In 1493 Pope Alexander VI (Roman Pontiff 1492-1503) (the father of Cesare Borgia) decreed the Papal Bull *Inter Caetara* which divided the lands of the New World between Spain and Portugal, and guaranteed the safety of Christian missionaries.[74]

Around this time the King of England, Henry VII (r. 1457-1509) authorized in 1496, the right to "conquer, occupy, and possess" the lands inhabited by "heathens and infidels". In 1578 and again in 1584, Queen Elizabeth I (r. 1588-1603) authorized the seizure of "remote heathen and barbarous lands". Purportedly, these Elizabethan colonizers had received plenty of training already as Elizabeth worked to finish the mission of her father Henry VIII in conquering Ireland.[75]

These Papal Bulls and laws were recognized by the US Supreme Court in cases brought by Native Americans against US encroachment, as for example in, *Johnson v. M'Intosh* (1823), *Cherokee Nation v. Georgia* (1831) and *Worcester v. Georgia* (1832), *Tee-Hit-Ton v. United States* (1955), and others.[76]

---

[70] Malcolm Billings, *The Cross & The Crescent: A History of The Crusades*, (New York, Sterling Publishing, 1988) p208
[71] Quoted in Francis Jennings, *The Invasion of America*, (New York, W.W.Norton & Company, 1976) p44
[72] Jennings, p4
[73] Howard Zinn, *A People's History of the United States*, (New York, HarperCollins, 1980)
[74] Jennings, p5
[75] Jennings, p5, 45-46
[76] Links to the full (translated) texts of the Papal Bulls *Romanus Pontifex* and *Inter Caetara*, can be accessed through the website of the Jesuit Spring Hill College. www.shc.edu/thelibrary/docs.htm Peter Nabokov's *Native American Testimony* reveals how through the 19th century these and other "documents became thinly disguised bills of sale, transferring ancient tribal lands into white hands," though of course the US was not in the jurisdiction of the Holy Roman Empire. (Revised Edition, New York, Penguin Books, 1991, p118) Edward Conrad Smith notes that when the US Supreme Court did side with the Native Americans, as for example, in *Worcester v. Georgia*, both the state of Georgia and President Andrew Jackson refused to obey or enforce the courts decisions and by 1835 most Cherokees had been exiled. (*The Constitution of the United States, With Case Summaries*, 11th edition, ed. Edward Conrad

In the 19th century, as in centuries before, Native Americans, or Indians, were forcefully converted to Christianity from their own religion.[77] One Kamia Indian named Janitin wrote about the coerced conversion he underwent in California, being imprisoned and whipped daily. In 1865 the US government made formal arrangements for Protestant groups to administer government-owned boarding schools for Indians, which is said to have helped vanquish their own tradition and native identities.[78]

Shortly after the Civil War African-Americans were barred from attending churches that were reserved for whites only.[79] This would last for over a 100 years during which time restrictions against African-Americans were extended, also known as 'Jim Crow' laws. The so-called 'Jim Crow' laws which worked to segregate African-Americans from European-Americans often worked in fusion of church and state. The great Muslim teacher Malcolm X (1925-1965) wrote in his autobiography: "Sunday mornings in this year of grace 1965, imagine the 'Christian conscience' of congregations guarded by deacons barring the door to black would-be worshippers, telling them 'You can't enter *this* House of God!'"[80] Martin Luther King, Jr., said that, "We must face the shameful fact that the church is the most segregated major institution in American society, and most segregated hour of the week is... eleven o'clock on Sunday morning."[81]

Clearly in America there are advantages to being religious, though as we see it depends upon one's particular brand of religion, of course. People whom are religious get tax write-offs on many expenses. While a Muslim like Muhammad Ali was thrown in prison for refusing to fight, many religious people are exempt from the draft because they are religious. During the Vietnam War while 17 Jehovah's Witnesses were each given a 2-year sentence for refusing to register for the draft, an African-American was given a 5 year sentence.[82]

One clear instance of church and state intermingling, if often unnoticed, is the USA PATRIOT Act. This is an acronym standing for: Uniting and Strengthening America by Providing Appropriate Tools Required to Intercept and Obstruct Terrorism Act. Under this law, which was passed in the House of Representatives with only one vote opposing, that of Russell Fiengold of Wisconsin, the President is given power that cannot be checked by the Supreme Court or the Senate. This of course violates the system of checks and balances which the Founding Fathers had put in place to head-off a relapse into dictatorship, monarchy, and the Divine Right of Kings.

Under the USA PATRIOT Act thousands of American Muslims have been arrested, harassed, and had their homes and activities put under surveillance, without any

---

Smith, New York, Barnes & Nobles, 1979), p88. The Onondaga tribe of New York (and others) have asked the Vatican to revoke these Papal Bulls. Check Philip P. Arnold's, "Challenging the 'Doctrine of Discovery': Religious Roots of Cultural Imperialism and Environmental Destruction", July/August 2005. www.peacecouncil.net/NOON/articles/pnl744doctr.html

[77] Russell Thornton, *American Indian Holocaust and Survival: A Population History Since 1492*, (Norman, University of Oklahoma Press, 1990) p84
[78] Nabokov, p59-60, 53
[79] Phillips, p151
[80] *The Autobiography of Malcolm X*, (New York, Ballantine Books, 1992) p425
[81] Martin Luther King, Jr., *Strength To Love*, (Philadelphia, Fortress Press, 1963) p101-102
[82] Zinn, p506

"The Separation of Church and State" 59

indictments, with only one conviction.[83] As Nancy Chang, who is the senior litigation attorney at the Center of Constitutional Rights in New York City, shows, such anti-terrorist laws, like the laws which exist in England and which have helped to discriminate against Catholics and Muslims, work along such vague lines that they are a danger to religious-freedom and civil liberties. It is fairly clear that Bush has targeted Muslims and Arabs and not Terrorists per say.[84]

After the 2006 election, U.S. Congress Representative Virgil H. Goode ostensibly violated Article VI of the constitution, though no one has yet offered legal precedent. This Congressman sent out letters to voters with the claim that, Keith Ellison, the first Muslim elected to Congress posed a serious threat to the nation's values. He warned voters if they didn't "wake up", there will "likely be more Muslims elected to office demanding the use of the Koran."[85] Moreover, Goode's argument isn't just anti-constitutional, it is racist toward the newly elected Congressman and anti-Semitic in its scope. Republican Oklahoma state representative Sally Kern, who seems to know very little about the classical rule of divide and conquer believes that the only greater threat to the United States than Islam is homosexuality.[86] Senator John McCain, who has a 50% chance of winning the 2008 presidential election has said that he would never vote for a Muslim because he believes the US is a Christian nation.[87]

The War on Terror
There is a link between such policies as the USA PATRIOT Act and the US support of Israel. The religio-political word to describe this connection is called Zionism. However, Zionism was not originally a militant movement, but a movement for solidarity, peace and justice. (Isaiah 2:3-4) As the French-Jewish philosopher Emmanuel Levinas (1906-1995) points out, it is more accurate to speak of 'Zionisms' rather than of one single doctrine.[88]

Levinas finds that a purely political interpretation of Zionism "offers no clarification" because the conflict between the Israeli's and the Palestinians, like all conflicts, is dependent upon moral factors. Nor should giving a non-political explanation or going beyond politics give "recourse to any supernatural or miraculous dimension."[89] Levinas hoped that Zionism could offer a politically innovative non-universalism: that "the State of Israel will be the end of assimilation" A "State that should embody a prophetic morality and the idea of its peace… peace is a concept that goes beyond purely political thinking."[90]

---

[83] Nancy Chang, *Silencing Political Dissent*, (New York, Seven Stories Press, 2002) p15; As'ad AbuKhalil, *Bin Laden, Islam, and America's New 'War On Terrorism'*, (New York, Seven Stories Press, 2002) p86
[84] Chang, p67
[85] "Congressman Criticizes Election of Muslim", by Rachel L. Swarns in, *The New York Times*, December 21, 2006
[86] Hailey R. Branson, *New York Times*, 3/19/08
[87] Stephen Labaton, *New York Times*, 9/30/07
[88] Emmanuel Levinas, "Zionisms", trans. Roland Lack, from *The Levinas Reader*, ed. Sean Hand, (Oxford, Blackwell Publishers, 1989)
[89] Levinas, p277, 278
[90] Levinas, p287-288, 283. In a 1982 interview, published under the title "Ethics and Politics", Levinas sought to denounce "confusion between Zionism and messianism", and to separate Zionism "from the simplistic image of messianism, which is dangerous as a political principal." In light of the violence that year between Israel and Lebanon, Levinas concluded, "A person is more holy than a land, even a holy land,

The Zionism that sponsors militarization and the walls of segregation has been that of a Judeo-Christian doctrine to the exclusion of Islam and other religions. Some argue, the US War on Terror is really a War on Islam and find one of the most apparent marriages of 'church and state" in the U.S. sponsorship of the Israeli military.

While almost all U.S. senators and congressmen are Christian, only about a quarter of the U.S. electorates are Christian evangelicals (i.e., "fundamentalists").[91] There are probably less than 5 or 6 non-Christian senators and congressmen. Why is this significant? Most Christians believe Jesus' second coming will be in Israel. It should be remembered that it was because of a Christian majority in the United Nations vote of 1947 that Israel was granted nationhood. The English and French had colonized and occupied much of the Middle East following their victory in World War I, and the UN decision was just a continuation of the Balfour Declaration of 1918, which had been drafted by England, and granted them hegemony.

By the 1970's, the U.S. Congress was giving an annual loan to Israel of more than $500 million. After 1973 the U.S. increased its loans and grants to over 2.1 billion dollars, much of which was used to "buy swords" (Matthew 10:34, Luke 12:51, 22:36), i.e., weapons and tanks.[92] The biggest advocates of Israel have been the Christian Coalition and more recently by the Christians United for Israel.[93] It is realistic to see not only this religious justification but also the need for an ally in the Middle East. After all, as the satirical slogan asks, "why is our oil under their soil?"

The US enjoys a privileged position within the United Nations and it was the US who vetoed the attempt to make Palestine a state in 1976. This has only led to more war, more deaths, shattered families and lives. The white evangelical elected officials in the US believe that the support for Israel is a battle between Good versus Evil.[94]

Religion and Law
Although historically when linking church and state together we think of the Crusades or the Inquisition, today the Pope is still the infallible leader to millions of people around the world. The Catholic Church, which is based in the Vatican, still uses laws that are based upon Empire.[95] The Canon Law, if not a state law beyond the

---

since, faced with an affront made to a person, this holy land appears in its nakedness to be but stone and wood." Trans. Jonathan Romney, from *The Levinas Reader*, p295, 297

[91] Rachel Swarns, *The New York Times, December, 21, 2006*

[92] Ian Buruma, "How to talk about Israel", *The New York Times*, 8/31/2003

[93] David D. Kirkpatrick, "For Evangelicals, Supporting Israel Is 'God's Foreign Policy", *The New York Times*, November 14, 2006

[94] Kirkpatrick, *The New York Times*

[95] Nelson Mandela discusses the reaction by the various churches to the Bantu Education Act of 193. This was a law passed by the government forcing religious schools to hand over all matters of education to the state. Here the Catholic Church was not swayed by the state. He writes: "With the exception of the Dutch Reform Church, which supported apartheid, and the Lutheran mission, all Christian churches opposed the new measure. But the unity of the opposition extended only to condemning the policy, not resisting it. The Anglicans [Church], the most fearless and consistent critics of the new policy, had a divided policy... Despite their protests, all the other churches did the same with the exception of the Roman Catholics, the Seventh-Day Adventists, and the United Jewish Reform Congregation –who soldiered on without state aid. Even my own church, the Wesleyan Church, handed over their two hundred thousand African students to the government. If all the other churches had followed the example of those who resisted, the government would have been confronted with a stalemate that might have forced a compromise. Instead, the state

Vatican, is binding on all Catholics around the world. If the pope declares war, all Catholics must enlist.[96]

In 2007 Reverend Ruben Capitanio testified before a court in Argentina that the church was linked with atrocities, particularly a Reverend Christian von Wernich. Capitanio said, "The attitude of the church was scandalously close to the dictatorship", killing over 15,000 people, torturing tens of thousands of others, "…to such an extent that I would say it was of a sinful degree."[97]

Knowing the election year was coming, US bishops published a voting guide for American Catholics, titled *Forming Consciences for Faithful Citizenship*. The document raises the question of whether the church ought to deny communion to politicians who support abortion, which is an intrinsic evil.[98] In the election for Prime Minister in Spain, the Catholic Church urged Spanish voters to avoid all candidates who were socialists or who negotiate with socialists.[99] However, this seems redundant because in 1949 Pope Pius XII (p.1939-1958) excommunicated every communist in the world.[100]

Although numbers range well into the thousands, it is questionable whether Priests and Nuns involved in scandals will ever be charged as an average citizen would, for the sexual abuse of children. In a 2007 case involving sexual abuse by Nuns, one catholic woman said that she thought this was "just the tip of the iceberg".[101] In 2007 a Jesuit order in Alaska agreed to pay $50 million to over 100 natives of Alaska.[102] In 2006 a Roman Catholic Diocese in Iowa had filed bankruptcy when a jury awarded $1.5 million to a victim. In 2007 the diocese reached a $37 million settlement for 156 victims. In 2007 the Diocese in San Diego had filed for bankruptcy but was denied by a judge. The diocese had agreed to pay 133 claimants $183 million for sexual abuse. The Archdiocese in Portland, Oregon, came out of bankruptcy after settling to pay $51 million to 133 claimants, with $20 million extra for possible future victims. In 2007 the Diocese in Spokane, Washington came out of debt after a $48 million dollar settlement for 180 claimants. In 2006 the Tucson Diocese temporarily went into bankruptcy after paying over $22 million to 50-plus claimants.[103] In 2007 the Los Angeles Superior Court approved $660 million for a settlement between 500 victims and the archdiocese, making this the largest settlement in US history.[104] However, most or all of the clergy and nuns involved in all these cases were most likely defrocked as punishment.

In the US oftentimes there are state laws still writ from centuries ago which are not currently enforced for one reason or another. This does not mean that they are decriminalized, necessarily, but what should be understood is that these laws may be enforced again someday, given the circumstances.

---

marched over us." *Long Walk To Freedom: The Autobiography of Nelson Mandela*, (Boston, Little, Brown and Company, 1994) p167-168
[96] By order of Pope Pius IX's 1870 declaration "Pastor Aeternus". (Carroll, p441)
[97] Alexei Barrionuevo, "Argentine Church Faces 'Dirty War' Past", *New York Times*, 9/17/07
[98] Peter Steinfels, "Effort to Adopt Election-Year Statement Challenges Catholic Biships", *New York Times*, 10/27/07; Neela Banerjee, "Catholic Bishops Offer Voting Guide, Allowing some Flexibility on Issue of Abortion", *New York Times*, 11/15/07
[99] *New York Times*, 2/1/08
[100] Carroll, p44
[101] Catrin Einhorn, "Nun Pleads No Contest In Sex Abuse", *New York Times*, 11/13/07
[102] AP Press, *New York Times*, 11/19/07
[103] Dan Frosch, "Diocese in Iowa Settles With Abuse Victims for $37 Million", *New York Times*, 12/4/07
[104] Rebecca Cathcart, "Cardinal Tells of Assault Over Sexual-Abuse Cases", *New York Times*, 12/5/07

As we saw earlier the Protestant Reformation began the modern era of the centralized state. The National Church of the United States in Washington DC is an Episcopal one. One particularly bad link between church and state is the indiscriminate use of the word "evil". President Bush has called those opposed to US foreign policy "evil-doers". Whether or not evil actually exists or not, there is a very strong connotation, especially when used by politicians because it designates something which cannot be tolerated and which from necessity must be eradicated. If someone or something is evil, it cannot, by biblical definition, be negotiated with or reformed.

Blasphemy Laws

To this day 'democratic' countries such as England, Finland, New Zealand, Switzerland, the Netherlands, Germany, Austria, and Spain all have blasphemy laws.[105] Spain, for example, celebrates holidays which are viewed by many as anti-Semitic. Such celebrations involve portraying the Muslims by doing black-face painting and celebrate the defeat of the Muslims by Christian conquerors.[106]

However, in true unison of church and state, these blasphemy laws do not recognize the rights of all religions and beliefs. When at the outbreak of the First World War the atheist Bertrand Russell (1872-1970) preached pacifism, the Christian government of England had him arrested (1918). The American philosopher Robert Audi sites another example in his work, *Religious Commitment and Secular Reason*: "In 1988, when British Muslims petitioned their government to ban Salman Rushdie's *Satanic Verses*, they discovered the existing blasphemy law did not prohibit insults to the Prophet Muhammad. It protected only Christianity."[107]

Ever since Henry VIII declared himself head of church and state in the 1500's, there has been a strong connection between church and state in England for nearly 500 years. Although the 17th century philosopher John Locke is credited as one of the first thinkers to make a separation between church and state, he of course had to flee England because of persecution. Is was during his exile in Amsterdam that he studied the political writings of Benedict Spinoza, a 17th century Dutch-Jew who had written extensively on the connection between church and state. Spinoza's lengthy *Tractatus Theologico-Politicus*, was published in 1670. Locke may have never come across the writings of Spinoza, if only because they were banned in 1674 by the slow-witted Prince of Orange, on the charge that Spinoza had blasphemed God, the Trinity, the divinity of Christ and His promise of salvation. Spinoza's work was tautologically labeled 'dangerous poison' by Orange, either to avoid redundancy, or so as not to confuse it with a more benign poison.[108] In 1688 the Prince of Orange became 'King Billy', King of England as William III, ushering in what doesn't just seem to be an epoch of conformity and stupidity.

---

[105] www.Wikipedia.org/wiki/Blasphemy, accessed 1/8/07. Though nationalists and anarchists alike loathe reference to Wikipedia, I have taken the liberty here and perhaps one other place in this book and take full responsibility for all errors.
[106] Akbar S. Ahmed, *Islam Today*, (London, I.B.Tauris & Co Ltd., 1999) p72; Carroll, p324
[107] Peter van der Veer and Hartmut Lehmann, *Nation and Religion*, quoted in Robert Audi, *Religious Commitment and Secular Reason*, (Cambridge University Press, 2000) p221-222
[108] W.H. White in his Translator's Preface to Benedict Spinoza, *Ethics*, (Hertfordshire, Wordsworth Editions Limited, 2001) XXIII-XXIV

Blasphemy laws still exist in England, and cases surface occasionally. To this day England still maintains their monarchy. The Queen of England is the head of the Protestant Anglican Church, and English 'Lords' are still referred to as the 'Lords Spiritual', and have more political clout than your average Englishman. Former Prime Minister Winston Churchill (r.1940-1945, 1951-1955) is quoted as having said, "I see no hope for the world, I am a man without hope", before praying with American Reverend Billy Graham.[109] Former Prime Minister Tony Blair (r.1997-2007) recently converted to Catholicism. Although there over two dozen mosques in London, plans to build one were recently sent back, which may be due in part to hostility by many toward Muslims.[110] The archbishop of Canterbury recently called on the British government to adopt aspects of the Islamic Law, or Shariah, in an effort to demonstrate equality, though he believes that Parliament and the courts of course have the last say. The archbishop, Reverend Rowan Williams, was highly criticized for his speech by many English citizens and officials.[111] The English government created a research panel which recommends that English children attending public schools be made to pledge allegiance to the Queen, as well as participate in citizenship ceremonies. This research was commissioned by Prime Minister Gordon Brown in an effort to get Scottish and Muslims in England to be more patriotic and nationalistic.[112]

In Russia, which had a centuries long history of persecuting Muslims under the Soviet regime, President Vladimir V. Putin has worked to increase religious tolerance in Russia. While the Russian occupation of the Muslim state of Chechnya has not helped things, in the past year Putin has set up government funding to assist any of the able-bodied Russian Muslims, who number up to possibly 23 million, on the hajj to Mecca. Putin has also used $60 million dollars in Russian money to support Islamic culture in Russia, (Russia has over 4000 mosques), as well as Islamic science and education, and state-accredited Muslim schools and universities.[113]

Blasphemy laws still exist in the books of state law, in some American states. For example the Massachusetts General Law states that denying the existence of God is punishable by imprisonment for up to a year, or a fine of $300 dollars. In Maryland, blasphemy gets you $100 dollar fine and/or 6 months in prison.[114]

As recently as 1960 a case was brought before the U.S. Supreme Court because the Constitution of the State of Maryland barred atheists and agnostics from holding public office. *Torasco v. Watkins* ended in a unanimous decision on the unconstitutionality of Maryland's state law, though both Maryland's Circuit Court and Court of Appeals had ruled against Torasco. Pennsylvania, Tennessee, and Arkansas either hold or have held until the 1960's that office holders must believe in God and can be impeached if they do not.[115]

---

[109] Edward Rothstein, "At Billy Graham Library, Man and Message Are One and the Same", *New York Times*, 11/10/07
[110] Jane Perlez, "A Battle Rages in London Over a Mega-Mosque Plan", *New York Times*, 11/4/07
[111] John F. Burns, "Top Anglican Seeks a Role For Islamic Law in Britain", *New York Times*, 2/8/08
[112] Sarah Lyall, "Britain: Pledging Allegiance To Her Majesty", *New York Times*, 3/12/08
[113] Michael Schwirtz, "Putin Opens Mecca Path For Muslims", *New York Times*, 12/17/07
[114] Massachusetts General Law, Chapter 272, Section 36 www.mass/gove/legis/laws/mg/272-36.html; Maryland Article 72, Section 189
[115] Walter Kaufmann, *The Faith of a Heretic*, p28-29

Many members of the Christian terrorist group, the Ku Klux Klan have held important public offices, though their level as 'active' members while holding office in many cases may be doubted. It is said that President Harry S. Truman (r.1945-1953) had very briefly been a dues-paying Klan member, though it should be remembered that he desegregated the US army. It is said, probably falsely, that President Warren G. Harding (r.1921-1923) had been sworn in to the Klan right inside the White House.[116] Democratic Senator Robert Byrd of West Virginia was a member of the Klan, though probably many other senators have been in the past.[117] Both U.S. Supreme Court Justices Edward Douglass White (j.1910-1921) and Hugo Black (j.1937-1971) were Klan members, though it can be said on behalf of Chief Justice Black that he wrote for the court's unanimous decision in the aforementioned *Torasco v. Watkins*.[118]

Capital Punishment

There has been a stereotype ever since the writing of the New Testament that 'the Jews', meaning every Jew still living today, are somehow responsible for the execution of Jesus. While this claim has been refuted in different studies, most influentially, by the Quran itself, it is not the intention of this study to make another rebuttal. The subject being one of church and state, however, it is pertinent to this discussion.

While the notion of an 'eye for an eye' did not originate with Judaism, the law is found in the Torah. Be that as it may, 'the Jews' have only practiced Capital Punishment once since Palestine became a Roman province, some hundred and twenty or so years before the birth of Jesus.[119] This single execution in the last 22 centuries was that of the War criminal, Adolf Eichmann, who was hung in Jerusalem in the 1950's.

Although for Christians there has always been at least one political execution that is necessary, for the Catholic Church there has been some reform. The medieval theologian Thomas Aquinas (1225-1274) had been a supporter of the death penalty and in 1953 Pope Pius XII had clarified that "the most important function of the punishment" is the "expiation of the crime committed".[120] Pope John Paul II (p.1978-2005) wrote in the encyclical *Evangelium Vitae* (3/25/1995) that only if nations are financially capable of putting people in prison, is it recommended to forego execution. In so many words, the church is not against capital punishment.[121]

One of the high points for Capital Punishment came during the Christian Spanish Inquisition, which began in the 15th century, though the church had programmed other

---

[116] John Corrado, "Was Warren Harding inducted into the KKK While President?", 11/8/05 www.straightdope.com/columns/read/2229/was-warren-harding-inducted-into-the-kkk-while-president
[117] Eric Pianin, "A Senator's Shame: Byrd, in His New Book, Again Confronts Early Ties to KKK", *Washington Post*, 6/19/05
[118] In his work *The Metaphysical Club*, Louis Menand mentions that Chief Justice White had been a Klan member after the Civil War, that President Woodrow Wilson watched the Ku Klux Klan's propaganda film, *The Birth of a Nation*, right inside the White House. (p387) Supreme Court Justice Hugo Black's membership is noted as well as the speculation of President Warren G. Harding by Roland G. Fryer, Jr., and Steven D. Levitt in their study, "Hatred and Profits: Getting Under the Hood of the Ku Klux Klan", 9/1/2007.
www.economics.harvard.edu/faculty/fryer/files/Hatred%20and%20Profits,%20Getting%20Under%20the%20Hood%20of%20the%20Ku%20Klux%20Klan.pdf
[119] Louis Ginzberg, *On Jewish Law and Lore*, (New York, Atheneum, 1955) p6
[120] Walter Kaufmann, *The Faith of a Heretic*, p183-184
[121] www.vatican.va/edocs/ENG0141/_INDEX.HTM

inquisitions before. The first Inquisition was established in 1231 by Pope Gregory IX (p.1227-1241), wherein people convicted of heresy were either burned at the stake or had their tongues removed. In 1252 Pope Innocent IV (p.1243-1254) decreed that torture is permitted. In 1484 Pope Innocent VIII drafted the Papal Bull *Summis Desiderantes*, which gave legal enforcement to witch-burning, a tradition that was not protested by the Protestant Reformation. The Spanish Inquisition began in or before the year 1492 at the request of the Divine monarchs Ferdinand and Isabella. The Grand Inquisitor Torquemada burned 2000 humans at the stake in the first 8 years of the inquisition and thousands more died in the decades to come. The Spanish Inquisition lasted 300 years, only being interrupted by Napoleon who shut it down upon conquering Spain. The Roman Inquisition began in 1543 by Pope Paul III (p.1534-1549) wherein dozens were executed and books were burned. In 1659 the Spanish Inquisition sent spies to Amsterdam to investigate the philosopher Benedict Spinoza. It was during the Spanish Inquisition that the church introduced the torture technique of 'waterboarding'[122], a technique that is still used on Muslims to this year in Guantanamo Bay, the center for the US Inquisition.

The Protestant Founding Fathers –Martin Luther, John Calvin, and King Henry VIII were all proponents of capital punishment. When Adolf Hitler was trying to get moral support for his practice of capital punishment, (or mass-extermination of some 18 million people, 6 million of which were Jewish), he widely distributed the writings of Martin Luther, such as Luther's pamphlet, "On the Jews and Their Lies". Luther had written in 1543 that Jews ought to "forbidden on pain of death to praise God, to give thanks, to pray, and to teach publicly, among us and in our country".[123]

John Calvin had sent at least one person to the Inquisition to be executed, a physician named Michael Servetus who denied the trinity and was thus charged with heresy. Calvin believed it was the job of the state to punish the bad.[124] Henry VIII had at least two of his wives executed by the state and had others, such as the philosopher of *Utopia* Sir Thomas More (1478-1535), beheaded.[125]

In 1841 de Tocqueville wrote that if one looked "for the key to the social enigma presented to the world by the United States", a gander at the pre-Revolutionary legislation of the colonies is the both the most "peculiar" and "instructive". He goes on to quote laws from the colonies of Massachusetts and Connecticut and finds that capitol punishment is rampant. According to these state laws a person is to be executed for worshiping false gods, blasphemy, sorcery, adultery, and rape. Moreover, various forms of corporal punishment were rampant. De Tocqueville writes: "Thus the legislation of a rough, half-civilized people was transported into the midst of an educated society with

---

[122] Carroll, p307, 317, 373, 411, 355-357
[123] Quoted by Carroll, p367
[124] Ronald H. Bainton, *Christian Attitudes Toward War and Peace: A Historical Survey and Critical Re-evaluation*, (Nashville, Abingdon Press, 1960), p145
[125] Charles Dickens wrote of the king, "Henry the Eighth has been favored by some Protestant writers, because the Reformation was achieved in his time. But the mighty merit of it lies with other men and not with him; and it can be rendered none the worse by this monster's crimes, and none the better by any defense of them. The plain truth is that he was a most intolerable ruffian, a disgrace to human nature, and a blot of blood and grease upon the history of England." Charles Dickens, *Child's History of England*, (New York, The Federal Book Company) p251-252. Originally published in 1851.

gentle mores; as a result the death penalty has never been more frequently prescribed by the laws or more seldom carried out."[126]

The Scottish were probably the first Western culture to get rid of the death penalty for the charge of heresy. This meant that the Scottish drew a distinction between divine justice, or what a god thinks one deserve on the one hand, and natural or social justice on the other, or what the community thinks one deserves.

In 1695 a young Scotsman named Thomas Aikenhead was the last person given the death penalty for violation of Blasphemy laws. Aikenhead had publicly doubted the veracity of the story of the resurrection of Jesus, the existence of Moses, saying among other things that Muhammad was better than them both. England had passed the Act of Toleration in 1689, which had been influenced by Locke's popular *A Letter Concerning Toleration*, published earlier that year. However, in 1832 a nine-year old child was executed in England for smashing a window and stealing some paint.[127] The last 'witch'-burning in Scotland occurred in 1722. Other countries followed: Switzerland and Spain burned 'witches' for the last time in 1782, Germany in 1793.

The Scottish, French, and Israelis have abolished the death penalty, while more than 75% of the United States still hold it as legal.[128] Notoriously, religious fundamentalism is greater in the U.S. than in all those nations which do not believe in capital punishment. The Algerian philosopher Albert Camus (1913-1960) wrote in his "Reflections on the Guillotine":

"Capital punishment, in fact, throughout history has always been a religious punishment. When imposed in the name of the king, the representative of God on earth, or by priests, or in the name of a society considered as a sacred body, it is not the human community that is destroyed but the functioning of the guilty man as a member of the divine community which alone can give him his life... Religious values, especially the belief in an eternal life, are thus the only ones one which the death penalty can be used, since according to their own logic they prevent that penalty from being final and irreparable: it is justified only insofar as it is not supreme."[129]

Although President Bush II is directly or indirectly responsible for the deaths of tens of thousands of innocent people in Afghanistan and Iraq (among other places), as the Governor of Texas Bush sent hundreds to the electric chair.[130]

For certain kinds of religious people like President Bush, killing people is a way of "bringing them to justice". In other words, to kill them is to do them justice. This is much along the lines of the Spanish Inquisition where executioners thought they were 'saving' heretics by torturing and killing them.

---

[126] Alexis de Tocqueville, *Democracy in America*, trans. George Lawrence, ed. J.P. Mayer, (New York, HarperCollins, 2000) p41, 42
[127] Walter Kaufmann, *Without Guilt and Justice*, p43-44
[128] It is probable that Venezuela was one of the first nations to abolish capital punishment.
[129] Albert Camus, "Reflections on the Guillotine", in *Religion From Tolstoy to Camus*, trans. *Evergreen Review* in, ed. Walter Kaufmann, (New York, Harper & Row, Publishers, Incorporated, 1964) p443-444.
Camus' *The Rebel: An Essay on Man in Revolt*, discusses the significance of the French Revolution and the dilapidation, or 'murder' as he puts it, of the 'king-priest'. This event "consummated what has significantly been called the passion of Louis XVI. Undoubtedly, it is a crying scandal that the public assassination of a weak but good-hearted man has been presented as a great moment in French history. The scaffold marked no climax: far from it. But the fact remains that, by its results and consequences, the condemnation of the king is at the crux of our contemporary history... The revolutionaries may well refer to the Gospel, but in fact, they dealt a terrible blow to Christianity from which it has not yet recovered." Trans. Anthony Bower, (New York, Alfred A. Knopf, 1954) p92
[130] Phillips, p 242

Some minority of churches in the U.S. are opposed to capital punishment, as for example the Methodists, Amish, Quakers, as well as some individual Catholics, although most churches do support the death penalty.[131] The Mormon Church holds as the 12th Article of Faith, patriotism, be it allegiance to kings, presidents, rulers, and magistrates, whose law must be obeyed, honored, and sustained.[132] The Mormon Founding Father Joseph Smith (1805-1844) was against slavery (he was a Vermonter). However, his followers were not and Utah was a slave state and "supported the aims" of the pro-slavery Confederacy during the Civil War (1861-1865).[133] Since the time of the murder of Smith in 1844, (he was killed in an Illinois prison by an angry Christian mob), Mormons have held capital punishment to be retributive and to be carried out through a firing squad or simple decapitation.[134]

To the Shores of Tripoli and Beyond

If as some want, the US government and constitution were more closely based upon a "literal" reading of the bible, what might follow? What would come of our democracy, of women's rights, of African-American's rights, of the abolition of slavery, or the American incredulity to the right of monarchy?

Many well-educated and self-educated people would be quick to add –*which reading* of the bible ought we to rely on as being the one which is literal? A freethinker might add -what if we come across contradictions in the Bible, which version ought we to prefer or abide by? Moreover the New Testament makes up a very small portion of the Christian Bible, and the four gospels themselves tell the same story four times, though there are some variations therein. After the four-told gospel, are personal letters, the book of Acts, which like the Gospels is merely a narrative, and the book of Revelation, which is a story that is said to take place in the near future. Where does this leave us?

How about our four points of analysis: the Divine Right of Kings, Women's Rights, Slavery, and the Death Penalty –how would these be understood in a theological configuration of the United States? For one thing, we would understand George W. Bush's presidency as he himself understood it: as righteous divine appointment.

Both the Old Testament and the New Testament agree to the Divine Right of Kings, although the former was much more discriminate, believing that the King (or 'Messiah' in Hebrew) must be a genetic descendant of King David. The New Testament however, says that question of genealogy are unprofitable and Kings, of whatever nation, are to be honored as divinely appointed regardless of their ethics.

As for Women's Rights, these too differ within the Christian Bible, though they are much more limited in the New Testament than in the Old. President Bush seems to

---

[131] Martin Luther King, Jr., who was a Protestant Baptist, said that, "Capital punishment is society's final assertion that it will not forgive." In "Love in action", *Strength to Love*, p39
[132] http://scriptures/lds.org/en/a_of_f/1/
[133] Jon Krakauer, *Under The Banner of Heaven*, (New York, Anchor Books, 2003) p209n
[134] Martin R. Gardner, "Mormonism and Capital Punishment: A Doctrinal Perspective, Past and Present", in *Dialogue: A Journal of Mormon Thought*, Spring 1979.
http://content.lib.utah.edu/cdm4/document.php?CISOROOT=/dialogue&CISOPTR=4434&CISOSHOW=4312 B.H. Roberts, ed. *History of the Church of Jesus Christ of Latter-day Saints*, Volume 5, p296.
www.archive.org/stream/historyofchurcho05churrich/historyofchurcho05churrich_djvu.txt

have worked with some accuracy here as his department has worked to defeat international women's treaties.[135]

While slavery was limited in the Old Testament to a term of 6 years, the New Testament overrules any limitations to the practice of slavery. In fact US legal history stands in gross contradiction to the Old Testament, particularly concerning the Fugitive Slave Act. The Fugitive Slave Act was a law passed in 1850 that made it easier and officially authorized for slave owners to reclaim slaves who had fled to free-states. In fact, it seems those religious slave owners were not very scrupulous in their interpretations of scripture. The Fugitive Slave Act was also written to criminalize anyone helping a runaway slave. Compare to Torah:

"Thou shalt not deliver unto his master a bondman [or slave] that is escaped from his master unto thee; he shall dwell with thee, in the midst of thee, in the place which he shall choose within one of thy gates, where it liketh him best; thou shalt not wrong him." -Deuteronomy 23:16[136]

Capital Punishment, or the Death Penalty, is of course justified throughout the Bible. But how about Bush's attempt to close the US borders and strengthen the border patrol? The Old and New Testaments offer us a clue:

"And if a stranger sojourn with thee in your land, ye shall not do him wrong. The stranger that sojourneth with you shall be unto you as the home-born among you, and thou shalt love him as thyself; for ye were strangers in the land of Egypt: I am the Lord your God." -Leviticus 19:33-34

The New Testament teaches, "If anyone comes to you and does not bring this teaching, never receive him into your homes or say a greeting to him." (2 John 10)[137]

Hundreds, perhaps thousands, of prisoners have been kept at the U.S. prison colony in Cuba, Guantanamo Bay. For years none of these men have been charged nor have they been given the right to a trial. All of this violates international law. Aren't our bible-thumping politicians being hypocritical to the actual words of the bible which says, "Ye shall have one manner of law, as well for the stranger, as for the home-born; for I am the Lord your God." (Leviticus 24:22) Or perhaps we ought to treat these prisoners as Jesus was treated?

The Founding Fathers did however attempt to make one more stronghold for constitutional democracy, perhaps in the event that the majority of American's remained Christian, as they have. At the end of the 18th century as America was beginning its first years as a nation, reports were received that American merchant ships were being pirated in the Mediterranean Sea. When the U.S. Marines were deployed to the area it became known that much of the fighting would occur near Muslim nations and peoples. Although Bush II has declared the war against the Muslim nations a "crusade", the founding fathers were a bit more scrupulous. They wanted to avoid this terminology if by chance the war reminded the North Africans of the earlier Christian blunders, the Crusades.

In 1796, just before the end of his second term, President George Washington (r.1789-1797) drafted and signed the Treaty of Tripoli, weary of getting the U.S. involved in such a crusade or global war. On June 7, 1797, the Treaty of Tripoli was read before Congress and signed by President John Adams (r.1797-1801). Article XI of the Treaty of Tripoli states:

---

[135] Phillips, p240
[136] Torah trans. from the Masocretic text, (Philadelphia, The Jewish Publication Society of America, 1917)
[137] New Testament passages from *The New World Translation of the Holy Scripture*, trans. New World Bible Translation Committee, (Brooklyn, Watchtower Bible and Tract Society, 1961)

"The Government of the United States of America is not, in any sense, found on the Christian Religion."[138]

Although this is significant as an instance of great discernment and fastidiousness on he part of the Founding Fathers, it is even more significant within the United States itself because of an important clause in the U.S. Constitution. Article VI, Section 2 states:

"This constitution, and the laws of the United States... and all treaties made, under the authority of the United States, shall be the supreme law of the land."

Thus, when the Treaty of Tripoli says our nation "is not, in any sense, found on the Christian Religion", according to the U.S. Constitution this is "supreme law of the land". Notice that George Washington and John Adams do not single out Judaism or Islam (or Hinduism, Buddhism, or Taoism, etc..).[139] If church and state cannot be separated, and Christianity cannot be the basis for the US state by definition, which religion ought we to prefer?

In discussing the separation of church and state this essay has focused on four institutions: the divine right of kings, slavery, women's suffrage, and the death penalty. We have seen how the Scottish, French, and American figures of the Enlightenment did away with the divine right of kings. It took an extremely bloody war to end slavery in America. For women to gain the right to vote it took a lot of activism and many public demonstrations and sober protests. Chapter 3 will discuss further the issues of the Divine Right of Kings, Women's Rights, and Slavery as they are regarded by the popular monotheisms and other religions and philosophies.

As for the death penalty, we have seen the religious justifications and it is popular assumption that all religions hold to some form of capital punishment. This should be clarified in the case of the religion of Islam, however. While it is popular to point out that Muslims believe in 'an eye for an eye', the Islamic Law, Shariah, is not state law, so lawfully one cannot call the Death Penalty a state-law. Perhaps this separation of church and state is why the Renaissance and Enlightenment owe their origins to Islam. The Quran tells us, "No compulsion is there in religion."[140] (Surah 2:256) We will return the question of Capital Punishment and justice in Chapter 6.

A hundred years ago the pragmatist and pedagogical innovator John Dewey wrote the reason that

"the American tradition is so strong against any connection of state and church, why it dreads even the rudiments of religious teaching in state-maintained schools, the immediate and superficial answer is not far to seek. The cause was not, mainly, religious indifferences, much less hostility to Christianity, although the eighteenth-century deism played an important role. The cause lay largely in the diversity and vitality of the various denominations, each fairly sure that, with a fair field and no favor, it could make its own way; and each animated by a jealous fear that, if any connection of state and church were permitted, some rival denomination would get an unfair advantage."

Dewey did not believe the Founding Fathers had sought to separate church and state, but more significantly, to subordinate all churches to the state. He wrote: "Doubtless many of our ancestors would have been somewhat shocked to realize the full

---

[138] http://avalon.law.yale.edu/18th_century/bar1796t.asp
[139] Oddly enough, de Tocqueville was convinced that because the Koran was more scientific than the New Testament that Islam would not fair as well in the age of enlightenment and democracy. See, George E. Lawrence's trans., ed. J.P. Mayer, (New York, First Perennial Classics, 2000) p445 (Unabridged)
[140] From A.J. Arberry', *The Koran Interpreted*, (New York, Macmillan Publishing Company, 1955)

logic of their own attitude with respect to the subordination of churches to the state (falsely termed the *separation* of church and state)". Because he was so involved in public education, he was well aware of the questions and problems which inevitably arise in a country comprised of such broad diversities. He believed that if we decide to teach some religion in schools, the question then becomes "which" religion? Dewey did not think that even in the United States that just one religion could be taught. He said, "In America, at least, the answer cannot be summarily given even as Christianity in general... [But] even if it were a question of Christianity alone. *Which Christianity?*"[141] There are of course hundreds of Christian denominations in the United States alone.

Moreover, in a democracy separation of church and state might be impossible if a majority of citizens are religious in general. The democratic vote is after-all determined by the majority. This might be empirically verifiable. Such a general position is criticized by the American philosopher Robert Audi. In his work, *Religious Commitment and Secular Reason*, Audi writes: "Liberty and basic political equality are central among the ideals of free democracy, and some form of separation of church and state is essential to fulfilling the ideals." Audi holds that there isn't from necessity an incompatibility between the values of either church or state, but that in fact the "problem is particularly urgent today".[142]

Audi believes that a proper "separation of church and state provides a distinctive basis on which a free society can progress without undue strife even when there are irreconcilable differences among its citizens on...profound issues." Audi is a believer in the efficacy of human reason and the rational mind. He says that for those who hold "the idea that [human] reason is corrupt, I do not see how we can proceed in moral, political, and even religious matters without trusting reason to a high degree."[143]

After years of working to end the British occupation of India, as well as working with the millions of Muslims who live in India, (and the British had used the strategy against Hindu/Muslim unity of 'divide and conquer'), the great non-violent Hindu revolutionary Mohandas Gandhi (1869-1948) ended his autobiography by stating: "I can say without the slightest hesitation, and yet in all humility, that those who say that religion has nothing to do with politics do not know what religion means."[144]

Given these contrasting positions of Audi and Gandhi, either that a separation of church and state is integral to democracy or that such a separation is always illusory, which philosophy or religion should we as Americans understand as being the most democratic? Ought Americans to prefer one religion or philosophy over another? Are some religions more tolerant than others? Which religion is the most reasonable? Or most philosophical, or scientific? How will our choice here affect our understanding of such institutions as slavery, on women's rights, and incorrigibility toward the Divine Right of Kings? To these questions we immediately turn.

---

[141] John Dewey, "Religion and Our Schools", from *Essays on Pragmatism and Truth: 1907-1909*, The Middle Works, 1899-1924, Volume 4, ed. Jo Ann Boydston, (Carbondale, Southern Illinois University Press, 1977) p168-169, 171, 169
[142] Audi, p209-210
[143] Audi, p214-215
[144] Mohandas K. Gandhi, *An Autobiography: The Story of My Experiments with Truth*, trans. Mahadev Desai, (Boston, Beacon Press Books, 1957) p504. Gandhi had worked for years in the British colony of South Africa as well, and in 1914 he changed the British law (which echoed the Canon Law) so that non-Christian marriages would be recognized as lawful. (Called the *Indian Relief Act*.)

3

Why Islam is Greater Than Your Religion in Philosophy

The greatest thing about the love of wisdom is that it bears us and entreats us in face of hypocrisy. Hypocrisy –those who tell lies -will always try to forsake us, will always make us ask the wrong question or answer to an authority that is false. Honesty and wisdom are what maintain a true relationship with reality. Truth, wisdom, courage, tenacity, resilience, grit; in short –virtue, is what makes this world such a great place, is what makes reality its own reward. The rest is bullshit.

Not every belief is a true belief. Not every philosophy is a true philosophy. Not every question is a valid question, and not every answer has true-value or strength. The King of France isn't either bald or haired because there is no King of France. There is a real world around us –sometimes we have true knowledge of the world and sometimes we have false belief about the world. Socrates believed hemlock to be quite medicinal, but from what was written twenty-five centuries ago –I am convinced it is poisonous. Not all knowledge is gained through experience; some comes through reasoning.

If we believe that the world was created in six days some 6000 thousand years ago or was created 30 billion years ago, or differently, if we believed that the world was created *ex nihilo,* from nothing, as well as from preexisting matter –then logically our beliefs are contradictory. Our beliefs would be in contradiction to one another. Something can't both be true and not true simultaneously. Even if it turned out that one of our beliefs was in fact really the truth -say the earth really was created 30 billion years? The answer is still that we would not have true belief. This is because we would still lack the right kind of justification –we would only be right by chance, and not by faith alone.

Hypocrisy, like bullshit, is unconcerned with truth, even if it presents itself always as being unfailingly, the real truth. Whether or not there were weapons of mass destruction in Iraq, for example, as it turns out there were not, it would be hypocritical for a bullshitter to recognize their disagreement with fact. This is because hypocrites present their beliefs to be the 'real' truth, and like the neurotic, unwittingly believe that they cannot fail to know what is true, though some are just complacent in their own childish ways. However, unlike the liar, for whom the truth is of the utmost importance, the bullshitter is unconcerned with truth.

This disregard for the truth of the world around us is naïve, but is often a product of imperialism. However, imperialism is just as often masked as another 'ism' – relativism. Relativism is the corrosive idea that each person or culture has their own truths that for them alone are true. As some say in order to curtail disagreement and justify what is habitual and status quo: "Its all relative". On this relativist and imperialist account humans cannot know what is true in the sense of there being a world around them. What is true is true relative to one's own perspective and one's relatives. If the relativist believes that truth is just a kind of personal truth, the imperialist believes their own personal truth is the only real truth -even if some foreigners "just don't get it" and hold to their own personal false truths with undue fervency and ethical practicality.

Some beliefs are stronger than other beliefs, and some philosophies are greater than other philosophies. Reality, like gravity, is separate from any system of belief. Every system of beliefs is a philosophy, but not every philosophy is a belief system: some philosophies are more closely based on reality than others. The question of whether we are born a blank slate or whether we are representative of some race or culture is beside the point. There is a real world which we are part of so we cannot always choose what we believe. The true value of a belief is found in real life in its application in this world: to the extent that it is reasonable or intelligible or valuable or ethical and practical. This is the strength of philosophy over mere belief.

The question of philosophy is a question of true-value. Just as there are many philosophies, there are many kinds of values and many kinds of belief systems. Some systems of belief are called religions. Every religion is a philosophy, but not every religion is just a belief system –some are more or less practical and reasonable than others.

Although I believe that philosophy is greater than religion, some religions are greater than some philosophies. This is because some beliefs are more reasonable or more practical than others. If the strength of a belief cannot determine its truth, still some beliefs are greater than other beliefs in their value and coherence.

Even if we do not follow any religion in particular, and are non-religious like myself, I realistically accept that there is a world around me, which in some ways I know, and some ways I do not know. How do we learn about what we do not know? It is the purpose of this essay to literally demonstrate to the English speaker: we can only understand, by standing-under. Thus by understanding, we might be able to find out which religion is the most philosophical, which religion has greater practicality, consistency, and sustainability. This is the realm of philosophy and the wisdom of love.

Could someone who is not religious and who is a non-theist have anything to say about the philosophical hierarchy of theistic religions? Let us consider something that some might call a "trivial" matter, but which will demonstrate how quickly it can be understood as significant: translation.

Let's be realistic. We speak English. And if we can read, we read in English, too. If we cared to read something written by a foreigner, say in the Spanish or Dutch languages, we would read an English-translation. If we want to read something that is older than the Spanish or Dutch, or English languages, we must read a translation. If we want to read Beowulf or the Bible, or the ancient Sumerian *Epic of Gilgamesh*, we must read a translation. Translations are often done by a native English speaker who has learned a foreign language, or by a foreigner who has learned English in addition to their own native language. Many ancient languages no longer have native speakers, such as Sumerian, Babylonian, Abenaki, as well as thousands, though probably millions of other languages.

If we look for a copy of a book, for example, something written 2400 years ago in the language of ancient Greek, say Plato's book *Symposium*, we will find that there are several translations. How do we pick the best (or most sober) translation without having to learn the foreign language ourselves? This excursion would entail us becoming exegetical -comparing words and phrases in different contexts alongside the original untranslated text (which could take something like a very long-time)? Perhaps we should go to an authority on the matter, someone that is an expert in the area of translations? After all there are only thousands of languages, how could one person possibly find the time to learn them all?

Experts are notoriously good in their area of expertise. What 'translation manuals' do these expert translators use in this science of translation? Who, in turn, wrote these 'translation manuals' in the first place, what language was the translator's mother's tongue? As a reader should be able to see: we are left with only an infinite regress -the chicken and the egg. It seems if we want translation to be an exact science we will be faced with only impossibility. Shall we conclude that because the immaculate 'translation manual' doesn't exist that translation is impossible?

William Shakespeare, however many writers that is, knew less than 20 thousands words.[1] The English language itself has something like 400,000 words in it. A lot of the words Shakespeare used some 400 years ago are today unfamiliar to us. When we look for the meanings of these words in the dictionary, as well as the meanings of other words, we will find not only that some words have several different meanings (some of which are contradictory), but that most English words are in fact rooted in different, and often-times much older languages.

Etymology, the study of the historical development of words, reveals this history of variation. For example: take the word *coffee*. The English word 'coffee' originally comes from the Italian word *caffe*, which itself was taken from the Arabic word *qahwah*, which means, "a drink made from berries".[2] Or the word *America:* America is the French version of the name *Americus Verspucius*, which is a Latinization of the name *Amerigo Vespucci*, who was an Italian navigator who for some time was believed to have been the discoverer of the Americas in the year 1512. Even the word *neologism*, which means "new word", is compounded from the Greek words *neos* (new) and *logos* (word).

Who decides which words become part of the language and are accepted as the right and proper names of things? Some have argued that there is an initial baptism or 'naming ceremony' that is performed by a social group through something called 'ostension'.[3] This has led some to note the patriarchal nature of English, where masculine words are taken as paradigms, as for example 'person', 'human', and 'mankind'. In the Hebrew story of creation, the book of Genesis, we read that Yhwh (Hebrew for 'God') has Adam name all the creations on earth. Entire languages are sometimes invented, as for example in the beginning of the 20th century when the victors of the First World War dissolved the Ottoman Empire. The political leader Kamal Ataturk commissioned experts in linguistics to come up with a national language for modern Turkey.

Some ethicists have pointed out that translation is highly political. It involves comparing what is unique and different from the values of different traditions, different cultures, and especially different speakers and writers, all of whom wrote under different circumstances at different points in history. For most of us who are fluent only in

---

[1] Counting all lexemes. David Crystal, *The Cambridge Encyclopedia of The English Language*, (Cambridge, Cambridge University Press, 1995) p123
[2] William & Mary Morris, *Dictionary of Word and Phrase Origins, Volume II*, (New York, Harper and Row, 1967) p54
[3] Saul Kripke, *Naming and Necessity*, (Cambridge, Harvard University Press, 1980) p96-97

English, such as myself, we must rely on different translators as authorities over what is "literally" the truth, all ethics aside.

Many translation versions are contro-versial and there is debate between experts over which translation is most authoritative. Some have jumped from this phenomenon of disputation to argue that there is always a biased understanding of different languages –that a person's values and social environment be they a translator or a reader, will always affect how they interpret the world of others. This phenomenon was studied at length by the Algerian-born French philosopher Jacques Derrida, who wrote that:

"The battle of proper names follows the arrival of the foreigner and that is not surprising. It is born in the presence and even from the presence of the anthropologist who comes to disturb order and natural peace."[4]

In his study *Of Grammatology* Derrida uses the word 'logocentricism' to describe this prejudice. Like the word neologism, or "new word", 'logocentricism' is a big word that is easily translated into smaller ones. It comes from the Greek *logos* (word) and *centri* (center) and is the belief that one language, particularly one's own language, is superior to all others. For Derrida, logocentricism is just as often indistinguishable from ethnocentricism –the belief that one's own ethnicity is superior to others.[5]

As some revolutionaries have noticed, 'history is written by the victor.' Perhaps the only reason we know that Julius Caesar conquered Britain over 2000 years ago is because he wrote about it. Those who write and record and translate often have authority over what people are made to understand. Social theorist and activist Edward Said (pronounced *si-eed*) tells us:

"The authority of academics, institutions, and governments can accrue to texts [i.e., translations], surrounding it with still greater prestige than its practical successes warrant. Most important, such texts can *create* not only knowledge but also the very reality they appear to describe."[6]

The writers and translators creation of knowledge can have both good and bad effects. The latter phenomenon is well described in Said's book, *Covering Islam: How the Media and the Experts Determine How We See theWorld*. Said, who was an a n non-theist from a Christian background, discusses this power over translation:

"In [Britain and France] there has always been a cadre of Islamic experts, of course, with a longstanding advisory role in formulating –and even executing- government as well as commercial policy. But in both instances there was an immediate task at hand: the administering of rule in colonies."[7]

The ethnocentricism, or logocentricism, that we have been describing has a long history. For the ancient Greeks anyone who could not speak their language was called a *barbarian*. When William the Conqueror defeated the Anglo-Saxons in 1066, in the so-called 'Norman Conquest', the English language went through a Dark Ages of sorts and for the next few centuries all monarchs and clergy of Britain spoke and wrote only in French. By the 13th century some 10,000 French words had become standardized in the English language –almost exclusively words dealing with administration, law, science, fashion, and art. The English vocabulary as exists today is comprised of words from over 120 different languages from around the world.[8]

---

[4] Jacques Derrida, *De la Grammatologie*, trans. Gayatri Chakravorty Spivak, (Baltimore, Johns Hopkins University Press, 1997) p113
[5] The first 'logocentricist' and coiner of the term was the German philologist Ludwig Klages, whose use of the term in the 1920's is positive if uncritical.
[6] Edward Said, *Orientalism*, (New York, Vintage Books, 1979) (a) p94
[7] Edward Said, *Covering Islam*, (New York, Pantheon Books, 1981) (b) p144
[8] Crystal, p46-47, 126

Translation has many benefits and has probably saved many lives. Thomas Cahill's book *How The Irish Saved Civilization,* gives an account of how from the 5th-9th centuries, a time which is usually considered the heart of the Dark Ages of Europe, Irish monks translated and preserved books which would have otherwise been destroyed by the Northern European tribes, as for example most books and libraries were during the sack of Rome (though a greater number of books were destroyed by the church itself).

During this period of the European Dark Ages was the Golden Age of Spain, which at the time was known as 'Al-Andalusia' by the Muslims who thrived there. When Muslims conquered Spain in the year 710, like the Irish, they too safeguarded the Greek tradition, which was often otherwise destroyed by barbarians or burned by the church, by translating the ancient Greek works into Arabic. Historian of medicine Lawrence Conrad has written that these Arabic translations "saved many classical texts which might otherwise have been lost, and the Islamic world ultimately passed this heritage back to Europe when its medical works were translated into Latin."[9]

Translations have been of great benefit to some, though not always their messengers. The translation of an English version of the bible resulted in at least one death, that of William Tyndale, who was condemned as a heretic and burned at the stake in 1536 for translating the New Testament middle Greek into English. The bones of John Wycliff, who had translated the New Testament in the 14th century were dug up and burned 41 years after his death. When in 1611 the first English translation of the bible, the King James Version was completed, however inaccurate the translation really is, some argue that it still gave power to people who were not experts and thus had important political consequences. Martin Luther came to regret some of his own translations, lamenting, "It does not help the peasants' that they claim that in Genesis I and II all things are created free and common and that we have all been equally baptized."[10]

Other highly influential translations were those of the 19th century European philologists, as for example Max Muller, who began to translate Sanskrit books found in the European colonies in India. The ancient language of the Persians and Hindus, Sanskrit, contained a word that would go on to become the identity of Europeans during the late 19th and early 20th centuries: the word 'aryan'.[11] Though perhaps most English speaking people today still believe that the Sanskrit word 'aryan' is a European word, possibly of English or German origin, when in fact, the Middle Eastern country Iran can literally be translated as 'the Land of the Aryans', without *malapropos* or ethnocentricism.

Perhaps the maxim that 'history is written by the victors', should be tempered by something the philosopher Karl Popper (1902-1994) said in his book, *The Poverty of Historicism*[12], "history is affected by discoveries we will make in the future." Under this maxim it would seem that even our own understanding of ourselves, who we are, is

---

[9] Lawrence I. Conrad, "The Arab-Islamic Medical Tradition", in *The Western Medical Tradition: 800 BC to 1800 AD*, (Cambridge, Cambridge University Press, 1995) p93
[10] From *Werke*, Section XVIII, 358; trans. Walter Kaufmann. Quoted in Walter Kaufmann's, *The Faith of a Heretic*, (Garden City, Anchor Books, 1963) (a) p273.
[11] Max Muller (1823-1900) is quoted as having said of this malapropism, "To me an ethnologist who speaks of an Aryan race, Aryan blood, Aryan eyes and hair, is as great a sinner as a linguist would be if he spoke of a dolichocephalic dictionary or a brachycephalic grammar." In Paramahansa Yoganda's, *Autobiography of a Yogi*, (Los Angeles, Self-Realization Fellowship, 1946) p392n
[12] Karl Popper, *The Poverty of Historicism*, (New York, Harper & Row, 1957)

related to something greater than ourselves, namely, other people. So, if learning a language always depends on the sincerity of others, how are we to determine which translation is right and which is wrong? The American pragmatist philosopher Hilary Putnam gives us the quick on the matter:

> "...how do we know that a translation scheme 'works' if [individual] conceptions always turn out to be different? The answer to this question, as given by various thinkers from [Giambattista] Vico [1668-1774] down to the present day, is that interpretative success does not require that the translated beliefs come out the *same* as our own, but it does require that they come out *intelligible* to us."[13]

According to this definition of translation, translation can never be an exact science: the best translation will be the one that is the most intelligible or the most reasonable to us. This in some ways relates to the attempt to understand other peoples, which literally demands that we stand-under in order to understand, and by not imposing our own values and prejudices on what can never be seen as the same.

Another translation feat is occurring right now. There are some 300,000 Arabic books, some of which date back to the 12th century, now being translated for the first time, preserved by the Muslims of northern and central Africa.[14] These books deal with mathematics, science, medicine, and philosophy. One of the most popular ancient language today is Arabic, and there are almost a billion and half Muslims in the world, so Arabic is also one of the most popular languages in the world.

Be that as it may, Arabic, and the religion that has immortalized it, Islam, have had their share of critics. For all of its tolerance, Islam has been the most maligned religion in the world. In fact, more books and articles have been written in opposition to Islam than any other religion in world history.[15] This is especially true since the end of the Cold War with Russia and the need for a new scapegoat amongst us monolinguists.

A resentment of Islam began shortly after the death of the prophet Muhammad in the year 632. When in 638 Jerusalem was taken by Muslims, Jews were permitted to live in the city, drawing sharp criticism from many Christians. This was because the Christian Law or *Codex*, drafted one hundred years earlier by the Christian Byzantine Emperor Justinian I, continued the Roman tradition held since the 130's, which forbid Jews to live in the Holy Land. Thus the Muslims ended a 500-year exile of Jews from Jerusalem.

This led up to the 1st Crusade in the year 1096, which was issued by Pope Urban II in an attempt to reconquer 'Holy Lands' such as Jerusalem and Bethlehem. When the Christian crusaders reached Jerusalem in 1099 not a single person residing in the Holy Land was left alive, but every man woman and child was killed. The Christian Law was again reinstated, forbidding Jews [and Muslims] to live in Jerusalem. The Christians lost the 2nd Crusade, and every crusade to follow.

In 1187 the Muslim ruler from Egypt, Saladin recaptured Jerusalem. Saladin has become somewhat of a heroic figure in history for reasons other than his military prowess. He took Jerusalem by treaty and made compromises with the Christian King Guy for safe passage back to Europe. Where the Christians had destroyed the temples

---

[13] Hilary Putnam, "Philosophers and Human Understanding", in *Realism and Reason: Philosophical Papers, Volume 3*, (Cambridge, Cambridge University Press, 1983) (a) p195
[14] National Geographic, October 2007
[15] Seyyed Hossein Nasr, *The Heart of Islam: Enduring Values For Humanity*, (San Fransisco, HarperCollins, 2002) XIII

and mosques after the 1st Crusade, Saladin destroyed nothing, but rebuilt the mosque, and again allowed Jews to return to Jerusalem.

When the Christian poet Dante Alleghieri composed the celebrated and perverse epic The Divine Comedy in the 13th century, he depicted the prophet Muhammad as residing in hell. When Christians won the Battle of Grenada in 1492, Muslims and Jews were ordered to leave Spain. Those Muslims and Jews who were exiled from Spain found refuge in the Muslim nations of Africa as well as the Ottoman Empire, which was centered in modern day Turkey. Those who didn't make it that far east were detained in ghetto's. These ghettoes, such as the Roman Ghetto, were enclosed with walls by the Christian government, with only one entrance and exit. Ghettoes lasted until Napoleon (1769-1821) conquered Europe and tore down the walls. However, once the Frenchman died, they were rebuilt.[16]

The man who for the time being is said to have discovered America, the highly celebrated Christopher Columbus, did not love his neighbor Muslims. In a letter to the Spanish Queen Isabella, the very queen who had expelled all Jews and Muslims from Spain in 1492, the very year Columbus purportedly discovered America, Columbus wrote:

"Your Highness, as Catholic Christians and princes devoted to the holy Christian faith and the furtherance of its cause, and enemies of the sect of Mohammed and of all idolatry and heresy, resolved to send me, Christopher Columbus, to the...regions of India."[17]

In the 16th century the Protestant Father Martin Luther declared there were two archenemies of Jesus Christ: the Pope and the Prophet Muhammad.[18] In 1835 a British Lord Macaulay declared the languages of Arabic and Sanskrit to be held in contempt.[19] Or the psychologist E. Shouby whose 1951 essay, "The Influence of Arabic as a language on the Psychology of Arabs", argued that Arabic is marked by "General vagueness of Thought", "Overassertion" and "Exaggeration".[20]

The 16th century Dutch satirist Erasmus called for Christians to crusade against the Turks –"The Scourge of Christendom". The 17th century German mathematician, part-time alchemist and full-time courtier Barron Gottfried Leibniz criticized Islam as inspiring fatalism, or *fatum mahumetanum*.[21] The 18th century French satirist Voltaire wrote a book critical of Islam titled, *Fanaticism, or Muhammad the Prophet*. The 19th century French writer Ernest Renan who wrote a very successful biography, *Life of Jesus*, said that a Muslim is "incapable of learning anything or of opening himself to a new idea"[22] The 20th century Dutch painter M.C. Escher admitted to having made a career out of subrogating and deviating Arabic and Muslim art. Unlike the expressionless figures without qualities that Escher enjoyed representing in his work, he showed his gratitude by saying, "What a pity it is that Islam did not allow them to make 'graven images'."[23]

---

[16] James Carroll, *Constantine's Sword*, (Boston, Mariner Books, 2002) p416, 418
[17] Christopher Columbus quoted in Akbar S. Ahmed, *Islam Today*, (London, I.B. Tauris, 1999) (a) p71
[18] Ahmed, (a) p28
[19] Akbar S. Ahmed, *Islam Under Siege*, (Cambridge, Polity Press, 2003) (b) p76
[20] Said, (a) p320
[21] Maxime Rodinson, *Islam and Capitalism*, trans. Brian Pearce, (Austin, University of Texas Press, 1978) p109
[22] John L. Esposito, *Islamic Threat: Myth or Reality?*, Revised Edition, (Oxford, Oxford University Press, 1992) p44, 46
[23] M.C. Escher quoted by Miranda Fellows in *The Life and Works of Escher*, (Bristol, Parragon Book Service Limited, 1995) p22

Muslims would not be allowed back into Europe for almost 440 years, until the Christian Spanish monarchy fell in 1931. Shortly thereafter, the Christian Military General Francisco Franco led a revolution in Madrid in 1936, with the help of Muslims hired from Morocco. At the beginning of World War II, Benito (Il Duce) Mussolini led the Italians to wage war on the Abyssinian Muslims because of their alleged "heresy" against Christianity.[24] However, thousands of Muslims remained in Europe, though dispersed. These were the Muslim Roma, or Gypsies, as they are more popularly known. Not all Roma were Islamic, but most of the 600,000 killed in the Holocaust were.[25]

As H.G. Wells put it in his *Outline of History*, "By 1900 all Africa was mapped, explored, estimated, and divided between the European powers."[26] At the end of the First World War, the Muslim Ottoman Empire was for the most part, taken over by the victors of the war, in the Treaty of Sevres. "After the First World War, Britain, France, and Italy divided the Arab lands. Then, after the Second World War, the Europeans left behind artificial states and boundaries, often cutting tribes and nations in two."[27] France controlled the northern and western parts of Africa, as well as Lebanon and Syria, Britain controlled Palestine, Jordan, Iraq, the Gulf area, and the Indian subcontinent (contemporary Muslim nations like Pakistan, Afghanistan, and Bangladesh), as well as Southeast Asia, Malaya, Singapore, and more. The Dutch controlled Indonesia. By 1918 European countries occupied 85% of the globe.[28] Only two sovereign Muslim nations remained –Turkey and Iran.[29] Both of these nations were quickly modernizing as Ataturk moved to secularize Turkey, and the Shah of Iran was a puppet king to England and the United States. Ethiopia itself was a Muslim nation run by a corrupt Christian Emperor Haile Selassie (1892-1975).

Following the Second World War, the Cold War between the US and the USSR left Muslim peoples in very tough positions if only because their homelands so often had the oil which the opposing super-powers so badly needed. The bloody Russian-Afghanistan War has its roots in the Cold War, as does the Iraq-Iran War, both of which lasted roughly a decade and resulted in many, many deaths and economic relapses.

And in the past 20 years anti-Muslim violence has escalated. When the USSR collapsed in the 1990's, six new Muslim nations emerged. However, one former Soviet territory that was not freed was Chechnya. This is in all likelihood because Chechnya is oil-rich. However, the Muslim population of Chechnya, like the Muslim population of the Soviet Union, suffers from the foreign occupation, and some resist. In China the Uighur Muslims (of which there are 10 million) have suffered under government censorship. The Uighur live in the region of western China known as Xinjiang, where there are some 2000 mosques. Laws exist which limit religious practice, and which control and monitor the teaching of Arabic. Muslims are barred from joining the government. During recent demonstrations the government killed hundreds of Uighurs.[30]

---

[24] Bertrand Russell, *A History of Western Philosophy*, (New York, Simon and Schuster, 1945) (a) p369
[25] Bart McDowell, *Gypsies: Wanderers of the World*, (National Geographic Society, 1970)
[26] H.G. Wells, *The Outline of History*, Volume II, (Garden City, Garden City Books, 1956) p806
[27] Ahmed, (a) p133
[28] Said, (a) p123
[29] Esposito, p51
[30] Edward Wong, "New Protests Flare in Chinese City After Deadly Ethnic Clashes", *New York Times*, July 8, 2009

The bloody French conquest of Algeria in 1830 proved to be a disaster for Christian-Muslim relations. The French seized the Grand Mosque of Algeria and converted it into a catholic cathedral named Saint-Philippe. The archbishop of Algeria made it the Church's mission to convert Muslims from the "vices of their original religion generative of sloth, divorce, polygamy, theft, agrarian communism, fanaticism, and even cannibalism."[31] The French were finally ousted in the Algerian War of Independence (1954-1962), a war that led to the dissolution of the conservative French Fourth Republic. The French atheist philosopher Jean-Paul Sartre wrote of the French occupation of Algeria saying it was "a history of forceful conquest and colonization." "For a hundred years the French struggled to destroy the Arab language in Algeria; if they were not completely successful, they at least turned literary Arabic into a dead language that is no longer taught."[32]

In the former Yugoslavia, Slobodan Milosevic led Serbs on an attack of the Muslim Bosnians and tens of thousands were left dead.[33] Milosevic described his justification as an attempt to prevent the spread of Islam across Europe.[34] Moreover, in 94 concentration camps, at least 3,000 Muslims were slaughtered in a matter of weeks, their throats cut.[35] In some instances the sign of the cross was burned into the forehead of a victim and the body was crucified.[36]

Former Israeli Prime Minister Yitzak Rabin declared that Israel was the first line of defense against "the danger of extremist Islam".[37] Former Italian Prime Minister Silvio Berlusconi said the Islam was the main enemy of the West. Pope Benedict has read statements that declare Islam a violent religion. American media news anchor Bill O'Reilly equated the holy book of Islam, the Quran to Adolf Hitler's *Mein Kempf*. Anti-Muslim violence rose in the US from 2000-2001 by 15%.[38] And under the USA PATRIOT Act thousand of Muslims have been harassed, intimidated, arrested without charges, and had their civil liberties violated.[39]

Law professor Jack Balkin wrote: "Give a few dollars to a Muslim charity [Former Attorney General] Ashcroft thinks is a terrorist organization and you could be on the next plane out of this country."[40] The secretary general of NATO called Islam the new communism[41], and President Bush II called the US war on Afghanistan and Iraq a "Crusade". There are over 50 Muslim countries in the world today, many of which are in Africa. All of these nations and peoples have been colonized within the last hundred years and only recently gained their independence. However, in none of these countries has a civil war occurred as bloody as the American Civil War, which occurred 90 years after the colonial period ended.

---

[31] Esposito, p52-52
[32] Jean-Paul Sartre, "The Burgos Trial", *Life/Situations: Essays Written and Spoken*, trans. Paul Auster and Lydia Davis, (New York, Pantheon Books, 1977) p138, 147
[33] Michael Mandel, *How America Gets Away With Murder: Illegal Wars, Collateral Damage and Crimes Against Humanity*, (London, Pluto Press, 2004) p66
[34] Esposito, xiii
[35] Mandel, p120
[36] Ahmed, (b) p71
[37] Esposito, xiii
[38] Ahmed, (b) p25, 36, 39n9
[39] Nancy Chang, *Silencing Political Dissent*, (New York, Seven Stories Press, 2002)
[40] Noam Chomsky, *Hegemony or Survival*, (New York, Henry Holt and Company, 2003) p27
[41] Esposito, viii

What Is Honorable?

> The crusaders fought against something they would have done better to lie down in the dust before... -Friedrich Nietzsche[42]

Socrates was born and raised in the democratic city-state of Athens, and that's where he died when he was 70 years old. In his lifetime he had been a father, husband, mason, and soldier. In the last year of his life he was taken to court on the accusation that he believed in false gods and that his teachings about philosophy had corrupted the Athenian youths. Socrates was found guilty by a slight majority in a jury of 500 and sentenced to be executed.

While he is in prison awaiting the execution that will come within several days, he is visited by many of his friends. They try to persuade him to escape and tell him that everything is arranged and that the guards have been instructed to let this occur. Only, he would never be permitted to return to Athens once he'd escaped. Socrates, however, is resolved to comply with the sentence, though he does let his friend Crito try to persuade him otherwise.

Crito tells him, "...the majority will not believe that you yourself were not willing to leave prison while we were eager for you to do so."[43] (44c) Socrates replies, "My Good Crito, why should we care so much for what the majority think? ...They cannot make a man either wise or foolish, but they inflict things haphazardly." (44d) According to Socrates, those who care about reputation, "belong to those people who easily put men to death and would bring them to life again if they could, without thinking; I mean the majority of men." (48c)

For Socrates it is a matter of honor and duty that he abides by the decision of the court. He believes escaping from Athens would be hypocritical; a violation of his word, and dishonesty toward his life long commitment to Athens. Do the law and the constitution that he spent his life defending now have to make an exception for him? He tells Crito: "One should never do wrong in return, nor injure any man, whatever injury one has suffered at his hands... that neither to do wrong or to return a wrong is ever right, not even to injure in return for an injury received." (49d)

For both Socrates and his student Plato, honor does not come before duty but, just as they are both virtues, they are in an important sense, one and the same thing. In Plato's *Republic* it is said there are three basic kinds of lives: the lover of wisdom or learning, the lover of honor or victory, and the lover of profit or money. (581c) The lover of profit or money believes being honored and learning are valueless, unless one can make money from them. (581d) The lover of honor thinks money-makers are vulgar, and learning is nonsense. (581e) The lover of wisdom however does not reject these lesser interests, but goes beyond them in the pleasure of contemplation. As Socrates says, "[T]he pleasure to be gained from the contemplation of reality cannot be tasted by anyone except the philosopher."[44] (582c)

Aristotle was a friend and student of Plato's for some 20 years, until Plato's death, eventually opening his own school of philosophy in Athens, the *Lyceum*. Aristotle's

---

[42] Friedrich Nietzsche, *The Antichrist*, trans. R.J. Hollingdale, (London, Penguin Books, 1968) (a1) 60
[43] Plato, *Crito*, trans. G.M.A. Grube in *Five Dialogues*, (Indianapolis, Hackett Publishing, 1981) (a)
[44] Plato, *Republic*, trans. G.M.A. Grube, (Indianapolis, Hackett Publishing, 1974) (b)

ethics are often called 'virtue ethics' because of the central place the virtues play in his philosophy. However, for Aristotle, honor is not a virtue. In fact, the virtuous or magnanimous person does not "regard honor as the greatest good" (1124a16).[45] This makes them seem arrogant (a20). However, magnanimity "is the virtue concerned with *great* honor." (1125a35) If this seems paradoxical, it is because Aristotle believes that magnanimity is a mean, or middle-position between honor and dishonor. The excess of magnanimity is vanity, and the deficiency is pusillanimity, or timidity (1107b24).

Aristotle says that:

"...where there is excess and deficiency there is also an intermediate condition; and since people desire honor both more and less than is right, it is also possible to desire [honor] in the right way. This state, then, a nameless mean concerned with honor, is praised." (1125b20)

Aristotle believes that politicians, for example, value honor over virtue. This desire for honor makes one superficial and insincere since it depends more upon those who bestow honor, and depends upon the good of someone else rather than that of ourselves. Those who seek being honored by others do so "to convince themselves that they are good". Thus virtue itself is superior to honor (1095b25-30).

Despite what many think –neither Socrates, Plato, or Aristotle, nor most other classical philosophers up until the Stoics- were proponents of empire. The philosophies of Plato and Aristotle in particular made use of the city-state as the model for the ideal society and the ideal setting in which the philosophers played an important role, like Socrates himself.

During Aristotle's life-time his native Kingdom of Macedonia would go from being a Greek city-state to conquering most of the known world. This was through the impetus of Aristotle's one-time student, Alexander the Great. Aristotle's father Nicomachus had been court physician to Alexander's father King Philip.

When Alexander had died in 323, much of the world, particularly the regions around the Mediterranean, had been '*Hellenized*' or influenced by Greek culture. After his death Alexander's empire splintered into smaller kingdoms, which over the next few centuries became parts of the Roman Republic. This Republic became the Roman Empire in the 1st century BCE under the rule of Julius Caesar and his adopted son, Augustus. During Caesar's reign he gave himself such titles as "Son of God", and "Savior of the World", before dying in the 44th year before the birth of Jesus, (or Before the Common Era, BCE).[46]

Just a few centuries after the death of Jesus, Christianity became the official religion of the Roman Empire. This occurred by decree of Constantine the Great. Constantine had converted to Christianity in the year 312, when on his way to battle he saw the crucifix in a cloud upon which it was written 'Hoc Signo Vinces': "In this sign you will conquer." Soon afterward, Constantine had printed on the Roman coin, "To the unconquered sun my companion".[47] However, it would take over a thousand years to convert the rest of Europe to Christianity, and this period is generally referred to as the 'Dark Ages'.

The wars of religion in the dark ages are usually epitomized in a man who is often called the "Father of Europe": Charles the Great, or Charlemagne. Charlemagne was a

---

[45] Aristotle, *Nicomachean Ethics*, trans. Terence Irwin, (Indianapolis, Hackett Publishing, 1985) (E)
[46] Carroll, p80n36, 84
[47] Carroll, p178

French or Frankish King who was crowned emperor of the Holy Roman Empire in the year 800. Although he and his grandfather, Charles 'the Hammer' Martel, were responsible for halting Muslim armies in France and Spain, one of Charlemagne's biggest achievements was the defeat and forced conversion of the Saxons, or Germans. The Saxon Wars, as they are called, are referred to as particularly 'bloody', and culminated in the edict "Saxon Capitulary". Under this law, "Refusal to be baptized became a capital offence."[48]

These traditions of wars of conversion are most famously to be found in the Christian Crusades, which began in the 11th century, and the Inquisition, which was temporarily stopped by the conquests of Napoleon at the beginning of the 19th century. Of each of the three popular monotheism's, which is perhaps 3 to 4 billion people living today, each is burdened with histories of warfare. Quite easily, Islamic countries have been by any standard, the most tolerant of all, especially toward minorities. What is more: at its height the Muslim Empire was much more expansive than the Holy Roman Empire. This lasted up until the 16th century.[49]

As Bertrand Russell puts it in his *History of Western Philosophy,* Islam spread (to what is its current general global arrangement) within twenty years, "without much severe fighting", and with "little destruction". Within 100 years Islam reached from Spain, to all of Northern Africa, to Persia, Byzantine, India, and beyond. In this 'Golden Age' of Islam, Muslims reigned in Spain for nearly 800 years as well as most of Africa, the Middle East, as well as much of the Indian sub-continent.[50] This was only briefly interrupted when the Mongols of eastern Asia under the sons of Genghis Khan took Baghdad in 1256. Shortly thereafter most Mongols adopted Islam as their religion.[51]

"The conquests destroyed little: what they did suppress were imperial rivalries and sectarian bloodletting among the newly subjected population. The Muslims tolerated Christianity but they disestablished it; henceforth Christian life and liturgy, its endowments, politics, and theology, would be a private not a public affair. By an exquisite irony, Islam reduced the status of Christians to that which the Christians had earlier thrust upon the Jews, with one difference. The reduction of Christian status was merely judicial; it was unaccompanied by either systematic persecution or blood lust, and generally, though not everywhere and at all times, unmarred by vexatious behavior."[52]

By the 12th century, the Sufi Muslims were creating international networks around the world. The Sufis are ascetic Muslim men and women who celebrate the world and the divine, through study and love for what is mystic. "In Africa and Southeast Asia Islam was spread primarily by Sufi brotherhoods and merchants rather than the armies of Islam." The spread of Islam has also been aided by "schismatic" Christians and by Jews, seeking the protection of Muslims, from the empires of Europe.[53]

In those societies where there has least often been intolerance there has been a practice of honor and respect. However, in today's world of the modern and industrial age we find preponderance with class struggle, rather than the practice of any virtue, especially honor. It is somewhat difficult to imagine someone that is concerned with the

---

[48] Richard Fletcher, *The Barbarian Conversion*, (New York, Henry Holt, 1997) p193, 195, 215
[49] Rodinson, p56
[50] Russell, (a) p420
[51] David Waines, *An Introduction to Islam*, (Cambridge, Cambridge University Press, 1995) p183
[52] Francis E. Peters, "The Early Muslim Empires: Emayyads, Abbasids, Fatimids," in Marjorie Kelly, ed., *Islam: The Religious and Political Life of a World Community*, (New York, Praeger, 1984) p79. Quoted in Esposito, p39
[53] Esposito, p37, 39

protestant ethic or the Darwinian struggle, or the socialist/anarchist class-war, to have time or patience to care about honor, or virtue for that matter. As Alasdair MacIntyre remarks after discussing the varying ethical traditions of people's ranging from the Icelandic settlers, the Bedouin of the Western desert, the Celts of Britain, as well as the ancient Greeks, in his book *After Virtue*:

"In many pre-modern societies a man's honor is what is due to him and to his kin and his household by reason of their having their *due* place in the social order. To dishonor someone is to fail to acknowledge what is thus due. Hence the concept of an insult becomes a socially crucial one and in many such societies a certain kind of insult merits death… [I]n modern societies we have neither legal nor quasi-legal recourse if we are insulted. Insults have been displaced to the margins of our cultural life where they are expressive of private emotions rather than public conflicts."[54]

MacIntyre thinks the marginalization of honor has occurred in the modern or Western world because of the separation of law from morality. In some ways this stems from the rejection of Aristotle, made by his rebellious student, Alexander the Great. How did the "West" ever reject Aristotle, if ever? Wasn't Aristotle, after all, a European thinker, and what of Alexander's "hellenization" of the known world?

The Roman Empire, which in some ways came out of the conquests of Alexander, was, as we saw, converted to Christianity sometime in the 4th century. By the year 431 of the Christian Era, the writings of Aristotle, as well as geometers Euclid and Archimedes, and the physicians Hippocrates and Galen, were all banned from Europe. Their writings were 'smuggled' to the Middle East and eventually translated into Arabic.[55]

The study of Aristotle did not return to the West until Arabic and Islamic philosophers began to teach him and the other exilic writings in Spain, then called *Al-Andalusia*. The first Christian European to become a full-blown Aristotelian (since Boethius had been condemned and executed in 524) was the 13th century German philosopher Albertus Magnus, sometimes called *Albertus Teutonicus*. He taught the philosophy of Aristotle and that of the Muslim philosophers Avicenna and Averroes in Paris, Strasbourg, and Cologne. His student, the Italian Thomas Aquinas, helped to bring the philosophy of Aristotle, as well as Jewish, Muslim, and Christian philosophy together and Aquinas was aware that it was still illegal then in the 13th century to study Aristotle. Aquinas studied the Latin translations of the Arabic translations of Aristotle. Oddly enough, in 1263 Pope Urban IV repeated that there was a prohibition against Aristotle, and then proceeded to commission first-hand Greek to Latin translations of Aristotle's writings.[56]

The second-coming of Aristotle was short lived, however. Aristotle fell out of repute once again in the 15th century, just a couple of hundred years after his reentry to the West. This period of change, from the 15th to 17th centuries MacIntyre calls the "Enlightenment project". The Enlightenment attempt to create a rational foundation for a universalized or secular ethics, was in a sense non-historical, non-traditional, non-cultural, and thus could not include the "study" of the virtues.[57] It was during this time that Aristotle's ethics were repudiated and discarded because the process of 'Enlightenment' entailed universalism, where Aristotle had emphasized the many particularities; secularization, where Aristotle had highlighted the norms of organic

---

[54] Alasdair MacIntyre, *After Virtue*, (Notre Dame, University of Notre Dame Press, 1981) p116
[55] Josef Pieper, *Scholasticism*, trans. Richard and Clara Winton, (New York, McGraw-Hill, 1964) p103
[56] Pieper, 108
[57] MacIntyre, p117

societies; and modernization, where Aristotle had concentrated on the ethics of the community.

MacIntyre sees the 19th century philosopher/philologist Friedrich Nietzsche as both a great commentator on the failure of the Enlightenment project to repudiate the virtue ethics of Aristotle. This is because as a philologist Nietzsche had a greater historical sense and understanding of the power of cultural traditions, than did the secularists of the enlightenment such as David Hume, Immanuel Kant, and Jeremy Bentham.

When his health had permitted it, Nietzsche had been a philologist. A philologist is a kind of historian of literature –they locate writings in history and authenticate ancient texts, identifying when, where, and by whom they were written. Nietzsche noted how the 'uses and abuses of history'-the story that we believe is history –is one often told in the interest of political power, as for example, in gaining the consent of the populace.

In his study, "On the Uses and Disadvantages of History for Life", Nietzsche wrote that we need history "for the sake of life and action, not so as to turn comfortably away from life and action." Happiness comes from "the ability to forget or, expressed in more scholarly fashion, the capacity to feel *unhistorically*…" While a lack of historical sense makes one "least capable of being just", an excessive study of history is harmful as well. History should never become a "pure science" like mathematics, but should stand in the service to life. Hence Nietzsche introduces the supra-historical, saying that "*the unhistorical and the historical are necessary in equal measure for the health of an individual, of a people and of a culture.*"[58] Nietzsche new all-too well the power that history can have over peoples and nations:

"We know, indeed, what history can do when it gains a certain ascendancy, we know it only too well: it can cut off the strongest instincts of youth, its fire, defiance, unselfishness and love, at the roots, damp down the heat of its sense of justice, suppress or regress its desire to mature…"[59]

The study of history ought to "inspire and lend the strength for the production of the great man." This is because, "In truth, no one has a greater claim to our veneration than he who possesses the drive to and strength for justice." Thus, the goal of history cannot be the modern Enlightened state. "No, the goal of humanity cannot lie in its end but only in its highest exemplars."[60]

Thus, Nietzsche envisaged that certain traditions create great and noble individuals. It is thus that several years later he came up with the idea of the *Superman*. The Superman is the person who has overcome themselves and the cultural-moral schemes of the 'herd-morality'. As MacIntyre deftly shows, this radical libertarian position of Nietzsche's was itself, like the Enlightenment/Universalist ethics that he rejected, "nothing other than an historical sequel to the rejection of the Aristotelian tradition." Moreover, Nietzsche's illegitimate child, the Superman, , a construction that was an "absurd and dangerous fantasy", was in a sense a bastardized form of Aristotle's 'magnanimous soul'. MacIntyre believes, however, that Nietzsche's construction came from a "genuine insight".[61] Sometimes this is so.

---

[58] Friedrich Nietzsche, "On the Uses and Disadvantages of History for Life", *Untimely Meditations*, trans. R.J. Hollingdale, ed. Daniel Breazeale, (Cambridge University Press, 1997) (b) p59, 62, 64, 67, 63
[59] Nietzsche, (b) p115
[60] Nietzsche, (b) p111, 88, 111
[61] MacIntyre, p118, 113

In his book, *Beyond Good and Evil*, an aphorism says:

"Signs of nobility: never thinking of degrading our duties into duties for everybody; not wanting to delegate, to share, one's own responsibility; counting one's privileges and their exercise among one's duties."[62]

In the companion piece to *Beyond Good and Evil* called, *On the Genealogy of Morals*, Nietzsche attempts to trace back the origins of what is noble and the origins of what is ignoble. Nietzsche makes use of the crude phrase 'master morality' to describe the ethics of nobility, and he uses the term 'slave morality' to refer to the ethics of the ignoble. By using these terms 'master' and 'slave' it is clear throughout that Nietzsche is not attempting to come up with, or trying to describe an ethics for a slave-owner to follow, or for that matter, trying to describe an ethics for slave to follow. In fact, Nietzsche believed that the 'slave morality', rather than the master morality, had already been victorious over the West. He wrote: "…consider to whom one bows down in Rome itself today, as if they were the epitome of all the highest values –and not only in Rome but over almost half the earth…"[63]

What Nietzsche is doing here is drawing genealogical conclusions from his study of ancient languages in philology. Early in his study Nietzsche notes that: "It was this *pathos of distance* that first seized the right the create values and to coin name for values".[64] The *pathos of distance*, or the mindset of distance, means something like that predisposition of nobility, or self-mastery. The 'slave morality', which Nietzsche believed to have become the normality of the modern world, was marked by self-deception and resentment. Nietzsche always uses the French word for resentment, *ressentiment* (even though he wrote in German), because the French version has a more emotional resonance.

Nietzsche writes:

"The slave revolt in morality begins when *ressentiment* itself becomes creative and gives birth to values: the *ressentiment* of natures that are denied the true reaction, that of deeds, and compensate themselves with an imaginary revenge. While every noble morality develops from a triumphant affirmation of itself, slave morality from the outset says No to what is 'outside', what is 'different', what is 'not itself'. … [I]n order to exist, slave morality always first needs a hostile external world… [because] its action is fundamentally reaction."[65]

According to Nietzsche people who come from the tradition of *ressentiment* "crave to be *hangmen*"; "There is among them an abundance of the vengeful disguised as judges, who constantly bear the word 'justice' in their mouths like poisonous spittle…this will to power of the weakest!"[66]

Of the noble traditions, Nietzsche believed that Arabs and Muslims belonged, alongside others. Several times Nietzsche mentions the Arab and Muslim tradition of nobility, writing that: "What an *affirmative* Semitic religion, the product of a *ruling* class,

---

[62] Friedrich Nietzsche, *Beyond Good and Evil*, trans. Walter Kaufmann, (New York, Vintage Books, 1966) (c) 272
[63] Friedrich Nietzsche, *On The Genealogy of Morals*, trans. Walter Kaufmann and R.J. Hollingdale, (New York, Vintage Books, 1967) (d) First Essay, Section 16, p53
[64] Nietzsche, (d) First Essay, Section 2, p26
[65] Nietzsche, (d) First Essay, Section 10 p36-37
[66] Nietzsche, (d) Third Essay, Section 14 p23

looks like: the law-book of Mohammed, the older parts of the Old Testament."[67] Referring to the pre-modern Muslim culture of Spain, Nietzsche says:

> "The wonderful culture of the Moors in Spain, which was fundamentally nearer to us and appealed more to our senses and tastes than that of Rome and Greece… had to thank noble… instincts for its origin – because it said yes to life, even to the rare and refined luxuriousness of Moorish life!"[68]

For a writer who as MacIntyre points out, illegitimately borrowed and used philosophers such as Aristotle's ideas without paying credit, here he was forthright. A thinker who is critical of Nietzsche, the sociologist Akbar Ahmed, has touched upon the ascendancy of noble traditions, noting: "One reason for Islam's tolerance is that… from its early days Islam emerged as the dominant ruler of the area."[69] From early on, Muslims controlled their own destiny and did not have to contend with any empire, but were often greeted as peace-makers and liberators. In fact, the people of Yathrib pleaded for Muhammad to come and arbitrate over their own disputes and make the peace.

For a true Muslim there is a virtue held which honors other non-Arabic speaking peoples and religions. The Arabic word to describe this custom is *adab*. *Adab* are the norms, traditions, and habits of Muslims and is part of what makes for civility or *asabya*. This social solidarity or *asabya* is what has historically made Islam one of the most tolerant societies toward those who are different

In his work *Islam Under Siege*, Ahmed discusses the concept of 'honor' as it is understood in 20th and 21st centuries, in both the US and around the world. Is honor understood as the same thing around the world, or is it something that is in scarcity in certain societies? Ahmed makes use of a theory developed by 'the father of sociology', Abd al-Rahman ibn Khaldun, who lived in northern Africa in the 14th century. Khaldun discussed what the implications that honor and dishonor reveal about a society. Accordingly, Ahmed suggests we are entering a "post-honor" world, believing that:

> "the dangerously ambiguous notion of honor –and the even more dangerous idea of the loss of honor –propels men to violence. Simply put, global developments have robbed many people of honor. Rapid global changes are shaking the structures of traditional societies…No society is immune. Even those societies that economists call 'developed' fall back to notions of honor and revenge in times of crisis."

> "The mass media invade the most private rooms in homes throughout the world with new disturbing and threatening images. The news itself, instantly replayed, heightens the sense of anger and outrage, which feed into atavistic prejudices. People respond by defending the honor of their group, culture, or religion. In some cases revenge and martyrdom are one expression of the response. Too many people believe that while they are people of honor, others are not. They point to the dishonorable behavior of the other or to historical events to bolster their arguments. Through a distorted and even perverted logic, the notion of honor is applied to acts of violence, and innocent civilians are often the victims."[70]

Ahmed argues that in order to "reverse the movement that has brought us into a post-honor world we need to rediscover the dialogue with, and understanding of cultures other than our own. We need to advance a morality that emphasizes justice and compassion for all." Ahmed thinks this ability to show honor is not something non-intellectual, but involves great study and discipline. "I do not suggest that we accept each other's or all religions uncritically but that we understand them in order to make sense of what is happening in global society." "The relationship between Islam and modernity is

---

[67] Friedrich Nietzsche, *The Will To Power*, trans. Walter Kaufmann and R.J. Hollingdale, (New York, Vintage Books, 1968) (e) 145
[68] Friedrich Nietzsche, *The Antichrist*, trans. H.L. Mencken, (Tucson, See Sharp Press, 1999) (a) 60
[69] Ahmed, (a) p26
[70] Ahmed, (b) p14-15, 57

much more complex than the simplistic clash of civilizations theories would have us believe."[71]

Modernity and Conformity

> If a premodern view of morals and politics is to be vindicated against modernity, it will be in *something like* Aristotelian terms or not at all. –Alasdair MacIntyre[72]

Both Nietzsche and MacIntyre are critical of modernization, or the modern era. For this reason Nietzsche is often refereed to as a 'post-modern' thinker. If modernity has various connotations and is difficult to define, post-modernity is famously even harder to define. Generally speaking, modernity is the belief that there is one true description of the world.[73] The 17th century philosopher Rene Descartes is often called the father of modern philosophy. For example –he believed that *thought* was the most fundamental and true description of reality. Descartes took skepticism as far as was realistically possible until he realized he couldn't doubt his own thinking. Charles Darwin, for example, is considered a modernist –he believed that the theory of evolution was the one true description of how species originated. Karl Marx is considered a modernist –at least when he said that "The history of all hitherto existing society is the history of class struggle."[74] Thus, Marx believed there was one true description of reality.

Some believe that modernity began when Muslims conquered Constantinople in 1453 by the use of heavy artillery, or in 1492 when Columbus sailed and the Inquisition forced all non-Christian religions out of Spain, or in 1517 when Luther nailed his 95 theses to the cathedral door at Wittenberg which began the Protestant Reformation, or when Copernicus' theory that the sun was at the center of the galaxy, was published posthumously in 1543 (although the ancient astronomer Aristarchus of Samos (Turkey) had said this in the 3rd century before the Common Era).

In 1864 Pope Pius IX wrote the "Syllabus of Errors", "a list of eighty mistakes of philosophy, theology, and politics" which were encyclically anathema. It turned down the notion that "the Roman Pontiff [or Pope] can and ought to reconcile and align himself with progress, liberalism, and modern civilization". "Modernism" would come to be regarded and condemned as "the synthesis of all heresies". Young clerics were forced to make an "Oath Against Modernism" into the late 1960's, even after Pope John XXIII's truce with modernism in 1962, during Vatican II.[75]

Modernization has had drastic consequences for most of the world. According to the sociologist Kevin Danaher the standard of living was greater in Africa, America, and

---

[71] Ahmed, (b) p16, 161, 47
[72] MacIntyre, p118
[73] The French philosopher Jean-Francois Lyotard wrote in 1979 in *The Postmodern Condition: A Report on Knowledge*, modern designates "any science that legitimates itself with reference to a metadiscourse... making an explicit appeal to some grand narrative, such as the dialectics of Spirit, the hermeneutics of meaning, the emancipation of the rational or working subject, or the creation of wealth." A paragraph later Lyotard writes, "Simplifying to the extreme, I define *postmodern* as incredulity toward metanarratives." (Minneapolis, University of Minnesota Press, 1984) xxiii, xxiv
[74] Karl Marx and Friedrich Engels, *The Communist Manifest*, (New York, Bantam Books, 1992)
[75] Carroll, p442, 444, 548

Asia than it was in Europe, where there were wars, crusades, plagues, and inquisitions. For example, Africa consisted of roughly 100 million people before the modern era of colonization. By 1619 a million Africans had been brought to South America as slaves. By 1800 10–15 million Africans had been brought to the new world as slaves, and in the process, the African population of Africa had decreased by 50 million, or by half.[76]

For many Muslims, modernity has caused a bit of trouble, and modernization is often associated with colonialism and Western imperialism. The modern Western empires did away with all Muslim states but the two most corrupted: that of the Shah and the Emperor. If we say that modernity began when Columbus sailed the oceans blue in 1492, that was the same year that Muslims (and Jews) were exiled from Europe, after having lived in Spain and Italy for almost 800 years. Sociologists (such as Danaher) have called the period of modernity, (roughly the last 500 years), the greatest demographic collapse in world history, or '500 years of violent redistribution of wealth'.[77] Some Muslims see modernism as "secularist fundamentalism", finding that it "seeks to destroy every other point of view", that modernism "is completely intolerant".[78] Many link the resistance to modernity with the resistance to imperialism[79], and have found that French and British mandates have created legacies of instability.[80]

The sociologist Max Weber is recognized as having described the modern era with accuracy. He said of the "tremendous cosmos of the modern economic order", that it has become an "iron cage".

"This order is now bound to the technical and economic conditions of machine production which today determine the lives of all the individuals who are born into this mechanism, not only those directly concerned with economic acquisition, with irresistible force."

"The modern man is in general even with the best will, unable to give religious ideas a significance for culture and national character which they deserve."[81]

Modernity is obviously the work of conformity. Modernity, or Globalization, as it is more popularly referred, seeks to impose a structure on the world and on thought, sometimes called, 'structural adjustment', or state-capitalism. This modern era is the belief that there is only one true description of the world, be it the Darwinian, Copernican, Marxist, or Weberian, or what have you. If modernity is connected with the assimilation of what is diverse, post-modern philosophers, most of whom are French, believe that there is *not* just one true description of reality. This seems to point in the direction of pluralism, the understanding that there are many different truths, values, perspectives, and lifestyles. Pluralism also points to the American philosophy of pragmatism, in which multiplicity is celebrated.

---

[76] Howard Zinn, *A People's History of the United States*, Revised and Updated Edition, (New York, Harper/Perennial, 1995) p26, 25, 29
[77] Kevin Danaher, "Alternatives to Globalization", delivered at Bowdoin College, Brunswick, Maine, 10/8/96. Recorded by Roger Leisner for Radio Free Maine. www.radiofreemaine.com
[78] Nasr, p109
[79] Oussama Arabi, *Studies in Modern Islamic Law and Jurisprudence*, (The Hague, Kluwer Law International, 2001) p189
[80] Esposito, p75
[81] Max Weber, *The Protestant Ethic and the Spirit of Capitalism*, trans. Talcott Parsons, (New York, Charles Scribner's Sons, 1958) p181, 183

Contemporary post-modern philosophers can learn a great deal from Islam's rejection of modernization. The 20th century French philosopher Michel Foucault wrote that:

> "Islam values work; no one can be deprived of the fruits of his labor; what must belong to all (water, the subsoil) shall not be appropriated by anyone. With respect to liberties, they will be respected to the extent that their exercise will not harm others; minorities will be protected and free to live as they please on the condition that they do not injure the majority; between men and women there will not be inequality with respect to rights, but difference, since there is a natural difference. With respect to politics, decisions should be made by the majority, the leaders should be responsible to the people, and each person, as it is laid out in the Quran, should be able to stand up and hold accountable he who governs."[82]

Foucault says, "These are the basic formulas for democracy, whether bourgeois or revolutionary."

Philosophy

> Except in the Mohammedan world, the claims of reason remained in abeyance until the eleventh century.[83] –Bertrand Russell

Why is it that Islam is so great philosophically, or greater than other religions philosophically? After all, wouldn't a religion that was started by a philosopher rather than a prophet be more philosophical, like say, Pythagoreanism, or Philoism? The answer is controversial and hopefully inspires a lot of education and debate.

The word *philosophy* itself is a Greek word meaning "the love of wisdom" and was probably coined by Plato or Socrates. They in turn were influenced by various Greek and Asian thinkers spanning back a couple hundred years. And of course Socrates and Plato had studied the poet Homer who may have lived or written in the 8th century BCE.

Originally Greek philosophy included mathematics and science and many philosophers have been great mathematicians and scientists. In the modern world philosophy is delegated to five harmless areas of study taught in pricey colleges: ethics, aesthetics, epistemology, metaphysics, and logic. Ethics is the study of decisions and action, aesthetics is the study of beauty and art, epistemology is the study of knowledge, metaphysics is the study of reality, and logic is the study of reason. Obviously all of these disciplines predate the Greeks, though the Greek writers and vocabulary dominate much of philosophy as we know it today in the English speaking world. Be that as it may, both Hindus and the Chinese studied logic before the Greeks, and ethics is perhaps as old as communication. Most of the philosophers before Socrates came from the cities in what is now called Turkey.

A sophistical dichotomy that can be used to discuss some of the main differences between the East and West is the difference between Plato and Aristotle. While this does provide a kind of model that historically does have some validity, it should also be noted

---

[82] Michel Foucault, "What Are The Iranians Dreaming About?" First published in *Le Nouvel Observateur*, October 16-22, 1978, in *Foucault and the Iranian Revolution: Gender and the Seductions of Islam*, by Janet Afary and Kevin B. Anderson, (Chicago, University of Chicago Press, 2005) Accessed online. www.press.uchicago.edu/Misc/Chicago/007863.html

[83] Bertrand Russell, "The Ancestry of Fascism", in *The Will to Doubt*, (New York, Philosophical Library, 1958) (b) p90-91

how similar Plato and Aristotle really are, as they were friends for over 20 years until Plato's death.

If Plato coined the term 'theology' while teaching at the Academy, the students of Aristotle at the Lyceum coined the term 'metaphysics'. Theology means something like "the science of God" and comes from the Greek words *theos*, which means 'divine', and *logos*, which means among other things, 'logic', 'reason', or 'study'. Metaphysics means something like "the nature of reality" and comes from the Greek words *meta*, which means 'about', and *physics*, which means 'nature'. Thus theology and physics are both branches of metaphysics.

The theology of Plato and Aristotle is very similar: God or 'the divine' is an all-perfect being that is all-good or omnibenevolent. The introduction of metaphysics reveals an even bigger canvas than the single scientific picture of theology. Whatever reality ultimately is, be it the Milky Way, the universe, or the spirit –even if our best science can't yet describe it- whatever it is, *is* metaphysics. For Aristotle metaphysics is first philosophy.

For Plato this world is an illusion, is illusory, and is an imperfect copy of the true world, which for us is only in ideal while we live on earth. Some of us have a better recollection or cognizance of this ideal than others, like the difference between those awake and those sleeping. True reality is formal, or made up of perfect forms, and if the carpenter always builds an imperfect copy of the perfect house, the artist's picture of this house is of even greater imperfection. This is the formula for dualism, or the separation of body and spirit, which to this day is the most popular philosophy in America.

For Aristotle this world is part of reality and the many different and diverse particular characteristics in this world are all in relation to the universe. Thus, Aristotle can rightfully be called a naturalist: justification is something available to all rational animals. This leads to another generality about the difference between Plato and Aristotle - that Aristotle liked science while Plato did not. This is mostly true though not altogether. Plato highly esteemed both the study of medicine and mathematics, beyond this his interests in science did not go beyond politics. Aristotle, however, was prolific in what consider today 'science' and is generally regarded as the first biologist, the first zoologist, and the first logician among Greeks.

Historically Christianity, via the philosophers Philo and Plotinus, has been closer to Plato, while Islam has been closer to Aristotle and the many traditions he bequeathed, except in theology. While for both Plato and Aristotle (and Socrates) the divine is perfect, according to Aristotle the divine is unconcerned with this world or anything external to itself, though for Plato and Socrates the divine does occasionally interact with the world. Socrates in particular on his deathbed is delighted that he will soon meet the gods.

Whereas as some religions have devoted much of their intellectual efforts toward theology, or the science of God, such as discovering proofs for the existence of God, or proving certain scriptural idiosyncrasies, Islam, like Aristotle, has historically been more concerned with reason and virtue. We can thus make a rough comparison between Socrates, Plato, and Aristotle, on the one hand, and the three Abrahamic monotheism's on the other. In Islam, as in Judaism (and in Aristotle), we never see or represent the face of the divine. This is evident in Jewish and Muslim art where the divine is never represented. Christianity is much closer to the understanding of Socrates and Plato that the divine has a knowable Form and that ostensibly, humans can come face to face with the divine.

The question of whether humans have freewill or if reality is determined or predetermined is not so easily summarized, and neither Plato nor Aristotle or Socrates had worked out that aspect of their philosophy.[84] In Judaism unequivocally there is freewill –Yhwh designed humans so that they have freedom of choice, belief and action. Christianity on the other hand has been interpreted in two opposing ways. While Catholicism holds that people have freewill (otherwise why confess?), some Christians have said that reality is pre-determined: such as the 5th century theologian Augustine, as well as the 16th century Protestant reformers Martin Luther and John Calvin.

Islam on the other hand, at least for a pragmatist like myself, is difficult to determine, if only because there is very little theology, and consequently very little writing on the matter. More Islamic literature has been devoted to jurisprudence than any other field of study.[85] Some of the Islamic legal traditions, in particular one of the main schools of law, *Hanbalis*, have been opposed to theology in principal.[86] The Holy Book of Islam, the Quran says to the extent that humans have the freewill required for moral responsibility. Because the divine is all-knowing, everything is written in a book, which might mean that everything is predetermined. The Quran says, "No affliction befalls in the earth or in yourselves, but it is in a Book, before We create it; that is easy for Allah."[87] (Surah 57:22)

John Alden Williams' popular work *Islam* perhaps sums up the Muslim freewill debate, a debate that has been somewhat peripheral to the virtue ethics of Islamic philosophers. "Man is invited to believe, but in the end God is unknowable, except insofar as He has chosen to reveal Himself; the way to Him lies through His Book and devoted service to Him, and He enlightens and guides whom He will."[88] This is because theology is subordinate to metaphysics. Or as the prophet Muhammad said: "Knowledge that is not beneficial is like a treasure that you cannot spend."[89]

While the main of this argument deals with the relationship between philosophy and monotheism, it should be noted that the Greeks were not monotheists, nor are other popular religions such as Taoism, Hinduism, Buddhism, and Confucianism based upon monotheism, or, in some instances any 'theism' for that matter.

Confucianism is of course a highly philosophical religion, though we might call it a 'religious philosophy' if that is closer to the love of humanity. The *Analects* of Confucius are themselves a discussion between Confucius and other intellectuals covering a range of philosophical questions from ethics, politics, and aesthetics. Confucius taught that, "To love benevolence without loving learning is liable to lead to foolishness."[90] (17:8) His companion Tzu-hsia taught, "Learn widely and be steadfast in

---

[84] My thanks to Dutch-American philosopher Derk Pereboom for bringing this to my attention. His anthology on *Freewill* interprets Aristotle as holding to a general 'compatibilist' account in the freewill vs. determinism debate. Derk Pereboom, *Freewill*, (Indianapolis, Hackett Publishing, 1997)
[85] Waines, p74
[86] Nasr, p81
[87] Quran references from *The Koran Interpreted*, trans. A.J. Arberry, (New York, Macmillan Publishing, 1955)
[88] John Alden Williams, *Islam*, (New York, George Braziller, 1962) p40
[89] Robert Frager, *The Wisdom of Islam*, (Happauge, New York, Barron's Education Series, Inc., 2002) p131
[90] Confucius, *The Analects*, trans. D.C. Lau, (New York, Penguin Books, 1972)

your purpose, inquire earnestly and reflect on what is at hand, and there is no need for you to look for benevolence elsewhere." (19:6)

The holy book of Hinduism, *Bhagavad-Gita*, is a kind of ethical argument or philosophical dialogue between the mighty warrior Arjuna and the god Krsna. The discussion takes place on a battlefield. Arjuna refuses to fight this battle and is confronted by Krsna, who tells him: "There is nothing on earth equal in purity to wisdom. He who becomes perfected by *yoga* find this of himself, in his self in course of time."[91] (4:38) Arjuna, however is perplexed, and tells Krsna, "For the mind is verily fickle, O Krsna; it is impetuous, strong, and obstinate. I think that it is as difficult to control as the wind." (6:33) Krsna replies, "Without doubt, [Arjuna], the mind is difficult to curb and restless, but it can be controlled… by constant practice and non-attachment." (6:35) Wisdom is distinct from and greater than desire. "Enveloped is wisdom… by this insatiable fire of desire, which is the constant foe of the wise." (3:39)

The *Dhammapada* of Buddhism says: "People deficient in wisdom, childish ones, engage in awareness. But the wise one guards awareness like the greatest treasure."[92] (2:26) "He, truly, is supreme in battle, who would conquer himself alone, rather than he who would conquer in battle a thousand, thousand men." (8:103)

What is the role of wisdom in monotheism? Which of the three monotheisms is the most logical, or for that matter, most intellectual? In the beginning of Genesis we learn that the tree of life is permitted to humans but the tree of knowledge of good and evil is forbidden. (2:9) Some have taken this as meaning, in an important sense, that ethics is beyond good and evil.

In the book of Exodus we find that Moses is concerned that he is not wise enough to do what is right. "O Lord, I am not a man of words, neither heretofore, nor since Thou hast spoken unto Thy servant; for I am slow of speech, and of a slow tongue."[93] Yhwh replies, "Who hath made man's mouth? Or who maketh a man dumb, of deaf, or seeing, or blind? Is it not the Lord? Now therefore go, and I will be with thy mouth, and teach thee what thou shalt speak." (4:10-11) The final book of the Torah (the five holy books of Judaism, or the *Pentateuch*) Deuteronomy (4:6) says that wisdom and understanding are found in the observance of the laws of the Torah, of which there are 613.

Judaism has an ancient history like Hinduism, one filled with a long tradition of study. Not only do Jews study the Torah, but there is a vast literary tradition as well. For example, there are the Prophets, of which there are over a dozen, and the Writings (both which make up the Tanach, or Hebrew Bible, some of which is in the Christian Old Testament, some of which isn't). Only the Torah is considered to be divine and there is a long history of interpretation and commentary, some of which make up the Mishnah and the Talmud.

In the Talmud theology plays the smallest role.[94] The Talmud contains among other things advice on medicine and remedies for diseases.[95] Oddly enough, the Talmud

---

[91] *Bhagavad-Gita*, trans. Sarvepalli Radhakrishnan, in *A Source Book In Indian Philosophy*, ed. Sarvepalli Radhakrishnan and Charles A. Moore, (Princeton, Princeton University Press, 1957)
[92] *Dhammapada*, trans. John Ross Carter and Mahinda Palihawadana, (Oxford, Oxford University Press, 1987)
[93] All references to the Torah are translations of the Masocretic Text, (Philadelphia, The Jewish Publication Society of America, 1917)
[94] Louis Ginzberg, *On Jewish Law and Lore*, (New York, Athenium, 1955) p21-22

has been widely censored. When Pope Gregory IX began the first Inquisition in 1231, he ordered an investigation of the Talmud, calling it, "the chief cause that holds the Jews obstinate in their perfidy." In 1242 King Louis IX, or Saint Louis, had some 12,000 volumes of the Talmud collected and burned in Paris –taking almost 2 days for the fire to consume. This happened again in the Roman Inquisition of 1543, where Pope Paul III had all Talmuds burned. Pope Gregory's successor, Pope Innocent IV condemned the Talmud because it exceeded the size of the Christian bible, among other reasons.[96] This was repeated in the 20th century by the National Socialists, or Third Kingdom of God (Third Reich).

The Talmud (there are actually two Talmuds) is a work that demands study. This is a strong part of the *derekh eretz*, or 'deportment', the set of customs and norms of social relations that are part of the community. Scholars in particular were expected to be exemplars of this virtue of wisdom (*da'at*). The Talmud says, "a scholar in whom there is no *da'at* [is] worse than a carcass."[97]

The book of Proverbs says, "Wisdom crieth aloud in the street, she uttereth her voice in the broad places…in the city, she uttereth her words: 'How long, ye thoughtless, will ye love thoughtlessness?... And fools hate knowledge?" (Proverbs 1:20-22) "Whoso loveth knowledge loveth correction; but he that is brutish hateth reproof." (12:1) The most philosophical of the Jewish scriptural Writings is probably the book Ecclesiastes which says that, "The words of the wise spoken in quiet are more acceptable than the cry of a ruler among fools. Wisdom is better than weapons of war." (9:17-18) The man whom Aristotle asked to take over his school in Athens in 323 BCE, Theophrastus, said the Jews were an "especially philosophical" people.[98]

Of the three monotheisms Christianity is the only religion to explicitly refer to philosophy as such, as well as two different schools of philosophy, that of the Epicureans and the Stoics. (Acts 17:18) Be that as it may, the references are not endearing. More than once Jesus is said to have praised God specifically for having *not* revealed anything to those who are intellectual and wise. (Matthew 11:25, Luke 10:21)

Although Jesus spoke a Semitic language called Aramaic, the New Testament was written in Greek by his apostles and others. Moreover, the writers of the New Testament themselves often say how little they understood Jesus. This is because often-times Jesus spoke in parables, which are fictional stories told as analogies to moral issues that are real.[99] It seems Jesus uses parable so that some people will *not* understand.

"So the disciples came up and said to him: 'Why is it you speak to them by use of parables?' In reply [Jesus] said: 'To you it is granted to understand the sacred secrets of the kingdom of the heavens, but to those people it is not granted...'

"All these things Jesus spoke to the crowds by parables. Indeed, without a parable he would not speak to them." Matthew 13:10-11, 34

---

[95] Adin Steinsaltz, *The Essential Talmud*, trans. Chaya Galai, (New York, Basic Books, Inc., Publishers, 1976) p97
[96] Quoted in Carroll, p307-309, 373n34
[97] Quoted by Steinsaltz, p207
[98] Noted in Hilary Putnam and Martha Nussbaum's, "Changing Aristotle's Mind", in *Words and Life*, ed. James Conant, (Cambridge, Harvard University Press, 1994) (b) p51
[99] From the King James Version the English translator has used 'parable' and this has been the most influential. However, in the *New World Translation of the Holy Scriptures*, the word 'parable' is replaced with 'illustration'. This substitution is reversed here.

"By way of response Peter said to him: 'Make the parable plain to us'. At this [Jesus] said: 'Are you also yet without understanding?'" Matthew 15:15-16

"To you the sacred secret of the kingdom of God has been given, but to those outside all things occur in parables, in order that, though looking, they may look and yet not see, and, though hearing, they may hear and yet not get the sense of it, nor ever turn back and forgiveness be given to them." Mark 4:11-12

"[I]n reply to Jesus they [the priests] said: 'We do not know'. And Jesus said to them: 'Neither am I telling you by what authority I do these things.'" Mark 11:33

"But his disciples began to ask him what this parable might mean. He said: 'To you it is granted to understand the sacred secrets of the kingdom of God, but for the rest it is in parables, in order that, though looking, they may look in vain and, though hearing, they may not get the meaning.'" Luke 8:9-10

If Socrates said, "The unexamined life is not worth living", the principal writer of the New Testament, Saint Paul, replies, "I do not examine myself". (1 Corinthians 4:3) Paul said, "For the wisdom of this world is foolishness with God; for it is written: 'He catches the wise in their own cunning." (1 Corinthians 3:19) He warns us: "Lookout: perhaps there may be someone who will carry you off as his prey through the philosophy and empty deception according to the elementary things of the world and not according to Christ."[100] (Colossians 2:8)

"Where is the wise man? Where the scribe? Where the debater of this system of things? Did not God make the wisdom of the world foolish? For since, in the wisdom of God, the world through its wisdom did not get to know God, God saw good through the foolishness of what is preached to save those believing." 1st Letter to the Corinthians 1:20-21

"For you behold his calling of you, brothers, that not many wise in a fleshly way were called, not many powerful, not many of noble birth; but God chose the foolish things of the world, that he might put the wise men to shame; and God chose the weak things of the world, that he might put the strong things to shame." 1st Letter to the Corinthians 1:26-27

In Paul's letter to the Roman Emperor Titus, he mistakenly advises the dictator that: "A certain one of them, their own prophet, said: 'Cretans are always liars...'. This witness is true." (Titus 1:12-13) This of course, is a self-refuting statement. If a Cretan said that all Cretans are liars, they would, by their own claim, be lying. And thus, their witness could not possibly be true. James, the brother of Jesus, warns against the wisdom of the world, saying: "This is not the wisdom that comes down from above, but is earthly, animal, demonic." (James 3:15) According to the book of Revelation, the role of wisdom is satanic. "Here is where wisdom comes in: Let the one that has intelligence calculate the number of the wild beast, for it is a man's number; and its number is six hundred and sixty-six." (Revelation 13:18)

Some of the most influential Christians were those most opposed to the intellect. From early on mainstream Christianity had been very critical of philosophy. The second and third century church father Tertullian had written,

"Wretched Aristotle! who hath taught them the dialectic art... Away with those who have brought forward a Stoic, and a Platonic, and a Dialectic Christianity. To us there is no need of curious questioning now that we have Christ Jesus, nor of enquiry now that we have the Gospel."[101]

As we saw, by the 5th century the writings of Aristotle, Ptolemy, Archimedes, Galen, and Hippocrates had been banned from Christian Europe. While Christian laws forbid Jewish teaching[102], "Under the more tolerant rule of Islam, the Palestinian

---

[100] All references from the New Testament are translations by New World Bible Translation Committee, (Brooklyn, Watchtower Bible and Tract Society of New York, Inc., 1961)
[101] *De praescriptione haereticorum*, VII, 6, 9, 11-13. (Eng. Trans., *Tertullian*, trans. C. Dodgson, Oxford, 1842, p441-442). Quoted in Rodinson, p88
[102] Carroll, p177

academies were reopened".[103] However, an even greater enemy of reason and philosophy was Martin Luther. Luther referred to Aristotle as, "The buffoon who has misled the church".[104] Luther called reason "the devil's bride", or a "beautiful whore", or "God's worst enemy". He said: "There is on earth among all dangers no more dangerous thing than a richly endowed and adroit reason." And: "Reason must be deluded, blinded, and destroyed"; "faith must trample under foot all reason, sense, and understanding."[105] Or: "Whoever wants to be a Christian should tear the eyes out of his reason."[106]

The founder of the philosophy of existentialism, the Christian writer Soren Kierkegaard, was opposed to reason, and believed reason was synonymous with absurdity. While some people believe that skepticism or doubt is a greater crime against piety, Kierkegaard thought otherwise. He said: "The misfortune of our age –in the political as well as in the religious sphere, and in all things –is disobedience, unwillingness to obey. And one deceives oneself and others by wishing to make us imagine that it is doubt. No, it is insubordination."[107]

Martin Luther King, Jr., who was rich in practical wisdom, knew the importance of education and the moral development of the intellect.

"Nothing in the world is more dangerous than sincere ignorance and conscientious stupidity... [D]evoid of intelligence, goodness and conscientiousness will become brutal forces leading to shameful crucifixions. Never must the church tire of reminding men that they have a moral responsibility to be intelligent."

King's words stand as a correction to the past and a warning to Christians today.

"Must we admit that the church has often overlooked this moral demand for enlightenment? At times it has talked as though ignorance were a virtue and intelligence a crime. Through obscurantism, closemindedness, and obstinacy to new truth, the church has often unconsciously encouraged its worshippers to look askance upon intelligence. But if we are to call ourselves Christians, we had better avoid intellectual and moral blindness."[108]

Although the Quran of Islam makes no specific references to philosophy it has historically been understood as being highly compatible and adaptable with the love of wisdom. The French sociologist Maxime Rodinson wrote that Muslim intellectuals reason "with impeccable logic, taking up, thinking over afresh and completing Aristotle's philosophy and the whole heritage of Greek science... developing a body of historical writing that filled thousands of volumes and was based on a critical foundation..."[109]

The Quran tells us:

"He gives wisdom to whomsoever He will, and whoso is given the Wisdom, has been given much good; yet none remembers but men possessed of minds." Surah 2:272 [and 4:113]

"Call thou to the way of thy Lord with wisdom and good admonition, and dispute with them in the better way." Surah 16:126

"The servants of the All-merciful are those who walk in the earth modestly and who, when the ignorant address them, say, 'Peace'." Surah 25:64

---

[103] Ginzberg, p29
[104] MacIntyre, p165
[105] Martin Luther quoted from the *Samtliche Schriften*, ed. J.G. Walch, 24 vols.; (Halle, Germany, 1740-53), (XII, 1530; VIII, 2048; V, 1312; III, 215), and trans. by Walter Kaufmann, *The Faith of a Heretic*, (Garden City, Anchor Books, 1963) (a) p75
[106] Luther, (V, 425) quoted and trans. by Walter Kaufmann, *Critique of Religion and Philosophy*, (New York, Harper and Brothers, 1958) (b) 65
[107] Kaufmann, (a) p71
[108] Martin Luther King, Jr., "Love in action", *Strength to Love*, (Philadelphia, Fortress Press, 1963) p43-44
[109] Rodinson, p104

"By the Clear Book, behold, We have made it an Arabic Koran; haply you will understand; and behold, it is in the Essence of the Book, with Us; sublime indeed, wise." Surah 43:3-4

Muhammad (570-632) himself was a merchant in his lifetime, though he was respected by Muslims and non-Muslims alike for his judiciousness. The *hadith* or sayings of the prophet Muhammad reveal a great respect and love for wisdom:

"Seeking knowledge is better than worship." "One hour of contemplation is worth sixty years of worship." "The cure for ignorance is to ask and learn." "The most ignorant among you is the one who does not learn from the changes in the world. The richest among you is the one who is not entrapped by greed."[110]

One of the main philosophical differences between the three monotheisms can be shown in the realm of judgment. Not only do knowledge and reason depend upon good judgment, but so does justice. We must judge justly –this is where our ethical philosophy becomes applied and practical. In the fifth book of the Torah, Deuteronomy, Moses tells the Israelites that wisdom and understanding are found in observance of the laws of the Torah (4:6) and he elaborates on what he had said in the book of Exodus:

"Hear the causes between your brethren, and judge righteously between a man and his brother, and a stranger that is with him. Ye shall not respect persons in judgement; ye shall hear the small and the great alike; ye shall not be afraid of the face of any man; for the judgement is Yhwh's; and the cause that is too hard for you ye shall bring unto me, and I will hear it." 1:16-17

"Thou shalt not wrest judgement; thou shalt not respect persons; neither shalt thou take a gift, for a gift doth blind the eyes of the wise, and pervert the words of the righteous. Justice, justice shalt thou follow, that thou mayest live and inherit the land which the Lord thy God giveth thee." 16:19-20

In the New Testament of Christianity judgement in this world is prohibited. This is for several reasons. "However, the things proceeding out of the mouth come out of the heart, and those things defile a man." (Matthew 15:17)

"Stop judging that you may not be judged." Matthew 7:1

"Moreover, stop judging, and you will by no means be judged; and stop condemning, and you will by no means be condemned. Keep on releasing, and you will be released." Luke 6:37

"For God sent forth his Son into the world, not for him to judge the world, but for the world to be saved through him." John 3:17

"Therefore let us not be judging one another any longer, but rather make this your decision, not to put before a brother a stumbling block or a cause for tripping." Romans 14:13

"I solemnly charge you before God and Christ Jesus, who is destined to judge the living and the dead, and by his manifestation and his kingdom." 2 Timothy 4:1

Under such advice it seems we ought to refrain from ethical judgment. For Islam and Aristotle, but not Socrates and Plato, this worldly reality is not something from which we must be saved from or redeemed of. In Islam, as in Judaism, judgement is a central part of being human.

"Surely We have sent down to thee the Book with the truth, so that thou mayest judge between the people by that Allah has shown thee." Surah 4:106

"Indeed, We sent Our Messengers with the clear signs, and We sent down with them the Book and the Balance so that men might uphold justice." Surah 57:25

As the contemporary Aristotelian philosopher Alasdair MacIntyre tells of the virtues in heroic societies:

"To judge a man therefore is to judge his actions. By performing actions of a particular kind in a particular situation a man gives warrant for judgement upon his virtues and vices; for the virtues just are those qualities which sustain a free man in his role and which manifest themselves in those actions which his role requires."[111]

---

[110] Frager, p61, 63, 79, 125
[111] MacIntyre, p122

Where as the study of logic was banned from Christian Europe in the 5th century, logic was continued by Arabic philosophers in all centuries to follow. One of the first Muslim philosophers to do work on reason and logic was one Abu Yusuf al-Kindi, known in Latin as Alkindus, who lived from about 800-870. Known popularly as "the philosopher of the Arabs", al-Kindi wrote a very influential study called, *On First Philosophy*. Al-Kindi collected and studied the works of Aristotle as well as others thinkers, influencing a long tradition. This helped cement the historical relationship between Aristotle and Arabic philosophy.

Abu Nasr al-Farabi, who lived from 870-950, was another influential student of reason (or logic) and philosophy. Al-Farabi taught out of Baghdad on the subjects of logic and the study of Aristotle and he was particularly influential in setting a precedent of keeping theology separate from Islamic philosophy. In his work, *The Enumeration of the Sciences*, he discussed the limited role of the theologian.

"[T]he jurist takes the opinions and the actions stated explicitly by the founder of the religion and, using them as axioms, he infers the things that follow from them as consequences. The dialectical theologian, on the other hand, defends the thing that the jurist uses as axioms, without inferring other things from them."[112]

Probably the most celebrated of Muslim logicians and philosophers is one Ibn Rushd (or Averroes), who lived from 1126-1198, born in Cordoba, Spain. The philosophy of the European Renaissance has often been called "Averroism" because of the enormous influence he had on the West.[113] Averroes' interpretation of Aristotle was studied in Germany by Albertus Magnus, in Scotland by Duns Scotus, and in Poland, by Nicolas Copernicus. None less than the 'Father of Modernity', or the 'Copernican Revolution' the physicist Copernicus, was influenced by Averroes and wrote about the Muslim's discovery of sun-spots.[114]

The 'Copernican Revolution' held that the earth was not the center of the universe, which opened the flood gates for the research of Galileo (1564-1642). As has been pointed out, the Quran has been interpreted not with the belief that there is only one universe, in which case the earth would be the focal point of the cosmos, but that there are in fact a plurality of universes, as we see in Surah 6:75, 79.[115] This counters the anthropocentric view that humans are the center of the universe, and all pretensions to the ecological dominion of humans.

Because of Copernicus the Catholic Church held a few meetings over an 8 year period (1545-1563) which are known as the Council of Trent. This was done in order to properly decide on whether the church ought to acknowledge or condemn the ideas of Copernicus. By decree of Pope Urban VIII Galileo was censored and spent the rest of his life under house arrest.[116]

The Protestant Fathers Martin Luther and John Calvin were both conformists in deciding to condemn Copernicus. Luther called him an "upstart astrologer" and said of Copernicus's theory that the earth went around the sun and not vice-versa, "This fool wishes to reverse the entire science of astronomy." Calvin "demolished" Copernicus by

---

[112] Quoted in Waines, p116
[113] Pieper, p104
[114] Nicolaus Copernicus, "On the Revolutions of the Heavenly Spheres", trans. John F. Dobson and Selig Brodetsky, in *Theories of the Universe*, ed. Milton K. Munitz, (New York, Macmillan Publishing, 1957)
[115] The writings of Ahmed brought this to my attention.
[116] Carroll, p371, 384

quoting Jewish writings, "The world also is established, that it cannot be moved." (Psalms 93:1) And asking, "Who will venture to place the authority of Copernicus above that of the Holy Spirit?"[117]

While the Quran concurs with the Judeo-Christian tradition that the earth was created in 6 days, there has never been a conflict between Islam and science. A human day for Allah is 1000 years (22:47) or possibly 50,000 years.[118] (70:4) Metaphysics does not entail that humans can always know reality, whereas theology, or the science of the divine implicitly makes this claim.

Unlike Catholicism and many popular forms of Protestantism, there is no living person who is considered to be a divine authority, like the Pope or the King or Queen of England. Because of this lack of bureaucracy, Islam has been left to be interpreted by Muslim citizens and judges themselves. Like all intellectual traditions, Islam is based upon the book, and not upon a divine representative such as the Dalai Lama. The Quran encourages reading and studying (96:1-5) and the Arabic word for knowledge, *ilm,* is the second most used word in the Quran, after the name of God.[119]

When speaking about wisdom the prophet Muhammad's final speech usually comes up first, titled by his followers as the "Five Pillars of Wisdom". However, Muhammad had already said a great deal about the value of the intellect and the cultivation of knowledge. Some of the sayings or *hadith* of Muhammad reveal this. For example, "The first thing created by Allah was the intellect", or "Allah did not distribute to His servants anything more esteemed than Intelligence."[120]

The Sufi is probably the greatest example of the central place of wisdom in Islam. The Sufi emerged very early from the Muslim community as critics of affluence, materialism, and intellectual disinterest. As a protest to this they dressed in wool (*suf*) to mark themselves off as sincere and genuine in their intellectual pursuits. They made their goal to study the life of Muhammad, as well as other prophets. From early on Sufis have helped lay the foundations for Islamic Law.[121]

Muhammad said, "to know oneself is to know your Lord".[122] This has been the practice of Sufi's, who are in many ways philosophers. Recall that a central aspect to Greek thought was self-knowledge. Outside the Temple of Apollo in the city of Delphi was written, "Know Thyself". Socrates himself said, "The unexamined life is not worth living." For Plato and Aristotle, the intellectual life is a key aspect to living the good life.

The 13th century European Sufi Ibn Arabi believed there were four levels of Sufi practice: the first being the *Sharia* or path, which are the laws and morals of Islam, and the last being *Marifa* which means "deep wisdom", or in Greek 'gnosis'.[123] One of the earliest and most influential Sufis was an 8th century woman named Rabiah. By the 12th century, the Sufi's were creating international networks around the world. "In Africa and Southeast Asia Islam was spread primarily by Sufi brotherhoods and merchants rather than the armies of Islam."[124] A popular Sufi motto is *sulh-I-kul,* "peace with all".[125]

---

[117] Russell, (a) p528
[118] Ahmed (a) points this out.
[119] Ahmed, (b) p169
[120] Ahmed, (a) p30
[121] Williams, p137
[122] Waines, p139
[123] Frager, p75
[124] Esposito, p37

Science and Medicine

Before Socrates philosophized there was a school of thought in the city-state of Miletus called atomism, started by Leucippus and then continued by Democritus, who was from Thrace. As the name 'atomism' suggests these philosophers believed that reality consisted of atoms –the building block of nature. All that exists is 'atoms in the void'. This 'materialism', or belief that reality was absolutely physical was taken up again by one of the last schools of Greek philosophy, the Epicureans. Materialism obviously led to the belief in naturalism in science and medicine, or the belief that sickness and disease have natural causes and remedies, rather than supernatural. However, in the ancient world, and we might hesitate to say still today, this line of thinking was often exceptional.

Although both Socrates and Plato were dualists, believing that the body was a walking cadaver with a soul trapped inside it, they were not against medicine, unlike the more consistent dualists of the Christian Era. Some of Plato and Socrates' best friends were physicians, and both philosopher's held the medical practice in high regards.

In the *Republic* Socrates says in an ideal city there will be good physicians (408d). He and Plato both controversially believed that women can be physicians (455e), and that the physician should not be a capitalist.

"Surely no physician either, in so far as he is a physician, seeks or orders what is advantageous to himself, but to his patient? For we agreed that the physician in the strict sense of the word is a ruler over bodies and not a moneymaker." (342d)

Aristotle was scientifically innovative, introducing the studies of biology and zoology among many other advances in various disciplines. The 'v' shaped heart that represents love is derived from a sketch of the heart made my Aristotle, who believed the heart had two chambers.[126] The school that Aristotle had opened in Athens, the *Lyceum*, became fundamentally a school of biology. Therein works in anatomy and dissection took place, and Aristotle's work in logic provided the framework for much subsequent progress in science and medicine.[127] In his study of *Politics*, Aristotle says that in the ideal city-state health will be a central concern in its design.

"There should be a natural abundance of springs and fountains in the town, or, if there is a deficiency of them, great reservoirs may be established for the collection of rain-water... Special care should be taken of the health of the inhabitants, which will depend chiefly on the healthiness of the locality and of the quarter to which they are exposed, and secondly, on the use of pure water; this latter point is by no means a secondary consideration. For the elements which we use most and oftenest for the support of the body contribute most to health, and among these are water and air. For this reason, in all wise states, if there is a want of pure water, and the supply is not all equally good, the drinking water ought to be separated from that which is used for other purposes." *Politics*, 1330b5-15[128]

---

[125] Ahmed, (b) p164
[126] My thanks to the philosopher William E. Mann for teaching me this and other things about the love of wisdom (philosophy).
[127] Vivian Nutton, "Medicine in the Greek world, 800-50 BC", *The Western Medical Tradition 800 BC to AD 1800*, (a) p32
[128] Aristotle, *The Politics*, trans. Benjamin Jowett, ed. Stephen Everson, (Cambridge, Cambridge University Press, 1996) (P)

It is sometimes disputed whether the father of Western Medicine was either the Greek physician Hippocrates, who influenced Plato and lived some 4 or 5 hundred years before Christianity. (It is Hippocrates from whom today all doctors take the "Hippocratic Oath" –an oath to do their duty as physicians regardless of their feelings toward the afflicted.)

Or was it the Greco-Roman physician Galen, who was court physician to the last Stoic philosopher and Roman Emperor Marcus Aurelius, sometime in the 1st or 2nd century CE? The tradition of Hipppocrates and Galen holds that diseases are caused naturally, and not through magic or supernaturalism, and thus they sought non-supernatural cures for the various ailments.[129] This was perhaps one of the greatest causes for the spread of the so-called 'scientific method'. Galen himself said that "the best doctor is also a philosopher".[130]

The last school of pure Greek philosophy was that of the Skeptics. In the original meaning of the word in Greek, skepticism meant "inquiry", and the greatest proponent of Skepticism was a physician named Sextus Empiricus. By the time that Empiricus lived and worked sometime in the 2nd century of the Common Era, there were three medical schools: there was the Logical/Theoretical school, the Methodical school, and the Empirical School. Empiricus believed philosophical Skepticism was most aligned with the Methodical school of medicine, if only because the Logical/Theoretical and Empirical schools are dogmatically committed to either the evidential or the inevidential as causes for sickness or health. Empiricus thought the Methodical school was more practical (or pragmatic) and "take[s] from these whatever seems most expedient".[131] The Skeptical schools was closed in 529 by the Christian Roman Emperor Justinian I, due to Christian bigotry.[132]

Because of their attempt to naturalize medicine the writings and research of both Hippocrates and Galen were banned from Europe in the year 431 by the Holy Roman Empire.[133] These writings of philosophy, science, and medicine were 'smuggled' to the Middle East and there were preserved. Thereupon, the writings of the ancient Greek physicians were combined with the biological writings of Aristotle and were "systemized" for the first time.

Although many of the religions we have been considering as for example Hinduism, Judaism, Confucianism, Taoism, and Buddhism, predate much of the western medical tradition, they of course each have medical traditions of their own, whether they be acupuncture, or diet, etc... For example, each Native American tribe had a physician, and Native Americans had a cure for scurvy two centuries before Europeans (Native Americans helped in discovering insulin). Moreover, European colonists discovered that Native Americans had discovered over 200 indigenous medicinal drugs from the land

---

[129] Mary Lindemann, *Medicine and Society in Early Modern Europe*, (Cambridge, Cambridge University Press, 1999) p68
[130] Lindemann, p69
[131] Sextus Empiricus, "Outlines of Pyrrhonism", Book I, in *Selections from the Major Writings of Scepticism, Man, & God*, trans. Sanford G. Etheridge, ed. Philip P. Hallie, (Indianapolis, Hackett Publishing, 1985) p98
[132] Russell, (a) p277
[133] Pieper, p103

they lived in. Many colonists found that Native Americans were superior obstetricians as well.[134]

The last scriptural writings of the Hebrew Bible, Chronicles II, written in he 5th century BCE mentions the death of one 9th century Messiah Asa, who had preferred the assistance of physicians to faith-healing. Around the year 180 BCE, a Jewish man named Jesus ben Sirach had said, "Honor the physician for the good ye may have of him." By the end of the 4th century of the Common Era, by Jewish law, *Halachah*, all communities were required to have someone skilled in medicine.[135]

The 10th century Jewish physician Shabbetai Donnolo of southern Italy, wrote a *Book of Wisdom* which united Jewish and Greek medical thinking.[136] Although he wrote in Arabic, the Jewish philosopher, physician, and Talmudist Moses Maimonides wrote a great deal about medicine and had a great influence, particularly in 12th century Egypt. The late 15th century Pope Alexander VI, father of Cesare Borgia, had his own physician who was also a Jewish Rabbi.[137]

Jesus the Nazarene had rebutted the doctors, "Physician heal thyself" (Luke 4:23) The Gospel of Mark reveals the futilitarianism and ineffectuality of physicians, suggesting even a countervailing affect. (Mark 5:26) The greatest writer of Christianity, Saint Paul, had offered a medical tip to his friend in prison, Timothy. "Do not drink water any longer, but use a little wine for the sake of your upset stomach and your frequent cases of sickness." (1Timothy 5:23)

When the prophet Muhammad was asked, "Should one go the doctor?" He replied, "Allah sends down no malady without also sending down with it a cure." Moreover, Muhammad had his own physician, one al-Harith ibn Kalada.[138]

In spite of his rebellion against Rome, the Protestant father Martin Luther wrote of the hospitals there saying that they were the 'best'.[139] When the Protestant Reformation occurred in Europe during the 16th and 17th centuries, those states which broke with the church suffered grievously in loss of hospitals. In England, King Henry VIII "indiscriminately broke up cloisters, religious foundations, and charitable establishments and sold their lands."[140] Although there were thousands of "witch" burnings in the 16th and 17th century in Europe, often times some people would go to a witch before going to a doctor.[141]

It is not because the physician Michael Servetus confirmed the discoveries of the Arabic physicians -that blood moves through the lungs -that he was condemned by the Protestant father John Calvin. It was because he did not believe in ghosts. Calvin had Servetus executed in the Inquisition. The father of Methodism, John Wesley (1703-1791)

---

[134] Francis Jennings, *The Invasion of America*, (New York, W.W. Norton & Company, 1975) p52
[135] Vivian Nutton, "Medicine in Late Antiquity and the Early Middle Ages", *The Western Medical Tradition 800 BC to AD 1800*, (b) p73
[136] Vivian Nutton, "Medicine in Medieval Western Europe, 1000-1500", *The Western Medical Tradition 800 BC to AD 1800*, (c) p139-140
[137] Carroll, p364
[138] Conrad, p98, 101
[139] Andrew Wear, "Medicine in Early Modern Europe, 1500-1700", *The Western Medical Tradition 800 BC to AD 1800*, p248
[140] Lindemann, p129
[141] Wear, p243

was critical of the medical practices and developed his own healing method called, "physick".[142]

Historically, Muslims have respected and honored many different philosophies, more so than any other religious tradition. For example in medieval Cordoba there were more books in libraries than in all other libraries in Europe combined.[143] Many of the most influential Muslim and Arabic philosophers were often even more influential in other areas such as medicine, surgery, mathematics, astronomy, and science. In the area of medicine the Western world is eternally indebted to the Islamic tradition.

In 832 a central medical school was established in Baghdad called the *Bayt al-Hikma,* or "House of Wisdom". Many scholars worked there in translating texts into Arabic from languages as diverse as Syriac, Pahlavi, Sanskrit, and Greek. Probably the first ever comprehensive medical compendium ever was made by a Jewish convert to Islam, Rabban al-Tabari, who lived around the year 850 in North Persia, or modern day Iran. His work is titled *Firdaws al-hikma,* or "Paradise of Wisdom", and consists of some 350 chapters summarizing all the medical knowledge from Arabic, Persian, Greek, and Indian cultures.[144]

The 13th century Arabic physician Ibn al-Nafis discovered blood-circulation in the lungs.[145] The first ever treatise on smallpox was done by the Muslim polymath Razi in his work, *Fi l-hasba wa-l-judari,* or "On Smallpox and Measles". This work was still being translated into English in the 19th century.[146] Razi's other works, some 200 titles on a vast array of subjects from anatomy to surgery, to logic and mathematics were published into Greek, Latin, and Hebrew for centuries after his death.

Two of the most influential Islamic doctors were Haly Abbas Majusi and Ibn Sina. Majusi was from southern Persia and died sometime in the 10th century. His work, *Kamil al-sina'a al-tibbya,* or "The Complete Medical Art" was a very early and influential history of medicine. The *Kamil* has been translated into Latin twice. Ibn Sina, or in Latin, Avicenna, is considered one the greatest doctors and writers of medicine. Of over 250 titles, his most recognized work is the *Al-Qanun fi l-tibb,* or "Canon of Medicine". Ibn Sina's genius lay in organizing the works of the 2nd century Greek physician Galen, which have been described as "diffuse" and "tentative", and arranging these works according to the science and logic of Aristotle. Ibn Sina's systemization of medicine, the *Qanun*, was translated into Latin in the 12th century Spain as "The Canon", and again in 16th century Venice. This latter translation was reprinted more than 30 times over two centuries, and was translated into Hebrew as well. Commentaries written on the *Qanun* in Latin and Hebrew cannot be numbered, and some medical historians say that the *Qanun* is probably the most studied medical work ever. The 13th century English philosopher Roger Bacon said of al-Kindi's *De gradibus* ('On the Grades of Drug Action') that it "demanded knowledge of mathematics well beyond his own contemporaries in philosophy and medicine."[147]

---

[142] Lindemann, p74, 212
[143] Ahmed, (b) p50
[144] Conrad, p105, 107, 112
[145] Lindemann, p74
[146] Conrad, p110, 138
[147] Quoted by Nutton, (c) p143; Conrad, p115

Some see the 'crowning achievement' of Islamic medical practice in the development of the hospital and medical school, which set the standards for modern medicine while most of Europe was still in the depths of the Dark Ages. The first Muslim hospital may have been established somewhere between 705-715 in Damascus, or in Baghdad around 805. By the 12th century a hospital was an essential feature of any large Islamic town. A "Surgery" was the name of a kind of open-shop. Admission was free, payment to the physician was due at the end of treatment. The first medical school in Turkey appeared in the 13th century, which was then expanded into a college.[148]

Another way in which Arab and Islamic medicine came to influence the West was during the Arab settlements of Italy and Sicily that had begun in 950. While the study of medicine was "not in place" in the 11th century Cathedral schools of France, by 1150 translations of Arabic were widely spread in Italy and further. It was in Salerno, Italy, that a medical school was founded by 4 masters –one Latin, one Jewish, one Arabic, and one Greek –where Arab and Islamic Medicine became the model for the West. "…the New Arabic material was also far more advanced, conceptually and practically, than what was available through the Greek." The Arab-Islamic medical tradition accepted admittance of non-Muslims and many Jewish and Christian medical texts of this time were written in Arabic. "The heavy Arabism of many Latin translations tended to create a specifically medical vocabulary." It was here that Islam set the precedent for the formalization of medicine as we know it today.[149]

What is most amazing about Islamic philosophy and medicine is their attention to detail. Islam in an important sense developed the 'science of citation', or *isnad* as it was originally called in Arabic. This science of citation allowed for analytic study and argumentation to begin, which is crucial in showing the history of concepts, theories, and interpretations. Science and medicine are in a strong sense based upon history, and trial and error. Islamic developments in pharmacology are representative of this phenomenon. An Andalusian named Ibn al-Baytar who died in 1248 listed over 3000 plants, animals, and minerals, and lists over 250 sources. Modern Turkish libraries contain over 5000 classical medical manuscripts in Arabic, Turkish, and Persian.[150]

The influence of Arabs and Muslims in mathematics has been immense. By 10th century most of Europe had adopted Arabic numerals (1,2,3…etc.) and no longer made use of the cumbersome Roman numerals (I,II,III).[151] The whole 'realm of algebra' was theorized by the Muslim mathematician Mohammed ibn Musa al-Khowarizmi in the year 825. The word 'algebra' is taken from the words of his book's title, *ilm al-jabra wa'l muqabalah*, or "the science of reduction and cancellation".[152]

Some see the *hajj* or trip to Mecca, a duty of all Muslims who are able, as Muhammad did 14 centuries ago to bring peace, as the first "international scientific congress" or the "first international economic fair".[153] Skill in the crafts of agriculture came from working in places where there is a scarcity of water. The water works of

---

[148] Conrad, p130-132, 135
[149] Nutton, (c) p140, 143, 146; Conrad 127, 125
[150] Conrad, p119, 122
[151] W.V. Quine, *Quiddities: An Intermittently Philosophical Dictionary*, (Cambridge, The Belknap Press, 1987) p239
[152] Isaac Asimov, *Realm of Algebra*, (New York, Fawcett Publication, 1961) p12. Khowarizmi also did work on the Hebrew calendar.
[153] Nasr, 138

Spain are called a work of Muslim "engineering genius".[154] Russell says in his *History of Western Philosophy*, "To this day Spanish agriculture profits by Arab-irrigation works."[155]

The only bathhouses in Europe during the medieval times were made and run by Muslims.[156] When Muslims were ordered to leave Cordoba, all 270 bathhouses were closed by the Christian *reconquista*.[157] The Christians who colonized America were both astonished and frightened to find that the Natives bathed on a daily basis.[158] Well before the toothbrush was invented, Muslims were using the *siwak* or *miswak*. Soap itself is an Arab invention, whereas the Greeks and Romans scraped dirt from their bodies using flat pieces of metal, called a strigel.

Medicine or Poison?

If only wisdom were like water… -Socrates[159]

The desert is dry. One thing which separates the Quran from both the Hebrew and Christian bibles is the prohibition against alcohol. The Quran tells us that both wine and gambling are distracting and sinful (Surah 2:216, 5:90-91) and are to be avoided. Muslims instead, are instructed to drink water. "We send down out of heaven water, then We give it to you to drink, and you are not its treasurers." (Surah 15:23)

Although Noah on one occasion is described as a confused drunk (Genesis 9:22), the Torah prohibited alcohol for Aaron and his family when coming near the holy writ. (Leviticus 10:9) When a Nazirite makes a vow, they must abstain from alcohol until the vow is fulfilled. (Numbers 6:3) The book of Deuteronomy permits us to buy alcohol (14:26), though Moses later praises the Israeli's for abstaining from alcohol. It helped them to understand things better. (Deuteronomy 29:5) The Hebrew Bible, or Tanach is filled with dozens of references to wine and alcohol, some positive, some negative. Isaiah says that a "drunken man staggereth in his vomit." (19:14) The book of Proverbs says, "Wine is a mocker, strong drink is riotous; and whosoever reeleth thereby is not wise." (Proverbs 20:1)

One of the most interesting things about the ancient writings of Hinduism, in particular the *Rig Veda*, are the many discussions about a fruit or vegetable juice called *soma*. In Sanskrit the word soma means 'pressed' and is a juice made by pressing different plants, although the exact ingredients are to this day vary, though it is described in places as being mixed with milk and honey. (4:27) Soma is believed to be a divine plant which could bestow anything from wisdom to immortality for those who performed the ritual of Soma.[160]

---

[154] Carroll, p323
[155] Russell, (a) p423
[156] Nasr, p130
[157] Nietzsche, (a) 21
[158] Jennings, p50
[159] In Plato's *Symposium*, trans. Alexander Nehamas and Paul Woodruff, (Indianapolis, Hackett Publishing, 1989) (c) p5
[160] David M. Knipe, "Soma", *The Perennial Dictionary of Religion*, ed. Keith Crim, (New York, HarperCollins, 1981) p698-699

The *Dhammapada* of Buddhism says: "And the man who engages in the drinking of intoxicants, right here in this world he digs up his own root." (247) According to the Buddha, intoxicants cause us to see fault in others, to be always readily disdainful (253), to never be contented with ourselves (272), but to be vain, heedless (292), and never achieving our goal. (420)

The ancient religion of Confucius teaches us that those who are wise rejoice in water (6:23). Although Confucius never set a rigid limit for wine, he never drank to the point of becoming confused (10:8), and he teaches that those who find the most pleasure in food and drink are losers. (16:5)

In the Christian New Testament we find several attitudes regarding alcohol. In the Gospel according to John we find that Jesus turns water into wine (John 2:9), and in the Gospel of Matthew Jesus instructs his followers not to put new wine into old wine skins. (Matthew 9:17) At the Last Supper Jesus passes out glasses of wine to his disciples that will forgive them of sin, though he says he personally will not drink wine again until he is in heaven. (Matthew 26:29) In the book of Acts we are told that "men of Judea" came to believe that the Apostles were drunk. Peter stood up and replied that they were, "in fact, not drunk, as you suppose, for it is the third hour of the day." (Acts 2:15) We are left to wonder at what hour drinking begins in a 24 hour day. In Paul's letters he writes that servants should not drink too much wine (1Tim 3:8), though, as we saw, he tells Timothy not to drink water again, but to drink wine for his frequent cases of sickness. (1Tim 5:23) Paul tells the Ephesians to abstain from alcohol because it leads to sex. (Eph 5:18) He tells the Galatians to avoid "drunken bouts" and "revelries", which are works of the flesh. (Galatians 5:21)

Historically, one of the most central sacraments to the church has been the drinking of wine, in a ritual called 'transubstantiation'. Accordingly, Christians of all ages drink some wine as a symbolic gesture of drinking the blood of Jesus. The spread of Christianity throughout Europe by the Roman Empire has been described as an encounter between "wine and beer"[161], and where there was not warfare, tales of miracles such as wine-cellars being multiplied through faith in Jesus, helped to convert the pagan.[162]

While some of the newer Christian Protestant sects such as the Mormons and the Seventh-Day Adventists abstain from alcohol, the founding father of Protestantism, Martin Luther, was a notorious drunk, having written poems about wine, and having had drinking contests with the devil. In a letter to one his admirers, Luther wrote:

"Whenever the devil pesters you with these thoughts, at once seek out the company of men, drink more, joke and jest, or engage in some other form of merriment. Sometimes it is necessary to drink a little more, play, jest, or even commit some sin in defiance and contempt for the devil in order not to give him an opportunity to make us scrupulous about trifles. We shall be overcome if we worry too much about falling into some sin. So, if the devil should say, 'Do not drink,' you should reply to him, 'On this very account, because you forbid it, I shall drink, and what is more, I shall drink a generous amount.' Thus one must always do the opposite of that which Satan prohibits. What do you think my reason for drinking wine undiluted, talking freely, and eating more often, if it is not to torment and vex the devil who made up his mind to torment and vex me?"[163]

---

[161] Fletcher, p13

[162] Fletcher, p182

[163] Martin Luther, "Letter to Jerome Weller, July, 1530", in *Briefwechsel*, vol. 5, trans. T.G. Tappert. Quoted in Kaufmann, (a) p233-234. Both founding fathers of Protestantism, Luther and John Calvin were copious drinkers. Check out Jim West's, *Drinking With Calvin and Luther!: A History of Alcohol in the Church*, Revised and Expanded Edition, (Lincoln, Oakdown, 2003)

In Islam alcohol is prohibited because it gets us distracted and makes us forgetful. (5:90-91) When Islamic revolutions occur, as for example when Muammar Muhammad Qaddafi ousted the conservative Libyan monarchy of King Idris in 1969, he did not propose a toast to his revolutionary power, but banned alcohol and gambling. In 1971 the Shah, or King of Iran celebrated 2500 years of Persian monarchy, by far the longest standing monarchy in world history. For this celebration the Shah spent over $200 million for a weak-long party, with caterers from Paris, and 25,000 bottles of wine.[164] Shortly after the Iranian Revolution of 1978-1979 led by Imam Ayatollah Khomeini, alcohol was temporarily banned though this was soon lifted for the 1/2 million Christians, 50,000 Jews, and 30,000 Zoroastrians living in Iran.[165] When Gaafar Muhammad Nimeiri took control in Sudan in 1983, though he was backed by the United States, he threw a grand celebration which was glorified when 11 million dollars worth of alcohol was dumped into the Nile River.[166] While the Boston Tea Party was probably less deleterious to the environment, still an ecologically worse prohibition was that prompted by John D. Rockefeller in order to get automobiles to run exclusively on oil and not alcohol.[167]

One lesser known accomplishment is the Sufi invention of *hashish*. Hashish is an Arabic word that may derive from the name of a group called the *Hashishin*, although other legends exist. Most likely, hashish was "discovered", that is invented in the year 1260 by a Sufi named Sheik Haidar, who was a farmer.[168] Hashish is a product derived from the Asian plant *Cannabis Sativa*. The ancient Sanskrit word for Cannabis (a Greek word) is *Ganja*. The male version of which is called simply 'hemp' (from Old English), and the female is called 'marijuana' (a Spanish-Mexican coinage).

The practice of ingesting or consuming *Cannabis* goes back thousands of years and many of the world's cultures, past and present, have made use of the strong hemp fiber. Archeologists have found evidence of the use of *Cannabis* in ancient China, anywhere from three to six thousand years ago. Remnants of cloth and paper made from hemp thousands of years ago have been discovered, some of which are medical documents which discussed the uses of *Cannabis*.[169] One of the earliest acknowledgements of *Cannabis* by a European writer was done by the ancient Greek historian Herodotus, some 2500 years ago. Herodotus reported that a Persian tribe called the 'Scythians' used to delight in burning the plant inside enclosed tents. This would cause the Scythians to shout with joy and sing and dance.[170]

Jack Herer's excellent book, *The Emperor Wears No Clothes*, tells of the many religions around the world which make use of *Cannabis*. The Hindu God Shiva brought *Cannabis* from the Himalayan mountains "for human enjoyment and enlightenment".[171] In the *Bhagavad-Gita* the god Krsna says, "I am the medical herb". (9:16) In India today a kind of holy person called a "Sadu" may smoke *Cannabis* on a daily basis, with little

---

[164] Esposito, p80-81, 104
[165] Dilip Hiro, *Iran Under the Ayatollahs*, (New York, Routledge & Keegan Paul Inc., 1987) p222
[166] Esposito, p89
[167] David Blume, *Alcohol Can Be a Gas!*, (Santa Cruz, International Institute for Ecological Agriculture, 2007); or watch the DVD by the same title.
[168] Robert Connell Clarke, *Hashish!*, (Los Angeles, Red Eye Press, Inc., 1998) p24
[169] Clarke, p9-10
[170] Clarke, p18-19
[171] Jack Herer, *The Emperor Wears No Clothes*, (Van Nuys, California, Hemp Publishing, 1990) p53

harm done to their body.[172] Buddhism has made use of *Cannabis* for thousands of years and supposedly, the Buddha himself ate nothing but hemp for six years prior to the formulation of his philosophy.[173]

The Japanese religion of Shintoism uses *Cannabis* during wedding ceremonies, and was believed to create laughter and happiness in marriage. The Persian religion of Zoroastrianism has made use the *Cannabis* plant since its origin some 2700 years ago. The ancient Jewish sect known as the 'Essenes' used hemp medicinally, as did the 'Theraputea' of ancient Egypt, from whence we get the word "therapeutic". The book of Genesis says that Yhwh has given all the seed-bearing plants to humans for use (Genesis 1:29), and the Talmud of Judaism discusses the properties of *Cannabis*.[174] African peoples, ancient and present, have also made use of *Cannabis* such as the Bantus, the Pygmies, the Zulus, and the Hottentots, who use the plant as medicine.[175]

However, when the Christian Inquisition began in the 12th century, *Cannabis* became illegal. And by the 13th century *Cannabis* was illegal in France. One of the accusations leveled at Joan of Arc in the 1431 was that of using *Cannabis*, for which she was eventually burned at the stake. In 1484, Pope Innocent VIII outlawed *Cannabis* use for both consumption and medicine. The Holy Roman Empire claimed that *Cannabis* is unholy and Satanic. Pope John Paul II lent assistance to First Lady Nancy Reagan in the US War on Drugs.[176] In 2008 the Catholic church reaffirmed its condemnation of such 'mind-altering' drugs though this deprecation did not include alcohol.[177]

So it seems, we are left with an opposition between the "juicers" and the "dopers". The Christian crusaders were said to have been kept in a perpetual drunken stupor. According to the philologist Friedrich Nietzsche one of the two greatest means of corruption is alcohol.[178] He calls alcohol "European poison", calling the middle ages the alcohol poisoning of Europe and Nietzsche believed alcohol to be the most lethal narcotic that Europe bequeaths to "savage tribes".[179]

Nietzsche believed that the "alcoholic poisoning of Europe" had throughout European history, "gone strictly in step with… political and racial hegemony."[180] The pilgrims who colonized America despaired drinking water and preferred beer. Francis Jennings writes in *The Invasion of America: Indians, Colonialism, and the Cant of Conquest*, "Alcoholic drinks, introduced by the Europeans, created mass drunkenness and demoralization."[181] The Iroquois of New York who looked down on drinking "staved off cultural disintegration".[182] Bertrand Russell wrote in his book, *The Conquest of Happiness*: "Drunkenness… is temporary suicide: the happiness that it brings is merely negative, a momentary cessation of unhappiness."[183]

---

[172] Clarke, p109, 297
[173] Herer, p53
[174] Clarke, p35
[175] Herer, p53
[176] Herer, p56, 210
[177] A.P. Press, *New York Times*, March 11, 2008
[178] Nietzsche, (a) 60
[179] Friedrich Nietzsche, *The Gay Science*, trans. Josefine Nauckhoff, (Cambridge, Cambridge University Press, 2001), (f) 42, 134, 147
[180] Nietzsche, (f) 143
[181] Jennings, p33, 34
[182] Peter Nabokov, *Native American Testimony*, (New York, Penguin Books, 1999) p173
[183] Bertrand Russell, *The Conquest of Happiness*, (New York, Bantam Books, 1968) (c) p11

Anyone who drinks regularly is an alcoholic. It should be noted that before the great *Symposium*, or 'Drinking Party' of Plato begins, everyone has sobered up. As the All-American Football and Lacrosse player Jim Brown put it simply in his autobiography, "Anyone who knows booze knows it gets you talking some dumb, convoluted shit –and believing it."[184]

Slavery

Just about every religion that I am familiar with tolerates slavery, or has tolerated slavery up until the last 140 years or so. Slavery probably still exists in some places, and some have argued that under some systems of slavery, the slaves were often more free than someone who is poor in a capitalist society. Under the current economic structure people are starving and millions are denied health care. Such conditions would have been tantamount to a bad investment under slavery. Once slavery was abolished in America, the industrial revolution was already in full swing and young children were forced to work in dirty and unsafe factories. They started in infancy and worked there for their whole lives or until they died on the job. Compulsory education, which put an end to a lot of the exploitation of child-labor, has sometimes had the effect of enslaving the minds of our youths and has bred and still breeds a great deal of conformity.

While I do not think slavery can be justified, there have been societies where slaves were treated better or worse, according to the laws. Socrates discussed mathematics with a slave and treated him with respect, the Stoic philosopher Epictetus was born into slavery but was later freed and went on to open his own school of philosophy.

Socrates, Plato, and Aristotle, like all Athenians and most ancient Greeks, were not against slavery. This does not mean that because their philosophy isn't in some sense universal that it is useless. In fact, their philosophies can in an important way be seen as a critique of what was then considered to be ethical common-sense about slavery and slaves.

We see in a dialogue named after *Meno* that Socrates engages a slave in discussion of mathematics, in order to prove that all people have reason and intellectual ability. In Plato's lengthy study *Laws*, we find Plato at his most generous, "And the right treatment of slaves is to behave properly to them, and to do to them, if possible, even more justice than to those who are our equals".[185] (VI, 777) Aristotle believed that slaves were part of the family, and that because slaves are human beings, they can be our friends too. (E, 1161b5) Thus, while the philosophical trinity were not opposed to slavery, they were aware of the need for common humanity.

Perhaps the most famous story related to Judaism is their enslavement by an Egyptian Pharaoh, and their own successful bout for freedom. This constitutes the largest book of the Pentateuch or Torah, the book of Exodus. The Babylonian Exile, over a thousand years later, is also understood as a period of enslavement, until Persian victory

---

[184] Jim Brown, *Out of Bounds*, (New York, Kensington Publishing Corp., 1989) p82
[185] Plato, *Laws*, trans. by Benjamin Jowett, *The Dialogues of Plato*, Volume II, (New York, Random House, 1937) (d)

over Babylon and the subsequent release of the Jews. These two events helped to shape the Jewish attitude toward slavery.

In the book of Genesis we learn that Joseph had been sold as a slave to some Egyptians by his brothers because they were jealous that their father Jacob loved Joseph the most. Shortly after reaching Egypt Joseph helps the Pharaoh understand a recurring dream he had been having and which no one could interpret. In turn the Pharaoh rewards Joseph by making him one of the most powerful men in Egypt, inviting the rest of his family to live in Egypt as well.

"Now there arose a new king over Egypt, who knew not Joseph." These are words that appear early on in the book of Exodus which tells of the enslavement of the descendents of Joseph and his family. By the time the Exodus occurs, the Jews living in Egypt number some 600,000 (12:37) and had been enslaved for 430 years. (12:41)

The Jewish population had multiplied since Joseph had arrived and the Pharaoh sought to kill off the infants, one of whom was Moses. Moses had been born unto slavery and was hidden in the banks of the Nile to save his life. He was discovered by the Pharaoh's daughter and was raised as an Egyptian Prince. When he got older, Moses witnessed an Egyptian soldier mistreating a Hebrew slave. Moses kills the Egyptian and flees the country. After settling and marrying into the Midian tribe, Yhwh commands Moses to return to Egypt to end slavery.

After their confrontation with the Egyptian sorcerers, Moses and his brother Aaron successfully lead the Jews out of Egypt. At Sinai Moses gives the law concerning slavery: slaves are only to be kept six years and are to be released on the seventh-year. (Exodus 21:2) Slave owners are to be punished if they kill a slave, and must let a slave go if they are physically damaged by their owner. (21:20, 26-27)

The final book of the Torah, Deuteronomy strengthens this law. According to Deuteronomy when a slave is released at the end of the six year period they are not to go empty-handed but shall be furnished "liberally". (Deuteronomy 15:14)

According to Deuteronomy any fugitive slave that is found is to be treated as free. They are not to be reported or returned to their owner, but are to be given accommodations amongst one's own dwelling and they shall not be wronged. (Deuteronomy 23:16) Anyone caught selling their brethren as a slave shall be put to death. (Deu 24:7) As the Torah says many times, "Love ye therefore the stranger; for ye were strangers in the land of Egypt." (Deu 10:19)

During the time of the second Commonwealth (6th-1st centuries before the Common Era), slave-holding was no longer practiced among Jews living in Palestine. However, Jews living under the Persian and Roman governments occasionally adopted the state law which allowed slavery.[186] After the Roman defeat of the 2nd Commonwealth, the Jewish state would not come into existence again until the Khazars of Russia converted their empire.

In Christianity slavery is treated as inabolishable. There are dozens of places in the New Testament where slavery is supported. This is for several possible reasons. As we have seen the Torah sanctioned the practice, if putting laws and limits on it. The New Testament was written in conformity to Roman Law which had even stricter laws on slavery. As Peter Gomes says in *The Good Book*,

---

[186] Ginzberg, p15-16

"Not only did New Testament morality fail to liberate the slaves or even to mitigate their lot in this life, but it required of the slaves obedience to their masters…and these arrangements were ordained by God, sanctioned by the patriarchs, tolerated by Jesus, approved by Paul, and enshrined in the Bible."[187]

In the New Testament, Jesus tells slaves that while they cannot serve two masters, if they remain loyal to one master, they will be rewarded in heaven. Jesus offers a parable which tells of a slave who thought his master had disappeared and he stopped working and became sinful. The parable ends when the master returns and Jesus says, "Throw the good-for-nothing slave out in the darkness outside. There is where weeping and gnashing of teeth will be." (Matthew 25:30) The point of this parable is demonstrate this ethics:

"Who really is the faithful and discreet slave whom his master has appointed over his domestics, to give them their food at the proper time? Happy is the slave if his master on arriving finds him doing so." (Matthew 24:45-46)

The letters of Paul, who was a Roman citizen, say as much about slavery. Paul writes that although slaves are equal according to Jesus (Galatians 3:28), they should remain as slaves and respect their owners (1Timmothy 6:1-2). They should not rebel against their owners (1Corinthians 7:22), though owners should not threaten them too much (Ephesians 6:9). Paul tells the slaves: "You slaves, be obedient to those who are your masters…" (Ephesians 6:5) Paul's letter to the Roman Emperor Titus informs the ruler of Christian tolerance for slavery. "Let slaves be in subjection to their owners in all things, and please them well, not talking back." Titus 2:9

The African slave trade began in 15th century by dint of two Papal Bulls of two different Popes. On January 8th of 1455 Pope Nicholas V added to the Canon Law, *Romanus Pontifex*, which called for the 'perpetual' enslavement of all Africans discovered. On May 3rd of 1493 Pope Alexander VI added to the Canon *Inter Caetera*, the instructions to conquer and colonize those non-Christian lands and peoples. Laws of the same nature were written by Henry VII in 1496 and by Queen Elizabeth I in 1578 and 1584.[188]

A letter written in 1610 by a Brazilian priest reveals how casual and normal it was to own slaves:

"Your Reverence writes me that you would like to know whether the Negroes who are sent to your parts have been legally captured. To this I reply I think your Reverence should have not scruples on this point… Therefore we and the Fathers of Brazil buy these slaves for our service without any scruple…"[189]

In 1774, two years before he wrote the most popular book of the American Revolution, *Common Sense*, Thomas Paine wrote in opposition to *African Slavery In America*.

"The managers of that trade themselves, and others, testify, that many of these African nations inhabit fertile countries, are industrious farmers, enjoy plenty, and lived quietly, averse to war, before the Europeans debauched them with liquors, and bribing them against one another; and that these inoffensive people are brought into slavery, by stealing them, tempting kings to sell subjects…By such wicked and inhuman ways the English are said to enslave towards one hundred thousand yearly; of which thirty thousand are supposed to die by barbarous treatment in he first year; besides all that are slain in the unnatural wars excited to take them."[190]

---

[187] Peter J. Gomes, *The Good Book*, (New York, William Morrow and Company, Inc., 1996) p89
[188] Jennings, p4, 5, 45
[189] Zinn, p29
[190] Thomas Paine, "African Slavery In America", originally published in the *Pennsylvania Journal and the Weekly Advertiser*, March 8, 1775; from *The Complete Writings of Thomas Paine*, ed. Philip S. Foner, (New York, the Citadel Press, 1945) p16

And what about Lincoln during the American Civil War? While what we refer to as the "Bible Belt" fought on the pro-slavery side of the war, the anti-slavery Unionists were just as often Christian soldiers as well. Some of the southern clergy, who were often times Baptists and some Presbyterians, believed the war was theological, a war in opposition to the "Yankee heresy" of the northern Unionists.[191] Although 450 years before the Civil War, Catholics and Lutherans were sworn enemies, both churches remained neutral on the question of slavery during the civil war. Mormons on the other hand were pro-slavery. The main opposition was between Southern Baptists vs. Northern Baptists.[192]

In 1869, four years after Northern victory and the abolition of slavery, an entry in a Southern Baptist journal read: "Now I would certainly be opposed to the restoration of slavery in this country, but I have undergone no change on the righteousness of slavery, nor can I change until convinced that our Bible is not the book of God."[193]

Long an activist for racial and economic equality, Martin Luther King, Jr., was honest in his look at history. "In America slavery could not have existed for almost two hundred and fifty years if the church had not sanctioned it, nor could segregation and discrimination exist today if the Christian Church were not a silent and often vocal partner."[194]

Some have interpreted Islam, like the other two Abrahamic monotheisms, Judaism and Christianity, as supporting slavery. However, in Islam there is perhaps an even more ethical view than that found in its predecessors. Muhammad is perhaps the only prophet, short of Moses, to have released slaves. When the prophet Muhammad bought a Persian slave named Salman, he "immediately freed him". In Turkey, some slaves became Kings.[195] The Quran tells us to ransom slaves.

More than once the Quran recommends "ransoming a slave", or setting a slave free once an oath has been made. (5:91)

"It is not piety, that you turn your faces to the East and to the West. True piety is this: to believe in Allah, and the Last Day, the angels, the Book, the Prophets, to give of one's substance, however cherished, to kinsmen, and orphans, the needy, the traveler, beggars, and to ransom the slave, to perform the prayer, to pay the alms." Surah 2:172

"The freewill offerings are for the poor and needy, those who work to collect them, those whose hearts are brought together, the ransoming of slaves, debtors, in Allah's way, and the traveler; so Allah ordains; Allah is All-knowing, All-wise." Surah 9:60

"Have We not appointed to him two eyes, and a tongue, and two lips, and guided him on the two highways? Yet he has not assaulted the steep; and what shall teach thee what is the steep? The freeing of a slave, or giving food upon a day of hunger to an orphan near of kin or a needy man in misery; then that he become of those who believe and counsel each other to be steadfast, and counsel each other to be merciful." Surah 90:8-17

In Islam slaves are permitted to marry, and if they converted to Islam, "their former slave status was no stigma or impediment to power." In fact, a slave may purchase their freedom from their owner through installments, and slaves crimes were not punished with the severity that would be given to a legally-responsible Muslim.[196] A

---

[191] Kevin Phillips, *American Theocracy*, (New York, Penguin Group, 2006) p141
[192] Phillips, p123, 162, 124
[193] Gomes, p97
[194] Martin Luther King, Jr., *Strength to Love*, p101
[195] Nasr, p91, 181
[196] Waines, p98, 99. As we see, this is Plato's philosophy fulfilled. (*Laws*, VI, 777)

slave owner gives up his property if he mistakenly kills someone (4:93) or if he breaks an oath. (5:91) For as we saw above, the Quran tells us a true Muslim will not be a slave-owner. (2:172) In this respect Islam is far more advanced and greater than the ancient Greeks, as well as many other popular religions.

Feminism

Although the city-state of Athens was a democracy women were not permitted to vote. (It has been argued that women were in fact not even considered to be citizens, like slaves. This was not the case in Sparta.) For the greater portion of US history women were not permitted to vote, until 87 years ago. Although Plato, Aristotle, and Socrates were by no means feminists, they did go further than the majority of their contemporaries in esteeming women, even if their writings were often patriarchal. Socrates (and Plato) believed that men were equal to women, that anything a woman can do a man can do as well. (*Republic*, 455d, 540c) The only person to ever defeat Socrates in an argument is a woman named Diotima. She questions Socrates' understanding of love, and he admits to her superior wisdom of love, as we see in the *Symposium*. Diotima teaches Socrates that love does not desire just beauty, but propagation. (*Symposium*, 206E)

Plato, on the other hand, admired the Spartan society where men and women were trained together from childhood and were treated the same as guardians of the city. As Socrates says in the *Republic*: "We should not have one kind of education to fashion the men, and another for the women, especially as they have the same nature to begin with." (456c-d) Aristotle, on the other hand, was fairly critical of the Spartan state and in his book *Politics* says that women would not make good rulers. (*Politics*, 1269b35) Incidentally, the last ancient philosopher in Alexandria (a city in Egypt named after Aristotle's student, Alexander) was a woman named Hypatia.[197]

The first thing which usually comes to mind when thinking about women and the Bible is the story of Eve, who was tempted by the serpent and convinced Adam to violate the divine law forbidding the fruit from the Tree of Knowledge of Good and Evil. Or the laughter of Abraham's wife Sarah when she gives birth for the first time at the age of 70.

According to Talmudic Law, women were not permitted to get involved in politics.[198] However, its not that women didn't have rights. The Torah offers many laws that protect single women and single mothers. In the book of Deuteronomy we are told that Yhwh "doth execute justice for the fatherless and widow, and loveth the stranger". (10:18) At the end of every three years a tithe of one's profit is to be donated to the fatherless, the widow, the stranger, or the Levite (priestly class) (14:29), and anyone who "perverteth the justice due to the stranger, the fatherless, and the widow" is to be cursed. (27:19) If it is found out that a man has had sex with a virgin he must marry her and is he is never permitted to divorce her. (22:29)

The book of Numbers lists as marriage statutes that a woman may not marry without her father's permission, that a woman may not divorce without her husband's permission. (Numbers, 30) According to both the Torah and the Talmud, a contract must be written between a woman and man called a *ketubah*, before they are married. The

---

[197] Russell, (a) p368
[198] Steinsaltz, p137

ketubah offers the conditions of the marriage as well as legal matters concerning financing the raising of children, matters of inheritance and divorce. If a man divorces his wife, he must pay her a sum that is fixed in their *ketubah*. In the *Halachah* or Oral Law, which is the central part of the Talmud, both women and men are permitted to divorce, though it is not considered particularly ethical.[199]

In the New Testament divorce is not permitted at all. Anyone who marries a divorced woman commits adultery. (Matthew 5:31) Any man who divorces and marries another woman commits adultery. (Matthew 19:9, Luke 16:18) Any woman who divorces and marries another man commits adultery. (Mark 10:12) Paul in his first letter to the Corinthian tells us not to divorce. (1Corinthians 7:10-11) Paul also teaches that the law permits marrying one's own sister (1Corinthians 9:5), in contradiction to the laws of the Torah prohibiting incest. (Leviticus 18:6-8) If a woman is accused of harlotry, she is to be stoned. (John 8:7)

The founding father of Protestantism Henry VIII would have none of this and rebelled against the Catholic church. This enabled him to become head of both church and state, marry several times, and execute two of his wives. However, the tenets of the Christian Bible are still carried out in contemporary Egypt where Coptic Christians follow the Christian Bible literally and must convert to some other religion in order to legally divorce.[200]

Ostensibly, the rights of women are restricted even further in the New Testament than in the Old. The letters of Paul, which make up the majority of the books in the New Testament, says that women should be silenced, barred from teaching as well as from politics. This is because "…man was not created for the sake of the woman, but woman for the sake of the man." (1 Corinthians 11:9)

"…let the women keep silent in the congregations, for it is not permitted for them to speak, but let them be in subjection, even as the Law says." (1Corinthians 14:34)

"Let a woman learn in silence and full submissiveness. I do not permit a woman to teach or to exercise authority over a man, but to be in silence." "However, she will be kept safe through childbearing…" (1Timmothy 2:11-12,15)

Paul wrote a letter to the Roman Emperor Titus, advising him that women should be obedient to their husbands. (Titus 2:5) He repeats this in his letter to some people from Ephesia. (Ephesians 5:22) Peter's letter repeats that women should be in subjection to their husbands, and afraid, because wives are weaker. (1Peter 3:1,7)

While the Western media like the display of Arabic and Islamic women wearing a veil, it is very rarely mentioned that this is the practice that is prescribed by the Christian Bible. Both Peter and Paul write that women must dress modestly, telling them what they must and must not wear. (1Timmothy 2:9, 1Peter 3:3)

"…every woman that prays or prophesies with her head uncovered shames the one who is her head… For if a woman does not cover herself, let her also be shorn; but if it is disgraceful for a woman to be shorn or shaved, let her be covered." (1 Corinthians 11:5-6)

The poet Heinrich Heine recounts how the criminal judge for the Duke of Lorraine, Doctor Nicolas Remigus:

"conducted the prosecutions against…eight hundred women…who were burnt at the stake, after being convicted of witchcraft. Proof of their guilt was mainly established as wise: their feet and hands being bound together, they were thrown into the water. If they sank and were drowned, they were

---

[199] Steinsaltz, p131, 133-134
[200] Nadim Audi, "Egyptian Court Allows Return to Christianity", *New York Times*, February 11, 2008

innocent; but if they remained floating on the surface, they were pronounced guilty and were burnt. Such was the logic of the time."[201]

In 1431 a young woman named Joan of Arc was burned for witchcraft, though she is now considered to have been a saint, having rid France of the English. In 1484 Pope Innocent VIII issued the Papal Bull *Summis Desiderantes*, witch set out the legal condemnation of witchcraft. In 1486 the Dominicans produced a manual for witchhunting called *Malleus Maleficarum*. Christian Europe's 'leading witch-hunter' was the Protestant Dr. Benedikt Carpzov, who was a professor at Leipzig. In 1635 he drafted laws on the jurisprudence of witch-trials and it is said that he oversaw some 20,000 executions of 'witches'. Around this time the Catholic Prince-Bishop of Bamberg, Johan George II Fuchs von Dornheim burned some 600 witches in a house he constructed with a built in torture chamber. In 1612 the Pendle Witches of Lancashire, England were condemned. In America some 22 witches had been executed before 1692 by Puritans.[202] Other great witch-hunters were King James VI and I. From the Papal Bull of 1484 the practice of witch-burning continued on for 300 years. This came to a halt in the 18th century in part through the protests of the Jesuits of Bavaria, which had been a place of particular fanaticism in the burning of those accused to be witches.[203]

Cardinal Ratzinger, (now Pope Benedict) drafted new Canon laws in the 1990's which punish by excommunication anyone who affirms the right of women to become priests or anyone who questions the biblical prohibition against premarital sex.[204]

In the centuries following the rise and fall of Alexander the Great, many people from around the Mediterranean sea became "Hellenized", or influenced by the spread of Greek culture. This included many Jews who began to speak Greek. The first translation of the Tanach, or Hebrew Bible, was made into Greek in the 3rd or 2nd century before the Common Era, and is called the *Septuagint*. One mistranslation in this edition that would prove to be very influential occurred in a particular sentence in the book of Isaiah. Whereas the original Hebrew version of Isaiah 7:14 said a young woman will conceive a child, the Greek version mistakenly said that a virgin will conceive a child.

Although the religion of the Hellenistic Greeks and Romans was filled with many instances where Zeus or some other god had copulated with a mortal, for Christianity, the virginity of Mary became a symbol of pureness with an 'immaculate' ability to conceive. This has become a point of contention for biblical scholars, whether Yhwh would impregnate a woman. Whether or not this has "maculated conception" as Nietzsche says, the American Founding Father Thomas Paine found it curious in his book *The Age of Reason*, that so much ink was committed in the gospels according to Matthew and Luke, to proving the genealogical background of Mary's husband Joseph, when he wasn't, after-all, the father of Jesus. Joseph was resolved to divorce her when an angel told him how she became pregnant. (Matthew 1:19-20)

This is not a problem of Islam. Although Mary is discussed more in the Quran than in the Christian Bible, the question of whether or not she did or did not have sex, is of no import in the Quran. As the English scholar David Waines says, "For Allah to have

---

[201] Heinrich Heine, *Religion and Philosophy in Germany*, trans. John Snodgrass, (Albany, State University of New York Press, 1986) p30
[202] Jennings, p51
[203] Norman Davies, *Europe: A History*, (New York, HarperCollins, 1996) p437, 566-567
[204] Carroll, p319-320

a son was also an absurdity and an infamy in the Muslim's eyes."[205] The Quran says: "It is not for Allah to take a son unto Him. Glory be to Him! When He decrees a thing, He but says to it, 'Be,', and it is." (Surah 19:36)

As we saw earlier, both the Quran and Arabic and Islamic philosophy usually do not ponder theological questions. The omnipotence of Allah is emphasized over any particular characteristic or nomenclature. "He is Allah, One, Allah, the Everlasting Refuge, who has not begotten, and has not been begotten, and equal to Him is not any one." (Surah 112:2-5)

The Quran, unlike the New Testament, does not bar a divorced woman from marrying again. "There should be for divorced women provision honourable –an obligation on the godfearing." (Surah 2:242)

For well over a thousand years Muslim women have often had more rights than in any other religion or state. This changed when nearly every Muslim state was colonized and subject to European and Christian laws, which were much more oppressive toward women's rights. European and American women's rights have only broken out of this tradition over the last 80 or 90 years with the furthering of church and state in democratic nations.

The city of Baghdad marks the meeting of two rivers, the Tigris and the Euphrates. Tigris means 'temperance', Euphrates means 'fertility'. There are nearly 1.5 billion Muslims in the world, nearly a quarter of the world population. Thus, we are talking about 750 million women in the world, across every continent. This group of people the Western Media pretend to represent. It is little wonder that one of the biggest misunderstandings about Islam is the status of women. The Western Media delights itself in spreading the image of Muslim women as covered from head to toe in a veil as though they do not have any say in the world, especially in politics.

One stereotype about Muslim women is that they are sold into marriage by a dowry, or that the marriages are arranged against their will by their father. This stereotype goes right against the entire precedent of Islamic history. The first Muslim was a woman, not a man –her name was Khadijah. She proposed to Muhammad marriage, and he listened to her and agreed to marry. When the prophet Muhammad was asked what is a short-cut to paradise, he said it is "under the feet of the mother."[206]

Before a woman and man are married, they must negotiate a marital contract, or *nikah*. This is because marriage is seen as a legal agreement. Although the Quran permits a man to have 4 wives (some would say this law limits, rather than permits – compare the open laws on polygamy in the Judeo-Christian tradition –ten centuries Before the Common Era, Messiah Solomon had 700 wives and 300 concubines [1 Kings 11:3]). However, women may stipulate in the *nikah* that they remain their husband's sole wife.[207] The Quran says husbands have greater obligations than wives (2:228), but are treated as equals in the Quran. (33:35) The Quran says that if a husband cannot treat their wives with equal care to marry only once. (4:3) It should be remembered that Moses had two wives, Abraham had children with his wife's servant, and Mormon Christians have been persecuted in America for their belief in polygamy.

---

[205] Waines, p102
[206] Ahmed, (b) p116
[207] Waines, p94-95

Unlike traditional Judaism and Christianity, Muslim women are allowed to initiate divorce. (17:23-24) However, if a woman commits an indecency she is to be put under house arrest (4:19). The Quran instructs women and men to consort together honorably. (4:23) Sex out of wedlock results in a flogging. (24:5) While this may seem harsh to a non-Muslim, it should be remembered that both the Torah and the New Testament call for the death penalty in this situation, and not flogging. A husband may correct his wife himself, however, if there is a breach of the marital contract, a third party is to help "compose their differences". (4:39)

Not only was Muhammad a Prophet but he was a husband and father and he and his wife Khajira had a daughter named Fatimah. According to the law of the Quran men must always financially provide for their children (2:233) Like Judaism, Islam has many laws against incest. (4:27)

Perhaps the most 'controversial' subject matter for women in Islam, that is, controversial for us western liberators whose corporate media minds everyone's business except American business, is the veil. However, unlike the Christian Bible, the Quran does not order a woman to cover herself in a veil, but to use a veil to cover their bosom from strangers. (24:31) This is actually not a big controversy within Muslim nations. In fact, because there are over 50 Muslim nations spread around the world, the dress code we might see in the Arabic world may be totally different somewhere else, and has nothing to do with the Quran, or the prophet Muhammad.

There have been many famous and influential Muslim women. Even in the 21st century America has still not had a female president or vice president. However, there have been Muslim Queens and Empresses who ruled independently, such as Noor Jahan. There have been several female Prime Ministers, the first being Benazir Bhutto, who challenged a military dictator and died a martyr's death in 2007. The small country of Bangladesh has had several female Prime Ministers, and in 2001 a woman named Megawati Sukarnoputri became president of the largest Muslim nation in the world, Indonesia. When the lawyer and founder of Pakistan, Mohammed Ali Jinnah, died in 1948, the military General Ayub Khan declared martial law. It was Jinnah's sister Fatimah, who took a stand against the General.[208] Although the US has never had a female vice-president, Iran did in 1997, and women have worked in Iran's parliament for years.[209]

The achievements of women in Islam are various. The Arabic word *Alemah* means "learned woman". One of the earliest and most famous Muslim poets was the 8th century woman, Rabiah al-Adwiyyah, who was also a great Sufi. The 20th century Parwin Etesami stands as another famous female Muslim poet. Many towns and roads are named after Muslim women, and armies have been led by women, as for example, the 7th century Aisha bint Abu Bakr, and the 13th century Persian Sultan Razia al-Din.

Two points which are controversial are the rules of gender in inheritance, where sons are often given a greater inheritance (4:11), and in the *Shariah*, where the witness of two women is needed for a conviction. (2:282) The issue of the veil has occasionally raised legal issues. In Turkey for example it is illegal for a woman to wear a veil or covering.[210] In France women were thrown out of schools for wearing a veil.[211] Under

---

[208] Ahmed, (b) p118
[209] Ahmed, (a) p115, 158
[210] Nasr, p196

the White Revolution of Shah Pahlavi in Iran it became law that women could not wear the veil. As political protest against the Shah Iranian women began to wear the veil again.[212]

According to the sociologist Akbar Ahmed, the first misogynist laws began in the 19th and 20th century when Muslim countries began to become colonized by Europeans, as the wives and daughters of European colonists had few rights. As Ahmed makes clear, these laws against women "have nothing to do with Islam."[213] The legal scholar Rudolph Peters tells us, colonizers such as the British found the Islamic Law far too lenient.[214]

We've got to wonder whether Muslim women really want non-Muslim men and women telling them how they ought to live and feel. Muslims much more prefer an Islamic feminism than a Western feminism, finding it is much more pertinent to their own needs and tradition.[215] As it is, at Muslim University in Morocco there are more female students enrolled than men.[216]

A 19th century Muslim feminist Qasim Amin, who was both a lawyer and judge, wrote books such as *The Emancipation of Women* and *The New Woman*, arguing that subjugation of Muslim women was un-Islamic and was leading to the deterioration of family and society.[217]

The Muslim feminist Fatima Mernissi has written in her book, *Women and Islam*, "...if women's rights are a problem for some modern Muslim men, it is neither because of the Koran nor the Prophet, nor the Islamic tradition, but simply because those rights conflict with the interests of a male elite. The elite faction is trying to convince us that their egoistic, highly subjective and mediocre view of culture and society has a sacred basis... Islam was not sent from heaven to foster egoism and mediocrity."[218]

Until 1865, millions of American women were slaves. Even after that, Native American Women were deprived of their land and their rights. Some of the earliest feminists in the US have been far from supportive of liberation. The Women's Christian Temperance Union, organized in Cleveland in 1874 was instrumental in starting the prohibition against alcohol in the United States.[219] One of the biggest opponents of women's suffrage, or right to vote, were the brewing companies, who boasted of having shut down the women's movement on more than one occasion. In 1911, Mrs. Arthur M. Dodge formed the National Association Opposed to Woman Suffrage, in New York. The state which fared the worst in the women's suffrage movement was Massachusetts, which had the largest bloc of Catholic voters of any state. The pope was neutral on the issue. Perhaps the most influential American feminist was Charlotte Gilman.[220] She wrote

---

[211] Ahmed, (b) p104
[212] Esposito, p103, 111
[213] Ahmed, (b) p117
[214] Rudolph Peters, *Crime and Punishment in Islamic Law: Theory and Practice from the Sixteenth to the Twenty-first Century*, (Cambridge, Cambridge University Press, 2005) p120
[215] Nasr, p196-197
[216] Ahmed, (b) p102
[217] Esposito, p58
[218] Fatima Mernissi, *Women and Islam*, (Oxford, Basil Blackwell, 1991) Quoted in Waines, p257
[219] This was advanced by a 4 million dollar donation given to them by John D. Rockefeller who sought to monopolize oil fuel. See David Blume's, *Alcohol Can Be A Gas!*, (Santa Cruz, International Institute for Ecological Agriculture, 2007)
[220] Eleanor Flexner, *Century of Struggle: The Women's Rights Movement in the United States*, (Cambridge, Harvard University Press, 1975) p186-187, 307, 306, 280, 309

about eliminating all non-European races and creating an earthly paradise where only women lived. Such feminisms often lead to a caricature of masculinity.

The feminist bell hooks has noted how such stereotypes arise about manliness and she shows how such prevarications became part of a popular slander against a Muslim like El-Haj Malik El-Shabbaz, or Malcolm X. This usually begins with those who try to present Malcolm X as the opposite to Martin Luther King, Jr. King was a pacifist and seen as a good Christian, while El-Shabbaz is recreated and feared as something like a drunk father: ruthless and violent.

"One of the ways I feel we suffered the loss of Malcolm X is that many people do not realize, having only seen his participation in public life where he was a very forceful man, that in his private life his children have spoken about what a caring, gentle, nurturing presence he was. We need a sense that there is no monolithic construction of masculinity, that the whole person is capable of being strong at those moments of life which require a certain assertion of agency and strength but then also to be capable of generosity and quietude and nurturance in other areas."[221]

Recounting her days as a student, bell hooks recalls, "the years that I was at Stanford, the Black Muslims were a strong force on the campus." hooks believes that feminism can be rooted in religious faith, citing Isabel Humphrey, or Sojourner Truth, whose "emancipatory politics emerged from her religious faith.", and as being the first Black woman to "publicly link the struggle against racism with gender liberation."[222]

In her essay, "Democracy: Who is She When Is She at Home?," Arundhati Roy discusses the way in which nationalism, in particular, anti-Muslim nationalism, with disturbing neatness, "dovetails into fascism".[223] "The incipient, creeping fascism of the past few years has been groomed by many of our 'democratic' institutions", which work to suppress real issues such as "bonded labor, marital rape, sexual preferences, women's wages, uranium dumping, unsustainable mining, weavers' woes, farmers' suicides."[224]

Roy discusses how the US government and co-opted American media use feminism as a rhetorical device to mask imperialism. She discusses the message being put out about the United States War on Afghanistan.

"Its being made out that the whole point of the war was to topple the Taliban regime and liberate Afghan women from their burqas. We're being asked to believe that the US marines are actually on a feminist mission... Can we bomb our way to a feminist paradise?"[225]

One thing we should make note of when we are talking about an issue like this is the different scopes of our claims: whether we are looking for universalism or pluralism. Do we desire the rules of our community, or even further, of ourselves, to be the universal rule for all people, even against their will? Or should the plurality of beliefs and traditions be permitted to influence one another?[226]

bell hooks discusses the need for a 'Global Feminism' and a 'decolonized feminist perspective'. She points out a pernicious tendency among European and American feminists.

---

[221] bell hooks and Cornel West, *Breaking Bread*, (Boston, South End Press, 1991) p125-126
[222] hooks, p68, 51-52
[223] Arundhati Roy, *War Talk*, (Cambridge, South End Press, 2003) p36
[224] Roy, p36, 38
[225] Roy, p51
[226] The American Aristotelian philosopher Martha Nussbaum's feminism has been described as holding that "an effective international feminism must champion rights, eschew relativism, and study local traditions sufficiently closely to see their diversity." Henry S. Richardson, *Cambridge Dictionary of Philosophy*, Second Edition, (Cambridge, Cambridge University Press, 1999) p 622-623

"While feminists in the United States were right to call attention to the need for global equality for women, problems arose as those individual feminists with class power projected imperialist fantasies onto women globally, the major fantasy being that women in he United States have more rights than any group of women globally, are 'free' if they want to be, and therefore have the right to lead feminist movement[s] and set feminist agendas for all the other women in the world, particularly women in third world countries. Such thinking merely mirrors the imperialist racism and sexism of ruling groups of Western men."

"Yet even when large numbers of feminist activists adopted a perspective which included race, gender, class, and nationality, the white 'power feminists' continued to project an image of feminism that linked and links women's equality with imperialism. Global women's issues liked forced female circumcision, sex clubs in Thailand, the veiling of women in Africa, India, the Middle East, and Europe, the killing of female children in China, remain important concerns. However feminist women in the West are still struggling to decolonize feminist thinking and practice so that these issues can be addressed in a manner that does not reinscribe Western imperialism. Consider the way many Western women, white and black, have confronted the issue of female circumcision in Africa and the Middle East. Usually these countries are depicted as 'barbaric and uncivilized', the sexism there portrayed as more brutal and dangerous to women than the sexism here in the United States."

"Until radical women in the United States challenge those groups of women posing as feminists in the interest of class opportunism, the tone of global feminism in the West will continue to be set by those with the greatest class power who hold old biases... The goal of global feminism is to reach out and join global struggles to end sexism, sexist exploitation, and oppression."[227]

Having been brought up in New York, I personally prefer the Native American model practiced by the League of the Iroquois. The League of the Iroquois was a network of tribes and communities that included the Mohawks, Oneidas, Onondagas, Cayugas, Tuscarora, and the Senecas. In Iroquois society women played a very prominent role and families were matriarchal or run by the women. Women would decide if there was to be a divorce, simply by placing their (ex) husband's belongings by the door. The most senior woman in each village would choose who were their representatives, in both the village and the League, and women had the power to remove any man from office who became too variant to the desires of the matriarchs.[228] This reminds of the inspiring true Muslim legend of King Rahman V who 'enslaved himself to his wife'.[229]

The State

The political philosophies of Socrates, Plato and Aristotle are in many ways similar, but where they differ is sometimes significant. Both Socrates and Plato were citizens of the democratic Greek city-state of Athens where they taught. Socrates taught in the *Agon* or marketplace, and Plato taught at a school he founded called the *Academy*. Aristotle lived in Athens for 33 years but was never a citizen, being from another Greek city-state in the north, the Kingdom of Macedonia. He opened a school not far from the *Academy* called the *Lyceum*, where much work in biology was conducted.

The political climate of Ancient Greece was turbulent. It was during the lifetime of Socrates when the democracy was restored to Athens following a Greek civil war of sorts between city-states, the Peloponnesian Wars, which had resulted in a victory

---
[227] bell hooks, *Feminism is for Everybody*, (Cambridge, South End Press, 2000) p45, 46, 47
[228] Zinn, p19-20. For a different picture of America today check out Laura Flander's study, *Bushwomen: How They Won the White House for Their Man*, (New York, Verso, 2004)
[229] Ahmed, (a) p65

of Sparta over Athens. Within his own lifetime, Aristotle lived to see the small Kingdom of Macedonia conquer most of the known world, and then shatter once Alexander the Great died in his early 30's, 323 years before the Common Era.

The contemporary model for democracy is said to be taken from ancient Greeks. However, the Greek and American models differ considerably. In contemporary democracies, citizenship is automatically granted at birth, and all citizens can vote once they've reached a certain age of maturity. In ancient Athens (most Greek city-states were not democracies), democracy was not an inalienable birthright like it is said to be today. Women were not permitted to vote, neither were slaves, but probably only the property-owners, or aristocracy, could vote. Coincidentally those of the aristocratic class were the ones who had written these laws into the state constitution in the first place.

Philosophy was brought to Athens in the 5th century by an Ionian named Anaxagoras. He was probably invited there by the Athenian statesman Pericles, who had heard of the philosopher's intellectual acumen. Pericles' wife Aspasia convinced him that philosophy would help further the democracy. Anaxagoras taught in Athens for about 30 years, leaving a big impact on Socrates and others. But he had to leave Athens when the citizens began to accuse him of heresy. This would happen shortly thereafter to Protagoras, and then to Socrates 30 years later, though Socrates was executed.

While Socrates accepted the consequences of the democratic state, both Plato and Aristotle were fairly critical of the polity of democracy. Plato believed that the most primal and pure form of government was monarchy. This would ideally be a philosopher-king, though he thought an Aristocracy, or rule by the best, was on par. (*Republic*, 445d) All other forms of government are imperfect to varying degrees.

The next best thing to monarchy, or the most minimally corrupted form of government is something called Timarchy or Timocracy. Under a Timarchic government the military has all political power, and sometimes the wisdom of the philosophers (or the king) is ignored. Plato believed that Timarchy eventually leads to Oligarchy (which is sometimes referred to as Plutocracy). In an Oligarchy or Plutocracy the love of money dominates all political motives and the rich and wealthy rule the state. If the purpose of an Oligarchy is to become as rich as possible, democracy emerges from inequalities in wealth, when the disenfranchised long for revolution (555e) and in which the poor are victorious. (557a)

Because of the freedom of speech and the general permissiveness of democracy, which is an "an emporium of constitutions" (557e), the love of freedom and liberty becomes too strong and at last a dictator comes to power. (Perhaps, we might ask today, because of the need of Homeland Security to safeguard our freedom? Critics of the US might be justified in saying that American democracy has wavered between oligarchy and dictatorship.) Thus, Plato does offer some criticisms of democracy that are worth considering. In his lifetime, Plato's teachings became popular and he was invited by the tyrant Dionysius to design a new government for the city-state of Syracuse. However, the attempt proved too difficult and Plato returned to Athens.

The ideal state of Plato, the *Republic*, is a state run by the aristocracy or philosopher-king. In fact, Plato's model resembles in many ways the Hindu *Law of Manu* in its structuring in society so that each has a duty. However, Plato clearly had the Greek city-state of Sparta in mind as a model for the *Republic*. Particularly, Plato liked the Spartan belief that children not be raised by their parents but by professional nannies. A contemporary version of this might be called public schooling.

If for Plato, people exist for the state, for Aristotle on the other hand, the state exists for the people. For this reason, the best type of state will be the one that best fits a particular people or community. Thus, Aristotle referred to political philosophy as the 'Master Science'.

"Our purpose is to consider what form of political community is best of all for those who are most able to realize their ideal of life. We must therefore examine not only this but other constitutions, both such as actually exist in well-governed states, and any theoretical forms which are held in esteem, so that what is good and useful may be brought to light." *Politics*, 1260b27-31

Aristotle believed there was one best form of government –aristocracy, or rule by the best. (*Nicomachean Ethics*, 1181a34) However, over the rule of a single person, he thought that the laws or constitution of the community was more fundamental. At most, the best ruler will be a guardian of the law. (*Politics*, 1287a21) He did realize that this was not always the most practical and in this regards he was a pluralist, believing that the three best types of government were monarchy, aristocracy, and the constitutional state. Aristotle agreed with Plato that the three worst types of government are tyranny, oligarchy, and democracy. However, Aristotle believed that all political forms should be studied accordingly:

"...let us try to review any sound remarks our predecessors have made on particular topics. Then let us study the collected political systems, to see from them what sorts of things preserve and destroy cities, and political systems of different types; and what causes some cities to conduct politics well, and some badly." *Nicomachean Ethics*, 1181b17-21

In the *Nicomachean Ethics* Aristotle suggests that "collections of laws and political systems might also, presumably, be most useful if we are capable of studying them and of judging what is done finely or in the contrary way, and what sorts of [elements] fit with what." (*Nicomachean Ethics*, 1181b6-8) Bertrand Russell interprets 'the Philosopher' such that "Aristotle arrives at a defense of democracy; for most actual governments are bad, and therefore, among actual governments, democracies tend to be best."[230] During his teaching years in the democratic state of Athens, Aristotle either wrote or authorized some 158 constitutions or more, one being the *Constitution of Athens*.[231]

Without a great deal of analysis it is possible to point out a few fundamental characteristics of the three Abrahamic religions and the political. Or, as it is more popularly called, the relationship between church and state. One thing which distinctively separates all possible political forms is their tendency towards either the Mundane vs. the Divine Right of Kings. This has a few exceptions.

Just as Cain and Abel, Abraham and Isaac appeared before the Torah was revealed. The idea of the Messiah is not found in the Torah or in Jewish politics until the 11th century Before the Common Era. It is in the 5th book of the Pentateuch or Torah that Yhwh says that if the Jews should for some reason desire to be like everyone else and have a King, this King must be chosen by Yhwh and cannot be a foreigner. What is more, this King will neither be permitted to acquire wealth in gold, silver, or livestock, but is to read and study the law every day of his life. (Deuteronomy 14:19) In some ways

---

[230] Russell, (a) p190
[231] Noted by Stephen Everson in his introduction to Aristotle, (b) xii

this Hebrew Messiah will be like Plato's philosopher king, who has no possessions but who studies constantly.

As seems *a priori* to us Westerners, Judaism is still 'waiting for the Messiah'. This however, is not true. Shortly after the Torah was completed and the death of Moses, the Jews did indeed desire a Messiah and against the warnings of Yhwh, one is eventually anointed – a farmer named Saul. David and Solomon were both Messiahs as well, Solomon being known for his wisdom and his treatise on erotic love, David for the genetically inferior statue of him in Rome. In the 8th century BCE, two centuries before the end of the Jewish messianic era, the prophet Isaiah (a name meaning 'God's Salvation') wrote of a future messiah or 'expected one'. Although by no means the central aspect of Isaiah, this ideal Messiah would bring peace to the earth. There upon no more warfare occurs and all living species cease to harm each-other. (Isaiah 2:4, 11:6,9)

To look at the history of the monotheistic state, we must go back to the patriarch of the three monotheisms – Judaism, Christianity, and Islam- who is Abraham. Abraham was born in the Sumerian city of Ur (in the Euphrates valley, by the Persian Gulf) somewhere between the 18th and 16th century before the Common Era. Yhwh tells Abraham to begin traveling and continue on until he is told to stop: there he shall reside as a stranger. Yhwh promises to someday make Abraham's family a great nation. (Genesis 12:1-2)

For a time Abraham's wife Sarah was unable to conceive a child, so Abraham had a son with an Egyptian woman. They called him Ishmael. Eventually, as we saw, Sarah becomes pregnant and gives birth to a son, Isaac. Judaism and Christianity trace their lineage through Isaac, while Islam traces its lineage through Ishmael.

The first Jewish state began around 12th century BCE, following the Exodus from Egypt and the conquest of Canaan. During the 11th century Saul becomes the first Messiah, his reign is followed by his son David, and David's reign is followed by his son Solomon. It is around this time that a large temple is constructed in Jerusalem. The temple has become a kind of symbol, or metonym for the political status of Judaism.

After Solomon's death in the 10th century, the Jews split into two kingdoms: Israel in the north, and Judah in the south. There was some internecine war between the various tribes until the Israeli's are conquered by the Assyrian Empire. Judea continues the Jewish state until they are conquered in the Babylonian conquests of Nebuchadnezzar in the 6th century BCE. The temple is destroyed.

When the Babylonians are conquered by the Persians several decades later, King Cyrus of Persia allows the Jews to return to Jerusalem and rebuild the temple. This lasts until Alexander the Great conquers Persia in the 330's, and a series of different Hellenistic Kings rule over the area. After a victory against the Romans by the Jewish Maccabees in 2nd century, the Jewish state came to an end 63 years before the Common Era when Pompey took Jerusalem, and the temple is destroyed.

Around the time that Jesus lived, the Romans had put a puppet king in Palestine/Israel and this King Herod pleased both the Romans and Jews by rebuilding the temple. However, after several Jewish Wars, or Jewish rebellions against the Romans, Emperor Titus destroyed the temple in the year 70, and Jews are banned from living in Jerusalem 50 years later. Although the Romans, including Paul who was a Roman citizen, had once persecuted Jews, the entire empire converted from paganism to Christianity in the 4th century. Muslims took Jerusalem from the Christians in the 7th

century, inviting Jews to return though in place of the temple, where the Western wall remains to this day, was built a Mosque. In 1099 in the second year of the First Crusade, Christians took it back, killing every inhabitant of Jerusalem and destroying Jewish temples and Muslim mosques. Eighty-eight years later the Muslim leader Saladin was victorious over the Crusader states in 1187, taking Jerusalem on the 4th of July. Instead of annihilating the Christians, Saladin released them by treaty. Jews were reinvited to return and the mosque was rebuilt.

The Jewish state did not reemerge until they 9th century. This occurred spontaneously when the Russian Khazar Empire converted to Judaism. The Khazar lived alongside the Byzantine Christians and Persian Muslims, and had "been hesitating between Judaism, Christianity, and Islam", before converting to Judaism toward the end of the 9th century.[232] The Khazar messiah was titled *Khagan*. This messianic era lasted until the 11th when the Khazars were conquered by pagan Slavs.

In 1948 the United Nations voted the current state of Israel into existence, it having been previously won by the British in the First World War from Turkey. Many orthodox Jews living today who believe in the Torah as the word of Yhwh do not recognize the state (perhaps most Jews live in New York). Both men and women serve in the Israeli army by compulsion for two years. Only orthodox Jews are excused from this duty toward the state, if only because they don't recognize the state's existence. Many Jews follow Yhwh's commandment in Genesis that Abraham reside as an alien amongst gentiles. All that remains of the Temple today is the Western Wall.

The question of whether Jews believe in the Divine Right of Kings or not, is not an ontological or theological question, but one of an epistemological nature, all politics aside. This is because there have been many messiahs already. The Jewish pragmatist Hilary Putnam, for example, rejects the belief in the Divine Right of Kings as "irrational".[233]

In Christianity the Divine Right of Kings is unequivocal. Jesus is considered to be both Messiah and Christ, which is Greek for 'savior'. And as the Christ-ian aspect of the religion, the New Testament instructs the followers of Jesus that all kings and rulers on earth are divinely appointed by God and must be obeyed. This is because both Jesus and the Christians reject the Jewish law in favor of the Roman law, which is the joining of church and state. The New Testament teaches:

"Let every soul be in subjection to the superior authorities, for there is no authority except by God; the existing authorities stand placed in their relative positions by God." Romans 13:1

"I therefore exhort, first of all, that supplications, prayers, intercessions, offerings of thanks, be made concerning all sorts of men, concerning kings and all those who are in high station…" 1Timothy 2:2

"For the Lord's sake subject yourselves to every human creation: whether to a king as beings superior or to governors as being sent by to inflict punishment on evildoers but to praise doers of good… have honor for the king." 1 Peter 2:13-14, 17

Some Christians have tended toward anarchism, and the tradition is rich with martyrdom. For the anarcho-Christian belief in the Divine Right of Kings remains as a metaphysical form only to be established upon the second-coming of Jesus, which is similar to Plato's ideal world. The gospel according to John offers a clue to this where Jesus says, "My kingdom is no part of this world". (John 18:36)

---

[232] Fletcher, p353
[233] Hilary Putnam, *Ethics Without Ontology*, (Cambridge, Harvard University Press, 2004) (c) p114

"Next, the end, when he hands over the kingdom of his God and Father, when he has brought to nothing all government and all authority and power." 1 Corinthians 15:24

"Stripping the governments and the authorities bare, he exhibited them in open public as conquered, leading them in a triumphal procession by means of it." Colossians 2:15

"Because we have a fight, not against blood and flesh, but against the governments, against the authorities, against the world rulers of this darkness, against the wicked spirit forces in the heavenly places." Ephesians 6:12

In the very document which guarantees the infallibility of the pope, meaning that the pope is incapable of being mistaken, was a law ordering all Catholics to declare war at the word of the pope. Interestingly, the *Pastor Aeternus* was defined on the day following Napoleon III (not to be confused with Napoleon Bonaparte, his uncle) declaration of war on Prussia. Incidentally, the only army protecting the Pope (Pius IX) prior to the Franco-Prussian War was Napoleon III's army which was up until then had been stationed in Rome.[234] The *Pastor Aeternus* says:

"Hence we teach and declare that... all of whatever rite and dignity, both pastors and faithful, both individually and collectively, are bound, by their duty of hierarchical subordination and true obedience, to submit not only in matters which belong to faith and morals, but also in those that appertain to the discipline and government of the Church throughout the world... under one supreme pastor... the Roman Pontiff. This is the teaching of the Catholic faith, from which no one can deviate without loss of faith and of salvation."[235]

The 13th century Christian theologian Thomas Aquinas had already written, "it is necessary for salvation to submit to the Roman Pope."[236] However, the *Pastor Aeternus* was followed by Leo XIII's dictum against revolution.

"And if at any time it happens that the power of the state is rashly and tyrannically wielded by Princes, the teaching of the Catholic Church does not allow an insurrection on private authority against them, lest public order be only the more disturbed, and lest society take greater hurt therefrom. And when affairs come to such a pass that there is no other hope of safety, she teaches that relief may be hastened by the merits of Christian patience and by earnest prayers to God."[237]

Protestant Christianity, which emerged in the 16th century, is said to be what solidifies both modern nationalism and the Divine Right of Kings. Bertrand Russell claimed in, *The Ancestry of Fascism*, "The philosophy of the movement which culminates in the Nazis is, in a sense, a logical development of Protestantism."[238] Ronald Bainton discusses the various church's views toward warfare: "They talked in terms of 'inevitable necessity' (Lutheran), 'support of the constitutional authority' (Catholic), and 'unfaltering allegiance to the Government' (Episcopalian)."[239] As Martin Luther said, "Even if the government does injustice, as the King of Babylon did to the people of Israel, yet God would have it obeyed, without treachery…"[240]

Luther's mirror image, John Calvin, also justified the state:

"Those who domineer unjustly and tyrannically are raised up by him to punish the people for their iniquity… Even an individual of the worst character, one most unworthy of all honor, if invested with

---

[234] Carroll, p440
[235] Carroll, p441
[236] Carroll, p316
[237] Carroll, p675n32
[238] Bertrand Russell, "The Ancestry of Fascism", (b) p100
[239] Ronald H. Bainton, *Christian Attitudes Toward War and Peace*, (Nashville, Abingdon Press, 1960) p198
[240] Martin Luther, "Treatise on Good Works", Section XII, 263, from *Werke*, trans. Walter Kaufmann. Quoted in Kaufmann, (a) p282

public authority, receives that illustrious divine power....In so far as public obedience is concerned, he is to be held in the same honor and reverence as the best of kings".[241]

As we saw, the founder of the philosophy of existentialism, Soren Kierkegaard said that: "Objections against Christianity come from insubordination, unwillingness to obey, rebellion against all authority... The misfortune of our age –in the political as well as in the religious sphere, and in all things –is disobedience, unwillingness to obey. And one deceives oneself and others by wishing to make us imagine that it is doubt. No, it is insubordination."[242]

The Prophet of Mormonism, the Vermont Joseph Smith lists 'patriotism' in the top ten of its Articles of Faith, teaching to recognized and obey leaders whether the be democratically elected or not.[243]

Liberation Theology

A political movement has been stirring in South and Central America, where the majority of the world's Catholics live: a movement called liberation theology. The movement was initiated by a group of Argentinean philosophers, who had gone into exile because of the military oppression of that late 1970's and early 1980's. These philosophers taught about the need for an 'autochthonous Latin American movement' with an emphasis on liberation and cultural identity.[244] Liberation theology has also been furthered by Catholic priests, usually in Latin America, and is then based on the interpretation of the New Testament, though this is generally agreed to be somewhat of a "Marxist reading".[245] Liberation theology holds that priests ought to be aligned with the poor, the peasants, and the workers, and that the church should be against the big landowners, against the clear-cutting of the rain-forests, against government hitmen, as well as timarchy, or rule by the military.

Some have remarked that this kind of theology has been long overdo[246], or that it is just a rehashing of an ethic taught by the gospels but which is ignored by the majority of Christians. Some say that liberation theology is too exclusive, obscuring the message of salvation, i.e., the next world. Be that as it may, many Catholic priests and nuns have lost their lives or been arrested because of their opposition to their government or the military of the United States.[247]

---

[241] John Calvin, *Institutes of the Christian Religion*, Section 25, trans. John Allen; 7th American ed., rev. and ed. By Benjamin B. Warfield (Philadelphia, Presbyterian Board of Christian Education, 1936) Quoted in Kaufmann (a), p274
[242] Soren Kierkegaard, *The Journals*, Section 630, ed. and trans. by Alexander Dru, (Oxford, Oxford University Press, 1938) Quoted in Kaufmann (a), p71
[243] http://scriptures/lds.org/en/a_of_f/1/
[244] Jorge J.E. Gracia, "Latin American Philosophy", in *The Cambridge Dictionary of Philosophy*, Second Edition, ed. Robert Audi, (Cambridge, Cambridge University Press, 1999) p488
[245] Douglass F. Ottati, "Liberation Theology", *The Perennial Dictionary of Religion*, (San Fransisco, HarperCollins, 1981) p426
[246] Charles W. Mills, "Prophetic Pragmatism and Political Philosophy", in *Cornel West: A Critical Reader*, ed. George Yancy, (Malden, Blackwell Publishing, 2001), p200
[247] Check, for example, CAMINO's (Central American Information Office), *El Salvador: Background to the crisis*, which offers a chronology of the imprisonment and assassination of church officials and others. (Cambridge, Central American Information Office, 1982)

As Martin Luther King Jr. wrote: "Any religion that professes concern regarding the souls of men and fails to be concerned by social conditions that corrupt and economic conditions that cripple the soul, is a do-nothing religion, in need of new blood."[248]

Former Catholic priest James Carroll talks about "the Vatican's suppression of liberation theology, which is a religious affirmation of the political ideal of rights for all."[249] Pope John Paul II "condemned, silenced, and disciplined priests and nuns in Nicaragua, El Salvador, Guatemala, Brazil, Haiti, and Mexico because of their so-called political activity" and the Pope was "reticent about Oscar Romero, the bishop of El Salvador who was slain at the alter", who "was the first and only head of state in the world to recognize the legitimacy of the military junta that overthrew the democratically elected president of Haiti (and former priest) Jean-Bertrand Aristide."[250]

Having written a great deal about the struggles in Central and South America for several of decades, Chomsky reports that the

"famous School of the Americas, which trains Latin American officers to carry out their missions, proudly announces as one of its 'talking points' that the US Army helped to 'defeat liberation theology,' the heresy to which the Latin American Church succumbed when it adopted 'the preferential option for the poor' and was made to suffer its own 'terrors of the earth' for this departure from the good order."[251]

Some Christians think we need to get past liberation theology, that the "liberationist outlook obscures rather than clarifies the practical imperatives of Christian ministry."[252] One of the most influential 20th century Protestant theologians in the United States, Reinhold Niebuhr, wrote extensively in opposition of liberalism, and is marked from early on for his "denunciation of all forms of liberalism, and particularly of liberal Protestantism."[253]

Islam

In Islam, as mentioned before, there is no belief in the Divine Right of Kings. As Seyyed Hossein Nasr tells us in his book, *The Heart of Islam*, that while there have been caliphs and sultans, these authorities are not like popes, kings, clergy, priests, or emperors, for they cannot write laws or interpret them, only administrate. Thus there can be no Islamic theocracy like the kind we find in Europe or under the Bush regime, but only 'nomocracy' –rule of the Divine Law.[254]

What separates the Islamic state from other states is not a religious necessity, because as we have seen, citizenship does not depend upon being a Muslim, but the primacy of law over constitution. An Islamic state can be many different kinds of states, however, each possible state must adhere to the law, or *Shariah*. The Shariah does not determine the type of state to be put in place –this is done through something called *al-Shura*, or 'mutual consultation' of the people.

---

[248] Martin Luther King, Jr., "What Is Man?", in *Philosophy Looks To The Future*, ed. Peyton E. Richter and Walter L. Fogg, Second Edition, (Prospect Heights, Waveland Press, Inc., 1978) p133
[249] Carroll, p589
[250] Carroll, p589-590
[251] Chomsky, *Hegemony or Survival*, (New York, Henry Holt and Company, 2003) p91
[252] Ephraim Radner, "From Liberation to Exile: A New Image for Church Mission", (*The Christian Century*, October 188, 1989) p931. Quoted in Robert Bruce McLaren's, *Christian Ethics: Foundations and Practice*, (Englewood Cliffs, Prentice Hall, Inc., 1994) p93
[253] Walter Kaufmann, *Critique of Religion and Philosophy*, (New York, Harper & Brothers Publishers, 1958) (b) 68
[254] Nasr, p148

Al-Shura can be democratic but it mustn't necessarily be. Instead of rule by the masses, the *Shura* usually consists of only those people who are concerned, which are often legal experts, though different Muslims attend the consultation. The type of state therein-chosen is the one which best fits the needs of the community. If a ruler is put in place or assumes power without mutual consultation, the law instructs that there be a coup, and historically rulers have been overthrown because of their violation of this law.[255]

There can be Muslim Kings and Queens, and there have been Empresses, as we have seen. However, their rule is not divine. As for the 'Prince of Peace' or the 'King of the Jews', the Quran does not discuss or mention such a thing as the Hebrew 'messiah' or the Greek 'Christ'. The holy book of Islam, the Quran, discusses Jesus though it never refers to him by the Hebrew 'Messiah' or the Greek 'Christ' –he is a great prophet, like Muhammad.

The Quran says, "We have preferred some Prophets over others." (17:57) Muhammad was a ruler for a short time in Medina and he later took Mecca without bloodshed. However, he was not considered to be a King, but the seal of the prophets. At his death Muhammad said that the matter of choosing a state is to be left to Muslims themselves.[256] There is an Arabic word that gets used by Muslims but is not found in the Quran: the word *Mahdi* which means something like 'the Expected', or 'Awaited One'. However peripheral or central the belief in the Mahdi is by both Sunni and Shia Muslims, they do not believe a Mahdi will appear until peace and justice have been established on earth already.[257] Thus the Mahdi is not like a savior or redeemer, or a King for that matter.

When we look for political hints in the Quran we find perhaps the opposite of what the Westerner thinks: religious compulsion is ruled out - "No compulsion is there in religion." (2:256), imperialism and empire are ruled out - "If Allah had willed He would have made them all one nation." (42:8), "O mankind, We have created you male and female, and appointed you races and tribes, that you may know one another." (49:13)

One Muslim nation that has been considered to be part of the "axis of evil" by the United States is Iran. The US helped to overthrow the first democratically elected president in the history of Iran back in 1953. This was because he had nationalized the oil industry, which largely had been controlled by English and American governments and investors.[258]

The Shah had been a financial contributor to Richard Nixon's 1968 presidential campaign, and between 1972 and 1978 the Shah increased Iran's military budget from $1.375 billion to $9.940 billion, making some $20 billion in arms deals with the US and

---

[255] Muhamed S. El-Awa, *On The Political System of the Islamic State*, trans. Ahmad Naji al-Imam, ed. Anwer Beg, (Indianapolis, American Trust Publications, 1980) p90
[256] El-Awa, p27
[257] Waines, p167-168; Nasr, 72
[258] Hiro's *Iran Under the Ayatollahs*, gives a good chronology of events. Mussadiq was democratically elected in 1953 –2,043,300 to 1,300; - CIA began clandestine forces and British Secret Service; British lose power in Iran, tell CIA to overthrow Mussadiq; this is named Operation Ajax –led by the in CIA 1953; head of CIA Kermit Roosevelt secretly meets with Shah; Shah dismisses Mussadiq; Mussadiq rescued by the Iranian army; CIA coup fails; Shah flees Iran; then Mussadiq overthrown in CIA ploy; Shah returns; Mussadiq arrested and put under house arrest until his death. Hiro says the coup "destroyed any chance that Iran had of evolving as a Western style democracy". (p34, 34n22, p36, 36n29)

US companies. In 1978 the Shah formed a military government with the backing of the US.[259]

Two months later the Shah was overthrown through non-violent demonstrations, led by an exiled Muslim cleric named Ayatollah Khomeini. Though exiled for 16 years, the philosophy of Khomeini had become very popular throughout Iran by way of pamphlet and cassette recordings of his lectures. Thus, the Iranian Revolution is often called the 'Cassette Revolution', a name denoting the non-violent nature of the revolution.

Khomeini had delivered many lectures in opposition to monarchy, and said that, "Islam is fundamentally opposed to the whole notion of monarchy…" According to Khomeini's interpretation of the Quran hereditary power is un-Islamic, and the Shah's regime was oppositional to Islam, violated constitutional rights, destroyed agriculture, and squandered large sums of money on foreign weapons.[260]

Khomeini and a council of other revolutionaries drafted a constitution in 1979 to be voted on by the Iranian people, though the new Iranian government would not be a democracy. Khomeini said, "Democracy is another word for usurpation of God's authority to rule." "Do not use the word 'Democratic'. That is a western idea. We respect western civilization, but will not follow it."[261]

Khomeini said the great aim of Islam is "to prevent oppression, arbitrary rule, and the violation of the law…[and] to establish social justice." Ayatollah Shariatmadari similarly said, "It is not for the ulema (Muslim clerics) to involve themselves in politics, that is for the government. We must simply advise the government when what they do is contrary to Islam."[262]

The French philosopher and genealogist Michel Foucault spent time in Iran before and after the 1979 revolution. He wrote that Islam is "a religion that gave to its people infinite resources to resist state power." Although Foucault was both an atheist and an anarchist, witnessing these events compelled him to write that:

"I do not feel comfortable speaking of Islamic government as an 'idea' or even as an 'ideal'. Rather, it impressed me as a form of 'political will'. It impressed me in its effort to politicize structures that are inseparably social and religious in response to current problems. It also impressed me in its attempt to open a spiritual dimension in politics."[263]

The activist As'ad AbuKhalil writes that, "There is no such thing as a political language of Islam."[264] Islam has been practiced by nomads, Kings, Queens, Emperors, Empresses, democracies, and socialist governments. Whatever the political form, the Shariah, or Islamic Law remain the same.

---

[259] Hiro, p308, 95, 81
[260] Quoted by Hiro, p57, 334, 64
[261] Quoted by Hiro, p87, 91, 106, 108
[262] Quoted in Hiro, p46, 117
[263] Foucault, "What Are the Iranians Dreaming About?"
[264] As'ad AbuKhalil, *Bin Laden, Islam, and America's New "War On Terrorism"*, (New York, Seven Stories Press, 2002) p21

Anti-Semitism and the Jewish Question

> Some Christians pretend that Christianity was not established by the sword; but of what period of time do they speak? -Thomas Paine, 1794[265]

The history of what is known as 'The Jewish Question' has existed since at least the 19th century. The question was posed in 1842 by a 'liberal' Prussian scholar named Bruno Bauer and was made famous when Karl Marx wrote a lengthy review and critique of him, called "On the Jewish Question". Marx had just become the editor for a German newspaper, *Rheinische Zeitung*, in which this review was published. Both Bauer and Marx were disciples of the defamed Ludwig Feuerbach, whose atheism cost him his professorship. Feuerbach believed that, "The beginning, middle, and end of religion is man."[266] These young liberals believed the only way Jews would ever be given equal rights in Europe was if they renounced their religion, an identity which set them apart from northern European Christians for a thousand years, and apart from the new social (post-religious) and anthropological philosophy of socialism and the classless secular society.

The Jewish Question has become a reoccurring leitmotif to the political climate of the 19th and 20th centuries, culminating in the United Nations declaring that Israel was a sovereign state. At the end of the Second World War there was a question in the conscience of many European's and American's concerning the rights and reparations of the 33% of Europe's Jews who had survived the war but were uprooted, robbed, and dishonored. The majority vote between UN delegations gave away land that had been militarily occupied with an iron fist by Britain since the end of the First World War. Backed by the victors of the Second World War, the new state of Israel was militarily supplied by the West with training and support, a military support second only to the Shah of Iran, to pump the prime desert messiah: oil. In time this western 'Herodism' came to uproot many who were native to the area, the Palestinians, who before this were persecuted by the English for more than 30 years.

There is a sense in which the Jewish Question is very real, both historically as well as today as many Jews do not live in Israel. Historically, one of the most practical answers to this question was the *Al Dustur al-Madinah*, or the Constitution of Medina. This Constitution was drafted by the prophet Muhammad sometime in the 620's or 630's, at the request of some warring tribes that trusted Muhammad as an unbiased 3rd party who could arbitrate for them and end the conflict. The Constitution of Medina itself says that both polytheists (pagans) and Jews alike are part of the community of Medina. The Constitution is about 4 pages long and mentions the Jews nearly two-dozen times, saying that Muslim community will defend the Jews. This Constitution seems to have been upheld during World War II when the French Marshal Petain told the Moroccan King Mohammed V to send the Moroccan Jews to labor camps and Mohammed refused.[267]

---

[265] Thomas Paine, *The Age of Reason*, in *The Life and Major Writings of Thomas Paine*, ed. Philip S. Foner, (New York, Citadel Press, 1945) p596
[266] Ludwig Feuerbach, *The Essence of Christianity*, trans. George Eliot, (Amherst, Prometheus Books, 1989) p184
[267] Ahmed, (b) p103

Anti-Semitism has its roots in the New Testament.[268] This does seem paradoxical, because after all, Jesus was both Semitic and Jewish.[269] However, Jesus did not write the New Testament. The New Testament was by and large written by Saint Paul and the writers of the Gospels were in turn influenced by Paul's writings. The New Testament tells us that the Jews are really Satan-worshipers (Revelation 2:9, 3:9) and that tens of thousands of Jews must be killed in order for the second coming of Jesus to occur (Revelation 7:3-4).

As James Carroll tells us in his book, *Constantine's Sword: The Church and the Jews*, hatred of people whom are Jewish is so easily detected in the New Testament. While the phrase 'the Jews' appears 16 times in the first 3 gospels, it appears 71 times in the gospel of John. Moreover the gospel of John tells us that the Jews are all Satanic (John 8:44).[270]

Church history has confirmed this hatred for Jews. As Carroll says, "the 'Jewish problem'... remains a Christian problem.... A miscarried cult of the cross is ubiquitous in this story, from the Milvian Bridge to Auschwitz."[271] This has ranged from the church writing blood laws making sure even Jews who had converted to Christianity would not gain power in politics or the church. This started with Statute of Toledo in 1547, to the Papal bull *Cum Nimis Absurdum*, which made dress codes for all Jews in Rome and which began the ghetto. This Statute of Toledo became the law for the church in the 17th century, and Pope Urban VIII had Jewish children forcefully taken from their parents, often times kidnapped, and baptized through force.[272]

Paul's letter to the Roman Emperor Titus asks the leader to censor the Jews: "For there are many unruly men, profitless talkers, and deceivers of the mind, especially those men who adhere to the circumcision. It is necessary to shut the mouths of these..." (Titus 1:10-11). Peter makes a similar suggestion after teaching that God has placed the existing kings and governors on earth in order to punish the evildoers, that "For so the will of God is, that by doing good you may muzzle the ignorant talk of the unreasonable man." (1 Peter 2:15)

The biblical scholar and archaeologist Robert Eisenman inquires into the contradiction which is found in the New Testament. He asks: "How can a document be both philo-Semitic and anti-Semitic at the same time? This is the kind of question that is

---

[268] Martin Luther King, Jr., was convinced that "Christianity repudiates racism". However, he was well aware that "the church has been appallingly silent and disastrously indifferent to the realm of race relations, but even more to the fact that it has often been an active participant in shaping and crystallizing the patterns of the race-caste system. Colonialism could not have been perpetuated if the Christian Church had really taken a stand against it... It will be one of the tragedies of Christian history if future historians record that at the height of the twentieth century the church was one of the greatest bulwarks of white supremacy." From *Strength to Love*, p100, 101-102

[269] While Shakespeare helped to spread anti-Semitism through his play *The Merchant of Venice*, he seems to have been ignorant also that Moorish Muslims are Semitic as well. In *Othello*, Shakespeare's villain Iago repeatedly says, "I hate the Moor" yet his jealousy is often admiration, "The Moor [has] a free and open nature too, that thinks men honest that but seem to be so" (Act I, Scene iii). "The Moor (howbeit that I endure him not) is of a constant, noble, loving, nature" (Act II, Scene I)

[270] Carroll, p91-93

[271] Carroll reports that in 1998 when Jews protested the erection of the cross at Auschwitz, Catholics began planting homemade bombs to stop them. (Carroll, p4-5)

[272] Carroll, 250, 374, 384n68

asked in literary or historical criticism of the Bible. The answer, of course, is it cannot be. This is a contradiction in terms..."[273]

Bertrand Russell gives a rough summation of history demonstrating the vicissitudes of religious moralities:

"But has Christianity, in fact, stood for a better morality than that of its rivals and opponents? I do not see how any honest student of history can maintain that this is the case. Christianity has been distinguished from other religions by its greater readiness for persecution. Buddhism has never been a persecuting religion. The Empire of the Caliphs was much kinder to Jews and Christians than Christian states were to Jews and Mohammedans."[274]

For someone who is not religious I was struck by a chapter late in the Quran which stated simply: *To you your religion, and to me my religion.* (Surah 109:5) For a non-theist such as myself I did not think that one religion recognized the reality of another. Compare this to the second letter of John the Baptist: "If anyone comes to you and does not bring this teaching, never receive him into your homes or say a greeting to him." (2nd of John 10)

Muhammad had said that "Differences in my community is a mercy"[275] and this hadith is proven by the sunnah and Constitution of Medina. The point of the Constitution of Medina and of Muhammad's mission in general is not imperialism: not to make everyone the same or force everyone to become a Muslim. For example, a passage from the Constitution reads: "the Jews have their religion and Muslims have theirs" (25) and this goes for other religions such as pagans (20b) and different tribes as well.

In Islam, one cannot be forcefully converted or baptized. The Quran says:

"No compulsion is there in religion." Surah 2:258

"And if thy Lord had willed, whoever is in the earth would have believed, all of them, all together. Wouldst thou then constrain the people, until they are believers? It is not for any soul to believe save by the leave of Allah" Surah 10:99-100

"Yet, be thou ever so eager, the most part of men believe not." Surah 12:103

"We have not given them any Books to study, nor have We sent them before thee any warner." Surah 34:43

"If Allah had willed, He would have made them one nation." Surah 42:8

"And for his saying, 'My Lord, surely these are a people who believe not' –yet pardon them, and say, 'Peace!" Surah 43:87

"O mankind, We have created you male and female, and appointed you races and tribes, that you may know one another." 49:13

The sayings, or *hadith*, of the prophet Muhammad confirm this:

"There is no superiority for an Arab over a non-Arab nor for a non-Arab over an Arab, neither for a white man over a black man nor a black man over a white man except the superiority gained through consciousness of Allah [*taqwa*]. Indeed the noblest among you is the one who is most deeply conscious of Allah."[276]

Anti-Semitism is not just hatred of the Jewish people, but is hatred for the Semitic race. Abraham was a Semite, as was Moses, as was Jesus, as was Muhammad, as is one heck of a model-American: Ralph Nader.

---

[273] Robert Eisenman, *James the Brother of Jesus*, (New York, Penguin Books, 1997) p55
[274] Bertrand Russell, "Can Religion Cure Our Troubles?", in *Why I Am Not A Christian*, (New York, Simon and Schuster, 1957) (d) p201-202
[275] Quoted by Arabi, p23
[276] Ahmed, (a) p21

In the dedication of his work, *Otherwise Than Being, Or Beyond Essence*, Emmanuel Levinas writes believing there is one God,

"To The memory of those who were closest among the six million assassinated by the National Socialists, and of the millions on millions of all confessions and all nations, victims of the same hatred of the other man, the same anti-Semitism."[277]

Those who believe in a god need not conclude that this god only created some people and not others. We come to the problem of the One and the Many. If everyone is fundamentally the same why are there so many differences and struggles? Who comes first –the individual or society?

This is the classical Western opposition: the individual vs. society. How are we to determine which is right or better or more just? Are individual rights fundamental or is it society that decides what is to be honored and what is dishonorable? Is it the problem or the solution that is to be found in the individual or in society? Is such a dilemma found in all parts of the world, or do strong communities exist? To the philosophy of the community we immediately turn.

---

[277] Emmanuel Levinas, *Otherwise Than Being, Or Beyond Essence*, (1974), trans. Alphonso Lingis, (Pittsburgh, Duquesne University Press, 1981)

4

Living As If There Were No Tomorrow

A community of contemporary scientists theorizes that the world will end in about a million years. Accordingly this will be the result of either the explosion or burning out of the sun whereupon the earth will be destroyed or sent into some uninhabitable trajectory. Or quite possibly before this million-year lifecycle reaches completion the earth could collide with a decent sized meteor, asteroid, or comet and human life would cease to be. Much of the second half of the 20th century dealt with an ethic concerning the imminence of a nuclear holocaust. A nuclear holocaust is the name given to the aftermath of a nuclear war where possibly no person is left alive and because of radiation and 'fall out' the earth loses its capacity to sustain human life.

It seems the reaction that barbarians have when they learn the word 'eschatology' is one of agony. Surely there is no one alive today who has this ancient Greek word in their vocabulary that doesn't have a belief about its meaning. To find out that there is a study of the end of the world which predates modern physical science can be alarming to the uninitiated heathen. But, alas, what forsaken individual has ever been so naïve as to believe the world would never end?

The point of focus in this chapter will be the relationship between two basic forms of belief about the end of the world and their attendant eschatological practices: the scientific and religious eschatologies, which sometimes accompany and sometimes counteract one another. Many such theories exist and some are more or less reasonable than others. To avoid oversimplification and the use of generalizations, as well as for a better sense of accuracy, however, the words 'scientific and religious' will be replaced with the more philosophical jargon, 'epistemological and metaphysical'.

Coined by the students of Aristotle, metaphysics is a Greek word and concept that represents the study of the nature of reality. The Greek *physis* means 'nature' and the prefix *meta* means 'on' or 'after', so the word 'metaphysics' literally means 'after physics'. Epistemology is a Greek word and concept representing the study of knowledge and justification. The Greek *episteme* means knowledge and *logos* means explanation, so literally epistemology means 'the explanation of knowledge'.

A metaphysical eschatology is a study of the nature of the end of the world and an epistemological eschatology is a study of how we as humans come to know the end of the world, or whether such knowledge exists at all. While the more popular terms 'religious' and 'scientific' help simplify things, they will not give so neat a description as our more sophisticated philosophical jargon. Be that as it may, the traditional metaphysical eschatology of the ancient world often coincides with modern scientific realism in alarming and life-threatening ways. Once upon a time people believed the world was going to end, say through a natural disaster like a flood or storm. Today humans know we can end the world if we so choose the habitual path of the relative status quo.

While supernatural theories of the end of the world are not as explicit today as say in the year 999 AD, the contemporary experts on such impending matters are usually not religious experts, but environmentalists and ecologists. By use of the experimental or epistemological scientific methods of reason, a natural projection is made in estimating such things as likelihood's, probabilities, causes and effects. All of these are in turn used in the prediction of such things as geological history, sustainability, as well as weather patterns, temperature fluctuation, and climate change. Today the small community of environmentalists are fighting one the hardest battles in the question of our earth's survival. Under Western modernization the world is in a bad way and in the US, say, environmentalists make up one the smallest communities amidst the earth's largest consumer culture. More and more each day the seas are polluted, forests are clear cut, and every day the air is continually supplied with a growing number of toxins produced by planes, automobiles, factories, and the burning of fossil fuels such as coal and oil. The world's greatest consumer of natural resources, the United States, is dependent chiefly upon non-renewable resources in its current phase of modernization.

The United States is the most powerful member of a group of countries known as the 'G8'. The G8, or 'the group of 8' was formed in the early 1970's following the oil crisis, when the western world nearly come to an end because Arab and Muslim oil-rich nations stopped exporting oil. The G8 is made up of those countries that dominate and manipulate the global market so that it works to their interests and keeps the oil flowing.

Conspicuously most of these countries also form the base of the United Nations Security Council, which is the military branch of the United Nations. The United Nations Security Council is different from the United Nations General Assembly (which consists of almost 200 nations) in that just 5 nations have perpetual veto power over any proposed resolution, no matter whether there is a clear majority or nay. This amounts to hegemony of international power. Not inconspicuously these 5 nations also happen to be established nuclear powers, with thousands of nuclear warheads between them.

This group of nations also dominates the non-democratic institutions such as the World Bank and the International Monetary Fund, where the U.S. has the most influence among nations. All of these nations use the euphemistic 'free-market' economy misleadingly referred to as 'capitalism'. Under this model of colonization, or top-down globalization as it is called in its current manifestation, these nuclear nations try to restructure other similarly dictator-led national economies and trade-policies, as well as their landscapes. Although the government of China is considered a socialist republic, which would ideally work to the advantage of the people, their status as the U.S.' number one trading partner reveals the common acquisitiveness of the modern globalizing tendency. Nations that were for thousands of years self-sustaining and examples of perfection are now caught in the money swindle of comodifying nature and selling the poor to sweat shop labor.

It is becoming evident that modernization not only has a devastating impact on the earth's environment but upon human beings as well, particularly at the level of the community. Once upon a time the community was the basis for society, and the community made available a face-to-face relationship between the peoples. The 5 nations of the Iroquois, for example, had effectively realized America's first true democracy well before 1492, and had sustained their neighbors through mutual aid. Since then the face-to-face relationship has been steadily replaced by international monarchies, representatives, 'representation', nation-states over city-states, multinational corporations over small businesses, and of course the monopolied mass-media of television. We are seldom face-to-face with our representatives, be they actors or politicians. Local communities disappear when multi-national corporations set up shop and then move abroad for cheaper labor. When the laws that each community must obey are written and enforced by a moneyed centralized bureaucracy, or when Hollywood and the movie industry sell us our image, the many different communities disappear.

Commidifying Time

The American Founding Father Benjamin Franklin (1706-1790) variously wrote:
"Remember that time is money... Remember, that *credit* is money... Remember, that money is of the prolific, generating nature. Money can beget money, and its offspring can beget more, and so on... Beware of thinking all your own that you possess, and of living accordingly. It is a mistake that many people who have credit fall into."[1]

Benjamin Franklin was not the first person to equate time and money and the practice of comidifying nature goes back far in human history. The term for this practice of equating time and money is called 'usury', which is most commonly exercised in the form of lending money for profit or increase. Given the general acceptance of usury in our culture it is hard for us to imagine there ever having been a society wherein the practice of lending money for profit was not practiced. It almost seems like common sense. Why ought someone lend money if they can't expect something in return for their own generosity?

The ancient Babylonian King Hammurabi (18th century BCE –or Before the Common, or Christian Era), for example, had forbidden certain kinds of usury in his famous code of law. It is probable that similar restrictions were in place in other societies and states as well[2], though the democratic ancient Greeks of Socrates' time lent money on interest, or *tokos*, which also means 'child'.[3]

Since the medieval times of Europe when Jews were not permitted by the laws of the Holy Roman Empire to own land or join guilds, there has been a stigma attached to Jews and banking.[4] Be that as it may, the practice of usury is barred by the laws of the Jewish Holy book Torah (Exodus 22:24, Leviticus 25:35) though the last book of the Torah, Deuteronomy (23:20-21), only forbids usury amongst people who are not foreign to one another. In the 6th century BCE prophecy of Ezekiel we find that Yhwh is disgusted with the practice of usury: "[T]hou hast taken interest and increase, and thou hast greedily gained of thy neighbors by oppression, and hast forgotten Me." (Ezekiel 22:12) The Talmudist Rabbi Louis Ginzberg tells us in his work, *On Jewish Law and Lore*, of the ban on interest eventually becoming codified by the Rabbis.

---

[1] Max Weber quotes Franklin's essays *Necessary Hints to Those That Would Be Rich* (1736) and *Advice to a Young Tradesman* (1748), quoted in Max Weber, *The Protestant Ethic and The Spirit of Capitalism*, trans. Talcott Parsons, (New York, Charles Scribner's Sons, 1958) p48-49
[2] Maxime Rodinson, *Islam and Capitalism*, trans. Brian Pearce, (Austin, University of Texas Press, 1978) p240
[3] G.M.A. Grube points this out in his translation of Plato's *Republic*. (Indianapolis, Hackett Publishing Company, 1974) (a) p161n14
[4] According to church law, "Jews could not join guilds or own land". James Carroll, *Constantine's Sword*, (Boston, Mariner Books, 2002) p431-432

"The Biblical precept against usury and increase not only was turned into law by the Rabbis but was developed to an extreme which made dealings in futures almost impossible, and thus a curb was put on speculation, a clear case of legislation for the benefit of the farmer."[5]

If the Macedonian philosopher Aristotle (384-322 BCE) is taken to be one of the first economists[6], his lecture on ethics, *Nicomachean Ethics*, sets out to forbid usury and the lending of money with interest. Aristotle said that an "excess in giving without taking is proper to a foolish person" (1121a27).[7] In the *Politics* Aristotle decries usury as unnatural and against the common well being of the community.

"The most hated sort [of wealth-getting], and with the greatest reason, is usury, which makes a gain out of money itself, and not from the natural object of it. For money was intended to be used in exchange, but not to increase at interest. And this term interest, which means the birth of money from money, is applied to the breeding of money because the offspring resembles the parent. That is why of all modes of getting wealth this is the most unnatural."[8] (1258b2-8)

By the 5th century, however, Aristotle was banned from Europe[9] and in the 6th century the Christian Emperor Justinian had codified laws that barred only certain forms of usury, while permitting others, sometimes in different forms.[10] The Roman law or *Codex* was to go on to have enormous influence on Western law for centuries and is still influential today. Justinian himself had declared the law immutable[11], and the laws of usury in national and international trade still hold today. Debt is particularly profitable for the multinational banking agencies of the IMF and the World Bank whose loans to third-world countries can only be repaid through comodifying their natural resources such as in the fishing of coastlines, the mining of minerals, and the clearing of forests for lumber, all to pay back loans given to those in power.

Nominally the church condemned the practice of lending at interest, while widely maintaining usury in practice. The predominant economic model of medieval Europe was feudalism, which was itself a kind of lending with interest. Feudalism was much more prevalent than is usually considered by 'economists', and was the primitive norm wherever there were no economists, but simple kings, barons, and lords, which is often still the case wherever these institutions still exist. As the historian Francis Jennings writes of the pre-Adam Smith era,

"Feudal process was the incessant wrestling within and between these communities to establish relations of dominance and dependency. In such a world the ordering restraints of religion and law often become mere instruments for conquest, petty or grand."[12]

The 13th century church authority Thomas Aquinas (1225-1274) had used a sophistical argument in his work *Summa Thelogiae* to demonstrate the important utility of

---

[5] Louis Ginzberg, *On Jewish Law and Lore*, (New York, Atheneum, 1970) p16-17
[6] This is suggested by the philosopher and economist Amartya Sen in his work *On Ethics and Economics*. Sen also mentions the ancient Hindu thinker Kautilya, who lived around the same time as Aristotle. His work *Artha-Sastra* is translated as *Treatise on the Science of Economics and Politics*, written somewhere between 321-296 BCE. Amartya Sen, *On Ethics and Economics*, (Oxford, Blackwell, 1987) p3, 5
[7] Aristotle, *Nicomachean Ethics*, trans. Terence Irwin, (Indianapolis, Hackett Publishing, 1985) (E)
[8] Aristotle, *Politics*, trans. Benjamin Jowett, (Cambridge, Cambridge University Press, 1996) (P)
[9] This occurred at the Council of Ephesus in 431 CE. Check Josef Pieper's *Scholasticism*, trans. Richard and Clara Winston, (New York, Pantheon Books, 1960) p103
[10] Rodinson, p240
[11] A.P. d'Entreves, *Natural Law*, (London, Hutchinson & Co., 1951) p35
[12] Francis Jennings, *The Invasion of America: Indians, Colonialism, and the Cant of Conquest*, (New York, W.W. Norton & Company, 1975) p4

lending money at interest.[13] This foreshadowed the Protestant Reformation and inauguration of the era of modern states with centralized banking. It was not Martin Luther, but the Genevan Protestant co-Founding Father John Calvin who believed in the Divine Right of usury, and Calvin was highly successful in spreading the practice.[14]

Although the "Usury Act of 1660" had been written to reduce interest rates, one of the most influential jurists and authorities on the English Common Law, Sir William Blackstone (1723-1780), (a judge still studied and revered in both England and the United States), wrote in support of usury.[15] The jurist and Founding Father of the philosophy of utilitarianism, Jeremy Bentham (1748-1832) had written in support of usury in his essay, "Defense of Usury", and Benthamites have always found this to be for the greatest good as well.

The Prophet Muhammad (570-632) was himself by trade both a farmer and a merchant. The Arabic word *riba* is often translated as meaning 'interest' or 'increase' and in Islam the practice of lending money at interest is banned.[16] Around the time of the initial spread of Islam in Arabia a form of communism had been practiced in 5th and 6th century Persia (Iran). Before the prophet's death in 632, Muhammad had been accused of being a communist, or a follower of the 'non-Arab' Mazdak.[17] Into the 16th century the Muslim economy was greater and farther-reaching than the Western economy and trade reached from China to Timbuktu. This only changed with the discovery of America, the birth of the African slave trade, and new laws banning Islamic and Jewish banking in Europe.

The entity to emerge following 1492 and the beginning of the modern era is the modern state, as well as the resurgent belief in the Divine Right of Kings. The modern state is a centralized form of government that alone controls the currency, spirituality, military, and judiciary all in one. Pope Alexander VI (Roman Pontiff 1492-1503) declared the king and queen of Spain, Ferdinand and Isabella, "Catholic Monarchs".[18] King Henry VIII declared himself to be head of the Anglican Church in 1529. The English Common Law, which is a corporate law, became the standard of modern state-capitalism.[19] Even the founding father of Methodism, John Wesley (1703-1791) wrote: *"we must exhort all Christians to gain all they can, and to save all they can; that is, in effect, to grow rich."*[20]

However, the modern period is not replete with the celebration of Usury. In the 19th century Communism received a large renaissance through the work of Friedrich Engels (1820-1895) and Karl Marx (1818-1883) whose *Communist Manifesto* (1848) is

---

[13] Carroll, p244n16, 432. Check out Aquinas' letter to the James of Viterbo, "A Letter on Credit Sales and Usury", *On Buying and Selling*, trans. A. O'Rahilly, orig. pub. In "Notes on St. Thomas and Credit", *Irish Ecclesiastical Record*, XXXI, 1928, p164-165. Reprinted in *The Pocket Aquinas*, ed. Vernon J. Bourke, (New York, Washington Square Press, 1960) p223-225
[14] Weber, p111, 157
[15] From his four volume *Commentaries on the Laws of England*, 456-458. Noted by Justice Richard A. Posner in, *The Economics of Justice*, (Cambridge, Harvard University Press, 1981) p15n7
[16] The prohibition appears several times in the Quran. See Surahs 2:275, 276, 3:125, 4:159, and 30:38.
[17] Rodinson, p22-23
[18] Carroll, p363
[19] Albert Camus wrote that the only problem with the Bourgeois or 'capitalist class' is their advancement of mediocrity. A glance at the corporate world is testament to this. *The Rebel*, trans. Anthony Bower, (New York, Alfred A. Knopf, 1954) p179-180
[20] Quoted by Weber, p175; 77

perhaps the single-most influential political treatise in world history. The *Manifesto* has inspired countless revolutions as well as the movements syndicalism, anarchism, and international socialism.[21] The question of usury in a Communist state is of course obsolete, as is, at least in theory, the motivation behind usury: self-interest.

One of the most popular books written in 19th century America was Edward Bellamy's *Looking Backward* (1888). Written during the industrial revolution, this was a fictional novel about a man who fell asleep in 1887 and did not awake until the year 2000, only to find that the world had become a socialist paradise. Bellamy wrote:

> "It had been the effort of lawgivers and prophets from the earliest ages to abolish interest, or at least to limit it to the smallest possible rate. All these efforts had, however, failed, as they necessarily must so long as the ancient social organizations prevailed."[22]

However, the appraisal of self-interest has not always guided humanity. One of the first (known) economists in world history, Aristotle, believed that usury was unnatural and unlawful, and we find this message in the books of the Torah, Tanach, and the Quran as well. While some religions, cultures, and ideologies forbid the practice of making money off of money, others have supported the practice as a God-given right. What effects do these various practices have upon human relations and the world itself?

Ecology and Eschatology

The state of nature in the world is sustained through a process called homeostasis, which is like a natural give and take, high tide and low-tide, or the pumping of the heart. Time perhaps changes the structure of the world, and nature is changed over time. There is the formation and dissolution of mountains, rivers, seas, and deserts, etc. The world itself is sustained so long as it orbits around the sun and humans survive so as long as stray sizeable meteors, comets, and asteroids do not collide with us or we don't simply kill each other off through warfare or some massive plague.[23]

That the existence of peoples and life forms is dependent upon this world is a 'given' (the world is not a set of tools but is an "ensemble of nourishments"[24]). However,

---

[21] Camus found that Marx's "error only lay in believing that extreme poverty and particularly, industrial poverty, could lead to political maturity." (p186)

[22] Edward Bellamy (1850-1898), *Looking Backward*, (New York, Signet Classics, 1960) p26. This book was praised by many including John Dewey.

[23] In 1927 Bertrand Russell told his students: "... if you accept the ordinary laws of science, you have to suppose that human life and life in general on this planet will die out in due course: it is a stage in the decay of the solar system... I am told that that sort of view is depressing, and people will sometimes tell you that if they believed that, they would not be able to go on living. Do not believe it; it is all nonsense. Nobody really worries much about what is going to happen millions of years hence. Even if they think they are worrying much about that, they are really deceiving themselves. They are worried about something much more mundane, or it may merely be a bad digestion; but nobody is really seriously rendered unhappy by the thought of something that is going to happen to this world millions and millions of years hence. Therefore, although it is of course a gloomy view to suppose that life will die out –at least I suppose we may say so, although sometimes when I contemplate the things that people do with their lives I think it is almost a consolation –it is not such as to render life miserable. It merely makes you turn your attention on other things." Bertrand Russell, *Why I Am Not A Christian*, ed. Paul Edwards, (New York, Simon & Schuster, 1957) (a) p10-11

[24] Emmanuel Levinas, *Time and the Other*, trans. Richard A. Cohen, (Pittsburgh, Duquesne University Press, 1987) p63

people have many different relationships with the world and understandings of its nature. Some people believe that the earth is like a mother that nurtures us and sustains us and they call her Mother Earth. Some believe that it's not the earth but humanity that is the center of the universe, and the world is but a stage or playpen.

The holy book of Hinduism, the *Bhagavad-Gita* (4th century BCE) teaches that the earth is part of an Eightfold Division of Nature (7:4), and that the god Krsna alone is responsible for the world and its dissolution (7:6). The Hindu God teaches: "I am the beginning, the middle and the very end of beings."[25] (10:20) The *Gita* tells us that there are two types of beings created in the world –the divine and the demonaic. "The holy men...rejoice in doing good to all creatures..." (5:25) The demonaic believe the world to be unreal and they "rise up as the enemies of the world for its destruction". (16:8-9) "Bound by hundreds of ties of desire, given over to lust and anger, they strive to amass hoards of wealth, by unjust means, for the gratification of their desires." (16:12)

The Chinese philosopher and religious figure Confucius (6th-5th century BCE) teaches that: "The gentleman understands what is moral. The small man understands what is profitable." (4:16) Confucius praises the founder of the Shun dynasty, Yu, because "He lived in lowly dwellings while devoting all his energy to the building of irrigation canals. With Yu I can find no fault."[26] (8:21)

The *Tao Te Ching* (or 'Classic of The Way and Virtue') of Lao Tzu (6th century BCE) says that the person who is best, "loves the earth" (8) and that the "Earth is great... Man models himself after Earth. Earth models itself after Heaven. Heaven models itself after Tao. And Tao models itself after nature."[27] (25)

Another indication of people's attitude toward the world is their understanding of time. Plato for example believed that time was 'a moving image of eternity' and that the earth itself is like a nurse. The world is the divine's 'fairest creation' though it is of necessity an imperfect copy of a perfect world.[28] Plato's student Aristotle, on the other hand, believed that both time and the material world are infinite. He wrote, "Plato is the only thinker who ascribes an origin to time: it originated, he declares, simultaneously with the universe." Aristotle holds instead that "time must always have existed" and that "motion is something eternal". As the title of his book *Physics* suggests, he believed the physical world to be real, though he was not simply a monist (or 'one'-ist), that is, a 'materialist'.[29]

The categories of time –past, present, and future- are understood differently according to differences in tradition and belief. For example, a literal reading of the Bible will teach us that the world is several thousand years old. Differently, 'Big Bang theorists' and Darwinists hold that the world is much older. Whether the 'fossil-fuels' we use to power our cars come from decayed dinosaur bones from hundreds of thousands of years ago, or if God magically anointed the desert with this oil, which humans mislabel

---

[25] *Bhagavad-Gita*, trans. Sarvepalli Radhakrishnan, *A Source Book In Indian Philosophy*, (Princeton, Princeton University Press, 1957)
[26] Confucius, *The Analects*, trans. D.C. Lau, (New York, Penguin Books, 1979)
[27] Lao Tzu, *Tao Te Ching*, trans. Wing-Tsit Chan in *The Way of Lao Tzu*, (Indianapolis, Bobbs-Merrill Educational Publishing, 1963)
[28] Plato, *Timaeus*, trans. B. Jowett, from *The Dialogues of Plato*, Vol. I, ed. Jowett, (New York, Random House, 1937) (b) 37, 40, 29-30
[29] Aristotle, *Physics*, Book II, Chapter 8, 199a31. Quotations taken from Book VIII, Chapter 1, trans. Philip Wheelwright, in *Aristotle*, (New York, The Odyssey Press, 1935) (Ph) p49-50

as "fossil" fuel, conceptualizations of time vary widely. Thinkers as variant as the Catholic philosopher Friedrich Schelling (1775-1854), the Protestant Georg Hegel (1770-1831), the heretic Karl Marx (1818-1883), or the Chinese atheist Mao Tse-tung (1893-1976) –all believed that time is an unfolding process according to a determinant scheme, the course of which is apprehendable by the human mind. Some religions seem to agree with Socrates and Plato that time is just an image or [false] representation of the true reality that we only experience when we die. Still others believe that 'the time is short' and that judgement day is imminent and the destruction of the world is at hand.

We might say that these various conceptualizations of time loosely fit into two categories, however indiscreet. One conceptualization of time can be understood as being fundamentally metaphysical in its purport –it poses as being the only true definition or nature of time, purporting to be the one true description of ultimate reality. Metaphysical conceptions of time pose as exhaustive analyses of the nature of the world, and it is held they cannot be incorrect. Such things as correction and disagreement do not exist.

On the other hand, some conceptualizations of time are more epistemological. These conceptions relate more to the role that human reason and intelligence play in coming to know the true nature of time. Here there is room for disagreement, improvement, and success. This dichotomy of time-concepts -being either metaphysical or epistemological -can also be represented however generally, as the spiritual and supernatural beliefs about reality on the one hand, and on the other, the scientific and practical beliefs about reality. These disparate, if often times convoluted, conceptions come to a head in the analysis of the ends of time: eschatology.

Eschatology

Nearly every politician and policy maker in the United States believes in the creed that we should 'live as if there were no tomorrow'. This is evidenced in the inordinate stockpiling of thousands of nuclear weapons, a preponderant superfluity to annihilate the entire human race in a matter of hours, as well as the disrespect for the Mother Earth culminated in lawful environmental degradation and an attendant denial of global warming and species holocaust. This isn't just the result of profit-seeking corporate driven economic policies but is symptomatic of a conviction of the imminent end of the world.

Most of the politicians in the US are Christian and there has never been an American president who was not Christian. In the US it is the president, the commander in chief, who solely has authority to launch a nuclear attack, as was the decision of President Harry Truman at the end of the Second World War, who bombed Japan without the knowledge of Congress or the rest of the democracy. The United States is the only country to have ever used a nuclear weapon to attack an enemy. Hundreds of thousands of innocent people were killed instantaneously in Hiroshima and Nagasaki, more deaths than in any other terrorist attack before or since. There should be no doubt in anyone's mind that bombings like this as well as that of the English bombing of Dresden were intended to terrorize the populace.[30]

"Have no thought of tomorrow" is a teaching of Jesus the Nazarene, delivered in his brief yet "astonishing" Sermon on the Mount. (Matthew 6:34) This individual did not believe that it was the job of policy-makers or presidents or democracies to intervene in making the human relationship with the earth a sustainable one. He spoke about the imminent destruction of the earth.

"I came to start a fire on the earth...Do you imagine I came to give peace on the earth? No, indeed, I tell you, but rather division."[31] Luke 12:49,51

"Truly I say to you, this generation will by no means pass away until all things occur. Heaven and earth will pass away, but my words will by no means pass away." Luke 21:32-33

President George W. Bush was often criticized for acting-out these instructions verbatim.[32] Though he was elected in the second thousandth year period or second 'millennium' of the Christian calendar, Bush never shied away from such allusions as to the second coming of the Christian Messiah, Jesus, and Bush, who described himself as a war-time president, sites Jesus as his greatest moral influence. The man who received the third most amount of votes in both the 2000, 2004, and 2008 elections, the Arab-American Ralph Nader, wrote in 2004 that, "The president has implied that he occupies his current role by virtue of divine providence. [Bush's] messianic complex makes him as close-minded as any president in history."[33]

The Civil-Rights and anti-war activist Martin Luther King, Jr., worked and taught during the height of the Cold War when Americans were almost certain that an atomic war was inevitable. He was highly critical of the proliferation of nuclear weapons as well as the Military-Industrial Complex. Dr. King said, "…I am convinced that the church cannot be silent while mankind faces the threat of nuclear annihilation. If the church is true to her mission, she must call for an end to the arms race."

"Some men still feel that war is the answer to the problems of the world… They sincerely feel that continuation of the arms race will be conducive to more beneficent than maleficent consequences. So they passionately call for bigger bombs, larger nuclear stockpiles, and faster ballistic missiles. Wisdom born of experience should tell us that war is obsolete. There may have been a time when war served as a negative good by preventing the spread and growth of an evil force, but the destructive power of modern weapons eliminates even the possibility that war may serve as a negative good. If we assume that life is worth living and that man has a right to survival, then we must find an alternative to war… Yet there are those who sincerely feel that disarmament is an evil and international negotiation is an abominable waste of time. Our world is threatened by the grim prospect of atomic annihilation because there are still too many who know not what they do."[34] (40-41)

---

[30] Albert Einstein (1879-1955) was compelled to write in 1947: "I must frankly confess that the foreign policy of the United States since the termination of hostilities has reminded me, sometimes irresistibly, of the attitude of Germany under Kaiser Wilhelm II, and I know that, independent of me, this analogy has most painfully occurred to others as well." From "Military Intrusion In Science", *Albert Einstein: Out of My Later Years*, (Edison, NJ, Castle Books, 2005) p213
[31] All references to the New Testament are from *New World Translation of the Holy Scriptures*, (Brooklyn, Watchtower Bible and Tract Society of Pennsylvania, 1961)
[32] Albert Camus wrote that, "The end of history is not an exemplary or a perfectionist value: it is an arbitrary and terroristic principle." From, "State Terrorism and Rational Terror", *The Rebel*, p194
[33] Ralph Nader, *The Good Fight*, (New York, HarperCollins, 2004) (a) p222
[34] Martin Luther King, Jr., *Strength to Love*, (Philadelphia, Fortress Press, 1963) p153, 40-41. King said, "This hour in history needs a dedicated circle of transformed nonconformists. Our planet teeters on the brink of atomic annihilation; dangerous passions of pride, hatred, and selfishness are enthroned in our lives… men do reverence before false gods of nationalism and materialism. The saving of our world from

American history is somewhat rife (and replete) with eschatological expectations. James Russell, the founder of the Christian group the Jehovah's Witness's, saw his own faith in the end of times come to grief before his own fortuitous death. Christians such as the Adventists and Jehovah's Witness's have chosen such dates as 1843, 1844, 1874, 1878, 1881, 1910, 1914, 1918, 1920, 1925, and many others, to be the end of times, only to live to experience their own bad faith.[35]

Some Christians, most notably the Mormons, believe that Jesus will appear in America, while traditionally most believe that Jesus will appear in Jerusalem at the end of times. Former Republican strategist Kevin Phillips wrote in his assessment: *American Theocracy*,

"End-times prophecy fueled a fifth dynamic at work as the forces for the Iraqi invasion gathered, because many Christian fundamentalists dismissed worries about oil or global warming out of belief that the end times were under way. The Bible lands were what mattered. Events were in God's hands."[36]

Since the time of Plato or possibly Socrates there have been some who believe reality is split into two worlds: this world (earth) and the true world (heaven). According to this theory known as 'idealism', the earth is an imperfect copy of the true world. This 'two-ism' or 'dualism' is fundamental to idealism, the split between mind and body. Idealism is still one of the most popular beliefs in the Western world where it is a view generally held by religious and non-religious people, alike. Those who talk about the 'soul' or 'spirit' tend to believe in this kind of duality, though Aristotle is one of the few non-Athenian exceptions.[37]

Those who are not idealists have either emphasized the centrality of this world or believed in the existence of many worlds. Hinduism, for example, holds that there are three worlds. (Bhagavad Gita 1:35, 3:22) The Quran of Islam teaches that there are many universes (Surah 6:75,79) created by God (herein refereed to by the Arabic *Allah*) while emphasizing the importance of each human's relationship with planet earth. The Quran recites:

"Forget not thy portion of the present world; and do good, as Allah has been good to thee. And seek not to work corruption in the earth; surely Allah loves not the workers of corruption."[38] Surah 28:77

"Praise belongs to Allah, who has been true in His promise to us, and has bequeathed upon us the earth, for us to make a dwelling wheresoever we will in Paradise." Surah 39:74

"(Transgress not in the Balance, and weigh with justice, and skimp not in the Balance.) And earth –He set it down for all beings, therein fruits, and palm-trees with sheaths, and grain in the blade, and fragrant herbs. O which of your Lord's bounties will you and you deny?" Surah 55:7-12

"All that is in the heavens and the earth magnifies Allah; He is the All-mighty, the All-wise. To Him belongs the Kingdom of the heavens and the earth; He gives life, and He makes to die, and He is powerful over everything." Surah 57:2 (Surah's 62:2 and 64:2 repeat this first line.)

---

pending doom will come, not through complacent adjustment of the conforming majority, but through the creative maladjustment of a nonconforming minority." (p23-24)

[35] Michael Martin, *The Case Against Christianity*, (Philadelphia, Temple University Press, 1991) p118-119
[36] Kevin Phillips, *American Theocracy*, (New York, Penguin Books, 2006) p95
[37] The Christian philosopher and mathematician Baron Gottfried Wilhelm von Leibniz (1646-1716) wrote about there being many 'possible worlds' of which earth is the best, having been created by God. It usually goes unquestioned whether Leibniz believed that, given that the earth was the best of all possible worlds, whether the earth actually existed or was just a modality of possibility. Robert Adams finds that Leibniz's theory is epistemically neutral. See, Robert Adams, "Possible World", *Cambridge Dictionary of Philosophy*, Second Edition, ed. Robert Audi, (Cambridge, Cambridge University Press, 1999) p724-725
[38] All references to the Quran are from A.J. Arberry's, *The Koran Interpreted*, (New York, Macmillan Publishing Company, 1955). As a translator Arberry uses the English word for god, "God", though I have used the original Arabic word "Allah".

"Made We not the earth to be a housing for the living and for the dead? Set We not therein soaring mountains? Sated you with sweetest water?" Surah 77:25-27

"Let Man consider his nourishment. We poured out the rains abundantly, then We split the earth in fissures and therein made the grains to grow and vines, and reeds, and olives, and palms, and dense-tree'd gardens, and fruits, and pastures, and enjoyment for you and your flocks." Surah 80:24-32

The two-world theory, some argue, entails a turning-away from this world. Such a prejudice against the earth is emphasized in the belief in the imminent ending of this world, be it belief in the scrutability of an impending apocalypse, or some other form of misanthropy and lack of faith in humanity. The New Testament says that:

"Every tree not producing fine fruit gets cut down and thrown into the fire." Matthew 7:19
"Every plant that my heavenly Father did not plant will be uprooted." Matthew 15:13

There is the fable of the fig tree that was out of season.

"While returning to the city early in the morning, he [Jesus] got hungry. And he caught sight of a fig tree by the road and went to it, but he found nothing on it except leaves only, and [Jesus] said to it: 'Let no fruit come from you any more forever.' And the fig tree withered instantly." Matthew 21:18-19

"The next day, when they had come out from Bethany, he [Jesus] became hungry. And from a distance he caught sight of a fig tree that had leaves, and he went to see whether he would perhaps find something on it. But, on coming to it, he found nothing but leaves, for it was not the season of figs. So, in response, he said to it: 'Let no one eat fruit from you any more forever.' And his disciples were listening... And when it became late in the day, they would go out of the city. But when they were passing by early in the morning, they saw the fig tree already withered up from the roots. So Peter, remembering it, said to [Jesus]: 'Rabbi, see! the fig tree that you cursed has withered up." Mark 11:12-14, 19-21

The apocalypse seems like a theme of destruction:

"As he was going out of the temple one of his disciples said to him: 'Teacher, see! what sort of stones and what sort of buildings!' However, Jesus said to him: 'Do you behold these great buildings? By no means will a stone be left here upon a stone and not be thrown down." Mark 13:1-2

"Indeed, the ax is already in position at the root of the trees; every tree, therefore, not producing fine fruit is to be cut down and thrown into the fire." Luke 3:9

"For a good tree bringeth not forth corrupt fruit; neither doth a corrupt tree bring forth good fruit." Luke 6:43 (King James Version)

The book of Revelation offers an epic on the scale of the simplistic *Lord of the Rings*.

"And there occurred a hail and fire mingled with blood, and it was hurled to the earth; and a third of the earth was burned up, and a third of the trees was burned up, and all the green vegetation was burned up." Revelation 8:7

The Torah of Judaism teaches of only this one world that took God (herein refereed to by the Hebrew *Yhwh*) nearly a week to create (Yhwh rested on Saturday).

"Be fruitful, and multiply, and replenish the earth."[39] Genesis 9:1

"I establish a covenant with you, and with your seed after you; and with every living creature that is with you, the fowl, the cattle, and every beast of the earth. And I will establish My covenant with you; neither shall all flesh be cut off any more by the waters of the flood; neither shall there any more be a flood to destroy the earth... This the token of the covenant which I make between Me and you and every living creature that is with you, for perpetual generations." Genesis 9:9-12

The book of Psalms is particularly earth affirming:

"The righteous shall inherit the land, and dwell therein forever." Psalms 37:29

This message is changed in the New Testament, which teaches us of a looming world-expiration[40]:

---

[39] All references to the Tanach (Hebrew Bible) are from *The Holy Scriptures*, According to the Masocretic Text, (Philadelphia, The Jewish Publication Society of America, 1917). The translators use the English word for god, "God", though I have used the original Hebrew word, "Yhwh".

[40] The Protestant Theologian Rudolf Bultmann (1884-1976) has argued against the popular interpretation of the New Testament as an 'interim ethic' or "exceptional commands which only held for the last short

"Truly I say to you, There are some of those standing here that will not taste death at all until first they see the kingdom of God already come in power." Mark 9:1

"Truly I say to you that this generation will by no means pass away until all these things happen. Heaven and earth will pass away, but my words will not pass away." Mark 13:30-31

"Most truly I say to you, the hour is coming, and it is now." John 5:25

"...the ends of the systems of things have arrived." 1 Corinthians 10:11

"Afterward we the living who are surviving will, together with them [the resurrected], be caught away in clouds to meet the Lord in the air." 1Thessalonians 4:17

"Whoever, therefore, wants to be a friend of the world is constituting himself an enemy of God." James 4:4

"True, he was foreknown before the founding of the world, but he was made manifest at the end of the times for your sake." 1Peter 1:20

"Do not be loving either the world or the things in the world. If anyone loves the world, the love the Father is not in him...Furthermore, the world is passing away..." 1 John 2:15, 17

Such a perspective of an imminent and impending destruction of the world ought to be compared to that of the Prophet Muhammad, who lived 400 years later:

"They will question thee concerning the Hour, when it shall berth. Say: 'The knowledge of it is only with my Lord; none shall reveal it at its proper time, but He'." Surah 7:187

"Perish the conjecturers who are dazed in perplexity asking, 'When shall be the Day of Doom?' Upon the day when they shall be tried at the Fire: 'Taste your trial! This is what you were seeking to hasten.' Surely the godfearing shall be among gardens and fountains taking whatsoever their Lord has given them; they were good-doers before that. Little of the night would they slumber, and in the mornings they would ask for forgiveness; and the beggar and the outcast had a share in their wealth." Surah 51:10-19

"They will question thee concerning the Hour, when it shall berth. What are thou about to mention it? Unto thy Lord is the final end of it." Surah 79:43

The Spanish-born 12th century Muslim philosopher and physician Ibn Rushd (or in Latin, *Averroes*) (1126-1198) wrote a book against those who were anti-philosophical called *The Destruction of the Destruction*. The Spanish-born 12th century Jewish physician, jurist, and philosopher, Moses ben Maimon, or in Latin, *Maimonides* (1135-1204), seems to praise the wisdom of Surah 51:10 of the Quran in his study, *Laws of Kings and Their Wars*:

"Let no one think that the custom of the world will in any way cease to exist during the days of the messiah or that something new will occur in the Work of Creation... A man does not know how all these things and their like will take place until they do take place, for they remain sealed with the prophets. The wise men, too, have no tradition concerning these things; they can only decide by examining the verses, neither the sequence of these events nor the details concerning them are principles of the religion.... Nor should he regard them as having the status of a principle, for they bring about neither fear nor love. Nor should he calculate the end. The wise men said, 'May the spirit of those who calculate the end expire.'"[41]

Taoism teaches, "the end is not yet." (20) "Heaven is eternal and Earth everlasting. They can be eternal and everlasting because they do not exist for themselves, and for this reason can exist forever." (7)

---

interval until the end of the world. Rather, these imperatives are clearly meant radically as absolute demand with a validity independent of the temporal situation." In *Theology of the New Testament*, Vol. I, trans. Kendrick Grobel, (New York, Charles Scribner's Sons, 1951) p20. According to Bultmann, such an ethic necessitates the rejection of legal judgements in order to receive divine judgement and salvation. For a lengthier discussion of Bultmann, see Chapter 6: Many Forms of Justice.

[41] Moses ben Maimon, *Laws of Kings and Their Wars*, trans. Raymond L. Weiss in *Ethical Writings of Maimonides*, ed. Raymond L. Weiss w/ Charles Butterworth, (New York, Dover Publications, 1975) p175

Economics and Eschatology

Jesus is recorded as having said that his kingdom is not found in this world:
"I am no part of this world." John 17:14
"My kingdom is no part of this world." John 18:36

In his seminal work, *The Protestant Ethic and The Spirit of Capitalism*, sociologist Max Weber shows the path by which the 'otherworldliness' of Christianity became the foundation for modern state-based capitalism. Although Weber believed that capitalism as such had existed variously in different cultures throughout world history, he believed that the modern state economic system was descendent from the work of ascetic Christian Protestantism –particularly the Anglican, Calvinist, and Puritan traditions. Through propagation of the belief in a "calling" and a "justification by faith", the imperial economic license of state-capitalism was born. He wrote:

"[T]he intensity of the search for the Kingdom of God commenced gradually to pass over into sober economic virtue; the religious root died out slowly, giving way to utilitarian worldliness...

"The power of religious asceticism provided him in addition with sober, conscientious, and unusually industrious workmen, who clung to their work as to a life purpose willed by God.

"Finally, it gave him the comforting assurance that the unequal distribution of the goods of this world was a special dispensation of Divine Providence, which in these differences, as in particular grace, pursued secret ends unknown to men... This formulation of a leading idea of capitalistic economy later entered into the current theories of the productivity of low wages. Here also, with the dying out of the religious root, the utilitarian interpretation crept in unnoticed, in the line of development which we have again and again observed."[42]

Though he does not here discuss the implications such an economic system might have on democracy, Weber's conclusion now seems to have been an ominous prediction for the environment, though written in 1904.

"A man does not 'by nature' wish to earn more and more money, but simply to live as he is accustomed to live and to earn as much as is necessary for that purpose."

"The Puritan wanted to work in a calling; we are forced to do so. For when asceticism was carried out of monastic cells into everyday life, and began to dominate worldly morality, it did its part in building the tremendous cosmos of the modern economic order. This order is now bound to the technical and economic conditions of machine production which today determine the lives of all the individuals who are born into this mechanism, not only those directly concerned with economic acquisition, with irresistible force. Perhaps it will so determine them until the last ton of fossilized coal is burnt."[43]

Such findings ought to be contrasted with passages from the New Testament:
"Stop storing up for yourselves treasures upon the earth, where moth and rust consume, and where thieves break in and steal." Matthew 6:19
"No one can slave for two masters; for either he will hate the one and love the other, or he will stick to the one and despise the other. You cannot slave for God and for Riches." Matthew 6:24

There is Jesus' call to submit to the authority of the Roman Empire.
"Pay back Caesar's things to Caesar." Mark 12:17 (repeated in Matthew 22:17, Luke 20:25)

It is Saint Paul who offers the most famous formulation concerning the love of money. However, his letter to some 'Hebrews', may open the door for an eschatological capitalism, in indeed he too preached the end of the world.

"For the love of money is a root of all sorts of injurious things, and by reaching out for this love some have been led astray from the faith and have stabbed themselves all over with many pains." 1 Timothy 6:10

"Let [your] manner of life be free of the love of money, while you are content with the present things." Hebrews 13:5

---

[42] Weber, p176-177
[43] Weber, p60, 181

Weber points out that capitalism (when it existed) has existed variously over the course of history, from the Chinese and Hindus, as well as others, and Weber is concerned with its peculiar modern manifestation. He argues, for example, that modern capitalism is oppositional to cultural tradition, and in cases is oppositional to the traditional community.[44]

Martin Luther King, Jr., though a great critic of Communism, stands as one of Christianity's greatest critics of capitalism. He believed that while "Communism is Christianity's most formidable rival", the theory of Communism "challenges us to be more concerned about social justice." He said that, "Our unswerving devotion to monopolistic capitalism makes us more concerned about the economic security of the captains of industry than for the labouring men whose sweat and skills keep industry functioning."

Dr. King taught that truth is not to be found in capitalism and that many of the problems in America derive from the economic fears that are fundamental to capitalism.

"In the face of the communist challenge we must examine honestly the weaknesses of traditional capitalism. In all fairness, we must admit that capitalism has often left a gulf between superfluous wealth and abject poverty, has created conditions permitting necessities to be taken from the many to give luxuries to the few, and has encouraged smallhearted men to become cold and conscienceless so that... they are unmoved by suffering, poverty-stricken humanity... Surely it is unchristian and unethical for some to wallow in the soft beds of luxury while others sink in the quicksands of poverty. The profit motive, when it is the sole basis of an economic system, encourages a cut-throat competition and selfish ambition that inspires men to be more concerned about making a living than making a life... Are we not too prone to judge success by the index of our salaries and the size of the wheel base on our automobiles, and not by the quality of our service and relationship to humanity?"

In contradiction to Marxist theory, Martin Luther King taught that "Jesus never made a sweeping indictment against wealth... Nothing in wealth is inherently vicious, and nothing in poverty is inherently virtuous". However, "Only an irrelevant religion fails to be concerned about man's economic well-being."[45]

The Buddha (563-483 BCE) taught: "Truly, no misers get to the world of gods. Certainly, childish ones do not applaud giving. The wise one gladly approves giving; hence indeed is he at ease in the hereafter."[46] (177) Similarly the *Bhagavad-Gita* instructs: "He who abandons all desires and acts free from longing, without any sense of mineness or egotism –he attains to peace." (2:71) "Thou shouldst do works also with a view to the maintenance of the world." (3:20)

Confucius taught:

"[A]void excesses in expenditure and love your fellow men; employ the labour of the common people only in the right seasons." 1:5

"A gentleman takes as much trouble to discover what is right as lesser men take to discover what will pay."[47] 4:16

"A gentleman gives to help the needy and not to maintain the rich in style." 6:4

---

[44] Weber, p51-52, 60, 72, 58-59, 106

[45] Martin Luther King, Jr., *Strength to Love*, p96, 99, 28, 103, 116, 102, 67-68. King found that "the inseperable twin of racial injustice is economic injustice." (p150)

[46] Siddharta Gotama Buddha, *The Dhammapada*, trans. John Ross Carter and Mahinda Palihawadana, (Oxford, Oxford University Press, 1987)

[47] The different translation is intentional. *The Analects of Confucius*, trans. Arthur Waley, (New York, Vintage Books, 1938

According to Lao Tzu:
"When gold and jade fill your hall, you will not be able to keep them. To be proud with honor and wealth is to cause one's own downfall. Withdraw as soon your work is done." 9

"The sage does not accumulate for himself. The more he uses the more he has himself. The more he gives to others, the more he possesses of his own." 81

The sociologist Maxime Rodinson points out: the Quran is not "a treatise of political economy, and one would seek in vain to find approval or condemnation of capitalism as such." When capitalism emerged in the Islamic world in the 8th century, the economic classes remained separate from the political class. This, however, did not result in class stratification or class war as we find in the modern West. The Islamic system tends toward the nationalization of credit because of the Shariah (legal) precepts of giving money to the poor.[48] This seems to work the opposite in capitalist states where there is a personalization of credit and a nationalization of debt, and a large divide is created between the few rich and the many poor.

In the contemporary world most people struggle to pay their rent or pay off their mortgage. Rodinson points out how in capitalist societies the relation between landowners and tenants is one of exploitation. This is to be contrasted with the common theme of classical Arabic literature of the non-exploitive relationship between landowners and tenants, which takes place in a community and town level. Rodinson points out how these basic analyses of commodity economy escaped the notice of Marx and Engels as well as Weber's occasional hasty generalizations.[49]

As we have seen the Prophet Muhammad was during his own life labeled a communist though he was a merchant and farmer by profession, as well as a husband and father. Since the Cold War, that is, the ideological war between capitalism and communism, which began at the end of the World War II, every revolution or struggle for power had been measured according to allegiance to either of these economic structures: capitalism vs. socialism. However, this was not the case in the Islamic revolution of 1979, wherein the Shah was dethroned. The end of Islamic monarchy was almost entirely a non-violent event, compared to the end of the French monarchy, where the guillotine decapitated the former king and thousands of others. The Iranian revolution was neither capitalist nor communist.[50] Dilip Hiro has written of the Iranian revolution that: "In a world accustomed to thinking in bipolar terms of capitalism and socialism, Iran has caused much confusion."[51]

To understand the Islamic economic practices we do well to understand the history of Islam.

Community and Sustainability

Almost 1500 years ago there was a battle in the desert for the right to use an oasis. As everyone knows the desert is as arid as its inhabitants are sober –the oasis marks one of the few places where a people can live and sustain themselves and their camels.

---

[48] Quoted by Rodinson, p13, 55, 72
[49] Rodinson, p50, 97. He also points out (p76-77) instances of orientalism and racism in the writings of Weber.
[50] Dilip Hiro, *Iran Under The Ayatollahs*, (London, Routledge & Kegan Paul, 1987) p357, 359
[51] Hiro, p362

Although the Sumerians and Babylonians invented beer in the 'fertile crescent', the intervening five thousand years between then and 622 of the Common Era had maculated the crescent's fertility (but anointed it with oil some might add). The tribes that battled over this life-preserving oasis saw the need for a third party, an objective non-partisan thinker to help resolve the bloody conflict.

In the year 622 Muhammad was invited by his neighbors to come help resolve this dispute between these warring tribes. Thus residing as arbiter, Muhammad successfully drafted *Al Dustur al-Madinah*, or "The Constitution of Medina". The wisdom of this singular prophet shines through in this document as the constitution states the acceptance of people of all creeds and customs –pagans, Jews, and people of many other traditions. Muhammad showed no undue ethical partiality in his life-saving stint as judge.

This oasis in the desert was given the name 'Medina' and became the beginning of the first Muslim *ummah*, or community. Muhammad and the Muslims believe that the ummah is central for human's sustenance on the earth. They do not believe the world will end today or tomorrow. Although like most religions, Islam does have eschatology, the Quran is specific in its denial of a human vocation for divine omnipotence or global (nuclear) destruction. Muhammad said, "Protect and honor the earth, for the earth is your mother."[52]

When a dispute arose about the Black Stone and the reconstruction of the pagan Kabah shrine in Mecca, once again Muhammad was called upon to instill his own equanimity between the various peoples. Although the Muslims of Mecca had been persecuted for more than a decade, Muhammad became the recognized ruler without bloodshed and he was instrumental in maintaining and developing the Hajj, which among other things became the first international congress. Muhammad said, "No one is superior because he is an Arab or non-Arab, but only through his piety."[53]

Today Islam is practiced on every continent in the world with well over a billion practitioners. The Arabic word 'ummah' translates as 'community' or 'nation', tending more toward sociality than any kind of nationalism. Some regard the ummah as being the worldwide community of Muslims. A look today at the geography of those nations that are predominantly Muslim is testament to the lack of religious nationalism amongst the adherents.

The 14th century African writer named Abd al-Rahman ibn Khaldun (1332-1406) is recognized as the 'father of sociology'. Against the selfish call for personal salvation, he wrote that "Human society is necessary." Khaldun had been a politician and historian and is considered the first thinker to have made a science of the study of history and the first to have made a science in the study of human society. According to Khaldun, an individual unites their "efforts with those of his fellow men who by co-operating can produce enough for many times their number." Human co-operation fulfills "God's will of preserving the species. Society is therefore necessary to man…and it is society which forms the subject of this science."[54]

---

[52] Quoted by Robert Frager, *The Wisdom of Islam*, (Hauppauge, Barron's Educational Series, 2002) p137
[53] Quoted by Frager, p58
[54] Abd al-Rahman ibn Khaldun, *Kitab al-Ibar*, [The Book of Examples], trans. Charles Issawi, from *Anthology of Islamic Literature*, ed. James Kritzeck, (New York, Penguin Group, 1964) p275

The Prophet Muhammad was neither a king nor a politician, however two legacies that have been passed on by him are the disbelief in the Divine Right of Kings and a political science of mutual consultation or *al-Shura*. Neither Muhammad nor the Quran prescribe any kind of political state and it is understood that this was omitted so that the community could decide for itself specifically on what type of polity was best suited and most practical given the particular needs of the times or environment.[55] For a Muslim the community is in an important sense co-extensive with salvation. The Quran teaches us to love the earth and human society:

"O believers, consume not your goods between you in vanity, except there be trading, by your agreeing together." Surah 4:33

"Whoso desires the reward of this world, with Allah is the reward of this world and of the world to come." Surah 4:133

"It is He who produces gardens trellised, and untrellised, palm-trees, and crops diverse in produce, olives, pomegranates, like each to each, and each unlike to each. Eat of their fruits when they fructify, and pay the due thereof on the day of its harvest." Surah 6:143

"And on the earth are tracts neighboring each to each, and gardens and vines, and fields sown, and palms in pairs, and palms single, watered with one water; and some of them We prefer in produce above others." Surah 13:4

"And the earth –We stretched it forth, and cast on it firm mountains, and We caused to grow therein of every thing justly weighed, and there appointed for you a livelihood, and for those you provide not for... And we loose the winds fertilizing, and We send down out of heaven water, then We give it to you to drink, and you are not its treasurers." Surah 15: 16-20, 23

"And the cattle –He created them for you; in them is warmth, and uses various, and of them you eat, and there is beauty in them for you, when you bring them home to rest and when you drive them forth abroad to pasture; and they bear your loads unto a land that you never would reach, except with great distress." Surah 16:5-7

"It is he who sends down to you out of heaven water of which you have to drink, and of which trees, for you to pasture your herds, and thereby He brings forth for you crops, and olives, and palms, and vines, and all manner of fruit." Surah 16:10-12

"He who created the heavens and earth, and sent down for you out of heaven water; and We caused to grow therewith gardens full of loveliness whose trees you could never grow." Surah 27:61

"And the earth –We have stretched if forth, and cast on it firm mountains, and We caused to grow therein of every joyous kind for an insight and a reminder to every penitent servant. And we have sent down out of heaven water blessed, and caused to grow thereby gardens and grain of harvest and tall palm-trees with spathes compact, a provision for the servants, and thereby We revived a land that was dead. Even so is the coming forth." Surah 50:7-10

The city of Mecca where Muhammad was born and raised had long been a meeting place for many different tribes and peoples. Muhammad was influenced by the practice of providing water services for pilgrims, or *al-Siqayah*, and the housing of pilgrims, or *al-Rifadah*, as well as the *Hilf al-Fudul*, which was an alliance formed to relieve oppression and establish justice among communities.

While in the Western world there is a race to buy up and purchase by corporate giants like Coca-Cola and others all of the freshwater and drinking water around the world, this is in fact outlawed under Islamic law. (Surah 15:23) The services of providing water and housing are still provided for in Islamic society today.[56] Through the example of Muhammad, called the 'sunnah' -making commodities out of water, grass, and fire is prohibited.[57] One of the five pillars of wisdom for Muslims is to pay the *zakat*, or tax.

---

[55] Muhamed S. El-Awa, *On The Political System of The Islamic State*, trans. Ahmad Naji al-Imam, ed. Anwer Beg , (Indianapolis, American Trust Publications, 1980) p28, 34
[56] El-Awa, p5-7, 5n2
[57] Rodinson, p17

Each year all able Muslims must give to the poor according to fixed rates: 2.5% (or one-fortieth) of their wealth or assets. Farmers must give at least 5% of crops and a number of animals, and merchants 2.5% of the value of their goods.[58]

This attitude of sustainability is also found in the writings of Confucius, and it is from Confucius that we find one of the earliest formulations of the Golden Rule: Do unto others as you would have them do unto you. Confucius teaches:

"Virtue never stands alone. It is bound to have neighbors." 4:25

"A benevolent man helps others to take their stand in so far as he himself wishes to make his stand, and gets others there in so far as he himself wishes to get there. The ability to take as analogy what is near at hand can be called the method of benevolence." 6:30

"[Confucius] instructs under four heads: culture, moral conduct, doing one's best and being trustworthy in what one says." 7:25

"Make it your guiding principle to do your best for others and to be trustworthy in what you say, and move yourself to where rightness is, then you will be exalting virtue." 12:10

"The gentleman helps others to realize what is good in them; he does not help them to realize what is bad in them. The small man does the opposite." 12:16

"Do not impose on others what you yourself do not desire." 15:24

The *Tao Te Ching* teaches that the community is an important and distinct component of nature:

"When one cultivates virtue in his person, it becomes genuine virtue. When one cultivates virtue in his family, it becomes overflowing virtue. When one cultivates virtue in his community, it becomes lasting virtue. When one cultivates virtue in his country, it becomes abundant virtue. When one cultivates virtue in the world, it becomes universal. Therefore the person should be viewed as a person. The family should be viewed as a family. The community should be viewed as a community. The country should be viewed as a country. And the world should be viewed as the world. How do I know this to be the case in the world? Through this." 54

The Torah and Tanach of Judaism teach of the importance of community:

"Thou shalt not follow a multitude to do evil." Exodus 23:2

"Build ye houses, and dwell in them, and plant gardens, and eat the fruit of them, take ye wives, and beget sons and daughters; and take wives for your sons, and give your daughters to husbands, that they may bear sons and daughters; and multiply ye there, and be not diminished. And seek the peace of the city whither I have caused you to be carried away captive..." Jeremiah 29:5-7

The *Bhagavad-Gita* offers clues as to the sustenance of the community and it was this book that guided the Hindu lawyer and revolutionary Mohandas Gandhi, which teaches about "rejoicing in the welfare of all creatures..." (12:4)

"Fearlessness, purity of mind, steadfastness in knowledge and concentration, charity, self-control and sacrifice, study of the scriptures, austerity, and uprightness, non-violence, truth, freedom from anger, renunciation, tranquility, aversion to fault finding, compassion to living beings, freedom from covetousness, gentleness, modesty, and steadiness, vigour, forgiveness, fortitude, purity, freedom from malice and excessive pride –these O [Arjuna], are the endowments of him who is born with the divine nature." 16:1-3

The Problem of Community

He who gives no thought to difficulties in the future is sure to be beset by worries much closer at hand. -Confucius, *The Analects*, 15:12

The modern period has worked against the local community through the monopolization and homogenization of global economics. The centralized mass factory

---

[58] Akbar S. Ahmed, *Islam Today*, (New York, I.B. Tauris Publishers, 1999) p34

replaces the local handicraft or thrift shop, the factory farm replaces the local or family farm, the cinema replaces the local theater, the radio and television replace the live and local musician, the internet replaces the store clerk and worker from the customer. The list could go on without implying a moral indictment.

As many people are coming to realize -be they 'post-modernists' or 'primitivists' or what have you -just as with the philosophies of Plato, Aristotle, Socrates, Adam Smith, and Ralph Nader -the community ought to be understood as a fundamental entity or social institution. Despite the actions of power-worshiping Alexander the Great (d.323), the ancient Greek philosophers held no delusion that anything larger than a city-state, as for example the modern state or empire, is practical or sustainable.[59] This community view was held until at least the philosophy of the *Stoa*, for the Stoics embraced the Roman Empire. The last Stoic philosopher Emperor Marcus Aurelius seemed to be skeptical of the future of the community: "[E]very man lives only this present time, which is an indivisible point, and that all the rest of his life is either past or it is uncertain. Short then is the time which every man lives..."[60]

In the modern era, an environmental problem *per say* is the problem of community.

One of the most radical studies on the problem of community is that of the Christian pragmatist Josiah Royce (1855-1916). Josiah was born in California and educated in philosophy in Europe. Upon return the US he met Charles Peirce and befriended William James. A pragmatist was also his contemporary, George Santayana, said that as the heir to both Calvin and Hegel, Royce didn't look at causes and effects but at *motifs*.[61] In 1913 he delivered a series of lectures later published under the title *The Problem of Christianity*. In these lectures Royce attempted at making a theoretical solution to the problem of community. Royce states in the preface to the publication of his lectures that he "has *no* hypothesis whatever to offer as to how the Christian community originated."[62] Rather than a historical justification, Royce uses the philosophy of pragmatism to offer a solution to the problem of community.

"Historically speaking, the Christian church first discovered the Christian ideas. The founder of Christianity, so far as we know what his teachings were, seems not to have defined them adequately... Those, I say, are right who have held that the Church, rather than the person of the founder, ought to be viewed as the central idea of Christianity."

"Not through imitating nor yet through loving any mere individual human being can we be saved, but only through loyalty to the 'Beloved Community'."[63]

Royce begins his lectures by exposing this dilemma where it is held that many of the traditional definitions of the community (or kingdom) are found to be inadequate, ambiguous, or unknown.

"...the Kingdom of heaven appears, on it very face, to be some sort of social order, some sort of collective life, some kind of community. Yet the reported sayings do not, when taken by themselves, make perfectly explicit what that social order, what that community, is to which the name of Kingdom of Heaven

---

[59] Aristotle believed that "the best material of democracy is an agricultural population; there is no difficulty in forming a democracy where the mass of the people live by agriculture or tending of cattle." (P) *Politics*, 1138b6. However, ancient Greece had dozens of colonies, and of course, many slaves.
[60] Marcus Aurelius Antoninus, *Meditations*, trans. G. Long, in *The Stoic and Epicurean Philosophers*, ed. Whitney J. Oates, (New York, Random House, Inc., 1940) Book III, Section 10, p505
[61] George Santayana, *Character & Opinion In The United States*, (Garden City, Anchor Books, 1956)
[62] Josiah Royce, *The Problem of Christianity*, (Chicago, University of Chicago Press, 1968) p46
[63] Royce, p43, 45

is intended to apply. Tradition represents the earliest interpretation of the term by which the Disciples of Christ themselves, while he was yet speaking to them, as, in their own minds, more or less doubtful. Was the Master's kingdom to be of this world, or of some other?"

"But, at this point, we indeed meet the more baffling side of the doctrine of love. Jesus has no system of rules to expound for guiding the single acts of the philanthropic life…It is simply not the lover's task to set this present world right; it is his only to act in the spirit that is the Father's spirit, and that, when revealed and triumphant, at the judgement day, will set all things right."

"For the end of the world was very soon to come…The Lord has delayed his coming…The vision has become the Problem of Christianity."[64]

Royce seems to be trying to replace talk of a "Kingdom" which flickers with otherworldliness, with talk of "community". This community can be understood variously as a community of interpretation, a community of memory and hope, and a common understanding of it's own past and future. This is not metaphysical.

"Without presupposing any one metaphysical interpretation of experience, or of time, our definition shows where, in our experience and in our interpretations of the time-process, we are to look for a solution of the problem of the community."

"What is practically necessary is therefore this: Let your Christology be the practical acknowledgement of the Spirit of the Universal and Beloved Community."

"All else about your religion is the accident of your special race or nation or form of worship or training or accidental personal opinion, or devout private mystical experience –illuminating but capricious."

"Judge every social device, every proposed reform, every national and every local enterprise by the one test: *Does this help towards the coming of the universal community?*""

"We can look forward, then, to no final form, either of Christianity or of any other special religion. But we can look forward to a time when the work and insight of religion can become as progressive as is now the work of science."[65]

Another attempt at tackling the problem of community was made by the Christian theologian and physician Albert Schweitzer (1875-1965), who was awarded the Nobel Peace Prize in 1952. *The Conception of the Kingdom of God in the Transformation of Eschatology*, written in 1950, is Schweitzer's attempt to show how the belief in the 'imminent end of the world' can be transformed in a practical sense to the human community, or 'Kingdom' as he says. Schweitzer's attempt inevitably reveals how the relationship between faith and practice has developed over the last couple thousand years.

"The primitive Christian hope of an immediate coming of the Kingdom of God was based on the teaching of Jesus; yet the fact that it remained unfulfilled did not shatter Christian faith. How was this catastrophe dealt with? What transformation of the faith enabled it to survive the surrender of the original expectation?"

"In ancient and mediaeval times, Christians had not faith in progress, no urge to go forward, no idea that things could be moving onward and upward; yet it never occurred to them that they were in an unnatural situation so long as their religious life was based on the idea that the Kingdom of God lay far

---

[64] Royce, p71, 90, 92, 97, 98)
[65] Lectures IX and X quoted from *Classical American Philosophers*, ed. Max H. Fisch, (Englewood Cliffs, Prentice-Hall, Inc., 1951) p206, 241-242. Royce was a native of California and is quoted as having a hostile attitude toward Mexicans and Spanish Americans. "The life of a Spanish American in the mines in the early days, if frequently profitable, was apt to be a little disagreeable. It served him right of course. He had no business, as an alien, to come to the land God had given us. And if he was a native Californian, or 'greaser', then so much the worse for him. He was so much more our born foe; we hated his whole degenerate, thieving, landowning, lazy and discontented race. Some of them were now even bandits; most of them by this time were, with our help, more or less drunkards; and it was not our fault if they were not all rascals! So they deserved no better." Quoted by Roger Daniels in *Prisoners Without Trial*, (New York, Hill and Wang, 1993) p6

away in the future. It seemed obvious to them that passivity concerning the Kingdom was the only possible attitude.

"It is otherwise with those of the new age who are under the influence of the ethical affirmation of the world. What they think is that the Kingdom is something ethical and religious, to be conceived as developing in this world, and requiring ethical effort on the part of believers."[66]

Schweitzer sees the Protestant Founding Father Martin Luther (1483-1546) as carrying the torch in transforming the ideal of a heavenly Kingdom into the earthly political Kingdom, finding its ultimate fruition in the Protestant state. Schweitzer finds the seeds of modernization, capitalism, the sovereignty of the state, in the protest of Luther:

"[Luther] erects an ideal of Christian perfection which attaches real value to the state, to marriage, and to lawful occupations, and views daily labour, however humble, as service required by God. He feels himself moved to agree with the affirmation of life and the world, although he does not break away from the pessimistic judgement of the world which is involved in the later form of eschatology. In this he was prophetic of what was to happen later in the history of Protestantism."

"[S]o modern Protestantism substitutes its view of the Kingdom of God and its coming for the eschatological view which Jesus presented as if it really represented the original. Historically both are wrong; but religiously both are right."

"Only as it comes to be understood as something ethical and spiritual, rather than supernatural, as something to be realised rather than expected, can the Kingdom of God regain, in our faith, the force that it had for Jesus and the early Church."

"If Jesus thinks like his contemporaries about the world and what happens in it, then his view of the coming of the Kingdom of God must resemble that of later Judaism."

"We are no longer content, like the generations before us, to believe in the Kingdom that comes of itself at the end of time. Mankind to-day must either realise the Kingdom of God or perish. The very tragedy of our present situation compels us to devote ourselves in faith to its realisation.

"We are at the beginning of the end of the human race. The question before it is whether it will use for beneficial purposes or for purposes of destruction the power which modern science has placed in its hands."[67]

We can see that both Josiah Royce and Albert Schweitzer in their different ways tried to reinterpret Christianity so as to cast it into a solution for the problem of community. Schweitzer's work was written in a post-WWII Europe and he is careful not to interpret the impending threat of a nuclear holocaust as the fulfillment of a religious eschatology. For this reason, as we see, he favored the 'kingdom' as he configured it from the Hebrew Bible over that which can be ascertained from the New Testament. Royce believed that the formation of a 'universal community' ought to be the goal of Christianity. It doesn't seem, however, that Royce understood that the word 'catholic' already means universal. Bertrand Russell reached a similar conclusion when he predicted in 1930 in a study titled, 'Has Religion Made Useful Contributions to Civilization?' that "there is reason to suppose that a hundred years hence Catholicism will be the only effective representative of the Christian faith."[68]

The problem of community was also tackled by the American pragmatist John Dewey (1859-1952), particularly as presented in his 1927 lectures, *The Public and Its Problems* and 1934 lectures, *A Common Faith*. The metaphysical beliefs of Dewey are

---

[66] Albert Schweitzer, "The Conception of the Kingdom of God in the Transformation of Eschatology," in *Religion From Tolstoy to Camus*, trans. and ed. by Walter Kaufmann, (New York, Harper & Row, 1961) p407, 420
[67] Schweitzer, p418, 420, 420-421, 422, 424
[68] Bertrand Russell, "Has Religion Made Useful Contributions to Civilization?", in *Why I Am Not a Christian*, (b) p44

debatable, though it is known that he had worked hard to overcome the Calvinism of his childhood. Whereas Schweitzer believed that we ought to supplement the eschatological Kingdom of God for an earthly Kingdom, and Royce believed that the Christian message ought to be interpreted as the process of realizing a worldwide universal community, Dewey did not hold much faith in either the state or any kind of ideological absolutism.

In contrast to making the Kingdom of God a reality on earth, Dewey argued that there is "no such thing as religion in the singular. There is only a multitude of religions." Moreover, "Attempts to prove the universality prove too much or too little... [T]he differences among [religions] are so great and so shocking that any common element that can be extracted is meaningless." [69]

Dewey called the state, or earthly kingdom, a "pure myth", arguing that the "American democratic polity was developed out of genuine community life". While the search for the great community is not inconceivable, being fundamentally an intellectual problem and not one of political implementation, the great community "can never possess all the qualities which mark a local community". [70]

"The scientific revolution of the seventeenth century was the precursor of the industrial revolution of the eighteenth and nineteenth. In consequence, man has suffered the impact of an enormously enlarged control of physical energies without any corresponding ability to control himself and his own affairs. Knowledge divided against itself, a science to whose incompleteness is added an artificial split, has played its part in generating enslavement of men, women and children in factories in which they are animated machines to tend inanimate machines. It has maintained sordid slums, flurried and discontented careers, grinding poverty and luxurious wealth, brutal exploitation of nature and man in times of peace and high explosives and noxious gases in times of war." [71]

If both Royce's and Schweitzer's substitution for the Kingdom of God with a Kingdom of earth or modern state in its stead, they are not able to address the true dilemma facing us, according to Dewey's assessment. That is, neither a universal kingdom nor modern state handles the problem of community. Dewey writes:

"History is testimony to this fact. Men have never fully used the powers they possess to advance the good in life, because they have waited upon some power external to themselves and to nature to do the work they are responsible for doing. Dependence upon an external power is the counterpart of surrender of human endeavor... [Responsibility for human endeavor] involves no expectation of a millenium of good." [72]

"The problem of a democratically organized public is primarily and essentially an intellectual problem, in a degree to which the political affairs of prior ages offer no parallel.

"Our concern at this time is to state how it is that the machine age in developing the Great Society has invaded and partially disintegrated the small communities of former times without generating a Great Community." [73]

Through the advancements in the modern industrial era in production, distribution, and transportation, the public had been 'eclipsed', according to Dewey. A radical transformation that occurred in America led to the downfall of the local community. The public was eclipsed, or altered to such an extent as to be surmounted – in the modern age traditions and customs often disappear.

According to Dewey's assessment the problems facing communities in the modern era is the loss of organization and communication. Dewey believed that the

---

[69] John Dewey, *A Common Faith*, (New Haven, Yale University Press, 1934) (a) p7, 8
[70] John Dewey, *The Public and Its Problems*, (Athens, Ohio University Press, 1927) (b) p224, 111, 146, 211
[71] Dewey, *The Public and Its Problems*, (b) p174-175
[72] Dewey, *A Common Faith*, (a) p46
[73] Dewey, *The Public and Its Problems*, (b) p126-127

problem of community was at base "a moral one dependent upon intelligence and education." Instead of the antiquated individualism espoused by the philosophers of the Enlightenment, Dewey believed "the only possible solution" lies in something that seems simple:

> "[T]he perfecting of the means and ways of communication of meanings so that genuinely shared interests in the consequences of interdependent activities may inform desire and effort and thereby direct action."[74]

In this way, with greater communication and solidarity, might the community reemerge amidst the individual anonymity of the totalizing modern era. The battle between the universal community and the local community is often one of imperialism and secularism vs. tradition and culture. Solidarity and increased communication are what will safeguard the community in the age of monopoly and assimilation.

For similar reasons the Christian African-American scholars bell hooks and Cornel West emphasize the importance of the local community. The feminist bell hooks discusses the importance of building and sustaining communities as a means to solidarity and resistance.

> "When we talk about that which will sustain and nurture our growth as a people, we must once again talk about the importance of community. For one of the most vital ways we sustain ourselves is by building communities of resistance, places where we know we are not alone... It does not mean we can sit around and wait for God to take care of business. We are not alone when we build community together."[75]

The pragmatist Cornel West adds:

> "It is important to note the degree to which Black people in particular, and progressive people in general, are alienated and estranged from communities that would sustain and support us. We are often homeless. Our struggles against a sense of nothingness and attempts to reduce us to nothing are ongoing. We confront regularly the question: 'Where can I find a sense of home?' That sense of home can only be found in our construction of those communities of resistance bell talks about and the solidarity we can experience within them. Renewal comes through participating in community. That is the reason so many folks continue to go to church. In religious experience they find a sense of renewal, a sense of home. In community one can feel that we are moving forward, that struggle can be sustained. As we go forward as Black progressives, we must remember that community is not about homogeneity. Homogeneity is dogmatic imposition, pushing your way of life, your way of doing things onto somebody else. That is not what we mean by community. Dogmatic insistence that everybody think and act alike causes rifts among us, destroying the possibility of community. That sense of home that we are talking about and searching for is a place where we can find compassion, recognition of difference, of the importance of diversity, of our individual uniqueness."

Salvation vs. Propagation –An Either/Or?[76]

If in America there is an espousal of 'rugged individualism' the institution of the family is under siege. Divorce rates are higher in America than in any other country and that means there are a lot of single mothers. Along with the emphasis on individualism is the dishonor associated with families who stay together and who look after each other.

---

[74] Dewey, *The Public and Its Problems*, (b) p155. However, in 1939, Dewey was still asking, "Can society, especially a democratic society, exist without a basic consensus and community of beliefs?" In, *Freedom and Culture*, (Amherst, Prometheus Books, 1989) (c) p104
[75] bell hooks and Cornel West, *Breaking Bread*, (Boston, South End Press, 1991) p17
[76] My thanks to the philosopher William E. Mann for pointing out to me the similarities and differences between these two ideals.

Children are usually sent to day-care and then 12 years of public school, both parent's work, and the grandparents are put in a retirement home.

This is in part because many people don't like their parents and want to move away from "home" as soon as they can. Why is this the case today? Has this always been the case –that by nature families break up and brothers and sisters don't get along? The psychologist Sigmund Freud (1856-1939) did not think this was the case, and he never divorced nor did his children rebel against him. Freud helped rid psychology of the belief that women are susceptible to something called 'hysteria' and the disease 'neurasthenia, which were misogynist myths created by the European patriarchal structure. This naturalization of psychology has had benevolent political effects. Freud's daughter Anna became his greatest disciple and dedicated her life to continuing his work.

In discussing the family Sigmund used the thought-experiment of a primal family that had reached the "stage of communal life in the form of bands of brothers. In overpowering their father, the sons had made the discovery that a combination can be stronger than a single individual."[77] Freud does not see this 'event' of brotherhood as the dissolution of the family, but as the foundation of community, law, love, and renewed happiness.

Thus, rugged individualism, those who believe they are 'self-influenced' or 'self-invented', appears contrived and inauthentic alongside the brotherhood of strength. The salvation of the individual is trumped by the propagation of the family. While loners and rugged individualists love to site as a 'timeless' characteristic of 'human-nature' the 'sibling-rivalry' found in the story of Cain slaying Abel -thinking this story set some kind of universal precedent- when in fact, the Torah instructs us to *not* do such a thing, to *not* follow this example.

"And if thy brother be waxen poor, and his means fail with thee; then thou shalt uphold him: as a stranger and a settler shall he live with thee. Take thou no interest of him or increase; but fear Yhwh; that thy brother may live with thee. Thou shalt not give him the money upon interest, nor give him thy victuals for increase." Leviticus 25:35-37

"Hear the causes between your brethren, and judge righteously between a man and his brother, and the stranger that is with him. Ye shall not respect the persons in judgement; ye shall hear the small and the great alike; ye shall not be afraid of the face of any man." Deuteronomy 1:16-17

"And thou shalt keep His statutes, and His commandments, which I command thee this day, that it may go well with thee, and with thy children after thee, and that thou mayest prolong thy days upon the land, which the Lord thy God giveth thee, for ever." Deuteronomy 4:40

"And thou shalt rejoice in thy feast, thou, and thy son, and thy daughter, and thy man-servant, and thy maid-servant, and the Levite, and the stranger, and the fatherless, and the widow, that are within thy gates." Deuteronomy 16:14

The philosopher Bertrand Russell (1872-1970) saw something different when he read the Bible:

"In emphasizing the soul, Christian ethics has made itself completely individualistic. I think it is clear that the net result of all the centuries of Christianity has been to make men more egotistic, more shut up in themselves, than nature made them; for the impulses that naturally take a man outside the walls of his ego are those of sex, parenthood, and patriotism or herd instinct. Sex the church did everything it could to decry and degrade; family affection was decried by Christ himself and by the bulk of his followers; and patriotism could find no place among the subject populations of the Roman Empire. The polemic against

---

[77] Sigmund Freud, *Civilization and Its Discontents*, trans. James Strachey, (New York, W.W. Norton & Company, Inc., 1989) (a) p55. Although Freud had changed his mind many times over fundamental questions, to the chagrin of 'anti-Freudians', his theory of the community of brothers was recurring throughout much of his work.

the family in the Gospels is a matter that has not received the attention it deserves. The church treats the Mother of Christ with reverence, but He Himself showed little of this attitude. 'Woman, what have I to do with thee?' (John 2:4) is His way of speaking to her."[78]

Russell seems to be referring to such passages of the New Testament as:

"For if you love those loving you, what reward do you have?" Matthew 5:46

"Further, brother will deliver up brother to death, and a father his child, and children will rise up against parents and will have them put to death." Matthew 10:21

"Do not think I came to put peace upon the earth; I came to put, not peace, but a sword. For I came to cause division, with a man against his father, and a daughter against her mother, and a young wife against her mother-in-law. Indeed, a man's enemies will be persons of his own household. He that has greater affection for father or mother than for me is not worthy of me." Matthew 10:34-37

"And everyone that has left houses or brothers or sisters or father or mother or children or lands for the sake of my name will receive many times more and will inherit everlasting life." Matthew 19:29

"Furthermore, brother will deliver brother over to death, and a father a child, and children will rise up against parents and have them put to death." Mark 13:12

"And if you love those loving you, of what credit is it to you? For even the sinners love those loving them. And if you do good to those doing good to you, really of what credit is it to you? Even the sinners do the same." Luke 6:32-33

"If anyone comes to me and does not hate his father and mother and wife and children and brothers and sisters, yes, and even his own soul, he cannot be my disciple." Luke 14:26

"Truly I say to you, There is no one who has left house or wife or brothers or parents or children for the sake of the kingdom of God who will not in any way get many times more in this period of time, and in the coming system of things everlasting life." Luke 18:29-30

Russell concludes: "All this means the breakup of the biological family tie for the sake of creed –an attitude which had a great deal to do with the intolerance that came into the world with the spread of Christianity."[79]

The Chinese philosopher Confucius had taught two and a half millennia ago[80]:

"A young man should be a good son at home and an obedient young man abroad, sparing in speech but trustworthy in what he says, and should love the multitude at large but cultivate the friendship of his fellow men." 1:6

"When the gentleman feels profound affection for his parents, the common people will be stirred to benevolence. When he does not forget friends of long standing, the common people will not shirk their obligations to other people." 8:2

"Love your fellow men." 12:22

"While at home hold yourself in a respectful attitude; when serving in an official capacity be reverent; when dealing with others do your best. These are qualities that cannot be put aside, even if you go and live among the barbarians." 13:19

Lao Tzu taught of a benign relationship between the individual, humanity, and the world.

"The best man is like water. Water is good; it benefits all things and does not compete with them… The best man in his dwelling loves the earth. In his heart, he loves what is profound. In his associations, he loves humanity." 8

The Quran teaches of the importance of family relations, of looking after the poor, the stranger, and single women:

"[T]here shall be for divorced women provision honourable –an obligation on the godfearing." Surah 2:243

"To the men a share of what parents and kinsmen leave, and to the women a share of what parents and kinsmen leave, whether it be little or much, a share apportioned; and when the division is attended by kinsmen and orphans and the poor, make provision for them out of it, and speak to them honourable words." Surah 4:8-9

---

[78] Russell, "Has Religion Made Useful Contributions to Civilization?", (b) p34
[79] Russell, (b) p34-35
[80] Confucius, *The Analects*, trans. D.C. Lau, (New York, Penguin Books, 1979)

"Be kind to parents, and the near kinsman, and to orphans, and to the needy, and to the neighbor who is of kin, and to the neighbor who is a stranger, and to the companion at your side, and to the traveler, and to that your right hands own." Surah 4:40

"The Lord has decreed you shall not serve any but Him, and to be good to parents, whether one or both of them attains old age with thee; say not to them 'Fie' neither chide them, but speak unto them words respectful, and lower to them the wing of humbleness out of mercy and say, 'My Lord, have mercy upon them, as they raised me up when I was little.'" Surah 17:23-29

"And slay not your children for fear of poverty; We will provide for you and them; surely the slaying of them is a grievous sin." Surah 17:33

"And of His signs is that He created you of dust; then lo, you are mortals, all scattered abroad. And of His signs is that He created for you, of yourselves, spouses, that you might repose in them, and he has set between you love and mercy. Surely in that are signs for a people who consider. And of His signs is the creation of the heavens and earth and the variety of your tongues and hues." Surah 30:21

In the *Bhagavad-Gita* we find the Hindu warrior Arjuna addressing the deity:

"I do not long for victory, O Krsna, nor kingdom nor pleasures...

"Teachers, fathers, sons, and also grandfathers; uncles and fathers-in-law, grandsons and brothers-in-law, and other kinsmen. These I would not consent to kill, though killed myself...

"So it is not right that we slay our kinsmen... Indeed, how can we be happy... if we kill our own people?

"Even if these whose minds are overpowered by greed see no wrong in the destruction of the family and no crime in treachery to friends;

"Why should we not have the wisdom to turn away from this sin... we who see the wrong in the destruction of the family?

"In the ruin of the family, its ancient laws are destroyed: and when the laws perish, the whole family yields to lawlessness.

"And when lawlessness prevails... the women of the family become corrupted, and when women are corrupted, confusion of castes arises...

"And to hell does this confusion bring the family itself as well as those who have destroyed it.

"By the misdeeds of those who destroy a family and create confusion of *varnas* [castes], the immemorial laws of the race and the family are destroyed...

"Alas, what a great sin have we resolved to commit in striving to slay our own people through our greed for the pleasures of the kingdom!

"Far better would it be for me if the sons of Dhrtarastra, with weapons in hand, should slay me in the battle, while I remain unresisting and unarmed." 1:32, 34-35, 37-43, 45-46

The Buddha taught:

"For one in the habit of showing respect, of always honoring elder ones, four qualities increase: life, complexion, ease, and strength." 109

In Judaism the community and the family are fundamental entities. In the book of Genesis Yhwh instructs Abraham and his family to leave their native country of Sumer and 'wander'.

"Get thee out of thy country, and from thy kindred, and from thy father's house, unto the land that I will show thee. And I will make of thee a great nation, and I will bless thee, and make thy name great... and in thee shall all the families of the earth be blessed." Genesis 12:1-3

The Torah teaches that all human beings, regardless of race or skin color, are descendent of Adam and Eve. The Jewish people are Yhwh's 'chosen people' in that they are to reside amongst the non-Jewish nations and cultures, and are to be ethical while not being assimilated. The Jewish ethic is an 'international' one, in the sense that they believe the law ought be applied to others such as strangers and the weak.

"And if a stranger shall sojourn among you... ye shall have one statute, both for the stranger, and for him that is born in the land." Numbers 9:14

"One law and one ordinance shall be both for you, and for the stranger that sojourneth with you." Numbers 15:16

"For the children of Israel, and for the stranger and for the settler among them, shall these six cities be for refuge, that every one that killeth any person through error may flee thither." Numbers 35:15

"And when ye reap the harvest of your land, thou shalt not wholly reap the corner of they field, neither shalt thou gather the gleaning of they harvest. And thou shall not glean thy vineyard, neither shalt thou gather the fallen fruit of they vineyard, thou shalt leave them for the poor and for the stranger... Ye shall not steal; neither shall ye deal falsely, nor lie one to another... Thou shalt not oppress thy neighbor, nor rob him; the wages of a hired servant shall not abide with thee all night until the morning. Thou shalt not curse the deaf, nor put a stumbling block before the blind... Ye shall do no unrighteousness in judgement; thou shalt not respect the person of the poor, nor favour the person of the mighty; but in righteousness shalt thou judge thy neighbor. Thou shalt not go up and down as a talebearer among thy people; neither shalt thou stand idly by the blood of thy neighbor... Thou shalt not hate thy brother in thy heart; thou shalt surely rebuke thy neighbor, and not bear sin because of him. Thou shalt not take vengeance, nor bear any grudge against the children of thy people, but thou shalt love thy neighbor as thyself." Leviticus 19:9-18

"And when ye reap the harvest of your land, thou shalt not wholly reap the corner of thy field, neither shalt thou gather the gleaning of thy harvest; thou shalt leave them for the poor, and for the stranger." Leviticus 23:22

"Love ye therefore the stranger; for ye were strangers in the land of Egypt." Deuteronomy 10:19

"And the Levite, because he hath no portion nor inheritance with thee, and the stranger, and the fatherless, and the widow, that are within thy gates, shall come, and shall eat and be satisfied." Deuteronomy 14:29

"When thou reapest thy harvest in thy field, and hast forgot a sheaf in the field, thou shalt not go back to fetch it; it shall be for the stranger, for the fatherless, and for the widow... When thou beatest thine olive-tree, thou shalt not go over the boughs again; it shall be for the stranger, for the fatherless, and for the widow. When though gatherest the grapes of the vineyard, thou shalt not glean it after thee; it shall be for the stranger, for the fatherless, and for the widow." Deuteronomy 24:19-21

"Cursed be he that perverteth the justice due to the stranger, fatherless, and widow." Deuteronomy 27:19

"And the Lord will make thee overabundant for good, in the fruit of thy body, and in the fruit of thy cattle, and in the fruit of thy land." Deuteronomy 28:11

Similarly, the New Testament often paraphrases or quotes the Tanach, which makes up over eighty percent of the Christian bible, in addition to the ethic of Jesus.

"Honor [your] father and [your] mother, and, You must love your neighbor as yourself... If you want to be perfect, go sell your belongings and give to the poor and you will have treasure in heaven, and come be my follower." Matthew 19:19, 21 (the first sentence paraphrases Exodus 20:12)

"Do not murder, Do not commit adultery, Do not steal, Do not bear false witness, Do not defraud, Honor your father and mother... Go sell what things you have and give to the poor, and you will have treasure in heaven, and come by my follower." Mark 10:19, 21 (the first sentence paraphrases Exodus 20:13-16, 12)

"Also, just as you want men to do to you, do the same way to them." Luke 6:31 (Golden Rule)

"You must love your neighbor as yourself." Luke 10:27 (This quotation is from the Hebrew bible, Leviticus 18:19, and is recited again in the New Testament in Romans 13:9 and James 2:8.)

"Honor your father and mother... Sell all the things you have and distribute to poor people, and you will have treasure in the heavens; and come be my follower." Luke 18:20, 22 (Exodus 20:12)

"For you have the poor always with you, but me you will not have always." John 12:8

"[I]f your enemy is hungry, feed him; if he is thirsty, give him something to drink; for by doing this you will heap fiery coals upon his head." Romans 12:20 (copied from Proverbs 25:21)

"Now I say to the unmarried persons and the widows, it is well for them that they remain even as I am. But if they do not have self-control, let them marry, for it is better to marry than to be [burned]." 1 Corinthians 7:8-9

"Wherefore, now that you have put away falsehood, speak truth each one of you with his neighbor, because we are members belonging to one another." Ephesians 4:25

"Do not severely criticize an older man. To the contrary, entreat him as a father, younger men as brothers, older women as mothers, younger women as sisters with all chasteness.

"Honor widows that are actually widows. But if any widow has children or grandchildren, let these learn first to practice godly devotion in their own household and to keep paying a due compensation to their parents and grandparents... Certainly if anyone does not provide for those who are his own, and especially for those who are members of his household, he has disowned the faith and is worse than a person without faith." 1 Timothy 5:1-4,8

"The form of worship that is clean and undefiled from the standpoint of our God and Father is this: to look after orphans and widows in their tribulation, and to keep oneself without spot from the world." James 1:27

As with the communitarianism and tolerance wrought in the Constitution of Medina, the Quran teaches:

"They will question thee concerning the orphans. Say: 'To set their affairs aright is good. And if you intermix with them, they are your brothers." Surah 2:218

"Give the orphans their property, and do not exchange the corrupt for the good; and devour not their property with your property; surely that is a crime." Surah 4:3

"...secure justice for orphans." Surah 4:126

"There is no fault in the weak and the sick and those who find nothing to expend." Surah 9:92

"The freeing of a slave, or giving food upon a day of hunger to an orphan near of kin or a needy man in misery; that he become of those who believe and counsel each other to be steadfast, and counsel each other to be merciful." Surah 90:14-17

"As for the orphan, do not oppress him, and as for the beggar, scold him not." Surah 93:10-11

Sexuality and Power

As we see with the examples given above, the family structure plays a crucial role in the creation and maintenance of the community. Oftentimes this structure comes to play a political role over sexuality itself. In both ancient societies and in the US today sexuality plays a large role in political and social institutions such as the community and the state. In some states (as we see in the US) certain kinds of sexuality are normalized and others are outlawed.

Ancient Greece is usually taken for the model of a society tolerant of homosexuality. Though Socrates was married with children, the *Symposium* recounts him having sexual affairs with younger men and this is said to be true of Socrates' student Plato as well. While such instances are documented, it should be remembered that people like Socrates and Plato were not typical of their community if they were exceptional. Anaxagoras, Protagoras, and Socrates got in legal trouble in Athens for their religious beliefs. Aristotle left Athens because he feared something similar would happen to him. Contemporary philosophers such as Michel Foucault, Alexander Nehamas, and Paul Woodruff have disputed this particular notion that homosexuality was socially accepted in ancient Greece.[81]

The three Abrahamic monotheisms of Judaism, Christianity, and Islam all outlaw homosexuality. When instituted politically or compulsorily it can be said that these laws are anti-homosexual. Whether a community of people ought to be allowed to institute its own laws is not a question of logic but of politics. Homophobia, on the other hand -the fear and hatred of homosexuals -is a particularly modern and Western problem found almost exclusively in both democratic and fascist states, alike. For in both democratic and fascist states the morality that would guide such laws would be purely prejudicial and arbitrary, not being based upon nature or revelation. It is just as often that sexuality

---

[81] Check the interview "Why the Ancient World Was Not a Golden Age, But What We Can Learn from It Anyway", in *The Foucault Reader*, ed. Paul Rabinow, (New York, Pantheon Books, 1984) p344. And Alexander Nehamas and Paul Woodruff's Introduction to their translation of Plato's *Symposium*, (Indianapolis, Hackett Publishing, 1989) xv

becomes understood in terms of (political) power and the mystery of sexuality is exchanged for imperialism, or the secularization of desire and bias.

In the Tanach we find several references to erotic love. The book of Proverbs teaches, "A lovely hind and a graceful doe, let her breasts satisfy thee at all times; With her love be thou ravished always." (Proverbs 5:19) The Song of Songs (in the Old Testament called 'The Song of Solomon') describes in erotic detail a woman's body, including her navel, thighs, belly, and breasts. (1:13, 7:4, 7:7, 7:8, 8:10)

In the New Testament, however, erotic love is sinful, and the Greek word for erotic love, *Eros*, appears only once, malapropos. This might be because of the way in which Jesus was conceived –God impregnated a mortal woman and this stands as an example of an 'immaculate conception', much like Zeus had sex with a woman named Alcmene who bore Heracles. Some have argued that one immaculate conception maculates the rest.[82]

In the 'Sermon on the Mount' of the New Testament, Jesus says:

"But I say to you that everyone that keeps on looking at a woman so as to have a passion for her has already committed adultery with her in his own heart." Matthew 5:28

"Whoever marries a divorced woman commits adultery." Matthew 5:32

One aspect that separates Christianity from both Judaism and Islam is the non-imperative to circumcise. Though Jesus himself was in all probability circumcised, as were most of the apostles, something which separates Christianity from most other religions is the imperative given to all able-bodied Christian men. Jesus decrees:

"For there are eunuchs that were born such from their mother's womb, and there are eunuchs that were made eunuchs by men, and there are eunuchs that have made themselves eunuchs on account of the kingdom of the heavens. Let him that can make room for it make room for it." Matthew 19:12

As we later find out, this is for an important reason.

"[F]or in the resurrection neither do men marry nor are women given in marriage, but are as angels in heaven." Matthew 22:30

"[B]ecause, look! days are coming in which people will say, 'Happy are the barren women, and the wombs that did not give birth and the breasts that did not nurse!" Luke 23:29

Sex, translated here as 'fornication', itself is a sin.

"[A]bstain from things polluted by idols and from fornication..." Acts 15:20

"No the body is not for fornication, but for the Lord... Flee from fornication. Every other sin that a man may commit is outside his body, but he that practices fornication is sinning against his own body." 1 Corinthians 6:13, 18

"Neither let us practice fornication, as some of them committed fornication, only to fall, twenty-three thousand [of them] in one day." 1 Corinthians 10:8

"Let fornication... not even be mentioned among you... For you know... that no fornicator... has any inheritance in the kingdom of the Christ and of God." Ephesians 5:3,5

"Deaden, therefore your body members that are upon the earth as respects fornication, uncleanness, sexual appetite, hurtful desire, and covetousness, which is idolatry. On account of those things the wrath of God is coming." Colossians 3:5-6

"For this is what God wills, the sanctifying of you, that you abstain from fornication... [and] sexual appetite..." 1 Thessalonians 4:3,5

"[K]eep abstaining from fleshly desires..." 1 Peter 2:11

The Quran teaches of a different kind of paradise:

"There is no fault in you touching the proposal to women you offer, or hid in your hearts; Allah knows that you will be mindful of them; but do not make troth with them secretly without you speak[ing] honourable words." 2:235

---

[82] Claimed by Friedrich Nietzsche, *The Antichrist*, trans. H.L. Mencken, (Tucson, See Sharp Press, 1999)

In Paradise there will be gardens, green pastures, gushing and outpoured waters, spreading shade, fruit, palm-trees, thornless lote-trees, serried acacias, pomegranates, cool pavilions, and plenty of comfort. Spouses are purified there (3:13, 4:60), and there are good and comely maidens (55:56, 70), and chaste and amorous virgins (56:35-37).

The philosopher Emmanuel Levinas attempted to show how -just as with the human conceptions of 'time', 'parenthood', 'brotherhood', and other social institutions -sexuality often becomes understood in terms of power, rather than as an ethical relation. It is very often that just one teaching or one definition is taken as the complete and final definition of something: such is the rule of conformity. Under ideologies of conformity sexuality is reduced to a kind of knowledge or power, leaving no room for anticipation or hunger. Levinas wrote: "The unity of these situations –death, sexuality, paternity –until now appeared only in relation to the notion of power that they exclude."[83] Levinas reveals that love is not a modality of power or identification with some ideal or principle. Instead he shows how in the erotic there is an "absence of fusion". Instead of sexuality as power, there is something more than contact. This is the caress. Levinas writes:

"The seeking of the caress constitutes its essence by the fact that the caress does not know what it seeks. This 'not knowing', this fundamental disorder, is the essential. It is like a game with something slipping away, a game absolutely without project or plan, not with what can become ours or us, but with something other, always other, always inaccessible, and always still to come. The caress is the anticipation of this pure future, without content. It is made up of this increase of hunger, of ever richer promises, opening new perspectives onto the ungraspable. It feeds on countless hungers."[84]

The Talmudist Adin Steinsaltz (b.1937) wrote that:

"The sages treated the sexual urge as natural instinct like any other, rather than as something to be condemned... In general, the sages were aware of the power of the sexual drive, and their view is epitomized in the saying: *Ein epitropus le'arayot* (there is no guardian over sexual affairs)."[85]

Rabbis Morris Kertzer (1910-1983) and Lawrence Hoffman have written that:

"Unlike Christianity...Judaism never looked down upon bodily pleasure, and did not associate sex with sinfulness. Monasticism, chastity, and celibacy never became Jewish ideals... The Rabbis therefore regarded sex not only as necessary but even as desirable... Eventually it even became the custom to consider Shabbat a time when married couples could celebrate their love by having sex together."[86]

In his work, *The Heart of Islam*: the Shia scholar Seyyed Hossein Nasr (b.1933) wrote that, "In Islam, as in Judaism, sexuality itself is sacred and a blessing. Therefore, there is no need of a sacrament, in the Christian sense, to sanctify it." If it is believed that the Muslim paradise described above is just a reflection of people's erotic desire, Nasr tells us, "In reality every joy and delight here below, especially sexuality, which is sacred for Islam, is the reflection of a paradisal prototype, not vice versa."[87]

The psychologist Freud has written at length on the dangers of curtailing the natural sexual instinct. This is summed up in one of his last books, *Civilization and Its Discontents*, written in 1929.

"A factor... hostile to civilization must already have been at work in the victory of Christendom over the heathen religions. For it was very closely related to the low estimation put upon earthly life by the Christian doctrine."[88]

---

[83] Levinas, p92
[84] Levinas, p89
[85] Adin Steinsaltz, *The Essential Talmud*, trans. Chaya Galai, (New York, Basic Books, 1976) p141-142
[86] Rabbi Morris N. Kertzer, Revised by Rabbi Lawrence A. Hoffman, *What is a Jew?*, (New York, Collier Books, 1993) p147
[87] Seyyed Hossein Nasr, *The Heart of Islam*, (New York, HarperCollins, 2002) p184, 26
[88] Freud, *Civilization and Its Discontents*, (a) p38

"...civilization is a process in the service of Eros [erotic love], whose purpose is to combine single human individuals, and after that families, then races, peoples and nations, into one great unity, the unity of mankind. Why this has to happen, we do not know."[89]

Freud pondered the supposition that curtailing our sexual instinct can lead to aggression. He found that while this thesis could always be further examined and simplified, such a notion cannot be ruled out.[90]

"[T]he prevention of an erotic satisfaction calls up a piece of aggressiveness against the person who has interfered with the satisfaction..."[91]

This resembles what Freud had noted over 20 years earlier (1908):

"Our civilization is, generally speaking, founded on the suppression of instincts."

"The retardation of sexual development and sexual activity at which our education and culture aim is certainly not injurious to begin with... But in the majority of cases the fight against sexuality absorbs the available energy of the character..."[92]

Health and Economics

Another vital component of community is health. While each religion has its own particularities, rituals, and demands, some push for healthy living more than others. Some religions have fairly strict laws about food and diet in order to ensure health and safety. While the particular diets and prohibitions of certain belief systems may strike us in the modern world as arbitrary, this does not rule out a practical or pragmatic function.

In the Torah, we find the prohibition against eating flesh and blood.

"Only flesh with the life thereof, which is the blood thereof, shall ye not eat." Genesis 9:4

"No soul of you shall eat blood, neither shall any stranger that sojourneth among you eat blood." Leviticus 17:12

"Only ye shall not eat the blood; thou shalt pour it out upon the earth as water." Deuteronomy 12:16

"Thou shalt not eat any abominable thing." Deuteronomy 14:3

The book of Leviticus gives a list of animals that observant Jews ought not to eat. Camels, badgers, rabbits, pigs, any fish that is without fins or scales (11:4), vultures, falcons, ravens, ostriches, hawks, owls, pelicans, storks, herons, bats (11:12-19), swarming bugs (11:23), weasels, mice, lizards, crocodiles, and chameleons (11:29). The book of Deuteronomy adds to this list ospreys, gledes, semews (14:11), and tells us not to eat anything that died itself, though this may be given to a stranger. (14:21) If someone accidentally eats unkosher food, they are instructed to wash their clothes and bathe. (Leviticus 17:15)

If the story of Abraham and Isaac represents the end of human sacrifice, animal sacrifice became a central aspect of Judaism. According to the Talmudist Adin Steinsaltz, animal sacrifice, called the "laying on of hands", was a procedure done with

---

[89] Freud, (a) p80-81

[90] While Jesus believed wars occurred from necessity (Matthew 24:6), his brother James seems to hold to a view that sexuality is the cause of wars. He wrote, "From what source are there wars and from what source are there fights among you? Are they not from this source, namely, from your cravings for sensual pleasure...?" (4:1)

[91] Freud, (a) p103

[92] Sigmund Freud, "'Civilized' Sexual Morality and Modern Nervousness", trans. E.B. Herford and E. Colburn Mayne, in *Sexuality and Psychology of Love*, ed. Philip Rieff, (New York, Collier Books, 1963) (b) p25, 33

strict precision and with clean instruments to provide safe consumption.[93] Such precautions concerning health are absent in the New Testament.[94]

"To take a meal with unwashed hands does not defile a man." Matthew 15:20

"Thus [Jesus] declared all foods clean." Mark 7:19

"He that feeds on my flesh and drinks my blood has everlasting life, and I shall resurrect him at the last day; for my flesh is true food, and my blood is true drink." John 6:54-55

"Everything that is sold in a meat market keep eating, making no inquiry on account of your conscience." 1 Corinthians 10:25

It is for this reason that when the Black Plague struck Europe in 1348, within 3 years some 20-25 million people died, or one in every three Christians. Some have argued this ratio is much higher. Jews, however, did not die from the plague (which came from food contamination) because of their strict dietary laws.[95]

The Quran recommends a diet very similar to the kosher one, and is called *halal* in Arabic.

"These things only has He forbidden you: carrion, blood, and flesh of swine, what has been hallowed to other than Allah." Surah 2:167

"O believers, when you stand up to pray wash your faces, and your hands up to the elbows, and wipe your heads, and your feet up to the ankles. If you are defiled, purify yourself." Surah 5:8

"Allah loves those who cleanse themselves." Surah 9:109

As David Waines reports in his *Introduction To Islam*, animal sacrifice is something done to feed the hungry. "The sacrifice of animals and the distribution of the meat to the poor are performed not only in Mecca but throughout the world wherever Muslims celebrate away from the holy city itself."[96]

While we civilized westerners like to look down on animal sacrifice as barbaric, few of us know where our food comes from or what the conditions were like when it was either harvested or killed.[97] The consumers advocate Ralph Nader has done a great deal of work to expose the unsafe and unsterile conditions under which much of the US meat industry is maintained. In the 1960's Nader worked tirelessly (no pun intended) to get some legislation passed to increase the amount of health inspection required for the meatpacking corporations. Nader criticized the antiquated and highly inadequate Meat Inspection Act of 1906, siting research which found that the industry allowed meat to come into contact with such things as manure, pus, and filth; instruments were not cleaned, chemicals and preservatives were often used, as well as false and deceptive labeling on packages, among other things.[98] Nader's effort resulted in the 1967 Smith-Foley bill, which passed in the Senate on December 6.[99]

---

[93] Steinsaltz, p188-189

[94] James Carroll says that although the book of Isaiah (1:11) is against animal sacrifice, Jesus was not against animal sacrifice. (Carroll, p112-113). Saint Paul was critical of vegetarianism. Check his letter to the Romans 14:3, 20. The Gospel of Mark depicts Jesus as killing 2,000 pigs simultaneously by drowning them. (Mark 5:13)

[95] Carroll, p338, 403. The historian Francis Jennings writes that while Native Americans shared their food and crops with the European colonists, in time the Europeans began destroying the Native American's crops in an attempt to starve them and drive them out of the land. (Jennings, p19, 33)

[96] David Waines, *An Introduction To Islam*, (Cambridge, Cambridge University Press, 1995) p92

[97] A religion known as Santeria won a case in the US Supreme Court protecting their right to ritually sacrifice chickens. *Church of the Lukumi Babalu Aye v. City of Hialeah*

[98] Ralph Nader, "We're Still in the Jungle," originally published in The New Republic, 7/15/67. *The Ralph Nader Reader*, (New York, Seven Stories Press, 2000) (b) p263

[99] Justin Martin, *Nader: Crusader, Spoiler, Icon*, (New York, Basic Books, 2002) p68-69

As Nader would be quick to tell us –we have a long way to go. In 2002 he reported:

"[F]our giant companies control 83 percent of the nation's cattle slaughter and about 63 percent of the hog slaughter in the country... [T]hese large meatpackers are also moving into livestock production like those massive hog farms that lead to environmental havoc and pollute water... The meatpackers have reported record profits in the last four years as the rate of family farm loss continues to increase."[100]

Although in the spirit of the Common Law, American economic policies are written to protect corporations and the wealthy, Nader says our modern economic policies are morally impoverished.

"Economic theory is so empirically undernourished that economists ought to hit the road and see the other America –in devastated inner cities, the sprawling waste of the suburbs, the impoverished rural countryside with its closed or decrepit Wal-Marted main streets and shuttered family farms."[101]

In *The Good Fight* (2004) Ralph discusses some of the problems facing us in the 21st century. While the government sets aside millions of dollars to bail out failed corporations, Nader has been listening to what American engineers have been trying to tell the government and us citizens –that the American infrastructure is crumbling. For example, the American Society of Civil Engineers (ASCE) has estimated (2001 and 2002) that some 1.3 trillion dollars is urgently needed to repair the problems of our infrastructure. "These include schools, drinking water systems, solid waste, sewage systems, airports, dams, navigable waterways, public transit, bridges, and roads."[102]

"Federal policy over the past century has largely failed to promote an energy system based on safe, secure, economically affordable, and environmentally benign energy sources. The tax code, budget appropriations, and regulatory processes overwhelmingly have been used to subsidize dependence on fossil fuels and nuclear power. The result: increased sickness and premature deaths; depleted family budgets; acid rain destruction of lakes, forests, and crops; oil spill contamination; polluted rivers and loss of aquatic species; and the long term peril of climate change and radioactive waste dumps, not to mention dependency on external energy sources. There is an alternative."

"Our country has more problems than it deserves and more solutions than it uses. It is time for the United States to stop letting ExxonMobil, Peabody Coal, and Westinghouse shape our energy policy and for our misguided elected officials to adopt an energy strategy based on clean, renewable energy and conservation. Future generations will thank us for curbing our fossil fuel appetite."[103]

One enormous blind spot of modern economics is its dismissal of 'externalities'. Externalities, according to modern economic theory, are factors or results that do not figure into the kind of efficiency that is measured by the profit directed modern economic algorithm –they are non-market values. According to modern economic theory a tree standing has no value –it is only when we cut this tree down and turn it into something on the market that it has value. The rules of modern industrialism and capitalism do not seem to leave room for tomorrow or for there to be efficiency for the parts of this world that are natural –these realms fall 'external' to economic efficiency. Some critics of this popular Western economic ethic point out that this policy amounts to generational-

---

[100] Ralph Nader, "The Meat Monopoly," 5/25/02. *In Pursuit of Justice: Collected Writings 2000-2003*, (New York, Seven Stories Press, 2004) (c) p366-367
[101] Nader, *The Good Fight*, (a) p17-18
[102] Nader, *The Good Fight*, (a) p214; and "Rebuild Our Infrastructure", *In Pursuit of Justice: Collected Writings 2000-2003*, (c) p241-242. www.asce.org/reportcard
[103] Nader, "Dick Cheney and Energy Conservation", *In Pursuit of Justice: Collected Writings 2000-2003*, (c) p147, 148

discrimination. Our children and our children's children will be the ones who suffer the results that are 'external' to personal greed or laissez-faire, economic liberalism.[104]

Since 1995 during the Clinton administration, laws requiring corporations to clean work sites where they have the polluted the environment (called 'Superfund' sites) have expired and have not been renewed. President Bush asked the American taxpayers to pay for the more than 11,000 toxic Superfund sites in America, created by corporations. Nader estimated in 2005 that 1.27 billion dollars of taxpayer money would be needed to clean up all of the pollution that corporations have left behind as they move from place to place, wreaking havoc. Corporations are still allowed to use the General Mining Act of 1872 which allows companies to buy federal land for five dollars an acre and pay no royalties for gold, copper, zinc, and other minerals which are mined. It has recently been estimated that mines have polluted over 40 percent of the headwaters in Western watersheds.[105]

Once one of the most powerful men in the world, after losing the 2000 election to Bush, Al Gore published a book exposing the rate of US pollution. He wrote: "of every nation's relative contribution to global warming, the United States is responsible for more greenhouse gas pollution than South America, Africa, the Middle East, Australia, Japan, and Asia –all put together."[106]

Modern economics in practice can be seen to have had dismal effects in other developing nations as well. The IMF and World Bank have forever changed the landscapes of some of these undeveloped nations. Before the Iranian revolution of 1979 the US, Britain, and other countries attempted to instill Western economic policies in Persia. Dilip Hiro's study of the 1978-79 Iranian Revolution makes note of how the attempts to westernize Persia's economy inevitably effected much more.

In 1901 the King of Persia, the Shah, gave oil concessions to the British in exchange for monetary loans. Then came the Uniformity of Dress Law of 1928 that required men to wear Western-suits and specific hats and in 1935 the veil was banned. In 1953 the CIA spearheaded Operation Ajax, which was a successful attempt to overthrow the first democratically elected president of Iran, Muhammad Mussadiq. Mussadiq had nationalized Iranian oil, which until then had been controlled by Britain and Western interests. Following this event the Shah signed an oil consortium in favor of Western nations. Iranian farms began to use a great deal of chemical fertilizers and pesticides, under the Shah. From 1963-1977 more than 6,000 factories were built, while agriculture fell. In 1966 book censorship began, highways were built, and supermarkets replaced neighborhood shops, because corporations began receiving specialized interest rates.

Plans were made in the late-70's for France to sell Iran nuclear technology (as France had previously given Israel nuclear weapons). By 1978 Britain was chief weapon supplier to the Shah, and the Shah lent 887 million dollars to the IMF and World Bank, and 728 million dollars to Britain, France, and Denmark. Between 1953 and 1969, Iran "received as much US military support in grants as all other countries combined."[107]

---

[104] The Hindu philosopher and economist Amartya Sen has argued that whole modern use of externalities must be reconfigured given the interest of human well-being or welfare. Check his 1987 work *On Ethics and Economics*.
[105] Nader, *The Good Fight*, (a) p127-128
[106] Al Gore, *An Inconvenient Truth*, (New York, Rodale, 2006). Percentages by region stand at: U.S. 30.3%, Europe 27.7%, Middle East 2.6%, Africa 2.5%, Southeast Asia-India-China 12.2%" p250-251
[107] Hiro, p18, 26, 28, 34, 36, 38-39, 53, 54, 62, 309-310, 304

"While a minority prospered, a once agriculturally self-sufficient country was spending more than one billion dollars on imports."[108]

But as we see with the non-violent revolution of 1979 where the Shah was dethroned, Iran (which consists of a majority of Shia Muslims) is comprised of strong communities. For example, the strong Persian community's effectiveness became evidenced when in 1890 the Shah gave the British a "fifty-year monopoly of purchase, sale and manufacture of the entire tobacco crop of Iran". A near total boycott of tobacco by the Iranians ensued, which before then had maintained an annual tobacco consumption rate of 10,000 tons.[109] In 1978 the Shah censured the media, ordering two newspapers to keep quiet on government violence not unlike that which was legalized in the US under the Patriot Act. In response to the Shah's censorship every employee walked out of the job. When wealthy Iranians secretly sent abroad $2 billion dollars, and thirteen military officials exported $253 million dollars, the Central Bank of Iran (Bank Markazi) released this information to the press, which published the findings and caused an outrage amongst the people. The constitution that was drafted following the 1979 revolution banned usury and in 1983 a bill was passed for interest-free banking.[110]

The End of the World Revisited (Teleology Naturalized)

In his book *The View From Nowhere* Thomas Nagel surmises a possible motivation behind those who support nuclear weapons production and maintenance.

"The widespread willingness to rely on thermonuclear bombs as the ultimate weapon displays a cavalier attitude toward death that has always puzzled me. My impression is that whatever they may say, most of the defenders of these weapons are not suitably horrified at the possibility of a war in which hundreds of millions of people would be killed. This may be due to monumental lack of imagination, or perhaps to a peculiar attitude toward risk which leads to the discounting of probabilities of disaster substantially below 50 percent. Or it may be a mechanism of defensive irrationality that appears in circumstances of aggressive conflict. But I suspect that an important factor may be belief in an afterlife, and that the proportion of those who think that death is not the end is much higher among partisans of the bomb than among its opponents."[111]

Nagel's suspicion that those who support the creation, maintenance, and use of nuclear weapons are those who believe in immortality seems plausible and has been verified in my own personal experience.[112] One of the biggest opponents of nuclear weapons was the atheist Bertrand Russell.[113] Be that is it may, the nation of Israel has

---

[108] John L. Esposito, *The Islamic Threat: Myth or Reality?*, Revised Edition, (Oxford, Oxford University Press, 1995) p103
[109] This was instigated by Jamal al-Din al-Afghani (1838-1897) who was later put under house arrest. Ayatollah Hasan al-Shirazi issued the *fatwa* forbidding smoking. (Esposito, p56, 65)
[110] Hiro, p9, 94, 17, 78-79, 123, 259
[111] Thomas Nagel, *The View From Nowhere*, (New York, Oxford University Press, 1986) p230n4
[112] I can remember one late night discussion with one student in college who ended the argument by saying that he had faith and didn't need justification. He then gratuitously added that he was glad our missiles were all pointed in a certain direction.
[113] Though critics complain that Russell occasionally changed his mind, see for example his books of the 1960's *Has Man a Future?* (1961) and *Unarmed Victory* (1963), which were written when Russell was in his 90's (he was born in 1870). In *Unarmed Victory* which accounts for his important role as mediator during the Cuban Missile Crisis, Russell reveals what was hidden by the US media: the reasonableness of

quite the nuclear arsenal (even if it was received as a gift from France) and many Jews do not believe in immortality but believe in propagation, as we see in the Torah.[114]

In 2003 the US was the only country to vote against (thus vetoing) a nuclear Comprehensive Test Ban Treaty at the United Nations General Assembly. Only the US and one other country (India) voted against (and thus vetoed) attempts to eliminate nuclear weapons altogether.[115] In his popular book, *Hegemony or Survival: America's Quest for Global Dominance*, Noam Chomsky arrives at a different interpretation behind the desire for nuclear weapons. Oil rich countries realize that the US, France, Britain, and Russia (the victors of WWII) only attack those countries that do not have nuclear weapons (or other kinds of Weapons of Mass Destruction, WMD). This is true of the case of Iraq which the US invaded and where there were no WMD, to 'our' chagrin. Chomsky writes:

"For centuries, Europeans have devoted themselves to slaughtering one another, meanwhile conquering most of the world. By 1945 they realized that the game was over: the next time it was played would be the last. Western powers can still resort to violence against the weak and defenseless, but not against one another."[116]

It is noteworthy that two countries that were also listed on the US's 'Axis of Evil' alongside Iraq -North Korea and Iran -were not attacked. This is because these countries were "not defenseless"[117] and as soon as North Korea successfully created a nuclear weapon they were removed from the Axis of Evil. Countries with nuclear weapons are not invaded. Accordingly, countries whose goal it is to gain nuclear capability, like Iran for example, do-so in order that they are not attacked by an existing nuclear power such as the US or Britain. If we expect other countries to not produce nuclear weapons, shouldn't we make such an example ourselves?[118]

Teleology

A concept that I have not yet mentioned is that of 'teleology'. Teleology is the study of ends or goals. The Greek word *telos* means 'end' or 'purpose'. This word concept was used by Plato and especially Aristotle in their conceptions not just of human nature and purpose, but also the nature and purpose of all things, sentient or otherwise. For example, Aristotle believed that human's *telos* or purpose is *eudeimonea*, or well-being, flourishing, or happiness, and this was realized through living in accordance to the virtues, which were themselves purposive ends.

---

atheist Russian leader Premier Khrushchev as opposed to the aggressiveness and readiness for war by the Christian President Kennedy.
[114] The Jewish philosopher Emmanuel Levinas has written of Hamlet's question, "To be or not to be –this is probably not the question par excellence" in "Bad Conscience and the Inexorable", quoted by Richard A. Cohen. *Time and the Other*, p73n50
[115] Noam Chomsky, *Hegemony or Survival*, (New York, Henry Holt and Company, 2003) p244
[116] Chomsky, p71
[117] Chomsky, p151
[118] Martin Luther King, Jr., seems to have combined theory and practice when he taught Christians, "We must pray earnestly for peace, but we must also work vigorously for disarmament and the suspension of weapon testing. We must use our minds as rigorously to plan for peace as we have used them to plan for war. We must pray with unceasing passion for racial justice, but we must also use our minds to develop a programme, organize ourselves into mass nonviolent action, and employ every resource of our bodies and souls to bring an end to racial injustice. We must pray unrelentingly for economic justice, but we must also work diligently to bring into being those social changes that make for a better distribution of wealth within our nation and in the undeveloped countries of the world." *Strength to Love*, p132

Within Aristotle's own lifetime the communal Greek city-state that was the model for his philosophy, as well as the model used by his teacher Plato, and Plato's teacher Socrates, became part of Alexander the Great's Empire. After Alexander's death in 323 and Aristotle's death a year later, the Empire dissolved and the Greek and Roman world became heirs of vast kingdoms and fiefdoms around the Mediterranean and beyond.

This is the beginning of the 'Hellenistic' era. The most popular philosophy at this time was that of the Stoic, a discipline that began a century after Aristotle's death. Stoicism had continued into the new millennium and many argue, to this day in our Western world. The Stoic philosophy, named after the *stoa*, or porch where the stoics held discussions and lectures, had been one that used the colloquial and communal Greek city-state philosophy of Plato, Aristotle, and Socrates, and adapted it to the kingdoms and empires, which had become the norm in the Hellenistic world. In such an imperial and international format, the specific virtues became formalized according to a more general and universal program, rather than through the distinctive virtues of each community. Through this institutionalization of the virtues came belief in the supremacy of law and jurisprudence over the communal *telos*.

This pattern of esteeming universal law over teleology was noticed in 1908 by John Dewey in his *Ethics*, as well as the 'communitarian' Alasdair MacIntyre. In his study *After Virtue* (1981) MacIntyre noted that "Stoicism is not of course only an episode in Greek and Roman culture; it sets a pattern for all those later European moralities that invoke the notion of law as central in such a way as to displace conceptions of the virtues."[119]

Stoicism's most powerful proponent was none other than the Roman Emperor Marcus Aurelius (128-180 CE). In his *Meditations*, the Emperor mused over the universal law.

"If our intellectual part is common, the reason also, in respect of which we are rational beings, is common: if this is so, common also is the reason which commands us what to do, and what not to do; if this is so, there is common law also; if this is so, we are fellow-citizens; if this is so, we are members of some political community; if this is so, the world is in a matter a state. For of what other common political community will any one say that the whole human race are members? And from thence, from this common political community comes also our very intellectual faculty and reasoning faculty and our capacity for law; or whence do they come?"[120]

An administrative tool that was used in achieving and governing this universal law during the Roman Empire and onward was the *Pax Romana*. The Latin word *pax* means 'peace' or 'grace' and the *Pax Romana* was granted over those communities and states which surrendered to the Roman Empire and paid the tax. The Roman statesman Marcus Tullius Cicero (106-43 BCE) had written in his book, *De Republica* about the centrality of this universal law:

"It is a sin to try to alter this law, nor is it allowable to attempt to repeal any part of it, and it is impossible to abolish it entirely... And there will not be different laws at Rome and at Athens, or different laws now and in the future, but one eternal and unchangeable law will be valid for all nations and for all times, and there will be one master and one ruler, that is, God, over us all, for He is the author of this law, its promulgator, and its enforcing judge."[121]

---

[119] John Dewey, *Theory of the Moral Life*, (New York, Holt, Rinehart and Winston, Inc., 1960) (d) p27, published originally as part II in *Ethics* in 1908. MacIntyre, p150; quotation from p169. MacIntyre has subsequently rejected the label 'communitarian' to sum up his philosophy.
[120] Marcus Aurelius Antoninus, *Meditations*, Book IV, 4, p509
[121] Cicero, *De Republica*, III, xxii, 33. Quoted and trans. by d'Entreves, p21

The legal philosopher A.P. d'Entreves shows the extensive influence this concept of universal law has had,

> "This famous passage from Cicero's *Republic* clearly sets forth the doctrine of the law of nature which had been elaborated by the Stoics. Mankind is a universal community or cosmopolis. Law is its expression. Being based upon the common nature of men, it is truly universal. Being endorsed by the sovereign Lordship of God, it is eternal and immutable. The doctrine passed into the *ius naturale* of the Roman jurists as well as into the teaching of the Christian Church."[122]

This theory of a universal law, or natural (or general) law was practiced from the Greek and Roman times through the Middle-Ages or Medieval times, to the Enlightenment where belief in an immutable and universal law held primacy. MacIntyre writes that, "Stoicism remains one of the permanent moral possibilities within the culture of the West." The primacy of universal law has replaced the *telos* which was necessary in order that the virtues might really be practiced, and not just obeyed according to their institutionalization. MacIntyre writes:

> "The plurality of the virtues and their theological ordering in the good life –as both Plato and Aristotle and beyond them Sophocles and Homer had understood them –disappear; a simple monism of virtue takes its place. It is unsurprising that the Stoics and Aristotle's later followers were never able to live in argumentative peace with each other."[123]

Deprived of the virtues which were organic to the community and the city-state, the universal law of the modern world tends to produce two variations: 1) radical individualism (as we see in the two popular modern philosophies of empiricism and rationalism), or 2) conformity and totalitarianism (institutionalism, monotonization).

The norms of community under these two manifestations of Universal Law can be described thus:

1) *Individualism.* With the modern philosophy of the individual we see such positions held as empiricism (holding knowledge to be a product of personal experience), rationalism (holding knowledge to be an innate occurrence), anarchism and libertarianism (which hold that personal liberty is the greatest good), and mentalism (primacy of the personal will, as well as the belief that meaning, justification, and purpose are personal or internal).

2) *Totalitarianism.* The modern philosophy of totalitarianism can be found in bureaucratization (or the centralization of government away from the people), institutionalization (where opinions are formalized into universalities), communism (where all property and economics are handled by a centralized state), and fascism and majoritarianism (where the worship of power overrules the values of different peoples).

Two ways in which MacIntyre thinks we can regain the virtues are to either reacquire the concept of *telos*, or take up the concept of human nature. In these ways like the ways of Plato, Aristotle, and Socrates, we will recognize the importance of the virtues, and of justice in particular. Such a justice must not be merely liberal (promoting welfare) or libertarian (promoting rights) but must derive from the virtues of the community; particularly the idea of just deserts, or each receiving what they deserve. Whereas democracy promotes and highlights consensus among peoples, MacIntyre holds we need to step away from such generalizations and start looking more closely at the

---

[122] D'Entreves, p21
[123] MacIntyre, p169, 170

conflicts between rival versions of morality as they play themselves out in the modern world.[124]

The problem of the modern world stems from rival versions of morality and MacIntyre says our "culture of bureaucratic individualism" is a disjunction of those who believe in rights and those who believe in utility. MacIntyre finds these rival political views "incommensurable", which means that they are incompatible and oppositional. Disputes are irresolvable because "our pluralist culture possesses no method of weighing, no rational criterion for deciding between claims based on legitimate entitlement [rights] against claims based on need [welfare]."[125]

"[M]odern politics cannot be a matter of genuine moral consensus. And it is not. Modern politics is a civil war carried on by other means…"

"[T]he tradition of the virtues is at variance with central features of the modern economic order and more especially its individualism, its acquisitiveness and its elevation of the values of the market to a central social place."

Alasdair concludes:

"What matters at this stage is the construction of local forms of community within which civility and the intellectual and moral life can be sustained through the new dark ages which are already upon us. And if the tradition of the virtues was able to survive the horrors of the last dark ages, we are not entirely without grounds for hope. This time however the barbarians are not waiting beyond the frontiers; they have already been governing us for quite some time."[126]

MacIntyre's assessment, which was made shortly after the Iranian revolution and the beginning of President Reagan's reign in office, stands as a great criticism, not just of the modern world, but of the non-teleological 'Enlightenment' values such as rights-based ethics and liberalism. In their stead, MacIntyre espouses the community and Aristotelian city-state, wherein the virtues are organic and teleologically ordered.

American pragmatism offers an alternative approach. Pragmatists agree with MacIntyre's assessment that modernity has its share of problems, however, pragmatism is neither 'atavistic' nor a philosophy that holds in principal an absolutist stance on the unresolvability or incomparability of ethical problems. Impracticality is the opposite of pragmatism, which is a practical philosophy based upon capability, feasibility, and not just plurality.

In ancient Greek philosophy the *telos*, like the Forms (or *eidos*), was regarded as being fixed and permanent. Human nature (or form) and human purpose (or function, *telos*), say for the Spartan, were one and the same thing. Moreover, the *telos* of a rock was fixed and immutable, as well as the sun, the stars, and all life forms from algae to zucchini.

For pragmatists such rigid classifications can be a bit of a nuisance, particularly when experience and evidence contradict accepted beliefs and received notions. The many revolutions in scientific knowledge are testament to this. While it might be impractical to think of reality as flux, it is certainly not practical to think of nature as decided once and for all. Moreover, such stiff conceptualizations are not just recalcitrant to empirical evidence, but are in an important sense dogmatic, based seemingly upon something supernatural or at best, non-natural.

Teleology is not eliminated by pragmatism so much as it is naturalized and understood as something more reasonable or part of the mind's rationale. Construed

---

[124] MacIntyre, p254
[125] MacIntyre, p71, 246
[126] MacIntyre, p253, 254, 263

thus, teleology is not something fixed or absolute. This 'transcendentalism' is crystallized in the method used by John Dewey that he called variously 'instrumentalism', 'experimentalism', or sometimes 'functionalism'. Early on Dewey had adapted the term 'instrumentalism' from the radical empiricist William James (1842-1910) before coming to prefer 'experimentalism'.[127] Dewey's instrumentalism was never of the sort that we find among 'anti-realists' or 'mild realists' who hold that reality is our instrument, amenable by the always rational will, or intending mind.[128] Rather, Dewey regarded fallibility, or belief in the possibility of human error, as a central component in the method and practice of experimentalism. In one of his most personal and autobiographical writings titled "From Absolutism to Experimentalism" (1930), Dewey traced his philosophical development from his undergraduate studies at the University of Vermont to his mature and developed philosophy of educational reform. He wrote:

"I have enough faith in the depth of the religious tendencies of men to believe that they will adapt themselves to any required intellectual change, and that it is futile (and likely to be dishonest) to forecast prematurely just what forms the religious interest will take as a final consequence of the great intellectual transformation that is going on."[129]

He summarized the role of experimentalism and instrumentalism, finding it derivative from the progressive character of American life.

"Instrumentalism maintains in opposition to many contrary tendencies in the American environment, that action should be intelligent and reflective, and that thought should occupy a central position in life. That is the reason so for our insistence on the teleological phase of thought and knowledge. If it must be teleological in particular and not merely true in the abstract, that is probably due to the practical element which is found in all the phases of American life. However that may be, what we insist upon above all else is that intelligence be regarded as the only source and sole guarantee of a desirable and happy future. It is beyond doubt that the progressive and unstable character of American life and civilization has facilitated the birth of a philosophy which regards the world as being in continuous formation, where there is still place for indeterminism... It is the formation of faith in intelligence, as the one and indispensable belief necessary to moral and social life."[130]

In his work *Reconstruction in Philosophy*, Dewey argues that the main obstacle to pragmatism is the "inheritance from the classic tradition that has become so deeply engrained in men's minds…" and which holds to "the impossibility of reconciliation or compromise." For traditionalists, "The thought of looking ahead, toward the eventual, toward consequences, creates uneasiness and fear."[131]

The non-dogmatic or natural philosophy of pragmatism which Dewey espouses makes, instead of conformity to accepted notions of fate or destiny or calling, the practical goal of success as the *telos*. The intellectual or pragmatic "teleological theory of classification" is set up such that it "will promote successful action for ends."[132] In opposition to universalism, or an absolute teleology, Dewey wrote that:

---

[127] Joseph Ratner, in his Introduction to his Dewey collection, *Intelligence In the Modern World: John Dewey's Philosophy*, (New York, Random House, 1939) (e) p58
[128] For a refutation of instrumentalism and due to its incoherence check *Fodor's Guide To Mental Representations*, by Jerry Fodor in, *A Theory of Content*, (Cambridge, The MIT Press, 1990)
[129] John Dewey, "From Absolutism to Experimentalism", from *The Essential* Dewey, Volume I, ed. Larry A. Hickman and Thomas M. Alexander, (Indianapolis, Indiana University Press, 1998) (f) p18
[130] John Dewey, "The Development of American Pragmatism", (f) p12-13
[131] John Dewey, *Reconstruction in Philosophy*, (Boston, Beacon Press, 1957) (g) p158-159. Originally published in 1920, Dewey wrote the introduction (pages marked with Roman numerals) in 1947.
[132] Dewey, *Reconstruction in Philosophy*, (g) p154

"[T]he distinctive office, problems and subject matter of philosophy grow out of stresses and strains in the community life in which a given form of philosophy arises, and that, accordingly, its specific problems vary with the changes in human life that are always going on and that at times constitute a crisis and a turning point in human history."[133]

Dewey believed the modern era, which is dominated by corporations and industrialization, was split between an ethically neutral scientific world-view, and a regalement (or displacement) of ethics to 'spirituality'. This is the faith that justifies the suffering of the other, be it the status quo.[134]

"Man's physical command of natural energies has been indefinitely multiplied. There is control of the sources of material wealth and prosperity... But there are few persons optimistic enough to declare that any similar command of the forces which control man's social and moral welfare has been achieved. Where is the moral progress that corresponds to our economic accomplishments?... But where is there a corresponding human science and art?... [P]rogress has brought with it serious new moral disturbance. I need only cite the late war [WWI], the problem of capital and labor, [and] the relation of economic classes... [H]ow undeveloped are our politics, how crude and primitive our education, how passive and inert our morals. The causes remain which brought philosophy into existence as an attempt to find an intelligent substitute for blind custom and blind impulse as guides to life and conduct. The attempt has not been successfully accomplished. Is there not reason for believing that the release of philosophy from its burden of sterile metaphysics and sterile epistemology instead of depriving philosophy of problems and subject-matter would open a way to questions of the most perplexing and the most significant sort?"[135]

One of the secret strengths of Socrates and pragmatists alike is their belief in their own fallibility. The running suspicion, or more accurately – the supposition that even our best theories could be subject to error, bias, and prejudice –is the surest way to avoid dogmatism, absolutism, and imperialism. Accordingly, like the experimental scientist, the pragmatist holds that fallibilism is the best way to discover new values and truths. Dewey compared the pragmatist to the scientist:

"From the standpoint of scientific inquiry nothing is more fatal to its right to obtain acceptance than a claim that its conclusions are final and hence incapable of a development that is other than mere quantitative extension."[136]

Pragmatism and Ecology

It has been my purpose to show that there is a relationship between our social and physical environments, as well as our beliefs about metaphysics (whatever ultimate reality is) and the way we live our lives. There are many different beliefs and practices that exist in the world and there are thus many ways in which people relate to this world we live in, as well as to those whom we share it with. What can we predict about the future and the changing world we live in, physically and socially? Some lifestyles seem more compatible with the course of nature, while others seem less compatible or incongruous. People today can often feel adrift about who they are and what they ought to do with their lives, as the traditional models of family, society, and community disappear.

If anything is for certain, it is that we are not stuck between two options: rugged individualism or libertarianism, on the one hand, and on the other, patriotism, conformity,

---

[133] Dewey, *Reconstruction in Philosophy*, (g) V-VI
[134] Dewey, *Reconstruction in Philosophy*, (g) XXXII
[135] Dewey, *Reconstruction in Philosophy*, (g) p125-126
[136] Dewey, *Reconstruction in Philosophy*, (g) XV-XVI

and globalization on the other. The three-tenets of pragmatism –Naturalism, Fallibilism, and Pluralism -offer a model for solving the problems which face us today and which will face us tomorrow.

Naturalism. The philosophy of pragmatism is committed to naturalism. Naturalism is the practical belief that humans know certain things about themselves and about the world. Knowledge, explanation, and justification are natural parts of everyday life and by nature no human being is deprived of these abilities to know, explain, and justify. However, some methods and practices are more practical and more efficient than others, and the naturalist believes science, be it a human science like sociology, or a physical science like biology can truly describe reality, even if science does not offer the last word in many areas and even if it is not total knowledge, or omniscience.

Many of the beliefs and practices about the end of the world ignore the epistemological question concerning how we as humans come to know the nature of such a reality. Such shortsightedness is often called by the fancy word 'anthropocentricism'.[137] This big word, as the reader might tease out from its many syllables, means something like the belief that humans are the center of the universe, or that human's affairs, above those of all other species, are God's chief concern. It is anthropocentricism that has sponsored all of the genocides against earth's species such as the American Buffalo of the great plains, which were massacred in the thousands by the settlers, as well as the many rampant forms of discrimination against non-human species as animals, trees, and different peoples. According to such an anthropological-centrist view the earth's resources are so many tools and objects for man's being-in-the-world.

Naturalism is also a kind of humanism –the belief that humans are an integral part of the earth. The philosopher Peter Singer points out that there are in fact several different forms of humanism, in his seminal work, *Animal Liberation*. For example, the ancient Greek thinker, infidel, and legislator Protagoras (490-420 BCE) is famous for having stated that "Man is the measure of all things". However, we don't know if he meant for this to be the case for women as well, who could not vote in the democratic city of Athens, and from which Protagoras was eventually exiled. Protagoras' kind of humanism (he was not Athenian but from the region of Turkey), also known as sophistry, holds the rhetorical view that reality is a human construct –just as we invented the rules of basketball, humans create their reality in total. Another form of humanism is a religious humanism that holds that the human species are Gods favorite creation –the world was created for the use of people, who alone were created in the image of God. Still further, there is a humanism that holds to the belief in 'humanitarianism' and "the tendency to act humanely."[138]

If naturalism implies humanism, it does not imply a human-centered reality of nature. Naturalists believe that the external world exists independently of the human mind. Naturalism is also opposed to supernaturalism. From pragmatism's Founding Father Charles Sander Peirce (1839-1914) onward pragmatists have been expositors and utilizers of the natural sciences (physics) and the human sciences (sociology) and have sought natural explanations and phenomena apprehensible by all persons. As the

---

[137] Nietzsche defined 'anthropocentricism' as "the total denial of natural causes".
[138] Peter Singer, *Animal Liberation*, New Revised Edition, (New York, Avon Books, 1975) p198

mathematician and logician Peirce himself said, "Logic is rooted in the social principle."[139]

Fallibilism. If there were a hidden secret to the philosophy of pragmatism it is probably its fallibility, though I could be wrong. Fallibilism is the practical belief that even our best scientific theory, be it evolution, the atomic theory of matter, or for that matter alchemy -could be mistaken. Fallibilism is thus linked to naturalism in the belief that humans are part of earth, but also that humans can't possibly know everything there is to know about the earth, including the earth's future. A naturalist may try to predict the weather so they get their crops harvested at the right time or so they know the best and safest time to set sail. However, such naturalists know that even the best farmer or sea captain can be wrong from time to time and that such predictions about the future are fallible, or are capable of being wrong. We defy augury.

Fallibilism is in principal opposed to dogmatism. The dogmatist is the person who is a know-it-all and thinks they cannot fail to know the truth. They are certain. When a person's knowledge is infallibly justified there can be no difference between fact and opinion, or for that matter any room for doubt over what is right or wrong. Reason would be superfluous. The fallibilist, on the other hand, believes knowledge exists (a fallibilist cannot consistently think otherwise), and does not believe in the subjectivity of truth, as say the relativist might. Like the scientific method, which always starts with a hypothesis to be tested through experiment, the fallibilist never loses sight of the presuppositions and scaffolding which hold up our modern science and the fallibilist is the true discoverer and uncoverer of knowledge and values that hitherto had not existed.

Pluralism. Perhaps most controversially the pragmatist believes there are many true descriptions of reality. Some descriptions are based upon form, some are based upon function, and others are based upon aesthetic value, ethical value, etc... A chair for example, may be properly formed so that it can be sat in, and it may function better than other chairs, and be aesthetically pleasing –for better or for worse. A table is a mass of atoms, or a practical human invention, or something of beauty, depending upon the purpose of a given conceptualization or objective.

Pluralism is opposed to both monism and dualism, or the belief that there is only one true description of reality (or teleology) or perhaps just two such descriptions. Pluralists believe there are many descriptions. For this reason pluralism is an intellectual strength inviting diversity. Moreover, pluralism rules out relativism, the belief that value has no factual base. The pluralist does not think everything is the same or that everything is reducible to a single form or function. There are many ways to live life and the pragmatist rests on those philosophies and lifestyles which are most practical and open, and do not throw their hands up in the air or bury their head in the sand but get to work, whether such a task calls for doing some thinking, or acting upon our thoughts.[140]

---

[139] Charles Sanders Peirce, "The Doctrine of Chances", published in 1878, reprinted in *Philosophical Writings of Peirce*, ed. Justus Buchler, (New York, Dover Publications, Inc., 1955) p162

[140] In his book *Environmental Justice and The New Pluralism*, David Schlosberg writes: "Relations across differences are key to the emerging generation of pluralist theory. Secondly, an aura of partiality pervades these relations. We attempt to understand and relate to others different from ourselves, but in that we recognize difference as a key aspect to human agency, we acknowledge that understanding will never be complete... Once we give up on the necessity of universalism and embrace relations with others, ends, convergence, and finality remain forever distant... Agonistic respect calls for a constant cultivation of care

...and Democracy

What about democracy? Hopefully our democracy says as much about its communities as each community says about our democracy. If our government is of the people why should we expect the majority of citizens to converge on what is best for the world and us? Can we expect our government to do what is right for ensuring the well being of our communities and for providing a healthy and ethical relationship with the planet earth?[141] Pragmatism offers a good answer to these questions and practical solutions to these problems for a democracy's relationship with the world.

To conclude this discussion of the end(s) of the world I will set up three common attitudes that are popular in America with regard to the world and humans place in it. We will then see whether they are compatible with these three popular attitudes are with pragmatism, and if not, whether they can be rebutted using the three tenets of pragmatism mentioned above. These attitudes (which I have witnessed among socialists, capitalists, anarchists, and nationalists alike) will be that:

    1) Environmental problems such as global warming, pollution, and species genocide don't really exist.

    2) Environmental problems once existed or may still exist to a certain degree, but our government officials and experts either have already handled these problems or are dealing with them as they arise.

    3) Environmental problems are a serious threat to our survival and unless everyone gets on the right page, we are either doomed to failure or all of our attempts to set things aright will be ineffective.

1) "Environmental problems such as global warming, pollution, and species genocide don't really exist."

Answer: There are some who believe that the earth is our playpen and that talk of such things as global-warming and pollution is either exaggerated or uninformed. In a very real sense, these 'problems' don't really exist –either God controls the world or He is imperfect. God cannot be imperfect, therefore the problem doesn't exist.

While such a perspective is becoming less popular today, there are still plenty of people who take this view either explicitly and live their lives with no regard to their impact on the earth, or they believe so implicitly and do not think such issues have any relevance to their own well-being.

This perspective also violates the pragmatic tenet of naturalism. As we saw, naturalism holds that science is often-times correct (even it isn't the only description of reality) and many scientists, among them -all those who were awarded the Nobel Prize with Al Gore, have found that in fact Western market values have a malevolent affect on the natural environment.[142] The belief that environmental problems don't exist also

---

for self and others, intersubjectivity is ongoing, discourse is never-ending, and solidarity is forever creating new networks and mosaics." (Oxford, Oxford University Press, 1999) p103

[141] We can see in the meditations of Marcus Aurelius the tendencies which Europe inherited from the Stoics: "How quickly all things disappear, in the universe the bodies themselves, but in time the remembrance of them; what is the nature of all sensible things, and particularly those which attract with the bait of pleasure or terrify by pain, or are noised abroad by vapoury fame; how worthless, and contemptible, and sordid, and perishable, and dead they are –all this it is the part of the intellectual faculty to observe." - Marcus Aurelius Antoninus, *Meditations*, Book II, 12, p499

[142] In 2004 the Union of Concerned Scientists, which consisted of more than 60 preeminent scientists released the statement, "Restoring Scientific Integrity in Policymaking", which documented places where

violates the tenet of fallibility. The kind of faith that denies human's role in environmental degradation is akin to a kind of dogmatic skepticism, and pragmatism is opposed to this global doubt. The fallibilist necessarily believes that knowledge exists and therefore the faith in the denial of pollution also violates the tenet of pluralism. Pluralism might reveal that humans are not the most important species on earth or in the universe.

2) "Environmental problems once existed or may still exist to a certain degree, but our government officials and experts either have already handled these problems or are dealing with them as they arise."

Answer: This attitude seems to be the most prevalent of the three listed and is usually the result of either simple ignorance or plain indifference. Oftentimes people who understand the theory behind ecology and the human/environment reciprocation, do not know what they could do to help change the problems that exist short of relying on the experts and officials to take care of them. After all, our representatives are also our fellow citizens –they are either divinely appointed or democratically elected.

This second perspective of non-commitment and laissez-faire violates the tenet of pluralism. A problem which philosophers from Plato to Dewey were aware of is the potential dangers of majoritarianism. If the environmentalists in our community or country are a minority they cannot hope to change our government's policies except through educating the educators (and legislators), which could take something like a long time. A commitment to pluralism can mean showing due respect to differences of perspective and lifestyle. This isn't a mere tolerance for the status quo, but an active and practical approach to acknowledge what is different or new.

We ought not to look at our government officials and appointed 'experts' as infallible and omniscient –as though they were aware of all the hazards and threats. History is filled with examples where the experts believed something to be true only to have it overturned by some new discover or reasoning. Believe it or not, government officials and experts, call them 'representatives', aren't always infallible or altruistic. Accountability is key to any representation

3) "Environmental problems are a serious threat to our survival and unless everyone gets on the same page, we are either doomed to failure or all of our attempts to set things aright will be ineffective."

Answer: Some of the environmentalists I've talked to argue that unless we have an absolute view on reality or a dogmatic environmental position, either no one will listen to us, or our efforts simply must always prove ineffective. The time has passed for discussion. If we don't act now, it will be too little too late.

To the third perspective holding that unless we take a dogmatic view on the state of the environment or the human effect on the world, we are doomed to impotency and failure, the tenet of fallibilism is taken to be more practical and effective. Some would be quick to reject technology and make a philosophy of anxiety, or vice versa. There are more practical ways of changing the world than bombing or alienating oneself or others, and the fallibilist is the one who will find the best solution.

---

the Bush administration either suppressed, distorted, or manipulated scientific findings. Kevin Phillips, *American Theocracy*, (New York, Viking, 2006) p247

Those who believe it to be the 11th hour of the world inevitably set up a model of society and ethics that becomes one of class war. Education seems an ineffective tool in turning the tide and an inefficient way of making a last desperate move to save humanity from itself. Some of the environmentalists seem to magically know that our end-time has been reached –they seem to have infallible knowledge of the future and prescience of the earth's forecast. All that is left is the ideological war of class against class, the blind vs. those who see as gods.

Though the pluralist-committed does not deny the veracity of another's understanding, they are not the ones to point the finger at others alone and realize that responsibility begins with oneself. It's not about telling other people they are wrong and that we are right. As Gandhi said, we must "become the change we wish to see in the world." Only once others have seen our non-hypocrisy can we realistically hope to see them make the right decision. Most of the places Gandhi lived, from Phoenix, South Africa, to back in India, he set up communes, called *Ashrams*, and formed strong communities. This is a revolutionary movement in contradistinction to a war of class.

The monist classical teleology or monist eschatology which infallibly holds their to be rigid classes (or castes) ventures so far as to claim knowledge of the imminent end of the world. They offer no hope to the community. The pragmatic pluralist doesn't contemplate the end of the world, however, but the *ends* of the world -what we can do to work together to make this world a better and more just place. Aristotle said, "We deliberate not about ends, but about what promotes ends." (1112b11) As far as eschatology goes, the pragmatist will be committed to a natural science wherein claims will remain in the epistemological realm rather than the metaphysical. This goes for teleology as well, where pragmatism is committed to natural goals and purposes rather than some perverse theory of history, or biological justification of the status quo, or conviction that there is no tomorrow.

5

Black Nationalism and International Justice

When the Chinese philosopher Confucius (551-479) formulated the Golden Rule over 2500 years ago, he had in mind an ethic that was universal, or universalist. He taught, "Do not impose on others what you yourself do not desire".[1] This can be restated as the more contemporary: *Do unto others as you would have them to do unto you.* Such an ethic is found in the Torah of Judaism, the New Testament of Christianity, as well as the Quran of Islam. The Golden Rule is said to not just be an ethic that I alone could or should want to follow, but one that all other human beings could and should want to follow as well. For this reason this type of ethic is called universal: it is something that can be applied to all people alike and be universally functional. The great 18th century German philosopher Immanuel Kant (1724-1804) had this universatility in mind when he came up with a slightly different version of the Golden Rule called the Categorical Imperative. Kant states this ethical imperative: "*act only in accordance with that maxim through which you can at the same time will that it become a universal law*". Or, "*act as if the maxim of your action were to become by your will a universal law of nature.*"[2]

For many ethicists, especially those of the Western Enlightenment such as Kant, Thomas Paine (1737-1809), and the young Thomas Jefferson (1743-1826), morality is something revealed through human nature. According to these thinkers it is human nature to be ethical. Morality is understood through the use of common sense. Also, there are certain inalienable rights of man (and woman) that are hardwired into our design. For this reason ethics is something universal, or something commonly applicable to all human beings.

There are some, however, who disagree with the generalizations of the Enlightenment. Some believe, most famously the Englishman Thomas Hobbes (1588-1679) that humans left to themselves would amount to chaos, or a 'war of all against all'. This is similar to the not unpopular belief that human beings are fallen, corrupt, originally sinful, evil, or selfish. In accordance to this bad nature humans must be led by an institution such as a government or a religion, or perhaps a divine being, which alone can keep humans in check, curtailing their evil tendencies toward greed, avarice, and basic unfriendliness.

Modern philosophies such as state-capitalism, socialism, and anarchism are all equally guided by an ethic of universatility. Roughly, capitalists believe that people should realize we are all universally self-interested and that this understanding will make the world function properly. Socialism is also a universal ethic, holding that the natural history of humans is one of class struggle, a battle between the haves and the have nots, the bourgeois and the proletariat. Anarchists too hold this class war to be an essential

---

[1] Confucius, *The Analects*, trans. D.C. Lau, (New York, Penguin Books, 1979) 15:24
[2] Immannuel Kant, *Groundwork of the Metaphysics of Morals*, trans. Mary Gregor, (Cambridge, Cambridge University Press, 1998) 4:421, p31

component of human nature, and agree with socialists that this war must be escalated in order to achieve the ideal or universal/utopian society.

Modern states are guided by these visions of universality in their stewardship of foreign countries that are deemed 'third-world'. This act of charity is achieved in several ways. Traditionally, modern states would set up colonies in the third world in order to get access to natural resources and to save the souls of the pagans and heathen savages who had lived comfortably and peacefully for eons. But as a great deal of colonialism came to an end in the 20th century, the message of universality became spread through the multi-nationalization of economics. Modern states lend money and give weapons to the governments of former colonies. Through this paternal structure states are repaid with natural resources such as oil, lumber, and minerals. Modern weapons flood the market, currencies fluctuate and jobs are outsourced as multinational corporations keep on the constant lookout for cheaper labor and resources. Whole companies move overseas to set up base in a different country where the tax laws and environmental laws are less strict.

Another method of universalization is the democratization of select 'third-world' countries. This democratization occurs once a foreign dictator who was on the pay roll for years bites the hand of first world leaders, as in the case of bin Laden in Afghanistan and Saddam Hussein in Iraq. On more than one occasion the US has militarily deposed a foreign democratically elected official.

This program of universalization has not always been the ethics of the US government. The Founding Fathers, for example, fought against the global nationalization project of the British Empire –the United Kingdom. The British Empire sought to create a global kingdom under one universal law and one ruler. Those who would not volunteer for such a 'benevolent' cause were subjected to the imperialism of the British military. This was the same ideology of the Roman Empire that had ruled Britain for more than 450 years. The Roman Empire gave foreign peoples and countries the right to survive and be part of the Empire, under the *Pax Romana*, if only these Barbarians would submit and pay Caesar's tax.

The American revolution was an attempt to found a new nation free from these imperialisms of empires. The United States was a voluntary union of sovereign states, led by an elected President and other elected representatives. This excluded, however, the vast population of Native Americans and African slaves, who were not represented. In our post-revolutionary world, the revolutionary movement of those still under the yoke of foreign imperialism is called 'Black Nationalism', and the battle is over the right for self-determination against empire and totalitarianism.

Black Nationalism, Revolution and Counter-Revolution

The fight against oppression and political imperialism is a legitimization movement called Black Nationalism. Black Nationalism was perhaps first advocated by a Jamaican named Marcus Garvey (1887-1940) who taught this doctrine in New York City and around the world until his death. Garvey was born in Jamaica in 1887 and it was when he was growing up there that he learned of a movement called 'Back to Africa'. Although slavery had been abolished in Jamaica in 1833, (slavery was abolished throughout the British Empire in that year), the working and living conditions remained impoverished and destitute, as colonization and generations of enslavement had changed the landscape and left people uprooted and robbed.

If the US Declaration of Independence in 1776 stated that human rights were to be fundamental and universal, slavery was not abolished for another 89 years. This was not the case with the French Revolution of 1789 and the drafting of, 'The Declaration of the Rights of Man', which abolished slavery in all of the French colonies as well as ended laws which discriminated against Jews.

This news reached the French colony of Haiti, which had some 2 million African slaves. When people caught wind of the French Revolution and the new political Rights of Man, there was a coup d'etat. The Haitian Revolution of 1791 was led by a former slave named Touissaint L'Overture (1743-1803). L'Overture defeated the anti-abolitionist colonial settler as well as attacks from British military vessels stationed in Jamaica. Haiti became the third new republic of the Americas, 15 years after the United States (after the Republic of Vermont 1777-1791 was dissolved that year).

Napoleon sent a fleet of 22,000 troops from France to Haiti to reclaim the French colony. When his army reached Haiti in 1802 Touissant was captured and died in a French prison a year later. After a failed attempt to re-enslave the Africans of Haiti, another revolution occurred in 1804 and the French were driven into the sea.[3] Independence was declared once again and news spread around the world of this African victory. Many slave owners in America and the Caribbean became distraught that their own African slaves would learn of the event. Haiti became referred to as the "Black Menace"[4] by American slaveholders who feared of a similar event in their own time, which in some places did occur.

The Black Menace became the brainchild for Liberia. Liberia (from the word 'liberty') was a concept developed by the American Colonization Society in 1816, largely through the funding of Protestant churches and slave-sympathizers. The country of Liberia, located on the West African coast, had its first settlers arrive in 1821, thousands of which were former African-American slaves as well as African-Americans whom had been born free. "Well into the 20th century", Liberia and Ethiopia were the only independent nations in Africa.[5] For Africans abroad, things were only worse.

It was this global climate of imperialism and political exploitation that sparked the beginning of the 'Back to Africa' movement. Marcus Garvey himself was influenced by a Muslim of Sudanese and Egyptian descent, Duse Mohamed Ali (1866-1945). Ali had organized the First Universal Races Congress in 1911 and his writings on Africa were translated into many different languages. Following Ali's lead, Garvey formed both the Universal Negro Improvement Association (UNIA) and the African Communities League (ACL) in 1914 of which Ali was a member. With the Pan-African movement begun, the first International Convention of the UNIA was held in New York City in 1920 at Madison Square Garden with 25,000 in attendance.[6] During this convention some 122

---

[3] John Henrik Clarke, "The Caribbean Antecedents of Marcus Garvey", in *Marcus Garvey and the Vision of Africa*, ed. John Henrik Clarke with the assistance of Amy Jacques Garvey, (New York, Vintage Books, 1974) p25-27
[4] Joseph E. Harris, *Africans and Their History*, Revised Edition, (New York, Penguin Books, 1987) p105
[5] Harris, p107
[6] William Strickland, *Malcolm X: Make It Plain*, ed. Cheryll Y. Greene, (New York, Penguin, 1994) p17

delegates signed 'The Declaration of Rights of the Negro Peoples of the World'. The Declaration decries the many laws that existed in various countries that discriminated against Africans and it calls for the right of free immigration for all peoples of African descent living in foreign continents.

Marcus Garvey's major work, *Lessons From the School of African Philosophy*, provides an ethics for nearly every aspect of life. We find Garvey beginning the first of 21 lessons by instructing us: "You must never stop learning." The paragraph after that begins, "One must never stop reading", and eventually there is a section on 'How To Read'. Lesson 3 covers the 'Aims and Objects of the UNIA', and Garvey writes: "The Negro should not have but one nation, but work with the hope that these independent nations will become parts of [the] great racial empire. It is necessary, therefore, to strengthen the hand of every free and independent Negro state so that they may be able to continue their independence." He taught people to, "Establish Universities, Colleges, Academies And Schools For The Racial Education And Culture Of The People." For Garvey, need for Black Nationalism is fundamental. "Never be satisfied to always live under the government of other people because you shall ever be at their mercy." "Teach Negroes to look for honour in their own race and from their own nation and to serve their own race and nation to get such honours."[7]

Black Nationalism has also been inaugurated by people who might not be labeled as 'black'.[8] For example, the Hindu lawyer, Mohandas Gandhi (1869-1948). Gandhi first became known for his civil rights work in South Africa, where he had lived for 20 years. It was during this time that his method of non-violence was developed, a method that has become both loved and hated by many. Indians who lived in South Africa were subjects of the British Empire, whose realm stretched across much of the globe. However, Indians, like the native South Africans, were victims to many oppressive laws and free travel around the country was forbidden. Gandhi, who had studied the British Common Law in London, led a great march in demonstration against these unjust laws in South Africa and he was imprisoned by the British government. When this event became publicized around the world, the British government released Gandhi. Gandhi then had the laws of South Africa changed under the *Indian Relief Act*, which was passed in 1914. Non-Christian marriages were made lawful, a special tax was removed for indentured servants, the importation of indentured servants from India was banned, and Indians were allowed free travel to the Cape Colony.[9]

Before returning to India to successfully force the British Empire to quit their occupation of the Asian sub-continent -including India, Pakistan, and Bangladesh - Gandhi had written an influential pamphlet in 1908 called *Hind Swaraj or Indian Home Rule*. In this booklet Gandhi listed some of the central grievances from the British occupation of his country. *Indian Home Rule* sums up the uselessness of the industrialism being exported by the British Empire. Whereas workers once had dignity,

---

[7] From *Marcus Garvey: Life and Lessons*, ed. Robert A. Hill and Barbara Bair, (Berkeley, University of California Press, 1987) p184, 208, 209, 211, 212. My thanks to Ian for his gift of this book.
[8] The 'Black and Tans' on the other hand were a conformist, counter-revolutionary group set up to stop the Irish War for Independence. (1916-1921) My thanks to Terry McCue for discussing with me the term's origin.
[9] Homer A. Jack, *The Gandhi Reader*, (New York, Grove Press, 1956) p97

now machines do most of the work. Women, once queens in their homes, now work in factories. He concludes:

1. Real home-rule is self-rule or self-control.
2. The way to it is passive resistance; that is soul-force or love-force.
3. In order to exert this force, Swadeshi in every sense is necessary.
4. What we want to do should be done, not because we object to the English or because we want to retaliate but because it is our duty to do so. Thus, supposing that the English remove the salt-tax, restore our money, give the highest posts to Indians, withdraw the English troops, we shall certainly not use their machine-made goods, nor use the English language, nor many of their industries. It is worth noting that these things are, in their nature, harmful; hence we do not want them. I bear no enmity toward the English but I do towards their civilization.[10]

Despite Gandhi's achievement of Home Rule in India and Civil rights in South Africa, a system of apartheid remained in place in this African British colony into the 1990's. South Africa had first been colonized by the Dutch in the 17th century and then by the British in the 19th century, who eventually defeated the Dutch in the Anglo-Boer War (1899-1902). Although the population of South Africa today consists of some 85% native Africans, the apartheid system of the British Empire effectively disestablished and oppressed the majority for a century. It wasn't until the work of Black Nationalist groups that the native people were given equal civil rights.

Probably the most central figure to the Black Nationalist movement in South Africa is Nelson Mandela (b. 1918). At the age of 26 Mandela joined the grassroots movement known as the African National Congress (ANC), which sought to empower the native African people. His autobiography recollects: "African nationalism was our battle cry, and our creed was the creation of one nation out of many tribes, the overthrow of white supremacy, and the establishment of a truly democratic form of government. Our manifesto stated: 'We believe that the national liberation of Africans will be achieved by Africans themselves…"[11]

During the 1950's Mandela helped coordinate mass boycotting and civil disobedience. He was arrested with many others in 1956 on the charge of high treason. When the apartheid government censured and banned the ANC in 1961, Mandela covertly became involved in the resistance movement. In 1963, Mandela was arrested on trumped-up charges and was imprisoned for 27 years. Around this time the UN General Assembly passed resolutions to condemn and sanction the corrupt South African Government. These were vetoed by the US and Britain in the Security Council.[12]

Upon his release in 1990, Mandela completed his work of leading millions of people to overthrow the oppressive government, which over the years had killed many unarmed demonstrators. Once listed by the United States government as a terrorist, Nelson Mandela became the first democratically elected president in South African history and went on to receive the Nobel Peace Prize in 1993.

The principles of the African National Congress were summed up by Mandela in a speech he gave in Johannesburg in 1991.

(a) that all governments must derive their authority from the consent of the governed

---

[10] Mohandas K. Gandhi, *Hind Swaraj or Indian Home Rule*, (Ahmedabad, Navajivan Publishing House, 1938) p91-92. *Swadeshi* refers to the move to buy local goods and to boycott foreign goods.
[11] Nelson Mandela, *Long Walk To Freedom: The Autobiography of Nelson Mandela*, (Boston, Little, Brown and Company, 1994) p99
[12] Harris, p243-244

(b) no person or group of person should be subjected to oppression or domination by virtue of his/her race, gender, color, or religious belief

(c) all person should enjoy security in their persons and their goods against intrusions by secular or clerical authorities

(d) all persons should enjoy the right to life, unfettered by impositions from either secular or clerical authorities

(e) all persons should have the untrammeled right to hold and express whatever opinions they wish to subscribe to as long as the exercise of that right does not infringe on the right of others[13]

Black Nationalism defeated the White Revolution in Iran. Like Gandhi's successful bout for Home Rule, the Muslim cleric Ayatollah Ruhollah Khomeini (1902-1989) led a non-violent struggle against the Shah, or King of Iran in 1979. Khomeini's counter-revolution became known as the 'Black Reaction' to the Shah's White Revolution which had done away with the Islamic as well as Persian traditions of agriculture and grass-roots commerce.

The White Revolution had its origin in Iran, the Land of the Aryans. During the first week of 1963, the King of Iran, Shah Pahlavi, instituted the White Revolution in order to modernize or 'westernize' the nation of Iran. The White Revolution is sort of the metonym for the high tide of westernization in the world, though as we can still see today in Iran's western neighbor Iraq, the English and US governments are still trying to determine the politics of foreign peoples and states.

The White Revolution was the culmination of Westernization in Iran and had drastic consequences on the Iranian people. Just as with the centralized states of the Western world, where the government takes responsibility for the laws of trade, economics, and justice, so did the White Revolution in Iran work. As in the United States where many farms have disappeared because of centralized federal corporate rights and international trade agreements like the North American Free Trade Agreement (NAFTA), the International Monetary Fund (IMF), and the General Agreement on Tariffs and Trade (GATT), and the World Bank, so too in Iran the White Revolution worked to eliminate farms and local businesses. During the White Revolution more than 6,000 factories were built, highways were constructed, supermarkets replaced local shops, the military budget rose from 170 million annually to almost 2 billion, agriculture fell drastically, and under the Shah farmers began to use chemical fertilizers and pesticides.[14]

Monarchy had a long history in Iran and in 1971 Shah Pahlavi boasted of celebrating 2500 years of Persian monarchy. As early as the 1830's the Shah Muhammad Mirza gave trade concessions to the British and the Russians. This led to great decline in the local economy and alienated the clergy from him. Mirza's successor Shah Nasser al-Din secularized the school system in the 1850's, then gave trade monopolies to the British over Iranian goods in the 1890's. The people justly became outraged and demonstrations ensued. Because of popular protest and boycotts, the Shah was forced to change these bogus economic policies. However, again, in 1901, the Shah gave concessions to the British, this time in oil. By 1905, through the culmination of civil unrest and demonstrations against the Shah, the King was forced to allow the

---

[13] "Building a Political Culture That Entrenches Political Tolerance", Speech to Johannesburg Press Club, February 22, 1991, in *Nelson Mandela Speaks: Forging a Democratic, Nonracial South Africa*, (New York, Pathfinder Press, 1993) p78-79

[14] Dilip Hiro, *Iran Under The Ayatollahs*, (New York, Routledge & Kegan Paul, 1987) p52-63

establishment of a House of Justice (to ensure the judiciary remained separate from the state), and in 1906 the Shah conceded to agreements for the drafting of a new Constitution. Two years later the Shah terminated the new Constitution and Civil War erupted (1908). Shah Al-Din was forced to flee the country and he took to hiding in Czarist Russia. Russia then invaded Iran in 1911 and by the end of the First World War (1914-1918) both the British and Russians disputed control over Iran.[15]

In 1926 the sovereign monarchy was reestablished under the Pahlavi dynasty. Western style reforms would be enforced on the people –from Western style dress codes (men had to wear hats and ties, women could not wear a veil) to laws barring the haj, or trip to Mecca. During the Second World War (1939-1945) both the Russians and the British marched into Iran and did not leave until 1946. In 1953 a man named Muhammad Mussadiq was democratically elected Prime Minister of Iran. Mussadiq had successfully nationalized the oil to the disappointment of Britain, which had until then enjoyed favorable concessions. As a result the British and other nations boycotted Iranian oil.

It was under these circumstances that the United States Central Intelligence Agency (CIA) under the leadership of Kermit Roosevelt, Jr. plotted Operation Ajax. This ploy ousted Mussadiq and he was put under house arrest until his death. The Shah regained total power. The Indian journalist Dilip Hiro writes that this Coup "destroyed any chance that Iran had of evolving as a Western style democracy". The next year the Shah signed oil agreements with a Western consortium. In 1957 the Shah signed the US Eisenhower Doctrine which promised US military support to any Middle East government against "armed aggression from any nation controlled by international communism."[16]

The indefatigable Iranian people kept protesting the corrupt monarchy, and toward the late 1970's things were looking bleak for the Shah's regime. When in 1978 the Shah ordered the military to censor two newspapers in Tehran, over 4,000 workers walked out. The Shah was forced to lift the censor. Then the Central Bank of Iran, Bank Markazi, released a statement showing that some 177 wealthy Iranians (some of whom were military personnel) had sent some $2 billion dollars abroad. News of this move against the community caused greater civil unrest. The Shah declared martial law and instilled a military government that November. It became common knowledge that Washington backed the Shah. Under this tumultuous climate, the clergyman who had been exiled by the Shah for 16 years, Ayatollah Khomeini, returned home in 1979 and led the Iranians to a successful non-violent revolution, putting an end to both the Divine Right of Kings and Western intervention. Khomeini's 'Cassette Revolution' successfully spread the word how the White Revolution of the Shah was "hostile to Islam, violates constitutional freedoms, [and] destroys agriculture…"[17]

The centralization of the state which occurred in Iran under the Shah has been occurring in the Western world for some time. Just as we have seen in US history with the marginalization of the poor and disempowered, so we saw during Bush II's regime and still today, many democratic institutions have been violated. It is usually within the domain of state and empire that people are forced to fight for their rights.

---

[15] Hiro, p16-22
[16] Hiro, p26-41
[17] Hiro, p78, 81, 64

Civil Rights

Civil Rights originated in America, not with the Constitution, but following the Civil War. This period is known as the American Reconstruction. As the historians Eric Foner and Olivia Mahoney tell us in their work, *America's Reconstruction: People and Politics after the Civil War*, "For the first time, the national government assumed the basic responsibilities for defining and protecting America's civil rights."[18] This had occurred not without great struggle. The Civil War had been one of the bloodiest wars in world history, certainly the bloodiest war in US history.

In 1865, five days after the Confederate General Robert E. Lee surrendered his southern army President Abraham Lincoln was assassinated. This left Vice President Andrew Johnson with the task of reforming and reshaping the war-torn nation. Incidentally, Johnson had been the only southern senator not to join the succession movement into Confederacy. This created problems in the post-Civil War climate because the Senate was by and large made up of Northerners. While the North wanted the laws of southern states changed to their liking, Johnson was more set on putting the same southern political structure back in place, minus nominal slavery.

Southerners who had rebelled against the Union were put back in power by Johnson. New laws were written to control the lives of Africans in much the same way as the laws of slavery had. The "Black Codes" as they were called, granted the former slaves some rights, however. African-Americans were not permitted to vote, serve on a jury, or testify against a white person. Former slaves in the south were required by law to sign yearly labor contracts, and those who were unemployed were arrested, fined, or hired out to white landowners. In Florida, for example, disobedience was a criminal activity and if African-Americans broke labor contracts they could be whipped, pilloried, and sold for a year's worth of labor.[19] At the end of 1865, six months after the end of the Civil War, President Johnson declared the Reconstruction complete.

Northern senators became suspicious of this claim of Johnson's and established a Joint Committee in order to investigate the progress of Reconstruction in the south. In 1866 the senate passed two bills: one reestablishing the Freedmen's Bureau which worked to build schools for former slaves, and the Civil Rights Bill which defined US citizens rights in national terms, rather than in terms of race, as the Black Codes did. This went directly against the US Supreme Court's Dred Scott decision in 1857 which stated that no African could ever become a US citizen. Although both bills passed with a great majority in the Houses of Congress, to everyone's surprise President Johnson vetoed both bills, believing that African-Americans did not deserve the rights of citizenship. However, in April 1866 for the first time in American history a law was passed over a presidential veto, and the Civil Rights Bill became the law of the land. Two months later Congress passed the 14th Amendment to the Constitution, which stated that all citizens had equal protection of their rights. While it did not give African-

---

[18] Eric Foner and Olivia Mahoney, *America's Reconstruction: People and Politics after the Civil War*, (Baton Rouge, Louisiana State University Press, 1997) p11
[19] Foner and Mahoney, p74-75

Americans the right to vote, it threatened to diminish the political representation of the Southern states if they wouldn't allow freed slaves to vote.[20]

In early 1867 Congress, once again over the veto of President Johnson, adopted the Reconstruction Act, something which Johnson had pronounced finished in 1865. This marks the beginning of the period known as the Congressional or Radical Reconstruction, which lasted for ten years until 1877. Under the Reconstruction Act many former Confederates were barred from holding office, southern state governments were recreated, African-American men were given the right to vote, and hundreds of freed slaves were put into government positions. When in early 1868 President Johnson violated new laws passed by Congress he became the first president to be impeached, brought up on charges, and placed on trial by the House of Representatives. In Congress, the impeachment trial fell short by one vote needed for a two-thirds majority required to remove him from office.[21]

In 1868 the man who had defeated the Confederate General Robert E. Lee, Ulysses S. Grant was nominated as the new President of the United States. By 1870 a 15th Amendment was made part of the US Constitution, barring states from depriving citizens the right to vote because of race, though not according to gender. Although another Civil Rights Act was put into place in 1875 barring hotels, theaters, and railroads, among other things, from discriminating against African-Americans, this was changed by a Supreme Court decision in 1896, *Plessy v. Ferguson*, which stated that railroads could segregate people by race.[22]

Despite much of the Civil Rights legislation and enactment, a group of laws remained which segregated and discriminated against the Civil Rights of African Americans from the end of the Civil War in 1865 to the Civil Rights Act of 1964 passed by President Lyndon Johnson. These laws have become known as the Jim Crow laws. Jim Crow laws (named after an early racist folk song) made it so that white people and black people did not have to come into contact with one another, but each race would have its own public restroom, restaurant and church pew.

In 1965 President Johnson passed the Voting Rights Law, giving federal protection to minorities who wished to vote, but who had previously been threatened with violence when they had attempted. Riots and unrest ensued through 1966 and 1967. In 1968 Congress passed another Civil Rights Act giving even more protection to minorities against violence (Civil Rights laws also had been passed in 1957, 1960, and 1964). It was during this time that the Civil Rights struggle helped inaugurate the Vietnam anti-war movement.

The leading figure during the Civil Rights struggle of the 1960's was the Protestant Christian Reverend Dr. Martin Luther King, Jr. Martin Luther King, whose home was shot at and bombed on more than one occasion, had led many demonstrations in Alabama, Georgia, and Tennessee. He had been imprisoned a dozen or so times in these states and had survived a near fatal stabbing as well as many death threats.

In 1965 he wrote of the encouraging effects of civil disobedience, having marched with hundreds of thousands on Washington in 1963, and witnessing and participating in

---

[20] Foner and Mahoney, p78-79
[21] Foner and Mahoney, p81, 93, 85
[22] Howard Zinn, *A People's History of the United States*, Revised Edition, (New York, HarperPerennial, 1995) p194, 200

the solidarity that ought to guide democratic movements. He wrote that people are "imbued by demonstrations with a sense of courage and dignity that strengthens their personalities. Through demonstrations, Negroes learn that unity and militance have more force than bullets."[23] King believed that such movements were crucial to changing the laws in a democratic nation.

"Demonstrations, experience has shown, are part of the process of stimulating legislation and law enforcement. The federal government reacts to events more quickly when a situation of conflict cries out for its intervention. Beyond this, demonstrations have a creative effect on the social and psychological climate that is not matched by the legislative process."[24]

The Civil Rights struggle of the 1960's was the segue to the Anti-War movement, and both struggles helped change the nation's course toward better democratizing America. King showed that such demonstrations changed laws, and that such legal reforms did not depend upon the charity-conscience of a few sympathetic political softies or closet-racists. He wrote:

"The legislation was not a product of charity of white America for a supine black America, nor was it the result of enlightened leadership by the judiciary. This legislation was first written in the streets. The epic thrust of the millions of Negroes who demonstrated in 1963 in hundreds of cities won strong white allies to the cause. Together, they created a 'coalition of conscience' which awoke a hitherto somnolent Congress."

"*The overwhelming national consensus followed their acts; it did not precede them.*"[25]

A strong critic of the Civil Rights movement was also the most famous proponent of Black Nationalism in America: El-Hajj Malik El-Shabazz, or Malcolm X. Malcolm X's father, Reverend Earl Little, had been a Baptist minister, and supporter of Marcus Garvey, having worked as an organizer for the Universal Negro Improvement Association (UNIA). In fact, Malcolm's parents met each other at a Garvey rally in Canada. When Malcolm was 6 years old living in Nebraska, the Christian terrorist group, the Ku Klux Klan murdered his father.

Malcolm X preached a different message than Martin Luther King and the Black Nationalist movement seems to imply separatism or segregation. In 1964 Malcolm X gave a speech at Harvard University in which he said:

"When the black man controls the politics and the politicians in his own community, he can then make them produce what is good for the community… Our economic philosophy of Black Nationalism means that instead of our spending the rest of our lives begging the white man for a job, our people should be re-educated to the science of economics and the part that it plays in our community."[26]

For many Westerners, Black Nationalism can appear, if not racist, as being negative in its scope. However, Malcolm teaches that "the social philosophy of Black Nationalism doesn't in any way involve any anti-anything." Rather than implying racism, it is really about "brotherhood".[27]

Black Nationalism has two goals, one long term and one short term. The long-range goal is the Back to Africa movement, "to our homeland and to live among our own

---

[23] Martin Luther King, Jr., "Let Justice Roll Down", in *Uncivil War: Race, Civil Rights & The Nation. 1865-1995*, ed. Eyal Press, (New York, The Nation Press, 1995) p146
[24] King, p146
[25] King, p148, 152
[26] Malcolm X, "The Leverett House Forum of March 18, 1964", in *The Speeches of Malcolm X at Harvard*, ed. Archie Epps, (New York, William Morrow & Company, Inc., 1969) p140-141
[27] Malcolm X, p142, 158

people and develop it so we'll have an independent nation of our own."[28] The short-range goal is the aforementioned movement to putting political power of black communities in the hands of black leaders and politicians. Malcolm X says:

"And with this new approach and with these new ideas we think that we may open up a new era here in this country. As that era begins to spread, people in this country –instead of sticking under your nose or crying for civil rights- will begin to expand their civil rights plea to a plea for human rights. And once the so-called Negro in this country forgets the whole civil rights issue and begins to realize that human rights are far more important and broad than civil rights, he won't be going to Washington, D.C., anymore, to beg Uncle Sam for civil rights. He will take his plea for human rights to the United Nations. There won't be a violation of civil rights anymore. It will be a violation of human rights."[29]

The question of Civil Rights vs. Human Rights introduces an important dilemma and is relevant to the question of the different ethics used by Martin Luther King, Malcolm X and others. It is uncanny how many people believe that King and X represent opposite ends of an ethical duality. This is usually demonstrated as being the opposition of pacifism and violence, though the dichotomies get more crude.

As we see with Martin Luther King, he was an advocate of those methods used by the American naturalist and activist Henry David Thoreau. Thoreau believed in Civil Disobedience as a means of protesting against the American war on Mexico (1846-1848), as well as for against the institution of slavery, for which he was arrested in 1846. King also used the methods of the Hindu lawyer, Mohandas (Mahatma) Gandhi, who had fought both for civil rights in South Africa, and Home Rule (or Black Nationalism) in India. King wrote that "The Negro's weapon of non-violent direct action is his only serviceable tool against injustice."[30]

In his work, *Strength to Love*, King talks about the development of his political philosophy and its justification.

"The turn-the-other-cheek and love-your-enemies philosophies are valid, I felt, only when individuals are in conflict with other individuals; when racial groups and nations are in conflict, a more realistic approach is necessary.

"Then I was introduced to the life and teachings of Mahatma Gandhi... As I delved deeper into the philosophy of Gandhi, my scepticism concerning the power of love gradually diminished, and I came to see for the first time that the Christian doctrine of love, operating through the Gandhian method of non-violence, is one of the most potent weapons available to an oppressed people in their struggle for freedom."[31]

Those who believe in this dualism of King and X hold that while King followed the pacifism of Thoreau and Gandhi, Malcolm X represented violence and aggression. Many religious or spiritual Americans, as well as socialists and anarchists downplay the extent of Malcolm X's commitment to Islam, or more erroneously believe that in Islam Malcolm X found a justification for violence and aggression. Neither of these ignorant and racist assumptions could be more distant from the truth.

In a speech on December 16th, 1964, to the Harvard Law School Forum just a few months before he was assassinated, Malcolm X told people at Harvard University that he stood for peace, and that he was part of the peaceful group the Organization of Afro-American Unity (OAAU).[32] In his autobiography he recounted, "They called me 'a teacher, a fomenter of violence.' I would say point blank, 'That is a lie. I'm not for

---

[28] Malcolm X, p140
[29] Malcolm X, p143
[30] King, p148
[31] Martin Luther King, Jr., *Strength to Love*, (Philadelphia, Fortress Press, 1963) p150-151
[32] Malcolm X, "The Harvard Law School Forum of December 16, 1964", p175

wanton violence, I'm for justice."[33] Malcolm X did not see the point in fighting for civil rights but believed in fighting for International Justice, like the Black Nationalist Marcus Garvey.[34] It is little wonder that his whole life, from when he was the head of his class in 8th grade to his autobiography, Malcolm X had wished he had been a lawyer.

In this book he expressed his bent toward international justice:[35]

"...the United Nations proposes to insure the human rights of the oppressed minorities of the world. The American black man is the world's most shameful case of minority oppression. What makes the black man think of himself as only an internal United States issue is just a catch-phrase, two words, 'civil rights'. How is the black man going to get 'civil rights' before first he wins his *human rights?* If the American black man will start thinking about his *human* rights, and then start thinking of himself as part of one of the world's great peoples, he will see he has a case for the United Nations."

"...the American black man needed to quit thinking what the white man had taught him –which was that the black man had no alternative except to beg for his so-called 'civil rights'. I said that the American black man needed to recognize that he had a strong, airtight case to take the United States before the United Nations on a formal accusation of 'denial of human rights' –and that if Angola and South Africa were precedent cases, then there would be no easy way that the U.S. could escape being censured, right on its own home ground."[36]

International Justice

One may go back to the writings of the prophet Isaiah (8th century BCE) who predicted that the Hebrew god, Yhwh, would judge between the many nations and many peoples.[37]

"And He shall judge between the nations, and shall decide for many peoples; and they shall beat their swords into plowshares, and their spears into pruning-hooks; nation shall not lift up sword against nation, neither shall they learn war any more." Isaiah 2:4[38]

---

[33] Malcolm X, *The Autobiography of Malcolm X*, ed. Alex Haley, (New York, Ballantine Books, 1973) p421

[34] Even when Malcolm X was still with the Nation of Islam he was wary of the extent to which white people, be they nationalist, socialist, or anarchist, believed that either Islam or Malcolm X preached violence. In a speech he gave in the streets of Harlem in 1960 Malcolm X said, "You want peace. I want peace. Everyone craves for a world peace... The whole dark world wants peace. When I was in Africa last year I was deeply impressed by the desire of our African Brothers of peace, but even they agree that there can be no peace without freedom from colonialism, foreign domination, oppression and exploitation... The American so-called Negroes must recognize each other as brothers and sisters... stop carrying guns and knives to hurt each other..."

In an interview with Louis Lomax in 1963, Malcolm X again complained that Islam was being called a violent religion. "[T]he white man runs around here with a doctrine that Mr. Muhammad is advocating violence when he is actually telling Negroes to defend themselves against violent people." From Louis E. Lomax's, *When The Word Is Given... A Report on Elijah Muhammad, Malcolm X, and the Black Muslim World*, (New York, Signet Books, 1963) p130-131, 173-174

[35] King taught Americans, "Let us not join those who shout war and who through their misguided passions urge the United States to relinquish its participation in the United Nations." *Strength to Love*, p104

[36] Malcolm X, *The Autobiography of Malcolm X*, p207, 415

[37] Jane Addams wrote, "Isaiah's prophecy was remarkable in that it looked forward rather than backward, for the mythology of the ancients, including the dreams of the Greeks and Romans, had always placed the era of peace in the past, in a golden age of long ago which had been followed by other ages each harder than the last, until men fell upon the iron age of the present." With Emily Greene Balch, "The Hopes We Inherit", from *Building International Goodwill*, (New York, Macmillan, 1927). Reprinted in *Jane Addams' Essays and Speeches*, ed. Marilyn Fischer and Judy D. Whipps, (London, Continuum International Publishing Group, 2005) p279

However, the conception of International Justice probably has as its origin the theory of a World Government. Some might argue that it was probably the goal of every empire in history –from Alexander the Great (356-323), to the Roman Empire (27 BCE-1453), to Kublai Khan (1215-1294), to Napoleon Bonaparte (1769-1821), to both World Wars of the 20th century –to establish a kind of Super-National Justice under a single centralized government. The concept of World Government differs in that it is based upon the mutual consent of sovereign state-leaders and diplomats.

The ethical height of the Native American League of the Iroquois, which was a peaceful international treaty organization, of course precedes Western attempts at Internationalism. One may sight alongside the League of the Iroquois the Delian League which was a pact between well over a hundred Greek City-states who had banded together to fight off the Persian Empire in the 5th century BCE. Both the League of the Iroquois and the Delian were associations between peoples who shared a language.

The idea of a World Government of sovereign states is modern and wasn't attempted until the 20th century. There have been several intellectuals in history who have contributed to such a theory, a notable one being Immanuel Kant. In his work, "Eternal Peace", Kant discussed a "federalism of different states" which would form a non-compulsory association in "maintaining peace among themselves and toward other states, but not for the purpose of making conquests."[39] Although the early 17th century Dutch Jurist Hugo Grotius (1583-1645) had similar theories, Kant had called him a "miserable consoler", probably because Grotius's major work, *The Laws of Peace and War*, is by and large about the laws of war.

The idea of a World Government was also heavily discussed and written about by the English mathematician and philosopher Bertrand Russell (1872-1970). In 1951 Russell had concluded that "great wars cannot be avoided until there is a world Government"[40] and in 1963 he was still convinced of this. Russell saw the only way to avoid nuclear war to be through a World Government.

"The only ultimate and secure means of preventing wars employing methods of mass destruction is World Government. There are exactly the same reasons for World Government as there are for the internal governments of separate States... [I]f international law is to have any reality, it must be backed by international force, just as national law is backed by a national police."

Moreover, Russell finds that this international government, and not individual nations or militaries, ought to control the means of nuclear weapons production.

"The international Government should possess the raw materials necessary for weapons of mass destruction. This would prevent the possibility of the surreptitious production of such weapons by some rebellious State or group of States.

"There should be international criminal law and international criminal courts...

"Broadly speaking, the powers of the international Government should be only such as are required for the prevention of war. In all other respects, constituent States should retain their autonomy."[41]

Like the 'Justice League' of Comic books such as Superman and Captain America, the United Nations was not created by superheroes with supernatural powers, but was created by mortals; in this case by the governments that were victorious in World

---

[38] All translations of the Hebrew Bible, or Tanach, are according to the Masocretic Text by The Jewish Publication Society of America, Philadelphia, 1917
[39] Immanuel Kant, "Eternal Peace", in *The Philosophy of Kant: Immanuel Kant's Moral and Political Writings*, ed. and trans. Carl J. Friedrich, (New York, Modern Library Books, 1949) p472-473
[40] Bertrand Russell, *New Hopes For A Changing World*, (New York, Simon and Schuster, 1951) p95
[41] Bertrand Russell, *Unarmed Victory*, (Baltimore, Penguin Books, 1963) p119, 120

War II. The United Nations replaced the former League of Nations, which had been in turn formed by the victor government leaders of World War I. Today the United Nations is made up of more than 190 different nations, representing almost the entire population of the world.

World War I (1914-1918) marked the dissolution of three empires: the Austro-Hungarian Empire, the German Empire, and the Ottoman Empire. When the war ended in 1919, the leaders of the victor nations held a Peace Conference in Paris. By 1920, in the Treaties of Versailles and Sevres, lands formerly controlled and/or occupied by these three empires, were now occupied and controlled by the wars victors.[42] For example, from the dissolved Ottoman Empire, Britain took control of Palestine, Jordan, and Iraq, France took Syria and Lebanon. This pattern was followed throughout the world.

The League of Nations justly received a good deal of criticism. For the majority of Irish who gained their independence from Britain in 1920, the League of Nations was called "Britain's League". Irish nationalists had spent huge sums of money in campaigns to spread the word against the League of Nations in America.[43] Marcus Garvey became heavily critical of the League when it failed to defend Ethiopia in 1936 from the Italian war of aggression. Garvey became particularly critical of the then Emperor of Ethiopia, Haile Selassie, who fled the country for his own safety. Garvey said of Selassie, "The Emperor's reliance on the League [of Nations] was unfortunate, but more so was his reliance on his white advisors."[44]

The American pragmatist philosopher John Dewey (1859-1952) was critical of the United States entering the League of Nations, believing it to be part of a "legalized war system" offering only prospects for more war.[45] In 1923 he wrote: "The League [of Nations] is *not* honestly named. It is a League of governments pure and simple."[46] Following the Second World War and having witnessed the failure of the League of Nations, Dewey was pleased with the stir and controversy among people and politicians over what kind of authority the United Nations ought to have. He reminded people of its predecessor: "the main purpose of the League was to preserve the fruits of victory for the European nations that were on the winning side."[47]

Dewey had recommended the US instigate an agreement for the *Outlawry of War*. This was a proposal written by Salmon O. Levinson, who was the Chairman of the American Committee for the Outlawry of War in 1923. Dewey believed that people should promote such a cause over the creation of leagues of states and nations. As a

---

[42] W.E.B. DuBois points out that Marcus Garvey did ask the League to donate a former German colony in Africa for the Black Nationalist movement. See W.E.B. DuBois, "Back to Africa", in Clarke, p113
[43] Tim Pat Coogan, *The IRA*, Fully Revised and Updated, (New York, Palgrave, 2002) p99
[44] Marcus Garvey, "Italy's Conquest?", first published in the *Blackman* Magazine, August 1936, in Clarke, p364-365. Malcolm X seems to be clear of the mistake made by Garvey and the worshipers of the Christian Ethiopian Emperor, Haile Selassie. "Most people think Ethiopia is Christian. But only its government is Christian. The West has always helped to keep the Christian government in power." (*The Autobiography of Malcolm X*, p380) Most Ethiopians, like most Africans, are Sunni Muslims, though both Protestant and Catholic missions still riddle the continent. Islam is the fastest growing religion in the world.
[45] John Dewey, "On America's Responsibility", from *Characters and Events*, vol. II, published in 1926; quoted in *John Dewey's Philosophy*, ed. Joseph Ratner, (New York, Modern Library, 1939) p503, 508, 527
[46] From *The New Republic*, March 28, 1923. Quoted by Ratner in *John Dewey's Philosophy*, p503f
[47] John Dewey, "Afterword", *The Public and Its Problems*, (Athens, Swallow Press/Ohio University Press, 1954) p221

grassroots and non-bureaucratic movement the Outlawry of War had a better chance of succeeding than those laws written by military leaders, politicians, and representatives.

Dewey wrote:

"It denotes a general plan consisting of a few simple, understandable principles. War is not merely thought of and denounced as criminal; it is to be made a public crime by international law. It is not outlawed by rhetorical resolutions passed by either peace societies or parliaments. A judicial substitute for wars as a method of settling disputes is to be created in the form of a supreme court of justice of the world, which will be a real supreme court of justice for and of the world and not the kind of thing...[as] the so-called court of international justice. A judicial substitute for wars as a method of settling disputes is created in the form of a supreme court of the nations of the world, the court sitting and deciding cases under and by an international law that has made war a crime and the instigators or breeders of war as much criminals as any other kind of murderers that now infest the earth... I hope no one will take my word for the extent to which existing international law is bound up with the war system. Consult the texts and decide for yourselves."[48]

The feminist pragmatist Jane Addams (1860-1935) was also an early critic of the League of Nations. A lifelong pacifist, she had protested the Spanish-American War and the colonization that had ensued following US victory, as for example in the Philippines. Thus, when politicians in the United States debated the nation's entry into the First World War, Addams popularly became one of the greatest antagonists of war. In 1915 she headed a woman's movement in opposition to war called the Women's Peace Party. Though based out of Washington the party was international in its scope. In the same year she chaired for the International Congress of Women at The Hague. Then in 1919 the Congress became known as The Women's International League for Peace and Freedom (WILPF), in which she served as president until her death in 1935. The WILPF still exists today.[49]

Addams was critical of the League, particularly for the prominence it gave to military leaders over questions of world peace. She wrote: "The great danger ahead of the League of Nations is implicit in the fact that its first work involves the guaranteeing of a purely political peace and dependence upon the old political motives." She remained thoroughly convinced that the "League would have been a thousand times stronger if the possibility" of its utilization of military force had been removed. Though wary of this problematic fact, she decided that such an international institution could be made to be of some beneficial use, in particular, to alleviate starvation.[50]

Addams was the first American woman to be awarded the Nobel Peace Prize (1931). With her friend Emily Greene Balch, who was in turn awarded the Nobel Peace Prize in 1946, they wrote about how the existence of a World Court is necessary if any hope for World Peace is to be realized. Emily and Jane wrote:

"Arbitration treaties, a world court, an association of nations preventing aggression at once by world opinion and by providing non-violent methods of securing fair demands, -these are parts of the necessary machinery of world peace."[51]

The pacifist and atheist Bertrand Russell, who was arrested for protesting his nations entrance into World War I, found the League of Nations to be quite useless. He

---

[48] John Dewey, "International Law and the War-System", from *Characters and Events*, vol. II, in *John Dewey's Philosophy*, p513-514, 517
[49] www.wilpf.int.ch/
[50] Jane Addams, "Feed the World and Save the League", first published in *The New Republic*, (24 November, 1920). "How to Build a Peace Program", interview with William Hard, published by *Survey*, 68 (1 November, 1932) Reprinted in *Jane Addams' Essays and Speeches*, p217, 331
[51] Addams and Balch, "The Hopes We Inherit", p284

also thought that the League's successor, the United Nations to be defective as well. This is because of the veto power that some state leaders have over all others –particularly, those leaders who were victors in World War II.[52]

The United Nations was created in 1945 by the leaders of the then allied nations: the United States, the Soviet Union, France, and Britain. These four nations also make up a special branch of the United Nations known as the Security Council. Eventually this included China, in the 1960's (when their leaders too gained a Nuclear arsenal). The five nations of the Security Council are separate from the rest of other nations represented in the United Nations (all of whom constitute the General Assembly), because they have permanence in the Security Council. The permanent five nation members of the Security Council, as Russell pointed out, have veto power over all other national representatives, which in the General Assembly is over 185 votes.

Incidentally, the five members of the Security Council are also the biggest nuclear powers. The United States was the first nuclear power in 1945, and to date, the only nation to have ever used nuclear bombs in warfare.[53] The Soviet Union tested their own nuclear weapon in 1949. Against the council of Lord Bertrand Russell, the English became a nuclear power in the 1950's. The French tested their first nuclear weapon in 1960 and somewhere around then China developed nuclear weapons as well. Since then several other countries have been given nuclear weapons by one of the Security Council members, or have produced their own. For example, France gave some nuclear weapons to Israel. Canada gave a nuclear reactor to India, which they used to create a nuclear arsenal beginning in 1974. This was followed by Pakistan. Around this time South Africa developed Nuclear weapons, which were dismantled when the white government was ousted. In 2006 North Korea produced their own Nuclear weapons and were subsequently dropped from their membership amongst the Axis of Evil.

Being one of the five permanent members of the UN Security Council gives these representative governments a significant amount of clout when it comes to matters of International Legislation and Justice. This is because of the veto-power which members of the Security Council possess. Since the 1960's the United States has vetoed more Security Council resolutions than any other nation, with Britain in a close second.[54] Since 1966 the United States has had 76 of 138 vetoes in the Security Council.[55] Other members have far fewer –China, France, and Russia.

To name a few votes and vetoes: in 1976 the US vetoed a resolution on a Palestinian state. In 2003 the US was the only member to vote against a nuclear test ban treaty, and the reduction or elimination of nuclear weapons. When a resolution was passed 174 – 0 to prevent militarization of space, the US abstained from voting.[56]

---

[52] *The Autobiography of Bertrand Russell*, Volume III, 1944-1969, (New York, Simon and Schuster, 1969) p261.
[53] Truman gave the orders to drop the bomb without congress knowing. See Michael Mandelbaum's, *The Nuclear Revolution: International Politics Before and After Hiroshima*, (Cambridge, Cambridge University Press, 1981) p178
[54] Noam Chomsky, *Hegemony or Survival: America's Quest For Global Dominance*, (New York, Henry Holt and Company, 2003) p29-30
[55] Michael Mandel , *How America Gets Away With Murder: Illegal Wars, Collateral Damage and Crimes Against Humanity*, (London, Pluto Press, 2004) 17n44
[56] Chomsky, p168, 244

In his book, *Hegemony or Survival*, Chomsky tells us, "US abstention amounts to a veto: typically a double veto, banning the events from reporting and history. In the mainstream media, there was no mention of these failed attempts by the rest of the world to prevent serious threats to survival."[57] And in the case of the US War with Iraq, when the only other member of the Security Council to vote in favor of war was Britain, Bush II had said, "we don't need the Security Council".[58] Thus the US war with Iraq violates international law.[59]

World Court

A World Court was first planned in 1899 at the first Hague Conference in Holland. In 1900 The Hague Court of Conciliation and Arbitration was established. However, no cases were brought until 1902 when President Theodore Roosevelt got in a quarrel with the Mexican government over a property dispute. This was regarding the 'Pious Fund', where land had been sold between religious groups in Mexico and Southern California. The case went on for 15 years with the US getting the better end of the Hague decision. Roosevelt also brought a case between the US and Canada over rights to a Seal Fishery. Again The Hague Court decided in favor of the US, this time in a matter of weeks. In total, eighteen major cases were brought before The Hague Court as well as many lesser cases. The Court ceased to exist when the First World War erupted and thereafter.[60]

Jane Addams said that an important precursor to the modern conceptualization of a World Court was the establishment of the Universal Postal Union in 1875. She was 15 years old at the time, and she later recalled how exciting it was that with a 5 cent stamp a letter could be mailed anywhere in the world. This led to the laying of telegram cables, which stretched across borders and oceans. These types of advances made clear "how firmly established international activity" had become.

Addams believed that the establishment of a World Court would help further the cause of enfranchising women. She found that general discussion of a World Court was a good thing and that "there is a peculiar fitness in a woman's political organization going into this whole question of the World Court". It seems that such organized effort can get us past the old patriarchal structure and can

"get at some opinion which will not represent any individual opinion but will represent the opinion of a group trying quite honestly to act together in this new light that is opening before women as well as men that they may act as parties, as distinct groups, quite unlike the old individual action."[61]

After the First World War, the founding of the League of Nations eventually led to the reestablishment of a World Court. However, because of its political underpinnings the League of Nation's new World Court was quite unlike the previous and more

---

[57] Chomsky, p121
[58] Chomsky, p32
[59] Ralph Nader, *In Pursuit of Justice: Collected Writings: 2000-2003*, (New York, Seven Stories Press, 2004) p454
[60] Jane Addams, "The World Court", originally addressed to the Annual Meeting of the Women's Roosevelt Republican Club, in Chicago, January 14, 1926. First published by *Republican Woman* 3 (February 1926): 5, 7-8. Reprinted in Fischer and Whipps, *Jane Addams' Essays and Speeches*, p267-272
[61] Addams, "The World Court", p270

judiciary Hague Court, and as history has shown, this post-First World War court was highly ineffective.

The founding of the United Nations was followed by the United Nations War Crimes Commission in 1943, and the founding of the International Court of Justice (ICJ) in 1945. The first cases to be handled were the Nuremberg Trials and the lesser known Tokyo Trials. The penalty of death was meted out to some. While hundreds of Nazi's were executed in American and English military tribunals, several Americans, notably Lieutenant Colonel Murray C. Bernays who was a lawyer, Judge Samuel I. Rosenman, and Supreme Court Justice Robert Jackson pushed for a more judicial international war tribunal.[62] Their idea for an International Military Tribunal was at first met with opposition from the leader of England, Winston Churchill, and the leader of Russia, Josef Stalin, who believed such a trial was far too modest and that most Nazis ought to be executed summarily.[63]

While it was hoped by many that such an international court would remain in place long after the Nuremberg and Tokyo Trials, this would not be the case. Once the Second World War was over, a new ideological war had begun -the Cold War. During the Cold War, the world was again split along oppositional lines: instead of Axis vs. Allies it was capitalism vs. socialism, the US vs. the USSR.

Although Cold War as a subject doesn't sound like it would be too hot a topic, such summations are cool if intemperate. Like the Second World War, which it followed, the Cold War was a war that affected the whole world; undoubtedly helping in global warming's acceleration. After the fall of the Third Reich there was war between the two remaining super-powers ensued over the Third World, a kind Third-World War. Much of the Cold War was waged over whether the Third World had the right to form their own government, be it capitalist or socialist, or what have you. Whether it was in Korea, Vietnam, Afghanistan, or Cuba, it was a war between the US and the USSR. There have been few exceptions.

In 1949 the United States and other Western-European Second World War victors national leaders signed the North Atlantic Treaty, which then became an organization (NATO). NATO was designed to establish a collective military defense against those allied victors of WWII that were communist, known as the Eastern Bloc. According to Michael Mandelbaum in his study on *The Nuclear Revolution*, "Nuclear weapons have made NATO a defensive peacetime alliance."[64] The Eastern Bloc's response to this aggressive move is known as the Warsaw Pact, named after a treaty signed in Warsaw, Poland in 1955 by the allied communists. The Pact was for defense against NATO aggression.

For the second half of the 20th century, the Cold War might have otherwise been a stalemate between black and white, between NATO and the Pact of the Eastern Bloc, of two groups of military nations each with its own nuclear powerhouse (the US vs. the USSR). In 1955, however, a conference was held in opposition to both sides of this Cold War. This took place in the largest Muslim nation in the world, Indonesia, at the Asia-Africa Conference. With the initiative of five leaders -the Muslim President of Egypt Gamal Abdel Nasser, the Hindu President of India Jawaharlal Nehru, the Muslim

---

[62] Robert E. Conot, *Justice at Nuremberg*, (New York, Harper & Row, Publishers, 1983) p10, 14
[63] Mandel, p220n69
[64] Mandelbaum, p150

president of Indonesia Sukarno, the Pan-Africanist and Marxist Prime Minister of Ghana Kwame Nkrumah, and the atheist and socialist President of Yugoslavia Josip Broz Tito – the Non-Aligned Movement (NAM) was begun.

The basic idea behind the Non-Aligned Movement was a refusal to participate in the Cold War and the splitting of the world into two factions. Members of NAM refused to participate in the dualistic hegemony of NATO vs. Warsaw. The first conference of the Non-Aligned Movement was held in Belgrade in 1961. This was accomplished in large part through the work of President Tito, "who had expressed concern that an accelerating arms race might result in war between the Soviet Union and the USA"[65], a war between the Eastern Bloc and NATO. Today the Non-Aligned Movement has some 118 members and pushes for issues concerning Human Rights, the reform and democratization of the United Nations, the rights of peoples and nations to self-determine their own political identity, and the promotion of decolonization.[66]

With these permanent members of the Security Council battling in a 'Third-World' War, the idea of an International Criminal Court was not bothered with. However, the International Court of Justice (ICJ) remained in place as the judiciary organ of the United Nations. The ICJ can pass judgement in matters between nations, as for example, in questions of the exactitude of land surveys (which, for example, has occurred between Canada and the US, which share borders besides the Great Lakes and the 49th parallel). The ICJ, however, lacks the ability to enforce its decisions. This relies ultimately on the compliance of governments. If a government will not comply with the court's decision, the matter is passed over to the Security Council, which can vote on whether coercion by UN forces is justified. Given the veto-power of the Security Council this can be problematic if one of its members is the non-compliant government. This occurred in 1982 when the UN attempted to halt US aggression against Lebanon, only to be vetoed by the US. In 1986 the government of Nicaragua defeated the US government in the International Court of Justice, for having militarily funded a dictator. The US refused to enter the jurisdiction of the UN's international law. Because the US is on the Security Council, this nation "vetoed two Security Council resolutions affirming the court judgement and calling on all states to observe international law."[67]

The Cold War 'ended' (ideological wars never really end) in the late 1980's with the US victorious and the Russian President Mikhail Gorbachev setting in place the collapse of state-socialism, *Perestroika*, or 'restructuring', and *Glasnost*, or 'total transparency' . Then in the late 1990's trouble began in Kosovo with General Milosevic's religious and ethnic war of cleansing Europe to rid it of Muslims. For the first time ever NATO troops were deployed to the region. However, this was preceded by some of NATO's most hideous bombing tactics which killed mostly innocent civilians.[68]

---

[65] www.nam.gov.za/background/background.htm#1.1%20History
[66] www.nam.gov.za/xiisummit/chap1.thm#peace
[67] Chomsky, p167, 100, 14
[68] This bombing effort caused a lot of destruction and claimed innocent lives in the process. Fighting had already ceased in part through the efforts of the Kosovo leader Ibrahim Rugova's (1944-2006) strategy of passive resistance. Several Western writers were particularly proud of the NATO bombing campaign, including Salmon Rushdie, who was criticized by Tariq Ali as a "warrior writer" and as "the belligerati". (Mandel, p60)

An International War Crimes Tribunal was put in place to try Milosevic and others. This tribunal led up to the establishment in 2002 of a regular International Criminal Court (ICC). By 2003 89 state governments had ratified the ICC treaty, which was nearly half the members of the UN. Like the ICJ, the judges for the ICC come from a broad range of nationalities. The international laws that judges work with are found in a Statute that was voted on by the majority of UN governments called the Rome Statute. 120 governments voted in favor of the Rome Statute, 21 abstained from voting, and the US was one of seven governments that voted against the statute.[69]

From the Kosovo tribunals a model for the International Criminal Court was developed. In January of 2000, on President Clinton's last day in office he signed the ICC treaty but recommended that his successor, President Bush, not ratify it. When Bush began his first term as president he unsigned the treaty. This was because the ICC undermines the power of the Security Council. In fact, the US government had wanted ICC prosecution to be certifiable only by the Security Council.[70] This is much in the spirit of President Bush's own extension of the executive branch into the realms of the judiciary, something which violates the separation of powers guaranteed by the US Constitution.

Shortly after Bush nullified the US signature to the ICC, he passed a law that promised legal protection to any Congress-person who voted along with him. This was the ASPA –the American Service Members Protection Act, which was passed by a majority of house service members in August of 2002. The ASPA is a US law that protects all US government and military personal from being tried by the International Criminal Court. For this reason it is often jokingly called 'The Hague Invasion Act', because in effect it calls for the invasion of the courthouse itself in Holland. Moreover, the US government has argued for its own immunity from ICC prosecution, and each year this argument is renewed.[71]

Although the Rome Statute of the ICC is only prospective, meaning it will not deal with cases which occurred before July 1, 2002, intra-national crimes are out of its jurisdiction. Perhaps because of its involvement in the genocide in Rwanda, some government officials in Belgium changed their law system from being intra-national to being international in 1999. Shortly thereafter, many cases were brought to the Belgian courts from various peoples: Palestinians, Israelis, Iraqis against US General Tommy Franks and 'Operation Iraqi Freedom', as well as people against Castro and Saddam Hussein, President Bush, and Donald Rumsfeld. Shortly thereafter, Canada extended its law to being international in its scope. However, shortly after the Belgian and Canadian governments realized that their countries would be economically boycotted by the US, they changed the law so that each case had to first be consented to by the state, and after threats from the US, Belgian repealed its law in 2003.[72]

---

[69] Mandel, p207, 208
[70] Mandel, p211-212, 208
[71] Mandel, p209-210
[72] Mandel, p208, 211, 230-232, 232-233.

Human Rights and Civil Rights

"Kill the boys and the luggage! 'Tis expressly against the law of arms. 'Tis as arrant a piece of knavery, mark you now, as can be offert. In your conscience, now, is it not?"
—Fluellen, in William Shakespeare's *Henry V*, Act IV, Scene 7

The declaration of Human Rights goes back possibly to the ancient Persian Emperor Cyrus the Great (600-530). Cyrus the Great's religion was Zoroastrianism, a faith that is still practiced by some 200,000 people in the world, most of whom live in India. Shortly after Cyrus defeated the Babylonian Empire he commissioned a declaration of Human Rights to be drafted. This declaration still exists today, over 2500 years later, recorded on a clay cylinder in an ancient Semitic cuneiform script, Akkadian. Cyrus demonstrated his belief in human rights by tolerating other religions, freeing the Jews who had been enslaved by the Babylonians, and through his love of philosophy and the arts.

Although historically as we have seen there have been several movements for declaring human rights -as for example in the ancient Greek Cynic movement in philosophy, or in the theory of Natural Law advocated by the Greek and Roman Stoics, the English 'Magna Carta' of 1215, or as we have seen in the French Declaration of the Rights of Man and Citizen -the most significant work has been that done in the 20th century.

The Geneva Conventions consists of four treaties -the first of which was drafted in 1864, the second in 1929, and the third and fourth in 1949 –and are basically humanitarian laws. These were adopted by the UN in 1949 and are now adopted by almost 200 countries around the world. The 3rd and 4th conventions in particular deal with the ethical treatment of prisoners and victims of war.

The United States is signatory to a Universal Declaration of Human Rights (UDHR), which was passed unanimously by the General Assembly of the United Nations in 1948. The Universal Declaration of Human Rights consists of some 30 Articles proclaiming that all people have inalienable rights such as equality, protection of the law, freedom from discrimination based upon race, gender, or religion, the right to work, food, clothing, shelter, healthcare, and to an education, etc…[73] However, like the 'inalienable rights' described in the American Declaration of Independence, the articles of the of UDHR are not enforced, nor are they enforceable.

The Universal Declaration of Rights was approved without opposition by the General Assembly of the United Nations in late 1948, though not without a good deal of negotiation. This was achieved through the work of United Nations workers and representatives, the chairperson being the former First Lady of the United States, Eleanor Roosevelt. It seems to have been clear to those who did the drafting that they understood it purely as a declaration and not international legislation.

The UDHR is a fairly short and generalized list of declarations that in many ways resemble the laws set out in Western constitutional democracies. For example, the Preamble recognizes universal human characteristics such as, "inherent dignity", and "equal and inalienable rights". The Articles of the UDHR state that all humans are entitled to rights "without distinction of any kind, such as race, colour, sex, language,

---

[73] The UDHR can be accessed at www.un.org/Overview/rights.html

religion…" (Art. 2), slavery is prohibited (Art. 4), as well as torture (Art. 5), and arbitrary arrest or exile (Art. 9). All are innocent until proven guilty (Art. 11), all have the right to freedom of opinion and expression (Art. 19), "the will of the people shall be the basis of the authority of government" (Art. 21), all have the right to food, clothing, housing and medical care (Art. 25), education is to be free and compulsory and "shall promote understanding, tolerance and friendship among all nations, racial or religious groups", and shall further the maintenance of peace (Art. 26).[74]

Because the UDHR is a declaration and not a statute, treaty, or piece of legislation, the articles and entitlements are not legally binding. Leaders and representatives of different nations may sign the UDHR but can also violate one ore more of its articles without being disqualified or unsigned. Moreover, the articles of the UDHR are not enforceable. Governments which are members of the UN and are signatory to the UDHR can and do violate its letter without recrimination. One such nation is the US. Former US Attorney General Ramsey Clark has written that,

"The United States government pays lip service to the Declaration, but its courts have consistently refused to enforce its provisions reasoning it is not a legally binding treaty, or contract, but only a declaration. This ignores the fact that international law recognizes the provisions of the Declaration as being incorporated into customary international law which is binding on all nations."[75]

Take for example the War on (New York, Henry Holt and Company, 2003) that began in 2001. The adaptation of the USA PATRIOT Act of that year, which only one US Senator voted against, allows the government to override civil liberties.[76] Its violations of the Universal Declaration of Human Rights are manifold.[77] The Patriot Act allows for the arbitrary arrest of people based upon racial profiling and religious affiliation. Thousands have been arrested without charges based on such arbitrary criteria.[78] Such enactment also violates Articles 9 and 11 of the UDHR which prohibit arbitrary arrest, exile, and guilt without suspicion or proof. Racial and religious profiling goes against Article 2 of the UDHR, which decries such discrimination.

The War on Afghanistan which began in 2001 and the war on Iraq which began in 2003 stand as further violations of not just the UDHR, but the Geneva Codes and the International Laws of the United Nations as well. When the United States government sought permission from the United Nations to invade Iraq (though it had already invaded Afghanistan 2 years earlier) their request, as we saw, was denied by the UN Security Council. Nonetheless, in 2003 the US declared war on Iraq (though bombing had not stopped since the Persian Gulf war of Bush I, 10 years earlier).[79] The US has sought to

---

[74] http://www.un.org/Overview/rights.html
[75] Ramsey Clark, "On The Fiftieth Anniversary of The Universal Declaration of Human Rights", in Noam Chomsky and Edward Said's, *Acts of Aggression: Policing "Rogue States"*, ed. Greg Ruggiero, (New York, Seven Stories Press, 1999) p59-60
[76] The USA PATRIOT Act is an acronym: the Uniting and Strengthening America by Providing Appropriate Tools Required to Intercept and Obstruct Terrorism Act
[77] Its manifold violations of the US Constitution are revealed in Nancy Chang's, *Silencing Political Dissent: How Post-September 11 Anti-Terrorism Measures Threaten Our Civil Liberties*, (New York, Seven Stories Press, 2002)
[78] Chang, p69, 70
[79] The Algerian-born French Jewish postmodernist philosopher Jacques Derrida (1930-2004) said of President Bush II, "Bush speaks of 'war', but he is in fact incapable of identifying the enemy against whom he declares that he has declared war. It is said over and over that neither the civilian population of Afghanistan nor its armies are the enemies of the United States. Assuming 'bin Laden' is here the sovereign decision-maker, everyone knows that he is not Afghan, that he has been disavowed by his own

democratize Iraq (for violating the UN regulations) and Afghanistan which is in violation of Article 21 of the UDHR which gives a people the right to self-determination.

The US attitude toward Cuba, Korea, and Vietnam are great examples of interfering in other peoples right to choose their own government and self-determine, though perhaps these three are just the tip of the ice berg that has melted. The US gained Cuba as a territory in 1899 after defeating the Spanish in the Spanish-American War. Cuba was eventually granted autonomy. However, according to the Cuban-American Treaty of 1903 the US gained control of Guantanamo Bay. When 50 years later a revolution occurred in Cuba and the nation became socialist, the new Cuban government said that the US was no longer welcome to keep a base in their country. The Cuban government has sought to bring charges to the UN, arguing that the US is violating international law.

Whether the US occupation of Guantanamo Bay is in violation of International Law, what goes on there makes this violation pale in comparison. Though Guantanamo Bay was turned into a prison in the 1980's, in 2002 it became a primary detention camp for suspected terrorists. Although hundreds of people have been sent to the prison there, nearly all have been released, often half a dozen years later, and no charges were ever made.[80] Moreover, most, if not all of these hundreds of prisoners were tortured on a regular basis, just as with prisoners in US custody in both Afghanistan and Iraq.[81]

The use of torture by the US Government goes in violation to the Geneva Conventions, to the UDHR, as well as to a lesser known declaration, the United Nations Convention Against Torture (UNCAT) of 1984, which was signed by the US Government in 1988 and ratified in 1994.[82] A similar document –the Istanbul Protocol, became an official UN document in 1999.[83] The Istanbul Protocol was initiated in 1996 by the Human Rights Foundation of Turkey and the United States group Physician for Human Rights. The Protocol gives methods and rules for a guideline for doctors and lawyers who investigate prisoners and victims to see if they were abused or tortured. The Istanbul Protocol has been adopted by the European Union as well.

The combination of the UN Convention Against Torture and the Istanbul Protocol is another UN resolution titled the Optional Protocol to the Convention against Torture and other Cruel, Inhuman or Degrading Treatment or Punishment.[84] This "optional"

---

country (by every 'country' and state, in fact, almost without exception), that his training owes much to the United States and that, of course, he is not alone... As for states that 'harbor' terrorist networks, it is difficult to identify them as such. The United States and Europe, London and Berlin, are also sanctuaries, places of training or formation and information for all the 'terrorists' of the world. No geography, no 'territorial' determination, is thus pertinent any longer for locating the seat of these new technologies of transmission of aggression." From the October 22, 2001 interview with Giovanna Borradori, "9/11and Global Terrorism", trans. Pascale-Anne Brault and Michael Naas, in Borradori's, *Philosophy In A Time of Terror: Dialogues with Jurgen Habermas and Jacques Derrida*, (Chicago, University of Chicago Press, 2004). Excerpt accessed online at www.press.uchicago.edu/Misc/Chicago/066649.html
[80] www.amnestyusa.org/war-on-terror/86-days/guantanamo-fact-sheet/page.do?id=1051177
[81] Joan Walsh, "The Abu Ghraib Files", *Salon*, 14 March, 2006, www.salon.com/news/abu_ghraib/2006/03/14/introduction/index.html
Matthew Weaver, "CIA Waterboarded al-Qaida suspects 266 Times", *Guardian*, 20 April, 2009, www.guardian.co.uk/world/2009/apr/20/waterboarding-alqaida-khalid-sheikh-mohammed
[82] www2.ohchr.org/english/law/cat.htm
[83] http://physiciansforhumanrights/org/library/istanbul-protocol.html
[84] www2.ohchr.org/english/law/cat-one.htm

protocol was made in order to combine the Convention Against Torture and the Istanbul Protocol so that governments which volunteer, consent to allowing established international inspection of prisons and detention centers. This Optional Protocol, meant to give the Convention Against Torture some power, was adopted by the UN in 2002, and enforced in 2006. However, the US has not signed this Optional Protocol, which would have allowed international teams to search and report on abuses at Guantanamo Bay.

Some of the governments who have adopted these international treaties against torture and have opted to abide by international law, are critical of some of the articles of the 1948 Universal Declaration of Human Rights, however. Having been written by a specific group of human beings, be they representatives, generals, men, women, bourgeois, proletariat, have or have not, declarations which purport human universatility are of course fallibilistic.

It is understandable that it could be believed that a program for universal rights is either going to render the norms of the community as ineffectual or it is going to make the community obsolete. The writers of the UDHR certainly didn't intend for this. However, some of its provisions make it so. If for example the writers of the Old and New Testaments were pro-slavery, their community is at odds with Article 4 of the UDHR. Forms of pre-modern justice where it was illegal to insult someone or disrespect their beliefs run against Article 19 of the UDHR which says people should have a right to express any opinion. Moreover, the declaration of compulsory education runs against the philosophies of anarchism and libertarianism, which are against such federal regulation.

Muslim people are usually sighted as the greatest opponents of the UDHR, if only because Iranian officials and a few other Muslim national leaders have not signed the declaration. (There are over 50 nations with Muslim majorities). For example, the Islamic Law, Shariah, does not permit the visual representation of the prophet Muhammad, something which isn't unlawful according to the UDHR. However, Muslim governments are signatory to both the Constitution of Medina, written by Muhammad himself, and the Cairo Declaration of Human Rights in Islam (CDHRI), which was formulated in 1990.[85] Unlike the UDHR, this declaration is binding. So, while the US may violate the articles of the UDHR and pay no consequence, governments which are signatory to the CDHRI can get into real trouble.[86]

The United Nations has, however, come up with some good conventions, all of which point toward a meaningful international community. In 1966 the International Covenant on Civil and Political Rights was created.[87] The US ratified this covenant in 1992, but with 5 reservations, 5 understandings, and 4 declarations. This International Covenant has not been signed by the Vatican. In 1979 the Convention on the Elimination of All Forms of Discrimination Against Women was created.[88] While the US has signed this convention, it has yet to be ratified. The Convention is not signed by Iran, Sudan, the Vatican, and a few other small countries. In 2000 the Optional Protocol to the Convention on the Elimination of All Forms of Discrimination Against Women was

---

[85] www1.umn.edu/humanrts/instree/cairodecleration.html
[86] "Unlike the UDHR, the Muslim conventions are binding upon their signatories." Rudolph Peters, *Crime and Punishment in Islamic Law: Theory and Practice from the Sixteenth to the Twenty-first Century*, (Cambridge, Cambridge University Press, 2005) p174
[87] www2.unchr.org/english/law/ccpr.htm
[88] www.un.org/womenwatch/daw/cedaw/

created so that the UN law would have some enforcement.[89] The US has yet to sign this Protocol on Women's Rights. The 1989 United Nations Convention on the Rights of the Child has been ratified by every UN country except the US and Somalia.[90]

Rights vs. Responsibilities

The modern era has been one of human's achievement of rights. From the rise of democracy in France and America to the technological advances over nature –humans have gained more rights and powers over the external world. As we have seen, since the United Nations has sought to extend human rights. The modern philosophies that treat rights as the most fundamental value -in particular, individual rights -are capitalism, libertarianism, and anarchism.

While these philosophies have made the issue of rights or freedoms the central aspect of their ethical vision, others have pushed to the fore of ethics the question of responsibility. An analogy can help to point out this distinction. Is our vision of reality one of suspicion or one of trust? Do we think our rights are the most important thing to fight for, or do we think that something other than our individual selves, namely other people or the external world (or a divine being), to be more important?

The last half a century has been witness to a critique of this vision of the sovereignty of human rights. Influential ethicists such Rachel Carson and Peter Singer have emphasized ecological ethics or animal rights over human rights. Ecologists and environmentalists have been working in opposition to those who say that humans have a right to do with the earth whatever they want. Some want to argue that society and government ought to not interfere with the human rights of those who want to 'develop' or pollute the earth, or at least the part of the earth that they 'own'. Thus, some argue that when it comes to the earth and to other living creatures, responsibility overrides human rights.

In his work, *After Virtue*, Alasdair MacIntyre argues that the concept of human rights is a modern one and does not appear in literature or discourse until the 15th century. He writes: "the truth is plain: there are no such rights, and belief in them is one with belief in witches and unicorns." Accordingly, "every attempt to give good reason for believing that there *are* such rights has failed… In the United Nations declaration of human rights of 1949 what has since become the normal UN practice of not giving good reasons for *any* assertions whatsoever is followed with rigor.." This is because in actuality, "Natural or human rights then are fictions…"[91] MacIntyre thinks instead that for an ethic to be authoritative it must be grounded in the virtues of a given community or society. This is similar to the pre-modern view that responsibility is fundamental, rather than the exaltation of the individual, a la Rousseau and Nietzsche.

One thinker who believes that the universal conceptualization of human rights must be challenged is the Muslim scholar, Seyyed Hossein Nasr. Nasr writes that in Islam responsibility precedes rights and "even in the modern West, in many cases

---

[89] www1.umn.edu/humanrts/instree/cedawopprot-2000.hmtl
[90] www.unhchr.ch/html/menu3/b/k2crc.htm
[91] Alasdair MacIntyre, *After Virtue*, (Notre Dame, University of Notre Dame Press, 1981) p69, 70

responsibilities precede rights."[92] However, Nasr is not ignorant of the extent to which individual rights have overridden the natural world and the well-being of others.

"...the rapid destruction of both the natural environment and the social fabric of the most highly industrialized societies cannot but end in total disaster for the whole of humanity. Islam has a crucial role to play in bringing out the primacy of responsibilities over rights...

"The participation on a global scale by Muslims in the creation of awareness of human responsibilities to complement and precede human rights is itself a responsibility of primary order placed by God upon the shoulders of those Muslims endowed with sufficient knowledge combined with virtue to carry out such a task."[93]

Nasr holds that Universalist conceptualizations of human rights often bring results that are disharmonious.

"Islamic thought must also challenge on the highest intellectual level the current Western notion that the present-day Western understanding of human rights is universal, which in this context means global. Now, all values are related to the worldview, or *Weltanschauung*, within which they are understood, and not all worldviews are the same... These views can be easily correlated, but they cannot be harmonized with a view of the human being as an aggregate of molecules brought together by chance out of the original cosmic soup.

"Nor can human rights, which must of necessity be based on the concept of who the human being is, be considered global and universal because of such crass differences about what constitutes the human state."[94]

Any philosophy that downplays responsibility is guilty of attempting to speak for others, and such universalism is imperialist. This is both the strength and impediment of liberalism. Being strong enough to disagree with conformists but weak enough to impose one's duty of liberation on others, or belief in the primacy of human rights.

Universalism vs. Pluralism

As we have seen –many philosophies, be they ethical or political -seek to make themselves universal. By taking the view that universality is imperative, it is believed that our laws and principles will be like those of math and science. As we have seen in the realm of politics however, this universal standard has occasionally been one of imperialism or monotonization. One worldview is taken to be the only worldview. In education and in thought in general, this perspective is taught to be universal. Thus, for the diversity that exists in the world, universalization can be a threat. Could the universalization of ethics go hand in hand with imperialism?[95]

We probably shouldn't rush over to an anti-universalist alternative, however, perhaps substituting one form of imperialism for another. This is so in the case of the relativist who either abandons politics or worships of the status quo. The relativist cannot distinguish their own obedience from that of the conformist to universatility. This is the problem of the one and the many, or one over many where knowledge becomes

---

[92] Seyyed Hossein Nasr, *The Heart of Islam: Enduring Values for Humanity*, (San Francisco, HarperCollins Publishers, 2002) p278

[93] Nasr, p299-300

[94] Nasr, p303

[95] Albert Camus wrote of this universalization project: "The claim to a universal city is only supported, in this revolution, by rejecting two-thirds of the world and the magnificent heritage of the centuries, by denying, to the advantage of history, both nature and beauty and by depriving man of the power of passion, doubt, happiness, and imaginative invention –in a word, of his greatness." *The Rebel*, trans. Anthony Bower, (New York, Alfred A. Knopf, 1954) p210

necessary. If there are no universal truths, how is this truth determined? Here the relativist must plead skepticism or appeal to their relatives.

Ambiguity between the one and the many is broken and/or avoided by a respect for the multiplicity and non-reducibility of reality held by a philosophy of pluralism. Pluralism is the philosophical position that there are many truths, many perspectives, and many worldviews. This plurality does not mean that the many truths that exist are in some sense equal or the same. Rather than putting all of one's faith on some theory of the ultimacy of reality, the pluralist acknowledges the diversity of beliefs and lifestyles that actually exist. The pluralist respects the differences that exist and does not seek to convert everything that is different or external to their own sameness. Pluralism neither necessitates universality nor summons its contradiction.

Tendencies toward universalism can most easily be seen in political philosophy and religion. Philosophies like Marxism, Libertarianism, Capitalism, and Anarchism can all in some sense be both universalist and opposed to multi-culturalism and diversity. Pre-modern traditions and customs are found to be arbitrary and unauthoritative according to these universalist institutions. Religions, too, are oftentimes similarly against the plurality of traditions, beliefs, and cultures that exist. However, this is not always the case.

The ancient religions of Hinduism and Judaism, each going back several thousand years, do not believe in, or practice, universalization. Hindus believe there are many different peoples and many different destinies and duties. In the holy book, the *Bhagavad Gita*, it is written: "Devoted each to his own duty man attains to perfection... Better is one's own law though imperfectly carried out than the law of another carried out perfectly. One does not incur sin when one does the duty ordained by one's own nature." (18:45,47)

In the Torah of Judaism the word teaches adherents again and again to be kind to strangers, and only to convert them if they join your household. (Exodus 12:48) The Torah teaches that the Jews were chosen by God (Yhwh) to keep his law and commandments. (Deuteronomy 7:6) This is so even if Jews live in countries where they are the minority. (Genesis 12:1) The Jewish philosopher Emmanuel Levinas (1905-1995) believed that the Jewish people had a role outside of other nations, to reside amongst the gentiles and not be converted but to maintain their own law and tradition as an example of ethicality. In his work titled *Difficult Freedom* (1963), Levinas writes:

"A truth is universal when it applies to every reasonable being. A religion is universal when it is open to all. In this sense the Judaism that links the Divine to the moral has always aspired to be universal. But the revelation of morality, which discovers a human society, also discovers the place of election, which in this universal society, returns to the person who receives this revelation. This election is made up not of privileges but of responsibilities."[96]

In Christianity the ethic is a universal one. The mission has always been a particularly central aspect of Christian ethics as we see throughout common world history. This imperative to spread the word and convert every human being was given in the New Testament. The word 'catholic' itself means 'universal', while the superlative of Protestantism is the Universalist Church. The New Testament teaches:

---

[96] Emmanuel Levinas, *Difficult Freedom*, p21, trans. and quoted by Hilary Putnam in "Levinas and Judaism", from *The Cambridge Companion to Levinas*, ed. Simon Critchley and Robert Bernasconi, (Cambridge, Cambridge University Press, 2002) p33

"All authority has been given me in heaven and on the earth. Go therefore and make disciples of people of all the nations, baptizing them in the name of the Father and of the Son and of the holy spirit, teaching them to observe all the things I have commanded you." Matthew 28:18-20

"Go into all the world and preach the good news to all creation. He that believes and is baptized will be saved, but he that does not believe will be condemned." Mark 16:15-16

"For this very reason also God exalted him to a superior position and kindly gave him the name that is above every other name, so that in he name of Jesus every knee should bend of those in heaven and those on earth and those under the ground, and every tongue should openly acknowledge that Jesus Christ is Lord to the glory of God the Father." Philippians 2:9-11

"Who is the one that conquers the world but he who has faith that Jesus is the Son of God?" 1 John 5:5

"If anyone comes to you and does not bring this teaching, never receive him into your homes or say a greeting to him." 2 John 10

"And to him that conquers and observes my deeds down to the end I will give authority over the nations, and he shall shepherd the people with an iron rod so that they will be broken to pieces like clay vessels..." Revelation 2:26[97]

Perhaps the first international treaty ever signed which allowed for voluntary accession was the 7th century *Dustur al-Madinah*, or the Constitution of Medina.[98] This was written by the Muslim Prophet Muhammad who had been invited to Medina to reside as a judge. The Constitution of Medina was a document which rejected tyranny and injustice and swore protection and mutual aid to the cohabitants of Medina, whether they be pagans or monotheists, from the wars of aggression and empire. This alliance would prove fundamental in defeating the invading Christian armies during almost every Crusade.

In the Islamic tradition the Prophet Muhammad began the first *Ummah*, or community in the 7th century in Madinah. This community included Muslims as well as the followers of other religions and traditions. Neither Muhammad himself, nor those who followed his message and example, considered him to be a king. In fact Muhammad had been invited to live in Madinah and to maintain the peace of the community. Thus, when Muhammad died there was a meeting of the community, in which it became the tradition that the "establishment of order" would be left to the will of Muslims. Through 'mutual consultation' or *Al-Shura*, the community determines the political form they desire.[99]

Islam, like the philosophy of communitarianism, is resistant to certain attempts to universalize ethics. Communitarianism is a political philosophy that takes community to be the center of social and economic well-being. Communitarians believe that an ethics and law ought to be based upon the consensus of the community. It is held that this will alleviate the imperialism of class war, the assimilation of universalization, as well as the extremes of nationalism, or the duty of policing foreign peoples.

Like communitarianism, Islam is not pushing for a universal ethic. Like many religions they have their own system of law. However, they do not believe that it applies to everyone. The basis for the political life of Muslims is the Ummah, or community, and not the state as in the case of Christianity and Messianism in general. Islam, unlike

---

[97] All passages from the New Testament are from *The New World Translation of the Holy Scriptures*, trans. New World Bible Translation Committee, (Brooklyn, Watchtower Bible and Tract Society of New York, Inc., 1961)

[98] Muhamed S. El-Awa, *On The Political System of the Islamic State*, trans. Ahmad Naji al-Imam, ed. Anwer Beg, (Indianapolis, American Trust Publications, 1980) p21

[99] El-Awa, p34, 35

Christianity and some forms of Judaism, is not a Messianic movement and does not hold to credulity in the Divine Right of Kings.

Shortly after the fall of the Turkish Empire an Egyptian judge in the Shariah court wrote about the Islamic state:

"[I]t is inconceivable the whole world could be organized under one single religion and that the entire humanity could be regulated within one religious unity, but to put the whole world under the rule of one government and gather it in a single political unit would seem to be almost outside the scope of human nature and is not related to the will of Allah."[100]

The prophet himself said, "There is no superiority of an Arab over a non-Arab, and indeed, no superiority for a red man over a black..."[101] The Holy Book of Islam, the Quran, is written in the same spirit of pluralism as Muhammad's Constitution of Medina. The Quran says:

"No compulsion is there in religion." Surah 2:256

"And if thy Lord had willed, whoever is in the earth would have believed, all of them, all together. Wouldst thou then constrain the people, until they are believers? It is not for any soul to believe save by the leave of Allah." Surah 10:99-100

"Yet, be thou ever so eager, the most part of men believe not." Surah 12:103

"And of His signs is the creation of the heavens and earth and the variety of your tongues and hues." Surah 30:22

"If We had willed, We would have raised up in every city a warner." Surah 25:53

"If Allah had willed, He would have made them one nation." Surah 42:8

"O mankind, We have created you male and female, and appointed you races and tribes, that you may know one another." Surah 49:13

"To you your religion. To me my religion." Surah 109:5[102]

Pragmatism and Pluralism

The ethics of pluralism have been part of philosophical pragmatism since William James (1842-1910), who introduced the term to English-language philosophy. Even in the writings of pragmatism's founding-father Charles Sanders Peirce (pronounced 'purse', 1839-1914) we find him establishing multiple forms of reasoning. The pluralism of James has become the standard for all pragmatists to follow. James himself thought the word 'universe' ought to be replaced with his neologism, 'pluriverse'.[103]

Pragmatism is also opposed to imperialism. Not just the writer Mark Twain, but pragmatists from James to John Dewey, Jane Addams, among others were members of the Anti-Imperialist League. Around the turn of the century the Anti-Imperialist League had distributed more than a million copies of literature protesting US aggression in the Philippines, a country which had come into American hands with the defeat of the Spanish in 1898 in the Spanish-American war. The Philippine-American war would last until 1913, with hundreds of thousands of Filipino deaths.[104]

---

[100] Shaikh 'Ali 'Abd al-Razeq, *Al-Islam wa Usul al-Hukm*, (pub. 1925), quoted by El-Awa, p67
[101] El-Awa, p111
[102] All passages from the Quran are from *The Koran Interpreted*, trans. A.J. Arberry, (New York, Macmillan Publishing Company, 1955)
[103] Louis Menand, *The Metaphysical Club: A Story of Ideas in America*, (New York, Farrar, Straus and Giroux, 2001) p143, 88
[104] Zinn, p308, 310

In 1905 the pragmatist Supreme Court Justice Oliver Wendell Holmes (1841-1935) struck down the legality of President Roosevelt and William Howard Taft's taxation of, and tariffs on the Philippine people. Taft had crushed the Philippine rebellion in 1898 and had been the Civil Governor of the Philippines since 1901. Roosevelt appointed him Secretary of War in 1904. Holmes wrote the opinion for the court, defiant of the very president who had appointed him. However, Roosevelt and Taft later got passed by the Supreme Court a new Tariff for taxing the Philippine's, with Holmes' dissent.[105]

John Dewey himself had been very active in reforming and diversifying the American education system. Dewey helped create and sometimes lead such organizations as the American Civil Liberties Union (ACLU), the National Association for the Advancement of Colored People (NAACP), the League for Industrial Democracy, the New York Teacher's Union, the American Association of University Professors, and the New School of Social Research.[106]

Dewey also played a big role in international affairs, as for example in the Trotsky case. Dewey had previously denounced the trial and execution in 1927 of two anarchists, Sacco and Vanzetti, whom history has shown were innocent. Leon Trotsky was an exiled Russian socialist accused of plotting to kill Stalin among other similar acts of treason. During 'staged' trials held in Moscow in 1936, Trotsky was found guilty and was exiled. He moved from place to place in the search for political asylum.

When Dewey joined the American Committee of the Defense of Leon Trotsky, Dewey was 78 years old. He took a train to Mexico in 1937 where Trotsky was staying temporarily at the house of the artist Diego Rivera. Dewey sat as chairman for the Commission of this quasi-trial. The commission consisted of a number of participants including political activists and university professors, as well as two Christian and Jewish pragmatists, Reinhold Niebuhr and Lionel Trilling. After a week-long inquiry Dewey helped clear Trotsky of most of the allegations of which he had been found guilty by Stalin's court. Although Dewey was sympathetic with the man, in discussion he critiqued Trotsky's dogmatic and absolutist belief, shared amongst many socialists and anarchists alike, that "human ends are interwoven into the very texture and structure of experience."[107]

As we have seen, Dewey was also very active in the movement for the *Outlawry of War*. In "International Law and the War-System", he wrote of the need for a new direction in understanding how to oppose war.

"How long have we been taking steps to do away with war, and why have they accomplished nothing? Because *the steps have all ben taken under the war system*. It is not a step that we need, it is a right-about-face; a facing in another direction… No advance in human history that was of any great importance was ever made by taking steps along old lines. Think of that proposition. Taking steps along old lines *aids in perfecting principles and methods that are already established*, but they never initiate the great steps in human progress. These always come by finding a new method of attack upon the problem. I believe the fallacy which most paralyzes human effort today is the idea that progress can take place by

---

[105] Sheldon Novick, *Honorable Justice: The Life of Oliver Wendell Holmes*, (Boston, Little, Brown and Company, 1989) p278-280. Taft would go on to become president of the United States (1909-1913), and then Chief Justice to the Supreme Court (1921-1930).
[106] Menand, p235-236
[107] John Dewey, "Means and Ends", from *Their Morals and Ours*, ed. George Novick, quoted by Alan Ryan in *John Dewey and The High Tide of American Liberalism*, (New York, W.W. Norton & Company, 1995) p285, 304, 307

more steps in the old wrong direction. We can, if we please, take steps to perfect the international law and international courts under the old system, but let us not delude ourselves into thinking that in improving details of this system we are taking a single step toward the elimination of the war system of the world."[108]

The pragmatist Jane Addams (1860-1935) opened one of the first settlement houses in the US for the poor and for immigrants . From its beginnings in 1889, she lived-in and ran the Hull House in Chicago for over 40 years. The Hull House still exists today, and Addams helped create the trend for hundreds of other settlement houses. She was a prominent pacifist during the Philippine-American War as well as the First World War. She was involved with the women's suffrage movement and labor and union strikes in and around Chicago. Addams was member of the Civic Federation of Chicago, the Anti-Imperialist League, and as we have seen, was the first American woman to be awarded the Nobel Peace Prize (1931).

She was particularly critical of the lack of equality in American democracy as well as the paternal structure implicit in the charity-consciousness, which even today still helps to maintain the status quo. In "Charitable Effort" from her 1902 study, *Democracy and Social Ethics*, Addams wrote that "The most serious effect upon the poor comes when dependence upon the charitable society is substituted for the natural outgoing of human love and sympathy, which, happily, we all possess to some degree." She concludes:

"The Hebrew prophet made three requirements from those who would join the great forward-moving procession led by Jehovah. 'To love mercy' and at the same time 'to do justly' is the difficult task; to fulfil the first requirement alone is to fall into the error of indiscriminate giving with all its disastrous results; to fulfil the second solely is to obtain the stern policy of withholding, and it results in such a dreary lack of sympathy and understanding that the establishment of justice is impossible. It may be that the combination of the two can never be attained save as we fulfil still the third requirement –'to walk humbly with God,' which may mean to walk for many dreary miles beside the lowliest of His creatures, not even in that peace of mind which the company of the humble is popularly supposed to afford, but rather with the pangs and throes to which the poor human understanding is subjected whenever it attempts to comprehend the meaning of life."[109]

Pragmatism and Black Nationalism

The contemporary pragmatist Louis Menand has helped recover the relevancy of a great deal of the original movement behind pragmatism. Menand shows how the Cold War especially marked the disappearance of pragmatism from American thought. Much of the world was caught in an absolutist battle between two dogmatisms. Then in the 1950's there was the Civil Rights and Human Rights struggles of people like Martin Luther King and Malcolm X, which led to the anti-war movement of the 60's.

Menand questions whether the Civil Rights movement of Martin Luther King, Jr. could have approached success if it had been inspired by say Dewey and Holmes, rather than religious figures such as Reinhold Niebuhr and Mohandas Gandhi.[110] Whether or not

---

[108] Dewey, "International Law and the War-System", from *Characters and Events*, Vol II, in *The Philosophy of John Dewey*, p523
[109] Jane Addams, *Democracy and Social Ethics*, from *Pragmatism and Classical American Philosophy*, Second Edition, ed. John J. Stuhr, (New York, Oxford University Press, 2000) p635, 644
[110] Menand, p441. Menand also finds the classical pragmatists –Peirce, James, Dewey, and Holmes –to be modernists. (p439) Though there may be some truth to this claim, it has been argued in this book (see Chapter 1) that traditional modernists like Rene Descartes, Charles Darwin, and Karl Marx have all

this is so, it can be easy to underestimate the practicality of philosophical pragmatism given that most of its theorists have been white and Protestant. However, the 'prophetic pragmatist' and professor of Black Studies, Cornel West, finds that:

"The social movement led by Martin Luther King, Jr., represents the best of what the political dimension of prophetic pragmatism is all about... King was not a prophetic pragmatist. Yet... he was a prophet, in which role he contributed mightily to the political project of prophetic pragmatism."[111]

Cornel West also sees a lineage or theme between the experimentalism and improvisation of the naturalist Ralph Waldo Emerson that is

"thoroughly continuous with the great art form that Afro-Americans have given the modern world, which is jazz. And therefore to talk about America is to talk about improvisation and experimentation, and therefore to talk about Emerson and Louis Armstrong in the same breath."[112]

According to West, pragmatism helps the Black community "to understand that we have to interpret both American civilization and the modern West from our vantage point... It means we have to have a cosmopolitan orientation, even though it is rooted in the fundamental concern with the plight and predicament of African Americans." This is not a prophecy of there being one universal perspective but of one rooted in community. The prophetic pragmatism of West

"does not wallow in a cynicism or a paralyzing pessimism, but it also is realistic enough not to project excessive utopia. It's a matter of responding in an improvisational, un-dogmatic, creative way to circumstances, in such a way that people still survive and thrive. This is a great tradition intellectually, in fact, it has had tremendous impact on the way in which Americans as a whole respond to the human condition, respond to their circumstances."[113]

West has written of the Black Nationalist struggle, particularly of Malcolm X, that it had become pessimistic of the possibility of justice in a democratic society with a white majority. West writes that this impulse toward "internationalization of the black freedom struggle in the United States was a deep pessimism about America's will to racial justice, no matter how democratic America was or is."[114] This indicates how in an important sense Black Nationalism is an international solidarity movement.

According to Cornel West Black Nationalism is a "political and intellectual struggle for the redistribution of wealth and power" and a positive move to "place serious political reflection and action center stage" arising from "a need for community and all of its meanings: primordial bonding, support, sustenance, projection of a future and, of course, preservation of hope."[115]

---

believed there to be one true description of reality. This modern prejudice is notably absent in the pluralism of the pragmatists.

[111] Cornel West, *The American Evasion of Philosophy: A Genealogy of Pragmatism*, (Madison, University of Wisconsin Press, 1989) p234-235

[112] bell hooks and Cornel West, *Breaking Bread: Insurgent Black Intellectual Life*, (Boston, South End Press, 1991) p34

[113] West, p34

[114] Cornel West, *Race Matters*, (Boston, Beacon Press, 1993) p103. Malcolm X tells in his autobiography how he came to change his mind and embrace pluralism. "True Islam taught me that it takes *all* of the religious, political, economic, psychological, and racial ingredients, or characteristics, to make the Human Family and Human Society complete. Since I learned the *truth* in Mecca, my dearest friends have come to include *all* kinds –some Christians, Jews, Buddhists, Hindus, agnostics, and even atheists! I have friends who are called Capitalists, Socialists, and Communists! Some of my friends are moderates, conservatives, extremists –some are even Uncle Toms! My friends today are black, brown, red, yellow, and *white*!" *The Autobiography of Malcolm X*, p431-432

[115] West, *Breaking Bread*, p47, 93-94

In recalling some of her earliest recollections of Black struggle, feminist writer and activist bell hooks realized that, "Black people, nationally and internationally, are not joined ideologically, politically, or culturally by virtue of skin color but that, in fact, the question of ideology, and political stance would very much determine the degree to which we could be joined together." According to West, "Preservation of Black cultural integrity [and] acknowledgement of Black cultural distinctiveness... are important to a broader perspective on Black nationalism. These elements are indispensable for a progressive Black politics."[116]

Pragmatism and International Justice

Although pragmatism is committed to the tenet of pluralism, as we see, it is not opposed to justice, international justice, or solidarity movements such as the NAACP or Black Nationalist movements. All pragmatists alike have a stake in opposing imperialism and the monotonization and de-pluralization of the world.

For an international justice that is not just theoretical or nominal there must be some interest in its enforcement and sustenance. When, like an elected congress or parliament, an international movement becomes marked by representatives rather than the theorists and the activists, a sincerity is lost. Unfortunately, this sometimes happens to the United Nations. A man who has spent a lifetime fighting multi-national corporations and has started over 100 civic leagues is the attorney and activist, Ralph Nader. Nader points out how even the UN can become corporatized. Nader found that the UN was "veering down the road of commercialization and marginalization" and that under the UN 'Global Compact', "the UN would seek both to make it easy for companies to enter partnerships with UN agencies and to advocate for speeding up corporate globalization." Instead, Nader finds that:

"An effective United Nations must be free of corporate encumbrances. Its agencies should be the leading critics of the many ways that corporate globalization is functioning to undermine UN missions to advance ecological sustainability, human rights, and global economic justice, not apologists and collaborators with the dominant corporate order."[117]

Internationalism (call it globalization) has been accompanied by its share of organizations that have just as often helped the needy as they have furthered the wealthy and corrupt. Oftentimes this equation is disproportionate, and often there is no equation. For example, the Bretton-Woods institutions, (named after the Hotel in New Hampshire where they were created in 1944), organizations such as the World Bank and the International Monetary Fund, seem to have caused a good deal of complaint, even if they have sometimes helped.

The sociologist and activist Kevin Danaher has made a career out of promoting democracy in America and inspiring solidarity movements around the world. It has been said that one of the reasons apartheid ended in South Africa was because of Kevin Danaher's grassroots attempt to get small businesses, schools, and churches to divest from IMF funds and World Bank bonds. In 1994, decrying the bicentennial of the Bretton Woods institutions, Danaher compiled dozen's of articles written by critics of the World Bank and the IMF from around the world and from all different nationalities. In

---

[116] hooks, p68, West, p47
[117] Ralph Nader, "The UN –Cozy with Corporations", *In Pursuit of Justice*, p313-315

his introduction to *50 Years Is Enough: The Case Against The World Bank and the International Monetary Fund*, Danaher tells us of a basic principle of universalization: "The unwritten goal of the World Bank and the IMF –one that has been enforced with a vengeance –has been to integrate countries into the capitalist world economy."[118]

Something else that is obvious is that these wealthy international bankers never directly give money to poor people, but give huge sums of money to leaders of poor countries, regardless of their civil or human rights records, or their ecological intentions. This is in part purposive:

"...the central function of these multilateral lending institutions has been to draw the rulers and governments of weaker states more tightly into a world economy dominated by large, transnational corporations... For many in the Third World, this harkens back to colonial times... The Third World rulers get new infusions of cash... Without strong representative apparatus, it would be impossible to enforce the harsh policies dictated from Washington."

"A central problem with the structural adjustment policies is that they are developed and imposed in an undemocratic manner. Unelected elites from the North and South get together and devise these policies without any input from the poor majority who will be on the receiving end... It is telling that population groups and other living things that are relatively powerless tend to get trampled by the policies of the Bank and the Fund."[119]

When the US backed military leader of Sudan Gaafar Muhammad Nimeiri began working with the IMF and World Bank in the 1970's, local farmers lost all their subsidies and enormous demonstrations against the government as well as food riots, occurred in 1979 and 1982. In 1984 the US and the IMF froze a $114 million dollar loan to Nimeiri because they were critical of his use of Islamic law, rather than western corporate law. Only when he said he would no longer ban usury did Vice President George Bush visit Sudan and did the US and IMF resume their patriarchal monetary sponsorship if Nimeiri.[120]

The President and Founder of the bank for the poor, the Grameen Bank in Bangladesh, Muhammad Yunus, has written of the World Bank, "The World Bank is eager to assume all the responsibilities. They don't want to leave any responsibility for the borrower, except the responsibility for the failure of the project."[121]

International trade agreements such as NAFTA (the North American Free Trade Agreement) and the World Trade Organization (WTO), have been commented upon by Ralph Nader who calls them "international systems of autocratic governance."

"They are brilliantly suited to the long-held desire of mega-corporations to go around pesky domestic regulations into any arena they want to call their own. These agreements, enforceable upon their signatory nations, reverse priorities of social progress by subordinating worker, consumer, and environmental priorities to the supremacy of international commerce."[122]

One of the main difficulties with internationalism, be it of trade, human rights, or the meting out of justice, is that this is usually done through institutions and representatives. For example, the United Nations is a representation itself, made by

---

[118] Kevin Danaher, "Introduction", *50 Years Is Enough: The Case Against The World Bank and the International Monetary Fund*, ed. Kevin Danaher, (Boston, South End Press, 1994) p1-2

[119] Danaher, p2, 4. "Accordingly, Third World countries under IMF/World Bank tutelage have seen infant mortality rates increase, schools and housing deteriorate, unemployment skyrocket and the general health of the people decline." (p2)

[120] Esposito, p88, 90-91. Check out the Dambiso Moyo's study, *Dead Aid: Why Aid is Not Working and How There is a Better Way For Africa*, (New York, Farrar, Straus and Giroux, 2009)

[121] Muhammad Yunus, "Preface: Redefining Development", from *50 Years Is Enough*, xiii

[122] Ralph Nader, *The Good Fight*, p201

representatives and political elites. As we saw in the case of the League of Nations, so we see with the United Nations, as well as economic institutions like the World Bank and the International Monetary Fund -they are created by the victors of wars and by wealthy politicians. Justice which issues from the most powerful is often called 'victor's justice'. The International Laws themselves, not to mention the Security Council, are often written by those who won the last war or by those who have the most wealth.

Internationalism led by representatives also leads to the centralization of power. If a nation's president or prime minister is already a kind of central figure, then these international organizations are even further centralized. This means that they are even further out of touch with the majority of people. Moreover, as we see with institutions like the UN, in order to be represented at all one needs to be a state-leader. If a people do not have a state at all, then they seem to fall through the cracks of the international system. What can minorities such as Native Americans, who were once a sovereign nation or group of nations, hope to gain from international courts when their nation-status is in question? What could an international court do for those African-Americans whose families built this country and who have been robbed and violated for generations?[123]

Grassroots International Justice

One thing that is important to keep in mind about justice is that it is social. This is easily forgotten when a centralized state, bureaucracy, or international court poses as the ultimate arbiter of justice. Justice is not something that only happens in a courtroom or a guillotine, it is something that happens in society everyday. It is found in the family and in the community. Consideration of the social scope of justice is important in attempting to wrap our minds around something like international justice, and naivly succumbing to an imperial theory of justice.

If the English mathematician and logician Bertrand Russell was a great critic of pragmatism, yet he admitted that the American discipline had changed his mind in the course of his life more than once, and that philosophically he shared some affinities with pragmatism.[124] For example, Russell's mature philosophy shared the three basic tenets of pragmatism: pluralism, naturalism, and fallibilism. Russell was however, critical of pragmatist's epistemological claims, or lack-thereof, and he lived beyond all of the classical pragmatists, to see their philosophy eclipsed by the Cold War.

In his anti-war book *War Crimes in Vietnam*, Russell wrote, "To some, the expression 'U.S. imperialism' appears as a cliché because it is not part of their own experience. We in the West are the beneficiaries of imperialism. The spoils of exploitation are the means of our corruption."[125] He wrote of the international cooperation by state leaders complicit with the US war on Vietnam.

---

[123] There has been a movement in the US among the senate that is slowly gaining popularity, called HR40. This House Resolution seeks to recompense people whose families were formerly enslaved.
[124] Russell said he first became a pluralist in 1907. See Russell's "Revolt Into Pluralism" for a more technical exposition of his mature philosophy. From, *My Philosophical Development*, (New York, Simon and Schuster, 1959) p54-64
[125] Bertrand Russell, "Peace Through Resistance to U.S. Imperialism", from *War Crimes In Vietnam*, published in *Readings in U.S. Imperialism*, ed. K.T. Fann and Donald C. Hodges, (Boston, Porter Sargent Publisher, 1971) xi

"The fact that this naked aggression is condoned by the United Nations, and the ability of the United States to escape expulsion from the United Nations for its gross violation of the Charter, demonstrates that the United Nations has become a tool of American aggression of the kind displayed in the Dominican Republic. All my sympathy lies with the struggle of the people of the Dominican Republic, which continues at this very moment."

"The people of Vietnam are heroic, and their struggle is epic: a stirring and permanent reminder of the incredible spirit of which men are capable when they are dedicated to a noble ideal. Let us salute the people of Vietnam."

Though Russell was not a socialist and had been highly critical of both Marx and Lenin, he saved his greatest condemnation for the United States.

"In the course of history there have been many cruel and rapacious empires and systems of imperialist exploitation, but none before have had the power at the disposal of United States imperialism. This constitutes a world system of oppression, and represents the true threat to peace and the true source of the danger of world nuclear war."[126]

In 1966 Bertrand Russell set up what became known as the Russell Tribunals. These were in many ways like the Trotsky mock-trials which Dewey had chaired 30 years earlier. Russell had seen the limits of the reach of the United Nations and the International Court of Justice during the Cold War. Thus, he took hold of the social principal of justice and held International War Crimes Tribunals. As Russell was 94 years old at the time, he was greatly aided by the French philosopher Jean-Paul Sartre, (1905-1980) who was appointed as president. Sartre said, "We were hoping that the conclusions the tribunal reached would be taken up by the people, rather than simply remaining the conclusions of certain men who were following international law established by the Nuremberg Tribunal."[127]

In his speech at the first meeting of the member of the War Crimes Tribunal, in November of 1966, Russell said,

"I have lived through the Dreyfus Case and been party to the investigation of the crimes committed by King Leopold in the Congo. I can recall many wars. Much injustice has been recorded quietly during these decades. In my own experience I can not discover a situation quite comparable... May this Tribunal prevent the crime of silence."[128]

The Tribunal met for two sessions in 1967 –the first one in Stockholm, Sweden, and the second one in Copenhagen, Denmark. At these televised trials were more than two-dozen lawyers, writers, activists, and others from over a dozen countries from every continent in the world. These included: Russell, Sartre, Simone de Beauvoir, James Baldwin, and Stokely Carmichael among others.

The need to keep matters of peace and justice in the people's hands was felt by John Dewey as well. Dewey saw a need to safe-haven any International Laws by keeping them informed and driven by peace activists rather than politicians. He noted how "this proposition to outlaw war does put it up to the peoples of the world to find out whether they want the war system to continue or do not want it to continue."

"Here at last is a movement for peace which starts from the peoples themselves, which expresses their will, and demands that the legislators and politicians and the diplomats give effect to the popular will for peace... Just think what a difference it makes whether you begin with the people and end with the politicians, or begin with the politicians and end by putting something over on the people."

---

[126] Russell, "Peace Through Resistance to U.S. Imperialism", xv, xv-xvi
[127] Jean-Paul Sartre, "Self-Portrait At Seventy", *Life/Situations: Essays Written and Spoken*, trans. Paul Auster and Lydia Davis, (New York, Pantheon Books, 1977) p26
[128] Russell, *The Autobiography of Bertrand Russell*, Volume III, 1944-1969, p321

"[I]t is just as well to have no treaties which disguise the real situation and which lull lovers of peace into a wholly delusive notion of the prospects of peace."[129]

"I believe that if the energies of those who want peace were united to promote these measures, immensely more would be accomplished for peace than will be effected by keeping discussion and thought fastened upon the use of coercion."[130]

John Dewey's admonitions have a particular importance today when those government led international institutions are proving to be highly inadequate in many regards. As we have seen these politician and government run institutions are further centralized and relieved of democracy by the uncheckable power, as for example, of nuclear founders of the Security Council. Moreover, these international bureaucracies resort to either military intervention, bombing, or the sanctioning of people, including women and children. All of this leads to many innocent deaths as well as the bureaucratic preponderance for only passing resolutions on non-binding agreements.

Non-governmental organizations, on the other hand, seem to be the most hopeful alternatives. This is because they are run by people who are not representative to corporations, nations, or militaries. They are the people who deeply care about the issues and have dedicated their lives to these causes. Organizations like Global Exchange, for example, are effective in spreading grassroots internationalism because they work through the farmers, the activists, and the people in order to meet real needs, and not corporate or government needs. Here is where socialist and anarchist and feminist and environmental groups can be most effective, because what is not needed is for there to be one international power with the first and the last say.

This goes for international justice as well. If people like George Bush II, Dick Cheney, Donald Rumsfeld, and others are in fact guilty of war crimes or for lying, it does not seem likely that they will be tried at the Hague anytime soon. What about the plight of Chechnya or the Uighurs in China? Here grassroots movements and community movements can bring attention to the world and to help get the word out in people's struggles. For example, as we saw there is the instance of the Turkey Protocol which was a joint effort of doctors and jurists. Indian activist and writer Arundhati Roy has helped keep the movement for social justice moving forward in her participation in the World Tribunal on Iraq.[131]

For those who think that Black Nationalism is just a racist ideology, they do well to see the words of Stokely Carmichael. At a conference held by the Organization of Latin-American Solidarity (OLAS) in Havana Cuba in 1967, the Black Nationalist leader Stokely Carmichael delivered a speech titled, "Black Power and the Third World". He said:

"Black Power is more than a slogan; it is a way of looking at our problems and the beginning of a solution to them. It attacks racism and exploitation, the horns of the bull that seeks to gore us."

"No, we do not want to catch up with anyone. What we want to do is go forward all the time, night and day, in the company of man, in the company of all men."[132]

---

[129] John Dewey, from *Characters and Events*, vol. II, in *The Philosophy of John Dewey*, p523, 524-525, 546-547

[130] John Dewey, "Sanctions and the Security of Nations", from *Are Sanctions Necessary to International Organization?*, a discussion with R.L. Buell, published in a pamphlet by Foreign Policy Association, June 1932. From, *The Philosophy of John Dewey*, p600

[131] www.worldtribunal.org

[132] Stokely Carmichael, "Black Power and the Third World", from *Readings in U.S. Imperialism*, p350, 356

Whatever the scope of International Justice, it should keep to a separation of powers, and movements should be led by social groups rather than institutions. Black Nationalism pushes past the imperialist idea that there is only one form of justice in the world or that one state or empire can rule over many distinct peoples. This points to the notion that justice itself is a social institution. What is or isn't justice? Is there just one absolute justice? Is justice divine? Is justice personal? To these questions we immediately turn.

6

Many Forms of Justice

The Macedonian philosopher Aristotle was one of the first thinkers to separate questions of justice into two basic categories: Retributive Justice and Distributive Justice. Retributive Justice, or Retribution for short, deals with the justification of punishment. The most famous version of retribution, if not the most popular, is the 'law of talon' –'an eye for an eye', though retributive justice isn't just capital punishment but can exist as forms such as a monetary fine or a sentence of imprisonment. Distributive Justice deals with the distribution and allocation of resources or goods such as wages, welfare, and property (sometimes called Agrarian Justice) according to merit.

Aristotle would have warned against the US's attempt to democratize other countries. Not that he thought democracy was impractical, only that there are many forms of societies and governments, each constituted by a different and distinct community, each with its own tradition of justice. However, within Aristotle's own lifetime his one-time student Alexander the Great conquered many different peoples and for each instated his own form of government: empire. Although Aristotle outlived the emperor by a year, the post-Alexandrian, or Hellenistic world as it is called, gave birth to the Roman Empire and a justice formalized by universal law beyond theory and tradition.

As we still see in today's empires, justice is so universal as to be rhetorical. The concept of justice often becomes a matter of rhetoric even in democratic countries where the centralized law of a bureaucracy decides what is just for everyone. The justice of the community and the city-state is replaced by the justice decreed from a universal law; a law so universal that for some people 'justice' is thought of as a place where people are brought whom disagree with this law, much like Dante's concept of hell, call it prison.

If justice is universal, where is justice? Who is justice for? Where did justice come from? What is the relationship between justice and the universe? Where are the universal laws of justice writ? What is the relationship between the law and justice? Is justice a common universal concern or are there some who are indifferent to what is just? If some people support justice, are some opposed to it? If so, what has led people toward disbelief in justice?

This chapter will attempt to survey some answers to questions like these, while comparing and ranking the varying conceptions of justice that exist or are thought to exist. For example, some believe that justice is a convention of power –that 'might makes right'. Others say that justice is a gift from the Divine given to those who have the right faith or religion. Some believe that humans are incapable of being just and that a person should "realize his incapacity for good and learn to despair of himself."[1]

To simplify things these various theories will be related to three conceptions of justice, even if these occasionally overlap or contradict one another. These three conceptions are that justice is 1) cultural, 2) divine, or 3) personal.

---

[1] Martin Luther in *Samtliche Schriften*, St. Louis edition. Quoted and trans. by Walter Kaufmann, *The Faith of A Heretic*, (Garden City, Anchor Books, 1963) (a) p109

1) According to some ancient philosophers as well as some contemporary philosophers justice is a cultural phenomenon. By this it is meant that either all the cultures of the world have a tradition of justice and or that the content of such justice is informed by the values and customs of each particular culture. In some cases of this culturally informed form of justice there might exist a kind of judicial expert of sorts such as a ruler, legislator, judge, or representative who interprets and applies their culture's conception of justice.

2) The second general conception of justice is the belief that justice is of divine origin. This can mean either that the god(s) alone are just or s/he or they reveal justice to humans in the form of miracles or curses or through the revelation of divine laws or condemnations. Under this category we would list the many religious traditions or various spiritual beliefs, as for example the belief in karma or immortality, or some other form of cosmic retribution.

3) The third general conception of justice is the attitude that justice is a personal matter. Under this category would be the belief that justice is 'in they eye of the beholder'. That what someone takes to be just is purely subjective. What one person might regard as just will always be different from other people, except perhaps by chance. One man's utopia is another man's no place.

Many of the forms of justice we find in the world today fall under these three headings, though they occasionally may overlap with or without counteracting each other. To find where justice originated we might do well to look at some of the oldest recorded stories, disputes, or laws. An early account of how humans acquired or came to know justice can be found in ancient Greek poetry. 2500 years ago Hesiod meditated on justice, believing it was a gift from Cronus's son, Zeus:

"Listen now to justice, and forget, completely, violence. For Cronus' son set up this law for men. Fish, flesh, and fowl each other devour, for right is not in them. But right he gave to men, and for this is best by far."[2]

The first ancient Greek philosopher who attempts to account for the existence of justice doesn't get much further, though he offers perhaps a better answer. In his poem on "the One" Parmenides' recounts his journey of escape from the darkness (or ignorance). Waiting for him in the light (or knowledge) the Goddess of Justice, Dike, reveals that:

"For it is no evil fate that has set you to travel on this road, far from the beaten paths of men, but right and justice."[3]

We can gather from these two accounts the belief that justice is revealed to humans by the gods. We might interpret from Hesiod the belief that justice is on the one hand opposed to violence and on the other is related to 'rightness', or knowledge of truth. From Parmenides and Dike we might interpret the belief that 'rightness' and 'justice' are opposed to evil, which apparently is more common to men, though the Goddess does not mention women.

Many of the ancient religions that abounded (some of which are still faithfully practiced) in the world have a deity of justice in their pantheon. There is the Sumerian God of the Sun and Justice *Utu*, the Babylonian God of the Sun and Justice *Shamash*, the above mentioned Greek Goddess of Justice *Dike* (sometimes replaced with *Themis*), the

---

[2] Hesiod *Works and Days*, 1.16, quoted in *An Introduction to Early Greek Philosophy*, trans. and ed. James Mansley Robinson, (Boston, Houghton Mifflin Company, 1968) p18
[3] Parmenides "Prologue", trans. Robinson, *An Introduction to Early Greek Philosophy*, p108

Chinese God of Justice and Judgement *Gao Yao*, the African God of Hunting and Justice *Ochosi*, the Norse God of Justice *Forseti*, and finally and most famously, the Roman Goddess of Justice *Justicia*, who is represented as having worn a blindfold and holding a sword in one hand and scales in the other.

We can infer from these titles some characteristics or forms of justice. Many of these gods and goddess' are understood not only as representing justice but as embodying other forces as well. For example, 'justice and the sun' can be understood as the relationship between justice and intelligibility or the truth, or perhaps agriculture. Or 'justice and judgement' can be taken as the relationship between justice and justification. 'Justice and hunting' can be related to the connection between justice as desert, or getting what one deserves. Justicia's scales are used to represent equality in measurement and distribution, her blindfold represents impartiality or objectivity, and her sword represents retribution and deterrence.

One of the oldest recorded laws of justice, that of the Babylonian King Hammurabi was written some 3,800 years ago. King Hammurabi drafted a code of law written in an ancient Semitic script posted amongst the general public with the idea that it could be read and understood by all. The basic tenant of Hammurabi's law is what is commonly referred to as an 'eye for an eye'.

An 'eye for an eye' is one of first analytic formulations of Justice. What this means is that the concept of Justice was defined and predicated quantitatively, i.e., not according to partiality, which might be arbitrary. 'Eye for an eye' is opposed to aggressive violence, and because of its specificity, is opposed to mere opinion. An 'eye for an eye' is probably the most common forms of justice found amongst humans and is still popularly used in the United States today, where very few states do not have capital punishment. (See Chapter 2 for details.)

Before there was a written law there was an oral law. Moreover, not all forms of justice are laws. Most forms of justice that exist are not 'juridical' but are an admixture of tradition and personal preference in their scope. Personal justice is a matter of the conscience: only we know what is right and wrong for ourselves. Hamlet said, "nothing is good or bad but thinking makes it so."

Did King Hammurabi by recording and posting his ethics in effect make a step toward bureaucratizing justice? Do all such laws and theories of justice only impinge upon the individual's independence? Or could a written law or recorded theory of justice perhaps assist in setting a precedent, a standard or foundation from which all future understandings of justice can be built upon?

The Law of Manu stands as an example of a written law that overtime became bureaucratized and eventually believed by some to have been divinely revealed. Manu was a philosopher and not a prophet –moreover, he believed in social mobility. Popular representations of Hindus by the Western Media would have us believe the contrary, that there has always been a rigid caste system that has existed as the essence of the Hindu religion and culture. Such a prejudice is false and this ugly report of the Orient has thrived on dishonesty and robbery.

The Bhagavad-Gita of the Hindus teaches of a law that is both a divinely writ as well as personal, and thus not culturally informed:

"Better is one's own law though imperfectly carried out than the law of another carried out perfectly. Better is death in the fulfillment of one's own law, for to follow another's law is perilous." 3:35 (the first line is repeated in the last chapter, 18: 47)

"Therefore let the scripture be thy authority for determining what should be done and what should not be done. Knowing what is declared by the rules of the scripture, thou should do thy work in this world." 16:24[4]

A discussion between Socrates and his friend Polemarchus and others about the nature of justice leads to a conclusion that is structurally identical to that of the Hindu scripture Bhagavad Gita, as well as the philosopher Manu. This discussion is set out in Plato's *Republic*, which is considered to be one of the earliest Western philosophies of justice, and some say that Plato had been influenced by Hindu philosophers during his travels.

The *Republic* is perhaps one of the first scientific studies of justice to be found in literature.[5] It explores the three conceptions of justice listed above (cultural, divine, and personal) as well as many others, often criticizing some of the forms of justice that were popular around Plato's time.

In this dialogue we find the retired soldier Socrates in his late 60's hanging out with his friends discussing the virtues of aging and the question of what is just, or right conduct. His friend Polemarchus begins by offering as a definition of justice, "that it is just to give to each what is owed to him". (331e)[6] This is a very traditional and practical understanding of justice, sometimes referred to as "desert", and is still widely accepted as correct. So, for example, if I owe someone money it is unjust to not pay them back, because they deserve it.

Socrates replies to his friend, "what if he is out of his mind when he asks for it [back]?" (332a) He cites as an example a weapon. What if your friend has lent you his Tommy-Gun and you find later that they are drunk and outraged at someone (perhaps you). If, then they ask for their gun, according to Polemarchus, it is wrong and unjust to refuse to return it. Socrates does not accept this theory of justice, believing it to be a type of casuistry that is somewhat rhetorical, or as he puts it, "poetic".

Polemarchus reformulates his position and offers a different conception, this time saying that justice is "that which benefits one's friends and harms one's enemies." (332d) This conception can be taken as a form of a social or cultural theory of justice and is often used to justify war. Socrates wonders aloud, "[I]s it the part of the just man to harm anyone at all?" (335b) He uses as an example a horse. When we harm a horse it only makes the horse worse. "Shall we not say so about men too, that when they are harmed they deteriorate in their human excellence?" Socrates observes, "Then men who are harmed, my friend, necessarily become more unjust." (335c) and concludes, "…it is never just to harm anyone." (335e)

As the argument continues (it goes on for some 300 pages or papyrus scrolls) Thrasymachus, angrily interrupts the amiable discussion, "What nonsense have you two been talking, Socrates?" (336c) Thrasymachus is a military general from another city-state, which is run by a despot, or dictator. Socrates is startled by the general's indignation and trembling, he replies: "do not be hard on us, Thrasymachus, if we have erred in our investigation, he and I; be sure that we err unwittingly." (336e) Notice to 'err

---

[4] Bhagavad Gita, trans. Sarvepalli Radhakrishnan, *A Sourcebook In Indian Philosophy*, ed. Radhakrishnan and Charles A. Moore, (Princeton, Princeton University Press, 1957)
[5] The *Republic* of Plato is a discussion of justice and should not be confused with the *Republic* of Cicero which holds that justice is divinely revealed.
[6] Plato, *Republic*, trans. G.M.A. Grube, (Indianapolis, Hackett Publishing Company, 1974)

unwittingly' is another way of stating the unpopular belief of Socrates, that people only do bad from ignorance.

After warning Socrates and Polemarchus to be wary of their freedom to discuss the matter, Thrasymachus says he believes "the just is nothing else than the advantage of the stronger." (338c) This can be restated in the popular english usage as meaning 'might makes right' or 'nice guys finish last'. This is a form of a social or cultural conception of justice, and is often called "imperialism".

Thrasymachus now more confident and at ease continues:

"Yes, and each government makes laws to its own advantage: democracy makes democratic laws, a despotism makes despotic laws, and so with the others, and when they have made these laws they declare this to be just for their subjects, that is, their own advantage, and they punish him who transgresses the laws as lawless and unjust. This then, my good man, is what I say justice is, the same in all cities, the advantage of the established government, and correct reasoning will conclude that the just is the same everywhere, the advantage of the stronger." (338e)

Socrates asks the general, "Tell me, do you also say that obedience to the rulers is just?" (339b) Thrasymachus affirms this. Socrates asks, "And are the rulers in all cities infallible, or are they liable to error?" Thrasymachus replies that rulers are indeed liable to error. Socrates continues, "When they undertake to make laws, therefore, they make some correctly and make others incorrectly?" (339c) "Then, according to your argument, it is just to do not only what is to the advantage of the stronger, but also the opposite, what is not to their advantage." (339d)

Upon this rationalization Thrasymachus becomes confused. But he is stubborn. The general says that "complete injustice is more profitable than complete justice". (348b) This is the exact opposite of his original position. Thus, Thrasymachus went from believing that 'justice is the advantage of the stronger' to believing the 'unjust man is always at an advantage to the just'.

Socrates was a curious fellow and explores the general's new position. "What about the unjust man? Would he deem it right to outdo the just man and the just action?" (349c) When Thrasymachus replies with an affirmative to this question, both the arbitrariness and equivocality of his position is revealed. We can categorize Thrasymachus here as falling under the third conception of justice mentioned above, the individual or personal form.

What is wrong with holding that 'it is right for the unjust to outdo the just'? Why is this arbitrary and equivocal? To say it is equivocal is a polite way of saying it violates the classic law of logic known as the "law of non-contradiction". Something can't both be the case and not be the case simultaneously. To analyze Thrasymachus' argument it says: *The unjust are right to outdo the just.*

If this contradiction is not clear to the reader, imagine a person who tries to correctly do something incorrectly –they would have to correctly be incorrect to be incorrect correctly, otherwise they were incorrect incorrectly, in which case they failed. In Thracymachus' argument, as in all forms of imperialism, there is a breakdown in the relationship between knowledge and ethics. Someone can't do what is good or right unless they know what is good or right. Imperialism in both its cultural and personal forms is a kind of ignorance –it is unrealistic. Often times, imperialism is opposed to reality altogether.

Someone might respond: "Power doesn't care about truth. After all, imperialism is satisfied in its own self-confidence and feeling of its own infallibility that it is not concerned with external reasons. And if the just and the unjust have the same goal, which is power, then there really is no such thing as justice –it merely becomes a compliment we pay to ourselves." Note that this is the 3rd conception listed above, that is, the individual or personal conception of justice. We will return to this point shortly.

While it is not known to Thrasymachus that he has been defeated in argument he finally parts company with the philosophers. After all, how could he know of something of which he is ignorant?

Through the rest of the dialogue Socrates goes on to conceptualize an ideal city-state as being the place wherein Justice can be best defined. Socrates then sets a foundation from which to conceptualize a Republic as this ideal city-state. He uses a provisional definition of justice that can be stated as "each doing their duty". (441e) "In some way then possession of one's own and the performance of one's own task could be agreed to be justice." (434a) This was the position of the Bhagavad Gita. Socrates, however, despite the oracle of Delphi, (in which the god Apollo revealed that Socrates was the wisest among men), was a fallibilist and did not believe he always spoke for the divine:

"Do not let us, I said, take this as quite final yet. If we find that this quality, when existing in each individual man, is agreed there too to be justice, then we can assent to this –for what can we say? –but if not, we must look for something else." (434d)

Interestingly, Socrates never arrives at a final definition of Justice in the *Republic*, though this was the purpose of the dialogue in the first place. Socrates believes the definition should ceaselessly be arbitrated over by the philosopher kings.

"Cities will have no respite from evil... nor will the human race, I think, unless philosophers rule as kings in the cities, or those whom we now call kings and rulers genuinely and adequately study philosophy, until, that is, political power and philosophy coalesce, and the various natures of those who now pursue the one to the exclusion of the other are forcibly debarred from doing so." (473d)

"The struggle to be good or bad is important... much more important than people think, so that is not worth being led on by honours, wealth, or any office, or indeed by poetry, to neglect justice and other virtues." (608b)

Plato, like his friend and teacher Socrates, offers a highly theoretical and fallibilistic theory of Justice.[7] In the real world, however, this may be a luxury. In the real world teacher and pupil differ, as do the many cultures, nations, and religious traditions of the world. But what is important about the *Republic* is that it is an attempt to understand justice in a human way. The philosophy of dialogue is one of the most informative and constructive ways to discover truth and justice.

However influential Plato has been on the world, his philosophical method for understanding justice disappeared from the West for almost 2000 years. It wasn't until the 'Golden Age' of Spain when the Muslims and Jews revived the study of Plato and his pupil, Aristotle, and then the 'Enlightenment' era, when such freethinkers as Leibniz, Rousseau, and Kant continued the discussion of justice. In philosophy's stead, justice was either not questioned or not believed to be possible in this Western world outside of divine justice. Some of the most influential forms of justice found in the contemporary world are informed by the three main monotheisms: Judaism, Christianity, and Islam.

---

[7] We learn Socrates' theory of justice (as distinct from Plato's) in the dialogue *Crito*.

Judaism and Justice

Probably the two most famous events associated with Jewish history are the revelation of the Ten Commandments and the death of Jesus. The Ten Commandments, or Decalogue, were revealed to Moses on Mount Sinai some 3500 hundred year ago. Although most would be hard-pressed to list off all ten, the first one that usually comes to mind is, "Thou shall not kill."

Jesus was killed roughly 1500 years later for reasons that are not always clear. Some believe, "For God loved the world so much that he gave his only begotten Son, in order that…" (John 3:16)[8] For centuries Christians believed that Jesus was killed by his fellow Jews. The Catholic Church finally recanted this belief in 1965[9] though many people still believe the Jewish people were at least in part responsible for his death.

When we read the New Testament we find much resentment and blame for the Jewish people, but we also find the opposite as well. Probably all of the writers of the New Testament were Jewish in their upbringing (though apparently, a very Hellenized form of Judaism), with the exception of Luke. However, they all wrote in Greek and were influenced by the Greek syncretism, the collusion of Hebrew and Greek thought. Jesus once told a woman (according to Greek literature), "You worship what you do not know; we worship what we know, because salvation originates with the Jews." (John 4:22)

We find much compassion for Jesus by the Jewish people as well. We discover that they were concerned that Jesus was possessed by a demon (John 7:20) and that they were concerned that Jesus would commit suicide (John 8:22). What is more, the gospel according to John tells us the Jewish people did not have the death penalty, either. (John 18:31)

Some have inferred from the story of the brothers Cain and Abel that murder is not approved of by God. (Genesis 4:11) Abraham asked God (herein referred to by the Hebrew *Yhwh*) why he judges the wicked and the righteous (Genesis 18:23) yet later, we see that Abraham nearly sacrifices his own son in order to obey Yhwh's commandment. (Genesis 22:2) The revelation of the Ten Commandments occurred to Moses in the second book of the Torah, many generations after Abraham and Isaac.

Moses had killed an Egyptian guard and had fled Egypt before Yhwh appointed him to return and demand that Pharaoh "let my people go". Prior to receiving the Ten Commandments at Mount Sinai Moses had the heavy burden of arbitrating for many of the people. Upon the suggestion of his father-in-law Jethro, a better system is devised.

"And Moses chose able men out of all Israel, and made them heads over the people, rulers of thousands, rulers of hundreds, rulers of fifties, and rulers of tens. And they judged the people at all seasons: the hard cases they brought unto Moses, but every small matter they judged themselves."[10] Exodus 18:25-26

---

[8] All New Testament passages from *New World Translation of the Holy Scriptures*, trans. New World Bible Translation Committee, (Brooklyn, Watch Tower Bible & Tract Society of Pennsylvania, 1961)
[9] Set out in the Papal bull *Nostra Aetate*.
[10] All quotations from the Torah and Tanach are according to the Masocretic Text, trans. The Jewish Publication Society of America, (Philadelphia, The Jewish Publication Society of America, 1917)

Shortly thereafter the Ten Commandments were revealed to Moses on Mount Sinai. If it is popular in many Christian nations of Europe as well as the U.S. to proudly post the Ten Commandments, most do not realize that the Torah actually contains Six-Hundred and Thirteen Commandments. The five books of the Torah, or Pentateuch are considered by Jewish people to be the only books of the Hebrew Bible, the Tanach, which were divinely revealed. The remainder of the Tanach (Hebrew Bible) contains the Prophets and the Writings, neither of which were divinely revealed.

After Mount Sinai a basic code or set of rules are given to the people: "Now these are the ordinances which thou shalt set before them." (Exodus 21:1) The book of Exodus, or 'The Book of the Covenant' as it is called sets up the first code for the Jewish people. (They are listed from 21:1-22:23) This basic code contains some of the classic biblical ethics such as tolerance and good-will, as for example:

"And a stranger shalt thou not wrong, neither shalt thou oppress him; for ye were strangers in Egypt. Ye shall not afflict any widow, or fatherless child." Exodus 22:20-21

The third book of the Torah Leviticus is basically a priestly code. The sons of Moses' brother Aaron and the Levites were the priestly classes. The Levites in particular were not allowed to own any land but collected a tithe from the people. The book of Leviticus teaches:

"Ye shall do no unrighteousness in judgement; thou shalt not respect the person of the poor, nor favour the person of the mighty; but in righteousness shalt thou judge thy neighbor."

"Thou shalt not go up and down as a talebearer among thy people; neither shalt thou stand idly by the blood of thy neighbor...

"Thou shalt not hate thy brother in thy heart; thou shalt surely rebuke thy neighbor, and not bear sin because of him.

"Thou shalt not take vengeance, nor bear any grudge against the children of thy people, but thou shalt love thy neighbor as thyself..." Leviticus 19:15-18

"And if a stranger sojourn with thee in your land, ye shall not do him wrong.

"The stranger that sojourneth with you shall be unto you as the home-born among you, and thou shalt love him as thyself; for ye were strangers in the land of Egypt...

"Ye shall do no unrighteousness in judgement, in meteyard, in weight, or in measure." Leviticus 19:33-35

"Ye shall have one manner of law, as well for the stranger, as for the home-born..." Leviticus 24:22

The fourth book of the Torah is called the book of Numbers and is titled thus because it contains a record of all those people who were part of the Exodus. Yhwh supports a war against the King of Canaan (Numbers 21:3) and the Midianites (Numbers 31:2) wherein many people were killed.

It is in Deuteronomy, the final book of the Torah that we learn Yhwh wants all of his people to be self-ruling and to be well-acquainted with the law. Some view the ancient Hebrews as a tribe of lawyers and judges. As the Hebrew scholar and Talmudist Louis Ginzberg says in his essay, "The Codification of Jewish Law":

"It is characteristic of the 'Deuteronomic Code' that it is intended for the whole nation, and not for special classes –priest or judges. ...Nevertheless, it would be difficult to overestimate the importance of this code; it is not only a great reformative legal work, but it is also, in a certain sense, the first authoritative code...It is the first book of laws for the people, its predecessors being intended chiefly for judges and priests; and it retained this position as the people's code, although it underwent some changes in the course of time."[11]

---

[11] Louis Ginzberg, "The Codification of Jewish Law", *On Jewish Law and Lore*, (New York, Athenium, 1955) p155-156

The Hebrew word for justice *sedakah* can mean 'merciful love' or 'alms'. In Deuteronomy we find the first analytic formula for justice. This formula is similar to that of the Law of Hammurabi mentioned earlier, though there are differences. It should be noted that they are both of Semitic origin. In both the Deuteronomic Code and the Law of Hammurabi there is the belief that each person should know the law, and no adult can plead ignorance of it. This non-exemption through ignorance is still used today in the contemporary world.

The book of Deuteronomy is fairly exacting in its demand for justice:

"If there arise a matter too hard for thee in judgement, between blood and blood, between plea and plea, and between stroke and stroke, even matters of controversy within thy gates; then shalt thou arise, and get thee up unto the place which the Lord thy God shall choose. And thou shalt come unto the priests the Levites, and unto the judge that shall be in those days; and thou shalt inquire; and they shall declare unto thee the sentence of judgment." –Deuteronomy 17:8-9

"And the judges shall inquire diligently; and, behold, if the witness be a false witness, and hath testified falsely against his brother; then shall ye do unto him, as he had purposed to do unto his brother; so shalt thou put away the evil from the midst of thee. And those that remain shall hear, and fear, and shall henceforth commit no more any such evil in the midst of thee. And thine eye shall not pity: life for life, eye for eye, tooth for tooth, hand for hand, foot for foot." Deuteronomy 19:18:21

"The fathers shall not be put to death for the children, neither shall the children be put to death for the fathers; every man shall be put to death for his own sin.

"Thou shalt not pervert the justice due to the stranger, or the fatherless; nor take the widow's raiment to pledge." Deuteronomy 24:16-17

The Torah was either written by or given to Moses. Moses was not a king but a judge. It wasn't until a few centuries later that the Jewish people came to have a *messiah*, which is the title given to Hebrew kings. The 11th century BCE book of Judges attests to this, saying: "In those days there was not king of Israel; every man did that which was right in his own eyes." (Judges 21:25)

Judges were people of great wisdom who helped the tribes in times of distress and arbitrated over important decisions, as delineated by the law. The last of the judges in the tradition of Moses was a man named Samuel. Samuel was descendent from a long line of judges who helped maintain one of the twelve Hebrew tribes, Beersheba. As Samuel grew old and unable to work, his sons took over the job of judging. However, the people found the sons of Samuel corrupt and unjust.

The elders gathered together to find a solution for this problem and asked Samuel to make them a king to judge "like all the nations". (1Samuel 8:5) The people trusted Samuel and he warned them that kings were often corrupt and their decisions were arbitrary, as was the case in other kingdoms: "he will take your sons, and appoint them unto him, for his chariots, and to be his horsemen…and to make his instruments of war…" (1Samuel 8:11,12)

The people were stubborn. "But the people refused to hearken unto the voice of Samuel; and they said, 'Nay; but there shall be a king over us; that we also may be like all the nations…And the Lord said to Samuel: 'Hearken unto their voice, and make them a king'." (1Samuel 8:19-20, 22) Yhwh instructs Samuel to anoint a farmer named Saul to be messiah of Israel. (1Samuel 9:15)

In this classical messianic period of Jewish monarchy, which lasted nearly 500 years, no legal books were written: this was the time when the Jewish Prophets commenced. The Torah was canonized sometime before 350 BCE. Rabbi Louis Ginzberg writes that in consequence of this canonization of the five books, "the Law was for a period of time regarded as finished."[12] During this period were the Prophets. The Prophets were individual thinkers who were often critical of the messiah, and the Prophets emphasized the need to recognize the importance of social justice.[13]

"Wash you, make you clean, put away the evil of your doings from before my eyes, cease to do evil; learn to do well; seek justice, relieve the oppressed, judge the fatherless, please for the widow." Isaiah 1:16-17

"Execute ye justice and righteousness, and deliver the spoiled out of the hand of the oppressor; and do no wrong, do no violence, to the stranger, the fatherless, nor the widow, neither shed innocent blood in this place." Jeremiah 22:3

"Therefore turn thou to thy God; Keep mercy and justice..." Hosea 12:7

"And let justice roll forth like waters, and righteousness like a constantly flowing torrent." Amos 5:24

"It hath been told to thee, O man, what is good, And what the Lord doth require of thee: Only to do justly, and to love mercy, and to walk humbly with thy God." Micah 6:8

The messianic period of Judaism (which after Solomon split into two Kingdoms – Israel in the north and Judah in the south, with two messiahs) ended with the fall of Israel in the 8th century BCE to the Assyrians and the fall of Judah in the 6th century BCE to the Babylonians. When the Persians defeated the Babylonians some 50 years later, the Jews were freed from their exile but a messiah was not re-enthroned.

By the 4th century Alexander the Great had conquered Persia and Jerusalem. After Alexander's death in 323 the empire was split into smaller empires, wherein the Hellenistic kings reigned over Jerusalem: the Ptolemys who were based in Egypt ruled Jerusalem during the 3rd century, and the Seleucids who were based out of Persia ruled Jerusalem in the 2nd century. Outside of the bloody Maccabee uprisings and the autonomy granted to Jews in 142 BCE, from 63 BCE to the 7th century of the Common or Christian Era Jerusalem was controlled by the Roman Empire and after the 330's, the Holy Roman Empire.

As we can see from this disparate history the Jewish law and justice system often had to be maintained or adopted in times without political power or sovereignty. In the history of Judaism, going only back to Moses, 3200 years ago, the Jews only had 500 years of monarchy, not including the 500-year Jewish reign during the Khazar Empire of Russia, which in all likelihood had a messiah. Thus, the Jewish Khazar messiahs would have come to an end by pagan Slavs from the north in the 10th century of the Common Era. That means from the Torah to the Talmud, every legal book written by Jews was done when there was no messiah.

Although the word 'Torah' translates literally as 'the law', the Jewish Law proper is the *halakah*, which includes the Torah as well as the Oral Law, the interpretations of the Torah, and the practices and traditions which had been passed down from generation to generation. Halakah (ha–LAK-ah) translates as meaning 'the path' and first began to be written down and systemized in the 2nd century BCE.[14] These recordings were compiled in a book called the Mishnah in the 2nd century of the Common Era.[15]

As we saw, Jewish history since the 6th century BCE went through a thousand year period without a messiah or state. When the 523 chapters of the Mishnah were finished it completed the work of some 300 years of Jewish scholarship. With the

---

[12] Ginzberg, p158
[13] Kaufmann, (a) p203
[14] Adin Steinsaltz, *The Essential Talmud*, trans. Chaya Galai, (New York, Basic Books, Inc., 1976) p29,30
[15] Steinsaltz, p32. Ginzberg, p5

Mishnah, a need had been met so that the norms of the culture could be taught and recorded. When older codes become limited, "legislation comes to the rescue, abrogating obsolete laws and adding new ones which conform to the demands of the age." The Mishnah was not a book of law or the product of legislature, "but it was the work of judicial legislation" and was *de facto* and not *de jure*. The Mishnah was a textbook for students and a guide for teachers and many Mishnahs were written but only one survives.[16] It is comprised of six sections or orders dealing with the laws of agriculture, the Sabbath and holidays, family relations, property and court procedures, maintenance of the Temple, and proper ritual.

The Mishnah makes up a large portion of the Talmud. The Talmud was finished sometime in the 5th century CE, and the "completion of the Talmud signifies nothing less than the fixation of the entire Jewish law".[17] The purpose of the Talmud is the study of the Torah and is the last source material in Jewish literature. The Talmud is a primary source of Jewish law, however it cannot be cited as an authority for purposes of ruling. The Talmud completed some 800 years of work though in truth "The Talmud was never completed." This is because it is in many ways considered a living tradition. The Oral Law and Talmud were last codified by the Spanish-born Jewish philosopher Maimonides in the 12th century.[18]

There are actually two Talmuds, the Jerusalem or Palestinian Talmud and the Babylonian Talmud. Each differs according to the political climate under which the Jews lived. Talmudist Adin Steinsaltz shows the different histories, how the Babylonian Talmud became studied in North Africa and Spain while the Palestinian Talmud was studied in Italy, France, and Germany. Two schools of talmudic exegesis emerged: Sephardi and Ashkenazi. The Palestinian Talmud was unlocked by Lithuanian Jews. A "Jewish community which did not study the Talmud was condemned to attrition."[19]

The Talmud treats criminal law to be the same as civil law. There are three different kinds of courts, each with a different area of jurisdiction. Traditionally, the judiciary could consist of nobles, political leaders, and townsfolk. At the top were three ordained judges who decided upon cases of indemnity and other monetary issues, as well as corporal punishment. Then there was the court of three laymen, which often involved cases of arbitration, though one expert judge could take their place. There was no court of appeals. Capital offenses were handled by a panel of 23 expert judges. To be such a judge one could not be childless or well aged, and had to be impartial and without personal interest in the case. This court could pass the death sentence, but cases with political implications were passed by a supreme court made up of 71 judges and this court had the right to declare war. Its power extended beyond the national borders of the state and was considered to be the court of the entire Jewish population throughout the world.[20]

"In theory, the court can introduce ordinances and pass sentences that do not derive from the law of the Torah, but it is permitted to do so, on the explicit instructions

---

[16] Ginzberg, p4, 5, 7, 162
[17] Ginzberg, p28, 164
[18] Steinsaltz, p47, 64, 4
[19] Steinsaltz, p66, 83; Ginzberg, p 47-48
[20] Steinsaltz, p163, 164-166; Ginzberg, p25

of the Torah itself, in the general interest."[21] For example, prison sentences didn't exist in he Torah, but the court had this power.

Capital punishment ceased when Rome conquered Judea in the 2nd century Before the Common Era.[22] The Talmud discusses how difficult it became to give such a sentence. If the 23 judges found the defendant guilty of a capital offense, the Talmud ruled that the man must be acquitted.[23] The only way around this was for a king to appoint his own special court or if the community were in peril the court could be made into an administrative institution. No lawyers were allowed in criminal cases.[24]

"According to the Talmud, a court of twenty-three judges had been established to judge murder cases and to pass a sentence of death on the guilty... [I]f... the twenty-three judges voted unanimously for the death sentence, the Talmud ruled that the defendant must be acquitted! The Rabbis reasoned that if not one of the twenty-three could find some extenuating circumstance, the atmosphere of the trial must been charged with prejudice."[25]

As we have seen the Mishnah and the Talmud were produced when there was no messiah or Jewish state. These books in a sense teach Jews how to live according to the Halakah while residing in non-Jewish states. As Ginzberg tells us: "The Talmud made it possible for Judaism to adapt itself to every time and place, to every state and society, and to every stage of civilization." Jewish sages taught that "Jews should accept the rule of those gentile nations which opened the gates of their countries to them" though the sages did not extend this understanding to any gentile who occupied the 'Holy Land'.[26] This is because, as we saw, the Torah teaches that in their communities, Jews should apply their own law to strangers. As for residing in other lands the Tanach instructs:

"And seek the peace of the city whither I have caused you to be carried away captive, and pray unto the Lord for it; for in the peace thereof shall ye have peace." Jeremiah 29:7

Jews could, according to the "custom of the land" where they resided, waive some of the rights that Torah grants.[27] One major theme of those Jews who still live in Europe is the example set by Abraham who resided amongst the non-believer and acted according to law but was not assimilated.

"Get thee out of thy country, and from thy kindred, and from thy father's house, unto the land that I will show thee. And I will make of thee a great nation, and I will bless thee, and make thy name great; and be thou a blessing... And Abram journeyed, going on still toward the south." Genesis 12:1-2

Moses never reaches Israel but dies with it in his sight. (Deuteronomy 32:52) Walter Kaufmann (1921-1980) pointed out how the Jews existed for thousands of years before they had a state and Adam and Eve were created without a state. Kaufmann calls this position, "attenuated anarchy" saying that within the Hebrew Bible, the state "is not the natural condition of man."[28] Indeed, the book of Judges is fairly critical of monarchy. Before Saul was made messiah there was a man who became King named Abimelech who had asked, "Which is better for you, that all the sons of Jerubbal who are threescore and ten persons rule over you, or that one rule over you?" before murdering his brothers. (Judges 9:2,5) The one brother who escapes, Jotham tells the people of Abimelech's

---

[21] Steinsaltz, p146, 170, 172; Ginzberg, p14
[22] Ginzberg, p6
[23] Rabbis Morris N. Kertzer and Lawrence A. Hoffman, *What Is A Jew?*, (New York, Macmillan Publishing Company, 1993) p141
[24] Steinsaltz, p169, 171
[25] Kertzer and Hoffman, p141
[26] Ginzberg, p55, 88
[27] Steinsaltz, p146
[28] Kaufmann, (a) p198

treachery (though he reigned 3 years) and he mocks the people, comparing their desire for a king to the vegetable world.

"The trees went forth on a time to anoint a king over them; and they said unto the olive tree: Reign thou over us... And the trees said to the fig-tree: Come thou, and reign over us... And the trees said unto the vine: Come thou, and reign over us... Then said all the trees unto the bramble: Come thou, and reign over us. And the bramble said unto the trees: If in truth ye anoint me king over you, then come and take refuge in my shadow; and if not, let fire come out of the bramble, and devour the cedars of Lebanon."
Judges 9:8-15

The dishonest King Abimelech is eventually defeated in battle by a woman. He weakly says to one of his men, his armor-bearer, "Draw thy sword, and kill me, that men say not of me: A woman slew him.' And his young man thrust him through, and he died." (Judges 9:53-54)

The fact that no lawyers were traditionally allowed during criminal cases shows that there is a general understanding of the legal and justice system that is popular amongst the people. Even women were judges as we see in the case of Deborah, and this was the example set by Moses and Jewish legal philosophy. The fact that a King could appoint his own court if he was not happy with the existing judges, especially in the interests of homeland security is enough for one to prefer the judgement of the many judges, as opposed to the potential arbitrary judgments of a King. Even still, human judgement is not always perfect, even if it is perfectible.

Christianity and Justice

Of the popular monotheisms, Christianity poses the most difficult problem concerning the question of justice. Jesus was executed according to Roman Law. However, Christianity rejected the law of Judaism for that of its oppressor, Rome. The large influence of the Roman Law on the legal systems of the world today is due to Christianity. Perhaps in spite of serving two masters (Matthew 6:24), from the 6th century Emperor Justinian I to the 16th century Protestant Founding Fathers Henry VIII and John Calvin, all the way to the present day, the relationship between Christianity and justice has been a tenuous one.

For many Christians the books of the New Testament are not considered to have been divinely-revealed, with the exception of the book "Revelation". However, even someone as given to credulity as Calvin questioned this revelation's divine veracity. The New Testament instead is considered as 'the inspired words of God'. None of these books were written by Jesus and it is generally held that all of them were written after his death, in a language Jesus did not speak. Rather, Jesus as Christ, which is a Greek word meaning 'savior', is considered as divinely revealed. As the second greatest contributor to the New Testament (after Paul) John tells us, "the Word [of God] became flesh". The lamb whose death "takes away the sin of the world".

Modern Christian theologians have come to agree that there is a problem with regards to the teachings of the New Testament and their relationship with the social theory and practice of justice. Protestant theologians from Rudolf Bultmann (1884-1976) who wrote that Jesus "does not, as the prophets did, raise the demand for justice and right"[29]; Albert Schweitzer (1875-1965) who wrote, "These can have no hope for the world and its inhabitants; hopelessness about the present situation goes along with belief in the coming of the Kingdom of God at the end."[30] And Paul Tillich (1886-1965) concluded, "Therefore the divine justice can appear as plain injustice."[31]

The legal philosopher A.P. d'Entreves wonders in his book on *Natural Law*, "How could a Christian community be taught the elementary duties of good life and fellowship?" He reasons that it wasn't until the medieval philosopher (and citizen of the Holy Roman Empire) Thomas Aquinas that it was realized that, "The Christian community must be based on justice." This theory of justice is informed by Roman legal philosophy and jurisprudence. The Roman Law in turn comes by and large from the theory of Natural Law, which had been written about by the Stoics and neo-Platonists. Natural Law and the Roman Law are in many ways basically one and the same theory. D'Entreves writes: "The Thomist interpretation of Christianity is unthinkable without the notion of natural law."[32]

Thus, the Christian understanding of justice has undergone various interpretations and levels of relevance over time. This diversity comes to a head in a 1960 book called *Christian Attitudes Toward War and Peace: A Historical Survey and Critical Re-evaluation*, by a Yale professor Roland Bainton (1894-1984). Bainton discusses the various ways in which Christians have interpreted and understood the concept of justice, particularly regarding war and peace. Bainton says that, "Despite all the ambiguities in the New Testament, every one of the subsequent Christian attitudes to war and peace has relied on New Testament texts."[33]

These basic Christian attitudes according to Bainton are three: 1) Pacifism, 2) the war that is Just, and 3) the Crusade.

1) Pacifism. Bainton writes that "The Pacifism of the New Testament centers on the yielding spirit rather than on plans or philosophies of world peace."[34] Dicta such as 'turn the other cheek' (Matthew 5:39, Luke 6:29)[35] and the representations of the crucifixion are often taken as examples of this non-political, or passive pacifism. The New Testament tells us:

"For the entire Law stands fulfilled in one saying, namely: 'You must love your neighbor as yourself.'" Galatians 5:14 (This is a paraphrase of the Hebrew passage in Leviticus 19:18)

Be that as it may, the New Testament tells us that even thus, there will still be a lot of suffering and persecution, though this is necessary.

"Therefore do not become ashamed of the witness about our Lord, neither of me a prisoner for his sake, but take your part in suffering evil for the good news according to the power of God." 2 Timothy 1:8

---

[29] Rudolf Bultmann, *Theology of The New Testament*, Volume I, trans. Kendrick Grobel, (New York, Charles Scribner's Sons, 1951) p12
[30] Albert Schweitzer, *The Conception of the Kingdom of God in the Transformation of Eschatology*, trans. Walter Kaufmann in *Religion From Tolstoy to Camus*, ed. Walter Kaufmann, (New York, Harper & Row, Publishers, 1964) (b) p409
[31] Paul Tillich, *Love, Power, and Justice*, (Oxford, Oxford University Press, 1954) p66
[32] A.P. d'Entreves, *Natural Law: An Introduction to Legal Philosophy*, (London, Hutchinson & Co., 1951) p3842, 46
[33] Roland H. Bainton, *Christian Attitudes Toward War and Peace: A Historical Survey and Critical Re-evaluation*, (Nashville, Abingdon Press, 1960) p56
[34] Bainton, p64
[35] This is found in the book of Lamentations in the Hebrew Bible (or Tanach), 3:30

"I am suffering evil to the point of prison bonds as an evildoer. Nevertheless, the word of God is not bound." 2 Timothy 2:9

"In fact, all those desiring to live with godly devotion in association with Christ Jesus will also be persecuted." 2 Timothy 3:12

"Brothers, take as a pattern of the suffering of evil and the exercising of patience the prophets, who spoke in the name of Jehovah." James 5:10

"For if someone, because of conscience toward God, bears up under grievous things and suffers unjustly, this is an agreeable thing." 1 Peter 2:19

The Protestant Founding Father Martin Luther himself is recorded as having said, "to suffer wrong destroys no one's soul, nay, it improves the soul."[36]

2) The Just-War theory, or National War: The theory of a Just-War had been used by Greek philosophers and was later adopted for Christianity by such church founding fathers as St. Ambrose (337-397) and St. Augustine (354-430). Bainton writes: "The position of Augustine...continues to this day in all essentials to be the ethic of the Roman Catholic Church and of the major Protestant bodies."[37]

The 'Just-War' is purposively vague because it implies more than defense –it implies that any ideological justification occasions pre-emptive measures. The 'Just-War' is just a fancy way of saying that violence can be just, even if in reality this amounts to aggression. Bainton says, "For the Christian the most uncompromising demand of his traditional ethic is that a war to be just must be fought in the spirit of love."[38]

In the 330's the Roman Emperor Constantine (272-337) converted the empire to Christianity. Constantine's own conversion occurred on the way to battle in the year 312, in which he came to believe if converted to Christianity he would win the violent battle. More recently the Protestant Founding Fathers Luther, Calvin, and Henry VIII in particular have lent much authority to the Christian state. And there are injunctions for this conformist nationalism within the New Testament:

"You are going to hear of wars and reports of wars; see that you are not terrified. For these things must take place, but the end is not yet. For nation will rise against nation and kingdom against kingdom..." Matthew 24:6-7

"Continue reminding them to be in subjection and be obedient to governments and authorities as rulers..." Titus 3:1

3) The Crusade: There is a very important message in the New Testament: the world is about to end! Although the 'Crusades'-proper began near the end of the 11th century, the attempt to Christianize the world, the so-called 'Barbarian Conversion' began centuries earlier. Paul's letter to Rome says, "Jesus Christ our Lord, through whom we receive ...an apostleship in order that among all the nations they might be obedient by faith respecting his name." (Romans 1:5) His second letter to Timothy says as much:

"You, though, keep your senses in all things, suffer evil, do [the] work of an evangelizer, fully accomplish your ministry." 2Timothy 4:5

This mirrors the inspired message of Jesus according to the Gospels:

"All authority has been given me in heaven and on the earth. Go therefore and make disciples of people of all nations, baptizing them in the name of the Father and the Son and of the holy spirit, teaching them to observe all the things I have commanded you." Matthew 28:18-20

---

[36] From *Samtliche Schriften*, ed. J.G. Walch, (Halle, 1740-53). Quoted and trans. Kaufmann, (a) p293
[37] Bainton, p99
[38] Bainton, p246

"Go into all the world and preach the good news to all creation. He that believes and is baptized will be saved, but he that does not believe will be condemned." Mark 16:15-16

"But whoever stumbles one of these little ones that believe, it would be finer for him if a millstone such as is turned by an ass were put around his neck and he were actually pitched into the sea." Mark 9:42

"[A]n apostleship in order that among all the nations they be obedient by faith..." Romans 1:5

"Who is the one that conquers the world but he who has faith that Jesus is the Son of God?" 1 John 5:5

The American Revolutionary Thomas Paine in his two-part study *The Age of Reason*, rhetorically asks: "Some Christians pretend that Christianity was not established by the sword; but of what period of time do they speak?"[39] The Christian President Bush II declared the 21st century war on the Middle East to be a crusade as well. The Crusade is described by Bainton thus:

"The crusade suffers from the assurance not to say the arrogance of all elitism. It is the war of a theocratically minded community which seeks to impose the pattern of the Church upon the world... Those who have fought in a frenzy of righteousness against the enemies of God –or of the democratic way of life –are disposed to demand unconditional surrender, thus prolonging resistance by their refusal to state terms... The victors in war cannot administer disinterested justice, and least of all is this possible in the case of a crusade."[40]

It is argued the New Testament should be understood as beckoning a crusade. Thomas Paine wrote that, "As an engine of power, it serves the purpose of despotism."[41] The imminent return of Jesus and the ultimate battle between good and evil are central concerns in the New Testament. These advocates of wars have made appeals variously to New Testament dicta such as Jesus' statement in the Gospels of Matthew and Luke, "I did not come to bring peace". (Matthew 10:34, Luke 12:51)

More than once Jesus tells his followers to sell what they had in order to buy weapons. (Matthew 10:34, Luke 12:51, 22:36) Jesus tells his followers "he who is not for me is against me". (Matthew 12:30) Besides the injunctions to obey the nation-state, we should not underestimate the believed imminence of the apocalypse or 'end of times'. The book of 'Eschatology' (the end of the world) which is usually translated as the book of Revelations, is especially graphic regarding the second coming of Christ, or the Word of God become flesh.

"And I saw the heaven opened, and, look! a white horse. And the one seated upon it... the name he is called is the Word of God... out of his mouth there protrudes a sharp long sword, that he may strike the nations with it... the rest were killed off with the long sword of the one seated on the horse, which sword proceeded out of his mouth. And all the birds were filled from the fleshy parts of them." Revelations 19:11,13,15,21

Roland Bainton himself takes the attitude of pacifism but his appeal is made to humanitarianism and pragmatism and not according to the Bible. He concluded that: "All of the devices thus far considered for the elimination of war will be futile without the will to peace."[42]

"From every theological position divergent ethical applications have been deduced. Theism undergirds alike pacifism and the crusade... Some imitate the Christ upon the cross, and some the Christ on the rainbow at the judgement day. The expectation of the speedy coming of the Lord has led some to quietism, others to revolution to hasten the coming. The appeal to Christian love does not settle the case,

---

[39] Thomas Paine, *The Age of Reason*, in *The Life and Writings of Thomas Paine*, ed. Philip S. Foner, (New York, The Citadel Press, 1945) p596
[40] Bainton, p243
[41] Paine, p600
[42] Bainton, p248, 253, 259

because if God be love, then love and killing cannot be incompatible, since God in the end terminates every life, and often prematurely."

"The ethical teaching of Jesus is considered inapplicable because it was conditioned by the expectation of the speedy end of the age... The deepest source of reluctance arises from an aversion to all legalism so that even principles are rejected in favor of inspired hunches, and the Christian ethic comes to be devoid not only of predictability but even of coherence."[43]

These passages, though written some 50 years ago, describe the 21st century predicament of the United States with some accuracy. But because in this essay we are not only concerned with war and peace but with justice in general we might alter Bainton's tripartite model of Christianity slightly in accounting for Christian attitudes toward justice and violence. These three attitudes can be represented as:
a) Antipoliticism, b) Institutionalism, and c) Millenarianism.

a) Antipoliticism: When Jesus instructs us to 'turn the other cheek' he is telling us not to seek justice at all. Christianity does not instruct us to seek the justice for other people either. In the temple when Jesus' apostle Peter cuts off a priest's ear with his sword Jesus remarks, "Did you come out with swords and clubs as against a robber to arrest me?" (Mark 14:48) and nothing was said or done on behalf of the injured person. (Though when this story is retold years later by Luke, Jesus finally restores the priest's ear –but not in Matthew's version of this story. Some might argue that St. Peter never got what he deserved.)

I use the word antipolitical instead of pacifist for several reasons. One can be a pacifist and believe in the practice of an institutional or social law and justice. On the other hand, someone that is antipolitical is radically against compromise and opposed to appeals to social consensus.[44] Their misanthropy leaves them against all states of humanity, except perhaps the most primitive and perverse.

It is probable that among the first few centuries of Christianity an antipolitical view toward justice was held.[45] Bertrand Russell (1872-1970) gives as an example the church father Origen (185-254): "Christians, we are told, should not take part in the government of the State, but only of the 'divine nation', i.e., the Church."[46] If Christians could not identify with the Judaism as the New Testament tells us, they were certainly at odds with the Roman Empire for almost three hundred years.[47] The last Stoic

---

[43] Bainton, p238, 242

[44] Martin Luther King, Jr., taught, "Let us never succumb to the temptation of believing that legislation and judicial decrees play only minor roles in solving this problem. Morality cannot be legislated, but behaviour can be regulated. Judicial decrees may not change the heart, but they can restrain the heartless. The law cannot make an employer love an employee, but it can prevent him from refusing to hire me because of the colour of my skin. The habits, if not the hearts, of people have been and are being altered every day by legislative acts, judicial decisions, and executive orders." *Strength to Love*, (Philadelphia, Fortress Press, 1963) p33-34

[45] The International Jurist, Hans Kelsen writes that a believing Christian "holds his salvation –the fate of his soul in the hereafter –more important than earthly goods". *What is Justice?*, (Berkeley, University of California Press, 1957). Parts reprinted in *Justice: Hackett Readings In Philosophy*, ed. Jonathan Westphal, (Indianapolis, Hackett Publishing Company, 1996) p188

[46] Bertrand Russell, *A History of Western Philosophy*, (New York, Simon and Schuster, 1945) (a) p329

[47] Bainton writes that, "Paul enjoined Christians not to appeal to the Roman courts. Such injunctions and affirmations disclosed an aloofness from social participation and political involvement." (p60) Kaufmann noted that Jesus "rejects the courts altogether". (a) p182-183

philosopher, for example, Emperor Marcus Aurelius (who was also a Natural Law theorist) persecuted Christians. Others were fed to the lions.

The Protestant theologian Rudolf Bultmann claims in his study *The Theology of the New Testament,* that "Jesus' message is a great *protest against Jewish legalism*". Such a legalism according to Bultmann allows "no differentiation between religion and morality, nor are laws about worship and ethics separated from statutes of everyday law." "The real result is that motivation to ethical conduct is vitiated." "The error of Jewish legalism" is that it leaves room "for works of supererogation… capable of atoning for transgressions of the Law."[48]

Supererogation is a fancy word for doing something extra, beyond duty (or in spite of it). The one-time Protestant Walter Kaufmann notes of the supererogatory in Jesus' longest sermon, the Sermon on the Mount –its all rewards and threats: heaven or hellfire.[49] Bultmann concedes that if Jesus' gratuitous ethic is guided by a certainty "that God does reward faithful obedience".

"[H]is words are not without self-contradiction… Still the contradiction can probably be resolved in this way: The motive of reward is only a primitive expression for the idea that in what a man does his own real being is at stake –that self which he not already is, but is to become. To achieve that self is the legitimate motive of his ethical dealing and of his true obedience, in which he becomes aware of the paradoxical truth that in order to arrive at himself he must surrender to the demand of God –or, in other words, that in such surrender he wins himself."[50]

According to Bultmann's interpretation of Christianity –self-propagation (which in Christianity is immortality) is highlighted over divine and social laws. Bultmann holds Jesus as having taught that "the will of God is not an ethic of world-reform".[51] This is where personal justice goes beyond all politics. Accordingly, Jesus' supererogation discounts the law as something superfluous. The New Testament says:

"[B]y works of law no flesh will be declared righteous before him, for by law is the accurate knowledge of sin." Romans 3:20

"For we reckon that a man is declared righteous by faith apart from works of law." Romans 3:28

"Now the Law came in beside in order that trespassing might abound. But where sin abounded, undeserved kindness abounded still more." Romans 5:20

"[I]t means altogether a defeat for you that you are having lawsuits with one another. Why do you not rather let yourselves be wronged? Why do you not rather let yourselves be defrauded?" 1 Corinthians 6:7

"The sting producing death is sin, but the power for sin is the Law." 1 Corinthians 15:56

"We who are Jews by nature, and not sinners from the nations, knowing as we do that a man is declared righteous, not due to works of law, but only through faith toward Christ Jesus, even we have put our faith in Christ Jesus, that we may be declared righteous due to faith toward Christ, and not due to works of law, because due to works of law no flesh will be declared righteous… [I]f righteousness is through law, Christ actually died for nothing." Galatians 2:15-16, 21

"For all those who depend upon works of law are under a curse… Moreover, that by law no one is declared righteous with God is evident… Now the Law does not adhere to faith… Christ by purchase released us from the curse of the Law by becoming a curse instead of us." Galatians 3:10, 11, 12, 13

"You are parted from Christ, whoever you are that try to be declared righteous by means of law; you have fallen away from his undeserved kindness." Galatians 5:4

"[H]aving not my own righteousness, which results from law, but that which is through faith in Christ." Philippians 3:9

---

[48] Bultmann, p11, 12
[49] Kaufmann, (a) p210, 221
[50] Bultmann, p14-15
[51] Bultmann, p19

"But shun foolish questionings and genealogies and strife and fights over the Law, for they are unprofitable and futile." Titus 3:9

The philosopher Walter Kaufmann goes even further in his supervenient book *The Faith of a Heretic* and claims the Christianity of Jesus was a movement, not indifferent to social justice, but against social justice altogether. Kaufmann wrote: "For Paul, as for Jesus, social justice and political arrangements seemed irrelevant. He accepted the prevailing order, sometimes with contempt because it was merely secular, sometimes with respect because it was ordained by God."[52] Kaufmann points out how Calvin believed it was a 'Jewish vanity' "to argue for equality and liberty in this world."[53] Under this antipolitical view, to be like Christ is to be the victim of human justice (which is interchangeable with injustice). Jesus even accuses the Hebrew God: "My God, my God, why hath Thou forsaken me?" The gospels preach:

"Stop judging that you may not be judged; for with what judgement you are judging, you will be judged; and with the measure that you are measuring out, they will measure out to you." Matthew 7:1-2

"Woe to you who are versed in the Law, because you load men with loads hard to be borne, but you yourselves do not touch the loads with one of your fingers!" Luke 11:46 [This is in contradiction to what was revealed to Moses in the Torah where it says that if Yhwh were to someday appoint a messiah, he would have to well-versed in the law and study it everyday of his life. Deuteronomy 17:15,18,19]

"God, who has indeed adequately qualified us to be ministers of a new covenant, not of a written code, but of spirit; for the written code condemns to death..." 2 Corinthians 3:6

James' is perhaps the most authoritative writer found in the New Testament, having been Jesus' brother. His condemnation of human justice may well be representative, though we can wonder if he speaks through inspiration or compulsion.

"Quit speaking against one another, brothers. He who speaks against a brother or judges his brother speaks against the law and judges law. Now if you judge law, you are, not a doer of law, but a judge. One there is that is lawgiver and judge, he who is able to save and to destroy. But you, who are you to be judging [your] neighbor?" James 4:11-12

This sort of judicial and/or political pessimism fits in with the Christian idea of 'Original Sin'. According to the theory of original sin all humans are 'fallen' beings, incapable of good because of human's sinful nature. Humans are by nature incapable of getting social affairs right and one need seek redemption from this world of injustice. The Christian-existentialist theologian Paul Tillich points this out in his lectures, *Love, Power and Justice*. "The Stoic participates in the justice of the universe and its rational structure; the Christian expects the justice of the Kingdom of God". As we saw, Tillich was compelled to confess, "divine justice can appear as plain injustice."[54] Jesus preached:

"Jesus said to him, 'Why do you call me good? Nobody is good, except one, God." Mark 10:18 (repeated in Luke 18:19)

"The world has no reason to hate you, but it hates me, because I bear witness concerning it that its works are wicked." John 7:7

"My kingdom is no part of this world" John 18:36

"Keep your minds fixed on the things above, not on the things upon the earth." Colossians 3:2

"Do not be loving either the world or the things in the world. If anyone loves the world, the love of the Father is not in him...the world is passing away..." 1 John 2:15, 17

"He that is doing unrighteousness, let him do unrighteousness still." Revelation 22:11

---

[52] Kaufmann, (a) p222
[53] From Calvin's *Institutes of the Christian Religion*, trans. by John Allen; 7th ed., rev. and ed. by Benjamin B. Warfield, (Philadelphia, Presbyterian Board of Christian Education, 1936) 70. Quoted by Kaufmann, (a) p292
[54] Tillich, p61,66

b) Institutionalism: The most popular Christian attitudes toward justice are found in institutions: kingdoms, states, and empires. Institutionalism incorporates the Just-War theory of Augustine and Ambrose, and is accompanied by the conformism and disempowerment that is resultant of empires, bureaucracy and bureaucratization. D'Entreves wrote that with the theories of Augustine, "Christianity has ceased to be hostile to the world; it tends to be reconciled with it in a thoroughly Christian civilization."[55] Within the New Testament soldiers and generals are baptized and there is no injunction not to serve in the military.

"Let every soul be in subjection to the superior authorities, for there is no authority except by God; the existing authorities stand placed in their relative positions by God." Romans 13:1

"Now I exhort you, brothers, through the name of our Lord Jesus Christ that you should all speak in agreement, and that there should be divisions among you, but that you may be fitly united in the same mind and in the same line of thought." 1 Corinthians 1:10

"I therefore exhort, first of all, that supplications, prayers, intercessions, offerings of thanks, be made concerning all sorts of men, concerning kings and all those who are in high station..." 1Timothy 2:2

"For the Lord's sake subject yourselves to every human creation: whether to a king as being superior or to governors as being sent by him to inflict punishment on evildoers but, but to praise doers of good... [H]ave honor for the king." 1 Peter 2:13, 17

"If anyone comes to you and does not bring this teaching, never receive him into your homes or say a greeting to him." 2 John 10

We see in these quoted epistles that Christianity rejected the law of Judaism for that of Rome. Contemporary biblical scholars such as Robert Eisenman and James Carroll go out of their way to show that this preference for the more oppressive Roman Law was originally evinced because of both a conformism to, and a disempowerment resulting from, the hegemonic Roman Empire.[56]

In the *Theology of the New Testament*, Rudolf Bultmann discusses the importance of a Christian's obedience to the state. "As for *the Christian relation to the state*, here, too, it holds true that the Christian is to submit to it as a given order, for it was instituted by God. The Christian owes obedience even when, and precisely when, he is under its suspicion as a Christian." As for the Christian attitude toward the Roman Empire: "This order is simply not questioned, but it belongs, of course, to the transitory orders of the world."[57]

---

[55] D'Entreves, p38

[56] Robert Eisenman notes how the Greek language of the New Testament was written "to please not a Jewish audience but a Roman and Hellenistic one. This is also true of the presentation of the Jewish Messiah –call him 'Jesus' –as a politically disinterested, other-worldly (in Roman terms, *ergo*, harmless), even sometimes pro-Roman itinerant, at odds with his own people and family, preaching a variety of Plato's representation of the Apology of Socrates or the *Pax Romana*." Eisenman notes that even the defector and historian and author of the *Jewish War*, Josephus, noted "that all historical works from this period suffer from two main defects, 'flattery of the Romans and vilification of the Jews, adulation and abuse being substituted for real historical proof'." From *The Jewish War*, 1:1, trans. Eisenman, *James the brother of Jesus*, (New York, Penguin Books, 1997) XXI, XXII; James Carroll notes that "Intra-Jewish conflict served Rome's purposes... There is perhaps something craven in the Gospels' emphasis on 'Jews' as a threat to order in the empire, so opposed to 'Christians,' and it does not mitigate the Gospel writers responsibility for driving this wedge to note that they were responding to Roman oppression." Carroll also mentions how Paul changed his name from the Jewish 'Saul' to his Roman name. James Carroll, *Constantine's Sword*, (New York, Mariner Books, 2002) p87, 138

[57] Bultmann, Vol. II, p231

Then the Roman Empire was converted to Christianity early in the 4th century by the Emperor Constantine. Jews of the Roman Empire were exempt from military service, though Christians were not.[58] By the 5th century only Christians were allowed to serve in the army while Jews and pagans were forbidden.[59]

The legacy of Roman Law was preserved by the Byzantine Emperor Justinian I in the 6th century. Justinian made the first codification of Roman and Church Law, a work which had begun in the 4th century. The result was what is called today the Canon Law, which was completed in the year 534. The Canon Law interrelated the Natural Law of Rome and the Christian Church. Justinian declared this law "immutable" and we see that Canon Law still exists to this day, almost 1500 years later. D'Antreves writes that: "It is no exaggeration to say that, next to the Bible, no book has left a deeper mark upon the history of mankind."[60]

The Canon Law, as the law of the Holy Roman Empire, combined church and state. Much of what we know of this period is recorded in the *Digests* of the Roman jurists[61] and although legal histories are beginning to emerge not much has been written on this subject. We do know that Christianity from its inception (according to the New Testament) paid heed to the Roman Law. Jesus had told his followers to pay taxes to the Roman authorities, "Render unto Caesar what is Caesars." (Matthew 22:21, Mark 12:17)

With only Christians permitted to serve as soldiers in the Empire, even the clergy were armed.[62] The conversion of non-Christians was a coercive process. Contemporary legal scholar R.H. Helmholz tells of how this was accomplished legally. "The canonists brought this result into harmony with the requirement of free will in baptism by supposing that 'coerced volition is still volition'."[63] The Holy Roman Emperor Charlemagne's 8th century law, *Saxon Capitulary* decreed that all who would not covert to Christianity would be put to the sword.[64] Pope Urban VIII (1623-1644) had Jewish children forcefully taken from their parents and baptized. Many children were kidnapped and by 1870 the church still sanctioned such kidnappings.[65]

Other examples of Canon Law are the aforementioned crusade and the inquisition. Both legally justified the execution of some thousands. The Crusades were not limited to attacking the Middle East in the war against Muslims and Jews, but were used to convert all of Europe from their non-Christian religions (more remote countries such as Estonia and Finland were crushed and forced to convert, the Lithuanians were the least-conformist). Probably hundreds of thousands, but more likely, millions have been killed and burned through the legal system of the Church.

Passages from the New Testament used to justify capital punishment vary.
"[F]or all those who take the sword will perish by the sword." Matthew 26:52

---

[58] Constantine wrote an edict in 315 making it a crime for Jews to proselytize, or teach their religion to gentiles. Carroll notes that less than a century later this crime was punishable by death. (p177, 167)
[59] Bainton, p88
[60] D'Entreves, p17, 35. The only foreseeable refutation of this might be the Quran.
[61] D'Entreves, p19
[62] Bainton, p88
[63] R.H. Helmholz, *The Spirit of Classical Canon Law*, (Athens, University of Georgia Press, 1996) p225
[64] Richard Fletcher, *The Barbarian Conversion: From Paganism to Christianity*, (New York, Henry Holt and Company, Inc., 1997) p215
[65] Carroll, p384n68, 446

"It is unavoidable that causes for stumbling should come. Nevertheless, woe to the one through whom they come! It would be of more advantage to him if a millstone were suspended from his neck and he were thrown into the sea..." Luke 17:1-2

"Let him that is without sin be the first to throw a stone at her." John 8:7

"[I]t is to your benefit for one man to die in behalf of the people and not for the whole nation to be destroyed." John 11:50

"If anyone does not remain in union with me, he is cast out as a branch and is dried up; and men gather those branches up and pitch them into the fire and they are burned." John 15:6

"Although these know full well the righteous decree of God, that those practicing such things are deserving of death..." Romans 1:32

"If anyone practices killing with the sword, he must himself be killed with the sword. Here is where it means the endurance and faith of the holy ones." Revelation 13:9

"Yes, I saw the souls of those executed with the ax for the witness they bore to Jesus and for speaking about God..." Revelation 20:4

Helmholz gives an example of the Canon Law regarding the charge of heresy:

"First, although the decretal's terms left the question of the nature of the 'condign punishment' undefined, in fact no one doubted that the punishment being referred to was death. The canonists fully understood that death by burning was being authorized by the papal decretal, and they approved this understanding of the law."[66]

It wasn't until 1995 that the Church made the first steps away from capital punishment. However, under current Canon law execution is not illegal.[67] Most of the states in the US still carry a death penalty. Many nations still have laws against blaspheming Christianity as well as for heresy. Countries with blasphemy laws descendent from the Roman Law include New Zealand, Switzerland, Spain, the Netherlands, Germany, Finland, England, Austria, as well as the US state laws of Maryland and Massachusetts.[68]

Despite all of this, pacifism has remained a strong component of institutional Christianity, often as an apolitical wing.[69] For example, in the United States today there is a majority of Protestants -yet so little protesting is actually done. In a nation whose constitution allows citizens to gather to complain about the government, we might look to the Buddhists of Myanmar and Muslims of Pakistan to see less political apathy. The words of the New Testament teach us of a savior who suffers from the law and teaches us to consent to political authority –which seems a very passive pacifism.

Where the Canon Law was not accepted the state took its place. Although we might conclude that the laws of the Holy Roman Empire are imperialist, the British Common Law ought to be considered alongside of the Canon. The English used the medieval churches conception of natural law in order to defeat the "intransigent Augustinianism of the Puritans." D'Entreves notes that: "What is stressed is the duty of the State rather than the rights of the individual... It is more than a paradox that this

---

[66] Helmholz, p362
[67] www.vatican.va/edocs/ENG0141/_INDEX.HTM Affluent countries may sentence life-imprisonment instead. For more on his subject check Chapter 2.
[68] See Chapter 2
[69] Some have interpreted passages of the New Testament as pointing to an ethic of Collectivism, wherein an ethic is practiced and propagated. "For whenever people of the nations that do not have law do by nature the things of the law, these people, although not having law, are a law to themselves." Romans 2:14 "Let the stealer steal no more, but rather let him do hard work, doing with his hands what is good work, that he may have something to distribute to someone in need." Ephesians 4:28

notion should have provided the basis for the defense of the Church of England and indeed of what would nowadays be called the English way of life."[70]

D'Entreves notices how law as understood by the Protestant Founding Father of the English Common Law, an Anglican priest Richard Hooker (1554-1600), is "almost word for word the definition of Thomas Aquinas."[71]

"Protestantism did not necessarily lead to a complete break with the old tradition of natural law. The impact of the Reformation upon the continuity of legal and political thought is still the subject of controversy among scholars"

"The voluntarist bent of Protestant ethics may well afford an explanation of the comparative disparagement... of natural law in favour of the divine law of the Bible on one hand, and, on the other, of the positive law of the State conceived as ultimately grounded upon the will of God. That the 'divine right of kings' is a typical product of this age is certainly significant."[72]

Hooker argued against the Puritan assumption that scripture was the basis for law, and promoted in its stead the natural law, which he understood in the same way as the medieval scholastics.[73] In his book *Of the Lawes of Ecclesiasticall Politie*, Hooker wrote: "[U]nto Christian kings there is such dominion given...God does ratify the works of that sovereign authority which kings have received by men." Hooker also wrote that: "Kings by conquest make their own charter..."[74]

In 1645 a bill was passed in England which held that Unitarians and freethinkers could be executed and Baptists could be imprisoned. Hooker believed in the union of church and state. He wrote that "one and the same people are the Church and the Commonwealth" and "one and the self-same people were the Church and the Army."[75] And as we see over the last 100 years the contemporary Common Law of Great Britain discriminates against Catholics, Hindus, and Muslims.

The sociologist Max Weber said in his in his seminal work, *The Protestant Ethic and the Spirit of Capitalism,* the English or Common Law shows greatest distinction from the Roman Law which was "overcome by the power of the great legal corporations..."[76] Of the three main Protestant Fathers, John Calvin had the strongest influence on the laws of distributive justice, and is considered a father of modern capitalism.

c) Millenarianism: Millenarianism has attracted Christians across the political spectrum: anarchists, socialists, nationalists, crusaders, nazi's, as well as those against politicism altogether. Millenarianism also helps simplify the essence of Christianity, reducing it to the white vs. black battle of good vs. evil. Through this dualistic cosmology we are to believe:

"Next, the end, when he hands over the kingdom of his God and Father, when he has brought to nothing all government and all authority and power." 1 Corinthians 15:24

"Stripping the governments and the authorities bare, he exhibited them in open public as conquered, leading them in a triumphal procession by means of it." Colossians 2:15

---

[70] D'Entreves, p46, 47
[71] D'Entreves, p76-77
[72] D'Entreves, p69-70, 70
[73] David Wootton, *Divine Right and Democracy*, (Middlesex, Penguin Books, 1986) p214
[74] Richard Hooker, *Of the Lawes of Ecclesiasticall Politie*, quoted in Wootton, p223, 224
[75] Hooker, p172, 176, 164, 172
[76] Max Weber, *The Protestant Ethic and The Spirit of Capitalism*, trans. Talcott Parsons, (New York, Charles Scribner's Sons, 1958) p77 (Originally published in 1904.)

"Because we have a fight, not against blood and flesh, but against the governments, against the authorities, against the world rulers of this darkness, against the wicked spirit forces in the heavenly places." Ephesians 6:12

"He that conquers will by no means be harmed by the second death." Revelation 2:11

"And to him that conquers and observes my deeds down to the end I will give authority over the nations." Revelations 2:26

The second-coming of Christ is considered to be the most imminent and central concern for all Christians. In the book of Revelation (or Eschatology) it says Jesus will capture Satan and eventually murder him. The powers of Satan and evil have generally been applied to all that is not Christian. A list would be lengthy.

Millenarianism is basically the eschatological-purist wing of Christianity. It is believed to be one's duty to coercively usher in the kingdom of god. One such group of millenarians was the 17th century English militia known as the 'Fifth-Monarchy Men'. The Fifth Monarchists "believed in the imminence of the Second Coming and in their own right to rule until that event". Wootton writes that "The millenarians or Fifth Monarchists believed in the possibility of establishing a society of saints in short order." They are recorded as having believed: "The powers of this world are usurpations upon the prerogative of Jesus Christ; and it is the duty of God's people to destroy them in order to the setting Christ upon his throne."[77]

The former Catholic priest James Carroll notes:

"Crusading fever meshed with millennial fever, and soon enough the present moment was widely experienced as nothing less than the dawn of the apocalyptic age. Christ, ransomed by the sacrifice of his army, would return in triumph for the Last Day. Those embarked upon the rescue of Jerusalem were thus ushering in the End of Time."[78]

Carroll talks about how this worked into the mindset of the "millennialist Adolf Hitler".

"The Third Reich succeeded the First, the Holy Roman Empire (962-1806), and the Second, the Hohenzollern Empire (1871-1918), but below this literal chronology, Nazi mythology exploited the idea of the dawning of the messianic era. The Third Reich corresponded to the Third Age of the millenium. It was expected to endure, as Hitler said repeatedly, for a thousand years. Hitler worked to undermine the principles of Christian religion and targeted those who openly defended them, he perverted biblical hope by proclaiming himself the Messiah, but he also echoed the medieval Christian conviction that the obstacle to the inauguration of the glorious thousand-year reign, was the stiff-necked Jewish people."[79]

Another kind of millenarianism is known as 'antinomianism'. The philosopher William L. Rowe defines antinomianism as "the view that one is not bound by moral law; specifically, the view that Christians are by grace set free from the need to observe moral laws. During the Reformation, antinomianism was believed by some (but not Martin Luther) to follow from the Lutheran doctrine of justification by faith alone."[80]

According to an interpretation of the New Testament Christians have believed they are 'fulfilling the law'. In the Sermon on the Mount Jesus says: "Do not think I came to destroy the Law or the Prophets. I came not to destroy, but to fulfill." (Matthew 5:17)

Bultmann however holds that such passages in the New Testament which talk of this fulfilling of the law, "in view of other sayings of Jesus and of his actual practice

---

[77] Wootton, p175, 65, 124
[78] Carroll, p255-256
[79] Carroll, p256
[80] William L. Rowe, "Antinomianism", *Cambridge Dictionary of Philosophy*, Second Edition, ed. Robert Audi, (Cambridge, Cambridge University Press, 1999) p32-33

cannot possibly be genuine; rather it is a product of the Church coming out of the later period of conflict over the Law."[81]

Kaufmann notes this peculiarity in the New Testament and asks: "If 'he who eats me will live because of me' (John 6:57), why worry about loving one's enemies?"[82] If the law is fulfilled and Jesus already died for all human sins –why have social justice?

"Truly I say to you that all things will be forgiven the sons of men, no matter what sins and blasphemies they blasphemously commit." Mark 3:28

"Even if he sins seven times a day against you and he comes back to you seven times, saying, 'I repent,' you must forgive him." Luke 17:4

Where Rudolf Bultmann discusses "The Church's Relation to Judaism and the Problem of the Old Testament" he points out a popular interpretation of the bible. This interpretation says that, "The Old Testament with its Law is, accordingly, either an antiquated proclamation by a subordinate god or it is a Satanic Law. In either case, it is no longer valid for the Christian."[83] Many of the passages of the Roman citizen Saint Paul lead to such interpretations.

"For if those who adhere to law are heirs, faith has been made useless and the promise has been abolished. In reality the Law produces wrath, but where there is no law, neither is there any transgression." Romans 4:14-15

"For sin must not be master over you, seeing that you are not under law but under undeserved kindness." Romans 6:14

"But now we have been discharged from the Law…" Romans 7:6

"For Christ is the end of the Law, so that everyone exercising faith may have righteousness." Romans 10:4

"He will also make you firm to the end, that you may be open to no accusation in the day of our Lord Jesus Christ." 1 Corinthians 1:8

"Now to me it is a very trivial matter that I should be examined by you or by a human tribunal. Even I do not examine myself." 1 Corinthians 4:3 (This is antithetical to everything Socrates lived and died for.)

"All things are lawful for me; but I will not let myself be brought under authority by anything." 1 Corinthians 6:12

"Why then the Law? It was added to make transgressions manifest, until the seed should arrive to whom the promise has been made… [T]he Law has become our tutor leading to Christ, that we might be declared righteous due to faith. But now that the faith has arrived, we are no longer under a tutor." Galatians 3:19, 24-25

"[T]o that end that he may make your hearts firm, unblamable in holiness…" 1 Thessalonians 3:13

"If we confess our sins, he is faithful and righteous so as to forgive us our sins and to cleanse us from all righteousness." 1 John 1:9

In these passages from the New Testament we find the seed planted for those Christians who are against human moral responsibility. Martin Luther gave perhaps the best example of the belief that the law is fulfilled, even if he was not antinomial. "It is sufficient that we recognize through the wealth of God's glory, the lamb who bears the sin of the world; from this, sin does not sever us, even if thousands, thousands of times in one day we should fornicate or murder."[84]

A manual distributed to U.S. Army officers, *The Principles of War: A Strategy for Group and Personal Evangelism,* has written on the back cover, "In the light of the

---

[81] Bultmann, p16 It should be noted that if Bultmann is wrong and New Testament passages that talk of 'fulfilling the law' are not inauthentic, Bultmann's theory of supererogation is refuted.
[82] Kaufmann, (a) p221
[83] Bultmann, p110
[84] Letter from Martin Luther to Melanchthon, August 1, 1521; *Briefwechsel,* vol. 5, trans. by T.G. Tappert in *Luther: Letters of Spiritual Counsel.* Quoted by Kaufmann, (a) p232

approaching End of the Age, and the reasonable expectation of the heightening of this spiritual struggle, all militant Christians do well to read and ponder this message. What are their objectives? How can they mount the offensive?"

United States Colonel Granville A. Sharpe wrote in the forward "All except the most naïve know that the Christian is engaged in a warfare." [85]

Islam and Justice

The *Shariah* of Islam resembles in many ways the *Halakah* of Judaism. As Halakah means 'walking' Shariah means 'path'. Shariah is the body of Islamic Law and is the source of every Muslims ethics. It begins with the Quran and is followed by the precedent *hadith* or 'sayings' and *sunnah* or 'actions' of the prophet Muhammad. Islamic jurisprudence, or the science of legal reasoning is called *Fiqh*, and translates as 'knowledge' or 'understanding'

The Quran, which means 'reciting', was revealed to Muhammad on a mountain called Hira in the year 610. The Quran consists of 114 Surahs (or chapters) which contain 350 legal verses. The Quran instructs over a broad range of ethics from marriage to conduct, to community and health and is applicable to all subjects. The Quran teaches:

"Surely We have sent down to thee the Book with the truth, so that thou mayest judge between the people by that Allah has shown thee."[86] Surah 4:106

"Indeed, We sent Our Messengers with the clear signs, and We sent down with them the Book and the Balance so that men might uphold justice." Surah 57:25

As part of the Shariah, a Muslim will also be guided by the *sunnah*, or example set by the prophet Muhammad. Biographers report that Muhammad was a very gentle and wise man. Muslims believe he was a perfect human being. A Christian monk named Bakirah predicted Muhammad would become a prophet.[87]

While he lived Muhammad was called upon many times by various peoples and communities to arbitrate and judge over ethical disputes. Muhammad was beckoned in order to prevent a war, maintain peace, as well as guide in the rebuilding of a pagan temple, the 'Kabah', in all of which he was successful.[88] His achievement in the drafting of the *Al Dustur al-Madinah*, or Constitution of Medina, ended a conflict between some warring tribes. The tribes had agreed to call on Muhammad as an outside third party and he acquiesced as an impartial judge to make the peace.

The Quran teaches us to seek justice in this world:

"[W]hen you judge between the people, that you judge with justice." Surah 4:62

"O believers, be you securers of justice, witnesses for Allah, even though it be against yourselves." Surah 4:134

"And fill up the measure and the balance with justice. We charge not any soul save to its capacity. And when you speak, be just, even if it should be to a near kinsman." Surah 6:153

"Surely Allah bids to justice and good-doing and giving to kinsmen; and He forbids indecency, dishonour, and insolence, admonishing you, so that haply you will remember." Surah 16:92

---

[85] James I. Wilson, *The Principles of War*, (Annapolis, Christian Books in Annapolis, 1964)
[86] All quotations of the Quran are from the A.J. Arberry translation. *The Koran Interpreted*, (New York, Macmillan Publishing Company, 1995) Although Arberry translates the Arabic word for god into English, I have reverted it back when it is a proper noun.
[87] Seyyed Hossein Nasr, *The Heart of Islam*, (San Francisco, HarperCollins, 2002) p29
[88] Akbar S. Ahmed, *Islam Today*, (New York, I.B. Tauris, 1999) p14

"And those who believe, and do righteous deeds assuredly We shall admit them among the righteous." Surah 29:7

"We have appointed thee a viceroy in the earth; therefore judge between men justly, and follow not caprice, lest it lead thee astray from the way of Allah." Surah 38:25

"Transgress not in the Balance, and weigh with justice, and skimp not in the Balance." Surah 55:7

Within Islamic jurisprudence, or *Fiqh,* the laws of the Quran are primary, followed by the example (sunnah) set by Muhammad. While documents such as the Constitution of Medina are still extent, many biographies of Muhammad exist and there is sometimes disagreement regarding the interpretation or authenticity of the various *hadith*, or sayings of the prophet. Thus a great deal of jurisprudence deals with interpretation and independent judgement. However, any hypothetical rule (*al-akham al-zanniyya*) must preserve reason (*aql*) and virtue (*ird*).[89]

Whereas in Western monarchies and nations the laws are written by the state, *Fiqh* is "jurist's law". Muslim jurists, or *fuqaha*, determine the theoretical bases of law, or *usul al-Fiqh*. Since the inception of Islam in the 7th century there has been a special class of jurists known as the *mujtahid* who are qualified to logically interpret the law and arrive at an independent judgement where it is necessary.

An Islamic judge or *Mufti* is an individual with great expertise in jurisprudence and, like the mujtahid, do not exist for the state. Rather, a Mufti is an independent individual whose advice and authority is sought by jurists and members of the community. Differently, a government appointed judge is known as a *qadi* who decides on cases when there is a dispute over the Sharia.

Both the judges and the *mujtahid* will be learned in the methods of reasoning or *qiyas*. Qiyas means 'analogical reasoning', or 'reasoning by analogy' (*wa'l ijtihad al-qiyas*). If a dilemma occurs or a novel situation presents itself in legal matters where one is not able to draw from either the Quran, sunnah, or hadith, one will reason according to the best explanation or inference given what can be logically inferred. This is a creative or intellectual aspect of Islamic law and involves intellect, interpretation, and deliberation. However, only the *mujtahid* jurist is qualified to use the methods of *qiyas* in order to arrive at a fresh interpretation, or *ijtihad*. In some cases the entire community may be obligated to make such decisions.[90] This is called *ijma*.

The last and most telling aspect to Islamic law is the very civil *Ijma*, or law of consensus. Such laws are those which are decided upon either by consensus among legal scholars, or as with *ijtihad*, will be determined by the *ummah*, or community. It is rightfully said that the Western dichotomy of 'individual vs. society' does not stand up in Islam.[91] The norms or customs (*adab*)of the ummah which work to create and sustain the social bonds of the community are informed by the 'Five Pillars of Wisdom', which were taught in the final sermon of Muhammad.[92] A hadith of the prophet says: "My community shall never agree on error."[93]

There are well over a billion Muslims spread across every continent in the world and over 50 Muslim nations, or countries with a Muslim majority. Although there are

---

[89] Oussama Arabi, *Studies in Modern Islamic Law and Jurisprudence*, (The Hague, Kluwer Law International, 2001), p198
[90] David Waines, *An Introduction to Islam*, (Cambridge, Cambridge University Press, 1995), p76
[91] Nasr, p159
[92] Ahmed, p7, 117
[93] Quoted in Nasr, p121

many different kinds of Muslims, each with their own particular culture and garb (there were some 45 million Muslims in the USSR[94]) it is generally understood that most are Sunni and about ten percent of all Muslims are Shia. For these groups and others, differences are not very significant in the realm of the Shariah.

The greatest source of Islamic literature and the greatest portion of all Arabic writings is that made by the jurists or *fuqaha*, and the entire Muslim community is obligated to participate in disseminating the law. By the 10th century there were some 500 different schools (*madhahib*) of Islamic Law (though there are many more today). This multiplicity was then generalized by the 13th century Sunni scholar Ibn Khallikan as being representable by four *mujtahid* who were the heads of 4 different schools.[95] In order to make this synthesis Ibn Khallikan drew on the notices of over 800 Muslim men and women from around the world. In an important sense there are thousands of Islamic schools of law and each person affects the tradition.

The four basic schools of Shariah include the following. 1) The *Hanafi* school was founded in the 8th century by Imam Abu Hanafih. The Hanafih is the most popular legal school amongst the Sunni and is considered to be one of the most open of the four madhahib. 2) The *Malaki* school is a bit more conservative and is popular in North Africa. 3) The *Shafii* school is closest to Shia law and is to be found in Egypt and Southeast Asian countries such as Indonesia, Malaysia, Singapore, and Thailand. 4) The *Hanbali* school is a stricter school and is still used in Syria. An offshoot of Hanbali, *Wahhabism* is popular in Saudi Arabia.[96]

Hanafih was the student of a leader, Imam Jafar al-Sadiq, a man considered to be the sixth Imam of Shiism. Al-Sadiq was the founder of the Twelve Imam Shiite Law, the *Jafari*. The 'Twelve Imam' of Shiism is the direct descendent from the family of Muhammad. It is believed one of his descendents will someday affect great peace and justice to the earth, though he is not considered a Christ figure and is a human being.

The Shia scholar Seyyed Hossein Nasr says the differences between Shia and Sunni law are minor.[97] As in Judaism, Muslims hold there to be a supremacy of law over the state.[98] Although the first Muslim was a woman, Muhammad did not appoint himself king. He left it up to the community to decide which political form was best suited. This to this day is decided by a meeting of all concerned Muslims called *al-Shura*, 'mutual consultation'. The al-Shura determines which political form is best suited for the people. The 20th century Islamic theorist Shaikh 'Ali 'Abd al-Razeq wrote that: "*al-Risalah* (the Message of Islam) in itself required the Prophet to acquire some form of leadership and power over his people. But this is very far from the leadership of kings and their power over their subjects. Hence one must not confuse the leadership of *al-Risalah* with that of the king". Al-Razeq added that:

"it is inconceivable the whole world could be organized under one single religion and that the entire humanity could be regulated within one religious unity, but to put the whole world under the rule of

---

[94] Dilip Hiro, *Iran Under The Ayatollahs*, (New York, *Routledge & Kegan Paul Inc.*, 1987) p291
[95] Waines, p73, 74, 76
[96] Nasr, p68-69
[97] Nasr, p70
[98] Muhamed S. El-Awa, *On The Political System of The Islamic State*, trans. Ahmad Naji al-Imam, ed. Anwer Beg, (Indianapolis, American Trust Publications, 1980) VII

one government and gather it in a single political unit would seem to be almost outside the scope of human nature and is not related to the will of Allah."[99]

One of the difficulties of summarily describing Islamic Law, is that it is not something which is monolithic like the *Canon Law* of the Holy Roman Empire, (which did come under revision in the 20th century), nor is Islamic jurisprudence a corporate law like the Protestant Common Law which is still the basis of the British Empire, or Great Britain, as well as the United States. However, as the sociologist Maxime Rodinson points out, *Fiqh* "was more thoroughly systemized, unified and rationalized than was Western custom."[100]

In the most conservative of contemporary Islamic states there is a more fundamental split between church and state than in the most liberal Western democracy. This is because Muslim scholars most often do not attempt to codify the law as is done in our Western bureaucratic nations. Islamic scholars distrust the state. As we see today in our Western world the law is not formulated by scholars or professional jurists but by the centralizing bureaucracy of the state.

Accordingly the most conservative Muslim jurists are the ones most opposed to the codification of the law. As we see with the *halakah* of Judaism, Islamic jurisprudence does not admit allegorical interpretation.[101] Wherein codification has occurred, therein modernization has occurred as well. Thus, the codification of the law is identified with the centralized bureaucracy like we find in modern 'democracies'.[102] The Dutch legal philosopher Rudoph Peters has written that:

"Islamic jurisprudence, the *fiqh*, is, as we saw, essentially a legal doctrine formulated by scholars and not by the state. *Fiqh* is jurists' law. Judges applying the Sharia have to consult the scholarly works of jurisprudence, and to select, with regard to the case they must adjudicate, the most authoritative among several opinions with a bearing on the issue."[103]

While Western orientalist history is replete with willful misrepresentations of Islam, it is not my intention to add another, though I know as a *kafir* that my knowledge thereof will fall short. Because of the unfamiliarity found in modern democratic bureaucracies concerning the Islamic law it will help to dispel three popularly misrepresented components of Islamic jurisprudence and Shariah: 1) retributive justice, or *hudud*, 2) legal opinion, or *fatwa*, and 3) *jihad*, or 'effort'.

1) Retributive justice: *Hudud*

It has been a popular misunderstanding of us Westerners to teach that Islamic retributive justice is based upon things nearly as horrific as the forms of Christian retributive justice which were popular in Europe well into the 20th century. In fact, if torture is legal in the 21st century United States justice system, as we see that many Muslims have been tortured by the US government, torture has been permitted according

---

[99] Ali 'Abd al-Razeq, *Al-Islam wa Usul al-Hukm*, (Beirut, 1966) Quoted by El-Awa, p66-67
[100] Maxime Rodinson, *Islam and Capitalism*, trans. Brian Pearce, (Austin, University of Texas Press, 1978) p106
[101] Arabi, p196; Ginzberg, p127
[102] Rudolph Peters, *Crime and Punishment in Islamic Law: Theory and Practice from the Sixteenth to the Twenty-first Century*, (Cambridge, Cambridge University Press, 2005) p142-143, 148
[103] Peters, p147

to the Canon Law[104] and as we know from English treatment of Irish prisoners, that the Common Law permits torture as well.[105]

According to the Canon Law waterboarding is permitted and once upon a time peoples tongues were removed who would not accept Jesus Christ as their savior.[106] In Europe and America we are told that Muslim countries regularly de-limb criminals, castrate a rapist, or stone a murderer to death. In fact, in both Egypt and the Ottoman Empire, (based out of modern day Turkey), these forms of retributive justice ceased. When British colonization of Muslims nations began in the 17th century, the English found the Shariah to be too lenient and the English complained there were not enough capital offenses. The British then made all prosecution a matter of the state and increased number of public executions.[107]

If there is a precedent for dismemberment it is the New Testament. Jesus told his followers that if they had committed an offense to tear out their eye(s) or to cut off their hand(s) or to cut off their feet. This is beneficial. (Matthew 5:29-30, Mark 9:43, 45, 47) Men who were not born eunuchs and have the capacity ought to be castrated. (Matthew 19:12) Jesus said, "For everyone must be salted with fire." (Mark 9:49) This is in direct contradiction of the precedent set by Judaism which holds that "a man does not belong only to himself; just as he has no right to cause physical harm to others, so he has no right to inflict injury on himself."[108]

After praising these passages of the New Testament that instruct on dismemberment, Bultmann says such retribution "constitutes readiness for God's Reign, [and] is the fulfillment of God's will". "But this renunciation toward the world, this 'unworldliness', is not to be thought of as asceticism, but as simple readiness for God's demand."[109]

Once freed of the tyrannical British rule things changed for the better. When President Nixon's friend, the King of Iran, Shah Pahlevi was overthrown in a non-violent revolution led by the Ayatollah Khomeini, a new constitution was drafted which forbid torture.[110] In the 20th century the Muslim Brotherhood campaigned to suspend these forms of retribution (hudud) until poverty was eliminated and society was based upon the principles of social justice.[111]

Under the English and American Common Law there is little or no discretionary power, the judges must follow a formula in their decision, no matter what their own personal knowledge brings to the case. In Islamic Law, prosecution depends on the desire of the victim or the victim's family and heirs, and the state only plays the role of referee.[112]

---

[104] Pope Innocent IV decreed in 1252 that torture is permitted. (Carroll, p317)
[105] Tim Pat Coogan, *The IRA*, Fully Revised and Updated, (New York, Palgrave, 2002) p440
[106] Carroll, p356, 307. One of the earliest American critics of waterboarding was Mark Twain, who was outraged that this technique was used in by the US military in the Philippines in 1902. See William Saffire's, "Waterboarding", *New York Times*, 3/9/08
[107] Peters, p108-110, 119, 120
[108] Steinsaltz, p167
[109] Bultmann, p11
[110] Hiro, p123
[111] Peters, p184
[112] Peters, p111, 186

The prophet said: "better to err on the side of leniency than on the side of severity."[113] Peters tells of another legal measure, unfamiliar to the Canon and Common Laws:

"A very special form of exemption from punishment can in some cases be brought about by repentance. It is an interesting defense that does not fit in Western theories of criminal law, because it is connected neither with the *mens rea* nor with the unlawfulness to act."[114]

2) Legal Opinion: *Fatwa*

One area of ijma that has been repeatedly misrepresented by the Western media is the Arabic legal opinion, *fatwa*. According to popular misconceptions a fatwa is like a death sentence that can be given arbitrarily by any dictator. Fatwa, like most other aspects of Islamic law would undoubtedly be unknown to most Westerners if it had not been for a post-World War II quisling named Salmon Rushdie.

Contrary to popular opinion, fatwa is not a rigid sentencing, but is, as an aspect of ijma, a matter of consent. A fatwa can be issued over a variety of different subjects and does not have any legal status or extend beyond the community.[115] A fatwa can be issued but is not binding until there is the consent. The Muslim sociologist Akbar Ahmed teaches that:

"A *fatwa* can be delivered by any religious leader on a variety of topics. It does not have the status of law and, indeed, must be ratified in a proper court if it is to carry legal status. Its authority is also generally restricted to the cultural or geographical boundaries within which the Muslim divine who delivers the *fatwa* functions."[116]

After the non-violent Iranian revolution of 1979 led by the Shia Ayatollah Khomeini, the Western corporate media made sure that the public was outraged by these events: that a people could actually not want to be democratized or bureaucratized by Great Britain or the US. So when Muslims in Pakistan who protested Rushdie's ignominy were shot by the state, the corporate media began spreading the message that Khomeini had issued a fatwa against the simpleton. Muslims, however, know that such a legal opinion was not issued by Khomeini or any other official.[117] And as we have seen, even if such a legal opinion were written, it would have no jurisdiction over someone who lacked the courage to protest the divine right of the British monarchy. As the Palestinian exile Edward Said noted:

"Now everyone knows that to try to say something in the mainstream Western media that is critical of U.S. policy or Israel is extremely difficult; conversely, to say things that are hostile to the Arabs as a people and culture, or Islam as a religion, is laughably easy."[118]

Moreover, if Rushdie sought to criticize the religion of Islam and to celebrate free-speech safely within the confines of Great Britain, thousands of miles from any actual Muslim state, he did so without considering his own level of conformity. As the linguist Noam Chomsky summed up: "The point is, you defend freedom of speech when

---

[113] Waines, p81
[114] Peters, p27. There is a similarity found in Scots Law, which makes a provision for 'Compassionate Release'. See Reuters, "Scottish Court Lets Libyan Drop Lockerbie Appeal", *New York Times*, 8/18/09
[115] Ahmed, p8, 119. Ahmed points out that a fatwa can only be issued by a non-governmental organization or individual mufti.
[116] Ahmed, p8
[117] Mohamed Heikal points this out in his book *Illusions of Triumph: An Arab View of the Gulf War* (London, HarperCollins, 1992). Quoted in Akbar S. Ahmed, p118-119
[118] Edward Said, *Representations of the Intellectual*, (New York, Pantheon Books, p1994) p118

it's speech you like, and when you're sure there's a half-billion Western Europeans out there between you and Ayatollah Khomeini so you can be courageous."[119]

An example of a real Fatwa, and one that many Englishmen loathe to admit or even hear about, was that issued over a hundred years earlier in the 1890's by Ayatollah Hasan al-Shirazi. Al-Shirazi's fatwa forbade Persians to smoke tobacco when the king, Shah Nasir al-Din gave the British a complete monopoly over the sale and export of tobacco produced and consumed in Persia. What followed was a near total boycott by the Persians (Iranians) and the Shah was forced to cut the British out the deal, to the disappointment of both monarchies.[120]

3) Effort: *Jihad*

Many would like to think that the Arabic word *jihad* is synonymous with 'war' or 'crusade'. While it would be nice to have a single word which would sum up the Muslim resistance to American and European violence, the Arabic word which has been elected, jihad, is a malapropism. The Arabic word for war is '*harb*' and there is no Arabic cognate for the European word 'crusade'.

Jihad is most honestly translated as 'effort' or 'striving'. We find the word used in several contexts by Muslims. The prophet Muhammad told one of his followers to perform a "*jihad* for his parents" by which he meant for a person to *strive* to care for their parents.[121] Everyday forms of jihad found amongst Muslims are those such as praying, fasting, studying, and overcoming ignorance.[122] The prophet himself said that lawful and fair-trade is a jihad.[123] In Iran there is a jihad occurring. This is the *jihad i sazandigi*, or 'effort for construction': an organized *effort* to build houses for the poor.[124]

The prophet Muhammad himself said: "Jihad is not taking a sword and fighting on the way of Allah. Jihad is taking care of your parents and children and being free from needing others."[125]

If jihad is used in the context of war, it is only in the context of defense or for fighting against injustice. As the Shia scholar Nasr says, "There have been no Muslim *jihads* in non-Islamic lands. Those who carry out terror in the West or elsewhere in the name of *jihad* are vilifying an originally sacred term, and their efforts have not been accepted by established and mainstream religious authorities as *jihad* in the juridical and theological sense of the term."[126]

This difference between the crusade and jihad is made more obvious by looking at the ethics prescribed in the Quran which explicitly forbids acts of aggression.

"O believers, prescribed for you is retaliation... But if aught is pardoned a man by his brother, let the pursuing be honourable, and let the payment be with kindliness. That is a lightening granted you by your Lord, and a mercy; and for him who commits aggression after that –for him there awaits a painful chastisement." Surah 2:174

---

[119] Noam Chomsky, *Understanding Power*, ed. Peter R. Mitchell and John Schoeffel, (New York, The New Press, 2002) p271-272
[120] John Esposito, *The Islamic Threat*, Second Edition, (Oxford, Oxford University Press, 1995) p65, 102
[121] As'ad AbuKhalil, *Bin Laden, Islam, and America's New "War On Terrorism"*, (New York, Seven Stories Press, 2002) p28
[122] Nasr, p259-260
[123] Rodinson, p16-17
[124] Nasr, p257
[125] In Robert Frager, *The Wisdom of Islam*, (New York, Barron's Educational Series, Inc., 2002) p136
[126] Nasr, p263

"And fight in the way of Allah with those who fight with you, but aggress not: Allah loves not the aggressors." Surah 2:187

"Let not detestation for a people who barred you from the Holy Mosque move you to commit aggression. Help one another to piety and godfearing; do not help each other to sin and enmity." Surah 5:3

"And if they incline to peace, do thou incline to it." Surah 8:63

"Leave is given to those who fight because they were wronged" Surah 22:40

"Say: 'Surely I possess no power over you, either for hurt or for rectitude." Surah 72:21

Community and Difference

Muhammad had said that "Differences in my community is a mercy"[127] and this hadith is proven by the sunnah and Constitution of Medina. The point of the Constitution of Medina and of Muhammad's mission in general is not imperialism: not to make everyone the same or force everyone to become a Muslim. For example, a passage from the Constitution reads: "the Jews have their religion and Muslims have theirs" (25) and this goes for other religions such as pagans (20b) and different tribes as well. It says: "Each must help the other against anyone who attacks the people of this document. They must seek mutual advice and consultation, and loyalty is a protection against treachery."[128] (37a) Such laws are reflected in the Quran as well.

"Let there be one nation of you, calling to good, and bidding to honour, and forbidding dishonour; those are the prosperers." Surah 3:100

"These are the signs of Allah We recite to thee in truth, and Allah desires not any injustice to living beings." Surah 3:104

Muhammad had said: "Indeed, there is no superiority of an Arab over a non-Arab, and indeed, no superiority for a red man over a black except through *Taqwa* (fear of Allah)."[129]

Whereas we saw with Charlemagne's *Saxon Capitulary*, and the passages of the New Testament that each foreigner and proponent of another religion must be converted, this is not so in Islam. In fact, the Quran argues against such compulsion explicitly.

"No compulsion is there in religion." Surah 2:258

"And if thy Lord had willed, whoever is in the earth would have believed, all of them, all together. Wouldst thou then constrain the people, until they are believers? It is not for any soul to believe save by the leave of Allah" Surah 10:99-100

"Yet, be thou ever so eager, the most part of men believe not." Surah 12:103

"We have not given them any Books to study, nor have We sent them before thee any warner." Surah 34:43

"If Allah had willed, He would have made them one nation." Surah 42:8

"And for his saying, 'My Lord, surely these are a people who believe not' –yet pardon them, and say, 'Peace!" Surah 43:87

"O mankind, We have created you male and female, and appointed you races and tribes, that you may know one another." Surah 49:13

"To you your religion, and to me my religion!" Surah 109:5

There is a tendency in the Western world, which has fought for many years to spread Christianity, democracy, capitalism, or communism to think that there must be an Islamic equivalent. Muslims have always tolerated Christianity, say when they conquered Jerusalem –they only disestablish it, separating church and state.[130]

---

[127] Quoted by Arabi, p23
[128] *Al Dustur al-Madinah* (The Constitution of Madinah). Complete text reprinted in El-Awa.
[129] Quoted by El-Awa, p111
[130] Esposito, p39

Minorities have always had more rights in Muslim countries than Muslims have had when they are minorities, as we see with the current US and British laws. It is almost common knowledge that both Jews and Christians had more rights under the Muslim Ottoman Empire than in any Christian Empire.[131]

After Umar took Jerusalem in the 7th century the Muslim leaders allowed Christians and Jews who had been banned from Jerusalem for centuries (according to Christian law) to return. In the 11th century when the Christians took Jerusalem every man, woman, and child were slaughtered. When in 1187 Saladin recaptured Jerusalem by treaty on the 4th of July, he once again created a climate of religious tolerance.[132]

When the Spanish Muslims, the Moors, ruled during the 'Golden Ages' all religious forms were tolerated. This lasted until Christians gained the upper hand and inaugurated the Inquisition in 1492 and all Muslims were forced out of Spain. Minorities in the Middle East such as Zoroastrians, Druze, Yazidis, and Alawis have long survived amidst the Muslim ummah.[133] Indeed it is part of the adab of Islam to tolerate all religions. As Nasr says, "The Islamic system must be understood in terms of the premises of the Islamic conception of society, whose goal is to provide a just system and a beneficial environment for the spiritual and religious growth of human beings."[134]

"Had Allah not driven back the people, some by the means of others, there had been destroyed cloisters and churches, oratories and mosques, wherein Allah's Name is much mentioned." Surah 22:41

"It may be Allah will yet establish between you and those of them with whom you are at enmity love. Allah is All-powerful; Allah is All-forgiving, All-compassionate. Allah forbids you not, as regards those who have not fought you in religion's cause, nor expelled you from your habitations, that you should be kindly to them, and act justly towards them; surely Allah loves the just." Surah 60:6

As the Catholic sociologist John Esposito relates –the French and English [and Belgian] mandates over Muslim nations have created legacies of instability[135], from Rwanda to Uganda, to nearly every country in the Middle East, and to India and Asia. The universal laws of empire seem to create more problems than they solve. Whenever Islamic Law is reintroduced it is received enthusiastically as we see in 20th century Iran, Libya, and many others, and still today in countries like Bosnia.[136] Muslim legal scholar Oussama Arabi has written of the effects of modernity.

"Modern Islamic law is better viewed as what present-day Muslim jurists, legislators, judges, and theologians take to be Islamic provisions and rulings in the altered, complex world of today, rather than an *a priori*-constituted corpus that is conserved, albeit in an astonishingly rich variety, in classical legal manuals. Looked at from this perspective, *sharia* is a living law, flexible and responsive to new legal practices, and to the momentous changes in the larger social world that befall human existence."[137]

The principle of ijma, like the al-shura, is dialogue and compromise. This is much like the theory of democracy where law is made through interpersonal consent. The spread of Muslim law foreshadowed the European Enlightenment of the 17th and 18th centuries where there began a belief in human rationality. Moreover, Islam does not hold to the idea of 'original sin' but follows an ethic of virtue called, 'moral perfectionism'. As the Quran says, "We indeed created Man in the fairest stature." Surah 95:4

---

[131] Arabi, 16-17n46
[132] Ahmed, p60-61
[133] Nasr, p166
[134] Nasr, p167
[135] Esposito, p75
[136] Dan Bilefsky, "Islamic Revival Tests Bosnia's Secular Cast", *The New York Times*, 12/26/08; Peters, p146
[137] Arabi, p18

Justice and Democracy

The Constitution of Athens

Aristotle was never a citizen of the democratic state but since the 19th century he has been credited as the author of the Constitution of Athens. Aristotle was born in the Kingdom of Macedonia and came to Athens to study under Plato at the *Academy*, before opening his own school there, the *Lyceum*. At the Lyceum Aristotle and his students compiled over 150 constitutions for study.[138]

Aristotle's *Constitution of Athens* itself begins by recounting how there came to be Athenian democracy. The Athenians had originally consisted of 4 tribes, or *phylae*, each with administrative duties and each with a tribal king. Traditionally there were four kings, or *Archons*, whose ascension was based upon heredity and wealth. In the early 6th century BCE when the wealth became unevenly distributed and the majority of citizens were poor, the many citizens came to oppose those in power. Eventually they agreed to appoint a single man as King Archon in 594 BCE, Solon. Solon (638-558) was a man of great reputation and was neither poor nor wealthy. Solon changed the existing constitution into that of a democratic one and passed laws limiting certain kinds of monopolies and sales. The Athenian people became a political sovereign-body called the *Ekklesia*, or The Assembly, which was open to all adult men. When attendance for the Assembly became less popular, citizens were paid if they showed up.

From each of the 4 tribes Solon instituted 100 men to form a council of 400 known as the *Boule*. The *Boule* were chosen by lot and had several jobs. These included the care for the public infrastructure, collecting taxes and revenues, running the navy, supervising the judges, and preparing topics to be debated by the *Ekklesia*. The *Boule* saw that the disabled were cared for and they had the right to take away a horse from someone if it was mistreated.

After Solon's reforms the position of King Archon became one of appointment with a term consisting of one year. A new king was appointed each year and over time the position's power diminished. In a more limited role the King Archon became judge of law over religious cases, disputes about religion, and charges of impiety.

An early 6th century politician named Cleisthenes changed the original 4-way tribal structure into 10 new *phylae*. This was done in order to dissolve a tribal division that had been emerging. Cleisthenes then (from 508-507) changed the *Boule* from 400 men into 500 men, 50 from each new *phylae* and these changes and others were intended to help make Athens more democratic. The Persian War began in 499 and lasted until 448.

Before the time of the democracy there had been a group of judges 'the elected magistracy' which decided legal cases. When the democracy was put in place these judges were kept in power. However, supreme power to courts of law was bestowed upon the Athenian citizens. The laws were guarded over by the *Areopagus*, who were a

---

[138] Noted by Stephen Everson in his introduction to Aristotle's, *The Politics and The Constitution of Athens*, trans. Benjamin Jowett, ed. Stephen Everson, (Cambridge, Cambridge University Press, 1996) (P) (xi, xii)

council made up of retired *Archons* and they decided on matters of the law regarding homicide, arson, battery, and impiety.

Originally the *Boule* had the authority to punish, fine, imprison, or execute any criminal. This right was taken away by the people after the Lysimachus case. The *Boule* had sentenced Lysimachus to be executed. However, a jury court, the *Dikasterion*, also the court of appeals, acquitted him. Lysimachus became known as 'the man who escaped the rod'. From then on if the *Boule* found someone guilty, a presiding council of nine appointed Archons the *Thesmothae*, brought the case before the *dikasterion*, or jury court. All jurors of the *dikasterion* were volunteers and had to be at least 30 years of age.

Prisoners were taken care of by a selected lot called The Eleven. It was also the job of The Eleven to execute convicted thieves, kidnappers, and brigands who pleaded guilty. Civil-suits were decided by a council called The Forty, consisting of four men picked by lot from each tribe. Bigger civil-suits were handled by the Arbitrators who were men aged 60 years (an individuals age was known by the Archons or the 'eponymous heroes'). Some civil and criminal proceedings were brought before the Archon, who in turn could introduce the case to the jury court, *dikasterion*, or before a group of guardians. These cases included ones against abusive parents, offenses against orphans, the plight of pregnant widows, and charges of insanity. A charge of conspiracy to murder, or of killing a slave, metic, or foreigner was brought before Court of the Palladium. Cases where a man admitted to homicide but claimed it was lawful were heard in a place called the *Delphinium*.

To make jury duty more popular the politician Pericles (495-429) instituted fees for jurors. (P, 1274a1-10) Pericles also imported philosophers from Turkey in order to help teach the Athenian citizens how to argue and disagree. Pericles fought and died in the Athenian war with Sparta (the Peloponnesian Wars 431-404). Sparta defeated Athens (with the support of Persians whom both Athens and Sparta had defeated less than a century before).[139] It was within Socrates own lifetime that the democracy was restored in Athens.

In time Pericles' guest philosopher from Turkey, Anaxagoras (500-428) became unpopular among the Athenians. He was charged with impiety and found guilty by a jury of Athenian citizens and was exiled in 450 BCE. Similarly, thirty years later, Protagoras (490-420) was put on trial by the Athenian citizens for charges of impiety. For his defense he claimed he knew nothing about the gods, and thus was he found guilty of heresy and was exiled.

The trial of Socrates is probably one of the most interesting cases in history, and is certainly the most tragic. Socrates (469-399) had been a soldier in the Athenian army, as well as a stone-mason, husband, and father. After he had defeated most of the Athenian statesmen in semi-formal public debates, charges were brought against him for impiety –charges which included not recognizing the Athenian gods, of introducing false gods, and for corrupting the Athenian youth (of whom Plato was a member). In his defense Socrates had famously said, "the unexamined life is not worth living". He was found guilty by the jury of 500 Athenians, the *Boule*. Socrates was then given the opportunity to adjudicate his own punishment, and many hoped he would suggest his own self-exile as a just punishment. When Socrates determined that his penalty ought to consist of free meals for life in the Prytaneum (the Athenian Town Hall), the *dikastrion*

---

[139] Norman Davies, *Europe: A History*, (New York, HarperPerennial, 1998) p98, 100

decided upon his execution. Although friends promised him a safe passage from Athens and his 'escape' from Prison was guaranteed, Socrates opted to stay for the execution, voluntarily drinking the hemlock which ended his life. He was 70 years old.

Aristotle: Judges vs. Kings

Aristotle taught that "all men cling to justice of some kind" though our conceptions are often imperfect and do not adequately express what is just. (P, 1280a10) In some ways "what we call just is whatever produces and maintains happiness and its parts for a political community." (E, 1129b19)[140] "For in every community there seems to be some sort of justice". (E, 1159b27) Therefore, "the salvation of the community is the common business" of all citizens. (P, 1276b29)

According to Aristotle, justice is not the end, but is a means. (E, 1134a1) In other words, "justice is the only virtue that seems to be another person's good, because it is related to another; for it does what benefits another, either the ruler or the fellow-member of the community." (E, 1130a5) Justice is something human. "What is just is found among those who have a share in things that unconditionally are good... this is why what is just is something human" (E, 1137a26, 31)

However, some people "think that being just is also easy, when in fact it is not." (E, 1137a6) For example, "Knowing how actions must be done, and how distributions must be made, if they are to be just, takes [much] work" (E, 1137a13) In solution:

"[C]ollections of laws and political systems might also, presumably, be most useful if we are capable of studying them and of judging what is done finely or in the contrary way, and what sorts of [elements] fit with what. Those who lack the [proper] state [of experience] when they go through these collections will not manage to judge finely". (E, 1181b6-10)

"Then let us study the collected political systems, to see from them what sorts of things preserve and destroy cities, and political systems of different types; and what causes some cities to conduct politics well, and some badly." (E, 1181b17-21)

To those who would impose their own form of government in foreign lands, Aristotle believed there were many forms of government and constitution.

"Our purpose is to consider what form of political community is best of all for those who are most able to realize their ideal of life. We must therefore examine not only this but other constitutions, both such as actually exist in well-governed states, and any theoretical forms which are held in esteem, so that what is good and useful may be brought to light." (P, 1260b27-31)

Aristotle held that historically the "first governments were kingships" when "men of eminent excellence were few." (P, 1286b9) "But when many persons equal in merit arose, no longer enduring the pre-eminence of one, they desired to have a commonwealth, and set up a constitution." (P, 1286b12) Aristotle holds that the "community is the constitution" (P, 1276b30) and the words 'constitution' and 'government' have "the same meaning." (P, 1279a25) There are many forms of constitutions. (P, 1291b14) "The goodness or badness, justice or injustice, of laws varies of necessity with the constitutions of states." (P,1282b9)

The "state is a community of freemen" and the "governments which have a regard to the common interest are constituted in accordance with strict principles of justice". (P, 1279a17-19, 21) "A constitution is the organization of offices in a state, and determines what is to be the governing body, and what is the end of each community."(P,1289a15-17)

---

[140] Aristotle, *Nicomachean Ethics*, trans. Terence Irwin, (Indianapolis, Hackett Publishing Company, 1985)

Aristotle considers many different forms of government -from monarchy (or rule by a king) to aristocracy (or rule by the best) to oligarchy (rule by the wealthy) to democracy (or rule by the majority, or the poor as he puts it) as well as others. "Since there are many forms of government there must be many varieties of citizens". (P, 1278a15) He finds that the two best forms of state are the constitutional monarchy and the constitutional aristocracy. (P, 1288b1) However, we ought to favor the best law over the best men, be they kings or aristocrats. "[E]ven if it be better for certain individuals to govern, they should be made only guardians and ministers of the law." (P, 1287a21)

Aristotle believed "there is more than one type of justice" (E, 1130b6) though he concentrated on two basic kinds of justice: "one unwritten, and one governed by rules of law." (E, 1162b23) Aristotle held that "people seem to have natural consideration, comprehension and judgement" (E, 1143b7), that humans are "by nature a political animal" (P, 1253a2) and that "all communities aim at some good". (P, 1252a3) Thus, human "convention is a sort of justice" (P, 1255a3) and the unwritten law is a kind of natural state of being. In an important sense, the unwritten law, call it custom, convention, or tradition, is in some ways superior to the written law.

"One part of what is politically just is natural, and the other part legal. What is natural is what has the same validity everywhere alike, independent of its seeming so or not. What is legal is what originally makes no difference [whether it is done] one way or another, but makes a difference whenever people have laid down the rule" (E, 1134b19-22)

Thus, "attention by the community works through laws, and decent attention works through excellent laws; and whether the laws are written or unwritten, for the education of one or of many, seems unimportant" (E, 1180a35-b2)

Aristotle seems to be pointing out the necessarily social aspect of justice.

"Hence it is evident that in seeking for justice men seek for the mean, for the law is the mean. Again, customary laws have more weight, and relate to more important matters, than written laws, and a man may be a safer ruler than the written law, but not safer than the customary law." (P, 1287b4-7)

For those who think that justice is identical to law, they are ignorant of the role that the reasoning mind plays in the pursuit of justice. Rather than the programmatic obeisance of laws, which is something machines do, justice is something involving great wisdom and foresight.

"[P]eople think it takes no wisdom to know the things that are just and unjust, because it is not hard to comprehend what the laws speak of. But these are not the things that are just, except coincidentally." (E, 1137a12)

This is because "the law has no power to command obedience except that of habit" (P, 1269a20) The "law is only a convention, 'a surety to one another of justice'… and has no real power to make the citizens good and just." (P, 1280b10-12)

Aristotle believed it possible to know what is the best form of government. In place of democracy, Aristotle thought that "the best must be that which is administered by the best" (P, 1181a34) -be it an aristocracy or king. Aristotle did not believe in the so-called Divine Right of Kings, saying that such a ruler "should at any rate be chose, not as they are now". (P, 1271a21) The ruler or rulers must obey the constitution for "he who has never learned to obey cannot be a good commander". (P, 1277b9, 13) Although "temperance and justice" will be characteristic of such a one(s), "practical wisdom is the only excellence peculiar to the ruler". (P, 1277b16, 26) "If, as I said before, the good man has a right to rule because he is better, still two good men are better than one". (P, 1287b12) Such sovereigns ought to do "nothing arbitrarily or contrary to law" (P, 1286b32) because the rule of law "is preferable to that of any individual." (P, 1287a20)

Thus, Aristotle rejects the reign of an 'absolute monarch' (P, 1287a9) for that of the law of the constitution. He wrote: "laws, when good, should be supreme; and that the magistrate or magistrates [judges or rulers] should regulate those matters only on which the laws are unable to speak with precision owing to the difficulty of any general principal embracing all particulars". (P, 1282b2-7)

Aristotle found the role of judges to be thus: "[T]he judge is intended to be a sort of living embodiment of what is just." (E, 1132a21) However, the jurists have a right to impeach any person in power who goes beyond the constitution. (P, 1255a8-9) "A constitution is the arrangement of magistracies [judges] in a state" (P, 1278b9) and "the laws must be adopted to the constitutions." (P, 1282b10) Because a "multitude is a better judge of many things than an individual" (P, 1286a30) "the law trains officers [judges]... and appoints them to determine matters which are left undecided by it, to the best of their ability. Further, it [the constitution] permits them to make any amendment of the existing laws which experience suggests." (P, 1287a26-29)

"For matters of detail about which men deliberate cannot be included in legislation. Nor does anyone deny that the decision of such matters must be left to man, but it is argued that there should be many judges, and not only one. For every ruler who has been trained by the law judges well; and it would surely seem strange that a person should see better with two eyes, or hear better with two ears, or act better with two hands or feet, than many with many". (P, 1287b22-28)

As for democracy, Aristotle held it to be a perverted form of constitutional government, just as a tyranny was a perverse form of monarchy and oligarchy a perverse form of aristocracy. (P, 1279b5) Aristotle held that democracy is against the common good (P, 1279b10), as it institutes ostracism for anyone who is different, or greater, or not equal to everyone else. "Ostracism is a measure... which acts by disabling and banishing the most prominent citizens." (P, 1284a19, 36) Aristotle was well aware that this had happened to Plato's teacher Socrates and before him Anaxagoras and Protagoras. However, for cities that have become very large democracy becomes necessary. In such cases "no other form of government appears to be any longer even easy to establish." (P, 1286b20)

American Justice: The Common Law

The American judicial system is based upon a system know as the Common Law. The Common Law became the law of Briton in the 11th and 12th centuries when it was conquered by the Normans. The Normans were Celtic people of northern France (Normandy) and many of the legal terms found in the Common Law are of French (and thus Latin) origin.

Briton had originally been inhabited by Celtic people before it was conquered by Julius Caesar 43 years before the birth of Jesus. When the Roman Empire was converted to Christianity in the 300's, the Ecclesiastical law of the church became the law of Briton. Because of the Germanic conquest of Rome in the year 410, the Romans abandoned Briton. Thereupon Scottish and Pictish peoples from the north and the highlands swept down in order to reclaim Briton. It was in 449 that the Celtic King Vortigern invited the Angles and Saxons to Briton as mercenaries.[141] By the 6th century these two Germanic

---

[141] David Crystal, *The Cambridge Encyclopedia of The English Language*, (Cambridge, Cambridge University Press, 1995) p6

tribes lay claim to Briton. They were accompanied by two other tribes: from Denmark, the Jutes; from the Netherlands, the Frisians. In 597 a Benedictine monk named Augustine arrived in Briton in order to convert the Angles and Saxons to Christianity. Though there may have been as many as a dozen kings in Briton at the time, within a year of Augustine's arrival he had converted King Aethelberht of Kent to Christianity, perhaps because the king's wife was a Celtic Christian already.[142] By the end of the 8th century Briton was converted to Christianity and the Ecclesiastical law was put in place.[143]

The Norman conquest began when William the Bastard (or William the Conqueror) took Briton in 1066. His great grandson Henry II (1133-1189) institutionalized the Common Law so as to displace the Ecclesiastical which had been English law for several centuries.[144] The reforms of Henry II partly separated the courts from the church while further empowering the monarchy. Henry II had appointed his boyhood tutor Thomas Beckett (1118-1170) to be Archbishop in order to clean up the church, which the king had found to be corrupt. Soon thereafter the Archbishop and the King came into quarrel over the legal reforms and the followers of the crown put Beckett to death.[145]

By the 15th century the English monarchy set up 'equity' courts to allow commercial interests to override the Common Law courts. Thus, when colonization of America began, "The Crown corporations were granted authority by the British monarch to govern the conquered territories. The difference is that now the corporations are almost completely sovereign in themselves."[146]

In time the British parliament modified the Common Law and enforced the Statutory laws of the state. As we saw, the 16th century priest Richard Hooker had done much to expand upon the Divine Right of Kings. Within the 17th century both King James I and Charles I "destroyed an independent judiciary and the appeal to law". Both of these monarchs were steeped in a belief in their own divinity. James had suspended

---

[142] Crystal, p10

[143] In 787 the Viking invasion of Briton began, lasting 200 years. There are some 1500 towns in eastern Briton with Scandinavian names.

[144] Although the Common Law and the Ecclesiastical Law are much like the Holy Roman or Canon Law it has been argued that in fact the Common Law is derived from Islamic Law. If the Common Law began to be used around the 12th and 13th centuries, its devotion to judicial precedent and separation of the courts from state politics may have come from the Arab-Norman culture of Sicily in the 11th century. Check John A. Makdisi's 1999 article, "The Islamic Origins of the Common Law", *North Carolina Law Review*, 77 (5): 1635-1739

[145] It was rumored that Beckett's mother was a Muslim. Because of the Crusading spirit, on the day of the coronation of King Richard I, Henry II's successor, all Jews who attended the cathedral ceremony that day were murdered by angry Christian mobs and violence was carried on throughout the day. Charles Dickens puts the number of women, children, and elderly that were murdered in the hundreds. The Muslim leader Saladin crushed the army of King Richard in the Third Crusade. Less than a century later, all Jews were expelled from England (1290). Dickens says of King Richard 'the Lion-hearted', "His heart whatever it was had been a black and perjured heart... more deficient in a single touch of tenderness than any wild beast's in the forest." Charles Dickens, *A Child's History of England*, (New York, The Federal Book Company) Orig. pub. 1851, p71, 94-95, 92

[146] Karen Coulter, "Corporations and the Public Interest: The Development of Property Concepts In the U.S. 'Just Us' System", originally presented at the Yale Law School, February, 1999, reprinted in, *Defying Corporations, Defining Democracy*, ed. Dean Ritz, (New York, The Apex Press for the Program on Corporations, Law & Democracy (POCLAD), 2001) p93, 96

Parliament and persecuted Catholics and Puritans (whence their pilgrimages to America in 1620). Charles was "impolitic" and declared Martial Law –many were killed and many had their ears removed.[147]

These modifications were observed and described by the 18th century English jurist Sir William Blackstone (1723-1780) whose *Commentaries on the Laws of England* are still sited and studied today in US court rooms. Blackstone also drafted the Penitentiary Act in order to increase the number of prisons. This was passed by the Parliament though none of these Blackstone Penitentiaries were ever built.[148]

The Common Law is different from the Roman or Natural Law in two fundamental ways. Like the older Shariah which draws upon 1500 years of precedent, the Common Law is based upon a 1000 years of precedent. This means that the decisions made by judges become the example from which future lawyers and judges use to argue their decisions. In the United States, for example, historical decisions made by the courts of England and America remain the laws today as past cases become 'precedent' (or in Latin *'stare decisis'*).

Another distinctive feature of the Common Law is that it is a corporate law. Much of Common Law jurisprudence is known as 'contract law' and is the basis for most business and legal matters. Contract law goes hand in hand with business and corporate law. The pragmatist philosopher and American judge Richard Posner writes of the "implicit economic structure" of the Common Law and the fact that a judge's decisions "maximize economic welfare". Posner notes moreover how "economists and economically minded lawyers have found that the [Common] law uncannily follows economics."[149]

In an important sense then, as with the theory English Common Law, the justice system is supposed to be separate from the legislative or political branch, as it is with the Shariah. As we have seen in this century, the Supreme Court has the power to elect presidents and many find the courts inexcusably tied in with the state. Bertrand Russell wrote in 1938 that:

"In the United States at the present day, the reverence which the Greeks gave to oracles and the Middle Ages to the Pope is given to the Supreme Court. Those who have studied the working of the American Constitution know that the Supreme Court is part of the forces engaged in the protection of the plutocracy. But of the men who know this, some are on the side of the plutocracy, and therefore do nothing to weaken the traditional reverence for the Supreme Court, while others are discredited in the eyes of ordinary quiet citizens by being said to be subversive and Bolshevik. A considerable further career of obvious partisanship will be necessary before a Luther will be able to attack successfully the authority of the official interpreters of the Constitution."[150]

In 1799 the US Supreme Court Chief Justice Oliver Ellsworth (1745-1807) noted that, "The common law of this country remains the same as it was before the Revolution."[151] A glance at the opening pages of the American legal dictionary, *Black's Law Dictionary* offers a history of the British monarchy from William the Conqueror in 1066 all the way into the 20th century. American historian Howard Zinn wonders:

---

[147] J. Bronowski and Bruce Mazlish, *The Western Intellectual Tradition*, (New York, Barnes & Nobles, 1960) p155, 156, 158, 169n17
[148] Clive Emsley, *Crime and Society In England: 1750-1900*, (New York, Longman Inc., 1987) p217-218
[149] Richard A. Posner, *The Economics of Justice*, (Cambridge, Harvard University Press, 1981) p4-5
[150] Bertrand Russell, *Power: A New Social Analysis*, (New York, W.W. Norton & Company, 1938) (b)p72
[151] Howard Zinn, *Declarations of Independence*, (New York, HarperPerennial, 1991) (a) p186

"English common law? Hadn't we fought and won a revolution against England? Were we still bound by English common law? The answer is yes. It seems there are limits to revolutions. They retain more of the past than is expected by their fervent followers."[152]

So, for example, in a landmark decision in *Johnson and Graham's Lessee v. William McIntosh* (1823), Chief Justice John Marshall wrote for the Supreme Court that, "The tribes of Indians inhabiting this country were fierce savages whose occupation was war...". Marshall believed the European "discovery gave an exclusive right to extinguish the Indian title of occupancy, either by purchase or by conquest."[153] Thus were the pre-revolutionary laws maintained.

The French lawyer Alexis de Tocqueville (1805-1859) was amazed at how little the revolution had changed the legal structure from English rule to American autonomy. Writing of his visit to the US in the 1840's, he noted the barrier that the inherited English Common Law set up for American democracy. He wrote:

"Visiting Americans and studying their laws, one discovers that the prestige accorded to lawyers and their permitted influence in the government are now the strongest barriers against the faults of democracy."[154]

De Tocqueville found that with the absence of the British aristocracy in America, the practitioners of the Common Law had assumed their class privilege. Alexis wrote:

"I do say that in a community in which lawyers hold without question the high rank in society which is naturally their due, their temper will be eminently conservative and will prove antidemocratic."[155]

Such a class structure, de Tocqueville found, led to an ideological conservatism which was in direct conformity to the patriarchal structure obeyed in England.

"This aristocratic character which I detect in the legal mind is much more pronounced still in the United States and in England than in any other land. This is not only due to English and American legal studies, but also to the very nature of the legislation and the position of lawyers as interpreters thereof in both these countries

"Both English and Americans have kept the law of precedents; that is to say, they still derive their opinions in legal matters and the judgements they should pronounce from the opinions and legal judgements of their fathers.

"An English or American lawyer almost always combines a taste and respect for what is old with a liking for regularity and legality."[156]

Because the legal system of the Common Law is so based upon history, precedent economics, and legislation, not to say anything about the abstract legal terminology with its roots in French and Latin, de Tocqueville saw the American lawyer as a kind of elite specialist, or a cryptographer of sorts. He wrote:

"Where lawyers are absolutely needed, as in England and the United States, and their professional knowledge is held in high esteem, they become increasingly separated from the people, forming a class apart. A French lawyer is just a man of learning, but an English or an American one is somewhat like the Egyptian priests, being, as they were, the only interpreter of an occult science."[157]

De Tocqueville noted how, because of the inaccessibility of the law to citizens of the democracy, different political ideologies and class structures emerged.

"In America there are neither nobles nor men of letters, and the people distrust the wealthy. Therefore the lawyers form the political upper class and the most intellectual section of society.

---

[152] Zinn, (a) p186
[153] Francis Jennings, *The Invasion of America: Indians, Colonialism, and the Cant of Conquest*, (New York, W.W. Norton & Company, 1975) p60n7
[154] Alexis de Tocqueville, *Democracy In America*, trans. George Lawrence, ed. J.P. Mayer, (New York, First Perennial Classics, 2000) p263
[155] de Tocqueville, p265
[156] de Tocqueville, p267
[157] de Tocqueville, p267

Consequently they only stand to lose from any innovation; this adds an interest in conservation to their natural taste for order.

"If you ask me where the American aristocracy is found, I have no hesitation in answering that it is not among the rich, who have no common link uniting them. It is at the bar or the bench that the American aristocracy is found."[158]

Although 16th century Spanish Courts had begun the 'legal' work of drafting treaties with Native Americans, the US made its first treaty with the Delaware Indians in 1778. The treaty promised the Delaware political sovereignty if they helped fight against the British. In 1787 Congress drafted the Northwest Ordinance, promising that "utmost good faith shall always be observed toward the Indians; their land and property shall never be taken from them without their consent." Soon thereafter, however, after his inauguration in 1829, President Andrew Jackson (r.1829-1837) began dishonoring all treaties. In 1830 he had passed by Congress the Indian Removal Act which forcefully exiled Cherokees from Georgia. In 1831 Supreme Court Chief Justice John Marshall condemned Jackson and his administration, though the President was determined to not be stopped. And he wasn't.

By 1868 some 374 treaties had been signed and Native Americans lost hundreds of millions of acres. In early 1871 Congress passed the Indian Appropriation Act which stated, "No Indian nation or tribe within the territory of the United States shall be acknowledged and recognized as an independent nation, tribe, or power with whom the United States may contract by treaty." By 1940 some 5000 laws had been passed by the US government to deal with Native Americans.[159]

Pragmatism and Justice

Just twenty years after Alexis de Tocqueville surveyed America there was a bloody Civil War, much as he had predicted in his study, *Democracy in America*. The re-unified country that emerged from this most bloody war was continental: railroads stretched from the Atlantic to the Pacific as corporations gained greater and greater strength and legal power over state laws. New dilemmas were facing the American citizens as industrial revolution swept across the land and science and technology became the engine of factories and economic profit for the old-boy network. America was becoming an economic empire. As westward expansion was completed the question of empire became evident.

It was in this climate that the American philosophy of pragmatism emerged and became influential in shaping the ethical agenda of the moral Reconstruction and post-Civil War era. Against the ancient precedent and the worship of history, a practical and natural philosophy began to emerge —one based upon tolerance and an ethics based on humanity.

Oliver Wendell Holmes, Jr. (1841-1935) was the pragmatist philosopher who attempted to reorient the American version of the Common Law. Holmes sought to make it less based upon history and the decisions of our forefathers, (or for that matter a posited

---

[158] de Tocqueville, p268
[159] Peter Nabokov, *Native American Testimony*, Revised Edition, (New York, Penguin books, 1999) p118-120, 148-149

universal laws of logic), and more based upon the needs and experience of the community.

Wendell Holmes is probably one of the most influential Americans to have lived, and he was raised by a loving mother and father who were affectionate, wise, and set against racism. When the Civil War started in 1861 he dropped out of Harvard University one semester short of getting his degree and volunteered to fight against the slave-states. During the war he was shot four times, two of which produced wounds nearly fatal. After his tour of duty he went to law school, eventually becoming the Chief Justice of the Massachusetts Supreme Judicial Court, of which he was a member for 20 years. In 1902 he was appointed US Supreme Court Justice, a position which he held for 30 years, into his 90's. We shall consider first his pragmatic philosophy of law and then his decisions as a judge.

When Holmes began studying law he found that the legal practice was steeped in English history. Because the law was based upon almost a 1000 years of precedent it helped maintain the belief that the law was rooted in such things as teleology, logic, divine authority, or some other kind of moral-political justification. Traditionally, as we have seen, the popular forms of Western Law were rooted in a religio-political foundation: the Canon Law is founded upon what is believed to be holy writ, and the Common Law was founded upon the divine right of the sovereign, in this case, Henry II. These legal systems were either led or accompanied by the supposition that the law is identical with logic and morality.

From very early on Holmes had been critical of such beliefs that the law is universal and eternal. As a student at Harvard at 18 years of age, he gave the elderly Ralph Waldo Emerson an essay he had written criticizing Plato. Emerson said in response, "When you strike at a king, you must kill him."[160] In one of Holmes' earliest publications (1870) in the *American Law Review*, titled "Codes, and the Arrangement of the Law", he showed the difficulties behind any endeavor at formalization of the law. Later, in Holmes' most celebrated work, in England and America, *The Common Law* (1881), he stated, "The life of the law has not been logic; it has been experience."[161] And in the mature philosophy of his lecture addressed to the Boston University School of Law titled "The Path of the Law" (1897), Holmes developed a pragmatic legalism in opposition to any fixed codification of law.

Holmes fought against the idea that the laws of justice are fixed and immutable. His work has helped overturn the notion that justice and the law are based upon formal laws of logic, or *a priori* principles. Holmes taught that legal systems are based upon the community and the judges they appoint, and not upon some universal or metaphysical structure behind the law. Although he was aware of how much of legal studies depended upon morality, history, politics, and logic, he did not think that these were the actual factors that ran the courts or aided judges in reaching their decisions.

In the spirit of the Common Law, Holmes believed that jurisprudence ought to remain separate from politics and political justifications. He was critical of those who believed that morality was based upon or derived from law, saying that we ought not to

---

[160] Quoted by Sheldon M. Novick, *Honorable Justice: The Life of Oliver Wendell Holmes*, (Boston, Little, Brown & Company, 1989) p28
[161] Oliver Wendell Holmes, Jr., "Lecture I: Early Forms of Liability", *The Common Law*, (Boston, Little, Brown, 1881); from Menand, p137

"get the cart before the horse". Holmes believed that if the law is part of morality, it is limited by it. In 1897 in "The Path of the Law", he argued that: "nothing but confusion of thought can result from assuming that the rights of men in a moral sense are equally rights in the sense of the Constitution and the law."[162] The belief that law and morality are synonymous is a central notion to Natural, Roman, and Ecclesiastical Law and Holmes was critical of this universalism, call it imperialism. In his study on "Natural Law", Holmes wrote:

> "It is not enough for the knight of romance that you agree that his lady is a very nice girl –if you do not admit that she is the best that God ever made or will make, you must fight. There is in all men a demand for the superlative, so much so that the poor devil who has no other way of reaching it attains it by getting drunk. It seems to me that his demand is at the bottom of the philosopher's effort to prove that truth is absolute and of the jurist's search for criteria of universal validity which he collects under the head of natural law."[163]

D'Entreves noted the truth of this passage, that the idea of a natural and universal law had inspired imperialism. He wrote in response to this passage of Holmes' that it was "not a very charitable judgement: but there is no doubt that natural law was the *belle dame sans merci* who inspired the crusading spirit of old-time jurisprudence."[164] The belief that one's own laws were the universal morality for all mankind had incurred a great deal of warfare and crusades. In fact, Holmes wrote that issues of right and wrong are not issues of praise or blame, and he wished to leave out this religio-ethical terminology from the law.[165]

Holmes criticized the traditional belief that deciding the law or judging a case are based solely upon deductive reasoning or the laws of logic. For those (such as legal positivists) who believe that thinking and reasoning are purely a deductive process, Holmes believed it erroneous to conclude that the law works like mathematics. It was fallacious reasoning to think that "the only force at work in the development of the law is logic." Holmes believed that even a bad legal system can improve –that logic is not the sole force behind its determination. He found that "certainty generally is illusion, and repose is not the destiny of man." [166]

Holmes view of the law can be stated simply thus: "The prophecies of what the courts will do in fact, and nothing more pretentious, are what I mean by the law."[167]

Instead of the single foundations of both ancient and modern laws, Holmes took a sociological view. In *The Common Law* Holmes had written:

> "The felt necessities of the time, the prevalent moral and political theories, intuitions of public policy, avowed or unconscious, even the prejudices which judges share with their fellow-men, have had a good deal more to do than the [logical] syllogism in determining the rules by which men should be governed."[168]

Holmes believed that the study of law was in many ways like the study of social development. He said: "The rational study of law is still to a large extent the study of history." However, Holmes believed there was a danger in respecting history and

---

[162] Oliver Wendell Holmes, Jr., "The Path of the Law", first published in *The Harvard Law Review* 10 (1897), 457-78. From *Pragmatism: A Reader*, ed. Louis Menand, (New York, Vintage Books, 1997) p148
[163] Holmes, "Natural Law", first pub. in *The Harvard Law Review* 32 (1918), 40-44; from Menand, p173
[164] D'Entreves, p96
[165] Holmes, "The Path of the Law", p150
[166] Holmes, "The Path of the Law", p154
[167] Holmes, "The Path of the Law, p149
[168] Holmes, "Lecture I: Early Forms of Liability", *The Common Law*, p137

precedent over reason and consequences. The overestimation of history can override human rationality. The law is not only historical but is theoretical. He found that the determination of ends and consequences to be more practical than the respect for history.[169]

According to Oliver, the law is not the limit of freedom, but of community. Our attitudes and judgements are based upon another implication –whether it be "the practice of the community or of a class, or because of some opinion as to policy, or in short, because of some attitude of yours upon a matter not capable of exact quantitative measurement, and therefore not capable of founding exact logical conclusions."[170] Because he believed the law is not fixed, Holmes had found that the traditional practice of law had obscured the important theory behind the law. He found that an interest and understanding in the theory of law are fundamental in changing the practice of law. The pragmatist Louis Menand notes that Justice Holmes' methods are empirical and behavioral, and not racial.[171]

Justice Holmes

Holmes' many years practicing and studying law and his 50 years as a judge, occurred during a time of great changes in America and the world. As pragmatists we should not rashly agree with all that Holmes decided as a judge. And as we have seen, his own legal philosophy makes clear that this should occasionally be so. What can be admired is his reasonability. The ability to change one's own mind and to change the minds of others –is the true sign of reason. In his position as Supreme Court Justice Holmes became known as the 'Great dissenter'. This means that he often disagreed with the majority opinion of the Court and that he was vocal in his dissention.

According to the US Constitution there are three branches of government –the president, or executive branch; the senate, or legislative branch; and the Supreme Court, or judicial branch. These three branches of government are kept separate so as to 'check' and 'balance' each other, though this doesn't always run smoothly. The president must get a majority of the senate to pass a law or amendment, and vice versa, the senate must get the signature of the president to pass legislation or amendments. The Supreme Court decides whether these laws are Constitutional, but they cannot do so unless a case is brought before the court. However, for most cases to reach the Supreme Court, they must have already gone through state and districts courts of appeals, though since 1921 even this is no guarantee. Since 1921 the Supreme Court Justices' get to pick which cases they handle.

A position as a Supreme Court Justice is available, according to the US Constitution, only through the appointment of the President. There are nine justices and their position is held until retirement or death. Five judges makes a majority and a lot of cases are decided 5-4.

Many of the cases that were handled by the Supreme Court after the Civil War were questions of state authority vs. federal authority, labor unions vs. corporations, corporations seeking to monopolize the market, as well as questions of civil rights and the legality of US colonization in other countries. Holmes had been the Chief Justice of

---

[169] Holmes, "The Path of the Law", p154, 158, 161, 162, 164
[170] Holmes, "The Path of the Law", p148, 155
[171] Louis Menand, *The Metaphysical Club*, (New York, Farrar, Straus and Giroux, 2001) p343, 345

the Massachusetts Supreme Judicial Court, where he had been justice for 20 years, when President Theodore Roosevelt appoint him to the US Supreme Court in 1902. It was thus that Holmes first dissent was unpopular.

In 1904 President Theodore Roosevelt attempted to break up the railroad conglomerate Northern Securities Company because of 'monopoly', or controlling the market to such an extent that competition is not possible. This was illegal according to the Sherman Antitrust Act of 1890. The Act itself had originally been written only to protect state power over mines and local industry, recognizing that corporations are chartered by individual states and are thus limited by state law. President Roosevelt was now stretching the Act to include questions of ownership. Although the Court decided in favor Roosevelt, Holmes dissented, to the outrage of the President. Holmes believed the case was an attempt to politicize the Court and give it power as a branch of government beyond its role as arbiter and settler of disputes.[172] Holmes' dissent was consistent with his belief that the court should be separate from the government.

The following year (1905) Holmes dissented against the Court majority in *Lochner v. New York*, again favoring state rights over federal rights. However, a year later he decided with the court to limit the power of corporations in *Northwestern National Life Insurance Co v. Riggs*. By 1907 Holmes' had begun to be believe "Congress could pass a statute reasonably restricting the size of companies in interstate commerce".[173]

1908 proved to be a pivotal year for questions of workers rights. When the Court decided against the rights of workers unions in *Adair v. United States*, Holmes dissented. In *Muller v. Oregon* Holmes decided with the Court in favor of women's rights in the workplace. In two cases of 1911 –*United States v. American Tobacco Company* and *Standard Oil Company of New Jersey v. United States* –Holmes decided against corporate monopoly. In 1915 in *Coppage v. Kansas* when the Court decided in favor of limiting the rights of workers unions, Holmes dissented. In 1918 when the Court refused to recognize child labor laws in *Hammer v. Dagenhart,* Holmes dissented. Holmes decided with the court in *Pennsylvania Coal Corporation v. Mahon* to limit corporate power. In 1923 in *Adkins v. Children's Hospital* when the Court decided against their being a minimum wage, Holmes dissented. In 1928 in the *Swift and Company v. United States* Holmes decided with the Court that through the Commerce Clause the government could stop a corporate monopoly.

Holmes had also stood up for the rights of minorities. Two of his first cases regarding racial minorities were abominable, however. In 1902 the state of Alabama had changed its constitution in such a way that it required the eligible voters (men) to pass certain tests. This was intended to keep African-Americans from voting. Such discrimination had been blocked after the Civil War by the constant presence of Republican (Union) soldiers in the south who made sure that African Americans could vote. This period is called the Reconstruction. At the end of the Civil War in 1865 racial tensions remained high in the south. Once the federal army was removed in 1877 whites in the south raced to reclaim their government from the African-Americans who had been empowered after the war. Thus, when Holmes wrote the opinion of the Court in the 1903 *Giles v. Harris* case, maintaining to the effect that the court was impotent to put troops

---

[172] Novick, p272
[173] Novick, p 461n

back in southern states to protect voting rights, Holmes was condemned by liberal Americans.[174] Holmes made a moral blunder in the same year when he decided with the Court that Congress had a constitutional right to void its contracts made with the oppressed Native Americans in *Lone Wolf v. Hitchcock*. These early bad decisions are not his legacy, however.

At the turn of the century the Supreme Court of the state of Washington had decided that the state law could limit or take away Native American's rights to hunt, fish, and exercise other freedoms. In 1905 in *United States v. Winans* Holmes overturned the Washington state court decision, leaving Native Americans unharassed by the state to hunt and fish, as well as other civil liberties. In 1906 in *United States v. Shipp* Holmes decided with the Court that a corrupt Sheriff from Tennessee who had permitted an angry mob to lynch an African American, would be prosecuted. This was the first criminal trial every handled by the Supreme Court.

Two poor decision of Holmes' involved his concurring with the court in 1908 in *Berea College v. Kentucky* that states had a right to keep schools segregated, and he made the same decision in 1927 in *Lum v. Rice*.[175] However, in 1915 in *Guinn v. United States* Holmes decided with the court that state laws could not be written in order to limit the voting rights of African Americans. In 1917 in *Buchanan v. Warley* Holmes decided with the court against segregated housing. In 1927 in *Nixon v. Herndon* Holmes helped strike down a Texas law which barred African Americans from voting in the primary.

Empire vs. Community
During the 20th century the question of whether America ought to be considered as an empire or just a union of free states was a central concern. Cases were brought before the Supreme Court on these very issues and Holmes had changed his mind against empire to one that reflected a social philosophy of community. When the United States defeated Spain in 1898 in the Spanish-American War, the terms of the peace treaty held that Cuba, Guam, Hawaii, the Philippines, and Puerto Rico now belonged to the US.

When US troops were sent to the Philippines to occupy and announce American sovereignty, war broke out, lasting from 1899-1913. Although victory was declared by the US in 1904 at one point there were as many 70,000 US troops in the Philippines. Hundreds of thousands of Filipino's were killed.[176]

It was around this time that a group of concerned Americans formed the Anti-Imperialist League which opposed US aggression overseas. The American Anti-Imperialist League (AAIL) included such pragmatists as William James, John Dewey, Jane Addams, the writer Mark Twain, the business giant Andrew Carnegie, and the former president Grover Cleveland. In 1905 Holmes delivered an opinion striking down the US tariff imposed on the Philippine Islands, to the outrage of President Roosevelt, the very man who had appointed Holmes to the Supreme Court.

---

[174] Novick, p259. Novick also notes how as a witness and veteran of the Civil War, Holmes was wary of rekindling old animosities and "was unwilling to renew the war with the South." Novick calls Holmes's decision "a bad one, perhaps his worst" and his argument, "specious". (p459n15)
[175] In 1921 Congress passed legislation barring immigration of all peoples from Asia and Africa.
[176] Howard Zinn, *A People's History of the United States*, Revised and Updated Edition, (New York, HarperCollins, 1995) (b) p308

To the advantage of pragmatism, there is a sense in which Oliver Wendell Holmes' appointment to the Supreme Court was due to anarchism. In 1901 President McKinley was all set to appoint a Boston lawyer named Alfred Hemenway to the Supreme Court. That year some anarchist assassinated McKinley. The Vice-President Theodore Roosevelt became president and in 1902 appointed Holmes to the Court.

Holmes had always been sympathetic to anarchists and socialists and had himself read Karl Marx's *Capital*. Holmes had employed socialists and had defended both socialists and anarchists during his life even though these groups had attempted to assassinate him. Two of Holmes' most famous, if unfortunate, cases involved the socialists Charles Schenck and the presidential candidate Eugene Debs. In *Schenck v. United States* (1919) a jury in Philadelphia had found Schenck in violation of the Espionage Act of 1917 for mailing leaflets protesting the draft. Holmes' written opinion for the Court included this passage: "The most stringent protection of free speech would not protect a man in falsely shouting fire in a crowded theater and causing a panic... The question in every case is whether the words are used in such circumstances and are of such a nature as to create a clear and present danger..." As Holmes' biographer Sheldon Novick says, "Holmes statement in *Schenck* would have allowed punishment of speech only when it amounted to an incitement or attempt to commit a crime."[177]

The Eugene Debs case was more "distasteful", however (*Debs v. United States*). Debs had protested the US involvement in the First World and President Woodrow Wilson, (a man whom Holmes despised) had pursued the prosecution of Debs. Holmes knew his duty as a judge was limited; it was not in the power of the court to either pardon or commute a sentence but only to decide on the legality of the prosecution. Debs was given a 10 year sentence and Holmes could only hope that the president would pardon him. Holmes wrote to a friend, "I had a disagreeable task in writing a decision against Debs... There was no doubt in my mind about the law but I wondered that the Government should have pressed the case to a hearing –as it enables knaves, fools and the ignorant to say that he [Debs] was really condemned as a dangerous agitator."[178]

The same year as the *Schenck* and *Debs* cases (1919), Holmes delivered perhaps his most important dissent when the court decided against free speech. In 1918 when the Court decided upon censure, Holmes had dissented in favor of the free speech of a newspaper that had criticized a court judge (*Toledo Newspaper Co. v. United States*). In *Abrams v. United States* (1919) Holmes dissented against the court decision to censure socialist pamphleteers. Holmes wrote:

"Prosecution for the expression of opinion seems to me perfectly logical. If you have no doubt of your premises or your power and want a certain result with all your heart you naturally express your wishes in law and sweep away all opposition. To allow opposition by speech seems to indicate that you think the speech impotent, as when a man says that he has squared the circle, or that you do not care wholeheartedly for the result, or that you doubt your power or your premises. But when men have realized that time has upset many fighting faiths, they may come to believe even more than they believe the very foundations of their own conduct that the ultimate good desired is better reached by free trade in ideas –that the best test of truth is the power of the thought to get itself accepted in the competition of the market, and that truth is the only ground upon which their wishes safely can be carried out. That, at any rate, is the theory of the Constitution. It is an experiment, as all life is an experiment. Every year if not every day we have to wager our salvation upon some prophecy based upon imperfect knowledge. While that experiment is a part of our system I think that we should be eternally vigilant against attempts to check the expression of opinions that

---

[177] Novick, p201, 328, 327, 472n70
[178] Novick, p307, 327-328

we loathe and believe to be fraught with death, unless they so imminently threaten immediate interference with the lawful and pressing purposes of the law that an immediate check is required to save the country."[179]

In 1925 in *Gitlow v. New York* Holmes dissented from the Court decision to enforce the censorship of anarchists and socialists. In the *Whitney v. California* case of 1927 Holmes again dissented against the Court decision to limit the free speech of communists. By his last year as a judge in 1931 Holmes, aged 91 years, had the Supreme Court behind him in supporting freedom of speech and freedom of the press.[180]

William Howard Taft was appointed to the Supreme Court in 1921 as Chief Justice. Formerly Taft had been the governor of the Philippines in 1901 and in 1904 he had been appointed by President Roosevelt as Secretary of War. In 1909 Taft was elected president. When Taft was appointed to be Chief Justice of the Supreme Court in 1921, he attempted to reform the Supreme Court and make it the most powerful branch of the government. This ran against Holmes' philosophy of a non-political court. Taft changed the Court so that the judges could pick and choose which cases they wanted to handle, whereas Holmes wished the Court to remain accessible as a Common Law court was meant to be.[181]

One of Holmes' most controversial opinions and one which has stained his legacy was his decision in the controversial 1927 case *Buck v. Bell*. Holmes, like many of his generation, had often believed in scientism, or the idea that the physical sciences offer the final and true description of reality. A position which came out of this scientific view of reality was something called 'eugenics' which was the idea that humans could be bred scientifically so as to perfect the race and eliminate crime. Both feminists and anarchists such as Charlotte Gilman and Emma Goldman had believed in the power of eugenics and in this context it should be no surprise that as the son of Harvard physician Holmes was aware of this scientific supposition. At the time a Virginia state law had held that a person could be scientifically found to be psychologically degenerate in such a way as to warrant sterilization. The case went to the Supreme Court and the opinion Holmes wrote strikes us today as a bit disturbing, though as we see it was shared by even the most 'radical', 'free', and 'pure' thinkers of his time. He wrote:

"We have seen more than once that the public welfare may call upon the best citizens for their lives. It would be strange if it could not call upon those who already sap the strength of the state for the lesser sacrifices, often not felt to be such by those concerned, in order to prevent our being swamped with incompetence. It is better for all the world, if instead of waiting to execute degenerate offspring for crime, or to let them starve for their imbecility, society can prevent those who are manifestly unfit from continuing their kind. The principle that sustains vaccination is broad enough to cover cutting the Fallopian tubes... Three generations of imbeciles are enough."

Despite the rhetoric of this opinion, Holmes went on to deliver very important dissents from the court regarding Civil Liberties and the check on executive power. When an immigrant woman named Rosika Schwimmer was denied citizenship because she was a pacifist, Holmes dissented. (*United States v. Schwimmer*, 1929)

When in the 1921 case of *Milwaukee Social Democratic Pub. Co. v. Burleson*, and in *Leach v. Carlile* in 1922. Holmes dissented against the Court decision to censure mail and publications. When in 1928 in *Olmstead v. United States* the Court decided that illegal wiretapping was okay, Holmes dissented writing that, "Apart from the

---

[179] Quoted in Novick, p331-332
[180] Check *Stromberg v. California* and *Near v. Minnesota*.
[181] Novick, p347

Constitution the government ought not to use evidence obtained, and only obtainable, by a criminal act... [F]or my part I think it a less evil that some criminals should escape than that the government should play an ignoble part."

Justice and Pluralism

Though we should not know what it was like to have fought in the Civil War or more probably, to have been a Justice or Chief Justice in the state and federal courts, Holmes' legacy is to be found in his pragmatist legal philosophy, which has inspired several jurisprudential and practical schools of thought. Legal Realism, as it has come to be called, closely resembles Holmes's legal philosophy. It too is predicated on the 'prediction theory of law' –of prophesizing what the courts and judges will actually decide, rather than taking formal laws and principles as fundamental. Legal Realism, like the pragmatism of Holmes is sociological and has thus been instrumental in rooting out the actual prejudices in the legal system that are based upon race, religion, class, or gender. Instead of obeying the idea that the laws of reason are fixed and innate, legal realists have revealed how such laws are used to oppress people based upon their gender, race, and class. Whereas minorities in a democracy could have little hope of changing legislation that is based upon the representation of the majority, Holmes has bequeathed a method by which people are able to use the law and the legal system to gain rights and the 'privileges' of equality.

Legal Realism has evolved into a legal practice called Critical Legal Studies. Critical Legal Studies is a new discipline that has helped theorists point out contradictions within the Common Law and make known several *aporiai* –places where the Common Law is inapplicable or tacit. This plays out in disputes between individuals and communities. These findings of Critical Legal Studies correspond to Holmes's own emphasis on community over ideology. Where the Common Law lends itself to a liberalism which highlights individual rights, the community and the environment become thought of as external. With the tradition of Holmes and Critical Legal Studies, the values of the community are weighed as collective goods, and this includes not just human well-being but the environment as well.

Still another legal philosophy to stem from the thought and practice of Holmes is called the Economic Theory of the Law, as used by Justice Richard Posner. Holmes had ended his lecture "The Path of the Law" by saying that, "every lawyer out to seek an understanding of economics. The present divorce between the schools of political economy and law seems to me an evidence of how much progress in philosophical study still remains to be made."[182] The Economic Theory of Law attempts to sponsor the application of the law in terms of a cost-benefit analysis, rather than the more religious judgement of guilt and innocence, or something non-social.

Two very revealing things that Holmes spoke about in "The Path of the Law" are his position on Tort Law and the development of law in general. Holmes held that "We have too little theory in the law rather than too much" and that "Theory is the most important part of the dogma of the law... The most important improvements of the last twenty-five years are improvements in theory."

---

[182] Holmes, "The Path of the Law", p164

"We do not realize how large a part of our law is open to reconsideration upon a slight change in the habit of the public mind. No concrete proposition is self evident, no matter how ready we may be to accept it, not even Mr. Herbert Spencer's 'Every man has a right to do what he wills, provided he interferes not with a like right on the part of his neighbor.'"[183]

One area that Holmes found in need of improvement, and which links him to Ralph Nader, is the emphasis on Tort. Ralph Nader is someone that has made wide use of Tort law. A tort is any wrong which occurs to a person that doesn't arise out of a contract. So basically, this area of law is immense as it covers all personal injuries, invasions of privacy, or things that happen outside the workplace. It is thus very connected with the virtues –something that is not typical to the Common Law.

Nader used the Tort law to fight against the mega-corporation General Motors when they hired a private investigator to spy on him and attempt to uncover something to tell the newspapers about Nader's personal life: that either he was paying female prostitutes or that he was a homosexual. Nader has used the Tort law again and again to fight corporations who were getting away with maintaining dangerous work areas and denying workers rights. Something which Nader has fought against again and again is "Tort reform" which is the corporate attempt to limit tort cases. So where a factory had been dumping toxic waste in the river and a number of babies were born with disabilities because the drinking water was contaminated –corporations want to limit how much compensation victims are entitled to receive according to a jury of their peers.

As Ralph Nader tells us –"There aren't too many lawsuits".[184] Very few people use the Tort system, if only because most people are kept ignorant of the law. We need to make the laws more available to people so that they can be part of the justice system. This is after-all a democracy. There is a movement called "the Plain English Campaign" which is a movement to make the law understandable by non-specialists so that our justice system is not run by bureaucrats but by the people. President Carter made an attempt to have the laws written in Plain English and in 1981 President Reagan had Carter's attempts revoked.[185]

The historian Howard Zinn has written of the strong affect that both the legislative and executive branches inevitably have on the judiciary. Accept for President Clinton who is considered by many to have been a moderate, in the last 30 years the US has been run by far right-wing conservatives. This began with the defeat of Carter.

"Reagan's victory, followed eight years later by the election of George Bush, meant that another part of the Establishment, lacking even the faint liberalism of the Carter presidency, would be in charge. The policies would be more crass –cutting benefits to poor people, lowering taxes for the wealthy, increasing the military budget, filling the federal court system with conservative judges, actively working to destroy revolutionary movements in the Caribbean.

"The dozen years of the Reagan-Bush presidency transformed the federal judiciary never more than moderately liberal, into a predominantly conservative institution. By the fall of 1991, Reagan and Bush had filled more than half of the 837 federal judgeships, and appointed enough right-wing justices to transform the Supreme Court"[186]

The Bush II administration was able to drastically change the judicial system and during his two terms the president was able to appoint two US Supreme Court Justices.

---

[183] Holmes, "The Path of the Law", p166, 168, 155
[184] Ralph Nader, "Tort 'Reform' Would Aid Wrongdoers", orig. pub. by the *San Francisco Examiner*, April, 21, 1995, from *The Ralph Nader Reader*, (New York, Seven Stories Press, 2000) p281
[185] Crystal, p377
[186] Zinn, (b) p561

During his 2nd term a scandal arose concerning a controversial plot to fire over 25% of the 93 United States attorneys. Between February of 2005 and December of 2006 nine US Attorneys were fired and a list surfaced revealing plans to fire 26 in total. Bush's Attorney General Alberto R. Gonzales testified to 8 of them before handing in his resignation in 2007.[187]

Speech Laws and Multi-Potency
Anarchist/socialist Noam Chomsky, a man who has been arrested on multiple occasions for assembling for a redress of grievances, has repeatedly declared America enjoys greater free speech than any other country in the world.[188] Our country was not designed that way by the Founding Fathers and it has taken a lot of struggle to get freedom of speech this far. In fact, it wasn't until the 1970's that Americans came to have the amount of free speech that we have now. Be that as it may, legislation over the last eight years has fought against the free speech movement with the government involved in illegal wiretapping and the USA PATRIOT Act enabling the government to profile, arrest, and censure regardless of civil liberties.[189]

As we saw with Holmes –in places he defended freedom of speech and in other places he voted for censorship. Are the individual rights of free speech more fundamental than the rights of the community, or is it vice versa? In our considerations of the right to free speech ought we to concentrate on personal justice? Or social justice? Or the justice of some religion? Which best promotes a just law of free speech? Chomsky seems to believe that if we take care of permitting and defending free speech, the common good will be maintained in the process.

Free speech was long defended by the pragmatist philosopher John Dewey. In his 1927 study, *The Public and Its Problems*, he had written:

"There can be no public without full publicity in respect to all consequences which concern it. Whatever obstructs and restricts publicity, limits and distorts public opinion and checks and distorts thinking on social affairs. Without freedom of expression, not even methods of social inquiry can be developed... [T]his application cannot occur save through free and systematic communication..."

John Dewey was not so naïve as to believe that the law has the last word on freedom of speech. He said, "The belief that thought and its communication are now free simply because legal restrictions which once obtained have been done away with is absurd."[190]

Dewey had long been a defender of free speech. When Bertrand Russell was barred from teaching mathematical logic at the City College of New York in 1940 because some Protestant Christians did not care for his tolerance of open marriages, John Dewey came to his defense, believing that the English pacifist Russell ought to be permitted to teach. Dewey wrote a piece defending Russell titled, "Social Realities *versus* Police Court Fictions". He also co-edited a book in defense of Russell, published in 1941, *The Bertrand Russell Case*. Dewey was 81 years old at the time, going on 82.

---

[187] Dan Eggen and Amy Goldstein, "Justice Weighed Firing 1 in 4", *Washington Post*, 5/17/07
[188] Noam Chomsky, "Freedom of Speech", *Understanding Power*, ed. Peter R. Mitchell and John Schoeffel, (New York, The New Press, 2002) p268-272
[189] See Nancy Chang's, *Silencing Political Dissent: How Post-September 11 Anti-Terrorism Measures Threaten Our Civil Liberties*, (New York, Seven Stories Press, 2002)
[190] John Dewey, *The Public and Its Problems*, (Athens, Ohio University Press, 1927) p167-168

Just the year before on his 80th birthday, he seemed prescient of the coming world war and cold war. He wrote:

> "For everything which bars freedom and fullness of communication sets up barriers that divide human beings into sets and cliques, into antagonistic sects and factions, and thereby undermines the democratic way of life. Merely legal guarantees of the civil liberties of free belief, free expression, free assembly are of little avail if in daily life freedom of communication, the give and take of ideas, facts, experiences, is choked by mutual suspicion, by abuse, by fear and hatred. These things destroy the essential condition of the democratic way of living even more effectually than open coercion, which –as the example totalitarian state proves –is effective only when it succeeds in breeding hate, suspicion, intolerance in the minds of individual human beings."[191]

Community Justice

One thing that we should not deceive ourselves over is the difference between free speech and hate speech. Being able to criticize the government and report injustice is a very different kind of thing from spreading a message of racism, sexism, homophobia, and hate. We may be against censorship but we might also be against those who spread lies or who plan on committing a crime, or who are just simple racists and homophobics spreading the message of jealousy, hate, and fear.[192]

Another example would be to cite the instance of cartoonists and artists who have drawn a picture purporting to be the prophet Muhammad. Such a thing is against the law where there is Shariah, but what should be the policy in America where Muslims make up a minority and the freedom of speech is lawful? One question which arises is whether we care to defend the law for people who are against the community? Is it reasonable if I didn't want my taxpayer dollars being used to protect the free speech of someone who cannot respect 25 percent of the world's population?

As a possible solution there is a sense in which it might be possible that the issues of freedom of speech ought to be more closely aligned with the Tort law. Tort law, as we have seen, deals with wrongs not arriving out of contract. Holmes argued against the tradition of the Common Law that held the law ought to only decide upon cased which are based upon contract and duty. Holmes believed that someday that small area of Tort ought to be increased and perhaps brought back to a pre-modern and more humanistic level. Holmes wrote:

> "Our law of torts comes from the old days of isolated, ungeneralized wrongs, assaults, slanders, and the like, where the damages might be taken to lie where they feel by legal judgement. But the torts with which our courts are kept busy to-day are mainly the incidents of certain well known businesses. They are injuries to person or property by railroads, factories, and the like. The liability for them is estimated, and sooner or later goes into the price paid by the public. The public really pays the damages, and the question of liability, if pressed far enough, is really the question how far it is desirable that the public should insure the safety of those whose work it uses... On the other hand, the economic value even of a life to the community can be estimated, and no recovery, it may be said, ought to go beyond that amount. It is conceivable that some day in certain cases we may find ourselves imitating, on a higher plane, the tariff for life and limb which we see in the *Leges Barbarorum*. [i.e., Medieval Law]"[193]

The kind of Tort reform which Holmes seems to be pointing at is the notion that we need the Common Law to begin covering interpersonal conflicts. This could cover

---

[191] John Dewey, "Creative Democracy –The Task Before Us", in *Classic American Philosophers*, ed. Max H. Fisch, (Englewood Cliffs, New Jersey, Prentice-Hall, Inc., 1951) p392-393
[192] Hans Kelsen wrote, "But the answer to the questions as to whether truth or freedom from fear is the higher value is not possible on the basis of a rational scientific consideration." (p188)
[193] Holmes, "The Path of the Law", p156

such things as racism, sexism, dishonesty, and defamation. So where someone has the right of free speech on the street to use racial epithets and to insult other bystanders, a Tort under Holmes conception could be used to legally fight against such bigotry. This may seem like small fries to some as we saw in chapter 3, honor, if not a virtue, plays an important role in the family and community. As any sociologist worth their salt will tell you, in every society there are codes of honor, which are not transmitted through written or verbal laws, are fundamental aspects to human social behavior.[194]

We can learn a lot from the laws of other cultures and peoples and see what works and what doesn't work. When a case is heard in court, it is very seldom that the victim or the victim's family can feel like they had a say in the justice which is determined. Though we might personally be against capital punishment, we should not always decide other peoples business when the justice that exists or does not exist is their business and not ours. Are we in a position to determine what best promotes justice –is it something personal, social, or religious?[195]

Can there exist many forms of justice along side one another? It seems that alongside such institutions of justice such as the state and supreme courts, another more immediate form of justice is needed.

Mark Twain (1835-1910) recounts in his autobiography how during the Civil War he had worked as the editor of newspaper in Nevada, called the *Territorial Enterprise*. He was 29 years old at the time. He recalls:

"In those early days dueling suddenly became a fashion in the new territory of Nevada and by 1864 everybody was anxious to have a chance in the new sport, mainly for the reason that he was not able to thoroughly respect himself so long as he had not killed or crippled somebody in a duel or been killed or crippled in one himself."[196]

Twain himself did all he could to avoid this battle of wits until his peers got the better of him and demanded he challenge the editor of another local newspaper. He was able to avoid the battle at the last moment, and because he was a lousy shot, he admitted that he escaped with his life. He wrote: "I have never had anything to do with duels since. I thoroughly disapprove of duels. I consider them unwise and I know they are dangerous."[197]

Surely today, more than a hundred years later when the 'wild west' is best identified with professional actors who pretend to shoot bullets, more people own guns. Guns are in a greater abundance today with the advances in manufacturing and distribution. On television and the cinema screen probably hundreds of thousands of people are gunned down each day. It is no wonder they are so popular today.

---

[194] A unique aspect of Scot's Law is 'Admonition', which is a punishment given to a guilty offender but which consists of a verbal warning and the offense is kept on the records.
[195] Martin Luther King, Jr., said that, "He who is devoid of the power to forgive is devoid of the power to love." (p48)
[196] Mark Twain, *The Autobiography of Mark Twain*, ed. Charles Neider, (New York, Perennial Library, 1975) p123. He continues, "I was ambitious in several ways but I had entirely escaped the seductions of that particular craze. I had had no desire to fight in a duel. I had no intention of provoking one. I did not feel respectable but I got a certain amount of satisfaction out of feeling safe. I was ashamed of myself, the rest of the staff were ashamed of me –but I got along well enough. I had always been accustomed to feeling ashamed of myself, for one thing or another, so there was no novelty for me in the situation. I bore it well."
[197] Twain, p129

Surely not every gun owner is the same frightened moron with his or her values based upon some meager code of honor. However, with the cult of the individual and the personalization of justice it seems more and more people are founding their values on fear. Those who threaten with guns and knives and violence in general are certainly among the greatest cowards and scum of the earth. Indeed it is hard to imagine any code of honor existing today given the prevalence of fear here generated. There is a chasm where individuality is extolled and justice is institutionalized.

One part of law that perhaps has not been explored enough is the general area of adjudication. To adjudicate means to judge, but as a school of jurisprudence it is akin to arbitration and other social forms of justice. Adjudication can be taken to mean justice through consent. For example, once Socrates was given the verdict of his guilt, he still had the chance to adjudicate a just penalty. And while the court did not agree with him, we might examine here more closely the possibility of extending some social principal of judgment that is similar, if more fair.

We should expand and combine the notions of Adjudication and Tort. Through combining adjudication and tort we might bring justice back to the people and bring back the social aspect of justice. Here justice occurs where there is no contract dispute or use of an outside party. People come together and if possible, determine justice in a social setting. Here the law and justice become more closely aligned with the values of the community.

Though the United States may or many not be an empire, the tendency of the modern state seems to politicize justice and bureaucratize it. Justice becomes more and more inaccessible to the people. Its not that American judges wear robes and wigs, but their area of expertise and experience is often foreign to the people and issues at hand. Through adjudication, however, it is the people who can argue and settle cases. Knowledge of the law would have value to all people and justice would become for everyone something familiar and worth fighting for. While we should admit that not everyone is trained in logic, ethics, economics, or the law, and agreement is not always to be reached, we run the risk of losing the public in questions of justice if we continue to bureaucratically institutionalize justice.[198]

One thing that we can see is emerging, albeit as a sport, is informal or multi-formed fighting. This is to be found in sports like Ultimate Fighting Championship and Mixed Martial Arts and others. These seem like a model that could be used, albeit not as a sport, but as a consensual method of settling disputes. While we should avoid Hollywood glamorization of 'fight clubs' and I personally do not enjoy watching people fight, these are models which can be used in an adjudicative case where there is consent. Such judicial battles could help to minimize class war, gang warfare, and perhaps will bring a sense of honor back to our society, before it is beyond being praiseworthy. We need to stop thinking of justice as something not available to humans, and more along the

---

[198] Hans Kelsen writes that, "The desire for justice is so elementary , and so deeply rooted in the human mind, because it is a manifestation of man's indestructible desire for his own subjective happiness." He says, "The particular moral principle involved in a relativistic philosophy of justice is the principle of tolerance, and that means the sympathetic understanding of the religious or political beliefs of others – without accepting them, but not preventing them from being freely expressed. It stands to reason that no absolute tolerance can be commended by a relativistic philosophy of values; only tolerance within an established legal order guaranteeing peace by prohibiting and preventing the use of force among those subjected to the order, but not prohibiting or preventing the peaceful expression of ideas." (p185, 203)

lines of thinking of it as the greatest virtue, something that ought to be the concern of all people.

In keeping the judicial process amidst the community and the needs of the people we will keep justice from being overly politicized. Though the penalty may never fit the crime according to state justice, a community justice will come closer to realizing what people deserve. Community justice will also steer clear of becoming antipolitical, which is a main problem with big states and empires, where the many are disaffected. As it is, a faith in political-coercion in our democratic society has had adverse effects upon our justice system. This is evidenced in the prison industrial complex where wealthy nations are able to imprison rather than address the roots of social conflict. In what way does our current political faith justify the suffering of others? To this question we turn.

7

The Politics of Faith and the Justification of Suffering

400 years ago the great English bard William Shakespeare played on a paradox in his comedy, *Twelfth Night, or What You Will*. This paradox will no doubt strike many as being somewhat of a cynical and immoral observation. The dialogue is between the Countess Olivia, who is mourning the death of her brother, and Feste the Clown, who is the court jester. When Feste begins to annoy the Countess, she tells the attendants to, "Take the fool away." However, the clown protests considerably, and works his trickery.

> *Feste*: Good madonna, why mournest thou?
> *Olivia*: Good fool, for my brother's death.
> *Feste*: I think his soul is in hell, madonna.
> *Olivia*: I know his soul is in heaven, fool.
> *Feste*: The more fool, madonna, to mourn for your brother's soul, being in heaven.
>   Take away the fool, gentleman. (Act I, Scene 5)

We see in this dialogue between the Countess and the Jester that Shakespeare is playing on a paradox.[1] A paradox is something that seems contradictory or against common sense but which may in fact be the case or in some sense be true. The paradox that Feste the Clown points out is the seemingly psychological contradiction of mourning death while maintaining faith in immortality. Surely this perspective will strike us as cynical, or at least a bit strange.[2] Be that as it may, these fictional characters drawn up by Shakespeare were divined some 50 years after the death of King Henry VIII (1491-1547), one of the most influential if ignoble of monarchs.

Around the time that Shakespeare lived (1564-1616) there was a civil war of sorts, or splintering, happening across Europe. This period of European history is generally called by historians the 'Protestant Reformation', which was the second greatest schism to occur in Christianity, after the split between the East and West in 1054, between the Greek and Latin churches. Two years after Shakespeare's death the Thirty-Years War would begin (1618-1648), which was a scattered war of church and state, resulting in the deaths of millions of Europeans.[3]

Roughly between the time of Constantine in the year 312 to the time of this reformation in the 16th century, there had been one empire ruling over Europe –the Holy Roman Empire.[4] Although it had become particularly weak at the time, a monk named

---

[1] My thanks to the Shakespeare scholar Andrew Barnaby for discussing this passage.
[2] This is the attitude which led the courts to decide in favor of executing the protagonist in Albert Camus', *L'Estranger*
[3] Norman Davies puts the population of Germany by the end of the Thirty Years War as having decreased by 7 or 8 million, in *Europe: A History*, (New York, HarperCollins, 1996) p568
[4] With intermittent rises and falls including the Eastern European Byzantine Empire based in Constantinople. (Davies, p242)

Martin Luther (1483-1546) believed breaking away from the Church was politically crucial in 1517. He was soon followed by many others, most notably the preacher John Calvin (1509-1564), and King Henry VIII. These apostasies from the church probably happened for more than one reason, though state-building and nationalism were possibly at the top of the list. With this rise of nationalism was a resurgent faith in the Divine Right of Kings.

Luther believed there were exactly ninety-five reasons for breaking away from the church, a chief one being the 'sale of indulgences'. An indulgence was a tax one could pay to the Church to guarantee one's place in heaven after dying. Luther believed this practice of selling indulgences was wrong. To the contemporary ear this may sound like nit-picking, when the practice of selling 'indulgences' is now televised. Luther, however, took it very personally and was compelled to proclaim the good news that Christians could achieve salvation through faith in Jesus alone. Luther called this ideology 'Justification by Faith', because after the diet of worms he physically "couldn't have done otherwise".

Almost 500 years later and the concept of 'Justification by Faith' is still a popular ideology. Its origin as a protest against an empire, however, is now one of support. The 'Justification by Faith' has become the justification for the status-quo, for the powers that be, for the Divine Right of Kings, rulers, and whatever cannot be questioned, interpreted, or understood. These are declared righteous. The role today of this justification by faith is one of complicity, unquestioning obedience, and a plucking of the eyes out of human reason.

'Justification' is a concept found variously in logic, mathematics, ethics, and jurisprudence and has two basic functions: one that is ethical and one that is epistemological. Epistemology is the study of knowledge, of how we as humans come to know things. When someone is 'epistemically justified' it means they have warranted knowledge, or justified true belief. Epistemology answers the question, "what is the relationship between belief and knowledge?"

Some believe that it isn't illegal to be naked in the Vermont Green Mountains. When that Vermonter actually goes outside naked in public and is not arrested (or if they just simply read the law), they would have epistemic justification. Similarly, if someone is 'ethically justified' their action or behavior is warranted or justified as right and correct. So, for example, someone may believe their being naked outdoors will not offend their neighbor. When they actually go outside and their neighbor is not upset, there is ethical justification.

Because 'Justification by Faith' is an 'answer', though not to questions of knowledge or ethics, the phrase ought to be understood as being a piece of rhetoric. Rhetoric isn't necessarily a bad thing and can, when properly used, be a kind of fertilizer. In this case, 'Justification by Faith' is used in order to guarantee oneself one's own salvation. The phrase 'Justification by Faith' might thus be correctly reworded as 'Sanctification by Faith'.[5]

Under the conditions that call for such a Justification, it seems knowledge and ethics are damnable states of affairs, and all that matters is a belief in one's rightful place in the next life. The need for this type of justification, or proof to oneself or to others of

---

[5] Following William Hasker in *The Cambridge Dictionary of Philosophy*, Second Edition, ed. Robert Audi, (Cambridge, Cambridge University Press, 1999) p458

one's posthumous status, seems to imply something about one's own sense of strength as well as something about one's own sense of place in this world. One is tempted to think that the reality of this world must be of some disagreement if it requires such a leap of faith to achieve justification of sanctity. What is apparent in the claim of 'Justification by Faith' is that something about the world or about the nature of humans is bad or is much worse. One must seek redemption from the world that is given, from nature. Also seemingly implicit in this attitude is the belief that damnation is a normal state of affairs and only one particular belief can redeem or excuse us from this false "reality". It is perplexing how seldom people stop to think about what a lack of faith is demonstrated by this need for rhetorical affirmation, or sanctification by faith.

In fairness, it should be said that this claim of 'Justification by Faith' was originally intended to be in contradistinction to a caricature made of Catholicism labeled, 'Justification by Works'. For Protestants, Catholic justification came by way of the Church, a Priest, or through paying the indulgence tax. Catholics, however, have believed justification is made possible through a belief in the sinful nature of humans, and a hope of God's mercy through the sincerity of faith.[6]

A famous version of the justification by faith is found in 'Pascal's wager'. The 17th century mathematician and philosopher Blaise Pascal wanted to demonstrate the truth of Christianity, or at least induce others to adopt a believing attitude of its truth. He used a demonstration to show that, even if one were convinced that something was false, one still had a choice to believe it was true. One could either believe in its truth with the possibility of being rewarded posthumously or one could doubt its truth in which case there was no reward either way. Add to this the persuasiveness of possible eternal damnation. Pascal wagered, therefore, it is better to believe in its truth. It is uncertain how many people have been converted by this argument alone. Pascal once said, "The heart has its reasons, of which reason is ignorant".[7]

One of the most influential "sermons" on the 'Justification by Faith' was given by the physician, psychologist and pragmatist philosopher William James in his lecture, *The Will to Believe*. (1896) Although James mentions his "common sense" preference for Protestantism, he tells us he really means "an essay in justification *of* faith, a defense of our right to adopt a believing attitude in religious matters…"[8]

James says that our duty as would-be knowers is to both "believe truth" and "shun error". Such is the nature of reason, these two points on a compass. Occasionally, however, there are dilemmas that occur wherein the truth cannot be determined and yet one must still choose. For example, one might wonder if it is better to run their car on vegetable oil or if they ought to use bio-diesel, or whether we should be religious or not. Depending upon who you are, James argues, you might in your life be faced with such a dilemma, as for example: 'Be an agnostic or be a Christian' or 'Be a theosophist or be a Mohammedan [Muslim]'. According to James, "Every dilemma based on a complete logical disjunction, with no possibility of not choosing, is an option of this forced kind."

---

[6] Hasker, p458
[7] Quoted in Bertrand Russell's, *A History of Western Philosophy*, (New York, Simon and Schuster, 1945) (a) p691
[8] William James, "The Will to Believe", in *Essays in Pragmatism*, ed. Alburey Castell, (New York, Hafner Publishing Co., Inc., 1948) p88

This "freedom to believe can only cover living options which the intellect of the individual cannot by itself resolve."[9]

One of the main features of James's argument is his reliance on and inflation of the 'disjunctive syllogism'. A syllogism is a kind of reasoning or analysis that deduces a conclusion from two premises. So, for example, the classical logical form 'Barbara' can be stated as: a) Socrates is man; b) All men are mortal; c)Therefore Socrates is Mortal.

A *disjunctive* syllogism is a bit simpler however, and can be stated as an either/or: *either a or b, not a; therefore b.* An example of a disjunctive syllogism might be, "He who is not for me is against me." One is left to wonder what purpose there is to the reasoning faculty of the mind when ethics is reduced to such simple black and white terms.

While this duality may seem rather benign and innocent in the care of the self, taken into the realm of ethics and politics there are some fairly drastic consequences in this justification by faith. Such an example is the creed of the Divine Right of Kings, a belief that gives unlimited political authority to someone who may not be infallible. The mathematician and philosopher Bertrand Russell made note of this slippery slope in his study on "The Ancestry of Fascism":

> "Poor William James, who invented this point of view, would be horrified at the use to which is made of it; but when once the conception of objective truth is abandoned, it is clear that the question, 'what shall I believe?' is one to be settled... by 'the appeal to force and the arbitrament of the big battalions,' not by the methods of either theology or science."[10]

As it turns out, not all dilemmas are so tidy and discreet as choosing between two ineffable futures. In fact, many ethical dilemmas are not simplistic at all. In a world with many choices it is possible that these neat instances (or conceptualizations) of either/or reasoning are both fallacious and unrealistic. This type of fallacious reasoning is known as a false dichotomy, where we are told there are only two options –this or that. But in fact there aren't just dilemmas in life but trilemmas and fourway-lemmas, etc...[11]

James seems to be committed to a theory of the self in which everyone is equally ignorant in ethical matters. He never suggests the possibility of appealing to a friend, teacher, or a book to find answers to a lack of one's faith or justification. What is more, adopting this belief places no burden on the inductee. One so justified with this facile piety no longer searches the truth, or reasons, or reflects, or pursues justice for that matter in order to ensure their own salvation.

An important problem with James's *Will to Believe,* as we see, is the blatant disregard for the reasoning faculty in the mind. It is the sole purpose of reason to identify truth and shun error, nothing more. Accordingly, it is illogical to think that reason has other roles. Everything else is a matter of faith –reason is defied by augury. As Russell puts it, "...strange to say, James, throughout his essay, never mentions probability, and yet there is almost always some discoverable consideration of probability in regard to any

---

[9] James, p89, 108
[10] Bertrand Russell, "The Ancestry of Fascism", in *The Will to Doubt,* (New York, Philosophical Library, Inc., 1958) p102
[11] My thanks to the philosopher and logician William Mann who introduced me to decision theory and the study of ethical dilemmas.

question."[12] Reasoning upon probability and likelihood is called inductive logic. With induction it is determined if the conclusions one arrives at are based upon the strength of reason, whereas with the syllogistic or deductive logic that James employs the conclusion always follows necessarily. This is why James' either/or forced decision appears so contrived and artificial: it is based on the assumption that reason is predicated upon mutual exclusion and not in the determination of what is greater according to reason, but according to force.

Because James considered himself to be a 'radical empiricist', he believes truth is something internal or psychological. Traditionally, the English philosophy of empiricism held that that people (or subjects) are born like a blank slate, or in Latin, *tabula rasa.* Through experience, people learn about the external world (which is objective). This is the traditional empiricist formulation that knowledge comes through experience. James was influential in his critique of this traditional or non-radical empiricism, which was overly-dependent upon the separation of subject and object, which is a kind of dualism. For James, talk of personal or 'pure experience' ought to replace talk of what is 'ineliminabley' subjective, namely 'consciousness'. For James', consciousness is not an entity but a function.[13] Instead of consciousness, 'Pure Experience' is the "only one primal stuff…in the world… of which everything is composed".[14] It is the Will that is the theater of this Pure experience.

Reason's role in determining truths thus becomes relegated to the will. Will says of truth, that it has "cash value". That is, James ostensibly believes that truth is just an instrument. He says that truths have "only this quality in common, that they *pay.*"[15] This psychological theory of truth is also called, 'mentalism' –the belief that justification is internally produced, independent of our environment.

It is typical of this 'psychologism' to not lend much credence to the various forms of logic. This is because the principal method of psychology is reduction, which is a form of deduction. Psychology is based upon the presupposition of there being a certain human nature that all behavior is representative of or reducible to –otherwise, what are

---

[12] Russell, *A History of Western Philosophy*, (a) p815. Russell goes on to say, "James's doctrine is an attempt to build a superstructure of belief upon a foundation of scepticism, and like all such attempts it is dependent on fallacies. In his case the fallacies spring from an attempt to ignore all extra-human facts."

[13] In 1904 James described 'Radical Empiricism' thus, "To be radical, an empiricism must neither admit into its constructions any element that is not directly experienced, nor exclude from them any element that is directly experienced." How this rules out solipcism is unclear. From, "A World of Pure Experience", from *The Works of William James –Essays in Radical Empiricism,* ed. Frederick Burkhardt, (Cambridge, Harvard University Press, 1976). Reprinted in *Pragmatism and Classical American Philosophy*, Second Edition, ed. John J. Stuhr, (Oxford, Oxford University Press, 2000) p182

[14] William James, "Does 'Consciousness' Exist?", orig. published in *Journal of Philosophy*, 1:477-491, Sept. 1, 1904. Reprinted in *Classical American Philosophers*, ed. Max Fisch, (Englewood Cliffs, Prentice-Hall, Inc., 1951) p148

[15] William James, "Pragmatism's Conception of Truth", from *Pragmatism. A New Name for Some Old Ways of Thinking*, Lecture VI (New York, 1907). Reprinted in *Essays in Pragmatism*, p168.

The philosopher Stephen Stich has written of James' instrumentalist or 'cash value' theory of truth, "A consequence of this proposal is that there is yet another sort of relativism lurking in our questions about the goodness or badness of reasoning, a relativism that turns on the purpose of the inquiry." Stephen P. Stich, "A Pragmatic Account of Cognitive Evaluation", *The Fragmentation of Reason*, (Cambridge, MIT Press, 1990). Reprinted in *Naturalizing Epistemology*, Second Edition, ed. Hilary Kornblith, (Cambridge, MIT Press, 1994) p422. My thanks to Hilary Kornblith for suggesting and discussing this essay with me.

we talking about? Such theories seem to posit some kind of psychological foundation that is fundamental and prior to the rational mind of the individual.

As Russell put it in the, *The Ancestry of Fascism*:

"Now the characteristic doctrines of modern irrationalists, as we have seen, are: emphasis on *will* as opposed to thought and feeling; glorification of power; belief in intuitional 'positing' of propositions as opposed to observational and inductive testing."[16]

Moreover, such reductions put into doubt any relationship between knowledge and ethics. Typically, it is held that do what is good one must know what the good is. Even for those who are less radical than James, empiricists typically hold that there is a disjunction between knowledge and ethics. James refers to this separation as being one between reason and faith. Science is what is provable or knowable while faith and morality are dependent upon the devotion of the will. For James, like many 18th, 19th and 20th century thinkers, the foundation that all psychology can be reduced to is the 'Will'.[17]

In philosophies based upon empiricism and, and its economic counterpart, utilitarianism, the good is construed variously as something purely instrumental, personal, subjective, and arbitrarily formalized. With a definition of human nature, be it that of a blank slate or of one pre-designed, ethics becomes subordinated or secondary. Because of the dogma that knowledge is gained only through experience, there is a sense in which each person is self-invented and self-transparent, so it is no wonder that this self is so righteous. Reality becomes a construction of the self. In its most radical form, this attitude posits an omnipotent will of seemingly insatiable desire, isolation, and consumption – a game of survival in a world of finite resources and commodities. Ethics becomes a pretense and instrument of power.

When James called himself "a radical empiricist" he is saying of a person that all their character and knowledge are gained through experience by the always choosing will. There is an important if unfortunate result then for empiricists in which they believe that in a sense, reality is a construct of the Will. Taken to an extreme, this can lead to a philosophy like that of the pessimist Arthur Schopenhauer who said in the opening lines of his thesis, *The World as Will and Representation*, "Knowledge is subordinate to the Will."

James should be understood then in *The Will to Believe*, as holding that we always choose what we believe. This has some rather drastic results when we consider the problem of suffering. Does pain exist? Do people only die, as Edgar Allen Poe held in *Ligeia*, from a weakness of the will? Let us consider the problem of suffering.

The Problem of Suffering

Job was a righteous man who praised God (or in Hebrew, *Yhwh*) and refrained from doing bad. Upon the prompting of an accuser who claimed that all humans are

---

[16] Russell, "The Ancestry of Fascism", (b) p98

[17] To do some name dropping and show how wide this psychologistic prejudice is found: empiricists such as the Irish-Catholic Bishop Berkeley (1685-1753) and the Scottish-agnostic David Hume (1711-1776), Protestant and Catholic Christian existentialists such as the Danish Soren Kierkegaard (1813-1855) and the German Martin Heidegger (1889-1976), as well as French atheist-existentialist Jean-Paul Sartre (1905-1980), and German atheists such as Arthur Schopenhauer (1788-1860) and Friedrich Nietzsche (1844-1900) have all held the Will to be fundamental.

equally corruptible, Yhwh tested Job –allowing the killing his children, his livestock, and the infesting of Job with pestilence. As Job suffers inexplicably (not knowing the will of God) his friends tell him that he must have done something bad in order to deserve such a condition. They say to the effect that 'he must have had it coming to him', as the popular phrase goes. Job's friends are often called 'Job's comforters' with some irony, because of their lack of sympathy or compassion for his suffering.

The 'Problem of Suffering' is as ancient as life itself, but stated as such comes either from Christian theology or its critics. The problem can be simply stated: if God is good, why is there suffering? Historically Christian theologians have dealt with this in several ways and explanations have varied. Some say that suffering exists because of Original Sin, others say suffering exists because of the Devil or because of evil, and still others say that suffering exists because, without it, humans could not know its opposite: the good. The attempts to explain human nature as faulty while defending or justifying the goodness of God is called, *theodicy*.

Theodicy

While it should by necessity not be a crime if someone believes their own suffering or sickness is the result of their sins or lack of faith, we must ask –Can such explanations of suffering inevitably work to justify the suffering of others? Could it be the case that in theodicy, faith and politics come together and ultimately work to justify the suffering, sickness, or death of other people? Immanuel Kant makes this argument in a lesser known yet important essay titled "Of the Miscarriage of all Philosophical Trials in Theodicy", and Emmanuel Levinas makes a similar argument in a rare essay, "Useless Suffering."[18]

We saw in the opening dialogue between Feste and Olivia that the fool chides the Countess for mourning her brother's death while maintaining that he is in heaven. The Pious Lutheran philosopher Immanuel Kant was very concerned with this type of vacuous ethics and saw his goal as combating the philosophy of empiricism, which he called "scandalous". From his grave we can hear Kant's reply to James' *Will to Believe.*

"Hence, if someone says to himself (or –what is one and the same in religious professions –before God) that *he believes,* without perhaps casting even a single glimpse into himself –whether he is in fact conscious of thus holding a truth or at least of holding it to some degree –then such a person *lies.* And not only is his lie the most absurd (before a readers of hearts): it is also the most sinful, for it undermines the ground of every virtuous intention."[19]

For Kant there is no subordination of the reasoning mind to faith, no primacy of faith over morals. To the contrary, Kant believed faith was a kind of reason and a very important kind at that. Kant's reply to the story of Job is revealing on this point.

---

[18] I'm indebted to Paul Davies essay, "Sincerity and the end of theodicy: three remarks on Levinas and Kant", in *The Cambridge Companion to Levinas*, ed. Simon Critchley and Robert Bernasconi, (Cambridge, Cambridge University Press, 2002) p161-187.

[19] Immanuel Kant, "On the miscarriage of all philosophical trials in theodicy", in *Religion Within the Boundaries of Mere Reason and Other Writings,* trans. and ed. Allen Wood and George d. Giovanni, (Cambridge, Cambridge University Press, 1998) p28

"For with this disposition [Job] proved that he did not found his morality on faith, but his faith on morality: in such a case, however weak this faith might be, yet it alone is of a pure and true kind, i.e., the kind of faith that founds not a religion of supplication, but a religion of good life conduct."[20]

Although the word *theodicy* comes from two Greek words *theos* or God and *dike* or justice, one of the first uses of this concept was perhaps made by the mathematician and philosopher Gottfried Leibniz in his treatise *Theodicy*, written in 1710. A short quote should suffice:

"Since all possible things have a claim to existence in God's understanding in proportion to their perfections, the result of all these claims must be the most perfect actual world which is possible."[21]

In brief: if God is good, perfect, and all-knowing then this must be the best of all possible worlds. In a famous response, the great French satirist Voltaire makes use of Leibniz's proof. "Candide, stunned, stupefied, despairing, bleeding, trembling, said to himself: -'If this is the best of all possible worlds, what are the others like?"[22]

The philosopher Emmanuel Levinas expands on Kant's argument in his essay, *Useless Suffering*.

"Western humanity has none the less sought for the meaning of this scandal by invoking the proper sense of a metaphysical order, an ethics, which is invisible in the immediate lessons of moral consciousness. This is a kingdom of transcendent ends, willed by a benevolent wisdom, by the absolute goodness of a God who is in some way defined by this super-natural goodness, or a widespread, invisible goodness in Nature and History, where it would command the paths which are, to be sure, painful, but which lead to the Good. Pain is henceforth meaningful, subordinated in one way or another to the metaphysical finality envisaged by faith or by a belief in progress. These beliefs are presupposed by theodicy! Such is the grand idea necessary to the inner peace of souls in our distressed world. It is called upon to make suffering comprehensible. These will make sense by reference to an original fault or to the congenital finitude of human being. The evil which fills the earth would be explained in a 'plan of the whole'; it would be called upon to atone for a sin, or it would announce, to the ontologically limited consciousness, compensation or recompense at the end of time. These supra-sensible perspectives are invoked in order to envisage in a suffering which is essentially gratuitous and absurd, and apparently arbitrary, a signification and an order"[23]

Because theodicy is presupposed by the belief that there is one God who is all-good and all-knowing: omnibenevolent and omniscient, the problem of suffering becomes unsolvable, or as Levinas writes, "…it makes waiting for the saving action of an all-powerful God impossible without degradation."[24]

When someone justifies another's suffering, they believe that suffering is a tool or method with which to teach others. Ethics becomes subordinated to power or force. The philosopher Walter Kaufmann teaches us that, "…having to use means to achieve ends is one of the features that distinguishes limited power from omnipotence."[25] In other words, if the suffering of others is justified as necessary to achieve some end, then God cannot be both omnipotent and omnibenevolent, without also being vulgar. But this is blasphemy, according to theodicy.

---

[20] Kant, p26
[21] Quoted by David Blumenfeld, "Perfection and happiness in the best possible world", in *The Cambridge Companion to Leibniz*, ed. Nicholas Jolley, (New York, Cambridge University Press, 1995) p382
[22] Voltaire's *Candide*, quoted by Blumenfeld, p382
[23] Emmanuel Levinas, "Useless Suffering", trans. by Richard Cohen, in *The Provocation of Levinas: Rethinking the Other*, ed. Robert Bernasconi and David Wood; (London, Routledge Classics, 1988) p160-161.
[24] Levinas, p159
[25] Walter Kaufmann, "Suffering and the Bible", in *The Faith of a Heretic*, (Garden City, New York, Anchor Books, 1963) p162

Levinas, however, is also concerned with the *end* of theodicy, or the belief that suffering is for nothing. If theodicy can be unethical, so can the declaration of its impossibility. Levinas asks,

"But does not this end of theodicy... at the same time in a more general way reveal the unjustifiable character of suffering in the other person, the scandal which would occur by my justifying my neighbor's suffering? So that the very phenomenon of suffering in its uselessness is, in principle the pain of the Other. For an ethical sensibility –confirming itself, in the inhumanity of our time, against this inhumanity –the justification of the neighbor's pain is certainly the source of all immorality."[26]

Levinas claims that "theodicy... is as old as a certain reading of the Bible."[27] Interestingly, the three Abrahamic religions–Judaism, Christianity, and Islam –deal with the problems of suffering, sickness, and death differently.

Judaism and Suffering

We find in the Torah that Yhwh has brought pain to women because of Eve's transgressions. "Unto the woman He said; 'I will greatly multiply thy pain and thy travail; in pain thou shalt bring forth children..."[28] (Genesis 3:16) In Genesis Yhwh "plagues" the Pharaoh and his house, until he releases Abraham's wife, whom Pharaoh had been misled to believe was actually Abe's sister. (12:17) Seven chapters later an angry mob is blinded and are not able to find the door to get at Lot's daughters. (19:11) When Yhwh destroys the city of Sodom, Lot is permitted to escape while it rains fire and sulfur. (19:24) In Exodus we find that Yhwh has empowered Moses and Aaron who are able to plague the pharaoh's sorcerers with volitions of gnats and gadflies (8:17, 24), then boils and blains (9:9), then hail and fire storms (9:24), then locusts (10:12), and then three days of darkness (10:22).

In the book of Exodus Yhwh says to Moses that if he obeys the Lord, and does what is right, following Yhwh's commandments, and keeping Yhwh's statutes "I will put none of the diseases upon thee, which I have put upon the Egyptians". (15:26) Under the same formula, none shall be barren or miscarry either. (23:25) Hornets will be sent to protect Yhwh's faithful. (23:28) Aaron wears a band upon his head to bear the iniquity of the people. (28:38) Yhwh's calls himself "merciful and gracious, long-suffering, and abundant in goodness and truth, keeping mercy unto the thousandth generation, forgiving iniquity and transgression and sin" (34:6-7)

For those who don't do all of the commandments, who rejects the statutes and ordinances, as well as break the covenant, one will be stricken with terror, consumption, fever, and blindness. (Leviticus 26:16) In the book of Numbers some people eat flesh, which is something that is forbidden, and are smote with plague. (11:33) Miriam is temporarily made a leper (12:10) and later thousands die from plague. (17:14)

In Deuteronomy it says that if one hearkens to the ordinances, and keeps the covenant, Yhwh will take away all sickness. (7:15, 28:59) If you are bad, Yhwh will curse you with pestilence, fever, consumption (28:22), itches (28:27), as well as madness. (28:28) Yhwh says, "And there is no god with Me; I kill, and I make alive; I have wounded, and I heal; and there is none that can deliver out of My hand." (32:39)

---

[26] Levinas, p163
[27] Levinas, p161
[28] All references to the Torah are translations from the Masocretic Text, (Philadelphia, The Jewish Publication Society of America, 1917)

Christianity and Suffering
In the New Testament, written some 1500 years after the Torah, a concept called 'Original Sin' emerges as the essence of human psychology and physiology. Both sickness and death are the result of sin and no human is immune, except those who have faith in Jesus. In fact, we find in the New Testament there is a relationship between sickness and sin. Whenever someone is sick, or blind, or paralyzed it is because they are sinners.

"And when Jesus saw their faith he said to the paralytic: 'Child, your sins are forgiven."[29] (Mark 2:5) "But in order for you men to know that the Son of man has authority to forgive sins upon the earth,' he said to the paralytic: 'I say to you, Get up, pick up your cot, and go to your home." (Mark 2:10-11. This also happens in Matthew 9:1-8, and Luke 5:17-26)

What is more, when someone dies, it is because they were sinners. "For the wages sin pays is death, but the gift God gives is everlasting life by Christ Jesus our Lord." (Romans 6:23) "The sting producing death is sin, but the power for sin is the Law." (1Corinthians 15:56) Jesus tells people, "you will die in your sin." (John 8:21) "If anyone observes my word, he will never see death at all." (John 8:51)

Throughout much of the New Testament we discover Jesus traveling from city to city curing many people's sickness. He heals lepers as well as paralytics, making the blind see. However, there is more than one occasion upon which Jesus refuses to save or give assistance. Consider Lazarus.

After Jesus was 'greased' and 'perfumed' by Mary and her sister Martha, they ask Jesus to cure their brother Lazarus. But Jesus refuses saying, "This sickness is not with death as its object, but is for the glory of God, in order that the Son of God may be glorified through it." (John 11:4) A couple of days later Jesus reports to the sisters, "Lazarus has died, and I rejoice on your account that I was not there, in order for you to believe. But let us go to him." (John 11:14-15) When Jesus and Martha get to the tomb she says, "Lord, by now he must smell, for he has been dead four days." (John 11:39) And only after the man's suffering and death does Jesus, believing now that God is glorified, care for Lazarus.

Although Jesus is said to have '*cured* many of sin' and to have exercised many demons and evil spirits from people, he rejects a gentile woman who's daughter was "heavily demonized". When she asks Jesus for help, he refuses saying, "I was not sent forth to any but the lost sheep of the house of Israel." (Matthew 15:24) Only when she converts to his religion does he rid her daughter of demons. A similar scene occurs in Mark's gospel (7:24). A Greek woman whose daughter is possessed by a demon, asks Jesus for his help. At first Jesus is reluctant to rid a woman's daughter of a demon. Only once she tells Jesus something about eating crumbs off the floor does he change his mind and exercise the demon.

In the Acts, when a certain man, Ananias, does not give all of his money to Peter but only some of it, the Apostle condemns him and he immediately dies. (Acts 5:5) Those who are sick are oppressed by the Devil. (Acts 10:38) King Herod is eaten up by worms and killed because a crowd of people believed that he was God. (Acts 12:23 -or are 'Nonbelievers' killed?)

---

[29] All references from the New Testament are translations by New World Bible Translation Committee, (Brooklyn, Watchtower Bible and Tract Society of New York, Inc., 1961)

Another instance of the justification of suffering is in Jesus' attitude toward the violence of others. For example, in the Gospel according to Mark, Jesus stands by as a Priest's ear is cut off. Jesus seems only concerned with his own safety when his response to this violence is: "Did you come out with swords and clubs as against a robber to arrest me?" (Mark 14:48) When one of Jesus' companions cuts off the priests ears in the gospel of Matthew, Jesus is more assertive: "Return your sword to its place, for all those who take the sword will perish by the sword. Or do you think that I cannot appeal to my Father to supply me at this moment more than twelve legions of angels?" (Matthew 26:52-53) Peter cuts off the right ear of a Priest's slave named Malchus. To this action Jesus says, "Put the sword into sheath. The cup that the Father has given me, should I not by all means drink it?" (John 18:10-11) Its only in the Gospel of Luke when someone strikes the ear off a slave that Jesus heals the man, though he does justify the event saying, "Let it go as far as this." (Luke 22:50-51)

Paul tells the Thessalonians to not mourn the death of others.

"Moreover, brothers, we do not want you to be ignorant concerning those who are sleeping [in death]; that you may not sorrow just as the rest also do who have no hope. For if our faith is that Jesus died and rose again, so, too, those who have fallen asleep [in death] through Jesus God will bring with him. For this is what we tell you by God's word, that we the living who survive to the presence of the Lord shall in no way precede those who have fallen asleep [in death]; because the Lord himself will descend from heaven with a commanding call, with an archangel's voice and with God's trumpet, and those who are dead in union with Christ will rise first. Afterward we the living who are surviving will, together with them, be caught away in clouds to meet the Lord in the air; and thus we shall always be with [the] Lord. Consequently keep comforting one another with these words." 1 Thessalonians 4:13-18

There is also a great abundance of occasions in which the writers of the New Testament warn the reader that suffering is necessary for salvation. Just a brief reference should suffice: "Consequently I reckon that the sufferings of the present season do not amount to anything in comparison with the glory that is going to be revealed to us." (Romans 8:18) The sufferings of Jesus are seen as a model to be worshiped and imitated, and the tradition is rich with martyrdom.

Islam and Suffering

The Quran was written some 500 years after the New Testament, and 50 or so years after the Plague of Justinian (541-542) decimated over half the population of Europe. Islam deals with the problem of suffering in quite a different fashion than the Bible. While Muhammad is not depicted as having the same powers over reality as Jesus, the Quran goes much further in not justifying suffering. If someone is sick or dies, before anyone could go ahead and say that this person deserves what happens to them, it is understood that the 'will of Allah' overrides theodicy.[30] This is one of the noblest aspects of Islam. The Quran says:

"If good fortune befalls thee, it vexes them; but if thou art visited by an affliction, they say, 'We took our dispositions before,' and turn away, rejoicing. Say, 'Naught shall visit us but what Allah has prescribed for us; He is our Protector; in Allah let the believers put all their trust.'"[31] Surah 9:50

"There is no fault in the weak and the sick and those who find nothing to expend, if they are true to Allah and to His Messenger." Surah 9:92

---

[30] This is noted by the Shia scholar Seyyed Hossein Nasr, *The Heart of Islam: Enduring Values For Humanity*, (San Francisco, HarperCollins, 2002) p10
[31] All references of Quran from *The Koran Interpreted*, trans. A.J. Arberry, (New York, Macmillan Publishing, 1955)

If this passage leaves open room for interpretation of theodicy, Surah 57 titled "Iron", clearly does not.

"No affliction befalls in the earth or in yourselves, but it is in a Book, before We create it"
-Surah 57:22

The concept of 'Justification by Faith' is not pronounced in Islam because one's works must be commensurate to one's faith. The Quran teaches: "And those who believe, *and do righteous deeds* assuredly We shall admit them among the righteous." (Surah 29:7, Italics mine)

Suicide is not permitted in Islamic Law, and the prophet himself said, "The ink of the scholar is more precious than the blood of the martyr."[32] Muhammad traveled with his own physician. When he was asked, "Should one go to the doctor?" Muhammad replied, "Allah sends down no malady without also sending down with it a cure."[33]

Karma, Dharma, and Ming

If the English language itself derives from dozens of other languages it isn't too infrequent that some of these borrowed words take on a different meaning. Since the English colonization of India in the 19th century, one popular justification of suffering used in the Western world is that done through the naive use of the word *karma*.

Oftentimes people refer to an occurrence of good fortune as 'good karma'. It is believed that good fortune will result from some unselfish act (such as being a good Samaritan). The striving for good karma becomes the moral imperative to anyone who wants good fortune. Likewise, those who are already sufficiently fortunate are contented that their blessedness is based upon their own good karma, whatever that might consist of.

Bad karma, on the other hand, is the cause of misfortune. Misfortune either results from or creates more bad karma. This is akin to the maxim that 'what goes around comes around', and implies a belief in the existence of some sort of cosmic justice or omnipotent divine judge.

Despite the different uses to which it is applied, most English uses of the word 'karma' are bad translations, often with moral repercussions. Karma is a Sanskrit word meaning variously: 'action', 'deed', 'work', or 'function'. The oldest holy books of Hinduism, the *Vedas* (14th-12th century BCE) give mention to the word. In the books of the *Rig Veda* ('Knowledge of the Verses') karma refers to the acts or deeds of the gods as well as religious acts such as sacrifice and ritual. There is no mention or connotation of karma as being linked to anything like rebirth or the fortune of events and happenings of our existence.[34]

In the Hindu book of wisdom titled *Upanishads* ('To sit near to'), written some 500 or more years after the *Vedas*, is the understanding that karma has a relation to the question of whether or not we are reborn. This connection of karma with rebirth is usually understood as being the standard interpretation of Hinduism. Be that as it may,

---

[32] Nasr, p270

[33] Lawrence I. Conrad, "The Arab-Islamic medical tradition", in *The Western Medical Tradition: 800 BC to 1800 AD*, (Cambridge, Cambridge University Press, 1995) p98

[34] This is according to James P. McDermott's entry on the concept in *The Perennial Dictionary of World Religions*, ed. Keith Crim, (San Francisco, HarperCollins Publishers, 1981) p401-402

while some may think it may be honorable to have had many past lives, in this non-anglicized context being reborn is not a sign of good karma. The Upanishads say:

"According as a man acts and walks in the path of life, so he becomes. He that does good becomes good; he that does evil becomes evil. By pure actions he becomes pure; by evil actions he becomes evil.

"And they say in truth that a man is made of desire. As his desire is, so is his faith. As his faith is, so are his works. As his works are, so he becomes. It was said in this verse: 'A man comes with his actions to the end of his determination.'

"Reaching the end of the journey begun by his works on earth, from that world a man returns to this world of human actions.

"Thus far for the man who lives under desire."[35]

The Hindu book *Bhagavad-Gita* ('Song of the Glorious One') (4th century BCE) says that karma originates with the *Brahman*, or divine power. Karma is "the name given to the creative force that brings beings into existence." (3:15, 7:3) According to the *Bhagavad-Gita* the gods have created a "fourfold order" of existents and karma is understood as one's function, and not as aptitude (*guna*), or birth (*jati*).[36] (4:13)

These references ought to be considered in context of the *Purusarthas* or Hindu Aims of Life, of which there are four: *Dharma, Artha, Kama,* and *Moksa.* Dharma means duty; Artha means wealth; Kama means sexual desire; Moksa means salvation.[37] Moksa is held to be a release from all karma. If all karmic activity leads to rebirth (*samsara*) then Moksa is the release from this cycle and from karma which perpetuates it.

The non-Hindu who makes use of the word karma usually thinks the word refers to something like cosmic retribution. If I stub my toe, for example, it isn't because I hit it on something. It is because I have done something wrong in the past (or in a past life) for which my now stubbing my toe is retribution. Until an appropriate misfortune occurs to me, there was something in the past that I "got away with", and only now that I stubbed my toe am I suffering the retribution of cosmic justice.

What the colonialist who uses the word karma does not realize is that their malapropism is comparable to someone who says something but has no idea of what they are talking about. Moreover, this colonial use of the word karma plays a political role in society. As karma came to be understood as a notion of universal justice, the anglicized version has become used in order to justify the status quo. A person must be poor because either they or someone in their family must have done something to deserve this condition. Similarly, those who are in charge or are Kings, are so because of karmic universal justice.

The problem this poses for the Westerner who uses the word karma but has no understanding of Hindu law and tradition, or *dharma*, is using the word vacuously. When the Hindu uses the word karma, they are referring to something specific in the way of ritual or conduct, whereas the Westerner uses the word with no extension – what cosmic order are Westerners referring to, and where are the laws of this cosmic order recorded?

---

[35] "The Supreme Teaching", *The Upanishads*, trans. Juan Mascaro, (London, Penguin Books, 1965) p140
[36] Sarvepalli Radhakrishnan and Charles A. Moore make note of this in Radhakrishnan's translation of *Bhagavad-Gita* in their volume, *A Sourcebook In Indian Philosophy*, (Princeton, Princeton University Press, 1957) p117n1
[37] Glenn E. Yocum, "Hindu Aims of Life (Purusarthas)", *The Perennial Dictionary of World Religions*, p299

Popularly, we like to think of karma as a solution to the problem of why evil exists. Bad karma explains the existence of evil. Bad things happen, not because of the divine, but because of some fall that is human nature. The Hindu's must have had a lot of bad karma in order for God to decide to have Christians conquer them.

This type of reasoning, however, leads to an infinite regress. After-all, if the gods created karma humans cannot be responsible for the existence of evil. Rather, karma should not be thought greater than another Sanskrit word with which it rhymes: dharma. Dharma may be the Sanskrit word that translates most closely as our Western word, "religion". Dharma can mean 'righteousness', 'duty', or 'law'. The word appears more than 130 times in the *Rig Veda*. The *Laws of Manu* (2nd century BCE) may be one of the greatest jurisprudential books on dharma, and the ordering of the ideal society according to duty and law.[38]

In the *Bhagavad-Gita* we are told that "righteousness (*dharma*) saves from great fear". (2:40) When the god Krsna talks to Arjuna, he emphasizes dharma rather than karma. "I am the strength of the strong, devoid of desire and passion. In beings am I the desire which is not contrary to law (dharma)." (7:11)

Dharma is emphasized in the Buddhist sacred writings titled the *Dhammapada* ('The Path of Virtue'). When discussing the prospects of the next life, the Buddha Siddhartha Gautama (560-480) emphasizes dharma, which here is spelled as 'dhamma'. "One should follow dhamma, which is good conduct, not that which is poor conduct. One who lives dhamma, sleeps at ease in this world and also in the next."[39]

We can estimate Confucius' (551-479) conception of the problem of suffering in a brief passage in the *Analects*. Confucius' friend Po-niu is ill and Confucius visits him and holds his hand. He says that while Po-niu's death may be destined, however, Confucius is uncertain and can only repeatedly question such knowledge. "We are going to lose him. It must be Destiny. Why else should such a man be stricken with such a disease? Why else should such a man be stricken with such a disease?"[40] (6:10) When we see Confucius' other comments on the concept of Destiny (*Ming*), his belief that it is unchanged by human efforts becomes explicit: "It is destiny if the Way prevails; it is equally Destiny if the Way falls into disuse. What can Kung-po Liao do in the defiance of Destiny?" (14:36) Confucius thought that humans ought to concentrate on 'moral cultivation' and virtue (*jen*) and realize that destiny (*ming*) is external to human efforts and deeds.[41] We can see that Confucius held no respect for theodicy in his attitude toward death. "You do not understand even life. How can you understand death?" (11:12)

The non-theistic writings of this ancient philosopher Confucius do not resemble that ugly misconception called *Orient* that exists in the English-speaking world like a parasite of ignominy (and which some have entertained at least at some point in our lives, including myself, most regrettably). On the contrary, the *Analects* stand as proof to the magnificence, sincerity, humanism, and respect for nature that are fundamental to the

---

[38] G.R. Welbon, "Dharma", *The Perennial Dictionary of World Religions*, p219
[39] Siddhartha Gautama Buddha, *The Dhammapada*, trans. John Ross Carter and Mahinda Palihawadana, (New York, Oxford University Press, 1987) Chapter XIII, #169
[40] Confucius, *The Analects*, trans. D.C. Lau, (Middlesex, Penguin Books, 1979)
[41] Ch'u Chai and Winberg Chai, *Confucianism*, (Woodbury, New York: Barron's Educational Series, Inc., 1973) p40-41

enterprise of philosophy and evaluative thought. The *Analects* teaches: "The gentleman helps others to realize what is good in them; he does not help them to realize what is bad in them. The small man does the opposite." (12:16)

The Palestinian refugee Edward Said's exposition of the history of *Orientalism* reveals the dishonesty, homophobia, and racism that are inherent in all Western versions of the Orient. In 1979 Said wrote,

"[T]he principle dogmas of Orientalism exist in the purest form today in studies of Arabs and Islam. Let us recapitulate them here: one is the absolute and systematic difference between the West, which is rational, developed, humane, superior, and the Orient, which is aberrant, undeveloped, inferior."[42]

Folk Psychology and Folk Medicine, Clairvoyance and Hypochondria

It is clear that Confucius does not believe in clairvoyance but believes that knowledge is something natural. What is clairvoyance? Clairvoyance is an ability to perceive things that are external to the mind 'extra-sensorially', or without use of the senses. So for example, someone with clairvoyance can detect objects that cannot be seen or touched. In popular science fiction someone who is clairvoyant can without any hindrances 'grasp', 'see', or explain the future, or the past, or some unperceivable object. The belief that this can be done is called 'the magical theory of reference'.

Imagine someone tells you all about a new car they just purchased. It has leather seats, a sun-roof, and a custom paint job. When you ask them if they would take you for a spin sometime you find out that only they can perceive the automobile. Should we just use our imagination as we pull onto the thruway and hope other cars see us?

The 'magical theory of reference' has been discussed by psychologists and philosophers, alike. Sigmund Freud (1856-1939) agreed with theorists before him that the 'magical theory of reference' resulted from believing our own imagination is the reality of the world external to us; or, as he puts it: "mistaking an ideal connection for a real one."[43] He calls this mental state 'neurosis'. The neurotic is the person who mistakes their thoughts with the reality of the external world.

According to Freud this magical theory is essentially a "misunderstanding which leads [one] to replace the laws of nature by psychological ones." Magical thinking, such as the belief in spirits and demons, are "only projections" of "emotional impulses". The neurotic "turns his emotional [investments] into persons, he peoples the world with them and meets his internal mental processes again outside himself". Such a thing is possible (as we have seen with the mind of President Bush II) because for the neurotic "agreement with external reality is a matter of no importance".[44]

The American pragmatist philosopher Hilary Putnam discusses 'the magical theory of reference' in his seminal work, *Reason, Truth and History*. (1981) The opening chapter titled "Brains in a vat" deals with these science fiction fantasies. Putnam discusses several theories of reference, or ways in which we as humans refer to the world, one being the popular stumper of Descartes: how do we know that we are not just

---

[42] Edward Said, *Orientalism*, (New York, Vintage Books, 1979) p300
[43] Sigmund Freud, *Totem and Taboo*, (first published in 1913) trans. James Strachey, (New York, W.W. Norton & Company, 1950) p99
[44] Freud, p104, 115, 108

dreaming? For example, I've had dreams of doing everyday things like waking and eating and reading: how do I know this present mental state of reading this sentence isn't in fact part of a dream? Putnam translates Descartes thought-experiment into a more computer-age example: how do we know we are not just brains in a vat? Could it be that our brain is being fed the stimulus that to us appears as these very words you are now reading...? This thought-experiment is found in many popular fictional stories, as for example, *The Matrix*, though of course, without Putnam's crushing refutation of this magical possibility. He writes:

"Some primitive people believe that some representations (in particular, *names*) have a necessary connection with their bearers; that to know the 'true name' of someone or something gives one power over it. This power comes from the *magical connection* between the name and bearer of the name; once one realizes that a name *only* has a contextual, contingent, conventional connection with its bearer, it is hard to see why knowledge of the name should have any mystical significance."[45]

Putnam offers as an example of the magical theory of reference the word 'influenza'. He writes: "Our word 'influenza' is a survival of this medieval way of thinking. Evil spirits were thought to exert an influence –*questa influenza*, in Italian –on the air which in turn influenced the sufferers of the illness."[46] Although medical doctors and nurses today still use the term 'influenza', the term's reference has changed with the increased understanding of the nature and diagnostics of how this disease is actually contracted. (Called the 'germ theory of disease'.)

Magical theories of reference inevitably touch upon questions of health and sickness. A great deal of Freud's work was dedicated to naturalizing people's understanding of mental sickness, and one area in which he was particularly influential was in dispelling the prejudice that women are by nature prone to 'hysteria'. However, the subject of faith healing is one with a great deal of history and precedent in the Western world.

Two thinkers who were near contemporaries that are often lumped together are the Danish Christian writer Soren Kierkegaard (1813-1855) and the German atheist and philologist Friedrich Nietzsche (1844-1900). Kierkegaard is regarded as the founder of the philosophy 'existentialism' and usually Nietzsche is understood has having thought along the same lines. This is probably because both thinkers applied psychology to philosophy and placed great emphasis on the will. If their methods are sometimes dissimilar, their findings here are not. In his work, *The Sickness Unto Death* (1849) Kierkegaard wrote:

"The possibility of this sickness is man's advantage over the beast; to be sharply observant of this sickness constitutes the Christian's advantage over the natural man; to be healed of this sickness is the Christian's bliss. So then it is an infinite advantage to be able to despair..."[47]

In his study *Human, All-too Human* (1878) Nietzsche comes to a similar conclusion in an aphorism titled "Hypochondria".

"*Hypochondria*. –There are people who out of empathy with and concern for another person become hypochondriac; the species of sympathy that arises in this case is nothing other than an illness.

---

[45] Hilary Putnam, *Reason, Truth and History*, (Cambridge, Cambridge University Press, 1981) p3
[46] Putnam, p75-76
[47] Soren Kierkegaard, *The Sickness Unto Death*, (originally published in 1849) trans. Walter Lowrie, (Garden City, New York: Doubleday & Company, Inc., 1954) p148

Thus there is also a Christian hypochondria such as overcomes those solitary, religiously inclined people who have the suffering and death of Christ continually before their eyes."[48]

For much of European history both the church and the state had a monopoly on special healing abilities. An example of this type of magical healing power is called the 'Royal Touch', which could heal any faithful nationalist instantaneously. Notorious examples of monarchs endowed with these stately magical healing abilities were people such as King Henry IV of France (1553-1610), Queen Elizabeth (1533-1603), Charles I (1600-1649), who "cured a hundred patients at a stroke in 1633", his son Charles II (1630-1685) had royal cure for scrofula, and Queen Anne (1665-1714) who had the healing power of the Royal Touch as well.[49]

The Catholic church has recognized faith healing for centuries. Thousands of people have been cured who have made a pilgrimage to Lourdes, France where the virgin Mary once appeared. In 1999 the church recognized Fifty-Eight "healings" as miracles by the church, though this number is probably higher today, 10 years later.[50]

Medical historian Mary Lindemann writes that: "Christian churches taught, and Christians believed, that illness came ultimately from God as punishment for sin." In 1544 the Church of England wrote a petition to God, "The Great Litany", asking that if it pleased God, though He knew that the English were sinners, could He stop sending plagues and "grievous sickness"?[51]

Not many agree that the Church of Christian Science has the correct interpretation of the New Testament that healing can only truly be performed through faith. Christian Science was developed by an American woman named Mary Baker Eddy (1821-1910), around the turn of the century.[52] The scientist Richard Feynman (1918-1988) has written of this faith:

> "It's possible that the faith healing isn't so good. It's possible –we are not sure –that it isn't. And it's therefore possible that there is some danger in believing in faith healing, that it's not a triviality, not like astrology wherein it doesn't make a lot of difference. It's just inconvenient for the people who believe in it that they have to do things on certain days. It may be, and I would like to know –it should be investigated – everybody has a right to know- whether more people have been hurt or helped by believing in Christ's ability to heal; whether there is more healing or harming by such a thing. It's possible either way. It should be investigated. It shouldn't be left lying for people to believe in without an investigation."[53]

In the United States, some 300 children have died in the last 25 years because medical treatment was denied on religious grounds. Often the health issues are very simple but the parents believe praying to be the only way to cure their children, who sometimes die extremely painful deaths from things such as juvenile diabetes, pneumonia, a urinary tract infection, and others. In America 30 of the 50 states provide

---

[48] Friedrich Nietzsche, *Human, All-too Human*, trans. R.J. Hollingdale, (Cambridge, Cambridge University Press, 1986) #47 (orig. pub. in 1878)
[49] Mary Lindemann, *Medicine and Society in Early Modern Europe*, (Cambridge University Press, 1999) p59; Freud, p53-54; *The Western Medical Tradition: 800 BC to 1800 AD*, (Cambridge, Cambridge University Press, 1995) p413
[50] James Carroll, *Constantine's Sword*, (Boston, Mariner Books, 2002) p481-482
[51] Lindemann, p207-208
[52] Mohandas Gandhi (1869-1948) stands as another example of someone who abstained from institutional medicine and sought holistic remedies.
[53] Richard Feynman, "This Unscientific Age", in *The Meaning of It All*, (Reading, Massachusetts, Perseus Books, 1998) p94

legal protection for parents whose children died because they erroneously believed in faith healing.[54]

The justification of suffering has over a 500 year history in America. When Christopher Columbus (1451-1506) discovered the peaceful Arawaks in 1492, he wrote: "They invite you to share anything they possess, and show as much love as if their hearts went with it… How easy it would be to convert these people –and to make them work for us."[55]

Estimates of the native populations in the pre-Christian Western Hemisphere vary from as low as 8.4 million up to 112.5 million as the high. The sociologist and author of the study on *American Indian Holocaust and Survival*, Russell Thorndike, arrives at an estimate somewhere around 72 million Native Americans before Columbus's arrival in 1492. By the 1890's there was a 96 percent decrease in the Native American population, dwindled down to 4 or 4 1/2 million Native Americans. While a vast amount of the Native American Holocaust was achieved by warfare, enslavement, and the exiling, forced relocations, and forced starvation of the native peoples, probably most of the killing was done by a handful of European diseases which were new to the Western Hemisphere.[56] These diseases included venereal syphilis, gonorrhea, measles, whooping cough, influenza, and smallpox among others.[57] Thornton writes that "The destructiveness of alcoholism is surely not far behind, and it has been linked to the current high mortality rates of American Indians from suicide, accidents, diabetes, and, of course, cirrhosis."[58]

When pilgrims aboard the *Mayflower* landed in Cape Cod in 1620, they found the results of a recent endemic amongst the Native Americans to be pleasing. One pilgrim wrote: "Thus farre hath the good hand of God favored our beginnings… In sweeping away great multitudes of the natives…, a little more before we went thither, that he might make room for us there". In 1631 a New England colonist named Increase Mather wrote: "About this time the Indians began to be quarrelsome touching the Bounds of the Land which they had sold to the English, but God ended the Controversy by sending the Smallpox amongst the Indians of Saugust, who were before that time exceeding numerous".[59] Francis Jennings' study on *The Invasion of America*, tells how Europeans "warred against Indians by destroying their crops, knowing that they thus destroyed the tribes' basic food supply." Between 1622-1629 Virginians destroyed Indian crops with this in mind.[60]

The Catholic writer James Carroll's historical study *Constantine's Sword* discusses how after the 4th century the popular Christian message became one of

---

[54] Dirk Johnson, "Trials Loom for Parents Who Embraced Faith Over Medicine", *New York Times*, 1/21/09 Johnson lists the group Children's Health Care Is a Legal Duty which is opposed to faith healing and the writer Shawn Peters, whose 2007 book is titled, *When Prayer Fails: Faith Healing, Children and the Law*.
[55] Quoted by Russell Thornton, *American Indian Holocaust and Survival*, (Norman, University of Oklahoma Press, 1987) p13
[56] Europe itself had just gone through the Black Plague (1348-1351) in the previous century, killing 1 of every 3 Europeans, or 20-25 million. (Carroll, p338)
[57] Thornton, p22-23, 25, 42, 41
[58] Thornton, p45
[59] Quoted by Thornton, p71, 75
[60] Francis Jennings, *The Invasion of America: Indians, Colonialism, and the Cant of Conquest*, (New York, W.W. Norton and Company, 1976) p19n15

'triumphalism', or as it is sometimes called 'supersessionism'. This is the attitude that because Christianity became an empire (which alas, fell a century later to pagans) this was proof that other religions, particularly Judaism and paganism, are false. This is basically the same thing as saying that 'might makes right'. Carroll writes with strong moral courage: "Christian faith can seem to triumph over every evil except Christian triumphalism."[61] Incidentally this justification of others suffering has frequently been part of 'civilization', 'democratization', and the forcing of other peoples to live according to one set of standards.

Another justification of suffering was exemplified in the contemporary world when the Christian Pat Robertson claimed the Prime Minister of Israel Ariel Sharone was made sick by God because he had tried to be fair to Palestinians.[62] Or in the 1980's when the Protestant teacher Jerry Falwell said that the AIDS virus was divine punishment for homosexuals. It was one of these simpletons who also claimed that Hurricane Katrina was divine justice on the heathen New Orleans, as if a city were a person.

In James' attempt to proselytize his audience he made science and history and progress plain: "Here in this room, we all of us believe in molecules and the conservation of energy, in democracy and necessary progress, [and] in Protestant Christianity..."[63] Here history and imperialism unite.

Prisons[64]

During World War II over 100,000 Americans of Japanese dissent were rounded up and put in concentration camps for the duration of the war. They were never recompensed. One of the greatest justifications of suffering today is in the prison system. This is a result of the economic ability to imprison rather than correct. Right now the United States has the highest jail population in the world. Oliver Wendell Holmes once asked,

> "What have we better than a blind guess to show that criminal law in its present form does more good than harm? I do not stop to refer to the effect which it has had on degrading prisoners and in plunging them further into crime, or to the question whether fine and imprisonment do not fall more heavily on a criminal's wife and children than on himself. I have in mind more far-reaching questions. Does punishment deter? Do we deal with criminals on proper principles?"[65]

The three most populated countries in the world are China with some 1.3 billion people, followed by India with 1.1 billion, and then the United States with just over 300 million. However, the United States jail population is the highest in the world with nearly 2.2 million people in prison. Roy Walmsley's "World Prison Population List (seventh edition) of 2007 shows the data. China follows with over 1.5 million people in prison, then Russia with 0.87 million people in prison. The second most populated country in

---

[61] Carroll, p12
[62] "Robertson Suggests Stroke Is Divine Rebuke", *New York Times*, January 6, 2006, written by The Associated Press.
[63] James, *The Will to Believe*, p93
[64] www.kcl.ac.uk/depsta/law/research/icps/downloads/world-prison-pop-seventh.pdf This website shows Roy Walmsley's 2007 reports on the world prison populations. While the New Testament tells of God helping some prisoners to escape (Acts 5:19), the Prophet Muhammad released many from prison. See Muhamed S. El-Awa's, *On The Political System of The Islamic State*, trans. Ahmad Naji al-Imam, ed. Anwer Beg, (Indianapolis, American Trust Publications, 1980) p93n1
[65] Oliver Wendell Holmes, Jr., "The Path of the Law", in *Pragmatism: A Reader*, ed. Louis Menand, (New York, Vintage Books, 1997) p160

the world, India, has just over 332 thousand prisoners. Per 100,000 people, the US has 738 in prison, China has 118 in prison, and India has 30 people per 100,000 in prison. As the Canadian jurist Michael Mandel reports, if Texas were its own country it would have the highest jail population per capita in the world.[66]

Sanctions

After the destruction of all of the Iraqi food supplies in the 1991 US Gulf War with Iraq, the US and the UN imposed sanctions on Iraq for years to come.[67] This means that the US blocks other countries from trading goods such as food and medicine to Iraq. People have called the US/UN Sanctions "an act of genocide".[68] As former US Attorney General Ramsey Clark wrote in 1998:

"Every UN agency dealing with health, food, agriculture, or children, including the World Health Organization, and Food and Agriculture Organization, the World Food Project, and UNICEF, has reported repeatedly and often graphically about tens of thousands of deaths annually resulting directly from the sanctions. UNICEF reported as of August 1991 that already at least 47,500 children had died as a direct result of sanctions."[69]

A 1995 *60 Minutes* special about Iraq said that more than 500,000 children had died because of US-forced sanctions. Clark writes:

"It is clear beyond a reasonable doubt that with the sanctions it forced on Iraq, the United States intended to destroy in whole, or in part, the people of Iraq, largely Arab and Muslim, by causing them serious bodily and mental harm and by inflicting on them conditions of life culcated to bring about their physical destruction in whole, or in part. Sadly, the complicity of the UN cannot be ignored, because in a time of moral crisis threatening the life of a nation, it did nothing to prevent tragedy."[70]

When Bush attacked Iraq in 2003 (though US bombing of Iraq had not ceased since 1991), Iraqi citizens didn't know whether to be afraid of being conquered by a foreign country or to celebrate the lifting of the sanctions. Similar US/UN sanctions still exist around the world as in the case of Cuba, which has been under US sanctions for decades, as well as Iran and Palestine and others.[71]

---

[66] Michael Mandel, *How America Gets Away With Murder: Illegal Wars, Collateral Damage and Crimes Against Humanity*, (London, Pluto Press, 2004) p249n208

[67] The Former US Attorney General Ramsey Clark has noted that, "Iraq's agriculture and food-processing storage and distribution system was attacked directly and systematically." All irrigation systems were attacked, three food warehouses in Baghdad were attacked, as well as others, a factory producing baby milk powder was hit, the same with vegetable oil and sugar factories, the nation's biggest frozen meat storage was destroyed, animal herds were decimated including 3 1/2 million sheep and two million cattle, 90% of poultry supply was destroyed, grain silos were hit, as well as tractor assembly plants and fertilizer plants. 28 civilian hospitals were bombed, 52 community health centers, 676 schools were bombed, and there was much more destruction. See Clark's, "The Devastation of Iraq By War and Sanctions", in *Challenge To Genocide: Let Iraq Live*, (New York, International Action Center, 1998) p11-12

[68] This is pointed out by Brian Becker and Sara Flounders in their preface, "The Iraq Sanctions Challenge"

[69] Clark, p23

[70] Clark, p29, 31

[71] "Security Council sanctions against Iraq, which are forced by the United States, have devastated the entire nation, taking the lives of more than 1,500,000 people, mostly infants, children, chronically ill and elderly, and harming millions more by hunger, sickness and sorrow. The sanctions destroyed the 'dignity and rights' of the people of Iraq and are the most extreme form of 'cruel, inhuman and degrading treatment', which are prohibited by the [UDHR]." Ramsey Clarke, "On the Fiftieth Anniversary of the

Healthcare

The United States is the only Western Democracy to not have a universal healthcare system for its citizens. The US is signatory to the UDHR, or Universal Declaration of Human Rights which was drafted by the former first lady Eleanor Roosevelt in 1945. It states:

"Everyone has the right to a standard of living adequate for the health and well-being of himself and of his family, including food, clothing, housing and medical care and necessary social services, and the right to security in the event of unemployment, sickness, disability, widowhood, old age or other lack of livelihood in circumstances beyond his control." –Article 25, Section 1[72]

In 2001 Ralph Nader reported that some 45 million American did not have the health insurance required to have proper healthcare. The World Health Organization ranks the United States 37th amongst nations in the overall quality of healthcare. Of the uninsured Nader writes: "They remain the powerless in a scary world where even a relatively minor illness or injury can mean economic disaster and where preventative medicine, like a physical checkup or blood test, is an unaffordable luxury."[73]

"The Institute of Medicine of the National Academies estimates that about 18,000 Americans die every year because they cannot afford to pay for diagnosis, treatment, or cures. That is 1,500 people a month! What about the preventable sickness, the pain, the family disruption?"[74]

Nader calls this a "silent form of preventable violence". The number one cause of bankruptcy in America is health-related. Nearly 1 of every 2 bankruptcies involves illness or medical debt. Nader writes:

"Many of the 200 million citizens counted among the insured are actually 'underinsured' with limited policies that often cover only catastrophic injuries or provide exclusions for a long list of health problems. There are serious gaps in many health policies that leave the insured with little or no coverage for prescription drugs and medical supplies and vision and hearing care. And many policies require large out-of-pocket 'co-payments' for the insured, which make care unaffordable for low- and moderate-income families. We can do better as a wealthy nation."[75]

War

It is estimated that in the first six months of the US attack on Afghanistan, which began in October 2001, 20,000 people were killed, half of which were non-combatant men, women, and children.[76] An English polling agency, Opinion Research Business has estimated that since the US invasion of Iraq in 2003 there have been over 1.2 million Iraqi casualties.[77] Moreover, the USA PATRIOT Act has legalized the harassment, surveillance, and arrest of thousands of people according to racial profiling, and many

---

Universal Declaration of Human Rights", in Noam Chomsky and Edward Said's, *Acts of Aggression: Policing "Rogue" States*, (New York, Seven Stories Press, 1999) p60

[72] http://www.un.org/Overview/rights.html

[73] Ralph Nader, "Patient's Rights Legislation", from *In Pursuit of Justice: Collected Writings 2000-2003*, (New York, Seven Stories Press, 2004) (a) p141

[74] Ralph Nader, *The Good Fight*, (New York, HarperCollins, 2004) (b) p207

[75] Nader, "Patient's Rights Legislation", (a) p141-142

[76] Mandel, p29

[77] Reported by National Public Radio (NPR on September 18th, 2007 on *Day to Day*).

have died during interrogation and torture by the US government in Guantanamo Bay, as well as US prisons in Afghanistan and Iraq.[78]

Democracy and Imperialism

Although Socrates (469-399) defended the democratic state of Athens to his death, he had once told his friend Glaucon that, "I think democracy comes when the poor are victorious, kill some of the other side, expel others, and to the rest they give an equal share of political power and offices..."[79] (557a) This progression of democracy is perhaps exemplified in the history of the American democracy which was founded once the Native Americans were decimated and powerless, the English landowners were expelled, and the African slave trade had been well established.

According to Plato and his student Aristotle politics must always issue an admixture of pleasure and pain.[80] Plato (427-347) believed that "common feelings of pleasure and pain bind the city together". (462b) Aristotle (384-322) had written that: "It is proper to the political philosopher to study pleasure and pain, since he is the ruling craftsman of the end which we refer to in calling something unconditionally bad or good."[81] (1152b1)

In contemporary political philosophy the terms pleasure and pain are replaced by 'freedom' and 'coercion'. Freedom is defined as a civil liberty or right, like the freedom of the press, or the aforementioned right of Vermonters to go outside naked without recrimination. Coercion, on the other hand, is political force or control. The most popular form of coercion is taxation. According to the policies of the United States, for example, an adult citizen must pay tax on their income or they are fined by the government, though there are many different taxes decided by the states themselves.

The only political philosophy that is against coercion is anarchism. For Anarchists the state is without justification. Moreover, Anarchists hold that the political state is responsible for the problem of suffering. Accordingly coercion cannot be justified and must either be eliminated or ignored. Choice in this matter tells us to what extent anarchism justifies the suffering of others.

Ideally the citizens vote on the policies of coercion that exist in a democracy. This is to minimize the amount of suffering that is justified by the political state. As we

---

[78] Nancy Chang and the Center for Constitutional Rights, *Silencing Political Dissent*, (New York, Seven Stories Press, 2002). The writer Thomas Friedman, who supported Bush II's Wars on Afghanistan and Iraq, commented recently on the legacy of US torture, finding it to be just. "We have the luxury of having this torture debate now because there was no second 9/11, and it was not for want of trying... So, yes, people among us who went over the line may go unpunished, because we still have enemies who respect no lines at all. In such an ugly war, you do your best." Thomas L. Friedman, "A Torturous Compromise", *The New York Times*, April 29, 2009

[79] Plato, *The Republic*, trans. G.M.A. Grube, (Indianapolis, Hackett Publishing, 1974)

[80] "The idea that because Plato and Aristotle are male and the products of a slave society they should be disqualified from receiving contemporary attention is as limited an idea as suggesting that *only* their work, because it was addressed to and about elites, should be read today." -Edward Said, "The Politics of Knowledge" (1991), from *Falling Into Theory*, Second Edition, ed. David H. Richter, (Boston, Bedford/St. Martin's, 2000) p189-198. My thanks to Andrew Barnaby for introducing and discussing this essay with me.

[81] Aristotle, *Nicomachean Ethics*, trans. Terence Irwin, (Indianapolis, Hackett Publishing, 1985)

can see, though, it is not perfect, as suffering is not eliminated. A decision reached by a majority of votes is not unanimous: minorities can and often do suffer in democratic states.[82] Moreover, democracy is not so neatly divided between the majority and the minority. Society is constituted more along the lines of family, community, religion, profession, gender, race, class, and types of aesthetic appreciation. The dualistic tendency in the democratic system often works to blur the distinctions of the diversity that exists in society. Sociologists call this 'assimilation', where one dominant culture white-washes away all others, be it through trends or acculturation. Civil Wars do occur, however, as well as the ongoing struggle for civil rights. A popular phrase used to describe such phenomenon is sometimes called 'class war', or as some of the media prefers to call it, 'the culture wars'.

'Class War' is a phrase coined by Karl Marx and Friedrich Engels to describe the civil unrest inevitable to democracy and other pre-socialist societies. This war consists of the struggles between the different classes of peoples, in particular the haves and the have nots, the rich and the poor. This war between class and class is understood as the precursor to the cultural revolution which does away with class distinctions and ushers in human equality.

According to Marx and Engels and the new philosophy of anarchism that they inspired, the Class war is something which must be enjoined and escalated in order to achieve the utopia where suffering is no more. To make this leap from the way the world is to the way the world ought to be, an ideological Class war is (further) waged and the armies are drawn between the bourgeois and the proletariat, often unbeknownst to the 'participants'. Another person's suffering is justified insofar as it is part to the revolutionary struggle necessary in achieving the classless society. This is imperialism.

Imperialism is the belief that there is one true description of reality or one correct way to live. It is the extension of political power beyond the realm of consent and the forcing of others to live according to an arbitrary or foreign set of rules or policies. If imperialism is inevitable, is there a political form that is least coextensive? If another person's suffering is inevitably justified no matter the kind of political theory employed, the question becomes one of not whether or not imperialism is right or wrong, but whether if it is not eliminable if it is reducible.

If pragmatists have been advocates for democracy, this does not mean that they believe that it is a democracies job to democratize all other countries -a form of imperialism. William James, John Dewey, Jane Addams, and Mark Twain, as members of the Anti-Imperialist League, were all against the forced-democratization of the Philippines and other countries. Rather, pragmatists are concerned with something more relevant, namely, what is most practical? What has greatest chances of success?

Whatever the answer, pragmatists are opposed to a form of imperialism known as anti-democracy. Anti-democracy (sometimes called 'antipoliticism') is the belief that either humanity cannot come up with its own policies and principles, or that humanity is so class-based that a majority will always seek the suffering of minorities. These claims, which are more radical than Plato and Aristotle's critiques of democracy, are so because they depend upon a non-humanist non-philosophical perspective, call it misanthropy.

---

[82] Thinkers as diverse as Plato, Machiavelli, Thomas Hobbes, Emma Goldman, and Hilary Putnam have warned against majoritarianism.

The international jurist Hans Kelsen once said that, "Democracy cannot defend itself by giving itself up."[83] Pragmatism by design does not squander reason or hold to some bad faith in themselves and others. A practical and intellectual step is taken to abandon thinking of humanity from a metaphysical or ontological perspective, (which after all, is only an idea in our minds), to one that does not see from a false perspective, call it fallibility, nor one opposed to the world, call it naturalism, nor one which claim's to be a god's eye perspective, call it pluralism.

While James's is pragmatism's founding father of pluralism, the problem of James's 'will to believe' is that it can have drastic consequences in the political realm of democracy when the majority of people might be habitually led by faith rather than some other explanation, be it that of a small group of scientists, or in lieu of the discovery of greater justification, or considerations for the livelihood of the lesser-off. Conversely, such belief can also be anti-democratic and opposed to the perspectives of others, be they a majority or a minority, rich or poor.

In fact, the concept of 'Justification by Faith' isn't used today in an ethical sense at all, but is used rather uncritically, in conformity with minimal reasoning and maximum self-righteousness. If in day to day life the practice of self-deception and naiveté can be 'thought' of as therapeutic, taken into the realm of politics, however, as we see with so many self-righteous rulers from Pharaoh to Bush II, it leads to moral bankruptcy and conformity. In this sense 'Justification by Faith' can be highly anti-democratic and imperialistic.

'Justification by Faith', as we saw however, is not an ethical justification or a justification of belief. It is a demonstration to oneself and a protestation to others that one is justified or warranted in believing oneself 'saved' because one believes it is true. This isn't just begging the question, because in fact, there is no way of testing the truth of this "justification" unless one goes to war. Only the victor is justified.

William James's 'will to believe' may be the closest that pragmatism can come to theodicy given the philosophies commitment to nature and naturalism. Russell called this work of James "a transitional doctrine" along the road to pragmatism, having gone from doing work purely in psychology to work in philosophy.[84] As we see, he places supreme importance on the 'will' taking it as the natural foundation for faith.

If this is a popular interpretation of Christianity in America, it is not the only interpretation. Martin Luther King, Jr., who was trained as a philosopher, finds in contradistinction to James that, "There is a corruption in man's will." Here Martin Luther King is going beyond many of the 19th and 20th century philosophies that vitiate between faith and inaction. Whereas philosophies of will and faith often deny the importance of the human body, King holds that "Christianity… contends that the will, and not the body, is the principle of evil."[85]

---

[83] Hans Kelsen, *What Is Justice?*, (Berkeley, University of California Press, 1957), chapter found in Hackett's Readings In Philosophy, *Justice*, ed. Jonathan Westphal, (Indianapolis, Hackett Publishing Company, 1996) p205. Though Kelsen here agrees with standard pragmatist dicta, he was not a pragmatist but a positivist.
[84] Russell, (a) p816
[85] Martin Luther King, Jr., "What Is Man?", orig. pub. 1963, reprinted in *Philosophy Looks To The Future*, Second Edition, ed. Peyton E. Richter and Walter L. Fogg, (Prospect Heights, Waveland Press, 1978) p133-134. He believed there was a relationship between reason and faith and did not believe one had

King was critical of the Protestant Reformation theology which "emphasized a purely otherworldly religion" and a "doctrine of human nature [that] overstressed the corruption of man." He says that a disregard for the sacredness of both the soul and the body "creates a tragic dichotomy between the sacred and the secular", i.e., abstention from social movements.[86] This is something missing in the philosophy of the will, or libertarianism –the priority of the other person's well-being over my own. There is an acknowledgement of other's needs, the community's needs, humanity's needs, the world's needs over the solipsistic philosophical theologies of the will. The childish person is the person who does not realize how they affect others or how they effect the world, or whether or not we justify the other person's suffering.

King is in agreement with Levinas in believing in the need for substitution, in the need of taking on responsibility, the need for suffering ourselves if it may alleviate the suffering of others.

"By recognizing the necessity of suffering in a righteous cause, we may possibly achieve our humanity's full stature. To guard ourselves from bitterness, we need the vision to see in this generation's ordeals the opportunity to transfigure both ourselves and American society. Our present suffering and our nonviolent struggle to be free may well offer to Western civilization the kind of spiritual dynamic so desperately needed for survival."

King said, "Recognizing the necessity for suffering, I have tried to make of it a virtue."[87]

These views seem to be in sharp contrast to the faith that promises disengagement with wars that are going on, and the ways in which existing institutions, besides war, justify the others suffering. King wrote:

"Some men still feel that war is the answer to the problems of the world. They are not evil people. On the contrary, they are good, respectable citizens whose ideas are robed in the garments of patriotism. They talk of brinkmanship and the balance of terror. They sincerely feel that a continuation of the arms race will be conducive to more beneficent than maleficent consequences. So they passionately call for bigger bombs, larger nuclear stockpiles, and faster ballistic missiles.

"Wisdom born of experience should tell us that war is obsolete. There may have been a time when war served as a negative good by preventing the spread and growth of an evil force, but the destructive power of modern weapons eliminates even the possibility that war may serve as a negative good. If we assume that life is worth living and that man has a right to survival, then we must find an alternative to war."[88]

King's emphasis on personal responsibility, wisdom, and virtue are what lead to his understanding that war is no good. However, this is not a popular view today when most Americans seem to be in favor of war as a means of solving the problems of evil.[89]

---

primacy over the other. "Reason, devoid of the purifying power of faith, can never free itself from distortions and rationalizations." (p148)

[86] Martin Luther King, Jr., *Strength to Love*, (Philadelphia, Fortress Press, 1963) p131-132. He does agree however that "Protestants must forever affirm" the doctrine "of the justification by faith". (130)

[87] King, *Strength to Love*, p92, 154

[88] King, p40-41

[89] King was highly critical of the popular churches in America which are either pro-war, or are indifferent to war. (Matthew 24:6) "What more pathetically reveals the irrelevancy of the church in present-day world affairs than its witness regarding war? In a world gone mad with arms buildups, chauvinistic passions, and imperialistic exploitation, the church has either endorsed these activities or remained appallingly silent. During the last two world wars, national churches even functioned as the ready lackeys of the state, sprinkling holy water upon the battleships and joining the mighty armies in singing, 'Praise the Lord and pass the ammunition.' A weary world, pleading desperately for peace, has often found the church morally sanctioning war." (p61)

It seems among people, regardless of religion, that their conceptions of the good life and the problem of evil affect their attitude toward war. For Christian pacifists such as Roland Bainton and Martin Luther King, it is pragmatism and wisdom which lead them to oppose war, and not just faith. Both were citizens of the US and thus members of a democratic state.

How is it with democracy today? What are our conceptions of good and evil? What is the good life in America today? How is it conceived ? Why are certain members of a democratic state more concerned with evil? Is evil problematic or does it exist out of necessity? Let us see examine our conceptions of the good life and the so-called problem of evil and see how they are played out in our democracy.

8

The Good Life and The Problem of Evil

Sometimes it feels like we are getting closer and closer to Utopia. Utopia is the dream world that we know could exist in reality if thing were a little bit different in the world. If people were just a little bit less selfish, a little less greedy; if people could just get along and reconcile their differences and realize that we are all the same -the world would be such a better place. Just think of the glorious kingdom that could exist on this beautiful earth!

One thing is for sure –if everyone were the same it would make things a lot easier. If people in the Middle East and other 'third-world' countries could just realize that we here in the Western world know the best way to live a good, meaningful life; -if these foreigners would just allow us to take their economy and oil under our wing -we could finally make this world into that peaceful Utopia that is so desired and then finally, finally we could all live as one.

Utopian ideals, like that of the National Socialists, or those attempts to democratize other countries for that matter, are often guided by a moral bankruptcy –a disregard for the wealth of diversity that exists in the world. Utopian ideals are often the product of a single perspective and are prejudiced by an ignorance of the many other outlooks, beliefs, and traditions of the many peoples and societies that exist in the world and that are not of yesterday but have flourished for hundreds, even many thousands of years.

Of course, the ultimate goal of utopia is peace –but at what price is it worth the while? We can still see in the world today, many are willing to go to war to attain or maintain this "peace", through so-called "pre-emptive" or 'preventive' wars. It seems the best way to secure peace and justice is through victory. A few days following 9/11 President Bush told America and the rest of the world just who the sides were in this fight between good and evil: 'If you are not for us, you are for the terrorists.' Similarly, and less trivially, many believe there is a war between 'classes' that is going on right now in America and which must be escalated in order to achieve this 'post-revolutionary' or utopian and classless society.

What is characteristic of these different visions of peace and utopia is the conviction that we are all fundamentally the same. Or more insidiously, it is claimed there is a certain human nature that 'we all' must (be made to) realize. Many philosophies and religions, utopian or otherwise, have held there to be a human nature, for better or for worse. Hedonists hold that a human's nature is to maximize pleasure, Darwinists hold that a human's nature is to struggle for survival, and capitalists hold that humans are all by nature self-interested.

Worse still, many in the Western world believe that humans are by nature bad or evil. And because of this natural tendency toward evil, people must be led or ruled-over by an authority, be they political, religious, or scientific- lest we should succumb to an instinctive anarchical violence, or as a concerned member of the British Empire quipped, a 'war of all against all'. It is more than a little disconcerting to think that this negative ideology is most commonly found in democratic countries, where one might hope a government "run by the people" would be made up of friendly and goodly constituents, committed to living the Good Life.

The Good, The Bad, and The Evil

What is the Good Life? Is it of necessity the product of freedom and democracy, or the right kind of faith? What is the relationship between the Good Life and good in general? Is 'good' definable like an object, something we can possess, or is 'good' just a compliment we can pay to the things we like, having no factual basis at all? Is Good something invented or created by humans or is it something that happens to us through chance or dumb luck? Is it possible for humans to be good and to live the Good life, or is it all 'relative' —one man's good is some other value for the next fellow? Are the many philosophical, religious, and political conceptions of good and the Good Life incompatible with each other or are they all somehow fundamentally the same? Could it be that some philosophies are greater than others, or is only one religion or philosophy, one conception of the Good the correct one, and all other religions and philosophies are false, or even in some sense bad or evil?

What is bad and what is evil? Does evil exist, and if so, where does it come from? Do all philosophies and religions believe in the existence of evil? Is evil natural to the world, or is it something supernatural? Is evil something human? Or is it in some way a combination of things? Could evil in some way be divine, something ultimate? If evil ultimately exists, is it a problem, and for whom is it a problem? Could the Problem of Evil ever be 'solved'? Can evil be annihilated?

If for some people it seems like there are a lot of questions and not enough answers, we should not conclude that this confusion is the same for others. For many people knowing what is Good and what is Evil is as simple as seeing the difference between black and white. For some there exists an extensive, everyday 'common sense' understanding of what the words 'Good' and 'Evil' mean. Moreover, in our government these conceptions of Good and Evil are often found as the justification for ethical, political and economic wars and sanctions, just and unjust. Who is right, if anybody? Many people disagree.

Let us trace back and examine what some of the world's most influential philosophies and religions have to say about these questions, and see what prospects they offer to the Good Life and the Problem of Evil.

Plato, Aristotle, Socrates: Morons?
Utopia is a theory of the good life. "The Good Life" is a phrase taken from the ancient Greeks. These ancient philosophers weren't just concerned with abstract theories of cosmic origins and a search for timeless truths. They were interested in the very real questions of how one is to live a life that is meaningful and good. This was not a particularity of the ancient Greeks, but is well documented and therefore widely influential.

The ancient philosophers wanted to know what types of beliefs and practices would enable one to live a life that is meaningful and good and achieve what Aristotle called, *Eudaimonia* –'peace of mind'. Preeminent thinkers such as Socrates, Plato and Aristotle did not believe it was realistic to think that one type of state or empire could exist, or should exist in order to police and govern the world. Aristotle especially saw a plurality in this regard. He believed the norms and traditions of each culture and city-state beckoned a distinct political form or polity, whether it be monarchy, aristocracy, oligarchy, or what have you.

For Socrates and his student Plato, Good is an eternal and unchanging Form or ideal, superior to all else. This corresponds to human nature: people pursue the Good. In a discussion between Socrates, a military general, and others concerning the question of justice and the Good Life, as written in Plato's *Republic*, Socrates says that the Good is something "every soul pursues, and all… actions are done for its sake."[1] (505e) The attraction and beauty of the Good is something greater than any other force in the universe. Socrates tells his companions, "…as for the objects of knowledge, not only is their being known due to the Good, but also their reality…" This is because "the Good is not being but [is] superior to and beyond being in dignity and power." (509b) Thus, the Good precedes existence and is something that all existents are guided by.

Throughout the many dialogues of Socrates there is a type of argument he uses called a 'dialectic'. The dialectic, or 'Socratic Method', consists of a series of questions and answers, each question attempting to examine what is implied or implicated by each answer. The Socratic method is both an intuitional and intellectual process of thought in which dialogical reasoning, or reasoning through argument, reveals the Good and the True, in the same way that two and two can be deduced to be the equal of four.

A conclusion implicates a premise. There is, as an example, the logical form of Barbara: it someone, say Barbara, believes that Socrates is a man and that all men are mortal; it follows necessarily that she must believe Socrates is mortal. Dialogue reveals and enables us to recollect the True and the Good and to realize the Life that is Good. Honesty and sincerity of reason cannot fail to reveal the Good, which is not entirely unlike Gandhi's *satyagraha,* or experiments with truth.

While Plato thought all people were motivated by the Good, he argued that people did Bad only through ignorance. This was stated most succinctly in his book on other polities called *Laws* in which he stated that, "…all bad men are always involuntarily bad…the unjust man may be bad, but that he is bad [is] against his will."[23] (IX, 860) Nor can the god be blamed for the existence of evil, because the divine is purely good. (379c)

Knowledge and ethics not only have a strong relationship but are in fact one and the same, just as the virtues, such as wisdom and honesty, are all one and the same. The word *philosophy* was probably coined by Plato, and literally means "the love of wisdom". To do good is to pursue the Good, and to do bad one must be ignorant. A moral maxim of Socrates says that, "The unexamined life is not worth living."

---

[1] Plato, *The Republic*, trans. G.M.A. Grube, (Indianapolis, Hackett Publishing Company, 1974) (a)
[2] Plato, *Laws*, trans. B. Jowett, in *The Dialogues of Plato*, Vol. II, (New York, Random House, 1937) (b)
[3] This is repeated in another dialogue titled *Protagoras*, "For no wise man, as I believe, will allow that any human being errs voluntarily, or voluntarily does evil and dishonourable actions; but they are very well aware that all who do evil and dishonourable things do them against their will." "[N]o man voluntarily pursues evil, or that which he thinks is evil. To prefer evil to good is not in human nature…" (345, 358) Plato, *Protagoras*, trans. B. Jowett, in *The Dialogues of Plato*, Vol. I, 1937) (c)

There is a responsibility as intellectuals, of which Socrates' own defense at his trial is exemplary, where no feasible possibility is left unconsidered. This is called 'fallibilism' and is the belief that human's are capable of error. Socrates tells us: "The struggle to be good or bad is important...much more important than people think, so that it is not worth being led on by honours, wealth, or any office, nor indeed by poetry, to neglect justice and other virtues." (608b)

Plato held to a vision of a philosopher-king who would run the city-state in a wise and just manner, securing peace and well-being for its citizens. Socrates prophesies:

"Cities will have no respite from evil...nor will the human race, I think unless philosophers rule as kings in the cities, or those whom we now call kings and rulers genuinely and adequately study philosophy." (473d)

Aristotle, who studied under Plato for 20 years, believed there to be a human nature as well: the pursuit of *Eudaimonia*, which is translated into English as meaning "happiness" or "peace of mind". In a work dedicated to his son, Nicomachus, called *Nicomachean Ethics*, Aristotle wonders how this peaceful state of mind is to be developed and achieved: "Is happiness acquired by learning, or habit[], or by some other form of cultivation? Or is [happiness] the result of some divine fate or even of fortune?" (1099b9-10)

Natural and supernatural possibilities such as divine intervention, fate, and fortune are weighed for their influence before Aristotle reaches his conclusion that "it is the activities expressing virtue that control happiness..."[4] (1100b10) 'Virtue Ethics' is often the title given to Aristotle's ethics because he held that becoming virtuous controlled happiness and well-being. And although happiness is blessed and reflects the quality and fortune of one's upbringing, Aristotle believed that "...the virtues arise in us neither by nature nor against nature. Rather, we are by nature able to acquire them, and reach our complete perfection through habit." (1103a25)

In an ethics based upon virtue, emphasis is placed on human excellence, good habits and character, as well as upon our ends or goals in life. Aristotle teaches us that "we cannot be intelligent without being good." (1144b) A virtue is a goal –a desire to become something or someone and to achieve excellence and perfection. He says that:

"...the happy person...keeps the character he has throughout his life. For always, or more than anything else, he will do and study the actions expressing virtue, and will bear [good or bad] fortunes most finely, in every way and in all conditions appropriately, since he is truly 'good, foursquare and blameless'." (1100b18-22)

Eudaimonia is not to be confused with pleasure. Aristotle believed the virtues brought pleasure and for the followers of Aristotle, the Aristotelians, the study of virtue and learning in general are pleasurable. This is so not only for philosophers, but for scientists and mathematicians as well. The arts of music and poetry are also pleasurable ways of learning and studying virtue. Through the tragic arts, for example, people experience something called a *catharsis*, or purgation of fear and pity. Aristotle believed that artistic expression could not fail to be concerned with ethics, because all human actions are either good or bad. Aristotle noted that, "The *objects* which the poet as mimetic [or imitative] artist represents are human beings in action. Such agents must be

---

[4] Aristotle, *Nicomachean Ethics*, trans. Terence Irwin, (Indianapolis, Hackett Publishing, 1985) (a)

either good or bad, for the diversities of human character are nearly always secondary to the primary distinction between virtue and vice."[5] (*Poetics*, 1448a1)

Where Plato believed that there was one universal Good, Aristotle held there to be many distinct virtues. For Aristotle what is Good and what is just become defined according to the social fabric of relations relative to each community or city-state. "What is just is found among those who have a share in things that unconditionally are good, [and] who can have an excess or a deficiency of them". (1137a30)

Some of the virtues Aristotle discusses are bravery, temperance (or being well-tempered), generosity, magnificence, magnanimity, wisdom, and justice -all of which ensure the Good Life and *Eudaimonia*. Different societies have held different virtues, however, though all societies probably celebrate excellence and character. The Romans, for example, centuries after Aristotle, held Honor to be a virtue and an important goal to strive after, to become honorable. Aristotle did not think so. He thought that as an end or goal, the desire for honor might lead to conformity -the wish to be praised by others; or elitism, a kind of ethical-fulfillment wherein honor relieves us of our moral and intellectual responsibility.

Where these ancient thinkers seem to ethically differ the most depends ostensibly upon their respective understandings of human nature. This is clearly shown by the different virtues that are found. Socrates and Plato, for example, did not believe that virtue could be learned and "den[ied] that virtue[s] can be taught" (*Protagoras*, 360) believing the virtues were "a gift from the gods".[6] (*Meno*, 100b) And although virtue cannot be taught, recall that Plato and Socrates did not believe badness or vice are blameworthy. This was because everyone seeks the good and only does bad from ignorance.

To his teacher's thesis, Aristotle in part agrees, but he raises a corollary. "Suppose…no one is responsible for acting badly, but one does so because one is ignorant of the end, and thinks this is the way to gain what is best for oneself… [I]f all this is true, then, surely virtue will be no more voluntary than vice?" (1114b5-10)

If we believe that virtue can be learned, could it follow that vice can be taught as well? If we believe virtue can be learned and taught doesn't it follow that people can be held morally responsible? If virtue is perfection and excellence and is praiseworthy, does it follow that what is contrary to this is blameworthy? For Aristotle, believing that virtue is something that can be learned or taught implies something about moral responsibility. Consider, for example, the angry or bitter person. Aristotle thought that, although anger is painful to oneself, anger is important and necessary at times.

"The person who is angry at the right things and towards the right people, and also in the right way, at the right time and for the right length of time, is praised. This, then, will be the mild person, since it is his mildness that is praised; for being a mild person means being undisturbed, not led by feeling." (1125b30)

"The excess [of anger] arises in all these ways –in anger towards the wrong people, at the wrong times, more than is right, more hastily than is right, and for a longer time. However, [the vices are] not all found in the same person; for they could not all exist together, since evil destroys itself as well as other things, and if it is present as a whole it becomes unbearable." (1126a10)

---

[5] Aristotle, *Poetics*, translated as "The Art of Poetry", and edited by Philip Wheelwright, in *Aristotle*, (New York, The Odyssey Press, 1951) (b) p292
[6] Plato, *Protagoras*, (c) 360; *Meno*, (d) 100b

Someone who believes that the opposite of good is evil might also believe the opposite of virtue is vice. Aristotle was not so simple-minded. Rather, virtue is the intermediary between excess and deficiency, which are both vices. When the virtues are exceeded or are deficient it is called by the Greek word *akrasia,* which means "incontinence", or lack of self-control. "Incontinence and continence are concerned with what exceeds the state of most people; the continent person abides [by reason] more than most people are capable of doing, the incontinent person less." (1152a25-27)

Incontinent people have bad habits, are often unreasonable, and are easily led by their emotions. Aristotle describes being incontinent as like being asleep or drunk and this type of person is said to be overly stubborn, ignorant, opinionated, and boorish.

Be that as it may, the incontinent person is not led by vice but by an error of reason. This is because Aristotle believed that human nature entailed a "rational principal". Although philosophers from Turkey, from before the time of Socrates, had believed the earth was round and that humans had evolved from sea-creatures, Aristotle believed that what set humans apart from animals was rationality –humans were a "rational animal".

As Aristotle says, "…actions caused by emotion and other feelings that are natural or necessary for human beings…[are not] thereby unjust or wicked, since it is not vice that caused him to inflict harm." (1135b20) "Incontinents through habituation are more easily cured than the natural incontinents; for habit is easier than nature to change." (1152a30)

Only the bad-tempered or intemperate person is unconditionally bad because of their immunity to reason. Aristotle, who was the son of a physician, finds intemperance incurable and describes the intemperate person as 'bestial', 'vicious', without good habits or character, abandoning themselves for appetite without regret.

Isms' and Ologies'

These ethics of Plato, Aristotle, and Socrates as well as their theories of the Good Life and *Eudaimonia* have not been as influential upon the Western world as one might have hoped. Still, these ancient philosophers have had an enormous influence in other areas of science and understanding, in disciplines which today are typically thought of as separate from ethics (albeit, with results deleterious). Aristotle, for example, is believed to have been one of the earliest biologists, zoologists, or psychologists -among other things. Between the two, both Plato's and Aristotle's philosophies have been particularly influential in such areas as logic, metaphysics, ontology, theology, and epistemology. Ironically, the popular Western ethic of Good vs. Evil circuitously became founded upon these seemingly 'pre-ethical' areas of philosophical thought.

'Metaphysics' was originally an ancient Greek word coined by the disciples of Aristotle. When Aristotle died in the year 322 Before the Common Era (BCE) his students found amongst his works a writing which came after his study of nature titled *Physics,* so they called it *Metaphysics.* 'Meta' means 'after' or 'about' and 'physics' means nature. In contemporary usage, metaphysics is like a fancy synonym for 'reality' or 'ultimacy'. Under this conception, whatever really ultimately exists, 'the furniture of the universe', is the metaphysic.

The most common versions of metaphysics are materialism and idealism. Materialism came from such philosophers as Democritus and Leucippus who held that reality was constructed of atoms. Thus, materialism holds that reality is ultimately physical. Idealism, on the other hand, holds that reality is ultimately spirit or mind. In this sense the mind or spirit are immaterial while what is 'external' to the spirit is just representation. A more popular name for idealism is dualism (or two-ism). The most popular dualism found in the world is the belief in the mortal body and the immortal soul. When metaphysical dualism becomes applied as a foundation for ethics, ethics popularly becomes idealized as being ultimately Good vs. Evil.

For Plato (who was an idealist) 'theology' was metaphysics, a term which he coined, that is usually translated as meaning "the science of God". Plato's theology, or science of the divine, holds that the divine is good and perfect. As Plato was critical of the many decadent (Western) forms of poetry, he believed theology should become the poet's task, eulogizing the divine. Or as he put it:

> "We shall compel the poets to deny that these [bad] deeds were [the god's] or to deny that they were [done by] children of the gods; they must not say both or attempt to persuade our young men that the gods beget evil and that heroes are not better than ordinary men. As we said earlier, these things are both impious and untrue, for we have shown that evils cannot originate with the gods." (*Republic*, 391e)

Plato, Aristotle, and Socrates all agree that evil could not originate with the gods or the divine. Aristotle did not believe that the divine was concerned with the world, which is an arena of change. As we saw in the *Nicomachean Ethics*, Aristotle taught that "evil destroys itself". Aristotle's theology was much like that of the American Founding Fathers who were Deists and were not necessarily conservative. For Aristotle the divine is an Unmoved Mover, unchanging and perfect. "...what It thinks of is what is most divine and most worthy of esteem. And in this It is unchanging...it is that which *thinks Itself*, and Its thinking is a thinking of thinking."[7] (*Metaphysics*, 12:9) Most theologies tend to be more tied in with one particular ethics, which in turn is founded upon a metaphysics or ontology.

'Ontology' is another concept that is associated with metaphysics and theology. Ontology is like metaphysics in that it is concerned with denoting ultimate reality. However, ontology is more specifically concerned with existence or 'being' as the central aspect of reality. Human nature, under this conception, is a kind of ontology. As we have seen for Plato and Aristotle there was a certain ontology or human nature –for Plato, people pursue the good, for Aristotle, there is a 'rational principle' or ability to use reason (or logic) which helps us achieve *eudaimonia*, or peace of mind.

Logos, which in Greek means "meaning", was for Plato a description of the *theos* or divine. Plato's combination of *theos* and *logos* came to have a big influence in popular Western philosophy, as for example in the personification of the divine, where the divine takes on a form. For Aristotle, the *logos* became logic: the science of reason. Around the same time in history logic had been developed by Hindu and Chinese logicians independently of each other. However, Aristotle was the first among Greeks to attempt to formalize or systematize logic, the science of reason.

---

[7] Aristotle, *Metaphysics*, trans. and ed. Philip Wheelwright, in *Aristotle*, (c) p102-103

Popular Philosophy: Religion

The proliferation of Aristotle is to the greatest extent due to Islam rather than Christianity or any other popular Western philosophy. From early on there had been a tension between popular Christianity and the followers of Aristotle. This resulted from some of the ways in which Aristotle differed from his teacher Plato, as for example in Aristotle's belief in the indivisibility of the soul and body.

The Council of Ephesus in the year 431 of the Common Era [CE] banned the teaching of Aristotle in Europe[8], though just a hundred years later all philosophy schools were banned from that continent. Around this time Aristotle's works had been taken by the Persian Nestorius and were translated into Syrian and taught at the school of Edessa in Syria. Eventually Aristotle's works were translated into Arabic. "By 800 [CE] Arabic had become virtually an international language of science. Once translated into Arabic, Aristotle penetrated to the limits of Islam's dominion —which meant, to the Indus in the East and to the Pyrenees in the West."[9]

Plato's theology came to be very influential in Europe and played a crucial role in the development of Western philosophy. At around the same time that Jesus lived there was a man who lived in northern Egypt named Philo, a Greek word meaning 'Love', as in *philo –sophia*, or the 'love of wisdom'. Philo worked diligently to interrelate popular Greek Platonic philosophy with Hebrew philosophy. He used the Greek Platonic conception of *logos* in order to translate the Jewish conception of God, which is monotheism.

In Judaism (and Islam) God cannot be represented and is only to be 'known' through revealed texts. In Judaism it is said, "Yhwh is the Torah", i.e., 'the written Word'. Philo's use of *logos* had a very big effect on Christianity, which maintains "the word became flesh". The beginning of the fourth gospel reads: "In [the] beginning the Word was, and the Word was with God, and the Word was a god... So the Word became flesh and resided among us, and we had a view of his glory, a glory such as belongs to an only-begotten son from a father."[10] (John 1:1,14)

Very differently, the *logos* of Aristotle came to have enormous influence on Arabic and Muslim philosophy. As a British logician has noted "…it was above all [Aristotle's] logic that Arabic philosophers thought important at first. Later, however, they studied also his *Metaphysics* and his *De Anima*."[11] By the time Aristotle was translated from Arabic into Latin in the 12th century by the Bishop of Toledo, his philosophy had acquired through Islam a "definite, systematic interpretation."[12]

The logic and ethics of Socrates have been very influential in Western legal philosophy and jurisprudence. American courtrooms make use of the dialectical method of Socrates (called 'the Socratic-Method') through cross-examining, questioning and answering. Socrates' thesis that knowledge claims must be justifiable is not dissimilar to

---

[8] Josef Pieper, *Scholasticism: Personalities and Problems of Medieval Philosophy*, trans. Richard and Clara Winston, (New York, McGraw-Hill Book Company, 1964) p103; among other writers –most notably the Greek physicians Hypocrites and Galen.
[9] Pieper, p104
[10] All references from the New Testament are translations by New World Bible Translation Committee, (Brooklyn, Watchtower Bible and Tract Society of New York, Inc., 1961)
[11] Bertrand Russell, *A History of Western Philosophy*, (New York, Simon and Schuster, 1945) (a) p424
[12] Pieper, p107

the legal standard: 'innocent until proven guilty'. However, the legacy of Plato's ethical influence has not been as profound as that of his teacher, Socrates, or for that matter, his pupil Aristotle. The European tradition that used Plato's philosophy didn't have much use for his ethics, or for that matter -his love of wisdom, or belief in the philosopher king. In contradistinction Plato's philosophy became combined with such notions as 'Original Sin' and the nature of man as 'Fallen'. For followers of this tradition it was a human's nature to sin and do evil. As Plato's theology was metamorphized, no room was left for his ethics. In its stead was placed a dualistic realm of good and evil.

a) Ethics and Theology

In fact, in the Western world the foundation for ethics became nothing dialogical at all, but became based on the realms of metaphysics, theology, and ontology. For example, a principal theological concept of Plato that was very influential in Western thought is the idea that the divine is good. This goodness is often identified with love. For example, the Christian God is often referred to as the 'God of Love' and the New Testament tells us that, "God is love". (1st Epistle of John 4:16)

The identification of God with love predates the existence of Christianity however, as well as Plato. The religions of the ancient Celts and Greeks offer good examples. In ancient Greece *Eros* was not just the word for love but was the God of Love. So too in the great religion of the Celts –the beautiful Irish Goddess *Aine* is the Goddess of Love.

The holy books of Judaism, the Torah, and the holy book of Islam, the Quran, abound with references to divine love. At the very beginning of Genesis Yhwh (which is the Hebrew name of God) referred to all of His creations at the end of each day as good. "And Yhwh said: 'Let there be light'…Yhwh saw…that it was good."[13] (Genesis 1:3-4) In the Torah, the love of Yhwh extends beyond creation. He says: "I will make all My goodness pass before thee…and I will be gracious to whom I will be gracious, and will show mercy on whom I will show mercy." (Exodus 33:19) "The Lord, the Lord, Yhwh, merciful and gracious, long-suffering, and abundant in goodness and truth." (Exodus 34:6) "The Lord is slow to anger, and plenteous in loving kindness, forgiving iniquity and transgression…" (Numbers 14:18) "For the Lord thy God is a merciful God." (Deuteronomy 4:31) "And the Lord will make thee overabundant for good…" (Deuteronomy 28:11)

For Muslims the holy book of Islam, the Quran, speaks eloquently of Allah's love. The Quran is made up of 114 Surahs or chapters, each beginning with the same phrase which reminds us of Allah's compassion: "In the Name of Allah, the Merciful, the Compassionate". The Quran is a guide for humans and tells us to love the world and do good. "And Allah gave them the reward of this world and fairest reward of the world to come; and Allah loves the good-doers." (Surah 3:141) "…and forget not thy portion of the present world; and do good, as Allah has been good to thee. And seek not to work corruption in the earth; surely Allah loves not the workers of corruption." (Surah 28:77) "…and be just. Surely Allah loves the just." (Surah 49:9)

---

[13] All references to the Torah are translations from the Masocretic Text, (Philadelphia, The Jewish Publication Society of America, 1917). The Tanach, or Hebrew Bible, says: "The Lord is gracious, and full of compassion; slow to anger, and of great mercy. The lord is good to all; and His tender mercies are over all His works." (Psalms 145:8-9)

The Quran teaches:
"It may be Allah will yet establish between you and those of them with whom you are at enmity love. Allah is All-powerful; Allah is All-forgiving, All-compassionate. Allah forbids you not, as regards those who have not fought you in religion's cause, nor expelled you from your habitations, that you should be kindly to them, and act justly towards them; surely Allah loves the just." Surah 60:7-8

b) Ethics and Ontology

Although popular religions uniformly hold to the love and goodness of the divine, there are differences concerning their ontology and general understanding of human nature. Just as theology and metaphysics became important realms for the foundation of ethics, so too did ontology. In Western philosophy, ontology, or the theory of human nature became a central and integral support for ethics. 'Original Sin', for example, is particular to Christianity and is neither found among the Greeks of antiquity, nor in Judaism or Islam. The ancient Greeks had no conception of sin at all, but believed the gods were concerned with *hubris*, or excessive pride, which makes the gods jealous.

'Original Sin' is the idea that all people are predisposed toward sin or vice because of the fallen nature of humans. Jesus asked his followers: "Why do you call me good?" only to tell them that, "Nobody is good, except one, God."[14] (Mark 10:18, Luke 18:19) 'Original Sin' is described in the New Testament: "…just as through one man sin entered into the world and death through sin, and thus death spread to all men because they had all sinned." (Romans 5:12) There is a story relayed several times in the New Testament in which Jesus comes across a child who is paralyzed. Jesus tells him: "Child, your sins are forgiven." (Mark 2:5) and the child walks away. Every time that someone is healed of a disability or sickness in the New Testament, it is because they have been forgiven of sin.

One example of sin is sex (translated here as 'fornication'): "Flee from fornication. Every other sin that a man may commit is outside his body, but he that practices fornication is sinning against his own body." (1Corinthians 6:18) This human susceptibility to sinning predates man, because first "the woman was thoroughly deceived and came to be in transgression." (1Timmothy 2:13)

In Judaism, however, there is no concept of original sin. The very first chapter of Genesis says that humans were made in Yhwh's image, "And Yhwh created man in His own image, in the image of Yhwh created He him; male and female created He them. And Yhwh blessed them… And Yhwh saw every thing that He made, and, behold, it was very good." (Genesis 1:27-28,31) Although Yhwh created all people out of Adam and Eve, the Jews are His Chosen People, bearing the Law and residing amidst the gentiles, or the non-Jew. (Genesis 12:1)

In Islam, original sin is absent as well. In fact, many Muslims believe perfection is attainable for humans, and some see the Imam as morally perfect. More than once the Quran teaches that, "Allah loves the good-doers." (Surah 4:128, 5:94) The Quran says, "We indeed created Man of the fairest stature." (Surah 95:4) And because humans are capable of being good and just, Allah says, "I am setting in the earth a viceroy." (Surah 2:28) "It is He who appointed you viceroys in the earth." (Surah 35:35) "Let there be one

---

[14] However, when this occurs in Matthew it stated differently. "Why do you ask me about what is good? One there is that is good." (Matthew 19:17) A chapter later Jesus asks, "Is it not lawful for me to do what I want with my own things? Or is your eye wicked because I am good?" (Matthew 20:15)

nation of you, calling to good, and bidding to honour, and forbidding dishonour; those are the prosperers." (Surah 3:100)

"Do not exult; Allah loves not those that exult; but seek, amidst that which Allah has given thee, the Last Abode, and forget not thy portion of the present world; and do good, as Allah has been good to thee. And seek not to work corruption in the earth; surely Allah loves not the workers of corruption." Surah 28:77

The Problem of Evil

As we can see for popular philosophy and religion alike, there is the belief that the divine is both good and loves the good. What about bad and evil? What are their origins according to popular religion? While we saw a common understanding of the ineffective nature of evil amongst the three popular philosophers, for the three popular monotheisms each has a different understanding of evil. In fact, the problem and the phrase itself, the "Problem of Evil" originated either with Christian theologians or their critics.

The problem can be stated fairly simply: if God is good, why is there evil? Through the centuries Christians have offered different answers to this question. Some Christians have held that evil is the product of Satan, the angel who would not obey God and was exiled from heaven and condemned to the earth where he can control humans. Some hold that because of original sin people have a tendency to be tempted by evil and susceptibility toward sinning and corruption. Many Christians follow a metaphysical dualism in which human flesh and the physical world are evil, while the soul and spirit are good. The gospel of Matthew says: "The spirit, of course, is eager, but the flesh is weak." (26:41)

Plato, Aristotle and Socrates all agreed that evil could not originate with the divine. Plato and Socrates held that bad or evil are just forms of human ignorance. Aristotle held that if evil existed it would have already destroyed itself. However, belief in evil began a long time ago and despite the efforts of philosophers, is still popular in the West today, because of religion.

Some of the earliest cosmogonies (or theories of the universe -cosmogony is another fancy word for metaphysics) have held that reality is a dualistic realm of good vs. evil. Such ancient religions as Zoroastrianism, Orphism, Manichaeism, and Mithras all held that reality consisted of this dual opposition of good vs. evil. Traditionally, the followers of the Persian prophet Zoroaster (7th century BCE) believed in two gods or supernatural forces. Contemporary Zoroastrians emphasize their commitment to one God, Ahura Mazda, the benevolent 'wise Lord' who, created the world. Ahriman was at one point considered as the maleficent God of Evil. For a certain kind of ancient Zoroastrian reality was understood as the battle between Ahura Mazda and Ahriman, between Good and Evil, a battle that would ultimately result in the victory of Good and the destruction of Evil.

Manichaeism is usually sited as the exemplar dualist cosmogony of Good vs. Evil. Manichaeism was the religion of the 3rd century Babylonian prophet Mani, who it is believed died in prison. For Mani, reality was a struggle between the forces of light and dark, between Good and Evil. As the philosopher Bertrand Russell wrote in his *History of Western Philosophy*, "Manichaeism combined Christian and Zoroastrian elements, teaching that evil is a positive principle, embodied in matter, while the good principle is embodied in spirit."[15]

This opposition of Good and Evil plays a very important role in Christianity and is the sole reason why Christians believe that they need to be 'saved'. Humans and the divine alike, struggle with evil. This is sometimes construed as God vs. the Devil. We are told in the New Testament: "…for with evil things God cannot be tried nor does he himself try anyone." (James 1:13)

However, the three popular monotheisms we have been dealing with handle the problem of evil differently. In Judaism the oppositional structure of Good vs. Evil is absent. In the Torah we are told of a tree of knowledge, "For Yhwh doth know that in the day ye eat thereof, then your eyes shall be opened, and ye shall be as God, knowing good and evil." (Genesis 3:5) Later in the Torah Yhwh reveals the extent of his omnipotence: "See, I have set before thee this day life and good, and death and evil…" (Deuteronomy 31:15)

The Tanach (or Hebrew Bible) offers examples of how evil is either understood or is questioned: "Now the spirit of the Lord had departed from Saul, and an evil spirit from the Lord terrified him." (1Samuel 16:14) "I form the light, and create evil; I am the Lord, that doeth all these things." (Isaiah 45:7) "Shall evil befall a city, and the Lord hath not done it?" (Amos 3:6) "What? Shall we receive good at the hand of Yhwh, and shall we not receive evil?" (Job 2:10) "Out of the mouth of the Most High proceedeth not evil and good?" (Lamentations 3:38)

The oppositional structure of good vs. evil is absent from Islam as well. The Quran embraces the fact that people err through ignorance. The Quran says of those who disagree: "Truly, they are the foolish ones, but they do not know… they are not right-guided." (Surah 2:11,15) "Allah shall turn only towards those who do evil in ignorance, then shortly repent." (Surah 4:22) "There is no fault in you if you make mistakes, but only in what your heart premeditates." (Surah 33:5)

The Quran itself can be studied in order to avoid evil. "Whoso does righteousness, it is to his own gain, and whoso does evil, it is to his own loss." (Surah 45:14) "[A]nd this is a Book confirming, in Arabic tongue, to warn the evildoers, and good tidings to the good-doers." (Surah 46:12)

Muhammad had taught people to be sincere in their ethics. He said, "Le not any of you become a lackey who says, 'I am with the people; if they do good I shall do good, and if they do bad I shall do bad.'"[16] The Quran says, "Allah likes not the shouting of evil words unless a man has been wronged; Allah is All-hearing, All-knowing. If you do good openly or in secret or pardon an evil, surely Allah is All-pardoning, All-powerful." (Surah 4:147-148)

The Quran tells us: "Whatever good visits thee, it is of Allah; whatever evil visits thee is of thyself." (Surah 4:82) This is because, "Allah changes not what is in a people, until they change what is in themselves. Whensoever Allah desires evil for a people, there is no turning back; apart from Him, they have no protector." (Surah 13:11)

In Islam as in Judaism, there is no cosmic battle or struggle for the divine. This is well put near the very end of the Quran.

---

[15] Bertrand Russell, (a) p325

[16] Quoted by Muhamed S. El-Awa, *On the Political System of The Islamic State*, trans. Ahmad Naji al-Imam, (Indianapolis, American Trust Publications, 1980) p106

"In the Name of Allah, the Merciful, the Compassionate. Say: 'I take refuge with the Lord of the Daybreak from the evil of what He created, from the evil of darkness when it gathers, from the evil of the women who blow on knots, from the evil of an envier when he envies." Surah 113

In the Quran we find the position that evil cannot be understood as corresponding to knowledge or the good. Knowledge cannot be evil, but is a product of good. This is similar to something that Aristotle had written -that "we cannot be intelligent without being good." (1141b1) Rather, as Seyyed Hossein Nasr tells us, the closest cognate to the Arabic word for evil, *qubh*, is 'ugliness'.[17] Allah being all-powerful, has bestowed upon humans a book to guide. The Quran says: "And what of him, the evil of whose deeds has been decked out fair to him, so that he thinks it is good? Allah leads astray whomsoever He will, and whomsoever He will He guides." (Surah 35:8)

a) Good vs. Evil

One particularity of monotheism which limits all possible theologies is the belief in omniscience and omnipotence. A god who is omniscient is all-knowing, a god who is omnipotent is all-powerful. A third concept that is often added is omni-benevolence, or all-goodness, which as we have seen is common in our three popular religions. Beyond these meager similarities monotheism and theology differ, sometimes radically.

What is emphasized in both the Torah and the Quran was the inscrutability of the divine will –a place where theology becomes impossible either because we as humans lack this omniscience or omnipotence, or because it is believed that humans are not gods themselves. Yhwh "will show mercy on whom he will show mercy". Allah will lead "astray whomsoever He will, and whomsoever He will He guides".

In Judaism, Christianity, and Islam alike there exists a type of a metaphysical being created by this all-powerful God, called an angel. For example, in Genesis we are told that Yhwh has sent an angel to visit Abraham to tell him that animal sacrifice shall hereafter replace human sacrifice. At the summit of Mount Hira the angel Gabrielle recited the Quran to the prophet Muhammad. In the New Testament we learn of an angel named Satan who controls a whole metaphysical realm -evil.

Because Satan was defiant of God he was cast out of heaven, demoted to living in the earth, roaming its surface, and dwelling in the earth's heart of darkness -hell. At some point in the history of time, logically speaking, sometime after the Tanach was completed and before the New Testament was written, it is believed a rupture took place in monotheism. Something created by God began to have power over the things created by God. In fact, the world is *ruled* by Satan, a being so powerful humans cannot be good or even teach each other to be good. The New Testament tells us that: "...the original serpent, the one called Devil and Satan...is misleading the entire inhabited earth." (Revelation 12:9) According to this conception, humans cannot even attempt to save one another from such a force as evil, and accordingly Jesus instructs us to "resist not evil". (Matthew 5:39)

The Christian version of the Tanach is called the Old Testament. While there are many differences between the Tanach and the Old Testament, one of the many important dissimilarities is the translation that posits a figure named Satan. According to such a translation, one might assume that Satan has existed since Genesis when we find in the utopian Garden of Eden that he is a serpent waiting to tempt Eve. And in the epic poem

---

[17] Seyyed Hossein Nasr, *The Heart of Islam*, (San Francisco, HarperCollins, 2002) p223

of Job we would suddenly find Satan obedient to God, depicted as having persuaded God to kill many innocent people and cause a lot of suffering. Be that as it may, any translation which posits an angel named Satan in the Tanach is fraudulent.

The Jewish people have believed in some thing called in Hebrew, *Yesta Hara*, or the 'evil inclination'. Yesta Hara is much like the bad that Plato says people do out of ignorance, and not a metaphysical being or ultimate evil force. Two contemporary Rabbis put is succinctly, "For Judaism is so strictly monotheistic that it resisted the temptation to enthrone any being other than God with authority for a whole metaphysical realm, even the realm of evil."[18] Or, as Adin Steinsaltz writes, "Where other faiths believed in dualism or in two divinities, one creating only good and the other generating evil, Judaism always believed in one all-embracing entity."[19]

In the New Testament we find that the Hebrew word for 'accuser' became personified as Satan, a metaphysical being with more power than all of humanity. Although Jesus did not speak Hebrew but spoke a Semitic language called Aramaic, the New Testament was written in Greek. The Greek of the New Testament identifies Satan with the Greek word *Diabolos*, which means 'slanderer'. Satan is also referred to as *Lucifer*, and the *anti-Christ* and has his own number and sign, *666*.

In Christianity it is understood that because everything in the earth is led by Satan, people are very often possessed by demons or Satan himself. What is more, as the New Testament tells us variously, there are many ghosts and evil spirits that exist and can "possess" and overpower anyone, especially people who lack the 'right' kind of faith.[20] This is where the Christ becomes a saving factor in the failed Straw Utopia of an 'Old' Testament. While it might seem Jesus' mission was to perform exorcisms and rid people of demons that control them, in fact, the execution of Jesus is believed necessary in order that God may subjugate and execute the Devil, who has power over all of God's creations. The New Testament tells us: "…through his death [Jesus] might bring to nothing *that one having the means to cause death, that is, the Devil.*" (Hebrews 2:14)

The power of Satan, a figure not present in Judaism, and given the precedent of an entire realm of existence in Christianity, can be said to be a distraction for Muslims. As a monotheism, the perfection and all-powerfulness of Allah are emphasized. In Islam, Satan, or *Shaitan*, is a *Jinn* named Iblis. The Jinn are a being unlike Allah, or the angels, or humans for that matter. In fact, Iblis is obedient to Allah who is always all-powerful. The Quran tells us Iblis is a "foe to man", and is disobedient to humans. He says: "I would never bow myself before a mortal whom Thou has created of a clay of mud moulded." (Surah 15:33) However, Iblis is obedient to Allah and is never destroyed. And because of the omnipotence and *tawhid*, or 'oneness' of Allah, there is no comic struggle between good and evil. Rather, in Islam, Evil is that which attempts to distract us when we are concentrating, pursuing justice, and living the Good life.

b) Evil and Epistemology
As we saw in the philosophies of Socrates, Plato, and Aristotle there is a relationship on the one hand between Truth and Good and on the other hand, the human

---

[18] Rabbi Morris N. Kertzer, Revised by Rabbi Lawrence A. Hoffman, *What is a Jew?*, (New York MacMillan Publishing Company, 1993) p120
[19] Adin Steinsaltz, *The Essential Talmud*, trans. Chaya Galai, (New York, Basic Books, 1976) p107
[20] Matthew 7:22, 12:24, 13:39, Mark 1:32, Luke 8:36, Revelation 16:14

capacity for ascertaining this Truth and Good. To do what is good presupposes knowing what the good is. For Socrates and Plato humans come to know the Good and the Truth through the dialectical method of questioning and answering. For Aristotle, it is the study and practice of the virtues that ensure us of *eudaimonia*. And as we find with popular religion, each has its own moral-epistemology, or theory of how we come to know what is good and what isn't good. To a greater or lesser extent, as the case may be, in each philosophy there is a correspondence between the understanding of ethics, or how one ought to live, and the understanding of nature and reality, or in the case of monotheism, the divine will.

The Socratic dialogue, *Euthyphro*, raises the question of how one comes to know the divine good. On his way to his own trial, Socrates' comes across a priest named Euthyphro outside the courthouse. Euthyphro tells Socrates about a case he intends to bring to court. Euthyphro believes that he is justified in seeking the death penalty against his own father because the gods believe it is good and pious to punish the wicked. Apparently a man whom Euthyphro's father had taken prisoner (the man had murdered a slave), died of exposure when he was fettered and left to sleep outside. Socrates shows the priest that the situation is in fact not so simple as it seems, and in earnest Socrates asks the self-righteous priest: "Is the pious loved by the gods because it is pious, or is it pious because it is loved by the gods?"[21] (*Euthyphro*, 10a)

For many who have studied Plato, this is a serious paradox. It can be restated: Is the good good because the divine says it is so, or is the good good because that's what good is, regardless of the divine opinion? In either case, to do what is good one must know what the good is –but how is that possible?

As we have seen, often times in popular religion the divine values and purposes become known through a revealed or holy book. This book is disseminated for people by experts of one sort or another. Sometimes religious experts offer different interpretations of what is required for correct observance or practice.

In Judaism and Islam alike, one studies the revealed book, be it the Torah or the Quran which taken together probably contain over a thousand laws of conduct and practice. The Torah and Quran tell us how to be good, and the relationship between faith and knowledge is established. Through practicing and studying the laws, as well as the long history of discussion, interpretation, commentary, and reinterpretation of these laws, one pursues the Good Life according to their commitment.

In some religions there is no revealed holy book *per se*, but there is a central human authority who best knows the divine will. For example, in Hinayana Buddhism, this position is occupied by the Dahlia Lama. In Catholicism it is the Pope, who cannot fail to utter the divine will. In Judaism as well as Islam, however, there is no single human authority who has infallible access to the divine will.

Thus, there can be a gap between faith and knowledge –of knowing what is demanded by the divine will. Thomas Huxley labeled this inscrutability of the divine presence, agnosticism. An agnostic may believe in the existence of God, and be convinced that the very existence of this God cannot be proven. (This is the reasoning of Immanuel Kant). For those who think they cannot fail to know the divine will, the distinction between faith and reason is made ambiguous, and ethics becomes arbitrary.

---

[21] Plato, *Euthyphro*, trans. G.M.A. Grube, (Indianapolis, Hackett Publishing, 1981) (e) p14

An ethic founded purely on faith, without the advantages of reason, is capricious. An ethic founded purely on faith alone can be autocratic and imperial.

In Christianity the relationship between ethics and knowledge is tenuous. The point of Christian ethics is not to be good or study the good, but, because humans cannot be good, to search for or have faith in metaphysical salvation. The Problem of Evil thus exists only for Christianity because ethics becomes an ethics of salvation, thoroughly steeped in the inescapable opposing metaphysical duality of Good vs. Evil.

As in Manichaeism, 'Good and Evil' becomes an ultimate metaphysical duality for Christians –the parameters for all possible and actual behavior. In ethical dualism 'good' and 'evil' are representatives of two opposing forces, like black and white, or night and day. This simple binary opposition reduces ethics to a kind of unmutual exclusiveness. Ethics becomes trivialized and there is no lack of justification for war when there is a belief that whatever is not good is evil, and vice versa.

If moral strength rests upon faith in some metaphysic of resurrection it seems ethics has become something very weak. When an ethic is so crudely applied and unthinkingly obeyed it creates a precedent in opposition to reason and intellect –that is, the link between knowledge and ethics become confused and obscured. When it is believed that one couldn't fail to know what is good and what is evil, the many different values are eliminated, and reason is eliminated. And there is a similar result when ethics is not linked with knowledge but is considered to be purely belief or faith -there becomes no way of ascertaining truth or justice. Indeed, in a world of black and white, there is no way to even acknowledge what is different except by assimilating or eliminating.

Following the dictum of Jesus: "He who is not for me is against me" (Matthew 12:30) each person who does not believe Jesus is the savior is labeled "antichrist", which is on par with being evil. Saint John the Baptist teaches: "Who is the liar if it is not the one that denies that Jesus is the Christ? This is the antichrist, the one that denies the Father and the Son. Everyone that denies the Son does not have the Father either." (1John 2:22-23) This either/or situation is typical of dualism and a belief in the opposition of good and evil.

What is more, the tendency of treating ethics as a metaphysical dualism leads us away from qualitative reasoning and valuing, as well as dialogue and of course, the virtues. This is because the scope of a conception such as Good vs. Evil is not one of ethics but of metaphysics. Metaphysics is the nature of existence, the 'furniture of the universe', and not an evaluative judgment which might be taken to be right or wrong, better or worse, according to human needs and well-being. It is little wonder that ethics guided by these theological and metaphysical systems moves away from questions of practicality and relevance.

In popular Western philosophy, politics, and law, so much life and limb has been cost over issues which are not in opposition to ethics -issues such as having the right political beliefs, the right faith, allegiances, and conformities. There is a certain kind of theological obscurantism that has made impractical questions a matter of life and death and distracted us from more important ethical questions, such as how to live a good life.

In America we can see this Western tradition manifested in the whole realm of crimes in which no one is wrongfully harmed, so called consensual-crimes. Another form is the belief in the importance of a class war. In this war of class against class the relationship between knowledge and ethics, understanding what is good, dissolves.

Similarly, the War on Terror deals only with symptoms and does not reflect inward to realize the cause.

Non-theological Philosophy

Less popularly in the Western world there has been non-theological philosophy, sustained thousands of years now, arising prior to most popular Western traditions. Non-theological ethics can be found in the religions of Jainism, Buddhism, Confucianism, and Taoism. In each of these philosophical religions there is neither a belief in theology, nor a separation of the question of knowledge from ethics.

The 6th century *Analects* of Confucius are still studied today and have been much more influential in Asia than in its jutting Western peninsula. Confucius' "supreme moral principle in human relations" is *jen* (humanity, goodness). *Jen* is the Chinese word for 'virtue' and the tradition inspired by the *Analects* is a 'virtue ethics'. *Jen* "is also a practical morality easy to attain."[22] Confucius instructs us, teaching us that our concerns ought to be practical: "You do not understand even life. How can you understand death?"[23] (*Analects* 11:12)

Confucius based his ethics upon the education of humanity, through discussions and dialogue with others. The *Analects* are in fact a discussion between Confucius and others intellectuals and contains perhaps the earliest formulation of the Golden Rule. *Do unto others as you would have do unto you.* Where the Golden Rule is found in popular monotheism, Confucius did not use a theological or theistic base but accumulated this wisdom through his own experience in the world.

Around the same time in 6th century BCE Nepal, Gautama Buddha told his disciples the way to nirvana. One of the main schools of Buddhism, the *Mahayana*, has been particularly influential in propagating a non-theological ethics. In the stead of theology are praised the ethics and virtues such as dharma (duty), truth, tolerance, endurance, and non-enmity (non-hatred). The sacred writing, *Dhammapada*, is a collection made by the disciples' recordings of the Buddha's wisdom, of which the 15th chapter *Sukha-vaggo* or, "Happiness" says:

"Ah, so pleasantly we live without enmity among those with enmity. Among Humans with enmity do we dwell without enmity. (15.1) Ah, so pleasantly we live without affliction among those afflicted. Among humans with affliction do we dwell without affliction. (15.2) Ah, so pleasantly we live without restlessness among the restless. Among humans who are restless do we dwell without restlessness. (15.3) Winning, one engenders enmity; miserably sleeps the defeated. The one at peace sleeps pleasantly, having abandoned victory and defeat. (15.5) The wise one, the insightful, and the learned, having the virtue of enduring, dutiful, noble, a person true, intelligent, with such a one as this, one would associate, as the moon the path of the stars." (15.12)[24]

The sage Lao-Tzu's masterpiece, *Tao Te-Ching*, maintains an ethic based upon the appreciation for nature and the way (tao). The *Tao* teaches us to become naturalists

---

[22] Ch'u Chai and Winberg Chai, *Confucianism*, (Woodbury, New York, Barron's Educational Series, Inc., 1973) "Confucius' doctrine of *jen*, essentially a man-to-man relationship, is a moral system which is both practical and practicable. Without a trace of the metaphysical and the supernatural, it is readily understood; its teachings, replete with wisdom and common sense, can be applied in all human relations." (p37)
[23] Confucius, *Analects*, trans. D.C. Lau, (New York, Penguin Books, 1979)
[24] Gautama Buddha, *Dhammapada*, trans. John Ross Carter and Mahinda Palihawadana, (Oxford, Oxford University Press, 1987)

and shows us that nature is the point of return. "Earth is great.... Man models himself after the Earth. Earth models itself after Heaven. Heaven models itself after Tao. And Tao models itself after Nature." (25)

"The best man is like water. Water is good; it benefits all things and does not compete with them... The best man in his dwelling loves the earth. In his heart, he loves what is profound. In his associations, he loves humanity." (8)

"By the heavy accumulation of virtue one can overcome everything." (59)
"The way of heaven has no favorites. It is always with the good men."[25] (79)

While the Greek philosopher Epicurus continued the materialist critique of theology, one of the strongest critics of theology (as well as metaphysics) was the physician and skeptic Sextus Empiricus who lived around the 2nd or 3rd century of the common-era (CE). Sextus wrote about the history of skepticism and it's origins as a discipline in the 4th century BCE. This first Greek school of skepticism had begun by a man from Elis named Pyrrho. During the time of Alexander the Great, Pyrrho had traveled to India and studied with Hindu philosophers, who are sometimes called 'the naked philosophers', whom he learned from and tried to emulate. Pyrrho's disciple Timon of Phlius (who is possibly Shakespeare's comedic *Timon of Athens*) recorded the words and actions of his teacher.

Skepticism takes the fallibility of Socrates' dictum: "All I know is that I don't know anything" and goes a step further claiming: 'I can't even know that I don't know anything'. This wasn't supposed to make us despair of knowledge claims, but was held to be therapeutic as an ethic. Through *epoche* or the suspension of judgment, one could achieve *ataraxia*, or absence of disturbance – a tranquility not too foreign from Aristotle's Macedonian *eudaimonia*.

In his *Outlines for Pyrrhonism*, Sextus Empiricus points out a paradox of theology. This paradox occurs when people attempt to describe the ethical nature of the divine, either by 'positing' a particular theology or with the certainty in which humans ascribe to the divine a specific ethical nature. Theology is tantamount to impiety and blasphemy. He writes:

"...those who positively assert the existence of God probably are necessarily guilty of impiety. For if they say that he takes thought of all things, they will be saying that God is responsible for what is evil, while if they say he takes forethought for some things, or even for nothing, they will necessarily be saying that God is either malicious or weak, which is manifest impiety."[26]

Sextus points out how those attempts to reconcile the existence of evil with a theology committed to an omnipotent and benevolent deity soon runs into contradictions. Moreover, some might add, the notion of a consistent monotheism clashes with the idea of God being the god of something in particular and not a being that is universally all-powerful. Even if only temporarily evil persists in a world created and guided by a God of Love, this would seem to point to an imperfection of the divine. If reality is a passion play or cathartic lesson, the perverse and decadent prevail. For when the means justify the ends, there is no omnipotence.[27]

---

[25] Lao-Tzu, *The Way of Lao Tzu (Tao-te ching)*, trans. Wing-Tsit Chan, (Indianapolis, The Bobbs-Merrill Company, Inc., 1963) The *Tao* teaches us to question the view that reality is black and white: "How much difference is there between good and evil?" – 20

[26] Sextus Empiricus, "Outlines For Pyrrhonism", *Selections from the Major Writings on Scepticism, Man, and God*, trans. Sanford G. Etheridge, ed. Philip P. Hallie, (Indianapolis, Hackett Publishing, 1985) p178

[27] This is well pointed out by Walter Kaufmann, *The Faith of A Heretic*, (Garden City, New York, Anchor Books, 1963) p162

One of the first modern western philosophers to attempt to give a non-theological account of the problem of evil was the German philosopher Immanuel Kant. Kant lived during the 18th century and died shortly after Napoleon and the French conquered the majority of Europe. In a work titled, *Religion Within the Limits of Reason Alone* (1793), Kant attempted to account for the existence of Good and Evil as far as they coexist in human nature. He concludes that they cannot.

Kant argued that if Good or Evil are innate, that is, are part of human nature, then we can't be held morally responsible. This is because we were not free in the first place to have chosen our nature, however good or bad our nature actually is. If on the other hand people are free, which is the requirement for moral responsibility, they still cannot be held responsible for either Good or Evil. This is because freedom is spontaneous, or non pre-meditated. Kant's way around this problem is found in his belief that humans contain a rational principal to seek the Good, which is the moral law, and avoid Evil, which is contrary to moral law. According to Kant, all people must be guided by a single moral goal, principal, law, or concern, without which men become evil. Neither Good nor Evil can ever be eliminated as human capacities, and we can be held accountable for the propensity of the latter.

Kant saw philosophy leading toward the idea of a universal society where theology had by itself been less successful. "The result is that the *philosophical utopianism*, which hopes for a state of perpetual peace based on a league of peoples as a world-republic, and the *theological utopianism*, which waits for the complete moral regeneration of the entire human race, is universally ridiculed as day-dreaming."[28]

Instead what is needed is that each person be made to understand, through force if necessary, that there is one law or principle of good which must be obeyed by all.

"As far as we can see, therefore, the sovereignty of the good principle is attainable, so far as men can work toward it, only through the establishment and spread of a society in accordance with, and [established] for the sake of, the laws of virtue, a society whose task and duty it is rationally to impress these laws in all their scope upon the entire human race. For only thus can we hope for a victory of the good over the evil principle."

According to Kant, each person needs an 'ultimate concern', for without this singularity we may succumb to the evil principle.

"Despite the good will of each individual, because they lack a principle which unites them, men abandon, through their dissensions, the common goal of goodness and, just as though they were *instruments of evil*, expose one another to the risk of falling once again under the rule of the evil principle."[29]

Another critic of theology was the German philologist Friedrich Nietzsche (1844-1900). A philologist is someone who studies ancient writings and languages in order to authenticate them and determine when, where, and by whom they were written. Although once a student of theology himself, Nietzsche wrote of a discovery in his book *Beyond Good and Evil*, that there were more distinct origins in the moral vocabularies which opposed 'good' with 'bad' than one who opposed 'good' with evil'. He wrote:

"In a tour of the many finer and coarser moralities which have ruled or still rule on earth I found certain traits regularly recurring together and bound up with one another: until at length two basic types were revealed and a basic distinction emerged. There is *master morality* and *slave morality* –I add at once

---

[28] Immanuel, Kant, "Religion Within the Limits of Reason Alone", trans. Hoyt H. Hudson and Theodore M. Greene, in *The Philosophy of Kant*, ed. Carl J. Friedrich, (New York, The Modern Library, 1949) p382
[29] Kant, p404, 407. Although there is "...for us no conceivable ground from which the moral evil in us could originally have come... We are accountable, however, for the propensity to evil..." (p391, 382)

that in all higher and mixed cultures attempts at mediation between the two are apparent and more frequently confusion and mutual understanding between them, indeed sometimes their harsh juxtaposition – even within the same man, within *one* soul."[30]

Although Nietzsche emphasized that this dichotomy was by no means conclusive, he believed that by contrasting these two different moral schemes: 'Good and Evil' vs. 'Good and Bad', he offered a valuable thought experiment with which to teach Europeans something about being ethical. The morality of 'Good vs. Bad' is marked by nobility –by strength, distinction, rank. The morality of 'Good vs. Evil is marked by resentment – suspicion of virtue, mistrust, anti-humanism, and as Nietzsche teaches, a general confusion of 'good' with 'stupidity'.

Nietzsche's follow-up to *Beyond Good and Evil* is a companion-piece and analytic study, *On the Genealogy of Morals*.[31] As the title suggests, various systems of moral judgment are traced back and examination is made of the ethical meanings found variously in both modern and ancient languages. Nietzsche wrote:

"Fortunately, I have since learnt to separate theology from morality and ceased looking for the origin of evil *behind* the world. Some schooling in history and philology, together with the innate sense of discrimination with respect to questions of psychology, quickly transformed my problem into another one: under what conditions did man invent the value-judgments good and evil? *And what value do they themselves possess?* Have they helped or hindered the progress of mankind? Are they sign of indigence, or impoverishment, of the degeneration of life? Or do they rather reveal the plentitude, the strength, the will of life, its courage, confidence, and future?"[32]

Nietzsche writes that those who have used the dichotomy of 'good and bad' are of noble origin. "On the basis of this *pathos of distance*, they first arrogated the right to create values, to coin the names of values." (I, 2) The "origin of the opposition between 'good' and 'bad' is with the "pathos of nobility and distance". (I, 2) On the other hand, those who have used the dichotomy of 'good and evil' have a "morality of resentment" – their action is reaction, they are dishonest with themselves and others, and only hold respect for cleverness. (I, 10)

Nietzsche is often credited as being the 'supreme life-affirmer' among philosophers.[33] He came up with the idea of the 'Superman' which is now of cinematic-proportions, and Nietzsche popularly said, "That which does not kill me, only makes me stronger." However, as an individualist he did not hold much hope in the power of philosophy to positively influence humanity. A collection of his notes, *The Will to Power*, sheds some light on why he believed this. In a note titled "Anti-Darwin" Nietzsche wrote:

"What surprises me most when I survey the broad destinies of man is that I always see before me the opposite of that which Darwin and his school see or want to see today: selection in favor of the stronger, better-constituted, and the progress of the species. Precisely the opposite is palpable: the elimination of the lucky strokes, the uselessness of the more highly developed types, the inevitable dominion of average, even sub-average types... That will to power in which I recognize the ultimate

---

[30] Friedrich Nietzsche, *Beyond Good and Evil*, trans. R.J. Hollingdale, (London, Penguin Books, 1990) 260. A particularly beautiful aphorism says: "Whatever is done from love always occurs beyond good and evil." (a) 153
[31] Nietzsche made this clarification: "...that dangerous slogan written on the body of my last book: 'Beyond Good and Evil'... This at the very least does *not* mean 'Beyond Good and Bad'." *On the Genealogy of Morals*, trans. Douglas Smith, Oxford, Oxford University Press, 1996) (b) I, 17
[32] Nietzsche, *On the Genealogy of Morals*, Preface, (b) 3
[33] Although there are plenty of people who would claim that Nietzsche was the antichrist or the devil, labels both Dante and Martin Luther leveled at the prophet Muhammad, people usually do not consider that Nietzsche nor Muhammad, ever broke the Ten Commandments.

ground and character of all change provides us with the reason why selection is not in favor of the exceptions and lucky strokes: the strongest and most fortunate are weak when opposed by organized herd instincts, by the timidity of the weak, by the vast majority...

In summa: growth in the power of the species is perhaps guaranteed less by a preponderance of its children of fortune, of strong members, than by a preponderance of average and lower types. The latter possess great fruitfulness and duration; with the former comes an increase in danger, rapid wastage, speedy reduction in numbers."[34]

The 20th century philosopher Walter Kaufmann makes several important distinctions in a chapter titled "Against Theology". Kaufmann had been raised a Lutheran Protestant before converting to Judaism, eventually becoming agnostic in his two-fold heresy. He calls theology "a comprehensive, rigorous, and systematic attempt to conceal..." and a "systematic avoidance... [and] deliberate blindness to most points of view other than one's own, a refusal to see others as they see themselves and to see oneself as one appears to others –a radical insistence on applying different standards to oneself and others."[35]

"Emphatically, theology does not closely resemble either a science or philosophy. The model of the law is far more illuminating. So is another model that may well be more than merely a model: literary criticism."

Kaufmann agrees with the Christian pragmatist Richard Niebuhr that theology is often a covering and shield of class interest, whether it be political or otherwise.

"How little people think about theology, how much it is a mere epiphenomenon of organized religion, has been shown in some detail by Richard Niebuhr in *The Social Sources of Denominationalism*. As long as Protestant denominations have existed, social status rather than theology seems to have decided in most cases to what church a family belonged –and 'doctrines and practices changed with the mutations of social structure, not vice versa'"[36]

"Theology, of course, is not religion; and a great deal of religion is emphatically anti-theological... An attack on theology, therefore, should not be taken as necessarily involving an attack on religion. Religion can be, and often has been, untheological or even anti-theological."[37]

What non-theological philosophies and religions seem to be commonly pointing out is how metaphysics and theology can become dogmatic, and reason and ethics become subordinated to something tyrannical. When ethics is taken out of the evaluative realm of good and bad and placed in a metaphysical or theological realm of good and evil, there is little need of intelligence, or for that matter, any point to acknowledging what is different, unless to conquer and assimilate, or annihilate.

The American revolutionary and Founding Father Thomas Paine wrote of theology in his 1794-1795 study, *The Age of Reason*.

"The study of theology, as it stands in Christian churches, is the study of nothing; it is founded on nothing; it rests on no principles; it proceeds by no authorities; it has no data; it can demonstrate nothing; and it admits of no conclusion. Not any thing can be studied as a science, without our being in possession of the principles upon which it is founded; and as this is not the case with Christian theology, it is therefore the study of nothing."[38]

---

[34] Friedrich Nietzsche, *The Will to Power*, trans. Walter Kaufmann and R.J. Hollingdale, ed. Kaufmann, (New York, Vintage Books, 1968) (c) 685
[35] Kaufmann, p104
[36] Kaufmann, p130
[37] Kaufmann, p114, 127-128. However, he finds, "Christianity is inescapably a theological religion..." (p130)
[38] Thomas Paine, *The Age of Reason*, from *The Life and Major Writings of Thomas Paine*, ed. Philip S. Foner, (New York, The Citadel Press, 1945) p601

Thomas Paine's linking of theology with nihilism is not far from a comment made by the Austrian philosopher Karl Popper in his autobiography, *Unended Quest*: "Theology, I still think, is due to a lack of faith."[39]

Ethics and Metaphysics

Where the ethics of theology has been most true to its Platonic origin has been in its commitment to metaphysical dualism. Dualism is the belief that reality is split into two realms –usually construed as the spiritual or mental on the one hand, and the physical or material on the other. Dualism is most popularly expressed in the belief in the mortal body and the immortal soul. Although Plato was a fallibilist and his last writings demonstrate a great maturity and self-critique, it doesn't seem he ever got beyond this dual realm.

Aristotle, who did have a theology, did not always believe in the dualism of his master. Though a discussion of his metaphysics would be lengthy, suffice to say that Aristotle did not believe the soul was separate from the body. The philosophers he inspired were very much involved in biology and medicine.

It was perhaps thus when the believers in dualism began to reap the benefits of the physical sciences, ethics was left (without the benefit of the Aristotelian virtues) to the spiritual.[40] And thus someone today who claims themselves to be 'spiritual' means to imply that they are ethical. This is because the physical world is in some sense not real, or at least not eternal like the soul.

Under this metaphysical dualism the world of science seems bereft of the ethical. The world of nature around us seems to be without a purpose and only has one when it is made into an image by its artificer. The material world is determinate and finite while the ethical world is desire, emotion, and patriarchal.

According to such a view the super-mundane interest in science and the subsequent adaptation of physicalism seems to leave morality to politics and economics. The hallmarks of science -disinterestedness and deduction -leave the evaluative realm of ethics in the lurch. The philosophy which epitomized the sciences, positivism, sought at the same time to criticize and eliminate all talk of metaphysics and (and sometimes ethics) as nonsense, since neither is verifiable in the way that gravity and mathematics are.[41]

a) Ethics and Ontology
By the beginning of the 20th century in Europe the belief in ontology had become more popular than metaphysics. This was due in large part by the ensuing colonialism of 'savages', or globalization, which influenced the human sciences in areas such as

---

[39] Karl Popper, *Unended Quest*, (London, Routledge Classics, 1992) p14. Popper also mentions how Isaac Newton had believed his greatest legacy as a scientist would be his natural theology.
[40] This is a point made by Alasdair MacIntyre as I understand him in his excellent book *After Virtue*, (Notre Dame, University of Notre Dame Press, 1981)
[41] See for example A.J. Ayers, "Critique of Ethics and Theology", *Language, Truth and Logic*, (New York, Dover Publications, 1936)

anthropology, psychology, and the new Darwinism and eugenics.[42] Truth and knowledge became instruments for predicating 'the being of beings', that is, a weapon in the fight over what is the ultimate nature of being. Ontological theories claim to know human nature to the extent that they can both describe it as well as predict human action.

20th century Christian theologians such as Martin Heidegger and Paul Tillich believed that understanding human nature, or ontology, is fundamental in answering all questions about the Good. As the Catholic theologian Heidegger stated in his major work, *Being and Time* (1927), "Ontological inquiry is indeed more primordial, as over against the ontical [or physical] inquiry of the positive sciences." This "gives to the question of Being an ontological priority which goes beyond mere resumption of a venerable tradition and advancement of a problem that has hitherto been opaque."[43]

Similarly, and more clearly stated, in his lectures titled, *Love, Power and Justice*, the Protestant theologian Paul Tillich claims that an ontology or understanding of human nature is a necessary precondition to understanding ethics and love. "…without [an] ontological foundation neither love nor power nor justice can be adequately interpreted."[44] This is because for Tillich, "Values are expressions of existence unable to judge existence from a place beyond it." In other words, values cannot be objective or related to truth. This kind of subjectivity is more commonly known as relativism.

Historically, relativism can be seen as having been both philosophical and anti-philosophical, or as it is called in the latter case, sophistical. Socrates' philosophy of Irony may have as its birth the reaction or attack on sophistry. In ancient Greece there arose a kind of pedagogue called a sophist. The Sophists were hired teachers who taught the wealthier youths of Athens and other city-states how to argue to win. As Socrates' said in his own defense during his trial, the Sophists can make the worse argument appear the better. (*Apology*, 18c) While one might think that any person, be they sophist or philosopher, would want to win their arguments, the sophist will try to win, even at the expense of truth, whereas the philosopher will accept what is true, regardless of their own predisposition. Socrates' irony is found in the way in which he would argue with the sophist, naïve in his questions, only to show the inconsistencies and contradictions of their supposed knowledge once the sophist was encouraged to elaborate. Socrates taught that if the job of philosophy is to change people's minds, then the philosopher is the person who most loves changing their mind.

In a way relativism seems harmless. It seems open-minded and tolerant. If, for example, someone claimed it isn't good to go frolicking naked in the forest, as relativists we would grant this person the right to their perspective, even if we thought there was no absolute right or wrong in the matter. However, there is a unforeseeable tendency with relativism in that it is conducive to, and acquiescent in imperialism. Why is this so?

The relativist is in an important sense a conformist –they support the status quo. Nothing is really good or bad or evil or right or wrong –reality is really all relative, so

---

[42] The German philosopher Ludwig Feuerbach (1804-1872), whose fame is secured by his enthusiasts Marx and Engels, seems to have been quite prescient in his short and concise *Principles of the Philosophy of the Future*, written in 1843. "The task of the modern era was the realization and humanization of God –the transformation and dissolution of theology into anthropology." Ludwig Feuerbach, *Principles of the Philosophy of the Future*, trans. Manfred H. Vogel (Indianapolis, Hackett Publishing, 1986) 1
[43] Martin Heidegger, *Being and Time*, trans. John Macquarrie and Edward Robinson, (New York, Harper & Row, Publishers, 1962) p31
[44] Paul Tillich, *Love, Power and Justice*, (Oxford, Oxford University Press, 1954) p107, 74

whatever is really real is relative. In this way, cultural relativism becomes 'cultural imperialism': indifference to the traditions of other cultures and the many kinds of lifestyles and ways of living the Good Life that exist. There is no real reason to oppose racism or war or violence —or to refrain from them.

Relativism is an extremely popular philosophical pose in today's Western bourgeois countries.[45] With the affluence and secularization of modern industrialism and corporatism, there comes the change away from tradition toward an attitude that is not concerned with learning or pursuing the virtues, whatever they might be. In this vacuum, truth becomes an instrument of power for those who go unopposed.

The more imperial form of relativism is most commonly found in rhetorical speech and reliance on ambiguous and equivocal language. Politicians, HMO's, and the corporate CEO's might be the sophists of today. They find that 'we the people' are more easily persuaded by means of vague reasoning or uncontroversial slogans, such as 'free-trade', 'freedom', or 'free-market'.

One of the oldest refutations of relativism was that performed by Socrates during a discussion he had with a sophist named Protagoras. What Socrates shows is that the relativist cannot distinguish between believing and knowing, between truth and opinion. Say, for example, I look at the moon. Do I believe I am looking at the moon or do I know I am looking at the moon? A thought-experiment like this, when taken into the realm of ethics and politics, where truth and knowledge play a critical role, demonstrates how relativism corrodes any relationship between ethics and reason.

b) Ethics and Anti-Intellectualism

There is a sense in which Western theology is a history of apologetics through the creation of a science of god as distinct from the problem of evil. In consequence there has been an identification of evil with ontology, or human nature. As we saw with the example of Kant, evil is seldom identified with metaphysics and theology, but with human nature and capacity.

As we saw, the sophist and the relativist teeter on being anti-philosophical. What keeps them from falling over immediately is their commitment to bullshitting rather than to dishonesty. The problem with this anti-intellectual framework of the relativist and sophist is the disregard for the possibility that one is wrong or another is right. It is this fundamental opposition to human reason that is called anti-intellectualism.

This is more popularly known as the opposition between faith and reason. When faith or belief can be justified without reason or the use of the mind, as we saw in the discussion between Socrates and Euthyphro, ethics becomes subordinated to something contradictory and which cannot be understood.

Where an important part of the ethics of Islam and Judaism is in study and practice, in Christianity faith is placed as the only means in the ethics of salvation. This of course sounds contradictory —having faith without knowledge. It is not surprising that the New Testament is critical of argument, of wisdom, and of the intellect. The New Testament records more than once an esteeming of ignorance. "I publicly praise you, Father, Lord of heaven and earth, because you have hidden these things from the wise and intellectual ones and have revealed them to babes." (Matthew 11:25, Luke 10:21)

---

[45] Albert Camus said the only fault with the bourgeois is their commitment to furthering mediocrity.

"Where is the wise man? Where the scribe? Where the debater of this system of things? Did not God make the wisdom if the world foolish? For since, in the wisdom of God, the world through its wisdom did not get to know God, God saw good through the foolishness of what is preached to save those believing." 1st Letter to the Corinthians 1:20-21

"For you behold his calling of you, brothers, that not many wise in a fleshly way were called, not many powerful, not many of noble birth; but God chose the foolish things of the world, that he might put the wise men to shame; and God chose the weak things of the world, that he might put the strong things to shame." 1st Letter to the Corinthians 1:26-27

"And I came to you in weakness and in fear and with much trembling; and my speech and what I preached were not with persuasive words of wisdom but with a demonstration of spirit and power, that your faith might be, not in men's wisdom, but in God's power." 1 Corinthians 2:3-5

"For the wisdom of the world is foolishness with God; for it is written: 'He catches the wise in their own cunning." 1 Corinthians 3:19

"Lookout: perhaps there may be someone who will carry you off as his prey through the philosophy and empty deception according to the elementary things of the world and not according to Christ." Colossians 2:8

"But shun foolish questionings and genealogies and strife and fights over the Law, for they are unprofitable and futile." Titus 3:9

As Karl Popper pointed out in his work *The Open Society and Its Enemies,* "In its beginning, Christianity, like the Cynic movement, was opposed to the highbrow Platonizing Idealism and intellectualism of the 'scribes', the learned men."[46] This of course has not always been the case.

c) Ethics, Love, and War

Although in ancient Greece there had been a school of philosophers called the Cynics, cynicism is much more pervasive in the world today than it ever was in ancient Greece. The long history of separating ethics and knowledge, faith and reason, (as we find in the popular forms of relativism, sophistry, anti-intellectualism, and belief in good vs. evil which have pervaded Western history for the past 2000 years), has led to modern cynicism or decadence. In such a scenario, ethics loses its reasonable attributes such as dialogue, inquiry, and fallibility and becomes something ideological and arbitrarily principled.

Ideology manifests itself in people unbeknownst to themselves as the class war. The class war was originally both a descriptive and normative theory of social history and reality made by Karl Marx. Following the dualist model, Marx believed that human history was marked by a struggle between the 'haves' and the 'have nots', the bourgeois and proletariat. More than a description of a reality bereft of intellect, Marx believed that class war should be escalated and heightened in order to bring about a revolution which would result in a classless society.

Although Marx had noticed that displaying wealth was one of the principal means to class war, it should not go unnoticed how wars of ideology aren't always so discreet. They manifest themselves as racism, sexism, as well as cultural imperialism. So many miniature battles, worries, and concerns –a vast micromanaging of the affairs of others, as we find in art, entertainment and the aesthetic industries –all working to distract people from the real ethical questions that exist.

We can see how in so many wars that conquering is achieved through dividing. The extent to which the English worked to divide the religious groups of India in order to more easily subjugate them, or in the Belgian colonization of Rwanda where groups were

---

[46] Karl Popper, *The Open Society and Its Enemies,* (Princeton, Princeton University Press, 1966) II:22

arbitrarily created so as to be set against one another, stand as so many means of disempowerment and empire. We can see in the current Iraq war how this is achieved by dividing the Sunni and Shiite Muslims against each other, ensuring that they cannot stand united against those who are occupying their country.

Many theorists believe that Marx got his theory of class war from his childhood Christian education.[47] The New Testament is in a sense catalyst to such a class war. The God of love seems to have inspired something.

"For if you love those loving you, what reward do you have?" (Matthew 5:46) "He that has greater affection of father or mother than for me is not worthy of me; and he that has greater affection for son or daughter than for me is not worthy of me." (Matthew 10:37) "If anyone comes to me and does not hate his father and mother and wife and children and brothers and sisters, yes, and even his own soul, he cannot be my disciple." (Luke 14:26) "And if you love those loving you, of what credit is it to you? For even the sinners love those loving them. And if you do good to those doing good to you, really of what credit is it to you? Even the sinners do the same." (Luke 6:32-33) "If anyone comes to me and does not hate his father and mother and wife and children and brothers and sisters, yes, and even his own soul, he cannot be my disciple." (Luke 14:26) "For what I am working out I do not know. For what I wish, this I do not practice; but what I hate is what I do." (Romans 7:15) "Do not be loving either the world or the things in the world. If anyone loves the world, the love of the Father is not in him." (1John 2:15)

Anyone who has read any thing as perverse as Dante's *Inferno,* or Flannery O'Conner's short stories, will know what is begotten by this God of Love. The New Testament tells us:

"...whoever says, 'You despicable fool!', will be liable to the fiery Hell." (Matthew 5:22) "Woe to you, scribes and Pharisees, hypocrites! because you traverse sea and dry land to make one proselyte, and when he becomes one you make him a subject for Hell twice as much so as yourselves." (Matthew 23:15) "Serpents, offspring of vipers, how are you to flee from the judgment of Hell?" (Matthew 23:33) "And throw the good-for-nothing slave out into the darkness outside. There is where his weeping and the gnashing of his teeth will be." (Matthew 25:30)

While Dante's *Inferno* says hell was created out of eternal love, the 13th century medieval theologian Thomas Aquinas saw it as a spectacle of joy. "In order that the bliss of the saints may be more delightful for them and that they may render more copious thanks to God for it, it is given to them to see perfectly the punishment of the damned."[48]

Be that as it may, Aquinas was instrumental in reintroducing Aristotle and virtue ethics into the Western canon, though at the time this was still illegal. For all his prejudices and intolerance, what is best in Aquinas is what he gained through three teachers: Aristotle, whom he called "the philosopher", Moses Maimonides, whom he called "the rabbi", and Averroes, whom he called "the commentator".[49]

Knowledge and Ethics

While the Christian theologian Thomas Aquinas helped bring the influence Aristotle back to Western philosophy, it should be remembered that The Philosopher's influenced had never ceased in certain parts of the world. Besides, Aquinas' critics tend to agree that much of Thomist philosophy is Platonic, especially regarding the soul. And

---

[47] Bertrand Russell, (a) p364
[48] Thomas Aquinas, *Summa Theolgiae,* III, *Supplementum,* Q. 94, Att. 1, in Friedrich Nietzsche's, *On the Genealogy of Morals,* trans. Walter Kaufmann, (b) p49n1
[49] Pieper, p108

although there is much that is similar in the philosophies of Plato and Aristotle, there is a fundamental difference in their understanding of the availability of good.
As we have seen with Plato, the good is a super-sensible form, something which cannot be seen but that we should believe in. There is a sense in which the good is super-natural, or supra-natural, or non-natural. This idea has been influential on people like Jesus, who thought that the good was literally out-of-this-world, and this belief about the good is found in 20th century Analytic British philosophers such as G.E. Moore whose work *Principia Ethica*, argued that the good is a 'non-natural property'.

Being more of a naturalist, Aristotle rejected this aspect of Plato's philosophy, believing that "when people do not look out for the common good, it is ruined." (1167b14) Aristotle argues that the good is many things and that there is no one science of the good, or formalization. He says: "Moreover, Good Itself will be no more of a good by being eternal" (1096a4) And "the good is not something common which corresponds to a single Idea." (1096b25)

Through respecting the availability of good, and the plurality of goods, Aristotle is better able to connect the relationship between knowledge and ethics, between reason and virtue. Ethical knowledge is different from the knowledge of universal forms in that it is based on practicality. Such knowledge is of particular things: character, action, and virtue.

"Our discussion will be adequate if its degree of clarity fits the subject-matter; for we should not seek the same degree of exactness in all sorts of arguments alike, any more than in the products of different crafts.

"Moreover, what is fine and what is just, the topics of inquiry in political science, differ and vary so much that they seem to rest on convention only, not on nature. Goods, however, also vary in the same sort of way, since they cause harm to many people; for it has happened that some people have been destroyed because of their wealth, others because of their bravery.

"Since these, then, are the sorts of things we argue from and about, it will be satisfactory if we can indicate the truth roughly and in outline; since [that is to say] we argue from and about what holds good usually [but not universally], it will be satisfactory if we can draw conclusions of the same sort." (1094b12-23)

"Further, each person judges well what he knows, and is a good judge about that; hence the good judge in a particular area is the person educated in that area, and the unconditionally good judge is the person educated in every area." (1095a1)

For Aristotle there is a strong relationship between knowledge and ethics.
"…an immature person, like an incontinent person, gets no benefit from his knowledge.

"If, however, we are guided by reason in forming our desires and in acting, then this knowledge will be of great benefit." (1095a9-10)

"…decision requires understanding and thought, and also a state of character, since doing well or badly in action requires both thought and character." (1139a35)[50]

Thus, for Aristotle, like Plato and Socrates, knowledge plays an important role in ethics. For Plato and Socrates this was achieved through contemplation of the universal form of good. For Aristotle, it is through practical knowledge, character, and through setting goals. Although such knowledge is not necessarily universal or eternal, it is rooted in our human biology and psyche. Thus, Aristotle in an important sense rests upon a certain understanding of human nature, or metaphysical biology. He believes that

---

[50] "…the human good turns out to be the soul's activity of expressing virtue." (1098a16) "the prize and goal of virtue appears to be the best good, something divine and blessed." (1099b17)

metaphysics is 'first philosophy', meaning it comes prior to and supports all other areas of philosophy, including ethics.

Levinas

The strongest critic of this metaphysical foundation is the 20th century Jewish philosopher, Emmanuel Levinas (1906-1995). Levinas makes use of the Platonic good, which he takes as something 'Otherwise Than Being', just as for Plato the good was prior to beings –it is something other, prior to and beyond existence. An aspect which is fundamental to Levinas's ethics is the priority of this Other over the desire of the self. For Levinas, the Other is metaphysical. In 1961, Levinas wrote:

"The relationship with the Other does not move (as does cognition) into enjoyment and possession, into freedom; the Other imposes himself as an exigency that dominates this freedom, and hence as more primordial than everything that takes place in me. The Other, whose exceptional presence is inscribed in the ethical impossibility of killing him in which I stand, marks the end of powers. If I can no longer have power over him it is because he overflows absolutely every *idea* I can have of him."[51]

This passage comes from *Totality and Infinity*, a title which itself reveals a good deal about the philosophy of Levinas. For Levinas, ethics cannot begin with knowledge, and cannot be understood in terms of the metaphysical sciences: theology, ontology, and the metaphysical program itself, which is a totalizing. Rather, ethics begins with an asymmetry, a disproportion, an encounter with something that cannot be grasped, or reduced to a category of knowledge or science. The Other is something that cannot be totalized but is infinite. "The Other alone eludes thematization."[52]

The sciences of knowledge are based upon correspondence and symmetry. In mathematics 2 and 2 are the same thing, and together are equal to 4. This is standard fair for truths: they are a known equation, deduction, and demonstration. For example, A = A. For Levinas this symmetry is absent in the ethical relation. Ethics is the asymmetrical responsibility one has for the other, which is like a relation with something that cannot be contained. He rejects theological and ontological foundations for what is good.

"The Place of the Good above every essence is the most profound teaching, the definitive teaching, not of theology, but of philosophy… The ontology of human existence, philosophical anthropology… [insists], with pathos, on finitude. In reality what is at issue is an order where the very notion of the Good first takes on meaning; what is at issue is society… Infinity opens the order of the Good."[53]

Levinas is the first philosopher to hold ethics as 'first philosophy' and he wrote an essay under this title, "Ethics As First Philosophy". This is in contradistinction to the philosophy of Aristotle, which holds to the primacy of metaphysics as first philosophy. This is not to say that the Virtue Ethics of Aristotle are in any way secondary. But Aristotle, like Plato, did not think the virtues could be taught. They can, however, be accumulated.

For Levinas, ethics is revealed not through identification with universal laws or forms, nor with biology, ontology, or metaphysics, but from 'the face of the other'. The other person's face is the place of meaning, truth, and revelation.

"The proximity of the other is the face's meaning, and it means from the very start in a way that goes beyond those plastic forms which forever try to cover the face like a mask of their presence to

---

[51] Emmanuel Levinas, *Totality and Infinity*, trans. Alphonso Lingis, (Pittsburgh, Duquesne University Press, 1969) p87
[52] Levinas, p86
[53] Levinas, p103-104

perception. But always the face shows through these forms. Prior to any particular expression and beneath all particular expressions, which cover over and protect with an immediately adopted face or countenance, there is the nakedness and destitution of the expression as such, that is to say extreme exposure, defenselessness, vulnerability itself...

"The Other becomes my neighbor precisely through the way the face summons me, calls for me, begs for me, and in so doing recalls my responsibility, and calls me into question."

"In the face of the other man I am inescapably responsible and consequently the unique and chosen one."[54]

The face of other cannot be thematized. "The relation with the face is not an object-cognition." In fact, we really only see its trace, if knowledge isn't just optics. We cannot have power over the other -whether the 'other' be some externality such as time, the world, death, or other people –without them no longer being 'other'. "A philosophy of power, ontology is, as first philosophy which does not call into question the same, a philosophy of injustice."[55] If ontology is categorical, the other, the truly other person shatters all of my categories. What is important is acknowledging the priority of the other person, making ourselves available to the their suffering.

"The Other remains infinitely transcendent, infinitely foreign; his face in which his epiphany is produced and which appeals to me breaks with the world that can be common to us, whose virtualities are inscribed in our *nature* and developed by our existence."[56]

Outside of this responsibility for the other person, knowledge and justice begin when one encounters the third person, when there is a plurality.

"Here, starting from this third person, is the proximity of a human plurality. Who, in this plurality comes first? Here is the hour and birthplace of the question: a demand for justice! Here is the obligation to compare unique and incomparable others; here is the hour of *knowledge* and, then, of the objectivity beyond or on the hither side of the nudity of the face; here is the hour of consciousness and internationality."[57]

Pragmatism and Pluralism

What the scientistic, religious, and relativist views and attitudes of reality all have in common is the notion that reality is either one or two things. So, some materialists, physicalists, and scientists hold that reality is fundamentally physical material. Some religious philosophies hold that reality is fundamentally spiritual, immaterial, or a combination or duality of the spirit and the body. Similarly, anti-intellectualists believe that reality is 'all relative', or differently, that it is non-cognitive. It is believed that morality is fundamentally and eternally subjective and incapable of being factual or formalized.

What all of these perspectives and convictions have in common is the idea that the world of value and of values is separate and unrelatable to the world of truths and facts – (be they material, spiritual, or things-in-themselves). This view became the base for all modern philosophers, from Descartes, Hume, Kant, Hegel, or Schopenhauer. The technical term for this phenomena is the 'Fact/Value dichotomy, where the realms of fact and value are thought eternally separated and foreign to one another. So, for example, it

---

[54] Levinas, p82-83, 84
[55] Levinas, 75, 46
[56] Levinas, p194
[57] Emmanuel Levinas, "Diachrony and Representation" in *Time and The Other,* trans. and ed. by Richard Cohen, (Pittsburgh, Duquesne University Press, 1987) p106

is believed that while the realms of the physical sciences are hard and objective, the realms of ethics and value are hopelessly subjective and soft. The consequences of this split have had drastic consequences in the realm of economics, law, and ethics in general.

One of the first philosophers to attack the dualist method of prejudice -the 'Fact/Value dichotomy' -was the pragmatist John Dewey. In his 1908 work *Ethics*, Dewey discusses the consequences of such a divide.

> "The need for constant revision and expansion of moral knowledge is one great reason why there is no gulf dividing non-moral knowledge from that which is truly moral. At any moment conceptions which once seemed to belong exclusively to the biological or physical realm may assume moral import. This will happen whenever they are discovered to have a bearing on the common good... The important point is that any restriction of moral knowledge and judgments to a definite realm necessarily limits our perception of moral significance."[58]

One hundred years later we are beginning to see the effects and long term consequences of separating the physical sciences from the moral sciences–in the form of global warming, pollution, resource depletion, and the constant state of war in the new millennia. For Dewey knowledge and ethics combine so that we can aim at a good that is valuable and not 'specious'.

> "For experience shows, as we have seen, that not every satisfaction of appetite and craving turns out to be a good; many ends *seem* good while we are under the influence of strong passion which in actual experience and in such thought as might have occurred in a cool moment are actually bad. The task of moral theory is thus to frame a theory of Good as the end or objective of desire, and also to frame a theory of the true, as distinct from the specious, good."[59]

Dewey sees an ethics based upon pragmatism as avoiding what leads to a morality which, because of its arbitrary construal, is either capricious or impractical. An ethics based upon matters unrelated to the issues of every day life can have negative consequences on mental health as well as moral responsibility. "Experience shows that the subordination of human good to an external and formal rule tends in the direction of harshness and cruelty."[60] Dewey says that there is a:

> "...tendency to regard morals as a set of special and separate dispositions. Moral goodness is quite commonly divided off from interest in all the objects which make life fuller, and is confined to a narrow set of aims, which are prized too often merely because they involve inhibition and repression. Experience shows that the effect of this attitude is to keep attention fixed upon the things which are thought to be evil. The mind becomes obsessed with guilt and how to avoid it. In consequence, a sour and morose disposition is fostered. An individual affected in this way is given to condemnation of others and to looking for evil in them."[61]

While many ethicists have worried that if the good is not formalizable then it is an empty concept, others have worried about attempts to make the concept of good objective. Being good is not the obeying of rules, but involves going beyond ourselves. "The good can never be demonstrated to the senses, nor be proved by calculations of personal profit. It involves a radical venture of the will in the interest of what is unseen and prudentially incalculable."[62]

In one of Dewey's more personal writings, titled *What I Believe* (1930), he wrote:

---

[58] I have made use of the 1932 version of the *Ethics*, published as *Theory of Moral Life*, (New York, Holt, Rinehart and Winston, 1960) p144-145
[59] Dewey, p36-37
[60] Dewey, p105
[61] Dewey, p55-56
[62] Quoted from the original 1908 version, *Ethics*, (New York, Henry Holt and Company, 1929) p413

"It is impossible, I think, even to begin to imagine the changes that would come into life –personal and collective –if the idea of a plurality of interconnected meanings and purposes replaced that of *the* meaning and purpose. Search for a single, inclusive good is doomed to failure."[63]

Iris Murdoch

Someone who was aware of the vacuum surrounding the modern conception of good was the novelist and philosopher Iris Murdoch. In 1967 Iris delivered a lecture to an English audience titled "The Sovereignty of Good Over Other Concepts". While she was not arrested for treason or for blasphemy, she did help set an unprecedented trend in Anglo-American thinking. Against the popular English philosophy of empiricism which holds that good is a subjective value created by the will, Murdoch writes:

"There is a false tendency, as there is a false unity, which is generated by modern empiricism: a transcendence which is in effect simply an exclusion, a relegation of the moral [ethical realm] to a shadowy existence in terms of emotive language, imperatives, behavior patterns, attitudes... It is then attached somehow to the human will, a shadow clinging to a shadow. The result is the sort of dreary moral solipcism which so many so-called books on ethics purvey."[64]

Murdoch is critical of the modern-empirical self that is ahistorical and self-omniscient. For a sort of person living in the age of corporations and petite-capitalism, the good is something invented by the self. The empirical self is the central location where all meaning and value are created. Iris summarizes the effects of the modern era upon morality in a celebrated essay she wrote titled, "Against Dryness":

"What have we lost here? And what have we perhaps never had? We have suffered a general loss of concepts, the loss of a moral and political vocabulary. We no longer see man against a background of values, of realities, which transcend him. We picture man as a brave naked will surrounded by an easily comprehended empirical world. For the hard idea of truth we have substituted a facile idea of sincerity."

"It is natural that a Liberal democratic society will not be concerned with techniques of improvement, will deny that virtue is knowledge, will emphasize choice at the expense of vision... A simple-minded faith in science, together with the assumption that we are all rational and totally free, engenders a dangerous lack of curiosity about the real world, a failure to appreciate the difficulties of knowing it. We need to return from the self-centred concept of sincerity to the other-centred concept of truth."[65]

For Murdoch, who makes use of the Platonic theory of the good, "The concept Good resists collapse into the selfish empirical consciousness. It is not a mere value tag of the choosing will…". Rather, the good is something of priority.

"I would suggest that the authority of the Good seems to us something necessary because the realism (ability to perceive reality) required for goodness is automatically at the same time a suppression of self. *The necessity of the good is then an aspect of the kind of necessity involved in any technique for exhibiting fact.*"[66]

Iris finds that the good is indefinable for political reasons. Instead of seeking for the laws of good, she thinks we need to celebrate the virtues (and not popular concepts such as 'freedom' and 'courage'). Rather than being administrative and institutional,

---

[63] John Dewey, "What I Believe", from *The Essential Dewey, Volume 1: Pragmatism, Education, Democracy*, ed. Larry A. Hickman and Thomas M. Alexander, (Bloomington, Indiana University Press, 1998) p25

[64] Iris Murdoch, "On 'God' and 'Good'", *The Sovereignty of Good*, (London, Routledge Classics, 2001) (a) p57

[65] Iris Murdoch, "Against Dryness", in *Existentialists and Mystics*, (London, Penguin Books, 1998) (b) p290, 293. Originally published in *Encounter*, January, 1961. She added: "The connection between art and the moral life has languished because we are losing our sense of form and structure in the moral world itself."

[66] Iris Murdoch, 'The Sovereignty of Good Over Other Concepts", in *The Sovereignty of Good*, (c) p90, 64

ethics is something much more. "The area of morals, and ergo of moral philosophy, can now be seen, not as a hold-and-corner matter of debts and promises, but as covering the whole of our mode of living and the quality of our relations with the world."[67]

"A genuine mysteriousness attaches to the idea of goodness as the Good... A genuine sense of morality enables us to see virtue as the only thing of worth; and it is impossible to limit and foresee the ways in which it will be required of us. That we cannot dominate the world may be put in a more positive way. Good is mysterious because of human frailty, because of the immense distance which is involved."[68]

Murdoch was critical of the Western tendency to identify good with love, which she takes to be not just common sense, but something so unedifying as to be stultifying. She writes:

"Of course Good is sovereign over Love, as it is sovereign over other concepts, because Love can name something bad."

"However I think that Good and Love should not be identified, and not only because human love is usually self-assertive. The concepts, even when the idea of love is purified, still play different roles. We are dealing here with very difficult metaphors. Good is the magnetic centre towards which love naturally moves. False love moves to false good."[69]

The Necessities of (True) Good: From Theory and Practice

There is a revival of pragmatism afoot, a kind of second enlightenment. The pluralism which was preached by the classical American philosophers is finding its way back into popular culture, where it was until the Second World War. This ethics of pluralism is finding its way back into the mainstream through mass-communication, mass transportation and migration, and through those post-modernists who reject the myth of the 'Grand Narrative', the belief that there is a meta-narrative which alone is the one legitimate story of reality.[70] The Good is no longer seen only as economic or political or national, but is understood as existing in so many forms and visions.

The Aristotelian and Thomist scholar Alasdair MacIntyre has written that American pragmatism provided the *praeparatio evangelica* for the philosophy of emotivism:[71] something which "has become embodied in our culture" with its individualist, corporate, bureaucratic, and managerial structure.[72] The philosophy of emotivism came from Britain in the late 19th century, and is the belief that all ethical statements are merely statements of personal preference. MacIntyre is not too far off the mark if we look back at the trends in psychology (and hence in politics and jurisprudence) that have dominated America for some time: mentalism and behaviorism. Behaviorism was the most popular psychological theory in the United States well into the

---

[67] Murdoch, (c) p101, 95
[68] Murdoch, (c) p96
[69] Murdoch, (c) p99, 100
[70] See Jean-Francois Lyotard's, *The Postmodern Condition: A Report on Knowledge*, trans. Geoff Bennington and Brian Massumi, (Minneapolis, University of Minnesota Press, 1984) The pragmatist Louis Menand says of postmodernism, that it is "the Swiss Army knife of critical concepts. It's definitionally overloaded, and it can do almost any job you need done." Louis Menand, "Saved From Drowning", *The New Yorker*, 2/23/09, p68
[71] Alasdair MacIntyre, p66. Dewey had refuted the 'intuitionism' that MacIntyre believes is the precursor to emotivism, in his 1930 essay, "From Absolutism to Experimentalism". While MacIntyre's *A Short History of Ethics* is highly supportive of Dewey's ethics, in *After Virtue* he writes that in contemporary American society, in "morals the ultimacy of disagreement is dignified by the title 'pluralism'." (p32) MacIntyre does not see emotivism as stemming from Calvinism, which is probable.
[72] MacIntyre, p22, 27

1970's, and as the name suggests, is the theory that the human mind is a product of learned behavior and external stimulus.[73] Behaviorism is thus a social psychology, and one that works well with the biology of Darwin's theory of evolution. According to this Darwinian theory the behavior of people is an adaptation by their species to their environment. Mentalism is the flip side to this coin and is as we have seen, based upon assumptions that meaning is internal and individually created.[74] Mentalism too has come to influence the political scene where it is held there is no need for external agreement and mere belief is taken to be the justification that can necessitate other people's suffering.

Contemporary pragmatism rejects these one-ist explanations for human nature and ethics. Instead, the non-reducibility of phenomena is enjoined with the pragmatic bent on naturalism. The philosophy naturalism, which was important to Aristotle, holds that truth, justification, and the good are normal, everyday things not requiring an elaborate explanation, nor a materialist or physicalist, or mentalist or spiritual foundation. It is held that the natural good of the world ought to be available to the many different peoples and species, and this naturalist justification leads to pluralism.

Pluralism is obviously a positive doctrine, however, it is distinct from its metaphysical predecessors monism and dualism. The pluralist will not hold to there being one good, no matter how ultimate, nor will it reject the good as something unavailable or noncognitive. While Guinness is good, it is not the only good. Dualism, as we have seen, holds that the good is in something that resists multiple identifications. Moreover, ethical dualism is that doctrine that holds that what is not good is incorrigible and irredeemable.

The Possibilities of Evil

Fallibilism is perhaps the greatest strength of philosophy –a commitment against dogmatism that does not resolve into the infinite regress and quicksand of relativism. The fallibilist is the person most like Socrates, who questioned his own ethics in order to consider and correct the ethics of his peers. So, for example, while I am inclined to agree with Franz Brentano (1838-1917) that there is no such thing as evil, I would not go so far as to dismiss or explain away or justify the others suffering and deny them their own theodicy.

When we ourselves inquire into the content of evil to find out what it represents we will find that it is a term used heavily by people concerned with power, particularly politicians. It is politicians who often pose as experts over exactly who and what is evil. Politicians use their enormous influence to tell us who the evil-doers are and what the remedy to this evil is. Of course, they have interest in getting a moral majority behind them when they begin their inquisitions. If evil exists, perhaps we ought not to leave it

---

[73] Behaviorism was advocated by W.V. Quine, a philosopher who had helped introduce ontology to analytic philosophy.

[74] Mentalism was advocated early on by Hilary Putnam who came to change his mind. His version of mentalism he called 'functionalism' (which is identical to computationalism, or the computer theory of the mind). In 1988 he wrote that functionalism, "if it were correct, would imply behaviorism! If it is true that to possess given mental states is simply to possess a certain 'functional organization', then it is true that to possess given mental states is simply to possess certain behavior dispositions!" Hilary Putnam, *Representation and Reality*, (Cambridge, MIT Press, 1988) p124-125

up to these politicians and generals to be the ones who educate us on this matter. Here the Quran tells:
> "Allah likes not the shouting of evil words unless a man has been wronged; Allah is All-hearing, All-knowing. If you do good openly or in secret or pardon an evil, surely Allah is All-pardoning, All-powerful." Surah 4:147-148

Philosophy, Poetry, and the Good Life

If Good isn't only one thing, what is necessary is the acknowledgment of the different values of the many different goods. This could warrant a critical reevaluation of many of our values and is particularly important in America today. One force that is exceedingly strong in America is the arts and entertainment industry. In American society it is the arts (commercial as well as recreational) that have the most influence over the public. It is a simple truism that more people watch television than go to a church, though this is probably a most scant of contrasts. I am guessing that less than 1% of the US population do not own a television –most homes have several and the 'home entertainment center' is usually a big investment for adults and kids alike. Televisions today are highly informative with up to date weather reports, 24-hour news broadcasts, as well as any number of educational, comedic, and environmental programs. Be that as it may, most of the programming is uninformative, and a good deal of it is politically corroborative and ethically vacuous, verging on maleficent of people's mental health and reasoning skills.

Criticism of the media is very important. This 'Fourth Estate' (as the media is called) has an enormous influence over what people believe. Such criticism does not presuppose that the media could ever be 'unmediated' –that is, presented from an absolutely objective perspective. Neither should we conclude that people are universally biased and that objectivity is impossible. Criticism –critical reporting, critical journalism, is the eyes and ears of the democratic public.[75]

As it is, art today in the age of representation is perhaps the largest informer of morals and politics. While parents and teachers have a direct influence on American youths, nothing is more steady and ubiquitous than the representations that inhabit our purview for much of our lives from childhood to death. Of course representations are not in themselves bad. Each representation has a degree of accuracy and inaccuracy and each transmits an image of reality, however beneficial or otherwise.

As Hilary Putnam wrote upon the election of the actor Ronald Reagan to President of the United States, "The arts have been exalted by us to a place much higher than any they occupied in Plato's day or in the Middle Ages. As a number of authors

---

[75] For those artistic minded people who were tired of hearing about "imperialism", Bertrand Russell noted this in his 1963 study, *War Crimes In Vietnam*, "To some, the expression 'U.S. Imperialism' appears as a cliché because it is not part of their own experience. We here in the West are the beneficiaries of imperialism. The spoils of exploitation are the means of our corruption. Because imperialism is not part of our experience we do not recognize the aptness of the description for the economic and political policies of what President Eisenhower termed 'the military industrial complex'. Let us consider briefly the nature of U.S. power." Bertrand Russell, "Peace Through Resistance to U.S. Imperialism", from *War Crimes In Vietnam*, published in *Readings in U.S. Imperialism*, ed. K.T. Fann and Donald C. Hodges, (Boston, Porter Sargent Publisher, 1971) xi. Russell was 91 years old when he wrote this.

have remarked, for a certain sort of educated person, art today is religion, i.e. the closest thing to salvation available."[76] We can see this trend only growing, with a growing entertainment industry, and as more and more people are elected not because of their mastery of political science, but because of their Hollywood clout.

One of the world's most thorough critics of artistic representation was Plato, in whose time the arts existed on a much smaller scale in society than in America today. While criticism of Plato's *Republic* is not surfeit, one thing that is not sufficiently appreciated of Plato is his attack upon myths and other popular legends. An understanding of Plato's politics and theology are helpful in understanding his views on art and representation, however, they are not necessary for reaping the benefits of his aesthetics. While I am critical of most of Plato's political theories, I do not find that their refutation invalidates his lessons on some of the social aspects of art. If Socrates criticized the Athenian patriarchs, Plato criticized those who eulogized them.

Popular misrepresentations hold that Plato was against poetry, that he wanted all poets banned from Athens. In fact, Plato thought that poetry was both powerful and charming. However, likes Socrates, he was critical of the myths and rumors that were popularly spread through this medium.[77] The poet whom he objects to most is Homer, whose nationalist poetry was for many Greeks a kind of moral code. Against the representations of the gods as being a bunch of lying, cheating, and conniving brats, Plato wished to persuade the poets to tell a different tune.

"We shall compel the poets to deny that these deeds were theirs... [T]hey must not say both or attempt to persuade our young men that the gods beget evil and that heroes are not better than ordinary men." (391d)

In particular, Plato was concerned with the way in which representations can mislead people and distract them from the virtues. He sometimes writes of the artist and actor as though they were a symbol of ignorance, disempowerment, and non-activism. However, Plato does seem to put honor on a high pedestal.

"...all poetic imitators, beginning with Homer, imitate images of virtue and of everything else they write about and have no contact with the truth... [T]he painter, though he knows nothing of leatherwork, makes a picture which appears to be a cobbler to those who have no knowledge either and judge by colour and shape." (601a)

"I think that, if he truly had knowledge of the things he imitates, he would much rather devote himself to actions than to the imitation of them, and that he would try to leave behind many fine actions as memorials of himself and be eager to be the subject of a eulogy rather than the author of it." (599b)

Moreover, Plato found that for artists it is not subjects like virtue and temperance that are their muse, but only what will bring them praise amongst the masses.

"So the imitator will have neither knowledge nor right opinion about the beauty or quality of the things he imitates...

"Nevertheless he will make his imitations, though he does not know whether a particular subject is good or bad, and he seems likely to imitate what appears beautiful to the ignorant majority." (602a, b)

Seeking reputation, the poet "relates to the excitable and varied character because it is easy to imitate." (605a)

Plato was critical of how much of art focuses on whatever is just emotional, particularly on tragedy and how a lot of art represents suffering and misfortune. Some might call the foul here to be 'over-acting' (or over-reacting on Plato's part) but Plato

---

[76] Hilary Putnam, *Reason, Truth and History*, (Cambridge, Cambridge University Press, 1981) p151
[77] Plato did however, believe there is one necessary myth. For an excellent study on this point in Plato's *Republic*, check out Aldous Huxley's, *Brave New World*, (1931).

genuinely thought that even displays of feigned-suffering can have such an affect on an audience, as to make them suffer as well, and this only increases the amount of suffering in the world, which is contrary to the good life. Moreover, Plato found that artist's predilection for representing such 'extremes' in behavior makes an audience insatiable, "unreasonable, idle and friendly to cowardice...

"Now this peevish [or spiteful] part gives many opportunities for all sorts of imitations, while the wise and quiet character which always remains pretty well the same is neither easy to imitate nor easy to understand when imitated, especially for a festival crowd, people of all sorts gathered in theatres. For them the imitation is one of suffering alien to them." (604d, e)

These simple observations aside, for Plato the most serious charge to be leveled against imitation is, "namely that it is able to corrupt even good men, with very few exceptions..." (605c)

Perhaps in a plea for an historical justification Plato claimed that there had always been a quarrel between philosophy and poetry. "[L]est we be charged with a certain harshness and boorishness, let us tell poetry that here is an ancient quarrel between it and philosophy..." (607b) Whether or not this itself was a myth, it was quickly dispelled by his greatest student.

Aristotle found it important to also talk about the positive aspects of art and representation. In particular, Aristotle was aware of just how much of human learning and education is dependent upon imitation and representation. In the *Poetics* he writes that:

"the desire to 'imitate or represent' is instinctive in man from childhood; in fact one of man's distinguishing marks is that he is the most mimetic of all animals, and it is through his mimetic activity that he first begins to learn. Moreover, such imitating and representing is always a source of delight, as experience plainly shows: for even where the objects themselves are disagreeable to behold –repulsive animals, for instance, or dead bodies –we take delight in artistically exact reproductions of them. The reason for this is that learning gives the keenest pleasure –not only to philosophers but even to the rest of mankind despite the scant attention they bestow on it. Hence the reason why men enjoy seeing a picture is that in contemplating it they are incidentally learning and inferring in their recognition of particulars..." (1448b5-20)

Aristotle held for example that tragic art helps humans by representing "incidents arousing pity and fear in such a way as to accomplish a purgation (katharsis) of such emotions." (1449b29) This *catharsis* is a kind of 'purification through art' where experiencing art can be beneficial to our constitution and our well-being. In this sense, art is interpreted as a form of therapy and care for the self in living the good life.

Story-telling plays a large role in the education of children by instilling lessons about right and wrong as through the example of characters in stories and narratives. In these ways art plays a fundamental role in society. In a sense, the arts are a social institution and accordingly must be treated as a science and with as formal an ethic as is found in any other discipline.

Aristotle was concerned with the ethics of representations and believed it was not right for fictional stories to represent injustice, which "merely offends us by its brutality." (1452b35) Moreover, "The poet, being a portrayer, like the painter or any other artist, must always portray one of three kinds of object: things as they really were or are, things as they are said or popularly supposed to be, or things as they ought to be." (1460b10)[78]

One thing which has happened which neither Plato nor Aristotle could have foreseen in our contemporary world is the modern exaltation of actors and 'celebrities'

---

[78] Aristotle, *Poetics*, (b) p293-294, 296, 306, 322

and 'personalities'. Perhaps since the time of Charlie Chaplin the actor has become one of the most idolized and celebrated persons in the United States and the world. Thousands of reporters, hundreds of publications, and millions of images and words are dedicated each day to the biographies and reporting on these actors. This is known as the 'Cult of Personality'.

The 'Cult of Personality' is the phenomena of hero-worship, idolization, and idolatry. This is much akin to the belief in the Divine Right of Kings and the belief in demigods, and the simple worship of power. This servile mentality holds that honoring a figure as a hero is the prerequisite of the good life. While it is true that good heroes are often absent in life, allegiance to and the adulation of heroes often leads to an ethic that is unthinking and uncritical. As any war-protestor knows, imitation, i.e., following rules, is not what morality comes down to. The Cult of Personality exists at the expense not just of moral responsibility, but also of our virtue and character. It is our character which properly developed, allows for a nature and temperament that is discerning and unique.

In his study *On The Genealogy of Morals*, Friedrich Nietzsche wrote about the political role that art inevitably plays, be it that of ushering in conformity or obedience to some authority. An unpopular poet himself, he was not afraid to turn the eye-ball inward and reevaluate his own values. He wrote that artists
> "have at all times been the valets of some morality... [T]hey have unfortunately often been all-too-pliable courtiers of their own followers and patrons, and cunning flatterers of ancient or newly arrived powers. They always need at the very least protection, a prop, an established authority: artists never stand apart; standing alone is contrary to their deepest instincts."[79]

In this light the popular resurgence of horror movies, popular during the Reagan era, are finding their back to popular art. This celebration of fear has its roots in the worship of power and the conformity to governmental control. The captive audiences to these fear-based movies are often the ones who play audience to other forms of intimidation and hatred in their acceptance of state terrorism and the war machine. Often times the advocates of psychological thrillers and devotees of films based upon irrationality are those people who have developed a tolerance for what is grotesque and appalling, such as is often found on television most of the day.

Some might say that the most obvious (and most repressed) reason why nearly every second of television is so perverse is quite possibly in the illegality of displaying nudity. This repression of beauty has led to a trend of decadence, where only what is grotesque holds peoples attentions. The industry of the erotic, in turn, has become the culture for the micromanagers and the disempowered. Truly, what passes for 'imagination' here is nothing but the most unpolitical of concerns (though those with an under-developed imagination certainly thrive on the miniaturism of concern, in their vocation for minding other people's business, instead of identifying in their own moral and political apathy the source of their boredom and simple satisfaction). In censoring nudity and representing brutality on television, are we trying to spread love or fear?

Someone who did not settle for this parade of ignominy and being-towards-pathetic was Emmanuel Levinas. When in 1948 he published an essay in a French journal criticizing the cult of representation, the editors saw it fit to warn the reader before witnessing such an indictment. In fact, Levinas links the lack of criticism of the

---

[79] Of his fellow pre-World War artists Nietzsche simply said, "Let us leave out of account whether in the *new* Germany an artist could have existed who lacked the milk of pious, *Reich*-pious sentiments." Friedrich Nietzsche, *On The Genealogy of Morals*, trans. Walter Kaufmann, (New York, Vintage Books, 1969) III, 5

arts to political disempowerment and acceptance of the status quo, as though we were all still fettered inside of a cave. This essay, titled "Reality and Its Shadow" discusses the ways in which representations, (just like representatives), go unchecked and accepted by the many. He writes that: "art, essentially disengaged, constitutes, in a world of initiative and responsibility, a dimension of evasion." He was critical of the way in which art often became institutionalized and then understood as existing in itself, or in French, *L'art pour l'art*. He wrote:

"The formulation is false inasmuch as it situates art *above* reality and recognizes no master for it, and it is immoral inasmuch as it liberates the artist from his duties as a man and assures him of a pretentious and facile nobility."

Levinas was also critical of the lack of literary and artistic criticism, finding that "alongside of difficult art, criticism seems to lead a parasitic existence."[80]

Next to television, which is based upon spreading corrigibility and consumption, as we see, criticism is next to nonexistent. Networks have billion dollar budgets and movies have multi-million dollar budgets –and only politicians need to earn as much money to run their campaigns. As former Supreme Court Justice Sandra Day O'Connor recently pointed out, more people can name the judges on American Idol than can name the three branches of government.[81]

Simply, there isn't enough money for criticism to compete with the art and entertainment industry, whose kitsch films are released on an international scale and are advertised on TV and the media thousands of times each day. Of course there is some criticism –the two thumbs up or two thumbs down, the 4 out of 5 stars or tomatoes or what have you. But what is absent is a real thoroughly ethical criticism, perhaps done along the lines of poetry, which seeks to ridicule the television and movie industry into producing something worthwhile, perhaps by the 22nd century.

According to the film critic Anthony Lane every movie has one thing in common. Lane is one of the best movie critics I'm familiar with in that he often brings down as much criticism as praise; something which is contrary to the boot-lickers that overcrowd his profession. In his review of Star Wars, Lane writes that while all movies bear a tint of "perversity" and "vulgarity", this film is unique in the "art of flawless and irredeemable vulgarity".

"What [George] Lucas has devised, over six movies, is a terrible puritan dream: a morality tale in which both sides are bent on moral cleansing, and where their differences can be assuaged only by a triumphant circus of violence. Judging from the whoops and crowings that greeted the opening credits, this is the only dream we are good for. We get the films we deserve."[82]

However, what kind of audience does Lane have in comparison to Star Wars, which is, if not just international, alas, intergalactic? Exceptional criticisms will certainly never reach the kind of audience of those who stand as witnesses to television and the cinema. That is, unless the rappers become philosophers or the philosophers become rappers. As things stand, intellectual criticism of popluar art plays too small a role to go noticed for the most part.

---

[80] Emmanuel Levinas, "Reality and Its Shadow", *Collected Philosophical Papers,* trans. Alphonso Lingis, (Pittsburgh, Duquesne University Press, 1987) p12, 2, 1
[81] On the Daily Show, March 3, 2009
[82] This could have been a review for *Lord of the Rings*. Anthony Lane, "Space Case", *The New Yorker*, May 23, 2005. Lane said of Episode III, "the profits that await it are unfit for contemplation".

A particular area of criticism that is needed today is of the representations made by the media and art and entertainment industries of those 'non-Western' peoples and people of 'third-world' countries. While catastrophes like the wars on Iraq and Afghanistan are of course under-represented by the media, what we more often see are just caricatures of these peoples and places.

The lack of criticism of such representations was brought to English reader's attention in a1978 study called *Orientalism* by the Palestinian refugee Edward Said (pronounced *si –eed*). Said's work stands as a great analysis of the Western medium, call it art, entertainment, politics, or the media. His work shows the flag waving and political obedience of hundreds of years of writers, poets, and artists, all of who were but products of a political and racist ideology. 'Original' 'free-thinkers' as various as Dante, Balzac, Lord Byron, Sir Richard Burton, Gustave Flaubert, Rudyard Kipling, Ernest Renan, Voltaire, and Joseph Conrad [to name very few], all fit into this common mold of political obedience.

Said writes:
"the fields of learning, as much as the works of even the most eccentric artist, are constrained and acted upon by society, by cultural traditions, by worldly circumstances, and by stabilizing influences like schools, libraries, and governments; moreover, that both learned and imaginative writing are never free, but are limited in their imagery, assumptions, and intentions..."

"So Orientalism aided and was aided by general cultural pressures that tended to make more rigid the sense of difference between the European and Asiatic peoples of the world. My contention is that Orientalism is fundamentally a political doctrine willed over the Orient because the Orient was weaker than the West, which elided the Orient's difference with its weakness."

"And yet despite its failures, its lamentable jargon, its scarcely concealed racism, its paper-thin intellectual apparatus, Orientalism flourishes today in the forms I have tried to describe. Indeed, there is some reason for alarm in the fact that its influence has spread to "the Orient" itself: the pages of books and journals in Arabic (and doubtless in Japanese, various Indian dialects, and other Oriental languages) are filled with second-order analyses by Arabs of 'the Arab mind', 'Islam', and other myths. Orientalism has also spread in the United States now that Arab money and resources have added considerable glamour to the traditional 'concern' felt for the strategically important Orient. The fact is that Orientalism has been successfully accommodated to the new imperialism, where its ruling paradigms do not contest, and even confirm, the continuing imperial design to dominate Asia."[83]

The history of Orientalism is thus a history of passing on myths, fabrications, and stereotypes. In this vane, we are taught that what exists outside of the Western world and what existed before the modern world is something called 'mythology'. *Mythos* is a Greek word meaning 'tale'. A 'myth' is usually taken to be a story or 'superstition' that someone or some group of people uncritically believe. It is said by historians that all

---

[83] The contemporary writer John Barth comments on Said's work that although "the Western tradition of 'Orientalism', a tradition whose ramifications have been most authoritatively documented by Edward W. Said... [T]he ongoing fascination of Western artists and their audiences with the exotic 'East' is an impressive and ambivalent phenomenon... Said's real subject, and the focus of his own ambivalence, is Orientalism as an academic discipline all too often allied, consciously or unconsciously, with the power structures of European colonialism." Barth says that "Western Orientalisms [such] as the Romantic arabesque may have their patronizing or otherwise questionable aspects, but they may also be manifestations of innocent curiosity, sympathy, and admiration." *Further Fridays*, (Boston, Little, Brown and Company, 1995) p319, 320. Said himself wrote that, "I certainly do not believe the limited proposition that only a black can write about blacks, a Muslim about Muslims, and so forth." *Orientalism*, (New York, Vintage Books, 1979) p201-202, 204, 322. Though Said was a non-theist from a Christian background, he wrote an excellent book titled, *Covering Islam: How the Media and the Experts Determine How We See the Rest of the World*, (New York, Pantheon Books, 1981)

ancient cultures and peoples had myths and this word is usually used to describe the beliefs of foreign peoples today. Thus, there is a strong connection between this anthropological use of the term 'myth' and a political use of the term, be it in inspiring nationalism or invigorating cultural imperialism.

We know these myths. Women are bad drivers, that Indians are unfair givers, that Jews are money-lenders, Black people are ungenerous, the Irish are not teetotalers, to never go in against a Sicilian when death is the on the line, etc… We know the power that myths play over the imagination of people and it is the nature of much political propaganda campaigns to foster and further spread such myths. Henry VIII, Mussolini, Hitler, and Stalin have been some of the greatest counterfeiters in history through the spread of myths, rumors, and other fabrications. And what about Bush? Perhaps someday WMD will be discovered in Iraq and their link to events in 2001.

Leaders of states around the world have always found use for mythical stories of their own lineage and the spread of nationalist mythologies to stir up the citizens and youths. They also find use in spreading myths about the beloved enemy. These myths are held to be self-evident truths while it is the traditions and very existence of people across the borders that are said to be based on an irrational mythology. We are told that the traditions of foreign and non-Western people are based upon pure myths, while our myths aren't really myths but are truths. It is said that certain races, nations, genders, languages, beliefs, and traditions are myth-laden, and that mythology is a central component of primitive or pre-modern society. There is a sense in which the thing described is the thing created, and myths are manufactured to inform us that certain people are good while other peoples and countries are evil.

Naturalists have always been opposed to myth. Aristotle himself had rejected the traditional myths about the gods, preferring instead rational proofs. In his work in *Metaphysics*, he wrote: "But is not worth our while to inquire seriously into the subtleties of the mythologists. The people we must cross-examine are those who speak of proofs." (*Metaphysics*, 1005a21)[84] The great physician and skeptic Sextus Empiricus had written that: "Mythical belief is an acceptance of unhistorical and fictitious events…"[85]

Pragmatists have long been opponents of myth, being committed to naturalism. Naturalists reject myth in favor of reason and knowledge in their explanations and justifications of history, causality, and meaning. It was the American pragmatist W.V Quine who began serious talk of refuting a 'museum-myth' of meaning –the idea that meanings are determined once and for all like objects on display in a museum. Quine had forerunners.

The Spanish-born American pragmatist George Santayana wrote in his four-part study, *The Life of Reason*, "That magic and mythology have no experimental sanction is clear as soon as experience begins to be gathered with any care. As magic attempts to do work by incantations, so myth tries to attain knowledge by playing with lies." Santayana was aware of the large role that myth played in the popular imagination. He warned that "…myths, the more currency they acquire, pass the more easily into superstitions." He knew the role that myth plays in obtaining compliance and obedience. "Mythical thinking… is no *vehicle* for knowledge; it cannot serve the purpose of transitive thought

---

[84] Aristotle, *Metaphysics*, quoted and trans. Terence Irwin, *Classical Philosophy*, ed. Terence Irwin, (Oxford, Oxford University Press, 1999) 101
[85] Sextus Empiricus, "Outlines For Pyrrhonism", p69-70

or action."[86] Like Socrates, Santayana sees a great obstacle to ethical reasoning in the propagation of myth. He describes this as ambivalence between ethics and mythology:

"But the chief source of perplexity and confusion in mythology is its confusion with moral truth. The myth which originally was but a symbol substituted for empirical descriptions becomes in the sequel *an idol substituted for ideal values.* This complication, from which half the troubles of philosophy arise, deserves our careful attention."[87]

One of the most famous and influential Orientalists and 'mythogenists' in 20th century America was the Catholic heretic Joseph Campbell (1904-1987). In such works as *The Hero With a Thousand Faces* (1949) and *The Power of Myth* (1986) among others, Campbell wanted to illustrate just how central myths are to all people in the world, past and present.[88] For Campbell myth is not just a history of rumors and hearsay, told and retold by people like himself. Myths are universalities. Myths "are the world's dreams. They are archetypal dreams… Myths tell me where I am." "What myths are for is to bring us into a level of consciousness that is spiritual."[89]

What Campbell wants us to believe with him is that these myths aren't just labels or even particularities of different peoples and communities in history and different parts of the world, but that they are universal structures or universal representations of some ideal and absolute 'archetypal' form. It is these spiritual archetypal forms which inform our myths and not vice-versa. Thus, every myth, rumor, stereotype, and label is in some way informed by this form of 'reality'.[90]

Moreover, this is both the way the world is and the way the world ought to be; both the right explanation and justification for existence. In fact, Campbell believed many of the problems facing the world in the modern era stem from the loss of myths among peoples and he believed that myths ought to be reintroduced as a solution to this problem.[91]

Campbell was modest enough not to call himself a specialist, or guru. More insidiously, he thought of himself as a generalist. As a generalist what he wants to do is put in the mouths of every person the same corrigibility and uncritical predilection for superstition. He wants to put in the minds of every intellectual and layman the same beliefs and weakness of reason. Through this method, Campbell can both label a foreign

---

[86] George Santayana, *The Life of Reason*, (New York, Dover Publications, 1980) Volume III, p127; II, 53; III, 129. Originally published in 1905. In the single volume 1953 edition, Santayana replaced the word 'knowledge' with 'experience'. (New York, Charles Scribner's Sons, 1955) p241
[87] Santayana, Volume III, p130. Italics mine.
[88] For a *reductio ad absurdum* of Campbell's work check out John Barth's, *Giles Goat-Boy*, (Garden City, Doubleday & Company, 1966). My thanks to the philosopher Kevin Lynch for pointing this out to me.
[89] Joseph Campbell, *The Power of Myth*, w/ Bill Moyers, ed. Betty Sue Flowers, (New York, Doubleday, 1988) p15, 14. Interviews taken in 1985 and 1986.
[90] MacIntyre finds that one particularly powerful archetype in America is the manager class, however, he rejects as *begging the question* that someone could choose aesthetics over ethics. (*After Virtue*, p40, 73)
[91] Santayana's insights seem to have foreshadowed the work of Campbell. George wrote: "Myth remains… a constituent part even of the most rational consciousness, and what can at present be profitably attempted is not so much to abolish myth as to become aware of its mythical character." (III, 128) However, unlike Campbell, he finds a natural separation between myth and reality. "To separate fable from knowledge nothing is therefore requisite except close scrutiny and the principle of parsimony." (III, 130) "A myth is an inverted image of things, wherein their moral effects are turned into their dramatic antecedents –as when the wind's rudeness is turned into his anger. When the natural basis of moral life is not understood, myth is the only way of expressing it theoretically…" (III, 141) To sum up, this is ethically opposite to Campbell.

tradition as 'myth' and say that he understands its mythical and tribal essence because it is but a manifestation of an archetypal form. This isn't about virtue but about power.

By institutionalizing an array of artifacts and familiar interpretations, Campbell trivializes the variety of veritable ethics and traditions and communities that exist amongst non-European peoples, as well as their distinctive virtues. In this way his generalization project is a form of imperialism and assimilation –standardizing Western archeology and anthropological stereotypes of these 'naïve' foreigners.[92] For such reasons, Joseph Campbell could never accept those religions that reject mythology and image-worship such as Judaism and Islam, or one in four.

Wary of the myth-industry that was quickly surrounding pragmatism and its practitioners, (a phenomenon which happens to any non-conformist, around whom rumors are spread by their shadows and the spirits of jealousy), John Dewey was critical of both institutional and unnatural myths. In "The Pragmatic Acquiescence" of 1927, Dewey wrote:

"There are myths and myths. Some are inspiriting; some are benumbing. Nature myths, at least in their first form, inspire because they are spontaneous responses of imagination to the scene that confronts it. Myths of literary criticism and historic interpretations are deadening. They do not enliven; they force subject-matter into ready-made patterns and dull sensitivity of perception. Such myths grow up in interpretations of past philosophies and always tend to overlay and conceal the realities of past reflection. They flourish in those literary versions by which the ideas of philosophers reach the public –for philosophers themselves are usually too much preoccupied with the technique, the professional rules, of their calling to have a public –except one another."[93]

An ethic that was general to the 20th century Christian theologian Rudolf Bultmann and the agnostic philosopher Walter Kaufmann was the 'demythologizing' project. As Kaufmann describes, demythologizing is the attempt to find out the "moral implications" of a text. It was during World War II that Bultmann coined the verb 'demythologize' as he saw a dire need to oppose the high tide of nationalist mythology. One way Bultmann did this was by interpreting scripture anthropologically.[94]

Demythologizing falls in line with a bent toward naturalism and literalness: taking a person at their word. The demythologist advocates sincerity, the idea that people can mean what they say and say what they mean, and that reality is in an important sense direct and present. While some would like to say that man without myth is disenchanted, even if one were so enlightened as to shatter the mythical chains which limit the conscious mind, we need not infer that because we are no longer fettered by myth, that the mythoclast and iconoclast is the redeemer.

Intellectual criticism need not imply imperialism. Demythologizing escapes negativity in the same way that the philosophy of deconstruction does not destroy. These two 'methods' of ethical reasoning work to examine what is often uncritically accepted and obeyed by myth-mongerers -call them cultural enforcers. In a demythologizing and deconstruction there is no censoring and there is no destroying.

Where such great 20th century French philosophers as Michel Foucault, Roland Barthes, and Jacques Derrida have put the authority of the 'author' in question, as we saw with Nietzsche and Said as well, it has been the goal of American pragmatists to

---

[92] Edward Said points out the link between archeology and nationalism in his lecture, *Freud and the Non-European*, (New York, Verso, 2003) p49. This work is banned in parts of Europe.
[93] John Dewey, "The Pragmatic Acquiescence", from *The Essential Dewey, Volume 1*, p33
[94] Walter Kaufmann, *Critique of Religion and Philosophy*, (New York, Harper & Brothers, 1958) #54, 55

'reconstruct' rather than delay, or separate practice from theory, or wait for some abstract myth to gain such ascendency as to become a self-fulfilling apocalypse. While some may worship at the alter of originality and others at the alter of destruction, pragmatists have not been concerned with firsts and lasts but with what is ethically diverse, intellectually multi-faceted, and what warrants reification, reconstruction, and is worthy of being reformed.

John Dewey said that "reconstruction is not something to be accomplished by finding fault or being querulous."[95] Being querulous means to be habitually complaining. Being predisposed toward complaint and being adversarial ostensibly are becoming popular trends in America today if only because of the super-fortunate phenomenon known as 'spoiled children' or because of some sense of entitlement that accompanies the cult of the individual. Certainly much of 'argument' today is childish banter, personal attacks, finger pointing, and this is often relayed in a vernacular that sounds something like the anthropomorphism of garbage, of which there is an excess. Very little of what is said to be argument and debate is actually of any philosophical worth if only because there is very little argument and debate –philosophy is simply not a skill in the age of commodities.

Reconstruction is needed in America. Not just the reconstruction of the physical infrastructure, of educational systems, of the health care system, but a reconstruction in philosophical virtues. Too often when political and economic power become isolated amongst the few, or allocated by a majority, there ensues an institutionalization of ethics and morals, both socially and politically. This may be an epiphenomenon of all big states and the isolation or centralization of political and economic power. Ideologies become institutionalized and the individual and the stranger become the objects of suspicion and derision in the age of the manager, the state, or Big Brother.

According to the ethic of reconstruction, social conventions and political institutions ought to be reinterpreted and reconstructed in such a way as to reintroduce the natural diversity of humanity and to reestablish the local community. It is at this level that the virtues flourish most naturally, as do the distinctive and particular values and goods of both individuals and societies.

We ought to resist the institutionalization of democracy. We forget that what is unique about the United States is that it is a 'voluntary' a union of separate sovereign states. Each state is distinct and particular and has its own constitution. Still further, these states often cover a vast array of terrains and communities, each with its own variety of environments and lifestyles. When morality becomes institutionalized according to state and federal legislation, or by a monarchy or majority for that matter, the virtues become institutionalized, much like they did by the Stoics during the Roman Empire. It is on such a grand scale that a picture of honor is codified amongst the virtues, and that the virtues, in their institutionalization, are divorced from ethics and intellect. It is for this reason that many call America a post-honor society.

Whether or not someone can attain honor on such a national stage is obviously not the question. Whether or not we become disaffected, disempowered, and become dishonorable guardians of the status quo is of greater concern. To support the status quo is to support the myth that the good life is the same thing for everyone and the virtues are

---

[95] John Dewey, *Reconstruction in Philosophy*, (Boston, Beacon Press, 1948) xxxvi. Dewey said, "In a verbal sense re-form and re-construction are close together." (xli)

all the same. Our great concern becomes a universal concern, and this universal concern is sometimes called the 'ultimate concern'.

It is traditionally held by believers of all sorts that everyone ought to have an ultimate concern. Someone without an ultimate concern is someone devoid of purpose: they are a nihilist. This ultimate-concernism is the reason to make everyone's business one's own business. Ultimately, this concern turns into the conviction that everyone ought to have the same beliefs, the same values, and same convictions as oneself. The very phenomenon of argument and disagreement invites suspicion of the human intellect and the rational mind in its ability to learn, change, and transcend, and we are left with an attitude of anti-intellectualism. Here it is that faith is done with reason and philosophical debate is politically cast aside.

The conviction that everyone ought to have some ultimate concern is a product of the institutionalization of morality in the age of empire and nationalism. This micro-management and personalism of concern is part of the institutionalization of the virtues and the misunderstanding of ethics as management and administration. It is here that myth becomes the powerful enforcer, and only whatever can be made compulsive.

Socrates was put to death by an Athenian jury of 500 because he had criticized the state myths. He had also criticized an oracle which had said he was the wisest among men. (Through her speech, Diotima taught him this was not the case for both sexes.) Socrates did not wish to leave Athens, even to save his own life, but he sought and found community wherever he could find it. This is the strength of philosophy, the love of wisdom –to be able to find community amongst individuals. It is this love of wisdom which entreats diversity and plurality over universalization and idealization.

In just the last 500 years, the continents of the world nearly lost their many distinctive virtues. In America, a re-adaptation of the Native American virtues are needed to show us how it was that communities once inhabited this land, and didn't just struggle to survive in the Darwinian sense, but flourished, complimentary to nature, complimentary of nature, and why the many distinct ways in which the Native Americans lived their lives and sustained themselves and this land for thousands of years were of necessity greater in virtue and distinction.

Reconstruction of the community will lead to the reconstruction of the good life – this is the recipe for renaissance, and for renewed enlightenment. Those who don't support reconstruction of the community don't necessarily support the status quo, but they do support a code of honor that is either based upon myth or is based upon obedience to power, though probably a bit of both. If honor is not something bestowed upon greatness by individuals or by the community, then, as some have pointed out, we are just worshipers of power and either quietly or noisily reside in a post-honor society.

Ethics is the way we live our lives. Plato, Aristotle, and Socrates all agreed that a life of study was necessary for living the good life. Aristotle imagined even the gods study. (1178b22) Through studying we learn what is good, what is valuable, and what is just. If we study ethics, we learn to bring out what is best in ourselves and in others, and how to live the life that is good. It is the love of wisdom, philosophy, that leads to a greater appreciation and acknowledgement of what is noble and what is honorable.

What is the status of philosophy in America today? Is there a pragmatic renaissance afoot in the US or can it be said that there is an American aversion to philosophy? Let us discuss this, then, starting from the beginning.

Acknowledgements

I would like to thank first and foremost my family for their love and support, particularly Daisy. The Yockel family, Liz being someone without whom this project may never have been completed. The Saul and Spitzer families, Quincy for having read an early draft and for his friendship and encouragement. The Serchan family for their wisdom and friendship. The Debevoise, Livingston, Wedell, Frank, Scully, Lahey, and Hayes families for their friendship and support. I would like to individually thank Tom McGrath, Shane McArdle, Lauren Finan, Marielle Bakian, John Van Hazinga, Patrick DiGiovanni, Brian Koloszyc, Alyssa Brown, Phin Sonin, Seth Schriener, Jason Velez, Tim Shepard, Sasha O'Connor, Katheryn Kelly, Jason Perkins, Nathan Curtis, Ian (for getting me into Marcus Garvey), Brendan Garvey, John Townsend, Eli Carrotheart, Shawn Smith, David Jacobs, Alanna Kessler, John Philpin, Greg Thoma, Julie McCoy, Sylvia Mucklevaney (5th grade at P.S. 25), Ms. Smith (high-school English), Sarah Cohen, John (Jack) Thetford, Madhav Naik, Mark Ciufo, Anas Maloul, Matthew Walker, Taifoor Jamil, Bob Immerman, Sarah Lee Slonsky, Bob Burke, Carleton (CT) Mayers, Corrina Collins, Terry McCue, Courtney Stevens, Macy Lawrence, Dennis Harleston, Marike Smith, Jimmy Lease, the Castleton Trinity –Kevin Lynch, Pat Standen, and Robert M. Johnson, as well as Robert Aborn, Jamey Hecht, University of Vermont professors William E. Mann, Derk Pereboom, Hilary Kornblith, Charles Guignon, Sidney Poger, Andrew Barnaby, Don Loeb, R. Thomas Simone, David Christiansen, and for their help in self-publishing –Mark Estrin, Christian Noll, and Steve Ekberg, and the library staff at the University of Vermont, the Vermont Law School, Middlebury College, and Norman Williams libraries, and the excellent staff at Lightning Source.

Index of Names

Abelard, Peter 31, 34
AbuKhalil, As'ad, 59, 128, 248
Adams, John, 68, 69
Addams, Jane, 4, 17, 48-49, 190, 193, 195, 207, 209, 264, 296
Ahmed, Akbar S., 21, 62, 77, 78, 79, 86, 87, 97, 98, 102, 115, 116, 117, 119, 129, 131, 150, 242, 243, 247, 250
Al-Adwiyyah, Rabiah, 116
Al-Afghani, 167
Albertus Magnus, 83, 97
Al-Farabi, 31, 97
Al-Khowarizmi, 103
Ali, Muhammad, 15, 16, 20, 40-41, 58
Ali, Duse Mohamed, 181
Al-Kindi, 31, 97, 102
Al-Razeq, 207, 244, 245
Al-Tabari, 102
Ambrose, 231, 236
Amin, Qasim, 117
Anaxagoras, 26, 120, 160, 252, 255
Aquinas, Thomas, 27, 31, 64, 83, 124, 136, 230, 238, 325
Arabi, Oussama, 88, 131, 243, 245, 249, 250
Archimedes, 83, 94
Aristarchus, 87
Aristotle, 5, 9, 26, 27, 30-31, 80-81, 83, 84, 86, 89-91, 94-95, 96, 97- 99, 100, 102, 108, 112, 119, 120, 121, 133, 136, 138, 139, 142, 151, 160, 168, 169, 170, 178, 217, 222, 251, 253-255, 295, 296, 301, 302-305, 306, 307, 308, 310, 312, 313, 314, 317, 321, 325-327, 332, 335, 339, 343
Armstrong, Louis, 210
Asimov, Isaac, 103
Audi, Robert, 62, 70
Augustine, 54, 91, 231, 236
Averroes, 31, 83, 97, 144, 325
Avicenna, 31, 44, 83, 102
Ayer, A.J., 321
Bacon, Francis, 17, 27
Bacon, Roger, 102
Bainton, Roland, 23, 25, 26, 65, 124, 230, 231, 232, 233, 236, 237, 299
Bakunin, Mikhail, 35
Balch, Emily Greene, 190, 193
Baldwin, James, 214

Barth, John, 338, 340
Barthes, Roland, 341
Bauer, Bruno, 129
Beauvoir, Simone de, 214
Bellamy, Edward, 138
Bentham, Jeremy, 30, 44, 84, 137
Billings, Malcolm, 57
Blackstone, William, 137, 257
Blume, David, 106, 117
Boethius, 31, 83
Bronowski, J., 53, 257
Brown, Jim, 108
Browne, John, 40
Buchanan, George, 44
Buddha, Siddhartha Gautama, 18, 104, 106, 146, 158, 287, 316
Bultmann, Rudolf, 143, 144, 229, 230, 234, 236, 240, 241, 246, 341
Burckhardt, Jacob, 42-43
Buruma, Ian, 60
Butler, Smedley, 1, 14
Calvin, John, 44, 65, 97, 98, 101, 102, 105, 124, 125, 137, 145, 229, 235, 239, 331
Campbell, Joseph, 7, 339-340
Camus, Albert 1, 21, 35, 66, 137, 138, 141, 204, 274, 323
Carmichael, Stokely, 214
Carroll, James, 23, 27, 30, 40, 53, 55, 61, 62, 65, 77, 81, 87, 93, 94, 97, 101, 103, 114, 124, 126, 130, 135, 137, 164, 236, 237, 240, 245, 290, 291
Carson, Rachel, 203
Chang, Nancy, 16, 21, 59, 79, 200, 269, 294
Chomsky, Noam, 21, 79, 126, 168, 194, 195, 197, 247, 269
Christian X, 40
Ch'u Chai, 287, 316
Cicero, 169, 170, 220
Clarke, John Henrik, 181, 192
Clarke, Ramsey, 200, 294
Clarke, Robert Connell, 106, 107
Columbus, Christopher, 57, 77, 291
Comte, Auguste, 35
Confucius, 30, 31, 91, 105, 139, 146, 150, 157, 179, 287, 288, 316
Conot, Robert E., 196
Conrad, Lawrence, 75, 101, 102, 103, 285

Coogan, Tim Pat, 192, 246
Copernicus, Nicolaus, 87, 97, 98
Crystal, David, 73, 74, 256, 268
Danaher, Kevin, 88, 211, 212
Dante, Alighieri, 77, 319, 325, 337
Darwin, Charles, 29, 35, 56, 87, 319, 332
Davies, Norman, 23, 40, 43, 114, 252, 274
Davies, Paul, 280
Dayan, Moshe, 21
D'Entreves, A.P., 54, 136, 169, 170, 230, 236, 238, 239, 261
Democritus, 99, 305
Derrida, Jacques, 74, 200-201, 341
Descartes, Rene, 27, 30, 43, 87, 209, 288, 328
Dewey, John, 4, 17, 36, 37-38, 39, 49, 69-70, 153-155, 169, 172, 173, 177, 192-193, 207, 208, 209, 214, 215, 216, 264, 269, 296, 329, 340-341, 342
Dickens, Charles, 5, 65, 256
Donnolo, Shabbetai, 101
Douglass, Frederick, 47
Dreyfus, Alfred, 39-40, 214
DuBois, W.E.B., 192
Duns Scotus, 31, 44, 97
Einstein, Albert, 19, 141
Eisenman, Robert, 130, 131, 236
El-Awa, Muhamed S., 127, 149, 206, 207, 244, 245, 249, 292, 311
Emerson, Ralph Waldo, 5, 210, 260
Engels, Friedrich, 29, 35, 137, 147, 296
Epictetus, 108
Epicurus, 317
Escher, M.C., 77
Esposito, John, 77, 78, 79, 82, 88, 99, 106, 117, 167, 212, 248, 250
Etesami, Parwin, 116
Euclid, 83
Everson, Stephen, 121, 251
Feuerbach, Ludwig, 129, 322
Feynman, Richard, 290
Fletcher, Richard, 82, 105, 123, 237
Flexner, Eleanor, 47, 48, 49, 118
Fodor, Jerry, 172
Foner, Eric, 186, 187
Foucault, Michel, 89, 128, 160, 341
Frager, Robert, 91, 96, 98, 148, 248
Frankfurt, Harry, 8
Franklin, Benjamin, 44, 45, 135
Freud, Sigmund, 29-30, 33, 34, 156, 162-163, 288, 289
Friedman, Thomas, 295
Galen, 83, 94, 100, 102, 307
Galileo, Galilei, 97
Gandhi, Mohandas, 2, 16, 18, 19, 20, 36, 70, 150, 178, 182-184, 189, 209, 290, 302
Garvey, Marcus, 180, 181-182, 188, 190, 192

Gilman, Charlotte, 18, 48, 118, 266
Ginzberg, Louis, 32, 64, 92, 94, 109, 135, 136, 224, 225, 226, 227, 228, 245
Goldman, Emma, 48, 266, 295
Gomes, Peter J., 109, 110, 111
Gore, Albert, 52, 166, 176
Grube, G.M.A., 135
Harris, Joseph E., 181, 183
Hegel, Georg, 30, 35, 140, 151, 328
Heidegger, Martin, 7, 279, 322
Heikal, Mohamed, 247
Heine, Heinrich, 113, 114
Helmholz, R.H., 237, 238
Henry, Patrick, 20
Herer, Jack, 106, 107
Herman, Arthur, 43, 44, 47
Hesiod, 218
Hippocrites, 83, 94, 100
Hiro, Dilip, 20, 106, 127, 128, 147, 166, 167, 184, 185, 244, 246
Hobbes, Thomas, 30, 179, 295
Hoffman, Lawrence A., 162, 228, 313
Holfstadter, Richard, 50
Holmes, Oliver Wendell, 4, 17, 208, 209, 259-271, 292
Homer, 89, 170, 334
Hooker, Richard, 239, 256
hooks, bell, 38, 118, 119, 155, 190, 210, 211, 218, 219
Hui Shih, 31
Hume, David, 30, 44, 84, 279, 328
Hutcheson, Francis, 47
Huxley, Aldous, 334
Huxley, Thomas, 35, 314
Ibn Arabi, 98
Ibn Khaldun, 148
Ibn Khallikan, 244
Jaimini, 31
James, William, 4, 9, 17, 27-28, 29, 34, 35, 36, 151, 172, 207, 264, 276-279, 280, 292, 296, 297
Jefferson, Thomas, 44, 45, 46, 50, 52-54, 179
Jennings, Francis, 33, 57, 101, 104, 107, 110, 136, 164, 258, 291
Johnson, Robert, M., 15
Josephus, 236
Kant, Immanuel, 9, 17, 30, 43, 84, 179, 191, 222, 280, 281, 314, 318, 323, 328
Kaufmann, Walter, 46, 53, 63, 64, 75, 105, 124, 125, 126, 153, 217, 226, 228, 230, 231, 233-235, 241, 281, 317, 320, 325, 341
Kautilya, 136
Kelsen, Hans, 233, 270, 272, 296
Kertzer, Morris N., 162, 228, 313
Khomeini, R., 20, 106, 128, 184, 185, 246, 247
Kierkegaard, Soren, 95, 125, 279, 289

King, Jr., Martin Luther, 16, 33, 36, 58, 67, 95, 111, 118, 126, 130, 141, 146, 168, 187-189, 209, 210, 233, 271, 297, 298, 299
Kirkpatrick, David D., 52, 53, 60
Kornblith, Hilary, 278
Knox, John, 44
Krakauer, Jon, 67
Kripke, Saul, 73
Krugman, Paul, 56
Lane, Anthony, 337
Lao Tzu, 139, 147, 157, 317
Leibniz, Gottfried, 30, 43, 77, 142, 222, 281
Leucippus, 99, 305
Levinas, Emmanuel, 13, 39, 59, 132, 162, 168, 205, 280-282, 298, 327-328, 336-337
Lindemann, Mary, 100, 101, 102, 290
Locke, John, 43, 62, 66
Luo, Michael, 52
Luther, Martin, 65, 75, 77, 94-95, 97, 101, 105, 124, 153, 231, 240, 241, 274-275
Lyotard, Jean-Francois, 87, 331
Machiavelli, Niccolo, 296
MacIntyre, Alasdair, 43, 83, 84, 86, 87, 95, 96, 97, 169, 170-171, 203, 321, 331, 340
Mahoney, Olivia, 186, 187
Maimonides, Moses, 31, 101, 144, 227, 325
Majusi, Haly Abbas, 102
Malcolm X, 30, 58, 118, 181, 188-190, 192, 209, 210
Mandela, Nelson, 2, 20, 60-61, 183, 184
Mandel, Michael, 79, 194, 196, 197, 198, 293, 294
Mandelbaum, Michael, 194, 196
Mann, William, 15
Mao Tse-tung, 140
Marcus Aurelius, 100, 151, 169, 176, 234
Martin, Michael, 142
Marx, Karl, 1, 29, 35, 87, 129, 137, 140, 147, 265, 296, 324, 325
Mazlish, Bruce, 53, 257
McDowell, Bart, 78
McKinley, William, 55, 265
McLaren, Robert Bruce, 126
Mead, George Herbert, 17, 49
Menand, Louis, 5, 37, 49, 64, 207, 208, 209, 260, 261, 262, 331
Meno, 9
Mernissi, Fatima, 117
Mills, Charles W., 125
Mohammed V, 129
Moore, G.E., 326
More, Thomas, 65
Moyo, Dambiso, 212
Muhammad, 131, 148, 249
Muller, Max, 75
Murdoch, Iris, 330-331

Nabokov, Peter, 57, 58, 107, 259
Nader, Ralph, 8, 131, 141, 151, 164, 165-166, 195, 211, 212, 268, 294
Nagel, Thomas, 167
Nasr, Seyyed Hossein, 25, 76, 88, 91, 103, 104, 111, 117, 126, 127, 162, 203, 204, 242, 243, 244, 248, 250, 284, 285, 312
Nehamas, Alexander, 160
Newton, Isaac, 321
Niebuhr, Reinhold, 208, 209
Niebuhr, Richard, 320
Nietzsche, Friedrich, 27, 29, 30, 80, 84-86, 87, 107, 114, 203, 289, 318-320, 336, 341
Novick, Sheldon, 208, 260, 263, 264, 265, 266
Nussbaum, Martha, 93, 118
Nutton, Vivian, 99, 101, 102, 103
Orwell, George, 13
Paine, Thomas, 15, 36, 38, 44-46, 110, 114, 129, 179, 232, 320-321
Parmenides, 218
Pascal, Blaise, 30, 276
Peirce, Charles Sanders, 3, 17, 151, 174-175, 207
Pereboom, Derk, 91
Peters, Francis E., 82
Peters, Rudolph, 117, 202, 245, 246, 247, 250
Peters, Shawn, 291
Phillips, Kevin, 34, 48, 53, 55-56, 58, 66, 68, 111, 142, 177
Philo, 89, 90, 307
Pieper, Josef, 31, 83, 97, 100, 136, 307, 325
Plato, 5, 9, 26, 30, 72, 80, 81, 89, 90, 91, 96, 98, 99, 107, 108, 112, 119, 120-122, 123, 139, 140, 142, 151, 160, 168, 169, 170, 177, 220-222, 251, 252, 260, 295, 296, 301-305, 306, 307, 308, 310, 313-314, 321, 326, 327, 333, 334-335, 343
Plotinus, 90
Polemarchus, 220, 221
Popper, Karl, 9, 75, 321, 324
Posner, Richard, 5, 137, 257, 267
Protagoras, 26, 120, 160, 174, 252, 255, 323
Ptolemy, 94, 226
Putnam, Hilary, 7, 33, 34, 35, 36, 76, 93, 123, 205, 288, 289, 295, 332, 333-334
Pyrrho, 317
Pythagoras, 26, 89
Quine, W.V., 5, 103, 332, 339
Randi, James, 33
Ratner, Joseph, 172
Ratzinger, Joseph, 79, 114
Razi, 102
Reid, Thomas, 44
Remnick, David, 41
Rivera, Diego, 208

Rodinson, Maxime, 33, 77, 82, 94, 95, 135, 136, 137, 147, 149, 245, 248
Roosevelt, Eleanor, 199, 294
Roosevelt, Theodore, 55, 195, 208, 263, 264, 265, 266
Rorty, Richard, 5
Rousseau, Jean-Jacques, 43, 203, 222
Roy, Arundahti, 118, 215
Royce, Josiah, 17, 36, 151-152, 153, 154
Rugova, Ibrahim, 197
Rushdie, Salman, 7, 62, 197, 247
Russell, Bertrand, 17, 18-19, 23, 30, 39-40, 62, 78, 82, 89, 98, 100, 103, 107, 112, 121, 124, 131, 138, 153, 156, 157, 167, 191, 193-194, 213-214, 233, 257, 269-270, 276, 277-278, 279, 297, 307, 310-311, 325, 333
Ryan, Mary, 48, 49
Said, Edward, 24, 25, 74, 77, 78, 200, 247, 288, 293, 295, 337, 338, 340, 341
Santayana, George, 5, 18, 38, 151, 339, 340
Sartre, Jean-Paul, 19, 30, 40, 79, 214, 279
Schlosberg, David, 175
Schopenhauer, Arthur, 27, 30, 279, 328
Schweitzer, Albert, 152, 153, 154, 230
Selassie, Haile, 78, 192
Sen, Amartya, 136, 166
Servetus, Michael, 65, 101-102
Sextus Empiricus, 27, 100, 317, 339
Shakespeare, William, 17, 73, 130, 199, 274, 317
Sheik Haidar, 106
Singer, Peter, 174, 203
Smith, Adam, 44, 136, 151
Socrates, 5, 8, 9, 26, 27, 71, 80, 81, 89, 90, 91, 94, 96, 98, 99, 104, 108, 112, 119, 120, 135, 140, 142, 151, 160, 169, 170, 173, 220-222, 252, 253, 255, 272, 277, 295, 301-308, 310, 313, 314, 317, 322, 323, 326, 332, 334, 339, 340, 343

Spencer, Herbert, 35, 268
Spinoza, Benedict de, 30, 44, 62, 65
Steinsaltz, Adin, 92, 93, 112, 113, 162, 163, 164, 227, 228, 246, 313
Stich, Stephen, 278
Strickland, William, 181
Taft, William Howard, 208, 266
Tertullian, 94
Thayer, H.S., 4
Theophrastus, 93
Thoreau, Henry David, 5, 15, 16-17, 18, 36, 38, 189
Thornton, Russell, 58, 291
Tillich, Paul, 230, 235, 322
Tocqueville, Alexis de, 46, 47, 54, 65, 66, 69, 258, 259
Trilling, Lionel, 208
Trotsky, Leon, 39, 208, 214
Twain, Mark, 207, 246, 264, 271, 296
Vico, Giambattista, 76
Voltaire, 43, 77, 281, 338
Waines, David, 25, 82, 91, 98, 111, 114-115, 127, 164, 243, 244, 247
Washington, George, 45, 52-53, 68, 69
Wear, Andrew, 101
Weber, Max, 33, 88, 135, 137, 145, 146, 147, 239
Wells, H.G., 25, 78
Wells-Barnett, Ida B., 47
West, Cornel, 5, 38, 118, 125, 155, 210
Williams, John Alden, 91, 98
Winberg Chai, 287, 316
Wittgenstein, Ludwig, 7, 28, 29
Woodruff, Paul, 160
Wootton, David, 239, 240
Yunus, Muhammad, 212
Zinn, Howard, 48, 55, 57, 58, 88, 110, 119, 187, 207, 257, 258, 264, 268, 269
Zola, Emile, 39-40

www.ingramcontent.com/pod-product-compliance
Lightning Source LLC
Chambersburg PA
CBHW032031150426
43194CB00006B/236